W9-AMM-396

LET'S GO

■ THE RESOURCE FOR THE INDEPENDENT TRAVELER

"The guides are aimed not only at young budget travelers but at the indepedent traveler; a sort of streetwise cookbook for traveling alone."

—*The New York Times*

"Unbeatable; good sight-seeing advice; up-to-date info on restaurants, hotels, and inns; a commitment to money-saving travel; and a wry style that brightens nearly every page."

—*The Washington Post*

"Lighthearted and sophisticated, informative and fun to read. [Let's Go] helps the novice traveler navigate like a knowledgeable old hand."

—*Atlanta Journal-Constitution*

"A world-wise traveling companion—always ready with friendly advice and helpful hints, all sprinkled with a bit of wit."

—*The Philadelphia Inquirer*

■ THE BEST TRAVEL BARGAINS IN YOUR PRICE RANGE

"All the dirt, dirt cheap."

—*People*

"Anything you need to know about budget traveling is detailed in this book."

—*The Chicago Sun-Times*

"Let's Go follows the creed that you don't have to toss your life's savings to the wind to travel—unless you want to."

—*The Salt Lake Tribune*

■ REAL ADVICE FOR REAL EXPERIENCES

"The writers seem to have experienced every rooster-packed bus and lunar-surfaced mattress about which they write."

—*The New York Times*

"A guide should tell you what to expect from a destination. Here Let's Go shines."

—*The Chicago Tribune*

"[Let's Go's] devoted updaters really walk the walk (and thumb the ride, and trek the trail). Learn how to fish, haggle, find work—anywhere."

—*Food & Wine*

LET'S GO PUBLICATIONS

TRAVEL GUIDES

Alaska 1st edition **NEW TITLE**
Australia 2004
Austria & Switzerland 2004
Brazil 1st edition **NEW TITLE**
Britain & Ireland 2004
California 2004
Central America 8th edition
Chile 1st edition
China 4th edition
Costa Rica 1st edition
Eastern Europe 2004
Egypt 2nd edition
Europe 2004
France 2004
Germany 2004
Greece 2004
Hawaii 2004
India & Nepal 8th edition
Ireland 2004
Israel 4th edition
Italy 2004
Japan 1st edition **NEW TITLE**
Mexico 20th edition
Middle East 4th edition
New Zealand 6th edition
Pacific Northwest 1st edition **NEW TITLE**
Peru, Ecuador & Bolivia 3rd edition
Puerto Rico 1st edition **NEW TITLE**
South Africa 5th edition
Southeast Asia 8th edition
Southwest USA 3rd edition
Spain & Portugal 2004
Thailand 1st edition
Turkey 5th edition
USA 2004
Western Europe 2004

CITY GUIDES

Amsterdam 3rd edition
Barcelona 3rd edition
Boston 4th edition
London 2004
New York City 2004
Paris 2004
Rome 12th edition
San Francisco 4th edition
Washington, D.C. 13th edition

MAP GUIDES

Amsterdam
Berlin
Boston
Chicago
Dublin
Florence
Hong Kong
London
Los Angeles
Madrid
New Orleans
New York City
Paris
Prague
Rome
San Francisco
Seattle
Sydney
Venice
Washington, D.C.

COMING SOON:
Road Trip USA

LG

LET'S GO

PUERTO RICO

RESEARCHER AND EDITOR
MICHELLE BOWMAN

NATHANIEL BROOKS MAP EDITOR
ARIEL FOX MANAGING EDITOR

ST. MARTIN'S PRESS 📖 NEW YORK

HELPING LET'S GO

If you want to share your discoveries, suggestions, or corrections, please drop us a line. We read every piece of correspondence, whether a postcard, a 10-page email, or a coconut. **Address mail to:**

Let's Go: Puerto Rico
67 Mount Auburn Street
Cambridge, MA 02138
USA

Visit Let's Go at **http://www.letsgo.com,** or send email to:

feedback@letsgo.com
Subject: "Let's Go: Puerto Rico"

In addition to the invaluable travel advice our readers share with us, many are kind enough to offer their services as researchers or editors. Unfortunately, our charter enables us to employ only currently enrolled Harvard students.

Maps by David Lindroth copyright © 2004 by St. Martin's Press.

Distributed outside the USA and Canada by Macmillan.

Let's Go: Puerto Rico Copyright © 2004 by Let's Go, Inc. All rights reserved. Printed in the United States of America. No part of this book may be used or reproduced in any manner whatsoever without written permission except in the case of brief quotations embodied in critical articles or reviews. Let's Go is available for purchase in bulk by institutions and authorized resellers. For information, address St. Martin's Press, 175 Fifth Avenue, New York, NY 10010, USA.

ISBN: 0-312-32009-4

First edition
10 9 8 7 6 5 4 3 2 1

Let's Go: Puerto Rico is written by Let's Go Publications, 67 Mount Auburn Street, Cambridge, MA 02138, USA.

Let's Go® and the LG logo are trademarks of Let's Go, Inc.
Printed in the USA.

ADVERTISING DISCLAIMER

All advertisements appearing in Let's Go publications are sold by an independent agency not affiliated with the editorial production of the guides. Advertisers are never given preferential treatment, and the guides are researched, written, and published independent of advertising. Advertisements do not imply endorsement of products or services by Let's Go, and Let's Go does not vouch for the accuracy of information provided in advertisements.

If you are interested in purchasing advertising space in a Let's Go publication, contact: Let's Go Advertising Sales, 67 Mount Auburn St., Cambridge, MA 02138, USA.

HOW TO USE THIS BOOK

ORGANIZATION OF THE BOOK

DISCOVER PUERTO RICO. Believe it or not, the island has much more than just beaches. The **Discover** chapter provides the tools to plan the perfect trip, from Caribbean beach getaways to amazing outdoor adventures.

LIFE AND TIMES. This chapter holds the answers to all your burning **questions** about Puerto Rico. Where did salsa come from? Does Puerto Rico really have the most beautiful women in the world? And once and for all, is Puerto Rico part of the US or not? Everything you've ever wanted to know about Puerto Rico is here, including an expanded section on the island's incredible **water sports.**

ESSENTIALS. The practical information involved in traveling can get downright pesky. Flip to this section to get the quick and easy guide to Puerto Rico, including getting there, getting around, finding a place to stay, and staying safe.

ALTERNATIVES TO TOURISM. After a trip to Puerto Rico, you may never want to go home. The Alternatives to Tourism chapter provides advice on what to do in Puerto Rico if you want to stay just a bit longer, be that **volunteering, working, studying,** or just being a responsible tourist.

COVERAGE. This book starts in the spirited capital of **San Juan.** From there, coverage works counter-clockwise around the island, culminating in a trip through the mountains along the **Ruta Panorámica. Vieques** and **Culebra** may be the last two chapters, but everyone knows that they are certainly not the least important. The **black tabs** will help you navigate the book quickly and easily.

GLOSSARY. English-speakers will have no problem getting around the island, but the handy glossary has an introduction to **Spanish,** Puerto Rico's native language. Look here to find out why *china* is more than just a country in Asia.

NOTES ABOUT LET'S GO FORMAT

SIDEBARS. Stylish black sidebars throughout the book have extra tidbits of knowledge, from informative **interviews** with locals to descriptions of the best **parties** in Puerto Rico.

GRAYBOXES AND ICONBOXES. Grayboxes provide quirky anecdotes about the fascinating Puerto Rican culture. **White boxes,** on the other hand, contain important practical information, such as warnings, helpful hints, and further resources.

PHONE CODES AND TELEPHONE NUMBERS. The area code for phone numbers is **787,** unless noted otherwise. Phone numbers are preceded by the ☎ icon.

A NOTE TO OUR READERS The information for this book was gathered by *Let's Go* researchers from November 2002 through May 2003. Each listing is based on one researcher's opinion, formed during his or her visit at a particular time. Those traveling at other times may have different experiences since prices, dates, hours, and conditions are always subject to change. You are urged to check the facts presented in this book beforehand to avoid inconvenience and surprises.

---

①②③④⑤
PRICE RANGES >> PUERTO RICO

Our researchers list establishments in order of value from best to worst; our favorites are denoted by the Let's Go thumbs-up (👍). Since the best value is not always the cheapest price, we have incorporated a system of price ranges for quick reference. Our price ranges are based on a rough expectation of what you will spend. For **accommodations,** we base our price range off the cheapest price for which a single traveler can stay for one night. For **restaurants** and other dining establishments, we estimate the average price of a full entree without beverages or appetizers. The table below tells you what you will *typically* find in Puerto Rico at the corresponding price range; keep in mind that a particularly expensive ice cream stand may still only be marked a ❷, depending on what you will spend.

ACCOMMODATIONS	RANGE	WHAT YOU'RE *LIKELY* TO FIND
❶	under $25	Primarily campgrounds or, more likely, large fields on which you can place a tent. A couple of extremely cheap guest houses—have no expectations.
❷	$25-59	Inexpensive guest houses, usually located in the owner's house. These vary greatly, from unadorned spare bedrooms to surprisingly well-equipped hotel rooms.
❸	$60-89	Mostly small, independent hotels. Rooms should be clean and have a private bath; some may have a kitchenette. Also includes rustic cabins for larger groups.
❹	$90-129	Nicer guest houses and small hotels in highly touristed neighborhoods. You should always get daily maid service and quality service. Most *paradores* fall into this category.
❺	over $130	Large chain hotels and very trendy inns. Expect the best, because you're paying for it.
FOOD	RANGE	WHAT YOU'RE *LIKELY* TO FIND
❶	under $6	*Panaderías* and *cafeterías* serving sandwiches and typical Puerto Rican food. Typically only open for lunch.
❷	$6-10	Inexpensive sit-down restaurants with waitstaff and relatively expensive *cafeterías* serving dinner.
❸	$11-15	The vast majority of tourist-oriented restaurants fall into this category. Almost all have a waitstaff, a sit-down dining area, and a full menu with appetizers and desserts.
❹	$16-20	A somewhat fancy eatery, including most seafood restaurants. All of the amenities from above, but slightly classier.
❺	over $20	The best restaurants in Puerto Rico. Expect either a very hip atmosphere or some of the best food on the island. Make a reservation and dress nicely.

CONTENTS

RESEARCHER-WRITER

Michelle Bowman

A former Editor for *Let's Go: Peru, Ecuador, and Bolivia 2002*, the Publicity Manager for the 2003 Let's Go series, and a two-time Researcher-Writer (for *Let's Go: Peru, Ecuador, and Bolivia 2001* and *Eastern Europe 2000*), Michelle has held almost every position imaginable at Let's Go. She both edited and researched *Let's Go: Puerto Rico 2004*, trekking through Puerto Rico's lush forests, off-roading on Vieques, and salsa-ing her way through San Juan's pulsing night life. Michelle then returned with the stamina to painstakingly push her book through to press. And all of this adventure was just another day's work for the Oregon native, whose travel resume includes India, Costa Rica, Russia, Europe, and the Dominican Republic. She will put this knowledge to good use in her future work in international development.

CONTRIBUTING WRITERS

Adrián Cerezo is an education policy and non-formal education specialist currently directing the Community Based Education Center at Sacred Heart University in San Juan. He has a BA. in clinical psychology from Sacred Heart University.

Derek Glanz was the editor of *Let's Go: Spain & Portugal 1998*. He is now pursuing his PhD in political science at the University of North Carolina, Chapel Hill. He is a freelance baseball writer contributing regularly to St. Louis Cardinals' *Gameday Magazine*. He has written for *Baseball America* and *Baseball Weekly* and appeared as a guest analyst on ESPN Radio and Colombia's *Telecartagena*.

Camille Lizarribar has a PhD in Comparative Literature from Harvard University and a JD at Harvard Law. She has most recently returned to Puerto Rico to clerk for a Judge at the Federal District Court in San Juan.

Iliana Pagán Teitelbaum received her BA in Latin American Studies from the University of Puerto Rico. She is currently finishing her dissertation and expects to receive a PhD in Romance Languages and Literatures from Harvard University.

ACKNOWLEDGMENTS

Let's Go Puerto Rico is dedicated to the memory of Haley Surti

MICHELLE THANKS: If there is one thing I've learned from this project, it's that you really can't go it alone. First and foremost, thank you to the amazing people of Puerto Rico, who welcomed me onto their beautiful island like a friend and helped me every step of the way. A special *gracias* to Sofia Velez, one of the most wonderful people I've ever met. Thank you for being a friend and the ultimate source in San Juan knowledge. To *Let's Go,* a company that has been my home for the last 5 years—it's been a blast. Ariel, you have no idea what a difference a well-timed mailstop can make. Thank you for being eternally helpful. Nathaniel, the best mapper *ever* (and I mean that). Whoever hired you originally was a genius. Julie Stephens—my greatest personal and professional support from day one. You made this happen. Anne, as always, I don't know what this place would do without you. Camille, for being a friend. The 2003 ME team and especially 7 Story St.—I hope you all share my fond memories. Matt and Brian—thanks for putting up with my insubordination and proving that bosses can also be friends. Adam, the optimism to my pessimism. Megan, for girl talk. Ankur, for remembering the good ol' days. Nitin, Jesse, and Jeff for last minute support. Prod 2004 (and especially Dusty)—I promise, no more questions. Thanks for the help and the fun times. Christina—NYC has never been so fun. Everyone who came and visited me on the road—Marla, Mom, Megan, Laura, Graham, Brian, Lizzie, Corey, and Christina. Molly, Tanna, and Sprint PCS for the long phone conversations that kept me going. And finally, Mom and Megan. As always, I could not accomplish anything without your love and support.

NATHANIEL THANKS: First and foremost, the amazing Michelle. Uber-RW/editor combo, possessed of marathon stamina and Yoda-like wisdom, she probably would've done my job too, if I'd let her. Next, the hardcore team in mapland, many of whom had a hand in the maps in this book. Finally, Megan and the rest of the crew at 241 Washington Street. Quaaaaaality porches!

Editor
Michelle R. Bowman
Managing Editor
Ariel Fox
Map Editor
Nathaniel Brooks

LET'S GO

Publishing Director
Julie A. Stephens
Editor-in-Chief
Jeffrey Dubner
Production Manager
Dusty Lewis
Cartography Manager
Nathaniel Brooks
Design Manager
Caleb Beyers
Editorial Managers
Lauren Bonner, Ariel Fox,
Matthew K. Hudson, Emma Nothmann,
Joanna Shawn Brigid O'Leary,
Sarah Robinson
Financial Manager
Suzanne Siu
Marketing & Publicity Managers
Megan Brumagim, Nitin Shah
Personnel Manager
Jesse Reid Andrews
Researcher Manager
Jennifer O'Brien
Web Manager
Jesse Tov
Web Content Manager
Abigail Burger
Production Associates
Thomas Bechtold, Jeffrey Yip
IT Directors
Travis Good, E. Peyton Sherwood
Financial Assistant
R. Kirkie Maswoswe
Associate Web Manager
Robert Dubbin
Office Coordinators
Abigail Burger, Angelina L. Fryer,
Liz Glynn
Director of Advertising Sales
Daniel Ramsey
Senior Advertising Associates
Sara Barnett, Daniella Boston
Advertising Artwork Editor
Julia Davidson
President
Abhishek Gupta
General Manager
Robert B. Rombauer
Assistant General Manager
Anne E. Chisholm

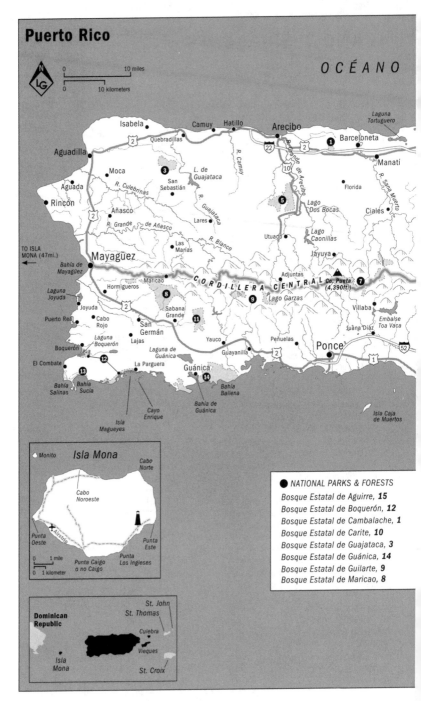

Puerto Rico

OCÉANO

NATIONAL PARKS & FORESTS
Bosque Estatal de Aguirre, **15**
Bosque Estatal de Boquerón, **12**
Bosque Estatal de Cambalache, **1**
Bosque Estatal de Carite, **10**
Bosque Estatal de Guajataca, **3**
Bosque Estatal de Guánica, **14**
Bosque Estatal de Guilarte, **9**
Bosque Estatal de Maricao, **8**

Isabela · Camuy · Hatillo · Arecibo · Barceloneta

Laguna Tortuguero

Manatí

Aguadilla

Quebradillas

Moca · San Sebastián · L. de Guajataca · Florida

Aguada

Rincón · Añasco · R. Culebrinas · R. Grande de Añasco · Lares · R. Guajataca · Lago Dos Bocas · Ciales

Las Marías · R. Blanco · Utuado · Lago Caonillas

TO ISLA MONA (47mi.)

Bahía de Mayagüez

Mayagüez · Jayuya

Laguna Joyuda

Hormigueros · Maricao · CORDILLERA CENTRAL · Adjuntas · Co. Punta (4,390ft.)

Joyuda · Sabana Grande · Lago Garzas · Villalba

Puerto Real · Cabo Rojo · San Germán · Embalse Toa Vaca

Boquerón · Laguna Boquerón · Lajas · Yauco · Juana Díaz

El Combate · Laguna de Guánica · Guayanilla · Peñuelas · Ponce

Bahía Salinas · Bahía Sucia · La Parguera · Guánica · Bahía Ballena

Cayo Enrique · Bahía de Guánica · Isla Caja de Muertos

Isla Magueyes

Isla Mona

Monito

Cabo Norte

Cabo Noroeste

Punta Oeste · Airstrip · Punta Este

Punta Caigo o no Caigo · Punta Los Ingleses

Dominican Republic

St. John
St. Thomas
Culebra
Vieques
St. Croix

Isla Mona

X

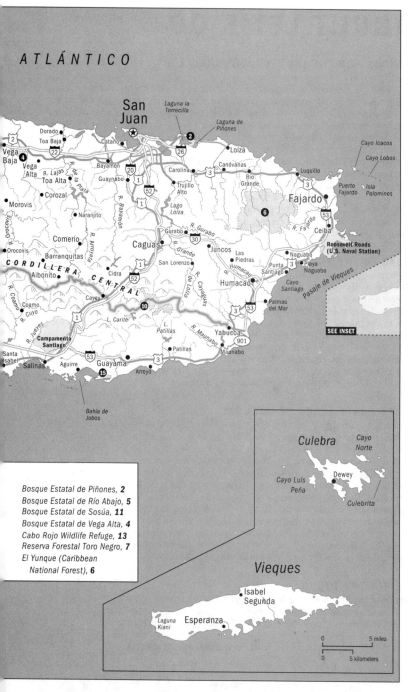

ATLÁNTICO

San Juan

Dorado
Toa Baja
Vega Baja
Vega Alta
R. Lajas
Toa Alta
Corozal
Morovis
Naranjito
Comerío
Orocovis
Barranquitas
Aibonito
CORDILLERA CENTRAL
Coamo
R. Cuyo
Santa Isabel
Campamento Santiago
Salinas
Aguirre
Guayama
Arroyo

Cataño
Bayamón
Guaynabo
Trujillo Alto
Lago Loíza
Gurabo
Caguas
San Lorenzo
Cidra
Cayey
L. Carite
L. Patillas
Patillas
Yabucoa
Maunabo

Laguna la Torrecilla
Laguna de Piñones
Loíza
Canóvanas
Carolina
Río Grande
R. Gurabo
Juncos
Las Piedras
Punta Santiago
Humacao
Palmas del Mar

Luquillo
Fajardo
Puerto Fajardo
Ceiba
R. Fajardo
Naguabo
Playa Naguabo
Cayo Santiago

Cayo Icacos
Cayo Lobos
Isla Palominos
Roosevelt Roads
(U.S. Naval Station)
Pasaje de Vieques

Bahía de Jobos

SEE INSET

Bosque Estatal de Piñones, 2
Bosque Estatal de Río Abajo, 5
Bosque Estatal de Sosúa, 11
Bosque Estatal de Vega Alta, 4
Cabo Rojo Wildlife Refuge, 13
Reserva Forestal Toro Negro, 7
El Yunque (Caribbean
    National Forest), 6

Culebra
Cayo Norte
Cayo Luís Peña
Dewey
Culebrita

Vieques
Isabel Segunda
Laguna Kiani
Esperanza

0   5 miles
0   5 kilometers

ABOUT LET'S GO

GUIDES FOR THE INDEPENDENT TRAVELER

Budget travel is more than a vacation. At *Let's Go*, we see every trip as the chance of a lifetime. If your dream is to grab a knapsack and a machete and forge through the jungles of Brazil, we can take you there. Or, if you'd rather enjoy the Riviera sun at a beachside cafe, we'll set you a table. If you know what you're doing, you can have any experience you want—whether it's camping among lions or sampling Tuscan desserts—without maxing out your credit card. We'll show you just how far your coins can go, and prove that the greatest limitation on your adventure is not your wallet, but your imagination. That said, we understand that you may want the occasional indulgence after a week of hostels and kebab stands, so we've added "Big Splurges" to let you know which establishments are worth those extra euros, as well as price ranges to help you quickly determine whether an accommo-dation or restaurant will break the bank. While we may have diversified, our emphasis will always be on finding the best values for your budget, giving you all the info you need to spend six days in London or six months in Tasmania.

BEYOND THE TOURIST EXPERIENCE

We write for travelers who know there's more to a vacation than riding double-deckers with tourists. Our researchers give you the heads-up on both world-renowned and lesser-known attractions, on the best local eats and the hottest nightclub beats. In our travels, we talk to everybody; we provide a snapshot of real life in the places you visit with our sidebars on topics like regional cuisine, local festivals, and hot political issues. We've opened our pages to respected writers and scholars to show you their take on a given destination, and turned to lifelong resi-dents to learn the little things that make their city worth calling home. And we've even given you Alternatives to Tourism—ideas for how to give back to local com-munities through responsible travel and volunteering.

OVER FORTY YEARS OF WISDOM

When we started, way back in 1960, Let's Go consisted of a small group of well-traveled friends who compiled their budget travel tips into a 20-page packet for students on charter flights to Europe. Since then, we've expanded to suit all kinds of travelers, now publishing guides to six continents, including our newest guides: *Let's Go: Japan* and *Let's Go: Brazil*. Our guides are still annually researched and written entirely by students on shoe-string budgets, adventurous travelers who know that train strikes, stolen luggage, food poisoning, and marriage propos-als are all part of a day's work. Even as you read this, work on next year's editions is well underway. Whether you're reading one of our new titles, like *Let's Go: Puerto Rico* or *Let's Go Adventure Guide: Alaska*, or our original best-seller, *Let's Go: Europe*, you'll find the same spirit of adventure that has made *Let's Go* the guide of choice for travelers the world over since 1960.

GETTING IN TOUCH

The best discoveries are often those you make yourself; on the road, when you find something worth sharing, please drop us a line. We're Let's Go Publications, 67 Mt. Auburn St., Cambridge, MA 02138, USA (feedback@letsgo.com).

For more info, visit our website: www.letsgo.com.

DISCOVER
PUERTO RICO

From the rumble of reggaeton to the beat of *bomba*, life on Puerto Rico pulsates to a constant cacophony of sound and movement. Hordes of cars weave across the island, commerce bustles at a pace comparable to any developed metropolis, and seemingly incessant *fiestas* ensure that nobody ever lacks a reason to celebrate. Not only sounds but sights fill the island; Puerto Rico is remarkable for the sheer amount of stuff that has managed to squeeze onto a space the size of Connecticut. In addition to four million people, this tiny plot of land holds some of the world's most beautiful beaches, the only tropical rain forest in the US, acres of coral reef, the world's third largest underground cave system, nine protected reserves, the world's largest radio telescope, and countless diverse ecosystems. Oh, and giant San Juan is the commercial capital of the Caribbean. Puerto Rico offers a diverse package of culture, commerce, and nature.

San Juan is an integral part of the island, but don't think that the capital city represents all of Puerto Rico—islanders from nearly every other town will quickly contradict you. Puerto Ricans hold deep pride, not only in their island but in each individual region: San Juan, Ponce, and Mayagüez battle for the title of Puerto Rico's supreme city, and *viequenses* and *culebrenses* both insist that there is really no reason to visit the other island. However, the prevalence of Puerto Rican flags and "Querida Boricua" stickers reveal that underneath these regional differences islanders are united by an intense pride in being Puerto Rican, or more accurately, Boricuan. The island's original Taíno name continues to serve as a password for the spirit of the island. Outsiders look at the question of Puerto Rico's status as the ultimate divisor, and in many ways it is. But underneath it all Puerto Ricans will continue to be Boricuan, regardless of whether the island is part of the United States or an independent country. Separated from the rest of the world by miles of water, Puerto Ricans unify their diverse heritage—Taíno, African, and European—to create a vibrant culture all their own.

Puerto Rico is simultaneously the poorest territory in the US and the richest part of Latin America, and these conflicting identities ooze through every aspect of island life. Visitors looking for the 51st US state will be disappointed; the language is Spanish, parts of the island look more like developing South America than the Caribbean, and the culture is decidedly Latin. However, others who believe that they're traveling to Latin America will be discouraged by the overwhelming presence of Wal-Mart and US flags. Only those who embrace Puerto Rico for what it is—a beautiful Caribbean island with some financial security and a spirited culture—will not fail to be impressed.

DISCOVER

FACTS AND FIGURES

OFFICIAL NAME: Estado Libre Asociado de Puerto Rico (Free Associated State of Puerto Rico)	**PERCENTAGE OF US RUM PRODUCED IN PUERTO RICO:** 80
CAPITAL: San Juan	**POPULATION OF PUERTO RICANS IN THE US:** 3.6 million
POPULATION DENSITY: 1112 people per sq. mi.	**NUMBER OF CITIES THAT CLAIM COLUMBUS LANDED THERE:** 6 (Combate, Guayanilla, Mayagüez, Boquerón, Añasco).
PER CAPITA GDP: $11,200	

WHEN TO GO

A variety of factors affect travel on Puerto Rico and there is usually a trade-off between perfect weather and steep discounts. No matter when you travel it will be low season on one part of the island. Most travelers escape to Puerto Rico between January and April when the weather up north is fairly miserable and the island's climate is at its prime. Unfortunately, hotels in San Juan, Culebra, and Vieques raise their rates during this season. The best solution is to travel to other parts of the island rarely visited by foreigners, such as the southwest. Puerto Ricans travel during school vacations—primarily Christmas (late Dec.), *Semana Santa* (the week before Easter), and summer (June-Aug.)—and fill up accommodations and beaches nearly everywhere outside of San Juan. Also, during the summer Puerto Rico is also at its hottest and most humid. **Hurricane season** officially lasts from June to November, but most storms are in August and September. Traveling during this time is risky; a hurricane will almost definitely ruin any vacation, but when there isn't a hurricane (most of the time) travelers will enjoy nearly empty beaches and steep hotel discounts. **Surf season** in Puerto Rico runs from November to mid-April.

THINGS TO DO

Many people travel to Puerto Rico just for the beaches—and the beaches are unbelievable—but the island easily has enough cultural and natural attractions to keep anyone busy for weeks. Whether you're looking for a taste of Caribbean culture, an off-the-beaten-track adventure, or just a relaxing vacation on the beach, Puerto Rico will not disappoint.

IN THE SEA

Ah, the gorgeous blue Caribbean. You haven't really seen Puerto Rico until you've explored the underwater world around it. Puerto Rico is a great place to swim with sharks, turtles, manatees, barracudas, dolphins, whales, lobsters, and hundreds of brightly colored fish. Everyone agrees that Puerto Rico's best diving is at **Isla Mona** (p. 195), which boasts hundreds of dive sites and visibility up to 180 ft. However, the 4hr. journey takes a lot of planning, and even more moolah. For a similar, but more accessible experience, try Rincón, where boats leave almost daily for **Isla Desecheo** (p. 185), an offshore island surrounded by thriving reefs. A completely different dive experience awaits off the southwestern coast of Puerto Rico. Six miles offshore a dramatic sea wall starts at 60 ft. then seems to disappear completely as a sheer cliff descends to over 150 ft. The best place to access The Wall is the spirited *pueblo* of **La Parguera** (p. 209). Slightly less advanced divers may want to head to the eastern side of the island—**Fajardo** (p. 257), **Vieques** (p. 292), and **Culebra** (p. 305) send divers to the hundreds of tiny cays in the Sonda de Vieques that appear more stereotypically Caribbean (white

sand, palm trees) than anywhere else in Puerto Rico.
Finally, one of Puerto Rico's most unique dive spots is
just off the coast of **Aguadilla** (p. 174), where hundreds
of old tires have been transformed into an artificial reef.

ON THE SAND

If it's beaches you're after, you've come to the right
place. From Culebra to San Juan to Isla Mona, Puerto
Rico has some of the most beautiful beaches in the
world. And the winner is...**Playa Flamenco** (p. 302), Culebra's public beach. With an enormous crescent of
white sand, aquamarine water, and medium-sized
waves, Flamenco is everything a beach is meant to be.
Culebra's other beaches are equally stunning, if not
more so, but a bit more difficult to reach. Flamenco
may win for overall effect, but the area's most unbelievable water is found far offshore at distant **Isla Mona**
(p. 195). The many beaches of **Vieques** (p. 290) come in
a close third, and supposedly some of the best coastline on the eastern half of the island is still closed.
Back on the mainland, many of the best beaches are in
southwest Puerto Rico. **Balneario Boquerón** (p. 199),
Playa Bahía Sucia (p. 204), **El Combate** (p. 203), and **Playa
Santa** (p. 219) could all tempt you to extend your vacation a bit longer. Luquillo's **Balneario Monserrate** (p.
251) receives a lot of public acclaim, much of it
deserved, but it must share the spotlight with fellow
north coast all-star beaches **Balneario Seven Seas** (p.
256), **Balneario Cerro Gordo** (p. 157), and **Balneario
Puerto Nuevo** (p. 162). In terms of aesthetics alone, the
dramatic coastline of northwest Puerto Rico is incomparable, although the rough waves in the area make it
difficult to swim. Almost any coastline drive will reveal
spectacular beaches, but some easily accessible areas
include **Playa Jobos** (p. 172), in Isabela, **Bosque Estatal
de Piñones** (p. 146), near San Juan, and **Las Ruínas** (p.
176), near Aguadilla. And, of course, if you're looking
for one of the best metropolitan beaches in the world,
the coastline around **San Juan** (p. 134) cannot be beat.

IN DA CLUB

It's no surprise that the song "Livin' La Vida Loca"
was created by a Puerto Rican. This island knows
how to party—on Friday and Saturday nights San
Juan's nightlife scene competes with the best in the
world. Traffic slows to a crawl as thousands of hip,
young *sanjuaneros* prowl the streets for the biggest and best party. **Old San Juan** (p. 140), and Calle
San Sebastian in particular, is without a doubt the
hippest scene on the island. If it's big clubs that
you're after, **Santurce** (p. 142) and **Isla Verde** (p. 143)
offer anything and everything: salsa, reggae, pop,
gay, straight, ritzy, and low-key. But San Juan is not

NO WORK, ALL PLAY

TOP 10 FESTIVALS

Puerto Rico has so many festivals
that it can be hard to keep track of
them all. To facilitate your planning, *Let's Go* lists the best below.

**1. Festival San Juan Bautista, San
Juan** (p. 138). Not surprisingly, San
Juan's patron saint festival is the big-
gest and best on the island.

**2. Festival de Santiago Apostle,
Loíza** (p. 148). This patron saint festival features *vejigante* masks (colorful masks with horns) and live
bomba music.

**3. Festival de la Calle San
Sebastian, San Juan** (p. 138).
It's an artisan festival, but many
consider this to be the island's
biggest street party.

**4. Festival de las Flores, Aibo-
nito** (p. 267). Flowers line the
streets in one of the world's most
beautiful harvest festivals.

5. Carnaval, Ponce (p. 230). This
pre-Lent party offers parades, *vejigantes*, and a hoppin' good time.

**6. Festival de las Máscaras,
Hatillo** (p. 168). It may be Puerto
Rico's third-best mask event, but
Hatillo's festival is still a party you
have to see to believe.

**7. Bacardi Feria de Artesanía, Cat-
año** (p. 139). This giant artisan festival features more than just rum.

8. Casals Festival, San Juan. (p.
139). This celebration of classical
music festival proves that festivals
can be more than just parties.

9. Fiesta del Café, Maricao (p.
277). Coffee-lovers will be the first
to arrive at this bean-filled party.

**10. Festival de Platos Típicos,
Luquillo** (p. 252). For all the fried
plantains you can eat, check out
Luquillo's festival of typical dishes.

the be all and end all of Puerto Rico's nightlife. **Ponce** (p. 220) has a lively bar scene and one of the best gay clubs on the island. During the surf season, **Rincón** (p. 178) and **Playa Jobos** (p. 170) host a good party any night of the week. University students liven things up in **Mayagüez** (p. 187), but on weekend nights they head to the coastal towns of **La Parguera** (p. 209) and **Boquerón** (p. 199). Puerto Rico has plenty of places to party, but keep in mind that Vieques and Culebra have almost zero nightlife scene.

ON THE EDGE OF YOUR SEAT

Find San Juan a bit tame? Is Vieques too "laid-back" for your vacation? Never fear, Puerto Rico has some first-rate adventures that offer an all-natural adrenaline rush. Start your engines and head to Arecibo's **Camuy Caves** (p. 166), the world's third-largest underground cave system. The faint-of-heart may take the guided tour, but several tour operators lead more rugged explorations, complete with spelunking, rappelling, rafting, and hiking. For adventure of an entirely different nature, arrange a trip out to the natural paradise of **Isla Mona** (p. 195), where enormous iguanas and hordes of hermit crabs greet every visitor. Navigating the rugged terrain of Puerto Rico's **Rúta Panorámica** (p. 261) may require some crafty driving skills, but the panoramic views, ample hiking, and numerous lakes provide more than enough reward. Speaking of driving, the greatest adventure of all may just be navigating the wild streets of **San Juan**.

▨ LET'S GO PICKS

BEST PLACE TO SALSA THE NIGHT AWAY: San Juan's glitzy clubs, especially Habana Club and Rumba (p. 140).

BEST PLACE TO BE AWE-INSPIRED BY NATURE: The peak of **Cerro de Punta** (p. 271), where you stand above the clouds; **Isla Mona** (p. 195) where animals still rule the roost; and **Cabo Rojo Lighthouse** (p. 204), where earth meets land in the most dramatic way possible.

BEST PLACE TO PLAY BALL WITH THE TAÍNOS: Utuado's **Parque Indígena Caguana** (p. 275) has a host of *batey* fields. Ponce's **Parque Indígena Tibes** (p. 234) has even more, but they actually originate with pre-Taínos. Jayuya's **Museo El Cemí** (p. 273) comes in a distant third.

BEST PLACE TO SEE MACHO PUERTO RICAN MALES WEAR DRESSES: Ponce's carnaval (p. 230), where masculinity takes a backseat to tradition.

BEST PLACE TO FORGET YOU'RE IN PUERTO RICO: San Juan's **Ocean Park** (p. 91), an American suburb if there ever was one. **Culebra** (p. 294), **Vieques** (p. 278), and **Rincón** (p. 178), where the American to Puerto Rican ratio is seriously skewed.

BEST PLACE TO HAVE A CAR ACCIDENT: Hwy. 3 (p. 94), the highly congested road that connects San Juan to Fajardo. Or perhaps Hwy. 2...or maybe Hwy. 52...

BEST PLACE TO FIND A VALENTINES DAY PRESENT: Aibonito's **Flower Festival** (p. 267), where countless bouquets of flowers fill the town every June.

BEST SUNSETS: The lighthouse at Rincón (p. 178), the coastline of Boquerón (p. 199), or, if you're in the mood for adventure, Playa Sardinera on Isla Mona (p. 195).

BEST PLACE TO WALK AMONG THE MANGROVES: Fajardo's **Las Cabezas de San Juan Nature Reserve** (p. 256), a guided tour over the mucky water; Aguirre's **Bahía de Jobos** (p. 236), the best place for independent exploration; and **Bosque Estatal de Boquerón** (p. 202).

BEST PLACE TO GET SLOSHED: San Juan's **Festival de la Calle San Sebastian** (p. 138), where the drinking never seems to stop.

BEST CARIBBEAN ISLAND: Puerto Rico, of course. As if you had to ask.

SUGGESTED ITINERARIES

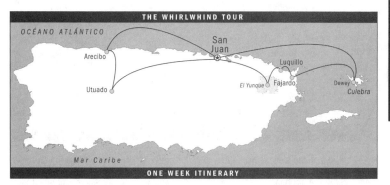

THE WHIRLWHIND TOUR

OCÉANO ATLÁNTICO

San Juan

Arecibo

Luquillo

Utuado

El Yunque   Fajardo

Dewey
Culebra

Mar Caribe

ONE WEEK ITINERARY

DISCOVER

THE WHIRLWIND TOUR (1 WEEK).
One week? Is that all the time you have? Well you better get started. Try to get an early morning flight, then spend the afternoon at a San Juan beach in **Condado, Ocean Park,** or **Isla Verde** (1 day; p. 134). If you arrived on a weekend, you're lucky: don't miss San Juan's incredible nightlife scene (p. 140). But don't stay out too late, because the next day you need to cover the sights and museums of **Old San Juan** (1 day; p. 123). For the next couple of days you'll need to rent a car. Wake up early and venture west for a daytrip to Arecibo's famous sights: the **Camuy Caves** and the **world's largest radio telescope** (1 day; p. 165). On the way home, stop by Utuado's **Parque Indígena Caguana** (p. 275). The next day it's time to say good-bye to San Juan (at least temporarily) and travel east, spending the morning at the only tropical rain forest in the US, **El Yunque** (½ day; p. 243). Don't miss the hike down to La Mina Falls. For an after-

noon of fun in the sun, stop by **Luquillo's** famous public beach (½ day; p. 251), before continuing east to Fajardo and a nighttime expedition through the magical **bioluminescent bay** (p. 258). It's been a busy four days, but you can't come to Puerto Rico without relaxing on the beach, so go straight to the best—**Culebra** (3 days; p. 294). Yes, Culebra is captivating, but don't forget to leave enough time to get back to San Juan and fly home.

PUERTO RICO ON PUBLIC TRANS-PORTATION (2 WEEKS). Some people say it's impossible, but traveling Puerto Rico on public transportation will give you a much more local perspective and save barrels of money. With a bit of persistence (and private taxi fees) you can get almost anywhere. This itinerary highlights the easiest destinations to research on *públicos* alone. Ninety-nine percent of visitors arrive at the airport in **San Juan** (3 days; p. 88), undoubtedly the most public transporta-

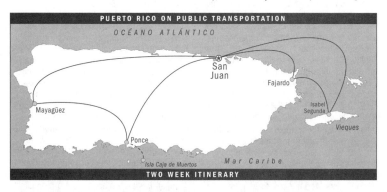

PUERTO RICO ON PUBLIC TRANSPORTATION

OCÉANO ATLÁNTICO

San Juan

Fajardo

Mayagüez

Isabel Segunda

Vieques

Ponce

Isla Caja de Muertos   Mar Caribe

TWO WEEK ITINERARY

tion-friendly city on the island. It will be easy to spend three days exploring the city; reserve one day for **Old San Juan,** don't miss the new art museum in **Santurce,** and, if you're really adventurous, check out the botanical gardens and market in **Río Piedras.** The next day is primarily a transport day, as the *público* to **Mayagüez** (2 days, p. 187) takes about 4hr. Once you make it to the unofficial capital of the west coast enjoy the island's largest zoo, more botanical gardens, and some of Puerto Rico's cheapest hotels. Next stop: **Ponce** (3 days; p. 220), the gem of the south. If you have time between navigating the turn-of-the-century streets and countless museums, journey out to **Isla Caja de Muertos** (p. 233), Puerto Rico's own Coffin Island. Get an early start on the next leg of the trip, as you'll take a *público* from Ponce to San Juan, then from San Juan to Fajardo. Before heading to **Fajardo** (2 days; p. 252), make a reservation to see Las Cabezas de San Juan, a nature reserve encompassing seven different ecosystems. You can visit the bioluminescent bay here or you can wait for your next stop: **Vieques** (3 days; p. 278), home to one of the best bio bays in the world. The off-shore island is also home to some of Puerto Rico's best beaches, and your last three days may be your best. Stay in Esperanza and transportation should never be an issue. Finally, take a ferry back to Fajardo where you can find a *público* to San Juan. Don't forget to tell you friends how much money you saved.

THE BEST OF PUERTO RICO (5 WEEKS).
Welcome to Puerto Rico; get ready to have a blast. The journey begins in **San Juan** (4 days; p. 88), one of the most exciting cities in the Caribbean. Take some time to wander the streets of Old San Juan, discover the museums of Santurce, and explore the market area of Río Piedras. And if you're looking for Latin-

flavored nightlife, it doesn't get much better than this. Then it's time to rent a car and venture west for the beginning of your island tour. Get an early start because it takes almost 2hr. to get to **Arecibo** (1 day; p. 163) and you'll want plenty of time to enjoy the world's largest radio telescope and the world's third-largest underground cave system. Then hop back in the car and enjoy the karstic scenery en route to **Bosque Estatal de Guajataca** (1 day; p. 173). It's easy to spend the day exploring the forest's cave and hiking the trail, but if you have extra time make a detour over to Lago de Guajataca. The next day continue the journey west to Playa Jobos in **Isabela** (2 days; p. 170). Finally, it's time to take a couple of days to relax and enjoy the spectacular northern coastline. If the surf bum lifestyle has you hooked, never fear; the next stop is Puerto Rico's premier surfing spot, **Rincón** (3 days; p. 178). Surfers may want to spend more time here. When you can tear yourself away, drive south to **Mayagüez** (1 days; p. 187) to explore nature of a more urban sense and mingle with the college crowd. Hopefully it's a weekend when you arrive in **Boquerón** (2 days; p. 199) and the town is partying in fine form. Even if it's not, the beach is still gorgeous. Stop by Puerto Rico's southwest corner to see the dramatic **Cabo Rojo Lighthouse** (1 day; p. 204) before continuing to **Bosque Estatal de Guánica** (2 days; p. 214). With hiking trails, water sports, and scenery galore, two days may not seem like enough. However, you need plenty of time in **Ponce** (2 days; p. 220), an urban center filled with southern charm. Get to know the city's rich history with a visit to **Parque Indígena Tibes** and **Hacienda Buena Vista** (1 day; p. 234); don't forget to reserve in advance. Skip past most of southeast Puerto Rico en route to **Rte. 901 Scenic Road** (1 day; p. 240), a superb place to rent a cute guest house room and indulge in succulent seafood dinners. Take a last look at the beach because you're about to head inland along the **Rúta Panorámica,** the scenic route traversing Puerto Rico's beautiful mountains. Pack a lunch because **Bosque Estatal Carite** (1 day; p. 261) has a great picnic area at Charco Azul. After a couple of hikes you'll have worked up an appetite for roast pork dinner at the famous *lechoneras.* **Barranquitas** (1 day; p. 267), the next stop on this cross-island path, is famous as the birthplace of Luís Muñoz Rivera, but its incredible mountain views are nothing to neglect. The views get even better as you brave the winding mountain roads en route to **Reserva Forestal Toro Negro** (1 day; p. 269), where you can ascend Puerto Rico's highest mountain. Time to leave the mountains and detour north for a visit to one of the island's best Taíno sites at **Utuado's Parque Indígena Caguana** (1 day; p. 275). The route may look a bit familiar as you spend one day traveling all the way east back to **El Yunque** (1 day; p. 243), Puerto Rico's tropical rain forest. **Fajardo** (1 day; p. 252) serves primarily as a departure point to the Spanish Virgin Islands, but it also contains one of the island's best nature reserves and a beautiful public beach. The trip is almost over and you haven't yet seen the highlight of Puerto Rico. Never fear. Hop on a ferry to **Vieques** (3 days; p. 278) for three days of exploring the jungle, the sights, and the beaches. Don't overdo the beach though, because practically perfect Playa Flamenco awaits on **Culebra** (3 days; p. 294). This island paradise is the ideal place to perfect your tan before heading home.

PUERTO RICO'S GREATEST NATURE RESERVES (2 WEEKS) Beaches,
shmeaches: Puerto Rico has some stunning inland scenery that easily makes a worth-

while destination all by itself. Escape the urban jungle of San Juan and head west to **Manatí** (1 day; p. 158), or rather, **Bosque Estatal de Cambalache.** If possible, bring a bike to try out one of the island's only mountain bike trails. Then don't miss an afternoon's worth of croc' hunting at **Laguna Tortuguero.** Avoid the congested Hwy. 2 and take the scenic drive through karst country en route to **Lago Dos Bocas** (1 day; p. 167), the perfect place to rent a kayak and enjoy the mountainside tranquility. Spend the next day at **Bosque Estatal de Guajataca** (1 day; p. 173), which has similar geography and a host of hiking trails. The topography changes completely as you travel south into the driest region of the island. Bird-watchers will love the salt flats and natural reserve along the **Cabo Rojo Scenic Drive** (1 day; p. 204). Puerto Rico's most spectacular natural area may be **Bosque Estatal de Guánica** (2 days; p. 214). Backtrack slightly to join up with the Rúta Panorámica and head to **Maricao** (1 day; p. 277), home of another forest and a peaceful fish hatchery. Take your time driving the windy roads to **Reserva Forestal Toro Negro** (2 days; p. 269). Located at the highest point of Puerto Rico, this forest reserve is completely different from Guánica, but almost as beautiful. For a true adventure, stop in Aibonito and get a guide to descend into **Cañón de San Cristóbal** (1 day; p. 265), Puerto Rico's very own Grand Canyon. The last stop in the Cordillera Central is **Bosque Estatal de Carite** (1 day; p. 261), preferably the Charco Azul area. You can't visit Puerto Rico's forests without going to the largest of them all—**El Yunque** (2 days; p. 243). Hiking to the peak of Puerto Rico's rainforest is a fitting end to a spectacular mountain trip.

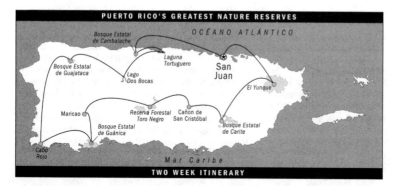

PUERTO RICO'S GREATEST NATURE RESERVES

OCÉANO ATLÁNTICO

Bosque Estatal de Cambalache

Laguna Tortuguero

San Juan

Bosque Estatal de Guajataca

Lago Dos Bocas

El Yunque

Maricao

Reserva Forestal Toro Negro

Cañón de San Cristóbal

Bosque Estatal de Guánica

Bosque Estatal de Carite

Cabo Rojo

Mar Caribe

TWO WEEK ITINERARY

LIFE & TIMES

THE GREAT OUTDOORS

LAND

Puerto Rico is located at the confluence of the Caribbean Sea and the Atlantic Ocean, 123 mi. southeast of Florida. The island serves as a barrier between the **Greater Antilles** to the east and the smaller islands of the **Lesser Antilles** to the west. At 3515 square miles, Puerto Rico is considered the smallest member of the Greater Antilles, which also include Cuba, Hispaniola (Haiti and the Dominican Republic), and Jamaica. Three sizable islands are also included in Puerto Rico's land area— Isla Mona to the west and Vieques and Culebra to the east. While the island only measures 100 mi. east to west and 35 mi. north to south, it does have a circumference of 311 mi. that becomes 700 mi. of coastline when all of the contours are accounted for—good news for visitors seeking sand and surf.

Three primary geographic regions cover Puerto Rico—the mountainous interior, the northern plateau (karst country), and the coastal plains. The first, dominated by the **Cordillera Central,** occupies 75% of the island's land area and includes Puerto Rico's highest peak, **Cerro de Punta** (1388m). With average temperatures 5-9°F colder than the coast, the mountainous interior is the coldest area on the island. Northern Puerto Rico is dominated by **karst country,** where water has dissolved limestone into a series of narrow canyons and deep **caves** (see p. 163). In this environment, the underground Río Camuy has created the third-largest system of subterranean caves in the world (see p. 166). The mountainous interior is surrounded by coastal plains, is the most fertile area of the island. Most agriculture (including sugar cane) was grown in this area; however, only 5% of the island is actually fertile and today less than 1% of the island's GDP comes from agriculture. Isla Mona, 50 mi. west of Puerto Rico, has an entirely different composition (see p. 195).

Puerto Rico contains over 1000 **streams** and 45 **rivers,** but they are all relatively small and unnavigable. The island does not have any significant natural lakes, but several rivers have been dammed to create artificial reservoirs. As a result of its strategic position at the mouth of the Caribbean, Puerto Rico has several shipping **ports;** San Juan (the 43rd busiest port in the US), Ponce, and Mayagüez are among the largest. Mona Passsage, the 80 mi. stretch of water between the Dominican Republic and Puerto Rico, is an important shipping lane to the Panama Canal.

CLIMATE AND HURRICANES

Ah, the weather in Puerto Rico; it's no surprise that many mainland US residents spend the winter here. The mild, tropical climate is pretty much perfect year-round. The record low is 40°F, but locals start grumbling when the temperature falls below 70°F. Even a north wind cold front in the winter, called a *nortes*, only drops the temperature to about 60°F. The temperature does differ slightly within the island; temperatures in the mountains usually hover about 3-5°F lower than temperatures on the coast. Northeastern trade winds drop all of the rain on the northern side of the island before clouds hit the mountains, thus leaving the south relatively arid and dry. Officially the dry season runs from December to March.

The much more important season to keep in mind is **hurricane season,** which officially runs from June 1 to November 30, but only poses a large threat from August to October. Hurricanes have plagued Puerto Rico throughout its history, destroying crops, causing floods, and taking lives. Statistically a hurricane brushes by San Juan every 3.85 years. Hurricane George, the worst storm in recent history, hit the island on September 21, 1998, causing almost $2 million in damage.

Temp. (°C/°F) Precipitation (mm)	January			April			July			October		
	°C	°F	mm	°C	°F	mm	°C	°F	mm	°C	°F	mm
Arecibo	23.8	74.8	120.7	24.7	76.5	14.8	26.9	80.4	111.8	26.5	79.7	142.8
Barranquitas	20.2	68.4	83.9	21.7	71.1	105.7	23.7	74.7	99.9	23.2	73.8	216.4
Fajardo	24.3	75.7	94.1	25.6	78.1	106.2	27.7	81.9	147.5	27.0	80.6	215.1
Mayagüez	23.8	74.8	56.7	24.9	76.8	141.5	26.5	79.7	261.3	26.2	79.2	255.9
Ponce	24.4	75.9	25.3	25.6	78.1	54.3	27.7	81.9	67.2	26.9	80.4	150.8
San Juan	25.0	77.0	75.3	26.3	79.3	94.9	28.1	82.6	4.5	27.7	81.9	139.9

FLORA & FAUNA

PLANTS

Due to environmental damage caused by industrialization, the vast majority of primary forest on Puerto Rico has been destroyed; however, much of it has been recultivated and **national reserves** now protect 90,000 acres of land. **El Yunque** (see p. 243) contains 75% of the island's scant virgin forest, including orchids, giant ferns, bamboo, and 240 species of trees. The reserve has both high altitude dwarf cloud forest and slightly lower altitude **rainforest,** consisting of sierra palms and epiphytes. Subtropical wet forest occurs at even lower elevations and, strangely, on mountains above 3000 feet. This vegetation, including open-crowned and canopy trees, can be found at Reserva Forestal Toro Negro (p. 269) and Bosque Estatal de Guilarte (p. 275). Found at an even lower elevation, subtropical moist forest is the most common type of vegetation on the island. Southwest Puerto Rico holds an entirely different dry forest, defined by low rainfall and arid vegetation, including bunch grass and many varieties of cacti. Although it's not indigenous, the brightly colored **flamboyán tree** is one of the most famous plants on the island. The flowering tree blooms from June to August at elevations below 2000 ft., especially along the Rúta Panorámica. Several types of **mangroves** grow on the calm waters around the southwest coast, the east coast, and Vieques.

ANIMALS

Don't come looking for lions, tigers, and bears—the most exciting animal in Puerto Rico is the **coquí,** a one-inch-long tree frog famous for its loud, distinct "ko-kee" call. Of the 16 species of coquí, 13 are endemic to Puerto Rico. The coquí is quite a tease—the first sound of the famous coquí call serves as a warning for other frogs to go away, but the second sound, the kee of male frogs, serves as an invitation for females to come reproduce. Puerto Ricans love their little mascot, and the coquí's image appears on merchandise throughout the island. The frogs themselves reside in any forest area.

Beyond that, most animals are birds and small, non-poisonous snakes. One bird of note, the **Puerto Rican parrot,** is among the 10 most endangered species in the world—the population once dropped as low as 14 parrots. Scientists have been working for 34 years to save the species, which initially suffered from deforestation, intense population growth, and humans who killed the parrots to protect their crops. Initial results have been moderately successful and in 2002 nine birds were released from captivity. Puerto Rican parrots, identifiable by their bright green body, red forehead, and blue wings, can be found in El Yunque.

Puerto Rico's most incredible wildlife is on small Isla Mona, 50 mi. west of the mainland. This uninhabited island has been referred to as the Galapagos of the Caribbean (see p. 195).

HISTORY

BEFORE THE SPANISH (PRE-1493)

AD 600
The Taínos, the first permanent inhabitants of Puerto Rico, refer to their island home as "Borinquén"

The first inhabitants of the area now known as Puerto Rico, the Arcaícos, came down through the Bering Straight, crossed North America, and settled around Loíza. They were soon followed by the Igneris people, who came up from Venezuela around AD 300 and inhabited the coastal areas. However, the Ostinoids soon replaced both of these tribes. By AD 1000, the Ostinoids on the island had evolved to become the **Taíno** civilization, the most influential group in the island's ancient history. Known for creating grinding tools and jewelry, these peaceful peoples lived in communities of 300-600 inhabitants, governed by one *cacique* (chief). The Taínos spent almost 500 years alone on the island, subsisting on domesticated tropical crops, when they were invaded by the more violent **Caribs** that came up from South America. These attacks sent many Taínos scrambling to the central mountains in retreat, but this turned out to be merely a precursor to the more lasting invasion to follow.

1300s
The violent Caribs land on Puerto Rico, threatening the Taínos' domination

POVERTY, DISEASE, AND ATTACK IN THE NEW WORLD (1493-1835)

1492
Christopher Columbus first sails the ocean blue

THE SEARCH FOR GOLD COMES TO THE RICH PORT. The face of Puerto Rico changed forever on November 19, 1493 when explorer **Christopher Columbus,** representing the government of Spain, landed on the island's western shore. Columbus was searching for gold and after dubbing the island "San Juan Bautista," he quickly moved on to find greater treasures on other islands. One man on this initial voyage, **Juan Ponce de León,** did not dismiss the island so quickly—he returned in July 1508 to search for gold and settle down. The Taínos, possibly looking for allies against their original foes, the Caribs, or possibly living up to their peaceful reputation, were relatively hospitable to Ponce de León and allowed him to explore the northern coast. Thus on August 12, 1508 the Spaniard established the first European settlement on the island, Caparra. By 1511 the settlement was renamed "Ciudad de Puerto Rico" and moved to the current site of San Juan.

1512
San Germán is founded as the second-oldest settlement in Puerto Rico

1515
Sugar cane is brought over from Hispaniola

This peaceful arrangement could not last forever. Under the auspices of the Repartimiento de Indos (Distribution of Indians) ordinance, Ponce de León instituted a system to control the native population by selecting an *hidalgo* to control each village, encouraging intermarriage between Europeans and Taínos, and converting the local population to Spanish Catholicism. This plan was intended to civilize the Taínos so they would not mind working as slaves for the Spaniards. However, the 30,000 Taínos were quite unhappy with the situation, which worsened when they began dying from smallpox, whooping cough, and other European diseases. In 1511 the Taínos joined with their former enemies, the Caribs, to rebel against the Spaniards but they could not hold up against the European pistols. Subsequent rebellions in 1513 and 1518 were equally unsuccessful, and by 1550 the few Native Americans who had not fled the island retreated to the central mountains.

FROM BAD TO WORSE. Meanwhile, the Europeans were dealing with the difficult reality of life on an undeveloped Caribbean island. They soon discovered that a settlement on a flat, swampy terrain was susceptible to both malaria-ridden mosquitoes and attacks. Thus they soon moved the capital to an island in front of a large, protected bay—this became known as **San Juan.** (In an unexplained mix-up, the capital city took the island's name and the island became "Puerto Rico," or "rich port.") As the native population dwindled, the Spanish had to find a new labor supply (they certainly wouldn't work the fields themselves), so they began importing West African slaves. The island was also plagued by persistent disease, unreliable crops, and hurricanes. Finally, the Spaniards realized that other European powers might attack the island in an attempt to disrupt Spanish trade. Preemptive construction on several **forts,** including **La Fortaleza** (p. 124), **El Morro** (p. 123), and **San Cristóbal** (p. 123), proved the islanders' foresight—the French raided San German in 1528, the English attacked in 1595, 1598, 1702, and 1703, and the Dutch attacked in 1625. Most of the attackers didn't get beyond the forts of San Juan; those with the ingenuity to attack other spots on the island were quickly conquered by island diseases.

LIFE IN THE FORTRESS. While the Spanish elite concentrated on keeping foreigners out, people actually living on the island focused on the much more practical concerns of colonial life. Suffering from a mercantile economy, islanders were supposed to trade only with the Spanish—they would send raw materials to Spain and receive finished goods in return. However, the Spanish placed heavy taxes on Puerto Rican goods and took profits for themselves while the islanders lived in poverty. To remedy the situation, islanders hidden from the watchful eye of the Spanish, outside of San Juan, began clandestine trade with other nations. By the 1760s the Spanish royalty got wind of this illegal trade and sent Irish-born Spaniard **Alejandro O'Reilly** to put an end to the practice. Upon arrival, O'Reilly found a population of 50,000 people (including 5000 slaves) and no government infrastructure. He quickly reformed the situation by lowering taxes, building roads and schools, encouraging urbanization, and developing the sugar cane industry. The changes were an immense success—within 50 years the population tripled and a Puerto Rican identity began to develop.

PUERTO RICO

1518
Portuguese and Dutch ships bring the slave trade to Puerto Rico

1533
The Spaniards begin constructing La Fortaleza to protect the island from invaders

1539
The Spaniards realize that they have made a major mistake constructing La Fortaleza too far inland and begin constructing El Morro— this time, in an appropriate place

1625
The Dutch lead the most successful attack on San Juan in history, burning the city before the Spanish turn them away

1635
A wall is built around San Juan to protect the city from invasion

1770
Puerto Rico has its first cockfight, starting a long tradition of rooster fighting

1791
A slave rebellion on Hispaniola sends shock waves to Puerto Rico

A REVOLUTIONARY WORLD. In the late 18th century the series of revolutions erupting around Latin America began to affect Puerto Rico. A 1791 slave rebellion on the neighboring island of Hispaniola caused foreign nations to turn to Puerto Rico for sugar and rum imports—this marked the beginning of the island's close relationship with the United States. Meanwhile waves of Latin American immigrants came to Puerto Rico in order to escape their own war-torn countries. By 1830 the population had jumped to 330,000 and Puerto Rico and Cuba were

1809
Puerto Rico finally gets a representative in the Spanish *Cortes*

the only two remaining Spanish colonies. The Spanish monarchy's fear of losing the islands, and their own tenuous position in Europe, prompted a series of reforms. In 1809 Puerto Rico was officially allowed to send a non-voting representative to the Spanish *Cortes*, and the abusive mercantilist system slowly came to an end as Spain cut tariffs and opened ports to foreign trade. Many white Spaniards migrated to the island and a significant agricultural industry developed, with large hacienda producing the cash-crops of **sugar cane, coffee**, and **tobacco.**

1835
For the first time Puerto Ricans lead a minor revolution against Spanish rule

FROM COLONY TO PROVINCE TO NATION TO COLONY (1835-1898)

REVOLUTIONARY PUERTO RICO. In spite of these preventative measures, a minor revolution erupted in 1835 and three years later native islander Buenaventura Quiñones was exiled for planning a second revolution. In the 1880s Ramón Emeterio Betances revived the independence movement, only to be exiled—twice. While Emeterio Betances continued his scheme

1868
The island's third "revolution" ends in a 1-month government

from nearby Santo Domingo, other Puerto Ricans initiated their own revolution in the town of Lares in September 1868. They declared a republic and elected a president, but people failed to join their plan and the "republic" died after a month and a half. Perhaps the most lasting contribution of the movement was the rallying cry "Viva Puerto Rico Libre!" which became the known as the **Grita de Lares** (Cry of Lares).

1873
Slavery is abolished in Puerto Rico

These revolutions failed, but changes came about nonetheless. In late September 1868 the Spanish military overthrew the monarchy and the next month a civil war broke out in Cuba. As a consequence of this turmoil, Madrid once again felt the call to improve the situation in Puerto Rico. Over the next 20 years Puerto Ricans were granted the rights to participate in the Spanish parliament, to form municipal councils, and to develop political parties. Moreover, the island finally achieved the status of a "province."

1881
A change in Spain's monarchy signifies the potential for change in Puerto Rico's status

A TEMPORARY VICTORY. In 1881 the election of the liberal **Práxedes Mateo Sagasta** as Prime Minister marked a new era in the Spanish government. Taking advantage of this opportunity, Puerto Rican **Luis Muñoz Rivera,** leader of the Autonomist Party, went to Madrid to politely ask for Puerto Rico's independence. Who knew that all they needed was someone to ask nicely? In 1897 Mateo Sagasta proclaimed Puerto Rico a self-governing, autonomous state. For the next year, Puerto Rico enjoyed its brief stint as an independent nation.

THE MISSING TRIANGLE The Caribbean has a legacy of exploiting slaves for mass agriculture production. However, Puerto Rico consistently maintained a much lower slave population than the other islands. The obvious question is, why did Puerto Rico stand out as such an anomaly? The island first started importing slaves from West Africa in 1518 to replace the departed indigenous population as agricultural laborers. By 1530 slaves constituted 50% of the island's population—but then again, that population was only 3000 people. As the white population increased, the black population failed to keep pace and the percentage of slaves hovered around 10-15%. However, on other islands, especially Jamaica and Hispaniola, African slaves grew to make up as much as 90% of the population. At its peak in 1845, Puerto Rico's slave population was 51,265—still less than 15% of the total population. What happened? Up until the 19th century Puerto Rico could not afford slaves—the island was extremely poor and lacked any significant cash crops, especially compared to its wealthy neighbor of Cuba. Consequently, on March 22, 1873 when slavery was finally abolished, there were only 31,700 African slaves on the island. Unlike most other Caribbean islands, Puerto Rico's strong African cultural heritage stems more from free blacks than slaves.

ENTER THE USA. Meanwhile, tensions were becoming heated in the rest of the Caribbean as the increasingly powerful US sought to protect its economic interests in the area. On February 15, 1898, the **US battleship Maine** mysteriously exploded in Havana's harbor. American journalists blamed the Spanish (although the accident remained a mystery and it was later suggested that the ship could have been blown up by war-hungry Americans) and public opinion persuaded President William McKinley to press for war. Under the pretense of freeing Cuba from colonialism, McKinley requested the immediate withdrawal of Spain from the island. On April 20, 1898 the US congress authorized the use of force in the Caribbean and the next day Spain declared war.

US troops attacked San Juan on May 12, 1898 with limited success, but within three months the Spanish forces surrendered in Cuba and the war was essentially over. When US troops landed at Guánica on July 25, the Spaniards barely put up a fight. Consequently, on December 10, 1898 Spain signed the **Treaty of Paris,** which granted Cuba independence and ceded Puerto Rico and Guam to the US. The war was over, but Puerto Rico was a colony once again.

SUGARVILLE, USA (1898-1942)

A ROCKY START. The first two years of American control were not particularly beneficial for either Puerto Rico or the US. Instead of creating a more sustainable economy, the US government sent military officials to govern the island, Protestant missionaries to convert the masses, and American corporations to take over the sugar and tobacco industries.

1897
Luis Muñoz Marín requests Puerto Rico's independence—and his wish is granted

April 1898
US congress authorizes the use of force in the Caribbean to "free Cuba from colonialism"

December 1898
After the US wins the Spanish-American war Puerto Rico once again becomes a colony

PUERTO RICO

1900
The US government
appoints Puerto
Rico's first
governor

Additional problems ensued when the Americans separated the Catholic church from the state, thus putting hundreds of priests and nuns out of work and necessitating a complete restructuring of the educational system. To make matters worse, a hurricane devastated crucial coffee crops in 1899. Americans did provide food for the hungry, import new vaccines, and build a network of roads on the island. But overall, the first two years of US occupation were not pretty.

1903
Universidad de
Puerto Rico is
founded

THE BOOM... This tenuous situation could not last, and in 1900 the US passed the **Foraker Act,** which formally established the island's civil government. Puerto Rico would have a governor, appointed by the US president, who would control a house of delegates (with elected representatives) and an upper legislature (with appointed officials). Residents of Puerto Rico would be taxed according to US laws, but they would not be considered American citizens. This was amended slightly with the 1917 **Jones Act,** which expanded the legislature to two houses, whose representatives would be elected by islanders. The Jones Act also finally gave Puerto Ricans American citizenship—coincidentally, this came right before they were eligible to be drafted for WWI.

1917-1919
20,000 Puerto
Ricans fight under
the US flag in
World War I

The economic situation was slightly more optimistic, as Puerto Rican industry was not taxed and the island could trade with the US without paying duties. As a result of this arrangement American investment increased and the Puerto Rican sugar industry boomed, leading to 30 years of relative property. The cigar, textile, coffee, and tobacco industries also expanded, but by 1920 75% of islanders depended on sugar for income. Wages rose, diseases decreased, education expanded, the government spent $50 billion on developing roads, and suddenly the population was increasing rapidly. Life on the island was great, but only a select few really reaped the benefits

1929
The Great
Depression sends
Puerto Rico's
economy crashing
to the ground

...AND THE BUST. Everything came crashing to an end as the 1930s approached. Devastating hurricanes in 1928 and 1932 ruined the consistent agricultural income, then the US Great Depression came rolling onto the island. Suddenly overpopulation became problematic as unemployment rose to 65%. Many Puerto Ricans attempted to solve their problems by migrating to the US. Others became increasingly dissatisfied with US control and joined the independence movement. The **Puerto Rican Nationalist Party (Partido Nacionalista Puertorriqueño; PNP),** headed by **Pedro Albizu Campos,** led protests declaring that Puerto Rico should be an independent nation. In 1936 the party was set back when four members were killed and others were jailed for murdering a chief of police, but the demonstrations continued. A year later, at the **Massacre de Ponce,** 19 people were killed at a PNP protest.

1932
Puerto Rican
women are granted
the right to vote

1934
The US passes a
law stating that
Puerto Rican sugar
production must
be cut in half

A more peaceful solution to the island's problems emerged in 1938 when **Luis Muñoz Marín** (grandson of revolutionary Luis Muñoz Riviera; see p. 12), founded the **Popular Democratic**

Party (Partido Popular Democrático; PPD). Marín was less concerned with the status of the island as a colony and more concerned with improving the quality of life for Puerto Ricans, especially the poor. This plan was well received; in 1940 the PPD won control of the legislature and Muñoz Marín became president of the senate. With this position he attempted to put an end to sugar monopolies and diversify the economy. The creation of the "Puerto Rican Development Company" was an attempt to create more public sector jobs. Though Muñoz Marín took the first steps toward reviving the economy, it would take a powerful outsider to finish the job.

OPERATION SAVE PUERTO RICO (1942-1999)

LET THE GOOD TIMES ROLL. In the early 1940s a few changes began to permanently alter Puerto Rico's position from "the poorhouse of the Caribbean" to a developed country. The first was that **Americans began to drink rum.** During WWII they couldn't get whiskey and suddenly rum became a major Puerto Rican export. The second, much more significant change, came when American President Franklin Delano Roosevelt (with input from Muñoz Marín and the PPD) realized that in order for Puerto Rico to be economically successful the island's economy would have to shift from agriculture to more lucrative manufacturing and tourism. This was the origin of **Operation Bootstrap,** the most successful economic revival campaign in the island's history. The American government encouraged US manufacturers to move their companies to Puerto Rico, where revenue was partially free from US income tax by **Section 963** of the US IRS code. Furthermore, Puerto Rico was promoted as a land of cheap labor. The program was overwhelmingly successful. By 1964 over 2000 American companies had relocated to Puerto Rico. The net income per capita rose from $121 in 1940 to $1900 in the early 1970s. Tourism boomed, especially after Cuba was closed to American tourists in 1961, and Puerto Rico was back in the fast lane.

OFFICIAL STATUS AT LAST. Political improvements soon followed. In 1948 the US offered the island a constitutional government that was approved by a 1951 vote, and in 1952 Puerto Rico became an official **commonwealth of the US.** As a commonwealth, Puerto Rico was similar to a US state, but residents could not vote in presidential elections, were not represented in Congress, and did not pay income taxes. Many Puerto Ricans, especially *independentistas* (supporters of independence), protested the island's new status. In 1951 these opponents attempted to assassinate both Muñoz Marín and US President Harry Truman. On the day the bill was signed, July 25, 1952, the *independentistas* opened fire on the governor's mansion in San Juan. Two years later, they

PUERTO RICO

1938
Luis Muñoz Marín founds the Popular Democratic Party, which later favors the commonwealth status

1939
The US Navy purchases 27,000 acres on Vieques, starting a long era of occupation

1940s
President Franklin Delano Roosevelt encourages economic development on Puerto Rico with Operation Bootstrap

1946
The US appoints the first native Puerto Rican governor, Jesus T. Piñero

1948
Puerto Rico participates in its first Olympic games with its own team

1952
Puerto Rico officially becomes a commonwealth of the US

1954
In the name of independence several Puerto Ricans open fire in the US House of Representatives

1967
For the first time Puerto Ricans are allowed to vote on their status—and the majority chooses a commonwealth

1970
The Conservation Trust of Puerto Rico is created to protect the island's natural resources

1971
The US Army takes over the majority of Culebra for training and testing purposes

1976
US IRS code Section 963 dictates that American companies operating on Puerto Rico do not have to pay taxes

1978
The police shoot and kill two young men accused of blowing up a TV tower in support of independence

started shooting in the US House of Representatives, reviving the old Cry of Lares as they shouted "Viva Puerto Rico Libre!" The attack wounded five American legislators.

The violence subsided, but this issue continued to dominate Puerto Rican politics as two parties alternated power. The **New Progressive Party (Partido Nuevo Progresista; PNP),** founded in 1968, advocated for statehood; the PPD supported the commonwealth; and a small but vocal minority continued to argue for independence. Responding to this controversy, in 1962 Muñoz Marín and US President John F. Kennedy worked together to create a "three-point program" that would first study the benefits of the three options, then allow Puerto Ricans to vote on the issue, and finally create two ad hoc committees to implement the results of the vote. After the study came to the indecisive conclusion that all three options were optimal, the issue was put to a vote in July 1967. With 65.8% voter turnout, 60.5% of Puerto Ricans supported commonwealth status, 38.9% wanted statehood, and 6% wanted independence. The status quo prevailed.

It's hardly surprising that islanders voted for the status quo, as the situation was quite favorable in the 1960s. "Operation Bootstrap" continued to support Puerto Rico's economy and education, literacy, life expectancy, and wages kept improving. Almost 100,000 people were visiting the island every year, and tourism was flourishing. The 1960s were a time of plenty.

THE SHIFTY SEVENTIES. Matters declined throughout the 1970s as the US recession increased the cost of imported fuels, raw materials, and consumer goods. Unemployment on the island was almost twice as high as it was on the mainland, reaching 25% in 1975. Meanwhile, the negative effects of "Operation Bootstrap" became apparent as people began to notice the environmental damage caused by excessive industrialization. As always, the faltering economy renewed interest in the Puerto Rican independence movement. In 1975 Governor Rafael Hernández Colón worked together with a US committee to create the **Bill to Approve the Compact of Permanent Union Between Puerto Rico and the United States,** which requested Puerto Rican control over immigration, the minimum wage, and environmental concerns; however, the bill was ignored when Gerald Ford, who supported statehood for the island, took over the presidency.

THE WATERGATE OF PUERTO RICO. Controversy wracked the island in 1978 when two alleged terrorists, both under 25 years old, were shot and killed by policemen on the mountaintop of **Cerro Maravilla** (see p. 271). The boys were attempting to blow up a television tower in support of independence, and in his 1980 reelection campaign, governor Carlos Romero Barceló said that the policemen who killed them were acting in self-defense and should be regarded as heroes. However, members of the opposing PPD reopened investigation in the issue and in 1983 it was discovered that the boys had already surrendered and were kneeling when the police shot them. Ten members of the Puerto Rican police force were convicted and, needless to say, Governor Romero Barceló was not reelected in 1984. However, many regard the crisis as a triumph of the Puerto Rican legal system.

ENVIRONMENTAL AND MILITARY CONCERNS. The economy improved slightly in 1978, but unemployment continued to be a pressing concern. Over 20% of the population was unemployed until 1986, when the figure finally dropped to 17%.

Environmental issues became prominent as the population continued to expand and industries continued to pollute. The new pharmaceutical, industrial, and thermoelectric plants were emitting hazardous chemicals into the air and sea, and Puerto Ricans realized that they had to do something about it. New organizations developed to combat these problems, such as the **Conservation Trust of Puerto Rico,** a non-profit created in 1970 to protect the island's natural resources.

But the foremost issue of the 1980s became the US military presence on the island. Puerto Rico's strategic position at the edge of the Greater Antilles and its proximity to the supposedly threatening island of Cuba made it the ideal position for the American military. The two most prominent bases have been the **Roosevelt Roads Naval Station,** located on the eastern coast, and the enormous naval base that occupies two-thirds of the island of **Vieques.** In 1984, 1500 Puerto Ricans marched in Washington, D.C. to protest these naval bases, but to no avail. Alarm grew throughout the 1980s as Puerto Ricans were particularly averse to the placement of nuclear weapons on the island. In 1986 US President Ronald Reagan declared his intention to begin training soldiers in El Yunque National Forest (p. 243) and Puerto Ricans were outraged. Although the governor dissuaded Reagan from his plan, Vieques and Roosevelt Roads continued to be controversial issues.

MORE VICTORIES FOR THE COMMONWEALTH. A 1993 plebiscite led by pro-statehood Governor Pedro Rosselló failed 48.4% to 46.2%, reaffirming that public opinion favored commonwealth status; however, the vote didn't have much political significance as the US Congress still had not agreed to allow Puerto Rico to become a state. In March 1998 the US House of Representatives narrowly passed a bill finally allowing Puerto Rico to have a federally authorized plebiscite. This indicated that if the advocates of statehood won, then Puerto Rico would actually be admitted into the Union. This victory revitalized Rosselló, who called for another plebiscite even after the Senate rejected the bill. Rosselló also led Puerto Ricans to believe that the US could revoke the commonwealth status at any time, and he created a four-choice ballot that did not include an option for maintaining the status quo. Anti-statehood Puerto Ricans protested and the pro-independence PNP and the pro-commonwealth PPD joined to create a **fifth column choice** for "none of the above." On December 13, 1998 almost 80% of the population turned up to vote and 51% chose this fifth column, demonstrating that Puerto Rico is not destined to become the 51st state any time soon.

1986
US President Ronald Reagan decides it's a good idea to train soldiers in El Yunque

1998
Puerto Rican independence suffers a resounding failure in yet another plebiscite

September 1998
Hurricane George devastates Puerto Rico, causing $2 billion in damage

1999
A stray naval bomb on Vieques accidentally kills civilian guard David Sanes

2000
48.8% of the island votes for Sila Calderón to be the first female governor of Puerto Rico.

2003
Calderón surprises the entire island by announcing that she will not run for reelection in 2004

PUERTO RICO

TODAY

Although the issue of statehood did not disappear, it has temporarily faded into the background. In 2000 Puerto Ricans elected the island's first female governor, **Sila Calderón**, who has focused on another pressing issue—the US military presence, especially on the island of Vieques. In April 1999 a bombing accident on the island accidentally killed a Puerto Rican security guard, prompting extensive protests. Thousands of protestors flooded the island and in June 2001 US President George W. Bush announced that the Navy would leave Vieques by May 2003. The Navy kept its end of the bargain, but then they also significantly downsized the Roosevelt Roads Navy Base, which dealt a tough blow to the island's economy. For more on both issues, see Vieques (p. 286) and Fajardo (p. 253).

Puerto Rico's general elections are scheduled for 2004, but the hoopla began well in advance. After declaring for months that she would run for reelection, Governor Sila Calderón shocked the island by changing her mind in May 2003 and leaving the field open to a wide variety of candidates. PNP president Carlos Pesquera and former Governor Pedro Rosselló started campaigning early to be the PNP gubernatorial choice. Meanwhile an unemployment rate hovering around 12.3% represents that Puerto Rico still has many domestic problems to solve as it looks toward the future.

ECONOMY

Puerto Rico is the secret economic success story of Latin America, all thanks to Operation Bootstrap. Within a time span of 60 years, Puerto Rico transformed from one of the poorest islands in the Caribbean, with a single-crop agricultural economy to one of the most prosperous, with a diversified industrial economy. The US is by far the island's largest trading partner and major exports include apparel, electronics, rum, and pharmaceuticals—Puerto Rico produces 50% of US pharmaceuticals. Today the $39 billion GDP breaks down as 54% services, 45% industry, and 1% agriculture. Increasing tourism has also played an important role in Puerto Rico's economic success.

But life on the island isn't all peachy. With a per capita GDP of $11,200, Puerto Rico remains much poorer than even the poorest US state. Unemployment continued to hover around 12% throughout 2002, almost three times as high as the mainland. So while Puerto Ricans certainly have nothing to complain about in comparison to some of the Greater Antilles, it's not easy being the underdeveloped cousin of the US.

GOVERNMENT

On July 25, 1952 Puerto Rico officially became a commonwealth of the United States. Ever since that day people have been asking, "what does this mean?" In many ways Puerto Rico resembles a state—the national American government handles foreign relations, defense, the postal service, and customs; Puerto Ricans are US citizens who are eligible for the draft; and the commonwealth is led by a governor who is popularly elected to a four-year term. Like the US, the Puerto Rican government is divided into executive, legislative, and judicial branches, with the governor choosing a cabinet and the judicial branch consisting of a supreme court and superior courts. However, some crucial differences fuel the intense debate over potential statehood. Like a state Puerto Rico sends a representative to the US House of Representatives, but a commonwealth representative cannot vote (until 2004 the seat was held by Anibal Acevedo Vila of

THE PPS OF PR When conversing with locals, knowledge of the Puerto Rican political parties will quickly prove that you're the most educated tourist around. And it ain't that hard:

New Progressive Party (Partido Nuevo Progresista; PNP). Endorses statehood.

Popular Democratic Party (Partido Popular Democrático; PPD). Supports commonwealth status.

Puerto Rican National Party (Partido Nacionalista Puertorriqueño; PNP). Endorses independence.

the PPD). While Puerto Ricans are citizens, they cannot vote in the US presidential elections and they don't have to pay federal taxes. It is these discrepancies that promote the constant debates over the island's status.

Additional aspects of Puerto Rico's government differ from a US state more in details and name than in functionality. The legislative branch of the government consists of two houses elected to four-year terms on the same cycle as the governor. Twenty-seven senators—two from each of eight districts and 11 at-large—and 51 representatives—one from each of 40 representative districts and 11 at-large—are elected every four years on the same cycle as the governor and constitute the legislative branch of the government. In an interesting quirk, at least one-third of the legislators must be from the minority party and if that does not happen, the houses are enlarged to make space for more representatives. Until November 2004 **the PNP controlled both houses of the legislature.** On a more local level, the island is divided into 78 municipalities, each with a mayor and an assembly.

PEOPLE

DEMOGRAPHICS

Like most Latin Americans, Puerto Ricans are an ethnic mix of their Spanish, African, and Native American ancestors. Today 80.5% of islanders classify themselves as white (of primarily Spanish origin), 8% as black, 0.4% as Indian, and the remaining 10.4% as mixed or other. However, almost everyone on the island has a darker complexion and dark hair, regardless of their self-classification. The African heritage is most prominent on the coast, especially the town of Loíza, and people of Indian ancestry remain predominantly in the central mountains, but racial discrimination is surprisingly limited.

Puerto Rico's population is defined less by ethnicity and more by abundance—the island is one of the most overpopulated regions in the world. The problem began in the early 19th century, when many Latin Americans immigrated to Puerto Rico in order to escape the revolutions in their own countries. They quickly found that Puerto Rico wasn't a bad place to live and stuck around for awhile. A high birth rate further aggravated the problem up until the mid-20th century. After the beginning of Operation Bootstrap the birth rate began to decline, but the death rate also declined and life expectancy rose accordingly. Furthermore, as Puerto Rico became relatively prosperous, residents of neighboring islands Cuba and Hispaniola began immigrating in floods. The resulting population of 3,957,988 on an island only three times as large as Rhode Island caused a staggering population density of 1780 persons per square mile. Luckily, the annual growth rate has finally fallen to 0.54% and the population seems to be leveling out.

PUERTO RICO

THE MOST BEAUTIFUL WOMEN IN THE

WORLD Do we have your attention yet? Like many Latin American countries, Puerto Rico hosts a plethora of beauty pageants and the island prides itself on having some of the most beautiful females in the world. Almost every major island festival elects some sort of queen or princess, from the Recycling Queen (who wears a gown made of recycled materials) to the more traditional Carnaval Princess. The crème de la crème go on to represent Puerto Rico in the annual **Miss Universe** pageant (Puerto Rico has a separate nominee from the US), where the island has had incredible success. Since the contest began in 1952 Miss Puerto Rico has won four times, an accomplishment surpassed only by the US (Miss Venezuela has also won four times). Islanders take great pride in the Boricuan beauties, who become a sort of island hero (see **A Match Made in San Juan,** p. 124). According to a survey in a popular Latin American women's magazine, 62% of people in Puerto Rico watch beauty pageants, more than any other country in the world. Clearly it's more than the nature that makes Puerto Rico the "Island of Enchantment."

Operation Bootstrap also caused Puerto Ricans to move to the cities, and today 71% of the population lives in urban areas, with almost one third in the greater San Juan area. In addition to the island population, currently almost three million Puerto Ricans live in the US, with at least one third in New York City.

LANGUAGE

Spanish and English are both official languages of Puerto Rico, but the vast majority of islanders take pride in their hispanic culture and prefer to speak Spanish. Spanish is also the official language of education, and students learn English as a foreign language. In San Juan almost everyone speaks English. It is polite for visitors who speak some Spanish to initiate conversations in that language, but many Puerto Ricans will answer in English. English continues to be much less common in rural areas of the island. However, almost everyone in the tourist industry speaks English—non-Spanish speakers should not have problems getting around.

The issue of language plays an important role in Puerto Rico's relationship with the US, as many Puerto Ricans oppose statehood because they do not want to sacrifice their Spanish-based culture. In 1991, when statehood again dominated the headlines, the Puerto Rican government officially abolished English as an official language in an attempt to prevent US cultural domination. The legislature revoked this policy two years later, but only after making a strong statement that Spanish is in Puerto Rico to stay.

RELIGION

Forty percent of Puerto Ricans retain their Spanish roots and practice Roman Catholicism. An equal number identify themselves as Protestant, though most major religions are represented on the island. As a commonwealth of the United States, Puerto Rico maintains a strict separation of church and state. **Santeria,** a blend of Catholicism and the religion of the Yoruba people who were brought to the Caribbean as slaves from Nigeria, continues to play a role in the island's African community. The juxtaposition first emerged in the slavery era when Africans continued practicing their own religions but substituted the names of Catholic saints to appease their masters. Practitioners of santeria generally worship a hierarchy of saints and believe that it is possible to divine the future. Over time, this form of religious worship has become increasingly accepted on the island.

CULTURE

FOOD

The wealth and diversity of restaurants in Puerto Rico, and especially San Juan, make it easy to visit the island without ever sampling regional cuisine. Don't make that mistake. Though similar to many other Latin American cuisines, Puerto Rican food (**comida criolla** or **cocina criolla**) offers a unique blend of spices and tastes that can satiate any palate. American cuisine, particularly fast food, has invaded the island in full force, and many locals have replaced traditional foods with Whoppers and Big Macs.

MAIN DISHES. The Puerto Rican day starts with **breakfast,** a casual meal enjoyed before work frequently in a local *cafetería.* For many locals, breakfast consists of a cup of hot *café con leche* (coffee with milk) and *tostadas* (toasted *pan de agua* with butter). Most restaurants also serve a larger American breakfast, including *huevos fritos* (fried eggs), *huevos revueltos con jamón* (scrambled eggs with ham), *tocineta* (bacon), *harina de avena* (oatmeal), *tostadas francesas* (french toast), *panqueques* (pancakes), and, from Spain, *tortillas españolas* (Spanish omelets; a mix of eggs, potatoes, and onions). Unlike Americans, Puerto Ricans also enjoy a good sandwich for breakfast. Sandwiches with *jamón, queso, y huevo* (ham, cheese, and egg) are popular, but so is just about every other type of sandwich; there's nothing like roast beef to start the day.

Sandwiches make a reappearance for lunch and this is one of the cheapest ways to fill up. Puerto Rican sandwiches are typically served on **pan de agua,** a fresh, tasty local version of French bread, and made with some kind of meat, cheese, lettuce, tomato, and mayonnaise or butter, then grilled in a press and served hot. Local favorites are the **cubano** and the **media noche,** two sandwiches made with roasted pork, *pepinillas,* ham, and swiss cheese. The difference is that a *cubano* is served on Cuban bread and the *media noche* on sweet bread. Other popular sandwiches include: *pollo* (chicken), *pavo* (turkey), *atún* (tuna), *pernil* (pork), and *bistec* (beef). The local fast-food chain **El Mesón Sandwiches,** based in Aguadilla, makes terrific sandwiches and has a couple vegetarian options.

Most Puerto Ricans head to a *cafetería* or an American fast-food restaurant for a quick lunch on the go. A **traditional lunch** includes a heaping pile of rice, either *arroz blanco* (white rice) by itself, or served with *grandules* (pigeon peas) or *garbanzos* (chick peas). Sometimes the rice comes mixed with *habichuelas rosadas* (red beans), other times the beans are served on the side. Next step is the meat; some common options include: *biftec encebollado* (strips of beef with onions), *chuletas fritas* (fried pork chops), *pollo frito* (fried chicken), *pechuga de pollo* (chicken breast), *biftec empanado* (breaded Spanish steak), *churrasco* (yet another type of breaded beef), and various types of *pescado frito* (fried seafood). Finally, add either *tostones* (dry, fried plantains; good with salt) or *amarillos* (fried sweet plantains) and a small *ensalada verde* (iceberg lettuce with tomatoes and Thousand Island dressing) to complete the meal.

Dinner tends to be a more formal affair eaten at home with the family, and smaller towns may not have any restaurants open late at night except fast food. More formal Puerto Rican restaurants tend to offer meals similar to those served at lunch with a few additional options. You can't leave Puerto Rico without trying the famous **mofongo,** mashed plantain served with meat or fish inside. This traditional dish has been referred to as "the poor man's food" (despite the fact that it can be quite pricey) and one serving will leave you stuffed for days. For less daring entrees, sample the relatively tame chicken options, such as *pechuga rellena* (chicken breast filled with ham and cheese). **Soups** are another popular option, and many are hearty enough to serve as a meal in themselves. *Asopao* is a thick stew served with either fish or chicken and occasionally pigeon peas. *Soncocho* is a salty, slightly thinner fish soup. Watch out for less traditional options such as *sopón de garbanzos con patas de cerdo* (chick pea soup with pig feet). During the **Christmas season** (Dec.) Puerto Ricans like to feast on *lechón asado* (pork roasted over an open flame) and *cuerito* (pork rind). Nothing says "Merry Christmas!" like roasted pork.

Puerto Ricans also love their **seafood,** though it's surprisingly expensive given that the island is surrounded by water. The unofficial national fish is *chillo* (red snapper), served in most nice restaurants as a whole fish, head and all. On the coast you will find a plethora of seafood restaurants serving the gamut of options, including *camarones* (shrimp), *carrucho* (conch), *pulpo* (octopus), *chapin* (trunk fish), *cangrejo* or *juey* (crab), and of course, *langosta* (lobster).

A few popular **spices** dominate Puerto Rican cuisine. The basic flavoring of most stews and soups is *sofrito*, olive oil seasoned with sweet chili peppers, onions, bell peppers, tomatoes, cilantro, oregano, and garlic. Meat dishes are typically marinated with the more simplified *adobo*, a mixture of vinegar, oil, black pepper, oregano, salt, and garlic. Many cooks also add a bit of *achiote*, a cooking oil made out of annatto seeds, to give the food a slight orange tint.

Vegetarians, especially those who do not eat fish, will have a hard time sampling local cuisine. Most beans are cooked with pork, many dishes are fried in lard, and almost everything comes with meat inside. There are **vegetarian cafeterías** in most big cities, but these typically only stay open for lunch. Puerto Rican restaurants can usually conjure up some type of vegetarian option, but be prepared for lots of plain *mofongo* and frozen vegetable medley. Restaurants that cater to tourists will typically have at least one vegetarian option. Good luck!

SNACKS. Mmm, fried food. Puerto Rico is not the place to travel if you want to lose weight, as it's hard to resist the delectable **fried snacks.** Small roadside stands, food kiosks, and some restaurants sell *empanadillas*, fried fritters filled with various types of meat, seafood, or cheese. For even more calories, try an *alcapuria*, fried plantains stuffed with beef or pork, or a *pinono*, a fried plantain wrapped around ground beef. *Bacalaítos*, flat, fried fritters with a bit of codfish flavoring, taste much better than they sound. To round out the fried family, *sorullitos de maíz* are fried sticks of ground corn that taste a bit like fried corn bread. Puerto Ricans go crazy for *pinchos*, hunks of meat barbecued on a stick like a kebab.

A couple of popular **frozen snacks** provide a great way to cool off during the day. Street vendors, mostly in big cities, sell *piraguas*, shaved ice with flavored syrup on top. Private individuals put up signs advertising the sale of *limbers*, frozen fruit juice. Puerto Ricans also enjoy their **pastries,** and at any *repostería* you'll find *quesitos* (long pastries filled with white cheese) and *pan mallorca* (sweet bread). These tasty treats can be eaten for breakfast, dessert, or just a snack.

DESSERT. Don't skip dessert. Puerto Rico utilizes its Latin heritage and its profundity of fresh fruits to create some delicious post-meal treats. The most common dessert is the popular *flan* (egg custard) served plain or with coconut or vanilla flavoring. Another dessert common throughout Latin America is *tres leches*, a sweet cake covered with condensed milk sauce. The **fruit** in Puerto Rico is so tasty that it is often served for dessert; look for *guayaba con queso* (guava with cheese). Puerto Ricans also serve a variety of fruit-flavored *helado*, a smooth **ice cream** that resembles Italian *gelato*. During Christmas season everyone serves *tembleque* (a gelatinous coconut milk pudding), although the dessert is available year-round. Finally, Puerto Ricans make their own style of *arroz con dulce*, sweet rice pudding frequently made with a coconut flavoring.

EATERIES. The cheapest place to dine is at one of the many **panaderías y reposterías** (bakery and pastry shops), found throughout the island. In addition to fresh bread and a variety of baked goods, these small shops usually serve sandwiches and some breakfast foods. The local eateries generally have long hours (typically open daily 7am-9pm), but rarely have English menus, and many are so small that they don't have tables. Another cheap, local option is the ubiquitous **cafetería,** found even in Old San Juan. At some *cafeterías,* those open for lunch only, you order from the glass counter filled with steaming hot entrees. Those open for dinner and breakfast as well are typically informal sit-down restaurants, but many have a $5-6 lunch special. The only type of international restaurant commonly found outside of San Juan (apart from generic American food and pizza) is Chinese food; however, most Puerto Rican Chinese restaurants serve more fried chicken than chow mein. Formal, sit-down restaurants are the most expensive option; even outside of San Juan it's hard to find an entree for less than $12. The Puerto Rican Tourism Company has recognized many of the best *comida criolla* restaurants around the island as **mesones gastronómicos.** These fancy eateries are a great place to splurge on a quality Puerto Rican meal; many are located in *paradores,* but check *Que Pasa* (see p. 78) for a complete list.

RUM

AND (SOMETIMES) OTHER BEVERAGES. Rum is more than a drink in Puerto Rico, it's part of being Puerto Rican. In the early 20th century Puerto Rico's thriving sugar industry produced truckloads of rum, and though the sugar industry has fallen, the rum industry continues to thrive (with sugar cane imported primarily from the Dominican Republic). Today, Puerto Rico produces three primary brands of rum: **Bacardi, DonQ,** and **Palo Viejo.** Bacardi has been based in Puerto Rico since the 1961 Cuban Revolution and continues to be the world's best-selling rum. However, Puerto Ricans prefer Don Q, which is still produced near Ponce at the Serallés Distillery. Real rum connoisseurs declare that Palo Viejo is the best Puerto Rican rum, but it is not as widespread. Since Governor Calderón took office a series of **alcohol taxes** have considerably raised the price of drinking, but that doesn't seem to stop anyone. The perennial bar favorite is the **Cuba libre,** commonly known as a rum and coke. And, of course, Puerto Rico is the birthplace of the **piña colada,** a blended mix of rum, pineapple juice, and coconut juice. During the Christmas season locals make **coquitos,** a mix of eggnog and rum named after the island's favorite frog.

ON THE MENU

YOHOHO AND A BOTTLE OF RUM

A positive attitude and a bottle of spirits are about all you need to have a good time in Puerto Rico. From classics to curious concoctions, the following rum recipes ensure that you enjoy your Puerto Rican vacation:

Piña Colada. This Puerto Rican favorite, invented on the island, mixes $1\frac{1}{2}$ oz. white rum, 1 oz. coconut cream, 2 oz. pineapple juice, and ice. Blend, then throw on a pineapple and a cherry for garnish.

Coquito. The island's favorite Christmas spirit makes an excellent drink year-round. For a full batch, mix 28 oz. coconut milk, 14 oz. condensed milk, 2 egg yolks, and 2 cups of Bacardi rum. Blend and drink.

Puerto Rican Sunrise. This Puerto Rican twist on the popular tequila sunrise is refreshingly easy to make: mix white rum, grenadine, orange juice, and stir. For a tropical twist, replace orange juice with passion fruit juice.

Fuzzy Pirate. Though it's not quite as well known as other beverages, the fuzzy pirate is a fruity tropical drink. Plus it's fun to order at a bar. Just take 1 oz. of peach schnapps, 5 oz. cranberry juice, 1 oz. of spiced rum, and add a dash of orange curacao. Serve over ice.

Cuba Libre. The name may be Cuban, but this common drink is extremely popular on the island of enchantment. Plus, it's one of the easiest mixed drinks to make—just mix rum and coke, and add a lemon. The quantities are up to your discretion. Drink responsibly and have fun!

But you can't survive on rum alone; sometimes Puerto Ricans drink **beer** as well. The locally produced **Medalla,** a light beer, is the cheapest and most authentic option, although Puerto Ricans drink many imports as well. When it's too early for alcohol, Puerto Ricans enjoy their **café con leche,** coffee served with a lot of milk and sugar. Although coffee production has decreased significantly over the last 50 years, the towns of Yauco and Maricao are still known for their fine brews. Another popular beverage is **mavi,** a fermented drink made from the bark of a mavi tree and frequently served out of a large barrel. Finally, Malta India, the producers of Medalla, also produce a popular local soft drink aptly called **Malta India.**

CUSTOMS & ETIQUETTE

Though many Puerto Ricans have spent time in the US, most retain a more Latin American sense of customs and etiquette. Puerto Ricans are generally very polite and friendly to travelers who treat them with similar respect. Most Puerto Ricans are very conscious of the discrimination that fellow islanders have been subjected to upon moving to the States and consequently go out of their way to welcome foreigners.

GREETINGS. The common greetings in Puerto Rico are *buenos días* (good morning; used anytime before lunch), *buenas tardes* (good afternoon; before dinner), and *buenas noches* (good night; used after dinner). It is polite to begin every conversation, in a personal or professional setting, with these phrases. Female friends often greet each other with a peck on the cheek or a quick hug. Sometimes men shake hands with women in a business situation, but the standard greeting between a man and a woman is a quick kiss on the cheek.

MEALTIME. Unless otherwise stated, Puerto Rican restaurants expect customers to come in and seat themselves. However, American chains in Puerto Rico (Chili's, Pizzeria Uno's, Denny's) generally ask that customers wait to be seated. Most waiters say **buen provecho** (bon appétit, or enjoy your meal) when they deliver food of any kind. It is polite to say *buen provecho* to anyone already eating when you enter a restaurant that is not too crowded, especially smaller Puerto Rican establishments. Waitstaff expect a 15% tip for sit-down service (20% for good service in a city), but it is unnecessary to tip at most *panaderías.* Customers sitting down and eating at any restaurant (even a *panadería*) should pay after they eat, unless a sign says otherwise.

TIMING. Puerto Ricans, especially those outside of San Juan and in every form of bureaucracy, have a much more laid back sense of time than most Europeans and North Americans. Things get done when they get done. With a dose of patience, this should not be too frustrating.

CHURCHES. It is respectful to wear pants or a skirt when visiting Catholic churches in Puerto Rico. The one exception is Old San Juan's Iglesia San Juan Baútista, where so many tourists enter that nobody enforces dress codes. Most church workers and worshippers also appreciate quiet voices.

OPENING HOURS. Restaurants, bars, and clubs in Puerto Rico do not maintain strict closing hours. Most will stay open as long as people are still around, even if this means staying open until 8am the next morning. On the flip side, if an establishment is empty, it will likely close early. Smaller establishments, even museums and stores, frequently change opening hours and will close if someone who's supposed to work happens to be sick or unavailable to come in.

THE ARTS

For an island of its size, Puerto Rico maintains a remarkably impressive tradition of art and culture. The **Instituto de Cultura Puertorriqueña** (http://icp.gobierno.pr), founded in 1955, has been greatly effective in preserving Puerto Rico's cultural heritage and opening it to the public over the last 50 years. This organization runs many of the island's museums. Check their online calendar for a list of upcoming cultural events.

VISUAL ART

HISTORY. San Juan's new Museo de Arte (p. 88) is the island's manifestation of a rich tradition of visual art. Most Puerto Rican artists have been strongly influenced by the island and their works tend to focus on the nature, history, and culture of Puerto Rico. The first prominent Puerto Rican artist, **José Campeche** (1751-1809) was born in San Juan as the son of a freed slave. Despite the fact that he never left Puerto Rico to be trained in the European schools, Campeche became an internationally renowned artist. Campeche focused primarily on religious subjects and portraits of prominent Puerto Ricans. Some of his most important works include: *San Francisco, San Juan Bautista,* and *La Sacra Familia.* Though Campeche worked with few outside interactions, the next prominent Puerto Rican artist, **Francisco Oller** (1833-1917), studied in Paris and was deeply influenced by the 19th-century Impressionist movement, particularly the work of Paul Cézanne. Oller used these European styles to portray nationalist scenes of Puerto Rican lands and people. In addition to depicting Puerto Rico's flora and fauna, Oller also painted more opinioned works about life on the island, including *El Velorio* (The Wake; 1893), a representation of a child's wake. Oller's hometown, Bayamón, maintains a museum devoted to the great painter (p. 150), and many of his works can be found in San Juan's Museo de Arte. These two men founded the idea of distinctly Puerto Rican art and inspired generations of later artists.

As Puerto Rico's economy began to flourish in the 1940s, so did its art scene. Around this time the government began subsidizing **poster art,** graphic arts initially dealing with social and political themes on the island, and later becoming announcements for cultural events and festivals. For six years graphic artist **Irene Delano** served as president of the graphics workshop of the Division of Community Education, and popularized the idea of using silk screen to create easily reproducible poster serigraphs. Another prominent poster artist and painter, **Lorenzo Homar** (1913-present), worked with fellow artists to found the **Centro de Arte Puertorriqueño,** designed the symbol for the Puerto Rican Institute of Culture, and established and ran a graphic arts workshop at the institute. Irene Delano's husband and photographer **Jack Delano** (1914-97) also played an important role in the Puerto Rican art scene. Delano was born in Pennsylvania and in 1941 he travelled to Puerto Rico, where he was captivated by the spirit, and poverty, of the island. Since then Delano has published several books of island photography.

TODAY. Though he was born in Brooklyn, **Rafael Tufiño Figueroa** (1922-present) moved to La Perla at an early age and is considered to be one of the island's most important contemporary artists. Tufiño used his background as inspiration to paint the scenes of poverty in Puerto Rico. In one of his most famous works, *La Perla,* Tufiño uses strong colors and lines to depict life in San Juan's most famous slum. *luquillense* artist **Tomás Batista** (1935-present) is one of the first Puerto Ricans to become famous for three-dimensional work, primarily woodwork. Trained in New York and Spain, Batista has spent much of his artistic time creating busts of notable Puerto Ricans that he had admired during his childhood, such as Eugenio de Hostos and Ramón Emeterio Betances. Batista has also created many of the statues adorning plazas in cities around the island, including Río Piedras, Ponce, and Luquillo. More recently Puerto Rico has seen the rise of a few female artists. Paving the way is **Myrna Báez** (1952-present), who uses a variety of media to represent the social issues and natural scenes of the island.

ARTS AND CRAFTS

The sheer number of artisans at any Puerto Rican festival demonstrates that *artesanía* is alive and well in Puerto Rico, though the island does have fewer traditional crafts than some other Latin American countries. One common form of folk art is the **santo**, a small religious figure carved out of wood by a *santero*. The tradition of making *santos* began as early as the 16th century, when Catholic Spanish colonizers placed saints on the mantel to protect their homes from harm (see p. 41). *Santos* vary greatly; larger ones are placed in churches while smaller ones remain in the home. They also vary in terms of quality; a high-quality *santo* is more complex, yet still carved out of one piece of wood. During the early 20th century *santos* decreased in popularity, but in recent years they have become trendy once again. *Santos* can be found at many tourist shops in Old San Juan in addition to almost any crafts fair.

Another popular Puerto Rican craft is the **vejigante mask,** a colorful mask with horns worn during *carnaval* celebrations. Some historians believe that *vejigante* mask-making originated in Spain, where the *vejigante* represents the Moors who fought with St. James. Others believe that it came from Africa with the slaves. Regardless, the art form now integrates both African and Spanish influences in a uniquely Puerto Rican tradition. There are two types of *vejigante* masks, each associated with a regional *carnaval* celebration. In **Ponce**, the masks are made out of *papier-maché* and contain larger horns painted with bright colors, frequently red and black (the colors of Ponce) or yellow and red (the colors of the Spanish flag). In the small northern town of **Loíza** the masks are made out of coconut shells and have smaller horns, teeth made out of bamboo, and exaggerated features to frighten spirits. Both types of masks are worn with a large coverall outfit with wide sleeves designed to look like wings. Several arts and crafts stores in Old San Juan and Ponce sell authentic *vejigante* masks, which start at around $25, but the price increases as the masks get larger, have more horns, and are made by more famous artists.

Finally, Puerto Ricans also excel in the art of **mundillo**, an elaborate lace made with a bobbin. This tradition also originated in Spain, then transferred to Puerto Rico; today only the two places produce authentic *mundillo*. Typically women will spend hours, or days, crocheting the intricate lace, which is then used to make baby clothes, doilies, hats, or numerous other items. This tradition is found primarily in the northwestern town of Moca (p. 177), where visitors can stop by and watch *mundillo* makers at work in their homes. Or stop by the Museo de Arte in San Juan (p. 132) to see the world's largest piece of *mundillo*.

LITERATURE

Puerto Rico's literary tradition originates in the mid-19th century, when people began writing about social and political themes distinct to the island. The first noted Puerto Rican author, **Manuel Alonso Pacheco,** was most well-known for his work *El Gibaro*. Like most of Alonso's work, this half prose, half poetry work discussed the life of rural peasants. The next 50 years were dominated by a few notable poets and essayists. **Alejandro Tapía y Rivera** (1826-82), namesake of Old San Juan's theater, was known primarily as a playwright but also scribed the allegorical poem *The Sataniad: Grandiose Epic Dedicated to the Prince of Darkness.* Following the world trend, late 19th-century Puerto Rico produced romantic poet **José Gautier Benítez** (1851-80) who during his short life wrote about both his love of country and his love of women. However, the most well-known author abroad during this area was philosopher, teacher, and political activist **Eugenio María de Hostos** (1838-1903) who composed everything from social essays to children's stories. He spent his life traveling throughout Latin America working for reform and the independence of Puerto Rico and Cuba. During this time he wrote his famous book *La Reseña Historia de Puerto Rico* (The Recent History of Puerto Rico; 1873).

Puerto Rican literature shifted focus after the American occupation of the island. During the first few decades of the 20th century the so-called **Generation of '98** began writing about the juxtaposition of American influence and traditional Latin American life. Most of these writers, including **Cayetano Coll y Toste, José de Diego,** and **Luis Muñoz Rivera,** were more well-known for their political work, but a few became renowned for their literary talents as well. Juana Díaz native **Luis Lloréns Torres** (1887-1945) used a variety of writing styles, but focused on his poems about the Puerto Rican landscape and spirit. Around the same time **Luis Palés Matos** (1899-1959) wrote verse about Puerto Rico's African roots. In 1898 **Manuel Zeno-Gandia** penned **Puerto Rico's first novel,** a story about the difficult country lifestyle.

The literary scene shifted after the Depression, when the **Generation of the Thirties** attempted to define Puerto Rico's evolving identity. The movement was ushered in by academic **Antonio S. Pedreira** (1899-1939), whose book *Insularism* looked at Puerto Rican values and culture under the influence of the US. Novelist **Enrique Laguerre** (1906-present) wrote about similar themes, focusing on the decline of Puerto Rico's agriculture system. In a look at the island's past **Tomás Blanco** composed *Historical Summary of Puerto Rico.* Around this time **Julia de Burgos** (1914-53) emerged as Puerto Rico's most famous female poet. After personally distributing her first works around the island then moving to the US, de Burgos attained international acclaim for her English-language poem *Farewell in Welfare Island.*

In the mid-20th century Puerto Rican literature switched focus from the main island to the quality of life of Puerto Ricans in New York. Foremost among this trend is Nuyorican **Pedro Juan Soto** (1928-present) who has authored several novels including *Spiks* (1956) and *Usmail* (1958). In the latter half of the 20th century a number of Puerto Rican playwrights have started turning the themes of identity into dramatic works. After studying in Mayagüez, Spain, and New York, **René Marqués** (1914-present) has gained notice for his play *La Carreta* (The Oxcart), which depicts a poor mountain family in Puerto Rico and their immigration to New York. Puerto Rico's most recent player in the international literary scene is **Esmeralda Santiago** (late1940s-present), a Nuyorican who narrates her Puerto Rican childhood in *When I Was Puerto Rican* (1993).

MUSIC

Music is the spice of life in Puerto Rico. From the gentle rhythm of salsa to the pounding thuds of reggaeton, this tiny island plays an exceptionally large role in the international music scene.

SALSA

The history of salsa is an unwilling love story between Cuban beats, Puerto Rican rhythms, and New York streets. Both Cubans and Puerto Ricans would like to claim to be the sole inventors of this contagious music, but most can agree that this popular genre of music originated among Caribbean immigrant populations in New York in the 1950s and only became identified by the term *salsa* in the 1970s. From the origins in mambo to the current popularity of artists such as Marc Anthony, salsa has evolved over the last 50 years to become the most popular form of music in Puerto Rico.

WHAT STARTS AS MAMBO... Throughout the 1920s Puerto Ricans and Cubans began immigrating en masse to New York, and they brought their music with them. In the 1940s Latin music became increasingly popular and **mambo** developed as a combination of Cuban, Dominican, and Puerto Rican rhythms with a bit of American jazz and big band music thrown in. The undisputed king of this early era was Puerto Rican **Tito Puente**, who studied percussion at Julliard, then formed one of the most famous orchestras in New York. His 1958 album *Dance Mania* popularized Latin music throughout the US and by 2000 he had recorded over 120 albums. Other popular Puerto Rican artists in the 1940s included **Tito Rodríguez, Charlie Palmieri**, and **Rafael Muñoz**. Meanwhile trumpeter **César Concepción** and percussionist **Rafael Cortijo** began incorporating the traditionally Puerto Rican sounds of *bomba* and *plena* into the New York Latin music scene.

...SOON BECOMES SALSA. By the 1960s the Latin/Caribbean influenced style of big band music that used congas, timbales, bass, güiro, bells, bongos, maracas, drums, a horn section, and several singers to create a new, rhythmic music was all the rage in New York, but had not yet caught on elsewhere. Still, in 1963 Nuyorican lawyer Gerald Masucci and big band leader Johnny Pacheco took advantage of this genre's increasing popularity to create **Fania Records,** a new record label that would sign unknown Boricuan bands, such as Nuyorican **Willie Colón** and Puerto Ricans **Ismael Miranda** and **Héctor Lavoe** and turn them into household names. As the music became increasingly popular, the word "salsa" also began to appear. In 1962 Joe Cuba released a song claiming that you need "salsa" to dance; this is the first recognized mention of the word *salsa*, which translates as "sauce," in relation to music. The next year Nuyorican **Charlie Palmieri** recorded an LP entitled *Salsa Na-Ma*. After **Carlos Santana** released the disc *Oye Como Va* in 1969, Latin music swept across the country and there was no turning back. **El Cheetah** nightclub in New York City became the gathering place for the Latin salsa scene and the new magazine *Latin New York* spread the idea of salsa throughout the US. By 1976 Billboard magazine was able to publish a 24-page article on the **Salsa Explosion,** solidifying salsa's position as a recognized musical genre.

It's had its ups and downs in the US, but salsa has been a driving force in Puerto Rico's music scene ever since. In 1962 **El Gran Combo** brought the New York sounds of salsa to Puerto Rico and they continued producing hits and winning awards for the next 30 years. **Gilberto Santa Rosa** has been another consistently popular Puerto Rican salsa star. Despite the fact that the younger generation is turning to the more contemporary music, such as rap and reggaeton, salsa continues to dominate Puerto Rican music. Pop musician **Marc Anthony** is actually better known in Puerto Rico for his salsa albums. Some other current popular Puerto Rican salsa artists include **Ismael Miranda, Tito Nieves,** and **Cheo Feliciano.**

CLASSICAL

DANZA. Puerto Rico's classical music tradition really starts in the 18th century. For years the colony had been adopting Spanish classical music traditions, but in the mid-19th century popular classical musicians began incorporating Caribbean rhythms to create *danzas*, a uniquely Puerto Rican style of minuet or waltz with an Afro-Caribbean slant. The music was initially limited to the lower classes until pianist and composer **Manuel Tavares** began creating more high-class versions of the *danza*. However, the *danza's* popularity did not really soar until Taveres's student, ponceño **Juan Morel Campos** (1857-96), developed to become the island's greatest *danza* composer. Due to Campos's success *danza* spread to urban areas throughout the late 19th century, becoming Puerto Rico's most popular form of music, and one of the first genres of island music to be recognized internationally. Many *danzas* continue to be popular today, including the island's national anthem *La Borinqueña*. Other notable *danza* composers include **José Ignacio Quintón** (1881-1925) and **José Enrique Pedreira** (1903-59).

THE 20TH CENTURY. Puerto Rico's first international classical music star was not a composer but an opera singer; around the turn of the century **Antonio Paoli** (1871-1922) rose to be one of the finest tenors in the world. Puerto Rico's music scene changed forever when Spaniard **Pablo Casals** (1876-1973) immigrated to Puerto Rico, his mother's homeland, in 1956. The talented cellist, composer, and conductor founded the renowned **Casals classical music festival** (p. 139) in 1957, then served as the first conductor of the **Puerto Rican Symphony Orchestra.** In 1959 Casals recruited a prestigious faculty to teach at Puerto Rico's first music conservatory, which continues to produce talented musicians today. Casals's legacy also lives on in the Symphony Orchestra, as the 76-piece orchestra continues to perform 48 weeks per year, primarily in San Juan's Luís Ferré Centro de Bellas Artes (p. 137). Other notable contemporary Puerto Rican composers include **Roberto Sierra, Ernesto Cordero,** and **Luís Manuel Álvarez.**

FOLK
Salsa may be more well-known internationally, but the real heart of Puerto Rico's music scene lies in its folk traditions. First popularized in the countryside, the island's folk music originates in Spanish and Moorish traditions from as early as the 16th century. Puerto Rican folk music centers on the **décima,** a 10-line rhyming verse with six to eight syllables per line. These stanzas can be either traditional songs or improvised, but both usually tell some kind of story about love, tragedy, or life lessons. There are two primary types of *décimas.* The most common is the **seis,** a simple melody performed with one to two singers, a row of male dancers facing a row of female dancers, and a band consisting of a **cuatro** (a Puerto Rican guitar), a güiro, a **tiple** (another type of Puerto Rican guitar), and sometimes bongo drums, maracas, claves, and a bass. The other form of folk music is the **aguinaldo,** which is similar to the *seis,* but more popular around Christmas. Many families go door-to-door singing *aguinaldos* to neighbors in the style of Christmas carols.

BOMBA Y PLENA
Puerto Rico has two traditional forms of music that originated directly from the island's African population. Though frequently grouped together as *bomba y plena,* the two are actually distinct musical genres.

LA BOMBA. This tradition came from Africa in the late 17th century and landed in the small, primarily Afro-Caribbean town of Loíza. In this complex song and dance, a group of people create a circle around three different drums. Everyone takes turns drumming and dancing in the center; meanwhile a caller or main singer is echoed by the larger chorus. The interactive music serves primarily as a background for the dancing, and the dancers take turns responding to the rhythms of the drums. In addition to singers and various drums, the *bomba* also uses one maraca and sometimes *palitos* (a type of stick). There are regional variations where either only women sing or only men sing, but the basic idea remains the same. The best place to see *bomba* music is at Loíza's carnival in late July (p. 148).

LA PLENA. Originating on the southern sugar cane zones around Ponce in the early 20th century, *la plena* initially served as a form of protest and expression for Afro-Caribbeans and peasants of all races. Referred to as a *periódico cantao* (a sung newspaper) the *plena* usually discusses, and sometimes satirizes, current events. In a *plena* one primary caller sings and then a chorus responds. Unlike the *bomba,* the *plena* does not require dancing, although it does occur sometimes. The most important instrument for singing a *plena* is the *pandero,* a handheld drum that looks like a tambourine without the bells; other common instruments include *cuatros,* güiros, guitars, accordions, cowbells, and maracas. Around 1950 the *plena* began moving into urban areas with the migrating population and temporarily became popular with all classes before falling out

RECENT NEWS

21ST-CENTURY SALSA?

If you've walked down Ave. Ashford on a weekend night, you've heard it—the bass-pumping beat of **reggaeton,** the newest music craze among young Puerto Ricans. Reggaeton is best described as a combination of hip hop and rap, with a bit of reggae flavor and Latin rhythms thrown in. And it's all in Spanish. In the early '90s reggaeton (also known as Spanish rap, or plain reggae) was perceived as underground music, popular in inner cities with hardcore fans. However, over the last 10 years reggaeton has hit the mainstream, despite its sometimes explicit lyrics focusing on sex, drugs, and, well, reggae. Almost all San Juan clubs (see p. 140) now play reggaeton at times —some don't play anything else. And in 2002 VI Music, one of the largest reggaeton music labels, signed an agreement with Universal Music to distribute reggaeton throughout the US and Puerto Rico. While many young Puerto Ricans, influenced by MTV and American hip [hop?], swear by reggaeton, others look at the new trend a different way—a 2003 San Juan Star article said it best with the headline: "Young people turn their backs on classic salsa." It may not be popular with everyone, but it looks like reggaeton is going to be a major force in Puerto Rican music. To hear some of the infectious beats, tune your radio to FM 107.7 (almost always reggaeton), pick up a cd by Tego Calderón, one of Puerto Rico's most famous reggaeton artists, or just stand on Ave. Ashford next Friday night.

of favor again. However, in the 1970s popular Nuyorican artists such as **César Concepción** revisited the beats of the *plena* and by the end of the millennium, the *plena* once again emerged as a popular expression of Puerto Rican culture.

POP

When the **Latin Invasion** hit the United States in the late 1990s, most of the invaders came from Puerto Rico. Long popular throughout Latin America, Puerto Rican **Ricky Martin** hit the English-language market with his hit single **Livin' La Vida Loca.** When Martin shook his bonbon on the 1999 Grammys, the world became transfixed, even though Martin had been performing since 1984 as a member of the boy band **Menudo,** Puerto Rico's version of the Backstreet Boys. After four solo albums in Spanish and two in English, Martin most recently returned to his native language, releasing another Spanish album in 2003.

She may just be Jenny From the Block, but **Jennifer Lopez** (a.k.a. **J. Lo**) is also of Puerto Rican descent and some of her early music was in Spanish. Another Nuyorican, **Marc Anthony,** started his career singing salsa music in Spanish, including a duet with fellow Puerto Rican salsa superstar **La India,** but in 1999 released an English-language album. One of the greatest guitarists of all time, **José Feliciano,** was born in Lares, Puerto Rico. Some current Puerto Rican pop superstars include **Giselle, Olga Tañón, Carlos Ponce, Chayanne,** and **Son By Four.** Puerto Ricans love the local band **Algarete,** although the four Boricuans have not yet made it in the international music scene.

FILM

The first Puerto Rican movie appeared 1912 when **Rafael Colorado D'Assoy** produced *Un Drama de Puerto Rico.* However, not much came of the island's film industry until the 1950s when **Maruja** was the first film to be distributed in the US. Other important films of the era included *Una Voz en la Montaña* (1952), directed by Amilcar Tirado, which won a prize at the Edinburgh Film Festival, and *Modesta* (1956), directed by Benjamín Doniger, which won first prize at the Venice Film Festival. Unfortunately the industry slowly died in the 60s and 70s as Puerto Rican filmmakers instead turned to joint productions in other countries.

Puerto Rico's film industry took a 180 in 1980 when **Jacobo Morales** wrote, directed, and starred in *Dios Los Cría* (God Created Them). Morales was already familiar on the big screen, as the Lajas native had appeared in Woody Allen's film *Bananas* (1971) and the 1972 film *Up the Sandbox,* but *God Created Them* was his first big film

WEST SIDE CONTROVERSY Ironically the most famous Hollywood movie related to Puerto Rico had nothing to do with the island itself. The 1961 film **West Side Story** took William Shakespeare's classic **Romeo and Juliet** and remade it in 1960s New York City, with a gang of second generation white Americans, "the Jets" as the Montagues and a gang of Puerto Ricans, "the Sharks" as the Capulets. While the movie did bring international attention to the growing Puerto Rican diaspora in New York City, many Puerto Rican immigrants were not happy with the film. Common complaints included: the film confused Mexican and Puerto Rican culture, the film only portrayed poor Puerto Ricans, most of the Puerto Ricans in the film were lawless and prone to criminal activity, and the Puerto Rican love interest (Maria) was portrayed by an American actress of European descent, while the more rough Puerto Rican woman was portrayed by Puerto Rican Rita Moreno. Despite the criticism, the film was an overwhelming success, winning 10 Academy Awards including Best Picture of the Year. The classic film continues to be one of the most widely viewed representations of Nuyoricans in American culture.

PUERTO RICO

in his native land. The movie, which related five stories questioning contemporary Puerto Rican society, was well received by critics and fans alike. Morales's second major film, *Lo Que Le Pasó A Santiago* (What Happened to Santiago) did even better; it won the **1989 Academy Award** for best foreign film. In 1994 Morales directed another film, *Linda Sara* (Pretty Sara), that was considered for the Best Foreign Film Oscar, though ultimately not nominated. Morales is still considered to be Puerto Rico's greatest film director.

In the mid-1980s another big name appeared in the Puerto Rican film scene. Director **Marcos Zurinaga's** first major movie, *La Gran Fiesta* (The Great Party; 1986), recounted the last days of San Juan's Casino, a great meeting spot of the rich and famous. Zurinaga directed two more major films, *Tango Bar* (1988) and *The Disappearance of Garcia Lorca* (1997), a mysterious look into the final days of Spanish poet Federico Garcia Lorca. Puerto Rico's most financially successful film of all time was **Luis Molina's** 1993 comedy *La Guagua Aérea* (The Arial Bus), which uses the pretext of a crowded flight to New York in the 1960s to explore the multitude of reasons that Puerto Ricans immigrate. Quite a few Puerto Ricans have made their names in the American entertainment industry, including Nuyoricans **Jimmy Smits, Rita Moreno, Jennifer Lopez,** and **Michael DeLorenzo** as well as Puerto Rican-born Oscar winner **Benicio del Toro.**

SPORTS AND RECREATION

DRY LAND SPORTS

BASEBALL. Forget soccer: Puerto Ricans shed their Latin American ties and choose baseball as the island's most popular sport. Every year from November to January six regional teams (Santurce, Bayamón, Carolina, Caguas, Mayagüez, and Ponce) play five to six games per week in competition for the series title. In February, the winning team participates in the **Caribbean Series,** playing against the Dominican Republic, Venezuela, and Mexico. Most of the top Puerto Rican baseball players eventually head to the US to play in the major leagues and this little island has had an enormous impact on American baseball. Ever heard of **Roberto Alomar, Bernie Williams, Juan Gonzalez, Carlos Delgado,** and **Iván Rodríguez?** All are Puerto Rican, along with over 200 other players in Major League Baseball history. The trend has become so strong that in the 1997 All-Star Game a Puerto Rican either scored or batted in every single run.

A few players stand out in Puerto Rico's illustrious history. In 1942 **Hiram Bithorn** (1916-51), a pitcher from Santurce, was the first Puerto Rican to be recruited by the Major Leagues. Ironically, *ponceño* **Francisco "Pancho" Coimbre** was actually considered the best Puerto Rican player of the era. Puerto Rico's most famous baseball player of all time, **Roberto Clemente** (1934-72), also had a long and illustrious career in the Major Leagues (see p. 38). During his 18 years with the Pittsburgh Pirates Clemente led the team to two World Series, was the National League MVP in 1966, the World Series MVP in 1971, and the National League Batting Champion four times. Puerto Ricans still hold this Carolina native in high esteem.

In 2003 Puerto Rican baseball fans had quite a treat when the **Montreal Expos** played a season at San Juan's Hiram Bithorn stadium. Seven major league teams headed down to Puerto Rico, allowing Puerto Ricans to see their favorite teams play at home. The temporary move was designed to increase the Expos's revenue and it is unlikely that they will move permanently to San Juan.

COCKFIGHTING. Though it's illegal in most of the US, cockfighting continues to be a popular tradition in Puerto Rico. Almost every city on the island has a cockfight arena, and fights are typically held every weekend, with as many as 40-50 games per day. Hordes of locals, primarily men, gather to watch, and bet on, the fight between two spur-wearing roosters. Though the tradition is primarily rural and private, San Juan does have one cockfight arena open to the public (see p. 137).

BOXING. Puerto Ricans has produced some of the world's best professional boxers. Most recently **Felix "Tito" Trinidad** ruled the ring as the champion of welter- and middleweight boxing after he beat superstar Oscar de la Hoya in 1999. With an impressive 41-1 record Trinidad retired in January 2003 to pursue other activities (such as a music career), despite de la Hoya's request for a rematch. In 2000 **John "The Quietman" Ruíz,** raised in Massachusetts and Puerto Rico by Puerto Rican parents, became the first Latino heavyweight champion. These talents come from a long line of professional Puerto Rican boxers. In the 1930s **Sixto Escobar** became the first Puerto Rican world boxing champion. Over the past 70 years Puerto Ricans have won six **Olympic medals** in boxing. In 1976 17-year-old welterweight fighter **Wilfred Benitez,** born in New York but of Puerto Rican descent, became the youngest boxer to win a world championship.

BASKETBALL. Puerto Rico also has an active basketball league, with 16 amateur and six professional teams. Internationally, the island has not fared so well since their gold medal at the 1991 PanAm games. However, several Boricuans have played for the NBA, including **Ramon Ramos, José Ortíz, Butch Lee, Carlos Arroyo,** and **Daniel Santiago.**

GOLF. Golf is the chosen sport of many tourists, and manicured green courses are spread across the islands—most often with luxury resort complexes in tow. However, tourists don't have all the fun; despite the significant expat population, 90% of the active members of the **Puerto Rico Golf Association** are Puerto Rican. Both the ladies and senior PGA tours end at one of Puerto Rico's magnificent golf courses. Puerto Rican golfers have also made their name internationally. The PGA Hall of Fame inducted Boricuan **Juan "Chi Chi" Rodríguez** in 1992 after a long career. **Kitty Michaels** is a well-known female golfer.

WATER SPORTS

With over 700 mi. of coastline and year-round water temperatures of 74-80°F, Puerto Rico is a paradise for water sports-lovers. From scuba diving to deep-sea fishing to surfing, Puerto Rico offers it all, with world-class conditions. Even beginners can dabble in many of the activities listed below.

> **SEA WARNINGS** Puerto Rico has its share of **fearsome sea creatures.** The most likely predators are **jelly fish, sea urchins,** and **sea lice,** small jelly-fish that resemble a tiny speck of predator. While painful, most of these ani-mals will do little permanent harm. When spending extensive amounts of time in the water (diving, surfing, windsurfing) it's best to wear a lycra or wet suit. There are **sharks** around Puerto Rico, but attacks are extremely rare. If you don't bother them, they most likely won't bother you. For more information, see **Environmental Hazards, p. 55.**

PUERTO RICO

SCUBA DIVING AND SNORKELING

Many people visit Puerto Rico exclusively for its superb diving and snorkeling. Numerous reefs surround the island, providing an arena to swim with hundreds of fish species large and small. **Snorkeling** is a relatively inexpensive, easy-to-learn activity. Snorkelers wear fins, a mask, and a snorkel (a short tube extending from the mouth out of the water), then swim on top of the water observing the marine life below. More advanced snorkelers can hold their breath while diving underwater to get a closer view (skin diving). Puerto Rico's best snorkeling is on Culebra, closely followed by Vieques and the islands off Fajardo, but there are ample snorkeling opportunities around the island. If you plan to do a lot of snorkeling on the island, it may be a worthwhile investment to buy your own gear; otherwise, it costs about $10-15 per day to rent.

Scuba diving is the act of swimming underwater for longer periods of time with a tank of oxygen (a Self-Contained Underwater Breathing Apparatus) attached to your back. In other words, it allows humans to have the incredible sensation of breathing underwater and swimming with the fish. In the late 1960s **PADI** (Professional Association of Diving Instructors) and **NAUI** (National Association of Underwater Instructors) formed to train divers and prevent injuries. Today all divers must be certified by **PADI, NAUI,** or **SSI** (Scuba Schools International) before they can dive alone. A certification course runs $150-600 and usually entails written work and up to four practice dives. The one exception to this rule is that professional instructors can accompany non-certified divers on an introductory dive, called **Discover Scuba** or a **resort course.** This intro dive is usually slightly more expensive, but provides an excellent way to try diving before investing in a full course. It is possible to get certified in Puerto Rico, but this takes up a significant portion of vacation time. Many travelers do the course work at home, then get a **referral** to do the certification dives in Puerto Rico.

Puerto Rico has over 40 certified dive shops that send expeditions to count-less sights. In choosing a dive shop, there are several important criteria to look at. Divers prone to seasickness frequently prefer large boats that remain more stable in the water. The majority of dives are done from boats, but some shops also do shore dives, where divers simply walk into the water. This can be a bit difficult with the cumbersome equipment and the strong shore currents, but it is typically less expensive. It is also a good idea to investigate how dive trips are organized. Some shops take divers and snorkelers out together, which means that divers get the majority of attention and snorkelers are left to fend for them-selves. Others have one divemaster for both certified and resort divers, which means that the experienced divers will have to go to a more shallow site at a slower pace. Finally, scuba diving requires a lot of equipment and many shops have a hidden surcharge for **equipment rental.** Or they will include equipment, but charge more for a wet suit. Others do not rent snorkeling equipment at all, so divers have to purchase it. If you are planning to do frequent diving in Puerto Rico, it's best to bring your own snorkel equipment at the least. Most dives are done over **coral reef,** where brightly colored tropical fish come to feed. Puerto Rico has some more unusual dive sites as well, including an artificial reef made out of tires and an enormous sea wall. For information about the island's best dive sites, see **In The Sea,** p. 2.

SURFING

Puerto Rico ranks among the best surfing destinations in the world, and is certainly the best in the Caribbean. Ever since the 1968 World Championships were held in Rincón, surfers from around the world, and particularly the US East Coast, have been descending upon the isle of enchantment to catch some world-class waves. **Rincón** continues to be the island's surfing paradise, with almost 20 breaks in a relatively small area, closely followed by Isabela's **Playa Jobos.** It is possible to surf almost anywhere along the north coast, but the southern, Caribbean coast does not have many waves. The prime surfing season runs from November to mid- April when a combination of low pressure and cold fronts creates excellent conditions. During the summer hurricane season (June-Nov.) waves tend to be more inconsistent, but still surfable, especially on the east coast. For current livecam images of surf in the Rincón area, check 🔲 www.ecosurfpuertorico.com, www.besidethepointe.com, or www.surfline.com. Private individuals in Luquillo, Dorado, Isabela, and Rincón teach lessons to surfers of all levels. Unlike many other surfing destinations, Puerto Rico has a fairly **local-dominated scene.** Visitors should respect of the local hierarchy and be careful not to break into the line.

Surfers use one of two types of boards: **long boards** (traditional style of board that can range as long as 10-12 ft.) and **short boards** (less than 9 ft. in length). Although beginning surfers generally start off on long boards, most surfers use short boards as well, as they have better maneuverability and are better for riding larger waves. Surfboards have two to three fins, called a **thruster,** which provide even greater maneuverability. The addition of a **leash** improved both the safety of surfing and its style. Before leashes were added, surfers spent a lot of time swimming out to retrieve lost boards after getting knocked off by waves. Lost boards would collide with reefs and rocks as well, resulting in significant board damage. With leashes, surfers can ride waves near rocks and reefs with greater security.

FISHING

Both the ocean and the numerous lakes and reserves throughout the island provide ample entertainment for fishermen. **Deep-sea fishing** is popular, but expensive, with half day boat charters starting at $150 per person or $400 per boat. Fishermen frequently return with mahi mahi, tuna, mackerels, sailfish, dorado, and blue marlin. Most **standing water** in Puerto Rico is actually man-made, but the DRN fills these with a variety of fish, including tilapia, catfish, sunfish, and large-mouth bass. Few charters supply equipment and almost nowhere on the island rents supplies (except some deep-sea charters), so fishermen should bring their own poles.

BOATING

Puerto Rico is the boating capital of the Caribbean, from yachting to sailing to kayaking. The largest **recreational ports** are in Fajardo and Salinas, while San Juan, Mayagüez, and Ponce have the primary **commercial ports.** Many boats in the Fajardo area (p. 257) take small groups out for day-long expeditions to nearby islands. Salinas (p. 235) is the best place to go if you're looking for **pas-**

sage on a boat headed throughout the Caribbean. Several companies scattered throughout the island **rent sailboats,** but usually require that renters have some sailing experience. **Kayaking** is a popular activity on many of the island's freshwater reserves and in the bioluminescent bays in Fajardo and Vieques.

WINDSURFING

In recent years windsurfing has exploded in popularity in Puerto Rico. The island's largest windsurfing shop, **Velauno** (p. 135), rents equipment, teaches lessons, organizes events, and pretty much dominates the oceans around Punta las Marías in San Juan. Other popular windsurfing areas include La Parguera and Guánica. For more information and current wave reports check www.windsurfingpr.com.

HOLIDAYS & FESTIVALS

Puerto Ricans love a good party; there is some kind of festival or event somewhere on the island nearly every week. The island has three primary types of celebration—patron saint festivals, harvest festivals, and national holidays. Almost every town celebrates at least one **patron saint festival** (see list, below) with singing, dancing, rides, religious processions, dances, concerts, and regional food spread out over 10 days. Typically held in the town square, these festivals are based on Catholic saints, but some incorporate elements of African culture as well. **Harvest festivals** are celebrated with similar festivities to commemorate the end of the harvest season. Despite the fact that agriculture has become increasingly unimportant in Puerto Rico's economy, many towns still host at least one harvest festival; see individual town write-ups.

The wise government of Puerto Rico has decided that it is necessary to commemorate both US and Puerto Rican holidays, so the island has a surplus of days off. However, most serve as little more than an excuse to take a three-day weekend. Many holidays, such as Memorial Day and important birthdays, are celebrated on the nearest Monday. Below is a list of the annual holidays celebrated in Puerto Rico; *italicized* holidays originated in the US.

Finally, Puerto Rico also has a smattering of additional festivities that do not fall into specific categories. San Juan (p. 88) hosts several festivals, from cultural events (San Juan CinemaFest and Heineken Jazz Festival) to events that are just an excuse to party (Gallery Nights, Festival de la Calle San Sebastian). The island also has three major festivals that incorporate *vejigante* masks. Though far from Río, Ponce's *carnaval* festival is still a major event. Loíza's *carnaval*, held in late July (p. 148), incorporates more African traditions, while Hatillo's mask festival (p. 168) in late December, is based on the island's Spanish heritage. One of the island's most unique festivals is Aibonito's spectacular Flower Festival, a modern-day variation on the traditional harvest festival (p. 265).

January 1 *New Year's*

January 3 Epiphany/Three Kings Day

January 11 Hostos Day (Eugenio María de Hostos's birthday)

January 19, 2004/January 17, 2005 *Martin Luther King Jr. Day*

February 16, 2004/February 21, 2005 *Presidents' Day*

March 22 Abolition Day

April 9, 2004/March 25, 2005 Good Friday

April 16 José de Diego's birthday

May 31, 2004/May 30, 2005 *Memorial Day*

June 23 St. John the Baptist Day

July 4 *US Independence Day*

July 17 Luis Muñoz Riviera's birthday

July 25 Constitution Day

July 27 José Celso Barbosa's birthday

September 6, 2004/September 5, 2005 *Labor Day*

October 11, 2004/October 10, 2005 Columbus Day

November 11 *Veteran's Day*

November 19 Discovery of Puerto Rico Day

November 25, 2004/November 26, 2005 Thanksgiving

December 25 Christmas Day

PATRON SAINT FESTIVALS

DATE	PATRON SAINT	TOWN
January 9	La Sagrada Familia	Corozal
February 2	La Virgen de la Candelaria	Coamo, Manatí, Mayagüez
February 3	San Blas	Coamo, Guayama
March 17	San Patricio	Loíza
March 19	San José	Ciales, Gurabo, Luquillo
March 31	San Benito	Patillas
April 29	San Pedro Martín	Guaynabo
May 1	Apóstol San Felipe	Arecibo
May 3	La Santa Cruz	Bayamón, Trujillo Alto
May 30	San Fernando	Carolina
June 13	San Antonio de Padua	Barranquitas, Ceiba, Dorado, Guayama, Isabela
June 24	San Juan Bautista	Maricao, Orocovis, San Juan
July 16	Virgen del Carmen	Arroyo, Barceloneta, Cataño, Hatillo, Morovis
July 25	Santiago Apóstol	Aibonito, Fajardo, Guánica, Loíza
July 31	San Germán	San Germán
August 30	Santa Rosa de Lima	Rincón
September 8	Nuestra Señora de la Monserrate	Jayuya, Moca, Salinas
September 29	San Miguel Arcangel	Cabo Rojo, Naranjito, Utuado
October 2	Los Angles Custodios	Yabucoa
October 7	Nuestra Señora del Rosario	Naguabo, Vega Baja
October 12	La Virgen del Pilar	Río Piedras
October 24	San Rafael Arcangel	Quebradillas
November 4	San Carlos Borromeo	Aguadilla
December 8	La Inmaculada Concepción de María	Humacao, Vieques
December 12	Nuestra Señora de la Guadalupe	Ponce
December 28	Día de los Inocentes	Hatillo, Morovis

ADDITIONAL RESOURCES

HISTORY

The Taínos: Rise and Fall of the People Who Greeted Columbus. Irvin Rouse (Yale University Press, 1993). The most informed and accessible history of Puerto Rico's first major civilization from their migration to the Caribbean to the decline of the civilization.

Puerto Rico: A Political and Cultural History. Antonio Morales Carrión (W.W. Norton and Company, Inc., 1983). A bit dry and overly academic, but one of the few comprehensive histories of Puerto Rico available in English.

Puerto Rico: A Colonial Experiment. Raymond Carr (New York University Press, 1984). Though it can be difficult to find, this work by British historian Raymond Carr is one of the standard reads about Puerto Rico's complex relationship with the United States.

SCIENCE AND NATURE

A Guide to the Birds of Puerto Rico and the Virgin Islands. Herbert Raffaele, Cindy House, and John Wiessinger (Princeton University Press, 1989). This is hands-down the best book for bird-watchers interested in learning about Puerto Rico's aviary species.

CULTURE

Puerto Rico Borinquen Querida. Roger A. Labrucherie (Imagenes Press, 2001). A photojournalist's account of the culture, history, and natural wonders of the island, highlighted with spectacular photos.

Stories from Puerto Rico/Historias de Puerto Rico. Robert L. Muckley and Adela Martínez-Santiago (Passport Books, 1999). Eighteen traditional Puerto Rican folk tales with short historical contextualizations. The book is part of the Bilingual Books series and all stories appear in both English and Spanish.

Puerto Rico Mio: Four Decades of Change. Jack Delano, Arturo Carrion, and Sidney Mintz (Smithsonian Institution Press, 1990). This widely-acclaimed work combines Delano's photographs from 1941, with photos of the same places in 1981 to illustrate the change, consistency, and beauty of island life.

Boricuas: Influential Puerto Rican Writings. Robert Santiago (Ballantine Books, 1995). With 50 short stories, plays, poems, and essays, this anthology provides a solid introduction to Puerto Rican writings of the 19th and 20th centuries, as well as a glimpse into the island's culture and history.

Clemente! Kal Wagenheim and Wilfrid Sheed (Olmstead Press, 2001). Using narrative and interviews, Wagenheim and Sheed detail the life and career of Puerto Rico's most famous baseball legend, Roberto Clemente.

FICTION

Juan Bobo Goes To Work: A Puerto Rican Folk Tale. Marisa Montes (Harper Collins Juvenile Books, 2000). This short children's book relates the misadventures of Juan Bobo, a Puerto Rican version of Foolish Jack. The protagonist, a popular Puerto Rican folk character, has his own statue on one of Condado's plazas.

When I Was Puerto Rican. Esmeralda Santiago (Vintage Books, 1994). Santiago recalls her childhood growing up in the Puerto Rican countryside and her move to Brooklyn at age 13. One of the most popular contemporary novels about Puerto Rican life.

The Rum Diary: A Novel. Hunter S. Thompson (Scribner Paperback Fiction, 1999). Though Thompson's first novel falls far short of his dream to create the great Puerto Rican novel, it does provide an interesting glimpse at Condado in the 1950s. Plotless, but interesting.

Paving the Latin Way Into Major League Baseball

The late, great Puerto Rican Roberto Clemente and Dominican Sammy Sosa share many traits. Both are right-fielders with shotgun arms and powerful swings who rose to superstardom playing America's national pastime. Both are black athletes from Latin America with flamboyant on-field demeanors. Like Clemente, Sammy takes his role as a Latin player seriously. But although they are two of the most beloved athletes of their times, their personalities will be remembered very differently by historians.

Clemente is considered by many to be the Jackie Robinson of Latin ballplayers. From 1955 to 1975 Clemente played for the Pittsburgh Pirates, and during this time he remained largely at odds with the press for what he considered racial bias. Clemente was openly miffed after finishing eighth in the MVP voting after the 1960 season, in which he hit .316 with 16 home runs and 94 RBIs. He believed the *Sports Illustrated* story about his hypochondriacal ways, which included an anatomical diagram of his myriad ailments, evinced a lack of respect that would not be shown a white North American star. The Pittsburgh press often quoted Clemente's broken English phonetically, which Clemente despised. Contrast this with the Sammy Sosa's press conference after signing a huge new contract with the Cubs, when the Dominican repeated the line from a 1980s *Saturday Night Live* skit— "Baseball been berry berry good to me." Different times, different persons.

Clemente carried himself above the fray, and while it rubbed some the wrong way, the fans loved Clemente. Baseball Commissioner Bowie Kuhn said of Clemente, "He had about him a touch of royalty." He was known to carry himself with an aristocratic air. Clemente was asked to appear in the movie *The Odd Couple* for $100; in the scene he would hit into a triple play. Clemente refused, citing the dollar figure and the triple play as disgraceful to him and to his native Puerto Rico. Clemente's relationship with the fans was a far different story. Pittsburgh fans rose to their feet and yelled *"Arriba!"* whenever Clemente stepped to the plate with runners on base. Today, a Clemente statue stands outside the stadium, and a nearby bridge bears the Hall of Famer's name.

On the field, Clemente was superior at everything. Legendary Yankees manager Casey Stengel said Clemente was the greatest right fielder he ever saw. Koufax said the best way to pitch to Clemente was to roll the ball. Pirates general manager Joe Brown said he was the most intelligent player he ever had. At the plate, Clemente wielded a leaden 36-ounce hunk of ash, which he used to hit .317 with 17 home runs and 119 RBIs in 1966 to earn his overdue MVP award. It was one of 13 seasons in which Clemente hit over .300. He led the Bucs to a 1971 World Series victory by hitting .414 with 2 homers and 4 RBI. In a live televised interview after the win he addressed his family in Puerto Rico in Spanish before starting the English interview. Clemente won 12 Gold Gloves for tracking down everything afield and for striking fear in opposing baserunners with his hose of a right arm. Clemente added plenty of mustard, too. He had a signature cock of the neck to click his ailing vertebrae in place before stepping in to the batters box. He turned a routine fly in the outfield into a little show, catching the ball and pirouetting suddenly to complete an underhand whip of a throw to second base.

Clemente's tragic death completed his legacy. In December 1972 he was heading to Nicaragua to manage an amateur Puerto Rican baseball team when an enormous hurricane rocked the country, killing 10,000 and leaving 250,000 homeless. Clemente could have put money and his name into the relief effort, as Sosa did after Hurricane George hit the Dominican Republic in 1998, but instead the Puerto Rican instead actually took part in the relief efforts by packaging and hauling supplies. When reports came through that two planeloads of supplies were not able reach the needy, Clemente boarded the third plane to Nicaragua himself. It was overloaded with material and manned by a shoddy pilot—the plane plunged into the sea minutes after takeoff. Clemente's epitaph was his own quote: "I want to be remembered as a ballplayer who gave all he had to give."

Today, Major League Baseball gives the Robert Clemente Award "to the player who best exemplifies the game of baseball, sportsmanship, community involvement, and the individual's contribution to his team."

Derek Glanz was the editor of Let's Go: Spain & Portugal 1998. He is now a freelance baseball writer contributing regularly to St. Louis Cardinals' Gameday Magazine. He has written for Baseball America and Baseball Weekly and appeared as a guest analyst on ESPN Radio and Colombia's Telecartagena.

Puerto Rico's Convoluted Relationship with the US

Tourists are often surprised to hear Spanish spoken on the streets of Puerto Rico. Puerto Ricans, patriotically known as Boricuas (for the indigenous name of the island, Borikén) are US citizens, but many identify themselves as part of a Latin American nation that is divided between support of the status quo, statehood, and independence. The political status issue brings Puerto Ricans to an intense debate—elections regularly draw 80% voter participation.

In its 1952 constitution Puerto Rico was labeled a Commonwealth or, as it is called in Spanish, *Estado Libre Asociado* (ELA; Free Associated State). To many, the ELA is a misnomer since Puerto Rico—an unincorporated territory of the US since 1898 and one of the longest standing colonies on earth, according to the United Nations—is neither free nor a state, and it lacks the power of a true "associate." Puerto Rico's economic dependency on the US interferes with the resolution of the ever-present political status problem. Democratic efforts such as referenda have been ineffective in clarifying the island's status. For example, fearing a vote for complete independence, President Wilson canceled the 1916 referendum on the imposition of US citizenship and military draft; in the 1993 political status referendum, options were ill-defined, so the majority of Puerto Ricans voted "None of the above."

Views on the political status of the nation depend on the degree of knowledge of Puerto Rican history and economics. Both the right-wing statehooders (who want Puerto Rico to become the 51st US state) and the left-wing *independentistas* (who favor Puerto Rico becoming an independent country) denounce the exploitation brought on by the colonial status of the island. Statehooders and the center-right status quo supporters differ only in the degree of political autonomy to be surrendered in exchange for US economic benefits. In their campaigns, all three groups emphasize the preservation of Puerto Rican nationality and culture, including the Spanish language, the Puerto Rican flag, and Puerto Rican representation in the Olympics and the Miss Universe pageant.

After four centuries under Spanish rule and one century under US domination, Puerto Ricans (on the island or in the US) are proud of their resistance and of their flexibility as a people. The Puerto Rican celebration of American Independence Day on July 4th can seem particularly confusing to outsiders. Some Puerto Ricans cheer for the US liberation from British colonial domination, while others demand the same freedom for Puerto Rico. Because a colonial government controls education, many aspects of Puerto Rican history are not taught in school. That is one reason why the independence movement, a majority from the 1920s to the 1950s, has diminished the same minority of the population. Still alive despite decades of criminalization, persecution, and infiltration by the FBI, the independence option is considered viable by less than 10% of the population, with only 5% voting for the Independence Party in what most *independentistas* consider to be fake colonial elections.

The environmental and economic effects of the US colonial regime have been devastating. As multinational cooperations profit $26 billion annually from the island, 60% of Puerto Ricans live in poverty and the per capita income is a third of the US average, or half that of the poorest state in the US. Many US industries have polluted land and water with impunity. The railroad that circumnavigated the island shut down in 1957, making Puerto Ricans dependent on cars. Fertile agricultural lands have been paved over in order to build giant car lots, shopping malls, and housing developments. Puerto Rico has been forced to rely on imports, and town centers are dying out as local merchants fail to compete with Wal-Mart.

With no vote in the US congress or the UN, Puerto Rico has been repeatedly utilized as an "Experimental Island." In 1930s experiments for the Rockefeller Institute, American Dr. Cornelius P. Rhoads injected cancerous cells into unknowing Puerto Ricans, killing eight people. In places like Vieques and El Yunque Rainforest, the US military has experimented with live artillery, radiation, napalm, Agent Orange, and depleted uranium. Today the US Department of Agriculture conducts more GM food experiments per square mile in Puerto Rico than in any US state, except Hawaii.

After decades of being not-quite-equal "associates" with the US, Puerto Ricans remain divided to this day as to what the best political alternative should be. The historical tension of a US-Puerto Rico relationship that seems unjust to some, but convenient or indispensable to others, has become part of daily life for Puerto Ricans.

Iliana Pagán Teitelbaum *received her BA in Latin American Studies from the University of Puerto Rico. She is currently finishing her dissertation and expects to receive a PhD in Romance Languages and Literatures from Harvard University.*

An Alternative Way to Explore Puerto Rico's Museum Culture

Signs of Puerto Rico's singular relationship with the United States are carved everywhere in the island. Carved in cement, literally. As in the continental US, cities have given way to suburbs and people have become dependant on cars to move from home to work, to school, and to shop. Today a great proportion of the island's land area is carved by streets and highways. At last count there where 2.2 million cars in Puerto Rico (about six for every ten residents)—three times the proportion of the US and many more times that of the European Community.

Sprawl and lack of urban planning have made it almost impossible to design a public transportation system that competes with the car. But in a country where the average per capita income is about $12,500, not everybody can afford a car. That is why many low-income families, students, recent immigrants, and elderly persons keep alive a network of *pisa y corre* (roughly translated to "stop and go") public vans, also know as *carros públicos* (public cars) to move from town to town every day. For $3-20 a traveler can tour all the towns of Puerto Rico and get a closer look at Puerto Rican culture along the way.

One great advantage of *pisa y corre* transportation is that the vans usually travel directly between town plazas. Because most of the museums, cultural centers, traditional stores, and market places are centered around theses plazas, you will get right to the action. If you ask, people will tell you how to walk from the van stop to any cultural spot or hotel in the area. If you are planning to go to a place between towns, talk to the van drivers and make sure the *pisa y corre* does drive past the area. To request a van stop tell the driver *"me deja"* (leave me here) and you will be dropped off.

Pisa y corre vans are not intended for tourism, and because the presence of a foreigner provides diversion from the drag of the daily commute, fellow riders and the driver will usually share information about the cultural highlights of a town, lessons and opinions about any subject imaginable, and a collection of life histories to fill many volumes. In other words, this is not the way to travel incognito. No matter how you look, people in small towns will know that you are new there, and at least somebody will want to know what you are doing. So, in a sense, *pisa y corre* transportation is a cultural activity.

The following is a possible museum trip using the *pisa y corre:*

On any given day (except Sunday) you can spend a morning in Río Piedras exploring the centennial campus of the University of Puerto Rico, with its small but beautiful museum. Then walk to the plaza and take the *pisa y corre* to Caguas. The van will take Rte. 1, the historic first road to cross Puerto Rico from north to south.

When you arrive in Caguas (about 1hr. later) you will be able to visit museums about *trovadores*, tobacco, and others on subjects related to the history and people of the town (see p. 149). From there take the bus to Cayey.

In Cayey ask around for directions to the college campus and visit their museum, which houses an impressive collection of modern print art. The main gallery is dedicated to the painter Ramón Frade and his masterful representations of everyday people and landscapes in early 20th century Puerto Rico. Next take the van to Guayama.

Right in Guayama you will find the Casa Cautiño Museum (see p. 239), a property co-managed by the Puerto Rican Institute of Culture and the Municipality of Guayama. It is an amazing example late 19th- century architecture that houses a collection of furniture and decorative arts of the same period. From there, on to Ponce…

Ponce is a good place to finally relax and spend the night. There are superb hotels close to the plaza where you can plan your visits to the city's many museums and cultural attractions.

Those who travel by *pisa y corre* soon discover that asking people is the best way to get around and, if you are lucky, to find some unexpectedly beautiful places and experiences.

Adrián Cerezo is an education policy and non-formal education specialist currently directing the Community Based Education Center at Sacred Heart University in San Juan. He has a BA in clinical psychology from Sacred Heart University. In 1998 Cerezo received a Distinguished Alumni Award for his contributions to education.

Celebrating a Traditional Art in the Context of Modern Culture

Sometime in the first two weeks of December, *santeros* (artisans of wooden saints made of wood; *santos de palo*) congregate in the small mountain town of Orocovis, home to one of the most talented and prolific carving families of the island, the Avilés family. In fact, the festival is set up across the street from the family museum. There are at least three generations of carvers in the family, and the oldest living member, Don Ceferino Avilés, has been recognized by the Smithsonian as a master artisan. They serve as the focal point of this unique festival that brings together established artisans and beginners, and people come to show, see, and buy only one thing: carvings of saints.

Puerto Rico's tradition of saint carvings is very old, inherited from Spain as part of the Catholic legacy. Originally, 16th-century Spanish clergy used polychrome sculptures and paintings to educate and convert. It is unclear when individuals began to make carvings, though some families, like the Espada family, are known to have specialized in religious images during the 17th and 18th centuries. It was only during the 19th century that local carvers became firmly established.

Saints were originally carved for devotional reasons, and the carvings emphasize the personal attributes of the saints, such as the saint's faith, virtues, or power. These unique traits can include a miracle or important event related to the saint, the specific causes for which the saint is invoked, or an instrument used to martyrize the saint. Thus, Saint Francis is accompanied by birds or small animals (he is the patron saint of animals), Saint Barbara holds a sword (she was decapitated by one), and Saint John the Baptist is accompanied by a lamb and water (evoking his baptism of Jesus).

Initially, these small carvings were placed on a shelf or small niche in the bedroom or living area of the home. They were sold by the carvers who traveled through the countryside selling their wares and offering repair and paint services for saints in need. Because of the saints' power as intermediaries, the carvings became objects of devotion and veneration. Thus, it was common for owners to have the saint repainted once a year before the saint's day, or as a way of showing gratitude when favors were con-

ceded. Today saints are kept for many reasons, not just devotion, and the art of carving has developed in many different directions.

The Orocovis festival offers a window into most recent developments of Puerto Rican culture and the many symbols of devotion that now appear around the island. With the beatification of Carlos Manuel Rodríguez, the first Puerto Rican candidate for sainthood, it is now common to see his image in suit and tie. Mother Theresa has recently become a favorite, as have representations of Jesus embracing the World Trade Towers in New York City. The carvings provide a medium for social and political expression as well, as evidenced by numerous representations of saints supporting the cause of peace and freedom for Vieques. It is worth noting the emergence of women carvers, who have become a stronger presence since the mid-1980s. In fact, there is a separate, all-female festival in the spring. Both women from established artisan families and newcomers have been able to establish their own style and interests.

Those who arrive at the festival early (around 7am) will see the hard-core collectors, who come to buy what they believe are the most valuable and unique pieces. (Collectors have been known to visit the Avilés family the day before the festival, "by mistake," in order to get first pick of the master carvers' pieces.) Both the speculators and the investors have inflated the prices of carvings, and it is now nearly impossible to find a $20 piece by one of the masters, as you could have several years ago. While this is good for the carvers in economic terms, it also has the negative effect of creating a gap between the saints and their most ardent devotees. Even those not interested in buying should try to arrive no later than mid-morning, as the pieces sell quickly.

Ironically, some of the best *santos de palo* are not found on the island, but in the United States. Teodoro Vidal, who held perhaps the largest and most valuable collection, donated it to the Smithsonian Institution in Washington D.C. But the saint carvings are only one part of the story, and there is much to be gained from watching the artisans show their most recent pieces and trade compliments and ideas. After all, they are themselves the intermediaries of our own devotion.

Camille Lizarribar has a PhD in Comparative Literature from Harvard University and a JD at Harvard Law. She has most recently returned to Puerto Rico to clerk for a Judge at the Federal District Court in San Juan.

ESSENTIALS

FACTS FOR THE TRAVELER

ENTRANCE REQUIREMENTS

Puerto Rico is a commonwealth of the US and treated like part of the US for immigration purposes. US citizens may enter Puerto Rico without a passport. All other citizens must follow the guidelines below.

Passport (p. 43). Required for all visitors.

Visa (p. 44). A visa is usually required to visit Puerto Rico, but can be waived.

Work Permit (p. 86). Required for all foreigners planning to work in Puerto Rico.

Driving Permit (p. 70). Not required. Most foreigners can use their home driver's license for up to 120 days.

EMBASSIES & CONSULATES

Contact the nearest US embassy or consulate for information regarding visas and passports to Puerto Rico. The **US State Department** provides contact info for US embassies and consulates abroad at http://usembassy.state.gov.

CONSULAR SERVICES ABROAD

US EMBASSIES

Australia: Moonah Pl., Yarralumla **(Canberra)**, ACT 2600 (☎02 6214 5600; fax 6214 5970; http://usembassy-australia.state.gov/embassy/index.html).

Canada: 490 Sussex Dr., **Ottawa,** ON K1N 1G8 (☎613-238-5335; fax 688-3091; www.usembassycanada.gov).

Ireland: 42 Elgin Rd., **Dublin** 4 (☎1 668 8777 or 668 7122; fax 668 9946; www.usembassy.ie).

New Zealand: 29 Fitzherbert Terr., Thorndon, **Wellington.** Mailing Address: P.O. Box 1190, Wellington (☎4 462 6000; fax 499 0490; http://usembassy.org.nz).

South Africa: 877 Pretorius St., **Pretoria.** Mailing Address: P.O. Box 9536, Pretoria 0001 (☎342 1048; fax 342 2244; http://usembassy.state.gov/pretoria).

UK: 24 Grosvenor Sq., **London** W1A 1AE (☎020 7499 9000; fax 491 2485; www.usembassy.org.uk).

US CONSULATES ABROAD

Australia: 553 St. Kilda Rd., **Melbourne,** VIC 3004 (☎03 9526 5900; fax 9525 0769); 16 St. George's Terr., 13th fl., **Perth,** WA 6000 (☎08 9202 1224; fax 9231 9444); MLC Centre, 19-29 Martin Pl., 59th fl., **Sydney,** NSW 2000 (☎02 9373 9200; fax 9373 9184).

Canada: 615 Macleod Trail SE, **Calgary,** AB T2G 4T8 (☎403-266-8962; fax 264-6630); Ste. 904, Purdy's Wharf Tower II, 1969 Upper Water St., **Halifax,** NS B3J 3R7 (☎902-429-2480; fax 423-6861); 1155 St. Alexandre St., **Montréal** QC H3B 3Z1, Mailing Address: P.O. Box 65, Station Desjardins, Montréal, QC H5B 1G1 (☎514-398-9695; fax 398-9748); 2 Place Terrasse Dufferin, **Québec City,** QC G1R 4T9 (☎418-692-2095; fax 692-4640); 360 University Ave., **Toronto,** ON M5G 1S4 (☎416-595-1700; fax 595-0051); 1095 W. Pender St., **Vancouver,** BC V6E 2M6 (☎604-685-4311; fax 685-5285); 860-201 Portage Ave., **Winnipeg,** MB R3B 3K6 (204-940-1800).

New Zealand: Citibank Building, 3rd fl., 23 Customs St., **Auckland,** Mailing Address: Private Bag 92022, Auckland (☎9 303 2724; fax 366 0870).

South Africa: Broadway Industries Center, Heerengracht, Foreshore, **Cape Town,** Mailing Address: P.O. Box 6773, Roggebaai 8012 (☎021 421 4280; fax 425 3014); Old Mutual Building, 31st fl., 303 West St., **Durban** 4000 (☎031 305 7600; fax 305 7691); 1 River St., Killarney, **Johannesburg,** Mailing Address: P.O. Box 1762, Houghton 2041 (☎011 644 8000; fax 646 6916).

UK: Queen's House, 14 Queen St., **Belfast,** N. Ireland BT1 6EQ (☎028 9032 8239; fax 9024 8482); 3 Regent Terr., **Edinburgh,** Scotland EH7 5BW (☎0131 556 8315; fax 557 6023).

CONSULAR SERVICES IN THE US

The United Kingdom and Canada have consulates in San Juan (see p. 97).

IN WASHINGTON, D.C.

Australia, 1601 Massachusetts Ave., 20036 (☎202-797-3000; fax 797-3168; www.austemb.org). **Canada,** 501 Pennsylvania Ave. NW, 20001 (☎202-682-1740; fax 202-682-7701; www.canadianembassy.org). **Ireland,** 2234 Massachusetts Ave. NW, 20008 (☎202-462-3939; fax 232-5993; www.irelandemb.org). **New Zealand,** 37 Observatory Circle NW, 20008 (☎202-328-4800; fax 667-5227; www.nzemb.org). **South Africa,** 3051 Massachusetts Ave. NW, 20008 (☎202-232-4400; fax 265-1607; www.saembassy.org). **UK,** 3100 Massachusetts Ave., 20008 (☎202-588-6500; fax 588-7870; www.britainusa.com/consular/embassy).

TOURIST OFFICES

The Puerto Rican Tourism Company, the island's official tourist center, operates offices in **Aguadilla** (p. 174), **Boquerón** (p. 200), **Ponce** (p. 222), and **San Juan** (p. 96). In addition there are regional offices in countries around the world. Any office will send you a complimentary issue of *Que Pasa* magazine (see p. 78). Most municipal **Alcaldías** (Mayor's Offices), located on or near the plaza of municipal centers, can provide a packet of historical information about the municipality.

Canada: 41-43 Colbourne St., Ste. 301, **Toronto,** ON M5E 1E3 (☎416-368-2680).

USA: 3575 W. Cahuenga Blvd., Ste. 405, **Los Angeles,** CA 90068 (☎213-874-5991); 901 Ponce de León Blvd., Ste. 101, **Coral Gables,** FL 33134 (☎305-445-9112); 666 Fifth Ave., **New York,** NY 10103 (☎212-586-6262).

UK: 67a High St., Walton-on-Thames, **Surrey,** KT 12 1DJ (☎0932 253 302; puertoricouk@aol.com).

DOCUMENTS & FORMALITIES

PASSPORTS

REQUIREMENTS. All foreign visitors need valid passports to enter the United States and to re-enter their own country. The US now requires that visitors have a machine-readable passport; if you do not, contact your local passport office. Returning home with an expired passport is illegal and may result in a fine. The US does not allow entrance if the holder's passport expires in under six months.

PASSPORT MAINTENANCE. Be sure to photocopy the page of your passport with your photo, as well as any travel insurance policies, plane tickets, and traveler's check serial numbers. Carry one set of copies in a safe place, apart from the originals, and leave another set at home.

If you lose your passport, immediately notify the local police and the nearest embassy or consulate of your home government. To expedite the replacement process, you will need to know all info from the previous passport and show ID and proof of citizenship. In some cases, a replacement may take weeks to process, and it may be valid only for a limited time. In an emergency, ask for temporary traveling papers that will permit you to re-enter your home country.

NEW PASSPORTS. File any new passport or renewal applications well in advance of your departure date. Most passport offices offer rush services for a steep fee. Citizens living abroad who need a passport or renewal should contact the nearest consular service of their home country.

Australia: Citizens must apply for a passport in person at a post office or an Australian diplomatic mission overseas. A 32-page passports cost AUS$144, children and seniors AUS$72; a 64-page passport costs AUS$216/$108. Adult passports are valid for 10 years and child passports for 5 years. Adults can request passport renewal forms by phone or online. For more info, call ☎ 13 12 32, or visit www.passports.gov.au.

Canada: Citizens must submit the application in person to any passport office or by mail to the central Passport Office, Ottawa, ON K1A 0G3. A 24-page passport costs CND$85, for ages 3-15 $35, for children under 3 $20; a 48-page passport costs CND$90/$35/$20. For info call ☎ 800-567-6868 or visit www.ppt.gc.ca.

Ireland: Citizens apply for a passport by mail to the Department of Foreign Affairs, Passport Office, Setanta Centre, Molesworth St., Dublin 2 (☎ 01 671 1633; fax 671 1092; www.irlgov.ie/iveagh). Residents of the Munster counties of Clare, Cork, Kerry, Limerick, Tipperary, and Waterford can apply to: 1a South Mall, Cork (☎ 021 494 4700). Obtain an application from a local *Garda* station, a post office, or a passport office. 32-page passports cost €57 and are valid for 10 years. 48-page passports cost €69. Citizens under 16 or over 65 can request a 3-year passport (€12).

New Zealand: Passport application forms are available online or from any travel agency or Link Centre. Applications should be sent to the Passport Office, P.O. Box 10-526, Wellington, New Zealand (☎ 0800 225 050 or 04 474 8100; fax 474 8010; www.passports.govt.nz). Adult passports (NZ$80) are valid 10 years; passports for children under 16 (NZ$40) are valid 5 years. Recent proposals would reduce the adult fee to NZ$71 and the children fee to NZ$36.

South Africa: Citizens must bring a completed application to a domestic Home Affairs office or a consulate abroad. Processing takes six weeks. Adult passports (ZAR120) are valid for 10 years. Passports for children under 16 (ZAR90) are valid for 5 years. Information and application documents are available at www.home-affairs.pwv.gov.za.

United Kingdom: Application forms are available at passport offices, post offices, travel agencies, and online (www.ukpa.gov.uk). Apply by mail, in person at a passport office, or at one of the High Street Partners. Adult passports (UK£33) are valid for 10 years; under 16 (UK£19) are valid for 5. The process takes about 2 weeks. For more info contact the UK Passport Agency at ☎ 0870 521 0410.

VISAS

Citizens of most European countries, Australia, and New Zealand can waive US visas through the **Visa Waiver Pilot Program.** Visitors qualify if they are traveling only for business or pleasure (*not* work or study) and are staying for fewer than 90 days. In addition, travelers must provide proof of intent to leave (such as a return plane ticket) and an I-94 form. Citizens of South Africa and some other countries need a visa in addition to a valid passport for entrance to the US.

All travelers planning a stay of more than 90 days (180 days for Canadians) need to obtain a visa; contact the closest US embassy or consulate. The US government charges $100 to apply for a visa. The **Center for International Business and Travel (CIBT),** 23201 New Mexico Ave. NW, #210, Washington, D.C. 20016 (☎ 202-244-9500 or 800-929-2428), secures **B-2** (pleasure travel) visas to and from all possible countries for a variable service charge (six-month visa around $45). If you lose your I-94 form, you can replace it at the nearest **Bureau of Citizenship and Immigration Services (BCIS)** office (☎800-375-5283; www.bcis.gov). **Visa extensions** are sometimes attainable with a completed I-539 form; call the forms request line at ☎800-870-3676. Be sure to double-check on entrance requirements at the nearest US embassy or consulate, or consult the Bureau of Consular Affairs' web site (www.travel.state.gov).

Entering Puerto Rico to study or work requires a special visa. For more information, see **Alternatives to Tourism,** see p. 80).

IDENTIFICATION

When you travel, always carry at least two or more forms of identification on your person, including at least one photo ID. Many establishments, especially banks, may require several IDs in order to cash traveler's checks. Never carry all your forms of ID together; keep them in separate places in case of theft or loss.

TEACHER, STUDENT, & YOUTH IDENTIFICATION. The **International Student Identity Card (ISIC)** is the most widely accepted form of student ID, but unfortunately Puerto Rican businesses rarely offers student discounts. The card may be for helpful for its 24hr. emergency helpline (☎877-370-ISIC) and insurance benefits for US cardholders (see **Insurance,** p. 55). Applicants must be degree-seeking students of a secondary or post-secondary school and must be at least 12 years of age.

The **International Teacher Identity Card (ITIC)** offers teachers the same insurance coverage as well as similar but limited discounts. For travelers who are 25 years old or under but are not students, the **International Youth Travel Card** (IYTC) also offers many of the same benefits as the ISIC. Each of these identity cards costs $22. Many student travel agencies (see p. 67) issue the cards; for a list of issuing agencies, or for more information, contact the **International Student Travel Confederation (ISTC),** Herengracht 479, 1017 BS Amsterdam, The Netherlands (☎31 20 421 28 00; fax 421 28 10; www.istc.org).

CUSTOMS

WOULD YOU LIKE RUM WITH THAT? US Residents returning from Puerto Rico may claim $1200 worth of goods, including 5L of alcoholic beverages and 1000 cigarettes. It is illegal to bring Cuban cigars into the US unless you have just returned from a legal State Department trip.

If you're entering Puerto Rico from outside the US, you must declare certain items from abroad and pay a **duty** on the value of those articles that exceed the allowance established by the US Customs Service (see below). Upon returning home, you must declare all articles acquired in Puerto Rico and pay a duty on the value of articles that exceed the allowance established by your country's customs service. Keeping receipts for larger purchases made abroad will help establish values when you return. Goods and gifts purchased at **duty-free** shops abroad are not exempt from duty or sales tax at your point of return; you must declare these items as well. "Duty-free" merely means that you need not pay a tax in the country of purchase. Upon leaving Puerto Rico your baggage will be inspected by the US Department of Agriculture if you are flying through the US. You are not allowed to take mangos, sour sops, passion fruits, or potted plants back through the US. For more information on customs requirements, contact the info centers below:

Australia: Australian Customs Information Centre (in Australia ☎1 300 363 263, from elsewhere 61 2 6275 6666; www.customs.gov.au).

Canada: Canadian Customs (in Canada ☎800-461-9999, from elsewhere 204-983-3500; www.revcan.ca).

Ireland: Customs Information Office (☎01 877 6200; www.revenue.ie).

New Zealand: New Zealand Customs Service (☎0800 428 786; www.customs.govt.nz).

South Africa: South African Revenue Service, Pretoria Customs and Excise (☎012 334 6400; www.sars.gov.za).

UK: Her Majesty's Customs and Excise, National Advice Service (☎0845 010 9000; www.hmce.gov.uk).

US: US Customs and Border Protection Service (☎202-354-1000; www.customs.gov).

MONEY

CURRENCY & EXCHANGE

DOLLAR ($)		
AUS$1 = US$0.66		US$1 = AUS$1.50
CDN$1 = US$0.74		US$1 = CDN$1.35
EUR€1 = US$1.14		US$1 = EUR€0.87
IR£1 = US$1.45		US$1 = IR£0.69
NZ$1 = US$0.58		US$1 = NZ$1.73
UK£1 = US$1.66		US$1 = UK£0.60
ZAR1 = US$0.13		US$1 = ZAR7.59

Puerto Rico uses the **US dollar (dólar),** which is divided into 100 **cents (centavos).** American paper money is green; bills come in denominations of $1, $5, $10, $20, $50, and $100. Coins are 1¢ (penny), 5¢ (nickel), 10¢ (dime), 25¢ (quarter), and $1. Puerto Ricans often refer to dollars as *pesos* and cents as *pesetas.* The currency chart above is based on July 2004 exchange rates between US dollars (US$) and Australian dollars (AUS$), Canadian dollars (CDN$), European Union euros (EUR€), Irish pounds (IR£), New Zealand dollars (NZ$), British pounds (UK£), and South African Rand (ZAR). Check the currency converter on web sites such as www.americanexpress.com or www.xe.com, or a large newspaper, for the latest exchange rates. Unless otherwise indicated, all currencies are listed in US dollars.

There is almost no reason why you should convert foreign currency in Puerto Rico, as traveler's checks and credit cards are very widely accepted and there are ATMs everywhere. Store most of your money in these forms, then carry only about $100 in cash. If you do decide to work in cash, banks are almost the only establishments that exchange money and the ubiquitous **Banco Popular** offers competitive rates. San Juan International Airport has a Banco Popular (open M-F during office hours), an ATM, and a currency exchange booth. It's wise to bring enough US dollars to last for the first 24 hours of your trip, including a taxi ride to your hotel.

TRAVELER'S CHECKS

Traveler's checks are one of the safest and least troublesome means of carrying funds in Puerto Rico. Most major hotels, restaurants, and stores accept traveler's checks as payment and will provide change in cash. **American Express** and **Visa** are the most widely recognized brands. Many banks and agencies sell them for a small commission. It is best to get checks in denominations of $20, as these are easier for businesses to exchange. Check issuers provide refunds if the checks are lost or stolen, and many provide additional services, such as toll-free refund hotlines abroad, emergency message services, and stolen credit card assistance.

While traveling, keep check receipts and a record of which checks you've cashed separate from the checks themselves. It also helps to leave a list of check numbers with someone at home. Never countersign checks until you're ready to cash them, and then always bring photo ID. If your checks are **lost or stolen,** immediately contact a refund center of the company that issued your checks to be reimbursed; they may require a police report verifying the loss or theft. Ask about toll-free refund hotlines and the location of refund centers when purchasing checks, and always carry emergency funds in another form (cash, ATM card, credit card).

American Express: Checks are available with commission at select banks, at AmEx offices, and online (www.americanexpress.com; US residents only). American Express cardholders can also purchase checks by phone (☎888-269-6669). AAA (see p. 73) offers commission-free checks to its members. *Cheques for Two* can be signed by either of 2 people traveling together. For purchase locations or more information contact AmEx's service centers: In the US, Canada, and Puerto Rico ☎800-221-7282; in the UK ☎0800 587 6023; in Australia ☎800 68 80 22; in New Zealand ☎0508 555 358.

Visa: Checks are available (generally with commission) at banks worldwide. For the location of the nearest office, call Visa's service centers: From the US and Puerto Rico ☎800-227-6811; from the UK ☎0800 515 884; elsewhere UK collect ☎44 20 7937 8091.

CREDIT CARDS

Credit cards are widely accepted throughout Puerto Rico, although smaller establishments only accept cash. Major credit cards—**MasterCard** (along with its European counterparts **Euro Card** and **Access**) and **Visa** (with its European counterparts **Carte Bleue** or **Barclaycard**)—are the most prevalent and can be used to extract cash advances in dollars from associated banks and teller machines. **American Express, Discover,** and **Diner's Club** are much less common, so make sure to have an alternative method of payment. Credit card companies get the wholesale exchange rate, which is generally 5% better than the retail rate used by banks and other currency exchange establishments.

CREDIT CARD COMPANIES. Visa (☎800-336-8472) and MasterCard (☎800-307-7309) are issued in cooperation with banks and other organizations. American Express (☎800-843-2273) offers a variety of cards, some of which have annual fees. Depending on the card, AmEx cardholders receive various services, including the ability to: cash personal checks at AmEx offices abroad, access a 24hr. emergency medical and legal assistance hotline (in North America call ☎800-554-2639, elsewhere call US collect ☎1 715-343-7977), and enjoy American Express Travel Service benefits (including plane, hotel, and car rental reservation changes; baggage loss and flight insurance; mailgram and international cable services; and held mail). The Discover Card (in US ☎800-347-2683, from elsewhere US ☎1-801-902-3100) offers cashback bonuses on most purchases.

ATM CARDS (CASH CARDS)

ATM (Automated Teller Machine) cards are widely used on Puerto Rico; even Culebra and Vieques both have one ATM each. Depending on the system that your home bank uses, you can most likely access your personal bank account from abroad. ATMs get the same low wholesale exchange rate as credit cards, but there is often a limit on the amount of money you can withdraw per day. **Banco Popular** limits withdrawals to $200 per day, but other banks have more flexible limits. Typically expect two surcharges of $1-2 per withdrawal; one by the bank you are using and one by your home bank. If your PIN is longer than four digits, ask your bank whether you need a new number. Also, always carry spare cash as ATM networks have been known to be temporarily out of service.

DEBIT CARDS

Debit cards are a hybrid between credit and cash cards. They bear the logo of a major credit card, but purchases and withdrawals made with them are paid directly out of your bank account. Using a debit card like a credit card often incurs no fee (contact the issuing bank for details), gives you a favorable exchange rate, and frees you from having to carry large sums of money. Be careful, though: debit cards lack the theft protection that credit cards usually have.

GETTING MONEY FROM HOME

If you run out of money while traveling, the easiest and cheapest solution is to have someone back home make a deposit to your credit card or cash (ATM) card. Another option is to arrange a **bank money transfer,** which means asking a bank back home to wire money to a bank in Puerto Rico. This is the cheapest way to transfer cash, but it's also the slowest, usually taking several days or more. Money transfer services like **Western Union** are faster and more convenient than bank transfers—but also much pricier. Western Union has a desk in almost every **Pueblo** supermarket. To find one, visit www.westernunion.com, or call the company (in Puerto Rico or the US ☎ 800-325-6000, in Australia ☎ 800 501 500, in Canada ☎ 800-235-0000, in New Zealand ☎ 800 27 0000, in South Africa ☎ 0860 100031, in the UK ☎ 0800 83 38 33). To wire money to Puerto Rico using a credit card (Visa, MasterCard, Discover), call ☎ 800-225-5227.

COSTS

Puerto Rico is not cheap, but with a bit of creativity it is possible to travel to your heart's desire and still stay on a budget. A car is necessary to reach many parts of the island, and travelers who plan on renting must include this expense in any daily budget (for information on car rental, see p. 71).

STAYING ON A BUDGET. Accommodations will be a major expense. Guest houses start at $25 per night, but in many places (especially along the Rúta Panorámica) it can be impossible to find accommodations for less than $70. You can cut costs significantly by sharing a room or, even better, camping ($0-10 per night). A sit-down **meal** costs about $8-12 depending on the region, though it's usually easy to get a filling breakfast and lunch for under $5. **Transportation** is another significant cost. Car rental runs about $30-45 per day and **gas** prices have risen to $0.40 per liter. A bare-bones day in Puerto Rico (camping, buying food at supermarkets, traveling on *públicos*) would cost about $25-30. A slightly more comfortable day (sleeping in guest houses and the occasional budget hotel, eating one meal a day at a restaurant, going out at night) would run $90-100. For a luxurious day, the sky's the limit; many of the nicest hotels have rooms that cost $4000 per night. Finally, don't forget to factor in emergency reserve funds (at least $200) when planning how much money you'll need.

TIPS FOR SAVING MONEY. Considering that saving just a few dollars a day over the course of your trip might pay for days or weeks of additional travel, the art of penny-pinching is well worth learning. The best way to save money is to **travel with companions;** splitting the costs of hotel rooms and rental cars will make your trip much more affordable. Wise travelers **pay close attention to high season.** San Juan hotel prices are much higher from November to May, while west coast hotels charge more from May to August. The weather is always good, so choose your destination accordingly. Travelers willing to brave the risk of hurricane season will find that everything gets cheaper in September and October. Of course **camping** is by far the most economical option; Culebra and Vieques have exceptionally nice campgrounds. The same principle also works for cutting down on the cost of **meals;** buying food in supermarkets is much cheaper than eating out. Recently imposed taxes have greatly increased the cost of **prepared alcohol** in Puerto Rico, but bottles still remain comparatively inexpensive. Making your own *cuba libres* on the beach is much cheaper than heading to a bar. With each bottle of water costing at least $1, keeping hydrated can add up quickly. Cut costs by filling **water bottles** in hotel sinks or potable water cisterns. Renting a car is convenient, but also very expensive;

planning a trip on **public transportation** can cut trip costs in half. Choose your sights wisely; many of the best museums, especially in Old San Juan, are free or cost less than $1. San Juan also has frequent **festivals** with live music or entertainment. These simple cost-saving tactics make Puerto Rico affordable for almost anyone.

TIPPING, BARGAINING, AND TAXES

In Puerto Rico, it is customary to tip waitstaff and cab drivers 15-20% (at your discretion). Tips are usually not included in restaurant bills. It is unnecessary to tip at most *cafeterías*, *panaderías*, and other small eateries where you pick up food at the counter. Porters expect at least a $1 per bag tip to carry your bags. Though not obligatory, it is also nice to give *público* drivers a small tip; about 10% should suffice. **Bargaining** is generally frowned upon and fruitless in Puerto Rico, but it does not hurt to ask hotel or guest house owners if they can offer a discount—many will lower rates if they are not full, especially if you are staying that day.

Get ready to shop; Puerto Rico has **no sales tax, restaurant tax, or Value-Added Tax.** There is a 9% **accommodations tax,** but unofficial guest houses frequently do not charge a tax. *Let's Go* indicates if tax is included in most accommodations listing.

SAFETY & SECURITY

Puerto Rico is generally considered a safe place; however, travelers should be sure to exercise the basic precautions described below. For information on transportation and driving safety, see **Getting Around** (p. 69). For more specific tips and information, see **Specific Concerns** (p. 75) or **Wilderness Safety** (p. 59).

> **EMERGENCY=☎ 911** For emergencies anywhere in Puerto Rico dial 911. In a few remote areas 911 may not work. If it does not, the Puerto Rico police department phone number is listed in every practical information section; it is generally the regional prefix plus 2020.

URBAN EXPLOITS. San Juan has gotten an unfair reputation over the last few years as a drug- and crime-filled city. Like any large metropolitan area, San Juan does have its share of crime, but it's no less safe than London or New York and most travelers do not have any problems. Most incidents are targeted and limited to specific areas; travelers should feel comfortable in Old San Juan, Condado, Ocean Park, and Isla Verde. At night it is best not to wander alone, especially in Santurce, Hato Rey, and Río Piedras. Travelers should also take caution in the metropolitan areas of Ponce, Mayagüez, Arecibo, Fajardo, and Aguadilla. There is usually less crime as the cities get smaller, but it's always good to keep your wits about you; Culebra and Isla Mona are the only really crime-free places in Puerto Rico. Unlike other major tourist destinations, Puerto Rico does not have a history of crime specifically targeting foreigners (except on the beach; see below); the biggest problem is being in the wrong place at the wrong time. Whenever possible, *Let's Go* warns of unsafe neighborhoods in every big city, but there are some good general tips to follow. When walking at night, stick to busy, well-lit streets and avoid dark alleyways. Keep in mind that a district can change character drastically between blocks and from day to night. Look for children playing, women walking in the open, and other signs of an active community. If you feel uncomfortable, leave as quickly and directly as you can, but don't allow fear of the unknown to turn you into a hermit.

BEACHES. Unfortunately, petty thieves have learned that travelers like to swim in the ocean and leave all of their valuables on the beach. **Do not take anything valuable to the beach.** This includes wallets, cell phones, cash, and jewelry. If you are traveling with a group, have one person stay on the beach and watch your stuff while the

ESSENTIALS

> **TRAVEL ADVISORIES.** The following government offices provide travel information and advisories by telephone, by fax, or via the web. Unfortunately, most of the regional information covers the US and not Puerto Rico. Take US info with a grain of salt and remember that Puerto Rico is a territory over 1000 mi. away from the mainland.
>
> **Australian Department of Foreign Affairs and Trade:** ☎ 13 00 555135; faxback service 02 6261 1299; www.dfat.gov.au.
>
> **Canadian Department of Foreign Affairs and International Trade (DFAIT):** In Canada and the US ☎ 800-267-8376, from elsewhere ☎ 1-613-944-4000; www.dfait-maeci.gc.ca. Call for their free booklet, *Bon Voyage...But.*
>
> **New Zealand Ministry of Foreign Affairs:** ☎ 04 439 8000; fax 494 8506; www.mft.govt.nz/travel/index.html.
>
> **United Kingdom Foreign and Commonwealth Office:** ☎ 020 7008 0232; fax 7008 0155; www.fco.gov.uk.
>
> **US Department of State:** ☎ 202-647-5225; faxback service 202-647-3000; www.travel.state.gov. For *A Safe Trip Abroad,* call ☎ 202-512-1800.

others swim. If you are traveling alone, the best thing to do is to put your hotel/car key in a waterproof bag, keep it with you when you enter the water, and leave absolutely nothing valuable on the beach. Another option is to ask a nearby beach-goer to watch your stuff while you swim, but this requires a bit of trust and a lot of luck. Less frequented beaches have become targets for car-jackings, especially along the north coast. When parking at the beach, do not leave anything in sight in your car and try not to store valuables in your trunk.

TERRORISM. In light of the September 11, 2001 terrorist attacks in the eastern US, the US government frequently puts the nation, and its territories, on an elevated terrorism alert. Puerto Rico has not had any attacks, or threats of attacks, but like the rest of the US the island has taken necessary precautions. Allow extra time for airport security and do not pack sharp objects in your carry-on luggage, as they will be confiscated. Monitor developments in the news and stay on top of any local, state, or federal terrorist warnings, but do not let fear of terrorism prevent you from enjoying your vacation.

PROTECTING YOUR VALUABLES. Though Puerto Rico does not have a notorious problem with petty theft, it is not unheard of. There are a few steps you can take to minimize the financial risk associated with traveling. **Carry as little cash as possible.** Don't put a wallet with money in your back pocket. **Keep a small cash reserve separate from your primary stash.** This should be about $50 sewn into or stored in the depths of your pack, along with your traveler's check numbers and important photocopies. Beware of **pickpockets** in city crowds, especially at festivals.

DRUGS & ALCOHOL

The drinking age in Puerto Rico is 18—when people bother to check. This is a culture based on rum and generally drinking rules are much more lenient here than in the US or even Europe. It is technically illegal to drive with a blood alcohol level over 0.8%, but it happens. Some cities do have specific rules about drinking in public. Except during major festivals, it is illegal to drink in the streets of Old San Juan (although it is legal in most other cities). It is also illegal to drink out of a bottle on the street in many cities, but bars will happily pour your beer into a plastic cup.

Narcotics such as marijuana, heroin, and cocaine are highly illegal in Puerto Rico, and this prohibition is much more strictly enforced. If you carry prescription drugs while traveling, keep a copy of the prescription with you.

Find (Our Student Airfares are cheap, flexible & exclusive) great Student Airfares everywhere at StudentUniverse.com and **Get lost.**

 StudentUniverse.com   **Student Airfares everywhere**

HEALTH

Common sense is the simplest prescription for good health. Drink lots of fluids to prevent dehydration and constipation, wear sturdy, broken-in shoes and clean socks, and use talcum powder to keep your feet dry.

BEFORE YOU GO

Though drugstores throughout the island carry every medical supply you could need, it's always best to be prepared. For minor health problems, bring a compact **first-aid kit** (see p. 56). Allergy sufferers might want to obtain a full supply of any necessary medication before the trip. While traveling, be sure to keep all medication in your carry-on luggage.

IMMUNIZATIONS & PRECAUTIONS

Travelers over two years old should make sure that the following vaccines are up to date: MMR (for measles, mumps, and rubella); DTaP or Td (for diptheria, tetanus, and pertussis); OPV (for polio); HbCV (for haemophilus influenza B); and HBV (for hepatitis B). For recommendations on immunizations and prophylaxis, consult the CDC (see below) in the US or the equivalent in your home country, and check with a doctor for guidance. Travelers spending extensive time in rural Puerto Rico should also consider getting vaccinated against typhoid fever, though the vast majority of travelers will not need this vaccination.

USEFUL ORGANIZATIONS & PUBLICATIONS

The US **Centers for Disease Control and Prevention** (**CDC;** ☎877-394-8747; fax 888-232-3299; www.cdc.gov/travel) maintains an international travelers' hotline and an informative web site. The CDC's comprehensive booklet *Health Information for International Travel*, an annual rundown of disease, immunization, and health advice, is free online or $30 from the Public Health Foundation (☎877-252-1200). For information on medical evacuation services and travel insurance, see the US government's web site (http://travel.state.gov/medical.html) or the **British Foreign and Commonwealth Office** (www.fco.gov.uk). For more information on travel health try the **International Travel Health Guide** by Stuart Rose ($25; www.travmed.com).

MEDICAL ASSISTANCE ON THE ROAD

Puerto Rico has the best medical system in the Caribbean. Every municipal center has some kind of health clinic or hospital, and all large cities have major hospitals with 24hr. emergency rooms. Travelers who have a minor medical problem in Puerto Rico can visit any hospital **clinic** and wait to see a doctor. Most hospitals have English-speaking doctors; smaller hospitals that do not should be able to find a translator. In an emergency, dial ☎**911** from any phone and an operator will send out paramedics, a fire brigade, or the police as needed. Alternatively, go directly to the nearest emergency room for immediate service. Puerto Rican hospitals take many American medical insurance plans, but most foreigners will have to pay for medical service. Almost all cities and towns have standard pharmacies. Culebra has much more limited medical services and in a real emergency you will have to be evacuated to Fajardo. Isla Mona has no medical services and is very remote.

Those with medical conditions (such as diabetes, allergies to antibiotics, epilepsy, heart conditions) may want to obtain a **Medic Alert** membership (first year $35, annually thereafter $20), which comes with a stainless steel ID tag, a 24hr. collect-call number, and other benefits. Contact the Medic Alert Foundation, 2323 Colorado Ave, Turlock, CA 95382, USA (in the US ☎888-633-4298; from elsewhere ☎1-209-668-3333; www.medicalert.org).

Don't be left out...

Get your travel on.
The International
Student Identity Card

International *Student* Identity Card
Carte d'étudiant internationale / Carné internacional de estudiante

STUDENT

Studies at / Étudiant à / Est. de Enseñanza
University of Student Travel

Name / Nom / Nombre
CHIN, S

Born / Né(e) le / Nacido/a el
23/06/1982

Validity / Validité / Validez
09/2003 - 12/2004

ISIC
S 000 123 456 789

$22 is all it takes
to save hundreds.

Accepted worldwide for awesome discounts!

The International Student Identity Card (ISIC) is a great
way to take advantage of discounts and benefits such
as airfare, accommodations, transportation, attractions,
theme parks, hotels, theaters, car rentals and more!

**visit www.ISICus.com to find out about discounts
and the benefits of carrying your ISIC.**

ISIC

Call or visit STA Travel online to find the nearest
issuing office and purchase your card today:

www.ISICus.com   (800) 474.8214

enough already...
Get a room.

Book your next hotel with the people who know what you want.

- » hostels
- » budget hotels
- » hip hotels
- » airport transfers
- » city tours
- » adventure packages
- » and more!

(800) 777.0112
www.statravel.com/hotels

WE'VE BEEN THERE.

Exciting things are happening at www.statravel.com.

ONCE IN PUERTO RICO

ENVIRONMENTAL HAZARDS

SURFING AND SWIMMING PRECAUTIONS Puerto Rican waves make for some of the world's best surf, but they can also be deadly. High surf can bring strong currents and rip tides, and each year lives are lost and endangered when surfers and swimmers fail to heed precautions. Know your limits and use caution when you swim or surf. The following are a few simple precautions:
Never swim alone.
Do not struggle against a **current** or **riptide;** swim diagonally across it.
Signal for help if you are unable to swim out of a strong current.
Use a **leash** for surf and boogie boards.
Keep your distance from other surfers and swimmers—a loose board can deliver a lethal blow.
Familiarize yourself with **beach and surf conditions,** as well as beach safety signs and symbols before you head out.
If you see **sharks,** get out of the water.

ESSENTIALS

Puerto Rico's hot tropical climate may be one of the island's biggest attractions, but it can prove harmful to travelers who don't take proper precautions.

Heat exhaustion and dehydration: It is important to watch out for dehydration—consciously drink more water than you drink at home. Heat exhaustion leads to nausea, excessive thirst, headaches, and dizziness. Avoid it by drinking plenty of fluids, eating salty foods (e.g. crackers), and abstaining from dehydrating beverages (e.g. alcohol and caffeinated beverages). Continuous heat stress can eventually lead to heatstroke, characterized by a rising temperature, severe headache, delirium, and cessation of sweating. Victims should be cooled off with wet towels and taken to a doctor.

Sunburn: Another extremely common affliction for unaccustomed visitors is sunburn. Always wear sunscreen with an SPF of at least 15, especially on boats. Even if you want to come home with that perfect Caribbean tan, you don't want to look like a lobster. If you get sunburned, drink more fluids than usual and apply an aloe-based lotion. Severe sunburns can lead to sun poisoning, a condition that affects the entire body, causing fever, chills, nausea, and vomiting. Sun poisoning should always be treated by a doctor.

INSECT-BORNE DISEASES

Many diseases are transmitted by insects—mainly mosquitoes, fleas, ticks, and lice. Puerto Rico has fewer mosquitoes than other tropical countries but they can still be a nuisance at best and a disease-carrying predator at worst. Use insect repellents that contain DEET and if you're planning some serious outdoors time, soak or spray your gear with permethrin.

Malaria: Travelers to Puerto Rico are not at risk of malaria.

Dengue fever: An "urban viral infection" transmitted by *Aedes* mosquitoes, which bite during the day. Early symptoms include chills, high fever, headaches, swollen lymph nodes, muscle aches, and, in some instances, a pink rash on the face. If you experience these symptoms, see a doctor, drink plenty of liquids, and take fever-reducing medication such as acetaminophen (Tylenol). *Never take aspirin to treat dengue fever.*

Other insect-borne diseases: The following diseases could occur in Puerto Rico, but are extremely unlikely. **Filariasis** is a roundworm infestation transmitted by mosquitoes. Infection causes enlargement of extremities and has no vaccine. **Leishmaniasis,** a parasite transmitted by sand flies, can occur in Puerto Rico. Common symptoms are fever, weakness, and swelling of the spleen. There is a treatment, but no vaccine.

FOOD- & WATER-BORNE DISEASES

Prevention is the best cure: be sure that your food is properly cooked and the water you drink is clean. The tap water in Puerto Rico is safe for drinking.

Traveler's diarrhea: Results from drinking untreated water or eating uncooked foods. Symptoms include nausea, bloating, and urgency. If afflicted eat quick-energy, non-sugary foods with protein and carbohydrates to keep your strength up. Over-the-counter anti-diarrheals (e.g. Imodium) may counteract the problems. The most dangerous side effect is dehydration; drink 8 oz. of water with ½ tsp. of sugar or honey and a pinch of salt, try uncaffeinated soft drinks, or eat salted crackers. If you develop a fever or your symptoms don't go away after 4-5 days, consult a doctor. Consult a doctor immediately for treatment of diarrhea in children.

Dysentery: Results from a serious intestinal infection caused by certain bacteria. The most common type is bacillary dysentery, also called shigellosis. Symptoms include bloody diarrhea (sometimes mixed with mucus), fever, and abdominal pain and tenderness. Bacillary dysentery generally only lasts a week, but it is highly contagious. Amoebic dysentery, which develops more slowly, is a more serious disease and may cause long-term damage if left untreated. A stool test can determine which kind you have; seek medical help immediately. Dysentery can be treated with the drugs norfloxacin or ciprofloxacin (commonly known as Cipro). If you are traveling in high-risk (especially rural) regions, consider obtaining a prescription before you leave home.

Hepatitis A: A viral infection of the liver acquired primarily through contaminated water. Symptoms include fatigue, fever, loss of appetite, nausea, dark urine, jaundice, vomiting, aches and pains, and light stools. The risk is highest in rural areas. Ask your doctor about the vaccine (Havrix or Vaqta) or an injection of immune globulin (IG).

Giardiasis: Transmitted through parasites (microbes, tapeworms, etc. in contaminated water and food) and acquired by drinking untreated water. Symptoms include swollen glands or lymph nodes, fever, rashes or itchiness, and digestive problems.

Schistosomiasis: Also known as bilharzia; a parasitic disease caused when the larvae of flatworm penetrate unbroken skin. Symptoms include an itchy localized rash, followed in 4-6 weeks by fever, fatigue, painful urination, diarrhea, loss of appetite, and night sweats. To avoid it, try not to swim in fresh water; if exposed to untreated water, rub the area vigorously with a towel and apply rubbing alcohol.

Typhoid fever: Caused by the salmonella bacteria; occurs occasionally in rural areas of Puerto Rico. While mostly transmitted through contaminated food and water, it may also be acquired by direct contact with another person. Early symptoms include fever, headaches, fatigue, loss of appetite, constipation, and sometimes a rash on the abdomen or chest. Antibiotics can treat typhoid, but a vaccination (70-90% effective) is recommended.

OTHER INFECTIOUS DISEASES

Rabies: Transmitted through the saliva of infected animals; fatal if untreated. By the time symptoms (thirst and muscle spasms) appear, the disease is in its terminal stage. If you are bitten, wash the wound thoroughly, seek immediate medical care, and try to have the animal located. A rabies vaccine, which consists of 3 shots given over a 21-day period, exists but is only semi-effective.

Hepatitis B: A viral infection of the liver transmitted via bodily fluids or needle-sharing. Symptoms, which may not surface until years after infection, include jaundice, loss of appetite, fever, and joint pain. A 3-shot vaccination sequence is recommended for health-care workers, sexually-active travelers, and anyone planning to seek medical treatment abroad; it must begin 6 mo. before traveling.

Hepatitis C: Like Hepatitis B, but the mode of transmission differs. IV drug users, those with occupational exposure to blood, hemodialysis patients, and recipients of blood transfusions are at the highest risk, but the disease can also be spread through sexual contact or sharing items like razors and toothbrushes that may have traces of blood on them.

AIDS, HIV, & STDS

For detailed information on **Acquired Immune Deficiency Syndrome (AIDS)** in Puerto Rico, call the **US Centers for Disease Control's** 24hr. hotline at ☎800-342-2437, or contact the **Joint United Nations Programme on HIV/AIDS (UNAIDS),** 20, Ave. Appia, CH-1211 Geneva 27, Switzerland (☎41 22 791 3666; fax 22 791 4187). **Sexually transmitted diseases (STDs)** such as gonorrhea, chlamydia, genital warts, syphilis, and herpes are easier to catch than HIV and can be just as deadly. **Hepatitis** B and C can also be transmitted sexually (see above). Though condoms may protect you from some STDs, oral or even tactile contact can lead to transmission. If you think you may have contracted an STD, see a doctor immediately.

WOMEN'S HEALTH

Women traveling in unsanitary conditions are vulnerable to **urinary tract** and **bladder infections,** common and very uncomfortable bacterial conditions that cause a burning sensation and painful (sometimes frequent) urination. Over-the-counter medicines can sometimes alleviate symptom vs, but if they persist, see a doctor. **Vaginal yeast infections** may flare up in hot and humid climates. Wearing loose-fitting trousers or a skirt and cotton underwear will help, as will over-the-counter remedies like Monostat or Gynelotrimin.

INSURANCE

Travel insurance generally covers four basic areas: medical/health problems, property loss, trip cancellation/interruption, and emergency evacuation. Although your regular insurance policies may well extend to travel-related accidents, you may consider purchasing travel insurance if the cost of potential trip cancellation/interruption or emergency medical evacuation is greater than you can absorb. Prices for travel insurance purchased separately generally run about $50 per week for full coverage, while trip cancellation/interruption may be purchased separately at a rate of about $5.50 per $100 of coverage. Call your provider to see if your home **medical insurance** covers costs incurred abroad. **Canadians** are protected by their home province's health insurance plan for up to 90 days after leaving the country; check with the provincial Ministry of Health or Health Plan Headquarters for details. **Homeowners' insurance** (or your family's coverage) often covers theft during travel and loss of travel documents (passport, plane ticket, etc.) up to $500.

   ISIC and **ITIC** (see p. 45) provide basic insurance benefits, including $100 per day of in-hospital sickness for up to 60 days, $3000 of accident-related medical reimbursement, and $25,000 for emergency medical transport. Cardholders have access to a toll-free 24hr. helpline (run by the insurance provider **TravelGuard**) for medical, legal, and financial emergencies overseas (US and Canada ☎877-370-4742, elsewhere call US collect ☎1-715-345-0505). **American Express** (☎800-528-4800) grants most cardholders automatic car rental insurance (collision and theft, but not liability) and ground travel accident coverage of $100,000 on flight purchases made with the card. Many budget travel agencies (see p. 67) offer travel insurance to supplement your basic coverage.

PACKING

Lay out only what you absolutely need, then take half the clothes and twice the money. If you plan to do a lot of hiking, also see **Camping & the Outdoors,** p. 62.

LUGGAGE. If you plan to use a lot of public transportation, then a sturdy internal **frame backpack** is unbeatable. (For the basics on buying a pack, see p. 60.) Toting a **suitcase** is fine if you plan to stay in one or two cities or if you have a car. In addition to your main piece of luggage, it is useful to bring a **daypack.**

CLOTHING. Puerto Rico's climate makes it easy to dress. Shorts and light t-shirts or tank tops suffice for almost any occasion. Puerto Ricans dress up to go out—women wear tight pants (usually jeans) with shirts that redefine scandalous and men wear slacks and button-down shirts. A long-sleeved t-shirt or a light jacket may come in handy for cooler nights in the mountains, though during the summer it's almost never needed. No matter when you're traveling, it's a good idea to bring a **rain jacket** for those sudden Caribbean downpours (Gore-Tex® is both waterproof and breathable). Remember also that if you visit churches, you'll need something besides tank tops and shorts to be respectful. If you plan to splurge on a chichi dinner at an exclusive restaurant, you may need to upgrade your wardrobe a smidgen.

CONVERTERS & ADAPTERS. In Puerto Rico, as in the rest of the US, electricity is 110 volts AC. 220/240V electrical appliances don't like 110V current. Visit a hardware store for an **adapter** (which changes the shape of the plug) and a **converter** (which changes the voltage; $20). Don't make the mistake of using only an adapter (unless appliance instructions explicitly state otherwise).

FIRST-AID KIT. For a basic first-aid kit, pack: bandages, pain reliever, antibiotic cream, a thermometer, a Swiss Army knife, tweezers, moleskin, decongestant, motion-sickness remedy, diarrhea or upset-stomach medication (Pepto Bismol or Imodium), an antihistamine, sunscreen, insect repellent, and burn ointment.

FILM. Film developing in Puerto Rico is expensive (about $6-8 for a roll of 24 color exposures), so consider bringing along enough film for your entire trip and developing it at home. Less serious photographers may want to bring **disposable cameras** rather than an expensive permanent one. Despite disclaimers, airport security X-rays *can* fog film, so buy a lead-lined pouch at a camera store or ask security to hand-inspect it. Always pack film in your carry-on luggage, since higher-intensity X-rays are used on checked luggage.

OTHER USEFUL ITEMS. Non-Spanish speakers will probably want a pocket Spanish dictionary. If you plan to spend a lot of time in the mountains, basic **outdoors equipment** (plastic water bottle, compass, waterproof matches, pocketknife, sunglasses, sunscreen, hat) may prove useful. Quick repairs of torn garments can be done with a **needle and thread.** Other things you're liable to forget include: an umbrella, sealable plastic bags (for damp clothes, soap, food, shampoo, and other spillables), an alarm clock, safety pins, a flashlight, earplugs, and garbage bags.

IMPORTANT DOCUMENTS. Don't forget your passport, traveler's checks, ATM and/or credit cards, adequate ID, travel insurance forms, a driver's license, and photocopies of all of the aforementioned in case these documents are lost or stolen.

ACCOMMODATIONS

With the exception of a couple of dorm-style rooms in Rincón, there are no youth hostels in Puerto Rico. Most travelers will end up staying in a combination of hotels, guest houses, and *paradores.* Groups of visitors staying in one place for a week or more can save money by contacting a realtor.

GUEST HOUSES

Guest houses are usually the most affordable type of accommodation in Puerto Rico, with a single room costing about $30-70, depending on the region. Generally owned by a private individual (as opposed to a company or chain), guest houses range from ramshackle rooms rented out on the second floor of a residence to charming hotel-style accommodations complete with a reception area and complimentary breakfast. Most accommodations of this type do not have a 24hr. reception area, so it is best to have a reservation if you plan to arrive late. Guest house rooms almost always have private bathrooms with hot water, but the furniture may be old or mismatched and the room itself may be aging. Guest house rooms rarely have daily maid service; instead rooms are cleaned after a guest leaves. The most important quality in a guest house is safety, as you will be trusting your life, and all your possessions, to the owner. Rooms are typically priced by the number of beds instead of the number of occupants, so a single person will pay the same as two people staying in one double bed and two people staying in separate beds will have to pay the price of a quad. Few guest houses accept credit cards. Guest houses are not always endorsed by the government, thus they do not always charge the 9% accommodations tax.

HOTELS

When Puerto Ricans refer to a "hotel" they are generally talking about the big, fancy, typically American chains. Wyndham (☎877-999-3223, outside the US and Canada ☎972-915-7070; www.wyndham.com) trumps the competition with six incredible resorts on the eastern half of the island. Marriott (www.marriott.com), Hilton (www.hilton.com), InterContinental (www.ichotelsgroup.com), Holiday Inn (www.holiday-inn.com), Embassy Suites (www.embassysuites.com), and Ritz Carlton (www.ritzcarlton.com) also have luxury hotels in the San Juan area with all of the amenities you could possibly imagine, from private beach areas to glitzy casinos. These hotels are not listed in *Let's Go*, but if you feel like breaking the bank, all of the above chains have web sites with full information: single rooms start at around $200 per night and go up from there. However, many offer discounts for army personnel, businesses, AAA members, frequent fliers, and a variety of other groups. Check the web sites for more details.

There are also a few **small hotels** in most urban areas (and quite a few in San Juan) that charge much more reasonable rates (singles $60-130 per night). These hotels usually have the regular amenities—bathrooms, daily maid service, 24hr. reception, sometimes continental breakfast—but few of the perks, like casinos and pools. These small hotels can get full so it is best to reserve in advance, especially during high season. Hotel employees almost always speak some English.

PARADORES

Paradores (roughly translated as "country inns") are small, independent hotels throughout the island that fit a set of specific requirements and are endorsed by the Puerto Rican Tourism Company (PRTC). A single room usually runs about $60-95 and the PRTC dictates that rates cannot change by season, making west coast *paradores* an excellent bargain during summer months. *Paradores* always have 24hr. reception, daily maid service, a wheelchair accessible room, an English-speaking staff, a restaurant, corporate discounts, and a variety of other features. Most also have a pool. Located primarily in the central mountains and on the west coast, *paradores* are very popular vacation destinations for Puerto Ricans. The Puerto Rican Tourism Company web site (www.gotopuertorico.com) and *Que Pasa* magazine both have a complete list of *paradores*.

VACATION RENTALS

Travelers staying for at least three days should consider consulting a realtor for information about vacation rentals. Most vacation rentals are either winter homes that the owners rent out during the rest of the year or permanent vacation homes that realtors rent out on a rotating basis. These units vary from timeshare condos in San Juan to luxurious houses on Culebra and Vieques. Most vacation rentals are quite classy and come with bedding, linens, and a fully equipped kitchen. Some also have air conditioning, pools, cable TV, and even jacuzzis. Always make sure you know exactly what amenities are included before reserving a vacation home, as units vary greatly and it is usually impossible to see a unit before reserving. Vacation rentals rarely have daily maid service, but usually offer unequalled privacy and a remarkably good deal for larger groups. *Let's Go* includes realtor information in San Juan, Luquillo, Vieques, Culebra, and Rincón. Many properties are also listed on the web. Search for "Puerto Rico vacation rentals" or try the following web sites: www.vacationhomes.com, www.prwest.com, www.surf-sun.com, www.10kvacationrentals.com, and www.a1vacationrentals.com.

CABINS AND VACATION CENTERS

When Puerto Ricans travel they frequently take the whole family, down to the last cousin. Several no-frills accommodations cater directly to these large groups. The Puerto Rican **Compañía de Parques Nacionales (CPN)** sponsors **centros vacacionales** (vacation centers) at beaches in Arroyo (p. 240), Boquerón (p. 201), Añasco, and Humacao, and in the forest near Maricao (p. 277). These vacation centers usually have two types of cabins. *Cabanas* are basic concrete structures with two bedrooms, bunk beds, a tiny kitchen area, no air conditioning, and no hot water. *Villas* have a similar structure, but are slightly more expensive and come with air conditioning and hot water. Almost all vacation center structures accommodate six people in a very small space. In addition to rooms most complexes also contain a pool, basketball courts, and a large beach. These are a great bargain for groups of travelers who plan to spend most time outside and don't mind cramped, cement rooms. All villas and cabins come with a full kitchen, but they **do not include sheets, towels, or kitchen supplies.** In 2003 the National Parks Company charged $60 per night for cabanas or $100 for villas plus 9% tax, with occasional promotional discounts. During low season (Sept.-March) it is usually possible to show up and get a room, but during major holidays (Holy Week, Christmas) and summer (May-Aug.) you must reserve well in advance either at the specific vacation center or at the San Juan office of the Compañía de Parques Nacionales, Apartado 9022089, San Juan, P.R. 00902-2089 (☎787-622-5200 ext. 355-369; fax 982-2107). Several private individuals have opened **cabanas** with a similar design; again, travelers must bring their own towels, linens, and kitchen equipment.

MOTELS

Motels are **not** traditional accommodations like they are in the US, but extremely private rooms rented out by the hour. See **The Luv Nest** (p. 159) for more info.

CAMPING & THE OUTDOORS

Camping in Puerto Rico can be a rewarding way to slash travel costs. Camping areas are generally in beautiful locations, either steps from the beach or deep in a tropical forest, and offer the same view that you find in five-star hotels. Puerto Rico's temperate climate only adds to the appeal of camping, which is feasible year-round. During the winter months (Sept.-May) very few Puerto Ricans go on vacation and most of the campgrounds are completely empty. The exceptions are major holidays, such as Christmas and *semana santa*. During summer months Puerto Ricans flock to campgrounds around the island and it is imperative to make reservations in advance.

There are two principal organizations that maintain camping areas in Puerto Rico. The **Departamento de Recursos Naturales** operates campgrounds at reserves primarily in the Cordillera Central, while the Compañía de Parques Nacionales allows camping at several of the public beaches *(balnearios)* throughout the island (see below). It is possible to camp in El Yunque, but you must first obtain a

ESSENTIALS

permit from park rangers. Puerto Rico has very few private campgrounds and those that do exist tend to be more expensive and less equipped than public camping areas. There are no camping areas in the San Juan area, though some people have been known to camp illegally in the Piñones area.

DEPARTAMENTO DE RECURSOS NATURALES (DRN). Puerto Rico's DRN operates camping areas in **Cambalache, Carite, Guajataca, Guilarte, Isla Mona, Lago Luchetti, Río Abajo, Sosúa,** and **Toro Negro.** However, at any given time at least two are usually closed for repairs. Good news first: most DRN campgrounds are safe, well-located, and well-equipped with a located gate, rustic showers, flush toilets, running water, covered picnic tables, outdoor grills, and trash cans. The bad news is that the camping process is enormously bureaucratic. Campers must first **get a permit** and **make a reservation** with a regional DRN office (see list below). To get a permit, you must pay $4 per person and provide the exact dates you want to camp. DRN officials asks that campers reserve at least two weeks in advance, but they sometimes make exceptions during low season. After obtaining a permit, campers need to check into the reserve's office during opening hours (usually M-F 7am-3:30pm) to get a key; campgrounds do not have attendants and campers use their own key for the front gate and the bathrooms. Almost none of the DRN camping areas are accessible without a car. Finally, few DRN officers speak English. If you can handle this governmental runaround, most campgrounds are gorgeous and peaceful, especially in the slow winter months. The main DRN office is located in San Juan next to the Club Naútico on Puerto de Tierra (see p. 97). Regional offices are in: **Aguadilla** (p. 174), **Arecibo** (p. 164), **Mayagüez** (p. 190), and **Ponce** (p. 223). For complete information (in Spanish), check the DRN web site at www.drnapr.com.

COMPAÑÍA DE PARQUES NACIONALES (CPN). The National Parks Company's oceanfront campgrounds afford travelers the opportunity to enjoy at a million-dollar view for mere dollars. The CPN allows camping at six public beaches around Puerto Rico, including **Cerro Gordo** (near Dorado), **La Monserrate** (in Luquillo), **Seven Seas** (in Fajardo), **Punta Guilarte** (near Arroyo), and incredible beach campgrounds on **Vieques** and **Culebra.** These campgrounds almost always consist of big grassy fields that transform into a sea of tents during big holidays. Camping areas usually have some type of picnic tables, outdoor showers, and flush toilets, though some bathrooms are not cleaned regularly. Only some CPN camping areas have 24hr. surveillance and unfortunately some of the others (Cerro Gordo and La Monserrate) have reputations of being less than safe. **Never camp alone at a camping area without a guard.** The CPN charges campers $10 per tent for up to six people, except at Playa Flamenco in Culebra, which recently increased prices to $20 per tent. Fortunately, the CPN is much less bureaucratic than the DRN and travelers can usually arrive any time and camp without a reservation. For more information contact the CPN main office in San Juan, Apartado 9022089, San Juan, PR 00902-2089 (☎787-622-5200 ext. 355-369; fax 982-2107). Spanish-speakers can find additional information on the CPN web site at www.parquesnacionalespr.com.

WILDERNESS SAFETY

THE GREAT OUTDOORS. The greatest danger while exploring Puerto Rico's outdoors is **heat exhaustion** (p. 53). Be sure to take a hat, sunscreen, sunglasses, and most importantly plenty of water on any outdoor excursion. Prepare yourself for an emergency by always packing rain gear, a first-aid kit, a reflector, a whistle, and high energy food. Check **weather forecasts** and pay attention to the skies when hiking, since weather patterns can change suddenly. Puerto Rico gets a lot of rain, even during the "dry season" and **flash floods** can knock out trees, bridges, and unsuspecting hikers. Whenever possible, let someone know when and where you are going hiking. See **Health** (p. 52) for information about outdoor ailments and basic medical concerns.

ESSENTIALS

WILDLIFE. Puerto Rico is lucky to have very few dangerous animals. There are no poisonous snakes and the only threatening land animal is the **rabid mongoose.** This species was originally imported to control the rat population and now runs wild, especially in **El Yunque.** If you see a mongoose, simply walk away as quickly as possible.

The waters of Puerto Rico are slightly more dangerous. Jellyfish and sea lice patrol the seas around Puerto Rico, but few are fatal. To protect yourself from jellyfish stings, wear protective clothing (a wet suit or lycra) when spending extensive amounts of time in the water. The **Portuguese Man-of-War** has been known to inhabit Caribbean waters. Purplish-blue in color with tentacles up to 30 ft. long, the Portuguese Man-of-War also has a painful and potentially dangerous sting, which has been know to cause anaphylactic shock, interference with heart and lung function, and even death. If you are stung by a Portuguese Man-of-War, rinse the sting with salt or fresh water and apply a cold compress to the affected area. If pain persists or if breathing difficulty develops, consult a medical professional. **Shark attacks** in Puerto Rico are extremely rare—Puerto Rico has had eight unprovoked shark attacks since 1749, and only two were fatal. Still sharks, especially small nurse sharks, do patrol the Caribbean. Surfers and spearfishers are at greatest risk, and swimmers are advised to stay out of the water at dawn and dusk when sharks move inshore to feed. Experts also advise against wearing high-contrast clothing or shiny jewelry and to avoid excessive splashing, all of which can attract sharks.

CAMPING AND HIKING EQUIPMENT

WHAT TO BUY...

Good camping equipment is both sturdy and light. Camping equipment is generally more expensive in Australia, New Zealand, and the UK than in North America. Puerto Rico does not have supply rentals, so travelers should come prepared.

Sleeping Bag: Most bags are rated by season ("summer" means 30-40°F at night; "four-season" or "winter" means below 0°F). They are made either of **down** (warmer and lighter, but more expensive, and miserable when wet) or of **synthetic** material (heavier, more durable, and warmer when wet). Prices range from $70-210 for a summer synthetic to $250-300 for a good down winter bag. **Sleeping pads** include foam pads ($10-30), air mattresses ($15-50), and Therm-A-Rest self-inflating pads ($45-120).

Tent: The best tents can be set up quickly, only require staking in high winds, and come with a rain cover. Low-profile dome tents are the best all-around. Good 2-person tents start at $90, 4-person at $300. Other tent accessories include a **battery-operated lantern,** a **plastic groundcloth,** and a **nylon tarp.**

Backpack: Internal-frame packs mold better to your back, keep a lower center of gravity, and flex adequately to allow you to hike difficult trails. **External-frame packs** are more comfortable for long hikes over even terrain, as they keep weight higher and distribute it more evenly. Make sure your pack has a strong, padded hip-belt to transfer weight to your legs. Any serious backpacking requires a pack of at least 4000 in.^{3} (16,000cc), plus 500 in.^{3} for sleeping bags in internal-frame packs. Sturdy backpacks cost anywhere from $125-420. This is one area in which it doesn't pay to economize. Fill up any pack with something heavy and walk around the store with it to get a sense of how it distributes weight before buying it. Either buy a **waterproof backpack cover,** or store all of your belongings in plastic bags inside your pack.

Boots: Be sure to wear hiking boots with good **ankle support.** They should fit snugly and comfortably over 1-2 pairs of wool socks and thin liner socks. Break in boots over several weeks before you go in order to spare yourself painful and debilitating blisters.

Other Necessities: A shatterproof plastic water bottle, water-purification tablets (for when you can't boil water), a first-aid kit, a pocketknife, insect repellent, calamine lotion, and waterproof matches or a lighter.

...AND WHERE TO BUY IT

The mail-order/online companies listed below offer lower prices than many retail stores, but a visit to a local camping or outdoors store will give you a good sense of the look and weight of certain items.

Campmor, 28 Parkway, P.O. Box 700, Upper Saddle River, NJ 07458, USA (☎888-226-7667; www.campmor.com).

Discount Camping, 880 Main North Rd., Pooraka, South Australia 5095, Australia (☎08 8262 3399; www.discountcamping.com.au).

Eastern Mountain Sports (EMS), 1 Vose Farm Rd., Peterborough, NH 03458, USA (☎888-463-6367; www.ems.com).

L.L. Bean, Freeport, ME 04033, USA (US and Canada ☎800-441-5713; UK ☎0800 891 297; www.llbean.com).

Mountain Designs, 51 Bishop St., Kelvin Grove, Queensland 4059, Australia (☎07 3856 2344; www.mountaindesigns.com).

Recreational Equipment, Inc. (REI), Sumner, WA 98352, USA (US and Canada ☎800-426-4840, elsewhere 253-891-2500; www.rei.com).

YHA Adventure Shop, 19 High St., Staines, Middlesex, TW18 4QY, UK (☎1784 458 625; www.yhaadventure.com).

ORGANIZED ADVENTURE TRIPS

In Puerto Rico various tour guides lead **organized adventure** trips throughout the island that include hiking, biking, canoeing, kayaking, rafting, and climbing. Most shorter trips are easy to organize from Puerto Rico, but longer adventures should be planned before you arrive on the island. One of the greatest adventures in Puerto Rico is exploring the limestone caves along the northern coast, either by foot, in a kayak, or by rappelling. See **Parque de las Cavernas del Río Camuy,** p. 166, for more information.

ENVIRONMENTALLY RESPONSIBLE TOURISM. The idea behind responsible tourism is to leave no trace of human presence behind. A campstove is a safer (and more efficient) way to cook than using vegetation. If you must make a fire, keep it small and use dead branches or brush rather than cutting vegetation. Make sure your campsite is at least 150 ft. from water supplies or bodies of water. If there is no toilet, bury human waste (but not paper) at least 4 in. deep and above the high-water line, and 150 ft. or more from any water supplies. Always pack your trash in a plastic bag and carry it to the next trash receptacle. For more information, contact one of the organizations below:

Earthwatch, 3 Clock Tower Place #100, Box 75, Maynard, MA 01754, USA (☎800-776-0188 or 978-461-0081; www.earthwatch.org).

International Ecotourism Society, 28 Pine St., Burlington, VT 05402, USA (01) (☎802-651-9818; www.ecotourism.org).

National Audubon Society, Nature Odysseys, 700 Broadway, New York, NY 10003 (☎212-979-3000; www.audubon.org).

Tourism Concern, Stapleton House, 277-281 Holloway Rd., London N7 8HN, UK (☎020 7753 3330; www.tourismconcern.org.uk).

Adven Tours (☎787-889-0251 or 831-6447; www.adventours.tk) offers a variety of tours leaving from San Juan, Mayagüez, and Luquillo and traveling throughout the island. Activities include city tours, hiking, kayaking, biking, bird-watching, and backpacking. Also offers specialty tours to coffee plantations, ecotours, and Hatha Yoga. Guides available in English, French, German, and sign language. Check the web site for full tour offerings and prices.

Expediciones Palenique (☎ 787-823-4354; www.expedicionespalenque.com) has 1-day trips to Ciales, Arecibo, Utuado, Adjuntas, Jayuya, and Camuy ($75-85), as well as 3- to 5-day trips to Isla Mona ($550-750). Includes high adrenaline activities such as rappelling and cliff-diving.

Las Tortugas Adventures (☎ 787-725-5169; www.kayak-pr.com), based in San Juan. One of the island's most comprehensive kayak tour operators. Offers trips to Cayo Santiago ($50), Río Espiritú Santo ($50), Laguna de Piñones ($50), Lago Matrullas ($70), Fajardo's bioluminescent bay ($40), and Isla Cardona ($65). Also has multi-day and snorkeling packages. Transport from San Juan available at additional cost.

Caradonna Caribbean Tours (☎ 407-774-9000 or 888-599-8400; www.caradonna.com) offers 7-night scuba dive packages at several resorts around the island ($720-1500). Some prices include airfare from Miami.

KEEPING IN TOUCH

BY MAIL

SENDING MAIL HOME FROM PUERTO RICO

Puerto Rico uses the good ol' US postal service and rates and speed are equivalent to the rest of the US. To mail a letter bring it to the post office or drop it in any blue US Postal Service drop box. The best place to buy stamps is at the post office. **Aerogrammes**, printed sheets that fold into envelopes and travel via airmail, usually cost the same as a postcard and provide much more writing space; pick them up at a post office. All letters and postcards are sent by **airmail**, which is also the fastest way to send a package. Sending a package **by boat** will be much cheaper, but it may take one to three months to cross the Atlantic and two to four to cross the Pacific—good for items you won't need to see for a while.

Regular airmail from Puerto Rico takes 3-4 days to the US and 4-7 days for any foreign country. A postcard from Puerto Rico **to the US** costs $0.23, a letter costs $0.37, and packages up to 2 lbs. cost $4.50. Rates **to Canada** are slightly higher ($0.50/$0.60/$13.25). Mail to **all other foreign destinations** costs the same amount, though package rates vary slightly ($0.70/$0.80/$15-22).

SENDING MAIL TO PUERTO RICO

Mark envelopes "air mail" or "por avión" or your letter or postcard will never arrive. In addition to the standard postage system whose rates are listed below, **Federal Express** (www.fedex.com; Australia ☎ 13 26 10; US and Canada ☎ 800-247-4747; New Zealand ☎ 0800 73 33 39; UK ☎ 0800 12 38 00) handles express mail services from most home countries to Puerto Rico; in 2 days they can get a letter from New York to San Juan ($17) or from London to San Juan (UK£28).

Australia: Allow 7-8 work days. Postcards up to 20g cost AUS$1; letters up to 50g AUS$1.65; packages up to 0.5kg AUS$14, up to 2kg AUS$50. **EMS** can get a letter to Puerto Rico in 5-6 days for AUS$35. www.auspost.com.au/pac.

Canada: Allow 6 work days. Postcards and letters up to 30g cost CDN$0.65; packages up to 0.5kg CDN$5.60, up to 2kg CDN$20.70. www.canadapost.ca.

Ireland: Allow 4-6 work days. Postcards and letters up to 25g cost IR£0.57; packages up to 0.5kg IR£5, up to 2kg IR£20. Add IR£3.60 for Swiftpost International. www.letterpost.ie.

New Zealand: Allow 7 work days. Postcards cost NZ$1.50; letters up to 200g NZ$2; small parcels up to 0.5kg NZ$20, up to 2kg NZ$58. www.nzpost.co.nz.

UK: Allow 5 work days. Postcards UK£0.42. Letters up to 20g cost UK£0.68; packages up to 0.5kg UK£4.77, up to 2kg UK£17.89. UK Swiftair delivers letters a day faster for UK£3.30 more. www.royalmail.co.uk.

US: Allow 3-4 days. Postcards cost $0.23, letters under 1 oz. $0.37; packages under 1 lb. $3.85. **US Express Mail** delivers overnight to most destinations and costs $13.65 for up to 8 oz. www.usps.gov.

RECEIVING MAIL IN PUERTO RICO

Mail can be sent to Puerto Rico via General Delivery. See the **Practical Information** section for each city to find out whether or not the post office accepts General Delivery mail. Address General Delivery letters like so:

Megan MONAGHAN
General Delivery
City, PR ZIP(POSTAL) CODE

The mail will go to a special desk in the central post office, unless you specify a post office by street address or postal code. It's best to use the largest post office, since mail may be sent there regardless. Bring photo ID for pick-up.

BY TELEPHONE

☎**AREA CODE** You must use the area code **(787)** before dialing any number in Puerto Rico, local or long distance. For telephone number information call ☎511.

Once again, Puerto Rico is considered part of the US. Calling between Puerto Rico and the mainland US is not an international call, but it is long distance. Most US **cell phone** plans with a nationwide plan get service throughout Puerto Rico. Coverage is fairly decent across the island except along the Rúta Panorámica and Rincón. If you plan to make any significant number of calls, either back to the US or within Puerto Rico, using a cell phone is by far your cheapest bet.

CALLING HOME FROM PUERTO RICO

Using a **calling card** is a relatively inexpensive and hassle-free way to call home. Calls are billed collect or to your account. You can frequently call collect without even possessing a company's calling card just by calling their access number and following the instructions. To **call home with a calling card,** contact the operator for your service provider in Puerto Rico by dialing the appropriate toll-free access number. Puerto Rico usually uses the same access number as the rest of the US.

You can usually also make **direct international calls** from pay phones, but if you aren't using a calling card, you may need to drop your coins as quickly as your words. (See **Placing International Calls,** p. 64.) Prepaid phone cards are another inexpensive way to make phone calls, especially to North America and the rest of the Caribbean. (See **Calling Within Puerto Rico,** p. 64.) Occasionally major credit cards can be used for direct international calls, but they are less cost-efficient. Placing a **collect call** through an international operator is even more expensive, but may be necessary in case of emergency. Phone rates typically tend to be highest in the morning, lower in the evening, and lowest on Sunday and late at night.

Let's Go has recently partnered with **ekit.com** to provide a calling card that offers a number of services, including email and voice messaging. Before purchasing any calling card, always be sure to compare rates with other cards, and to make sure it serves your needs (a local phonecard is generally better for local calls, for instance). For more information, visit www.letsgo.ekit.com.

PLACING INTERNATIONAL CALLS. To call Puerto Rico from home or to call home from Puerto Rico, dial:

1. The **international dialing prefix.** To dial out of out of Puerto Rico, dial 011; out of **Australia,** 0011; out of the **Republic of Ireland, New Zealand,** or the **UK,** 00; out of **South Africa,** 09.
2. The **country code** of the country you want to call. To call **Puerto Rico, Canada,** or the **US,** dial 1; **Australia,** dial 61; the **Republic of Ireland,** 353; **New Zealand,** 64; **South Africa,** 27; the **UK,** 44.
3. The **city/area code.** The area code for all of Puerto Rico is **787.** When calling internationally, if the first digit is a zero (e.g., 020 for London), omit the zero when calling from abroad (e.g., dial 20 from Puerto Rico to reach London).
4. The **local number.**

CALLING WITHIN PUERTO RICO

You must always dial the 787 area code when making phone calls in Puerto Rico. There are several different phone areas on the island, meaning that calling from the east coast to the west coast (or from San Juan to either coast) is long distance. The simplest way to call within the country is to use a coin-operated phone. Puerto Rican pay phones cost $0.25-0.50 for local calls, and start at $1 for long distance calls. However, only about 50% of pay phones actually work.

Another option is to use a prepaid telephone card, available at most newspaper kiosks, convenience stores, and drugstores. To use a prepaid phone card call the toll-free access number and follow the directions on the card. These cards can be used to make international as well as domestic calls.

TIME DIFFERENCES

Puerto Rico is five hours behind **Greenwich Mean Time (GMT),** on the same time as the US east coast. However, Puerto Rico does not participate in daylight savings time, so during the winter it is one hour ahead of the US east coast. During the summer Puerto Rico is three hours ahead of Vancouver & San Francisco, five hours behind London, six hours behind Johannesburg, and eight hours ahead of Sydney.

BY EMAIL AND INTERNET

Most large cities in Puerto Rico have some sort of public Internet access, but cyber cafes are not nearly as prevalent as they are in the US or Europe. Furthermore, Internet access in Puerto Rico is expensive ($5-15 per hr.). Most cafes offer better rates if you buy a card for a longer period of time. Internet cafes and the occasional free Internet terminal are listed in the **Practical Information** sections of individual cities.

Though in some places it's possible to forge a remote link with your home server, in most cases this is a much slower (and thus more expensive) option than taking advantage of free **web-based email accounts** (e.g., www.hotmail.com and www.yahoo.com). Travelers with laptops can call an Internet service provider via a **modem.** Long-distance phone cards specifically intended for such calls can defray normally high phone charges; check with your long-distance phone provider to see if it offers this option.

Find **(Our Student Airfares are cheap, flexible & exclusive)** great Student Airfares everywhere at StudentUniverse.com and **Get lost.**

StudentUniverse.com

Student Airfares everywhere

GETTING TO PUERTO RICO

BY PLANE

Puerto Rico is primarily accessible by plane and when it comes to airfare, a little effort can save you a bundle. If your plans are flexible enough to deal with the restrictions, courier fares are the cheapest. Tickets bought from consolidators and standby seating are also good deals, but last-minute specials, airfare wars, and charter flights often beat these fares. Several discount airlines also offer cheap flights into San Juan. The key is to hunt around, to be flexible, and to ask persistently about discounts.

AIRFARES

Puerto Rico is the airline hub of the Caribbean and flights are relatively inexpensive year-round, especially from the US east coast. Only San Juan's Luis Muñoz Marín International Airport has flights to North America and Europe. Most travelers will end up connecting somewhere on the US east coast, though **Iberia** also offers direct flights to Madrid.

Airfares peak between late December and April; holidays are also expensive. The cheapest times to travel are June to November. Midweek (M-Th morning) round-trip flights run $40-50 cheaper than weekend flights, but they are generally more crowded. Not fixing a return date ("open return") or arriving in and departing from different cities ("open-jaw") can be pricier than round-trip flights. Patching one-way flights together is the most expensive way to travel.

If Puerto Rico is only one stop on a more extensive globe-hop, consider a round-the-world (RTW) ticket. Tickets usually include at least five stops and are valid for about a year; prices range $1200-5000. Try **Northwest Airlines/KLM** (☎800-447-4747; www.nwa.com) or **Star Alliance,** a consortium of 22 airlines including United Airlines (☎800-241-6522; www.staralliance.com).

Fares for round-trip flights to San Juan from the US or Canadian east coast cost $220-600, from the US or Canadian west coast $500-800, from the UK, UK£410-810, from Australia AUS$3050-4100, from New Zealand NZ$3000-4000.

 FLIGHT PLANNING ON THE INTERNET. A plethora of flight-planning web sites allow travelers to find the cheapest airfare without paying a travel agent commission. This strategy lacks the guarantees and personal assistance of a travel agent, but with a bit of legwork you can find great deals on the web sites below. **Orbitz** (www.orbitz.com), **Expedia** (www.expedia.com), and **Travelocity** (www.travelocity.com) are the largest full online travel services. **Priceline** (www.priceline.com) allows you to specify a price, then obligates you to buy any ticket that meets it. **Travel Zoo** (www.travelzoo.com) lists the best deals from various different sources, with frequent cheap prices to Puerto Rico. **Skyauction** (www.skyauction.com) allows you to bid on both last-minute and advance-purchase tickets. Many airline sites offer special last-minute deals (see **Commercial Airlines,** p. 67) that don't appear on consolidators. Other sites do the legwork and compile deals for you—try www.bestfares.com, www.flights.com, www.hotwire.com, www.lowestfare.com, www.cheaptickets.com, and www.onetravel.com. The online *Air Traveler's Handbook* (www.cs.cmu.edu/afs/cs/user/mkant/Public/Travel/airfare.html) has a comprehensive list of links to sites with everything you need to know before you board a plane.

BUDGET & STUDENT TRAVEL AGENCIES

While knowledgeable agents specializing in flights to Puerto Rico can make your life easy, they may not spend the time to find you the lowest possible fare—they get paid on commission. All of the travel agencies below offer discounts for students holding **ISIC and IYTC cards** (see p. 45), but most also book budget airline tickets for the general public. However, booking directly through a discount airline (see **Commercial Airlines**, below) is usually cheaper. Most flights from budget agencies are on major airlines, but in peak season some may sell seats on less reliable chartered aircraft.

CTS Travel, 30 Rathbone Pl., **London** W1T 1GQ, UK(☎020 7290 0630; www.ctstravel.co.uk). A British student travel agent with offices in 39 countries including the US, Empire State Building, 350 Fifth Ave., Suite 7813, **New York,** NY 10118 (☎877-287-6665; www.ctstravelusa.com).

STA Travel, 7890 S. Hardy Dr., Ste. 110, **Tempe,** AZ 85284, USA (☎800-781-4040; www.sta-travel.com). A student and youth travel organization with over 400 offices worldwide. In the UK, 33 Bedford St., Covent Garden, **London** WC2E 9ED (☎0870 1 600 599). In New Zealand, Shop 2B, 187 Queen St., **Auckland** (☎09 309 0458). In Australia, 260 Hoddle St., **Abbotsford** VIC 3067 (☎03 8417 6911). Check their web site for a complete list of offices.

Travel CUTS (Canadian Universities Travel Services Limited), 187 College St., **Toronto,** ON M5T 1P7 (☎416-979-2406 or 800-667-2887; www.travelcuts.com). Canada's main student travel agent has offices throughout Canada and parts of the US. Also in the UK, 295A Regent St., **London** W1B 2H9.

USIT, 19-21 Aston Quay, **Dublin** 2 (☎01 602 1600; www.usitworld.com). Ireland's leading student/budget travel agency has 22 offices throughout Northern Ireland and the Republic of Ireland. Offers programs to work in North America.

COMMERCIAL AIRLINES

The commercial airlines' lowest regular offer is the **APEX** (Advance Purchase Excursion) fare, which provides confirmed reservations and allows "open-jaw" tickets. Generally, reservations must be made seven to 21 days ahead of departure, with seven- to 14-day minimum-stay and up to 90-day maximum-stay restrictions. These fares carry hefty cancellation and change penalties. The cheapest fare is usually on a direct flight; scan the airlines below that fly into San Juan's international airport to see which ones fly into your airport.

Air Santo Domingo (☎809-683-8006, in Puerto Rico ☎723-1015; www.airsantodomingo.com.do) flies to Santo Domingo.

Air St. Thomas (☎800-522-3084; www.airstthomas.com) flies to St. Barths, St. Thomas, and Virgin Gorda.

Air Sunshine (from Puerto Rico ☎888-879-8900, from North America ☎800-327-8900; www.airsunshine.com) flies to St. Croix, St. Thomas, Tortola, and Vieques.

American Airlines (☎800-433-7300; www.aa.com), is the largest airline flying into San Juan. Flights go throughout North America, Central America, and the Caribbean with connections to Europe.

ATA (☎800-225-2995; www.ata.com) has direct flights to Chicago and Orlando.

Cape Air (☎800-352-0714; www.flycapeair.com) flies to Ponce, St. Croix, St. Thomas, and Tortola.

Continental Airlines (☎800-523-3273; www.continental.com) has direct flights to Cleveland, Houston, and Newark.

Copa (☎800-359-2672; www.copaair.com) flies to Guatemala City, Panama City, and Managua.

Delta Airlines (☎800-221-1212; www.delta.com) flies to Atlanta and New York.

Iberia (☎800-772-4642; www.iberia.com) has direct flights to Madrid with connections to cities throughout Europe.

■ **Jet Blue Airlines** (☎800-538-2583; www.jetblue.com). This budget airline offers great deals to JFK airport in New York City.

Liat Airline (from the Caribbean ☎888-844-5428, from outside the Caribbean ☎868-624-4727; www.liatairline.com). The airline of the Caribbean flies to Antigua, St. Maarten, and Tortola.

Northwest Airlines (☎800-225-2525; www.nwa.com) flies to Detroit and Memphis.

■ **Song Airlines** (☎800-359-7664; www.flysong.com) is Delta's budget spin-off. No free food. From San Juan flights go to Orlando, where US connections can be made.

■ **Spirit Airlines** (☎800-772-7117; www.spiritair.com). This budget airline flies directly to Fort Lauderdale and Orlando.

Sun Country Airlines (☎800-359-6786; www.suncountry.com) flies directly to Minneapolis/St. Paul.

United Airlines (☎800-864-8331; www.ual.com) flies to Chicago.

USAir (☎800-428-4322; www.usair.com) flies to Boston, Charlotte, Philadelphia, and Pittsburgh.

STANDBY FLIGHTS

Traveling standby requires considerable flexibility in arrival and departure dates and cities. Companies dealing in standby flights sell vouchers rather than tickets, along with the promise to get you to your destination (or near your destination) within a certain window of time (typically 1-5 days). You call in before your specific window of time to hear your flight options and the probability that you will be able to board each flight. You can then decide which flights you want to try to make, show up at the appropriate airport at the appropriate time, present your voucher, and board if space is available. Vouchers can usually be bought for both one-way and round-trip travel. You receive a monetary refund only if every available flight within your date range is full; if you opt not to take an available (but perhaps less convenient) flight, you can only get credit toward future travel. Carefully read agreements with any company offering standby flights as tricky fine print can leave you in a lurch. To check on a company's service record in the US, call the Better Business Bureau (☎212-533-6200). It is difficult to receive refunds, and clients' vouchers will not be honored when an airline fails to receive payment in time.

TICKET CONSOLIDATORS

Ticket consolidators, or **"bucket shops,"** buy unsold tickets in bulk from commercial airlines and sell them at discounted rates. The best place to look is in the Sunday travel section of any major newspaper (such as *The New York Times*), where many bucket shops place tiny ads. Call quickly, as availability is typically extremely limited. Not all bucket shops are reliable, so insist on a receipt that gives full details of restrictions, refunds, and tickets, and pay by credit card (in spite of the 2-5% fee) so you can stop payment if you never receive your tickets. For more info, see www.travel-library.com/air-travel/consolidators.html. **Travel Avenue** (☎800-333-3335; www.travelavenue.com) is a US-based rebate travel agency that also works as a travel consolidator.

BY BOAT

FERRY

Unfortunately no public boats make the trip between Puerto Rico and the Virgin Islands. However, there is a ferry between Mayagüez, Puerto Rico and **Santo Domingo, Dominican Republic.** For more information see **Mayagüez,** p. 189.

CRUISE SHIP

Every year hundreds of cruise ships drop thousands of travelers off in San Juan bay to spend the day wandering the streets of Old San Juan. And despite popular conception, vacationing by cruise ship is no longer reserved for the rich and famous. During hurricane season, a seven-night cruise can be as cheap as $200 per person. Cruises generally depart from a major port (New York, Miami, Fort Lauderdale, San Juan) then spend four to seven days traveling throughout the Caribbean. Some cruise ships depart from European ports and head to the Caribbean, but these are much more expensive. Nights, and some days, are spent on board the ship, while most days are spent at various destination islands.

Cruise prices vary greatly. During hurricane season (June-Oct.) there are fewer ships to choose from, but they are also much less expensive. Also, there is always the possibility that a hurricane will delay or ruin your cruise. The most expensive places to buy a cruise is directly from the company's brochure or from a travel agent. All of the major online travel agents (www.expedia.com, www.orbitz.com, www.travelocity.com) offer highly discounted cruise prices (4-night cruises $200-800, 7-night cruises $300-1000). The individual cruise ship sites list regular fares with the occasional super special thrown in. Typically a cruise price includes accommodations, on-board meals and entertainment, and port taxes. However, travelers have to pay for their own transportation to the port of departure, meals and entertainment in the port city, casinos, gratuities, and alcoholic beverages. Price also varies with the type of accommodation: a suite or a cabin with a window is much more expensive than an interior cabin. **Carnival** (www.carnival.com) and **Royal Caribbean** (www.rccl.com) use San Juan as a home port year-round. **Princess** (www.princess.com) uses San Juan as a home port only during the high season. The other major cruise lines that stop in San Juan include: **Celebrity** (www.celebrity.com), **Costa Cruise** (www.costacruise.com), **Cunard** (www.cunard.com), **Holland America** (www.hollandamerica.com), **Norwegian Cruise Line** (www.ncl.com), **P&O Cruises** (www.pocruises.com), **Radisson Seven Seas Cruises** (www.rssc.com), **Seabourn** (www.seabourn.com), **Silversea** (www.silversea.com), and **Windstar Cruises** (www.windstarcruises.com). The following web sites also sell discounted cruises: www.bestpricecruises.com, www.1-800-cruises.com, www.allcruise-travel.com, www.cruisehotfares.com, www.beatanycruiseprice.com, www.caribbean-on-line.com, and www.acruise2go.com.

GETTING AROUND PUERTO RICO

BY PLANE

ONE-WAY TICKET TO PARADISE. There are several options for getting to the offshore islands of **Vieques** and **Culebra**. The fastest route is to fly directly from San Juan's Luis Muñoz Marín International Airport, but this is also the most expensive ($70 one-way). Slightly cheaper is to fly from Isla Grande airport, just outside Puerta de Tierra ($40 one-way). Larger groups may find it convenient to take a taxi from San Juan to Fajardo ($60 for four people), then either fly to an island ($20-25) or take the ferry ($2-2.25). By far the most economical option is to take a *público* from Río Piedras to Fajardo ($3.50), then hop on the ferry. Ask the driver to take you all the way to the dock (*la lancha*).

Most of Puerto Rico's internal flights connect San Juan, Fajardo, Culebra, and Vieques. All of the airline flying to the Spanish Virgin Islands use tiny planes and charge comparable rates. Note that flying into San Juan's international airport is significantly more expensive than flying into San Juan Isla Grande Airport. For information about flights see **San Juan** (p. 89), **Fajardo** (p. 252), **Culebra** (p. 294), or **Vieques** (p. 278). **American Airlines** operates flights from San Juan to **Mayagüez** (p. 189) and **Cape Air** flies from San Juan to **Ponce** (p. 221), but unless you're in a big hurry, it's much more economical to rent a car or take a *público*.

BY PÚBLICO

Very few Puerto Ricans travel by public transportation. Consequently there is no island-wide bus or train service. Instead you are stuck with *guaguas públicas* (public vans) or *carros públicos* (public cars), private vehicles that transport groups of people between cities. It is more than possible, albeit difficult, to travel around Puerto Rico using *públicos* alone, as long as you get used to the system.

On the plus side, *públicos* are cheap; the longest ride shouldn't cost more than $10. On the minus side, they are extremely slow, they have no schedule, and vehicles have absolutely no quality standards. Generally *públicos* wait either by a town's central plaza or in a *público* terminal starting early in the morning, then leave when they are full. This means that travelers have to wake up at the crack of dawn, then sit in a stuffy van waiting for enough to people to show up so they get to leave. Drivers usually leave for the day when passengers stop showing up, but this time varies, so if you come after 10am all the vehicles may be gone. The system is time-consuming and frustrating but relatively comprehensive. *Públicos* leave from almost every municipal center and travel to adjacent municipalities and smaller *barrios* within the municipality. The destination of the vehicle is usually written on the front of the windshield. For a higher price, most *público* drivers will act as taxi drivers and take you wherever you want to go. It is also possible to flag down a *público* mid-route, especially along Hwy. 3 (*públicos* traveling between San Juan and Fajardo) and Hwy. 2 (*públicos* traveling between San Juan and Arecibo). The best strategy is to wait at one of the big cement benches on the side of the road. It is polite to tip a *público* driver at least 10% per person and more if you have bags.

Let's Go lists *público* routes in the transportation section of each town, but information changes frequently so it's a good idea to stop by the *público* station the night before you leave to get an update. The transport times listed in *Let's Go* are estimates provided by *público* drivers and they are almost always overly optimistic. Theoretically it takes 1hr. to get from San Juan to Fajardo, but on a *público* it can take up to 4hr. when you include traffic and frequent stops to pick up additional passengers. Do not take a *público* when you are in a hurry.

BY CAR

Though car rental can be expensive, driving is the best and most efficient way to get around in Puerto Rico. Before hitting the road, make sure to read the **Hitting the Road,** p. 72.

A LICENSE TO DRIVE

The driving age in Puerto Rico is 16 with parental supervision or 18 years old without. All drivers must have a valid license. Puerto Rico accepts unexpired foreign licenses from any country that imposes requirements similar to Puerto Rico for up to 120 days (this includes the US, Canada, and many European countries). After 120 days you must apply for a Puerto Rican driver's license. Travelers with a foreign driver's license from a country that has established reciprocity with Puerto Rico (including the US) can get a Puerto Rican license by paying the $20 fee.

DRIVING DISTANCES (IN MILES)

	Aguadilla	Aibonito	Arecibo	Cabo Rojo	Fajardo	Luquillo	Mayagüez	Ponce	San Germán	San Juan
Aguadilla		95	33	26	112	108	17	63	31	81
Aibonito	95		61	72	59	62	78	32	66	42
Arecibo	33	61		58	79	73	49	52	62	48
Cabo Rojo	26	72	58		131	131	9	41	7	111
Fajardo	112	59	79	131		7	129	89	125	34
Luquillo	108	62	73	131	7		124	90	124	28
Mayagüez	17	78	49	9	129	124		46	14	98
Ponce	63	32	52	41	89	90	46		34	70
San Germán	31	66	62	7	125	124	14	34		104
San Juan	81	42	48	111	34	28	31	98	70	

ESSENTIALS

OBTAINING YOUR WHEELS

Puerto Rico has many local and US car rental agencies. Most travelers will rent a car in San Juan, then use it to get around the island, though there are car rental agencies in every major city. If you will spend most of your time in San Juan or other cities, a compact car works best to navigate the narrow congested streets. If you plan to drive the Rúta Panorámica, a car with 4WD may be the optimal choice for navigating the sharp turns and steep hills, though it's possible to get almost everywhere without 4WD. In general, cheaper cars tend to be less reliable and harder to handle on difficult terrain. Less expensive 4WD vehicles in particular tend to be more top heavy, and are more dangerous when navigating particularly bumpy roads.

RENTAL AGENCIES

During high season (Dec.-Apr.) you should always call ahead to rent a car. You can generally make reservations before you leave by calling major international offices in your home country. However, occasionally the price and availability information they give doesn't jive with what the local offices in your country will tell you. Try checking with both numbers to make sure you get the best price and accurate information. Cars with **automatic transmission** are common.

BUT OFFICER, REALLY, I'M 21. To rent a car from most establishments in Puerto Rico, you need to be at least 21 years old and have a major credit card. Some agencies require renters to be 25, and most charge those aged 21-24 an additional surcharge of $5-10 per day. Policies and prices vary from agency to agency. Small local operations occasionally rent to people under 21, but be sure to ask about the insurance coverage and deductible, and always check the fine print. Travelers under 21 will have to travel to Fajardo or Rincón to rent a car; San Juan car rental agencies do not rent to drivers under 21.

HOW MUCH FOR THE HOTROD? Rental car prices start at around $30-35 a day and rise during high season and major holidays. Expect to pay more for larger cars and for 4WD or at airport branches. The price also rises if you pick-up and drop-off the vehicle at different locations. Most rental packages offer **unlimited mileage,** although some allow you a certain number of miles free before the charge of $0.25-0.40 per mile takes effect. Quoted rates do not include gas or tax, so ask for the total cost before handing over the credit card; many large firms have added airport surcharges not covered by the designated fare. Return the car with a full tank of gasoline to avoid high fuel charges at the end.

THE FINE PRINT: INSURANCE. When dealing with any car rental company, be sure to ask whether the price includes insurance against theft and collision. There may be an additional charge for a collision and damage waiver (CDW), which usually comes to about $12-15 per day. Major **credit cards** (including MasterCard and American Express) sometimes cover the CDW if you use their card to rent a car; call your credit card company for specifics. Remember that if you are driving a conventional rental car on an **unpaved road,** you are almost never covered by insurance; ask about this before leaving the rental agency. Insurance plans usually come with a deductible of around $500 for conventional vehicles. This means you pay for all damages up to that sum, unless they are the fault of another vehicle. The deductible you will be quoted applies to collisions with other vehicles; collisions with non-vehicles ("single-vehicle collisions"), such as trees, will cost you even more. Generally, there is a sliding scale with regard to deductible—the more you pay, the more you're covered. All of the international agencies below have an agency in LMM international airport.

INTERNATIONAL AGENCIES

Avis (☎800-331-1212; www.avis.com). 25+. Under 25 with a corporate account.

Budget (☎800-527-0700; www.budget.com). 25+. Ages 21-24 $5 per day surcharge.

Dollar (☎800-800-4000; www.dollar.com). 25+. Ages 21-24 $5 per day surcharge.

Hertz (☎800-654-3131; www.hertz.com). 25+. Ages 21-24 $10 per day surcharge.

National (☎800-227-7368; www.nationalcar.com). 25+. Ages 21-24 $10 per day surcharge.

Payless Car Rental (☎800-729-5377). 25+. Ages 21-24 $5 per day surcharge.

Thrifty (☎800-367-2277; www.thrifty.com). 25+. Ages 21-24 $6 per day surcharge.

PUERTO RICAN AGENCIES

AAA Car Rental (☎787-791-2609). 25+. Ages 21-24 $8 per day surcharge.

Charlie Car Rental (☎800-289-1227; www.charliecars.com). 25+. Ages 21-24 $10 per day surcharge.

L&M Car Rental (☎787-791-1160; www.lmcarrental.com). 25+. Age 24 $4 per day surcharge at some locations.

HITTING THE ROAD

Driving in Puerto Rico is like navigating a three-ring circus—after all the animals have escaped. It's not impossible, but it is quite a juggling act. Roads are generally paved, well-marked, and developed, but Puerto Rican drivers can be classified somewhere between confident and absolutely insane. Traffic is heavy, many people disregard speed limits (especially on freeways), and markers such as stop signs are treated more like suggestions than laws. Aggressive urban drivers will feel right at home.

Puerto Rico's road system is very similar to the US road system. In this book "Rte." (as in "Rte. 1") refers to small, one-lane roads, and "Hwy." (as in "Hwy. 7") to highways and expressways; Puerto Ricans call almost all roads *carreteras*. Roads

NO HABLO SPANISH It seems that everyone in Puerto Rico speaks English—until you hit the road. All Puerto Rican road signs are in Spanish and if you get pulled over, the cop probably won't speak English either. Not that this prevents English-speakers from driving. Most of the road signs have the same design that you'll find in the US or Europe, and an 8-sided red sign isn't hard to decipher in any language. However, it's a good idea to brush up on your Spanish vocabulary before you hit the road. See the **Glossary**, p. 307.

are fairly easy to navigate, though signage varies. In San Juan remember that all signs pointing to "San Juan" eventually lead to Old San Juan. Puerto Rico has several good road maps, available for sale at most gas stations and drug stores. Hwy. 22, Hwy. 30, Hwy. 52, and Hwy. 53 are the island's only **toll roads.** These express freeways have intermittent toll booths charging $0.30-1. Use to the lane with the green "C" if you have correct change and the lane with the red "A" if you do not.

One confusing aspect of Puerto Rico's road system is the use of the **metric system** and the **imperial system.** Gas is measured in liters and the distance markers on the side of the road measure kilometers traveled. However, the speed limit is posted in miles per hour. Good luck. Gas costs about $0.40 per liter, but prices fluctuate.

Car jackings are common in Puerto Rico, especially in big cities. If you are in a big city hotel without a parking lot, it's a good idea to put your car in a garage. Ask the hotel receptionist for regional advice. Never leave anything visible in your car; people have been known to **break in** for something as small as a couple of tapes. Car jackings frequently occur at **beaches,** especially deserted beaches. When driving, keep doors locked and do not slow down for someone, especially at night.

Children under four years old should ride only in a specially-designed carseat, available for a small fee from most car rental agencies. While driving, be sure to buckle up—seat belts are **required by law** in Puerto Rico. The **speed limit** varies from region to region. Most of the highways have a limit of 65 mph, while residential areas can post limits as low as 20 mph.

AUTOMOBILE CLUBS

Most automobile clubs offer free towing, emergency roadside assistance, travel-related discounts, and random goodies in exchange for a modest membership fee. US citizens should contact the **American Automobile Association** (**AAA;** ☎ 800-564-6222; www.aaa.com), which offers service in Puerto Rico through a sister company; call ☎ 787-723-5177 for roadside assistance. Membership costs vary depending on which branch you join ($50-60 for the first year; less for renewals and additional family members).

> **DRIVING PRECAUTIONS.** Bring substantial amounts of **water** (a suggested one gallon per person per day) for drinking and for the radiator. In extremely hot weather, use the air conditioner with restraint; if you see the car's temperature gauge climbing, turn it off. Turning the heater on full blast will help cool the engine. If radiator fluid is steaming, turn the car off for half an hour. *Never pour water over the engine to cool it.* Never lift a searing hot hood. When traveling for long distances, make sure tires are in good repair and have enough air. It's a good idea to carry a **cell phone** in case of a breakdown. You should also carry **extra oil** and a **spare tire.** Learn how to **change a tire** before heading out, especially if you are planning on traveling in deserted areas. Blowouts on dirt roads are exceedingly common. If you do have a breakdown, **stay with your car;** if you wander off, there's less likelihood trackers will find you. *Sleeping in a car or van parked in the city is extremely dangerous*—even the most dedicated budget traveler should not consider it.

Find (Our Student Airfares are cheap, flexible & exclusive) great Student Airfares everywhere at StudentUniverse.com and **Get lost.**

 StudentUniverse.com

Student Airfares everywhere

BY TAXI

All major Puerto Rican cities have taxi services, which are listed in the **Practical Information** section. Puerto Rican taxi drivers are fairly honest, but they rarely use a meter. Agree on a price before you get in the cab just to be certain. San Juan taxis use regulated fares; see p. 96 for more information.

BY BICYCLE

Many travelers harbor romantic visions of biking around a Caribbean island, but that is really much more feasible on less developed islands. Heavy traffic and a huge mountain range running through the center of the island make it difficult to ride anywhere. Furthermore, the only bike rental stores are in San Juan and on Vieques and Culebra. For serious bikers, the best place to ride is on the southern half of the island where there are flat roads with less traffic. Many travelers try to get around Culebra and Vieques on bikes, but it is important to remember that both islands have mountains (or at least large hills) in the middle. It is far preferable to use bikes as a form of recreation rather than a mode of transportation.

BY THUMB

Nobody hitchhikes on mainland Puerto Rico because it is extremely dangerous. The few exceptions are major expat hubs, such as Rincón, Culebra, and Vieques. Of the three destinations only Culebra could be considered somewhat safe and it's just as easy to take a *público* or walk. Remember that hitchhikers are trusting their lives to strangers. *Let's Go* does not recommend hitchhiking.

SPECIFIC CONCERNS

WOMEN TRAVELERS

Women exploring on their own inevitably face some additional safety concerns, but it's easy to be adventurous without taking undue risks. Generally, it is safe for women to travel in Puerto Rico, but common sense still applies; women are targeted for muggings and swindlings, as well as general harassment. Stick to centrally located accommodations and avoid solitary late-night treks. Do not **camp** alone in Puerto Rico, as the campground will likely be completely deserted. Wherever you go, walk purposefully and self-confidently; women who look like they know what they are doing and where they are going are less likely to be harassed. When traveling, always carry extra money for a phone call, bus, or taxi. **Hitching** is never safe for lone women, or even for two women traveling together. Consider approaching older women or couples if you're lost or feel uncomfortable.

Puerto Rico is more like the US than Latin America in that women receive some catcalls, but they are generally harmless. Your best answer to verbal harassment is no answer at all; feigning deafness, sitting motionless, and staring straight ahead at nothing in particular will do a world of good that reactions usually don't achieve. The extremely persistent can sometimes be dissuaded by a firm, loud, and very public "Go away!" Don't hesitate to seek out a police officer or a passerby if you are being harassed. *Let's Go* lists emergency numbers in the **Practical Information** listings of major cities, and you can always dial **911**. The **rape crisis hotline** in Puerto Rico is ☎877-641-2004. An **IMPACT Model Mugging** self-defense course will prepare you for a potential attack and raise your level of awareness of your surroundings and your confidence. In the US **Impact, Prepare, and Model Mugging** can refer you to local self-defense courses (☎800-345-5425; www.impactsafety.org).

TRAVELING ALONE

There are many benefits to traveling alone, including independence and greater interaction with locals. On the other hand, any solo traveler is a more vulnerable target of harassment and street theft. As a lone traveler, try not to stand out as a tourist, look confident, and be especially careful in deserted or very crowded areas. If questioned, never admit that you are traveling alone. Maintain regular contact with someone at home who knows your itinerary. For more tips, pick up *Traveling Solo* by Eleanor Berman ($17) or subscribe to **Connecting: Solo Travel Network,** 689 Park Road, Unit 6, Gibsons, BC V0N 1V7, Canada (☎604-886-9099; www.cstn.org; membership $35). **Travel Companion Exchange,** P.O. Box 833, Amityville, NY 11701, USA (☎631-454-0880; www.whytravelalone.com; $48), links solo travelers with companions with similar travel habits and interests.

OLDER TRAVELERS

Puerto Rico is a fabulous destination for senior citizens. Cruises provide a relaxing and increasingly affordable way to travel without moving around constantly. THe island itself is more than prepared for older travelers. The government mandates that people ages 60-74 get half-price admission to most museums, sites, and entertainment facilities, and anyone over 75 gets in free. If you don't see a senior citizen price listed, ask, and you may be delightfully surprised. The books *No Problem! Worldwise Tips for Mature Adventurers*, by Janice Kenyon ($16) and *Unbelievably Good Deals and Great Adventures That You Absolutely Can't Get Unless You're Over 50*, by Joan Rattner Heilman ($13) are both excellent resources. For more information, contact one of the following organizations:

Elderhostel, 11 Ave. de Lafayette, Boston, MA 02111, USA (☎877-426-8056; www.elderhostel.org), occasionally organizes 1- to 4-week "educational adventures" to Puerto Rico for those over 55.

The Mature Traveler, P.O. Box 1543, Wildomar, CA 92595, USA (☎800-460-6676; www.thematuretraveler.com) publishes a monthly newsletter with deals, discounts, and travel packages for the over 50 traveler, including an annual review of cruise lines. Subscription $30.

BISEXUAL, GAY & LESBIAN TRAVELERS

Puerto Rico is one of the Caribbean's premier BGL destinations. The Condado area of San Juan is known for its active gay scene and has accommodations, restaurants, and nightlife venues geared specifically toward gay travelers. BGL travelers should have no problems traveling throughout the island, though urban areas are more accustomed to alternative sexuality than rural areas. For the latest info on Puerto Rico's gay scene do not miss **Puerto Rico Breeze** (www.puertoricobreeze.com), a Spanish/English newsletter that includes articles, advertisements, and a calendar of events related to the island's gay scene (available online and at most gay-friendly establishment in San Juan). The magazines **Colony** (www.colonypr.com) and **GXPR** (gneroX@aol.com) also contain information for Puerto Rico's gay community. Listed below are contact organizations, mail-order bookstores, and publishers that offer materials addressing some specific concerns. **Out and About** (www.planetout.com) offers a bi-weekly newsletter and a comprehensive web site addressing gay travel concerns.

Gay's the Word, 66 Marchmont St., London WC1N 1AB, UK (☎44 20 7278 7654; www.gaystheword.co.uk). The largest gay and lesbian bookshop in the UK, with both fiction and non-fiction titles. Mail-order service available.

Giovanni's Room, 1145 Pine St., Philadelphia, PA 19107, USA (☎215-923-2960; www.queerbooks.com). An international lesbian/feminist and gay bookstore with mail-order service (carries many of the publications listed below).

> **FURTHER READING: BISEXUAL, GAY, & LESBIAN**
>
> *Spartacus International Gay Guide 2003-2004*, Bruno Gmunder Verlag. ($33).
>
> *Damron Men's Travel Guide, Women's Traveller*, and *Accommodations Guide*. Damron Travel Guides ($14-19). For more info, call ☎800-462-6654 or visit www.damron.com.
>
> *Gay Travel A to Z, Men's Travel in Your Pocket*, and *Inn Places*. All by Ferrari Publications ($16-20).
>
> *The Gay Vacation Guide: The Best Trips and How to Plan Them*, Mark Chesnut ($15).
>
> *A Man's Guide to the Caribbean 1998-1999*, Senor Cardova ($19).

BGL CRUISES

Several cruise companies cater exclusively to gay and lesbian travelers; other companies book groups of gays and lesbians to cruise around on borrowed boats. Both allow groups of gay and lesbian travelers to experience the Caribbean in a comfortable environment. **RSVP Vacations** (☎800-328-7787; www.rsvp.net) and **Pied Piper Travel** (☎800-874-7312; www.piedpipertravel.com) offer cruises for both men and women; **Olivia Cruises and Resorts** (☎800-631-6277; www.olivia.com) offers cruises exclusively for women. BGL cruises leave less frequently than others, so it's best to plan early.

TRAVELERS WITH DISABILITIES

Puerto Rico is just as accessible to travelers with disabilities as the rest of the US. In big cities, most hotels and restaurants are wheelchair accessible, though this may not be the case in smaller towns or rural areas. All hotels endorsed by the Puerto Rican Tourism Company (listed in *Que Pasa*) are required to have at least one wheelchair-accessible room. Those with disabilities should inform airlines and hotels of their disabilities when making reservations; some time may be needed to prepare special accommodations. Major airlines will accommodate disabled passengers if notified at least 72hr. in advance. Call ahead to restaurants, museums, and other facilities to find out if they are handicapped-accessible. Playa Monserrate, Luquillo's public *balneario*, has Puerto Rico's only **handicapped-accessible beach** (see p. 251). Bosque Estatal de Cambalache, between Manatí and Arecibo, has a **wheelchair-accessible trail** (p. 159). For information on transportation availability in individual cities, contact the Puerto Rican chapter of the Easter Seals Society (☎787-767-6710; www.pr.easter-seals.org).

USEFUL ORGANIZATIONS

Society for the Advancement of Travel for the Handicapped (SATH), 347 Fifth Ave., #610, New York, NY 10016, USA (☎212-447-7284; www.sath.org). Publishes free online travel information and the magazine *OPEN WORLD* ($18, free for members). Most info focuses on the continental US. Annual membership $45, students and seniors $30.

Directions Unlimited, 123 Green Ln., Bedford Hills, NY 10507, USA (☎800-533-5343). Books individual and group vacations for the physically disabled; not an info service.

MINORITY TRAVELERS

Because the vast majority of Puerto Ricans have darker skin, and mixed Taíno, African, and European ancestry, there is relatively little discrimination on the island—in theory. In practice, many islanders still associate darker skin with lower economic levels. Minority travelers will most likely not experience hostility or outright discrimination, but some minor harassment is not unheard of. San Juan receives visitors from all over the world, but in the rest of the island it is quite rare to see travelers of African or Asian descent. Most likely minority travelers will experience more curiosity than aggressiveness.

TRAVELERS WITH CHILDREN

Puerto Rico is an extremely family-friendly destination. During the day streets are safe for walking and beach-going is a great family activity. Most museums, tourist attractions, and sights in Puerto Rico offer discounts for children under 12. Some of the best attractions for families include: Luís A. Ferré Parque de las Ciencias (Science Park), in Bayamón (p. 150); Museo del Niño, in San Juan (p. 129); Casa de Don Ramón Power y Giralt, in San Juan (p. 130); Parque de las Cavernas del Río Camuy, outside Arecibo (p. 166); and Zoológico de Puerto Rico, in Mayagüez (p. 192). Once a month Habana Club in San Juan has an alcohol-free children's salsa night (p. 142).

Family vacations often require that you slow your pace and always require that you plan ahead. If you rent a car, make sure the rental company provides a car seat for younger children. **Be sure that your child carries some sort of ID** in case of an emergency or in case he or she gets lost. Families on a budget may want to consider joining the Puerto Rican vacationers and staying in a **centro vacacional** (see p. 58), which offers excellent value for larger groups.

DIETARY CONCERNS

Vegetarians will not find it easy to survive on Puerto Rican food. Traditional island food centers around meat, beans cooked with lard, and sandwiches filled with meat. In San Juan the tourist-oriented restaurants will usually have at least one vegetarian option; unfortunately, there's not much variety and these restaurants tend to be more expensive. Outside of San Juan, some options include *mofongo* without meat inside, pizza *empanadillas*, and cheese sandwiches. Most major cities have at least one vegetarian *cafetería*, but these are typically only open for lunch. *Let's Go* tries to list any vegetarian options in the **Food** section of each city.

The travel section of the The Vegetarian Resource Group's web site (www.vrg.org/travel) has a comprehensive list of organizations and web sites geared toward helping vegetarians and vegans traveling abroad. The web site www.vegdining.com provides an excellent database of vegetarian and vegan restaurants worldwide. For more information, visit your local bookstore or health food store, and consult *The Vegetarian Traveler: Where to Stay if You're Vegetarian*, by Jed and Susan Civic ($16).

Travelers who keep **kosher** should contact synagogues in larger cities for information on kosher restaurants. Your own synagogue or college Hillel should have access to lists of Jewish institutions across the nation. If you are strict in your observance, you may have to prepare your own food on the road. A good resource is the *Jewish Travel Guide*, edited by Michael Zaidner ($17).

OTHER RESOURCES

Let's Go tries to cover all aspects of budget travel, but we can't put *everything* in our guides. Listed below are books and web sites that can serve as jumping off points for your own research.

USEFUL PUBLICATIONS

■ **Que Pasa** (☎800-246-8677; www.gotopuertorico.com). The official publication of the Puerto Rican Tourism Company (PRTC) includes accommodations, restaurants, nightlife options, feature articles, and maps. Call to have a copy mailed home or pick up a copy at any tourist office or hotel. Free. The PRTC also publishes **Go To Puerto Rico**, another magazine describing hotels and restaurants throughout the island. Free.

The San Juan Star (www.sanjuanstar.com). It may not be the best newspaper in Puerto Rico, but The San Juan Star is the only island paper to come out with a daily English edition. Also has a Spanish language version. $0.45.

Places to Go (www.coral-publications.com). Puerto Rican's favorite travel guide is a color brochure listing hotels and restaurants in every city on the island. Available in English and Spanish at most tourist businesses and offices on the island. Also publishes the less-popular *Bienvenidos* magazine. Free.

Puerto Rican Telephone Tourist Quick Guide (www.superpagespr.com). It's hard to find, but this is one of Puerto Rico's most helpful publications. Includes tourism-related articles and an abbreviated version of the yellow pages designed for tourists. Free.

WORLD WIDE WEB

Almost every aspect of budget travel is accessible via the web. Within 10min. at the keyboard, you can make a hotel reservation, buy plane tickets, or get advice on travel hotspots. Listed here are some budget travel sites to start off your surfing; other relevant web sites are listed throughout the book. Because web site turnover is high, use search engines (such as www.google.com) to strike out on your own.

OUR PERSONAL FAVORITE

🔲 **Let's Go:** www.letsgo.com. Our constantly expanding web site features photos, streaming video, online ordering, info about our books, a buzzing travel forum, and links that will help you find everything you ever wanted to know about Puerto Rico.

THE ART OF BUDGET TRAVEL

How to See the World: www.artoftravel.com. An online book of great travel tips, from cheap flights to self defense to interacting with local culture.

Travel Library: www.travel-library.com. A fantastic set of links to sites with general information and personal travelogues.

INFORMATION ON PUERTO RICO

Puerto Rican Tourism Company: www.gotopuertorico.com. The island's official tourism web site includes general info about Puerto Rico, top 10 destination lists, and lists of various hotels and restaurants.

Escape to Puerto Rico: http://escape.topuertorico.com. A variety of island-specific info, including a current event discussion forum, Puerto Rico e-cards, a search engine for island restaurants, and a history quiz.

Puerto Rico Herald: www.puertorico-herald.org. The island's only online English-language newspaper. A great source for current events.

CIA World Factbook: www.odci.gov/cia/publications/factbook/index.html. Tons of vital statistics on Puerto Rico's geography, government, economy, and people.

Welcome to Puerto Rico: www.welcome.topuertorico.org. A mini-encyclopedia of Puerto Rican culture, history, politics, and food. Check out the island recipes.

Music of Puerto Rico: www.musicofpuertorico.com. The ultimate site for anything you ever wanted to know about Puerto Rican music, including sound clips of popular songs in every genre.

The Puerto Rican Store: www.thepuertoricanstore.com. An online retail store selling products from around Puerto Rico, including coffee, books, souvenirs, and crafts.

Puerto Rico Magazine: www.prmag.com. Puerto Rico's first online travel magazine. Includes photos, maps, travel tips, island info, travel stores, and an online chat room.

Super Pages: www.superpagespr.com. Puerto Rico's yellow pages search engine.

Caribbean National Forest: www.southernregion.fs.fed.us/caribbean/index.htm. The official web site of El Yunque, with flora and fauna descriptions, forest facts, and recreation information.

E S S E N T I A L S

ALTERNATIVES TO TOURISM

Puerto Rico can seem like it was made for short-term vacationers. Let's face it, the prospect of a week relaxing on the beach can, and should, tempt anyone to hop on the next plane south. But when the last tourist leaves, Puerto Rico continues to be a living, breathing community, complete with social problems, a flourishing culture, a fragile economy, and almost four million permanent residents. Of course, tourism plays an integral role in Puerto Rico's entire society. Old San Juan was completely renovated in the last 20 years, due in large part to the desire to attract more tourists. Every year over 4.6 million people visit Puerto Rico, and the entire island—from the surfing culture of Rincón to the Vieques economy desperately seeking to attract foreigners—has been shaped by their influence. But tourism has the potential to mean much more than the struggle for foreign dollars. Motived by a desire to become more closely acquainted with island culture, or by an interest in giving something back to the island, many tourists choose to spend more time on Puerto Rico, interacting with the local culture. Through volunteering, working, studying, or just being a responsible tourist, everyone has the opportunity to improve the reciprocal relationship between travelers and the places they visit.

Volunteering can be one of the most rewarding ways to interact with and contribute to a different culture. One rising trend in travel, especially in places with such natural diversity as Puerto Rico, is ecotourism. **Ecotourism** focuses on conserving natural habitats and using them to build up the economy without exploitation or overdevelopment. In Puerto Rico the San Juan-based **Conservation Trust** is the best example of a private company that has been able to protect lands around the island by using them for tourist exploration. Many other organizations that work to protect the limited natural resources of Puerto Rico are usually looking for help. Puerto Rico offers a wealth of **volunteer opportunities,** from assisting in research at the world's largest radio telescope to preserving precious mangrove coastline. On p. 82, you'll find several organizations that can help you find the opportunities that best suit your interests, whether you're looking to pitch in for a day or a year.

There are any number of other ways that you can integrate yourself into the communities you visit. US citizens will find that Puerto Rico is an especially appealing destination to visit for a long period of time because they may stay on the island without procuring a visa or work permit. One option is to **study** on the island, either by enrolling in a university or participating in an exchange or language program. Another option is to find a short- or long-term job on Puerto Rico. Some travelers actually structure their trips by the **work** that they can do along the way—either odd jobs as they go, or full-time stints in cities where they plan to stay for some time. While Puerto Rico has a relatively high unemployment rate, fluent English speakers are usually in demand. Whether it's through volunteering, studying, researching, or working, interacting with Puerto Rico's welcoming community will inevitably make any trip more rewarding.

> **GIVING BACK.** Puerto Rico has several organizations that have made a special effort to better their communities. For information about some of the best look for our **Giving Back** features throughout the book: see **Going Green** (p. 275), **Saving Vieques** (p. 290), and **Turtle Time** (p. 304).

A NEW PHILOSOPHY OF TRAVEL

We at *Let's Go* have watched the growth of the 'ignorant tourist' stereotype with dismay, knowing that the majority of travelers care passionately about the state of the communities and environments they explore—but also knowing that even conscientious tourists can inadvertently damage natural wonders, rich cultures, and impoverished communities. We believe the philosophy of **sustainable travel** is among the most important travel tips we could impart to our readers, to help guide fellow backpackers and on-the-road philanthropists. By staying aware of the needs and troubles of local communities, today's travelers can be a powerful force in preserving and restoring this fragile world.

Working against the negative consequences of irresponsible tourism is much simpler than it might seem; it is often self-awareness, rather than self-sacrifice, that makes the biggest difference. Simply by trying to spend responsibly and conserve local resources, all travelers can positively impact the places they visit. Let's Go has partnered with **BEST (Business Enterprises for Sustainable Travel,** an affiliate of the Conference Board; see www.sustainabletravel.org), which recognizes businesses that operate based on the principles of sustainable travel. Below, they provide advice on how ordinary visitors can practice this philosophy in their daily travels, no matter where they are

TIPS FOR CIVIC TRAVEL: HOW TO MAKE A DIFFERENCE

Use public mass transportation whenever possible; outside of cities, take advantage of group taxis or vans. Bicycles are an attractive way of seeing a community firsthand. And enjoy walking—purchase good maps of your destination and ask about on-foot touring opportunities.

When renting a car, ask whether fuel-efficient vehicles are available. Honda and Toyota produce cars that use hybrid engines powered by electricity and gasoline, thus reducing emissions of carbon dioxide. Ford Motor Company plans to introduce a hybrid fuel model by the end of 2004.

Reduce, reuse, recycle—use electronic tickets, recycle papers and bottles wherever possible, and avoid using containers made of styrofoam. Refillable water bottles and rechargable batteries both efficiently conserve expendable resources.

Be thoughtful in your purchases. Take care not to buy souvenir objects made from trees in old-growth or endangered forests, such as teak, or items made from endangered species, like ivory or tortoise jewelry. Ask whether products are made from renewable resources.

Buy from local enterprises, such as casual street vendors. In developing countries and low-income neighborhoods, many people depend on the "informal economy" to make a living.

Be on-the-road-philanthropists. If you are inspired by the natural environment of a destination or enriched by its culture, join in preserving their integrity by making a charitable contribution to a local organization.

Spread the word. Upon your return home, tell friends and colleagues about places to visit that will benefit greatly from their tourist dollars, and reward sustainable enterprises by recommending their services. Travelers can not only introduce friends to particular vendors but also to local causes and charities that they might choose to support when they travel.

ALTERNATIVES TO TOURISM

VISA INFORMATION (LONG-TERM STAYS) All foreign travelers planning a stay of more than 90 days in Puerto Rico (180 days for Canadians) need to obtain a visa. **US citizens never need a visa to travel to Puerto Rico.** The Center for International Business and Travel (CIBT), 23201 New Mexico Ave. NW #210, Washington, D.C. 20016 (☎800-925-2428; www.cibt.com), or 6300 Wilshire Blvd., #1520, Los Angeles, CA 90048 (☎323-658-5100), secures "pleasure tourist" or B-2 visas to and from all possible countries for a variable service charge (6-month visa around $45). Visa extensions are sometimes attainable with an I-539 form; call the forms request line (☎800-870-3676).

RESOURCES

Several companies offer extensive information on sustainable travel and various volunteer, work, and study programs throughout the world. The web sites listed below are a good place to start researching various programs in Puerto Rico.

Go Abroad (☎720-570-1702; www.goabroad.com). The best web site for young people looking to study, work, volunteer, or intern abroad (including Puerto Rico). Includes numerous listings, in addition to general information about visas, permits, and requirements. Primarily for high school and college students.

Transitions Abroad (☎/fax 802-442-4827; www.transitionsabroad.com) publishes a bi-monthly online newsletter packed with various articles and resources related to working, studying, volunteering, and interning. The invaluable web site contains back issues and additional articles.

VOLUNTEERING IN PUERTO RICO

Though Puerto Rico is considered relatively wealthy in comparison to the rest of Latin America, there is no shortage of aid organizations to benefit the very real issues the region does face. From protecting the island's scarce natural resources to combatting poverty in the urban ghettos, there is a lot of work to be done on this little island. Furthermore, volunteering can be one of life's most fulfilling experiences , especially when combined with the thrill of traveling in a new place.

Most volunteer opportunities in Puerto Rico deal with some kind of nature preservation, either on land or in the sea. There are two principal types of programs. Local, smaller organizations frequently have less structured volunteer programs in which the work is catered to an individual's interest. These opportunities are typically free, but rarely provide room and board. Depending on the organization, working with a local group can either be extremely rewarding as they offer hands-on experience, or exceptionally frustrating as they tend to be less organized and ill-prepared for volunteers.

The other type of volunteer opportunity is a large, international volunteer service, most likely based in the US. Many of these companies charge a surprisingly hefty fee to participate, though they frequently cover airfare and most, if not all, living expenses. These large companies are usually more organized than smaller groups, frequently take care of logistical details, and provide a group environment and support system.

NATURE PRESERVATION

Almost all of Puerto Rico's native forests were destroyed in the island's agricultural days, and only in the last 50 years has there been a concentrated effort to preserve the island's natural resources. Several local and American organizations accept volunteers in their efforts to protect and revive Puerto Rico's incredible flora and fauna.

BEFORE YOU GO Before handing your money over to any volunteer or study abroad program, make sure you know exactly what you're getting into. It's wise to get the name of **previous participants** and ask them about their experience, as some programs sound much better on paper than in reality. Also, make sure the program itself is able to answer the following **questions:**
-Will you be the only person in the program? If not, what are the other participants like? How old are they? Will you interact with them?
-Is room and board included? If so, what is the arrangement? Will you be expected to share a room? A bathroom? What are the meals like? Do they fit any dietary restrictions?
-Is transportation included? Are there any additional expenses?
-How much free time will you have? Will you be able to travel?
-What kind of safety network is set up? Will you still be covered by your home insurance? Does the program have an emergency plan?

ALTERNATIVES TO TOURISM

US Fish & Wildlife Service (☎800-344-9453; www.fws.gov), has 3 offices around Puerto Rico. The **Cabo Rojo** office, Rte. 301 Km 5.1 (☎851-7258 ext. 35), participates in the **Student Temporary Employment Program,** which pays full-time students to spend 1 year working and studying on the reserve. Housing available. The office in **Vieques,** Rte. 200 Km 0.4 (☎741-2138; http://southeast.fws.gov/vieques), accepts volunteers on an individual basis, but has no housing or structured program. The office on **Culebra,** on Rte. 250 (☎742-0115), also accepts individual volunteers and has housing available. Check the federal web site for information about projects around the island not associated with any particular office.

Las Casas de la Selva, Rte. 184 Km 17.6 (☎839-7318; www.biospherefoundation.org/rf.htm), in Bosque Estatal Carite, outside of Patillas (p. 263), strives to demonstrate that it is possible to preserve a forest and simultaneously make the land economically profitable. Owned by the company Tropic Ventures and partially funded by Biosphere Technologies (the company that created Arizona's Biosphere Project). With over 1000 acres of land, this is one of Puerto Rico's most successful reforestation projects. Welcomes group and individual volunteers to help with its many projects, from clearing wood to building retaining walls to working in the nursery. Required to work 4hr. per day. $4 charge per day. Housing available. Food available at additional cost.

Vieques Conservation and Historical Trust, C. Flamboyán 138 (☎741-8850; www.vcht.com), Esperanza, Vieques (p. 290), works to protect and preserve the natural resources of Vieques. Accepts volunteers on a case-by-case basis to help with preservation projects, including a clean-up program, nature work, assisting with lab experiments, and occasionally helping with the marine life exhibit. No housing. Contact Sandra Ortíz or Mark Martin for more information.

Earthwatch Institute, 3 Clock Tower Place Suite 100, Box 75, Maynard, MA 01754, USA (☎800-776-0188; www.earthwatch.org) is an international non-profit organization that promotes the conservation of natural resources and cultural heritage around the world. Offers expeditions to Puerto Rico and 45 other countries primarily dealing in flora and fauna preservation. 1-2 week expedition $600-3000. Membership $45 per year.

Universidad de Puerto Rico Río Piedras Jardin Botánico (☎767-1710 or 250-0000 ext. 6578), San Juan (p. 127). Welcomes short-term volunteers to work in the gardens. No housing available. Call ahead for info.

ADDITIONAL OPPORTUNITIES

National Astronomy and Ionosphere Center, 504 Spaces Sciences Building, Cornell University, Ithaca, NY 14853 (☎607-255-3735; www.naic.gov), offers a 10-week research assistant program for 6-12 US citizens who are currently enrolled in an undergraduate college. Applications due early Feb. Housing and a stipend provided.

Habitat for Humanity (habitatpr@hotmail.com; www.habitat.org) builds houses around the world for low income families. Puerto Rico does not have an established volunteer program, but the local chapter welcomes volunteers for 1 day or 1 year. They do not provide room and board, but they can sometimes arrange for a small stipend.

Explorations in Travel, 2458 River Rd., Guilford, VT 05301, USA (☎802-257-0152; explore@volunteertravel.com; www.volunteertravel.com), places groups and individuals at a variety of diverse volunteer opportunities, including helping with an animal shelter and working at Casas de la Selva (see p. 83). Assists with obtaining university independent study credit. 18+ for individual volunteers. Application fee $35. Placement fee $975. Travel not included.

Volunteer Match (☎415-241-6855; www.volunteermatch.org), lists a few volunteer programs in Puerto Rico, though you are responsible for contacting the individual programs. Current listings include working with the American Red Cross and assisting homeless people and ex-addicts.

STUDYING IN PUERTO RICO

Study abroad means a host of different activities to different people, but most programs can be divided into two major categories. **University-level exchange programs** allow current college students to do coursework at another university, usually for credit. These programs last for at least one semester and usually cost about the same as college tuition plus traveling expenses and room and board. On the other hand, **language schools** allow travelers of all ages to take basic language and culture courses at private, usually non-accredited, teaching facilities for much shorter periods of time. Typically the former is only open to current university students, while the latter is open to everyone.

> **VISA INFORMATION (STUDYING)** Foreign students who wish to study in the US must apply for either an M-1 visa (vocational studies) or an F-1 visa (for full-time students enrolled in an academic or language program). The application process is time-consuming and expensive—start at least one year in advance. The international students office at the institution you will be attending can provide the specifics. For more information, check the Department of Education web site at: www.ed.gov/offices/OUS/international/USNEI/us/study-us.html.

UNIVERSITIES

Many students may find that studying at a Puerto Rican university is one of the best ways to get acquainted with the culture. Most university-level study abroad programs are meant as language and culture enrichment opportunities, and thus are conducted entirely in Spanish. There are two primary ways to attend college in Puerto Rico; either enroll directly in a university or participate in a foreign exchange program. If you are fluent in Spanish, you will find that **enrolling directly in a Puerto Rican university** provides the opportunity to interact with Puerto Ricans and avoid inflated program fees. Furthermore, the US government considers many Puerto Rico universities, including the University of Puerto Rico, to be domestic institutions and provides federal grants and loans for study there if you are American. (Call the school you are interested in and find out if they are a Title Four institution.) **Participating in a study-abroad program** is usually more expensive, but ideally the program takes care of all of the logistics and leaves your experience hassle-free.

Some university programs have large groups of foreigners, while others place students in classes with Puerto Ricans. You may feel more comfortable in a community of students who speak the same language, but you will not have the same opportunity to practice a foreign language or to befriend other international students. For accommodations, dorm life provides a better opportunity to mingle with fellow students, but there is less of a chance to experience the local scene. If you live with a family, there is a potential to build lifelong friendships with natives and to experience day-to-day life in more depth, but conditions can vary greatly from family to family. Think about what you're looking for in your experience and choose wisely, because a bad placement can ruin your entire trip. Whatever program you choose, plan well in advance—admission deadlines can come as much as six months before the program starts.

PUERTO RICAN UNIVERSITIES

Universidad de Puerto Rico, P.O. Box 364984, San Juan 00936 (☎250-0000 ext. 3208 or 3202; www.upr.edu), is the largest university system in Puerto Rico with campuses in Aguadilla, Arecibo, Bayamón, Carolina, Cayey, Humacao, Mayagüez, Ponce, Río Piedras, and Utuado. The central Río Piedras campus alone has 23,000 students. Students must have at least an intermediate level of Spanish to enroll. Tuition for nonresident students $2400 per year. Some dormitories available.

InterAmerican University of Puerto Rico, C. Galileo Final, urb. Jardines Metropolitanos, Río Piedras, San Juan; P.O. Box 363255, San Juan 00936 (☎766-1912; www.inter.edu). Campuses in Aguadilla, Arecibo, Barranquitas, Bayamón, Fajardo, Guayama, Ponce, San Germán, and San Juan. The original campus is in San Germán. With 38,000 students, this is the oldest and largest private university system in Puerto Rico. Most coursework is in Spanish, but the university offers a separate trimester program in English. Spanish immersion program available. Undergraduate tuition $120 per credit plus miscellaneous fees. Catalog available online in English. Many students live in dormitories on the San Germán campus.

Universidad del Sagrado Corazón, P.O. Box 12383, San Juan 00914 (☎728-1515; www.sagrado.edu), in the heart of Santurce. Known for its outstanding communications department. Established in 1880. Student population of 5000. Offers programs in humanities, communications, education, social sciences, business administration, and natural sciences. All classes are conducted in Spanish.

AMERICAN PROGRAMS

All of the following programs accept participants from other universities. For additional options, consult your school's study abroad office.

State University of New York Oswego, Office of International Education and Programs, 122A Swetman Hall #SW3, Oswego, NY 13126 (☎888-467-9346; www.oswego-abroad.com) sponsors 1-semester programs to study at UPR Río Piedras. Program includes tuition and room and board in a university residence hall. Total program cost: in-state $6771, out-of-state $9171. Scholarships available.

Temple University International Programs, 200 Tuttleman Learning Center, 1809 North 13th St., Philadelphia, PA 19122 (☎877-256-6913; www.temple.edu/studyabroad) has semester- and year-long programs to study at UPR Río Piedras. Students must enroll full-time. Students live in campus dorms with a meal plan. Program fees include tuition, room, and board. Tuition equal to the current fees at Temple University. Application deadline March 1.

State University of New York Albany, 1400 Washington Ave. LI66, Albany, NY 12222 (☎518-442-3525; fax 442-3338; www.albany.edu/intled), offers a semester- or year-long study abroad program at the Universidad del Sagrado Corazón in Santurce, San Juan. Spanish fluency required. Tuition includes housing, transportation, and meals. On-campus housing for women only. Approximate tuition in-state residents 1 semester $7842, 1 year $14,840. Out-of-state $10,292/$19,740.

LANGUAGE SCHOOLS

Language schools are frequently independently run international or local organizations or divisions of foreign universities that rarely offer college credit. This is a good alternative to university study if you desire a deeper focus on the language, a less-rigorous courseload, or if you don't speak any Spanish. Puerto Rico does not have many language schools, but a couple of options are listed below:

A2Z Languages, 5112 N. 40th St., Suite 103, Phoenix, AZ 85018, USA (☎800-496-4596; www.a2zlanguages.com), offers language programs for all levels in Hato Rey and arranges cultural tours. Price includes homestay. 1 week min. Max. class size 6. 1 week $425, with 2 meals per day $495; 4 weeks $1580/$1860. Private lessons available at an additional cost.

AmeriSpan, P.O. Box 58129, Philadelphia, PA 19102, USA (☎800-879-6640, outside of US 215-751-1100; www.amerispan.com), offers language programs for all levels in Hato Rey for anywhere from 1 week to 6 months. Price includes homestay with local family. Max. class size 6. Reserve at least 4 weeks in advance. $100 registration fee. 1 week $450, with meals $500; 4 weeks $1680/$1960.

Instituto Internacional Euskalduna, C. Navarro 56, Hato Rey, PR 00918 (☎787-281-8013; www.spanishinpuertorico.com), a division of New England School. Offers Spanish immersion classes for speakers of all levels. College credit offered through the University of Southern Mississippi. Classes 20hr. per week plus weekly excursions and cultural activities. Max. class size 6. Courses start at $300 per week. Home stays $150 per week, with 2 meals per day $220.

WORKING IN PUERTO RICO

As with studying, work opportunities tend to fall into two categories. Some travelers want long-term jobs that allow them to get to know another part of the world as a member of the community, while other travelers seek out short-term jobs to finance the next leg of their travels. Puerto Rico has a high unemployment rate, and very little work for travelers. Jobs traditionally done by foreigners (teaching English, working as an au pair) simply do not exist on the island. The only places you can even hope to find gainful employment are major tourist centers—San Juan, Rincón, Culebra, and possibly Vieques. Outside of these locations, it will be nearly impossible to find a job unless you are completely fluent in Spanish.

 VISA INFORMATION (WORKING) If you are a foreigner, you need a **work permit** or "green card" to work in Puerto Rico. Your employer must obtain this document, usually by demonstrating that you have skills that locals lack. Friends in the US can sometimes help expedite work permits or arrange work-for-accommodations exchanges. Obtaining a work visa may seem complex, but it's critical that you go through the proper channels—the alternative is potential deportation. People who wish to work on a **cruise ship** must obtain a US **C1-D visa** from the nearest US consulate. Normally you must have a job offer before you can obtain the visa. **US citizens** can work in Puerto Rico without any type of work permit or visa.

LONG-TERM WORK

If you are fluent in Spanish, the best way to find a job is to go to Puerto Rico and perform a thorough job search. All of the major newspapers have a help wanted section. Furthermore, businesses in major cities (especially San Juan) frequently place help wanted signs in the window. In San Juan, contact the **Departamento del Trabajo y Recursos Humanos,** Ave. Luis Muñoz Rivera 50 (☎754-5751), 15th fl., at C. Domenech, Hato Rey, for a list of office jobs. The job search process will be almost impossible for non-Americans.

TOURISM SECTOR WORK

Many restaurants, hotels, and other tourism industry companies hire new employees at the beginning of high season (usually Nov.-Dec. for places with lots of American tourists). The best way to find a job is to show up in a highly touristed city and ask around. The **Culebra Calendar,** available on Culebra or from P.O. Box 761, Culebra 00775 (☎742-0816; mcsculeb@coqui.net), includes a list of current job openings on the island. Most jobs will only be available during high season, and it is technically illegal for non-US citizens to work without a Green Card (see p. 86).

CRUISE SHIP WORK

Working on a cruise ship can be one of the best ways to make a living while traveling around the Caribbean. Cruise ship employees generally enter into contracts for three to nine months performing a variety of tasks, from housekeeping to entertainment work. In many ways, working on a cruise ship is just as **glamorous** as it seems—you travel the world, meet new people, and get a tan. Furthermore, citizens of some countries don't have to pay taxes when working on an international cruise ship. On the other hand, cruise ships are notorious for making their employees work long hours and live in small, windowless cabins. You typically do not get a plane ticket to the point of departure, and you only get a plane ticket home if you have completed your contract to the satisfaction of your employers. Cruise ship workers go months at a time without returning home, and most only get to communicate with the outside world on the rare days off at port.

If you decide that this is worthwhile, **applying** to work on a cruise ship can be a bureaucratic process. Cruise lines hire almost constantly, but most receive so many applications that they can disregard any applicant who does not follow their guidelines exactly. Pay close attention to the application directions and be sure to send your application to the right person. In order to work you usually must obtain a US C1-D visa from the nearest consulate. A few cruise ships post jobs on their web sites (see p. 69 for a list of cruise lines that dock in San Juan), but the majority hire through a separate online booking agent. Most of these agents charge a fee of $30-60 to even access the listings and there are reports that some of the web sites are scams. Some helpful web sites are: www.cruise-jobs.com, www.cruiselinejobs.com, www.funkycareers.com, www.cruiseshipjob.com, and www.shipjobs.com. However, *Let's Go* does not specifically endorse any web site.

FURTHER READING: ALTERNATIVES TO TOURISM
Alternatives to the Peace Corps: A directory of third world and US Volunteer Opportunities, by Joan Powell ($10).

How to Live Your Dream of Volunteering Oversees, by Collins, DeZerega, and Heckscher ($17).

International Directory of Voluntary Work, by Louise Whetter and Victoria Pybus ($16).

International Jobs, by Eric Kocher and Nina Segal ($18).

Overseas Summer Jobs 2002, by Ian Collier and David Woodworth ($18).

Work Abroad: The Complete Guide to Finding a Job Overseas, by Clayton Hubbs ($16).

Work Your Way Around the World, by Susan Griffith ($18).

ALTERNATIVES TO TOURISM

SAN JUAN

San Juan is not the most beautiful part of Puerto Rico, but it is undoubtedly the most vibrant. With over 25% of the island's population and 30,000 acres of land, the capital of the Caribbean defies classification. Ritzy Isla Verde, working class Santurce, and historic Old San Juan seem like different worlds, yet they are all part of the same city, less than 7 mi. apart. This diversity defines the city and provides it with a unique spirit of centricity. *Sanjuaneros* have been known to go their entire life without leaving the metropolitan area and it's easy to see why. Why leave, when everything you could ever want is here?

The pride of *sanjuaneros* is a legacy of the city's history. As soon as Juan Ponce de León moved the island's capital from Caparra to San Juan in 1521, the Spanish focused on little else on the island. A giant wall was constructed around the city with the sentiment that it was the only part of the island that needed protection. For the next 200 years San Juan served primarily as a military base, evident in the city's several military fortresses (El Morro, La Fortaleza, San Cristóbal, El Cañuelo). Meanwhile, Spain devoted most of her resources to more economically beneficial colonies, while San Juan suffered from numerous foreign attacks and regular hurricanes. Finally, in the 1760s, Irish-born Spaniard Alejandro O'Reilly came to implement economic reforms and modernize San Juan. The streets were paved with cobblestones and the capital began developing an urban infrastructure. Thus, in the 19th century, the city began to grow...slowly. Working class *sanjuaneros* migrated into Puerta de Tierra, while the white minority fulfilled their dream of a commercialized suburban area with the development of Santurce.

In the early 20th century the population of the city grew dramatically as Santurce blossomed, the university brightened up what was still the nearby village of Río Piedras, and at last San Juan became more than just a dusty port town. Meanwhile people began to inhabit the area between Santurce and Río Piedras, thus bringing about the development of Hato Rey. In 1951 Río Piedras was officially enveloped within the city limits and San Juan became the sprawling metropolis that it is today. Around the same time, tourism hit the city; when Cuba ignited in revolution, Condado became the new Caribbean hotspot. However, the next 30 years brought increasing industrialization and the city slowly entered an era of aesthetic decay that not even the Department of Culture, inaugurated in 1955, could combat. By the 1980s the government realized that something had to change. For the last 20 years San Juan has been experiencing somewhat of a revival, as Old San Juan has renovated almost all of its buildings and become tourist central, Condado has again become the Miami of the Caribbean, and Hato Rey has emerged as an international financial powerhouse. Once again, all eyes are on San Juan.

HIGHLIGHTS OF SAN JUAN

STEP BACK IN TIME to wander the cobblestone streets and explore the haunting forts of Old San Juan (see p. 123).

SHAKE YOUR BONBON with hundreds of other s*anjuaneros* at one of the city's unbelievable discos (see p. 140).

GAZE INCREDULOUSLY at the impressive collection of art in Santurce's new Museo de Arte (see p. 132).

LOUNGE with the rich and famous on the white sands of Isla Verde (see p. 134).

Old San Juan continues to be perceived as the heart of the city, both by visitors and by locals who flock to the former island on weekend evenings. Overflowing with culture, history, and charm, the old city has something to fit every traveler's desires. At times Old San Juan can seem like a Disneyfied cruise stop, with every business competing to impress the one-day visitors. But a walk down the quiet streets of Calle Sol and Calle Luna proves that underneath the hype, the real old city continues to shine. The rest of San Juan is undoubtedly the most American area of the island—it sometimes seems like you can't throw a rock without hitting a Burger King. Yet despite the commercialism, San Juan offers something a bit different, a little bit of Caribbean flavor that the mainland cannot compete with.

Perhaps San Juan can be best understood by sunset at the end of Paseo del Morro in Old San Juan. Under the shadow of one of the oldest forts in the new world, *sanjuaneros* go for an evening stroll surrounded by symbols of their island's status. Across the bay, the constantly working Bacardi factory serves as a reminder both of the island's economic prosperity and its international position. Cruise ships entering the harbor bring tourists to admire the city—and tourist dollars to fuel the city. Meanwhile, in the background, the Cordillera Central rises as an omnipresent reminder of the city's proximity to nature. And most of all the *sanjuaneros* themselves, who make the trip out to Old San Juan to appreciate and revel in their city's past and present, exemplify what makes the city unique.

■ INTERCITY TRANSPORTATION

Flights:

Aeropuerto Internacional Luis Muñoz Marín, on the eastern edge of San Juan in Isla Verde. The Puerto Rico Tourism Company regulates taxis leaving the airport. Go to a marked "Ground Transportation" booth outside baggage claim and an English-speaking official will provide a set fare (see p. 96) and a taxi. The cheapest way to get to and from the airport is by **bus.** Take bus B40 or C45 from the 2nd level in front of terminal C, then sit back and relax: the bus will complete its entire 45-60min. route before arriving in Isla Verde. From there, wait in front of Mall Isla Verde for bus A5, which goes through Santurce and Puerta de Tierra en route to Old San Juan. To get to the airport, take bus A5 to Isla Verde and get off at the end of Ave. Isla Verde, in front of the orange cockfight arena (40min. from Old San Juan). Then switch to bus B40 or C45 (5min.). The airport is a 5min. **drive** from Isla Verde, 20min. from Condado, and 30min. from Old San Juan. The Puerto Rico Tourism Company **tourist information office** is outside the lower level of terminal C. (☎791-1014. Open daily 9am-8pm.) Most major US airlines fly into San Juan. **Iberia** is the main European airline. For more information see **By Plane,** p. 66.

Aeropuerto de Isla Grande (☎729-8751), on the eastern edge of Puerta de Tierra, hosts several smaller airlines flying primarily to Vieques, Culebra, and Santo Domingo. Taxis usually wait out front when flights come in; if not, have the security guard call one. Open daily 5:45am-6pm.

Airlines:

Air Flamenco (☎724-6464) flies from Isla Grande Airport on demand only. Planes go regularly to **Culebra** (30min.; 2-3 per day; $40, round-trip $80) and sporadically to **Fajardo** ($25, round-trip $45) and **Vieques** (full plane charters only). MC/V.

Air Santo Domingo (☎723-1052 or 723-1013) flies from Isla Grande Airport to **Santo Domingo, Dominican Republic** (55min., 2-3 per day, round-trip $222-275). MC/V.

American Airlines, Ave. Ashford 1022 (reservations ☎800-433-7300). 1hr. free parking and long waits. American flies to major US cities as well as Mayagüez, Santo Domingo, Tortola, St. Thomas, St. Maarten, St. Lucia, St. Kitts, and St. Croix. Open M-F 9am-5pm. AmEx/D/MC/V.

Iberia, Ave. Ponce de León 760 (reservations ☎800-772-4642), sends flights from LMM airport to Santo Domingo and Europe via Madrid. Open M-F 9am-4:30pm. AmEx/D/MC/V.

ROM THE ROAD

A NATIONAL IDENTITY CRISIS

It all started in the airport. There I vas, at 5:30am, trying to stay awake n line when the airline representa-ives asked me, "Domestic or inter-1ational honey?" A fairly simple question, right? I had no idea. Nei-her did he. "We own it, right, so it should be domestic," was his guess. Sounded good to me. But he was vrong. In this instance, Puerto Rico vas considered a foreign country.

This was just the beginning of the confusion, as I confronted a question hat has plagued Puerto Ricans for he last 100 years. Is the island part of the US or not? We use the same currency, the same postal system and the same military. El Morro and San Cristóbal are managed by the JS National Park service. But then here's the whole language thing. And the drinking age is 18. And well, t just doesn't feel like the US. No vonder this has been the most hotly debated issue on the island for the ast 50 years.

Ultimately I decided that the issue does not have to be black or white. I enjoy the conveniences of not having o go through customs and being able to use my own currency, but I also love the constant beat of salsa hat you just don't hear on the main-and. Of course, I'm not Puerto Rican, so I don't have to worry about taxes, or being drafted, or having the right o vote for president. For islanders he issue is much more pressing. But or the average visitor, it's acceptable o just sit back and relax. There's always time later to figure out if you can still buy duty-free goods.

M&N Airlines (☎722-5980) flies from Isla Grande Airport to **Vieques** (30min.; 5 per day; $50, round-trip $90). AmEx/MC/V.

Vieques Air Link (☎888-901-9247 or 741-8331; fax 741-0101; valair@coqui.net) flies to **Vieques** from Luis Muñoz Marín International Airport (30min.; 3 per day; $69, round-trip $135) and Isla Grande Airport (30min.; 4 per day; $43, round-trip $80).

Públicos: *Públicos* (shared vans) are Puerto Rico's only public form of inter-city transportation. In San Juan, *públicos* congregate in Río Piedras and leave when full (6am-3pm). Arrive early for a faster departure. Drivers sit outside of the vans waiting for passengers; just tell any driver your destination and he'll point you in the right direction. The central **Terminal de Transportación Juan A. Palerm**, at the intersection of C. Arzuaga and C. Vellejo, near the market, houses *públicos* headed east to: **Fajardo** (1hr., $3.50) via **Luquillo** (45min., $3); and **Loíza** (30min., $1.75). Additional públiocs leave from Río Piedras's central plaza, 1 block south of Paseo de Diego. To: **Bayamón** (30min., $0.75); **Caguas** (30min., $1); **Guayama** (1¼hr., $7); **Guaynabo** (40min., $0.60); **Humacao** (45min.-1hr., $2.50); **Ponce** (1½hr. min., $10) via **Salinas** (1hr., $10). **Linea Boricua,** C. González 116 (☎765-1908) operates out of an unmarked parking lot. Walking downhill on C. González; the parking lot is on the right at the intersection with C. Jorge Romany. To **Arecibo** (1-1½hr., 2 per day noon-1pm, $8-10). **Linea Sultana,** C. Esteban González 898 (☎767-5205 or 765-9377), at Ave. Universidad, sends vans to **Mayagüez** (3½hr., every 2hr. 7:30am-5:30pm, $12). **Linea DonQ,** C. Brumbaugh 102 (☎764-0540) sends *públicos* to **Ponce** (1½hr., 3-4 per day, $10).

Cars: All of the major American car rental companies have a booth in the Luis Muñoz Marín International Airport. Some of the less expensive companies are listed below. For a complete list see p. 72. Unless otherwise stated, all price quotes are for compact cars with unlimited mileage.

AAA Car Rental (☎791-2609), in the Saint Tropez Condominium, Isla Verde. Nov. 24-May $35-45 per day; May-Nov. 23 $35; special deals as low as $27 per day. Ages 21-24 $8 per day surcharge. Open M-Sa 9am-6pm. AmEx/D/MC/V.

Charlie's Car Rental (☎728-2418, toll-free 800-289-1227; www.charliecars.com), on Ave. Isla Verde, across from the Marbella del Caribe building, Isla Verde. High season $44-51 per day; low season $26-30. Ages 21-24 $10 per day surcharge. Open 24hr. AmEx/D/MC/V.

Hertz, Ave. Ashford 1365 (☎725-2027 or 800-654-3131; fax 725-5537), Condado. $30-48 per day. Ages 21-24 $10 per day surcharge. Open daily 8am-noon and 1-5pm. AmEx/D/DC/MC/V.

ORIENTATION

San Juan is conveniently divided into a number of distinct neighborhoods, each with its own unique ambiance and almost all of which are dominated by one major thoroughfare that holds the majority of the shops and services. The neighborhoods normally frequented by visitors are described below.

> **NEIGHBORHOOD SAFETY** Although San Juan is generally safe, visitors should avoid a few specific neighborhoods. **La Perla,** on the northern edge of Old San Juan between the cemetery and San Cristóbal, continues to be dangerous despite increased police surveillance. **Puerta de Tierra** is fine during the day, but known to house drug dealers at night. In Santurce **Calle Loíza** and the surrounding areas should be avoided after dark. The neighborhood around Río Piedras's **Plaza del Mercado** also becomes a bit foreboding at night.

OLD SAN JUAN. Old San Juan is the tourist center of the city. From November to May, thousands of visitors disembark from cruise ships every day and land in this neighborhood lined with cobblestone streets and antique buildings. Almost all of the capital's museums and sights are located in Old San Juan, and any visitor to the island should plan to spend at least one day here. The old city is easy to navigate on foot and wandering through the small winding streets and alleyways is half the fun. As a general rule, streets go downhill as they go south.

CONDADO. In the 1950s tourists flocked to Condado, the hottest beach destination this side of Miami. **Avenida Ashford,** a one-way street running parallel to the ocean, has all the restaurants and services a traveler could need. The increasingly residential **Calle Magdalena** runs parallel to Ashford, but traffic goes in the opposite direction. The three blocks west of C. Condado between Ave. Ashford and the ocean constitute San Juan's gay district.

MIRAMAR AND SANTURCE. Lying directly south of Condado and Ocean Park, Miramar and Santurce used to be the centers of San Juan's business community, but over the years the two neighborhoods have slowly deteriorated. Today Miramar is more of a residential neighborhood with a few hotels, while Santurce continues to house many of the city's smaller businesses. **Avenida Ponce de León,** the major street that connects the two areas, houses most of the restaurants, hotels, and services. **Avenida Fernánez Juncos** is the street's parallel counterpart, with traffic running in the other direction. **Avenida José de Diego** and **Calle Roberto H. Todd** connect Santurce to Condado. By night, many of the city's major discos open in Santurce.

OCEAN PARK. Ocean Park proper is a gated community lying along the ocean between Condado and Isla Verde, but the term has come to encompass the surrounding streets as well. Most restaurants lie along **Avenida McLeary,** a continuation of Condado's Ave. Ashford, but it's necessary to head into Santurce, Condado, or Isla Verde to find many services. Recently this quiet residential area has been invaded by young Puerto Ricans in search of pristine sand and the perfect wave.

ISLA VERDE. Although technically it's within the city limits of Carolina, most people consider Isla Verde to be part of San Juan. Moving inland, Isla Verde consists of some of the best beaches in the city, bordered by an endless row of resorts and time-share condominiums, then the busy **Avenida Isla Verde,** then a row of shops and stores, then a freeway. This layered organization dominated by major roads can make Isla Verde a difficult area to navigate on foot. Many Isla Verde establishments do not have addresses; instead, they are identified in terms of the condo or building they reside in. If you get confused, ask a local; most have long since memorized the building names. Across the freeway, the small residential neighborhood

San Juan Overview

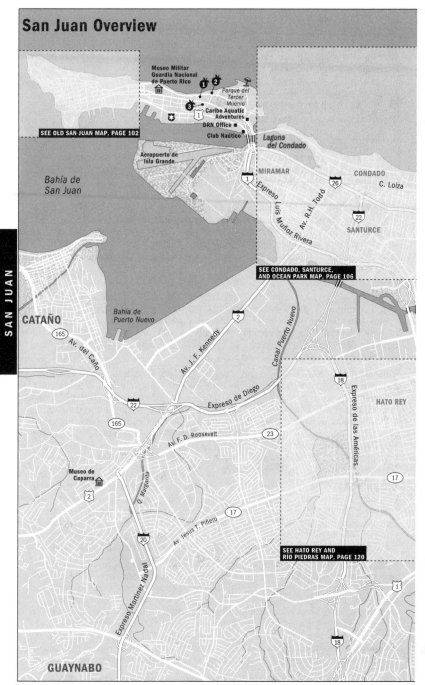

Museo Militar
Guardia Nacional
de Puerto Rico

Parque del
Tercer
Milenio

Caribe Aquatic
Adventures

DRN Office ■

Club Náutico

Laguna
del Condado

SEE OLD SAN JUAN MAP, PAGE 102

Aeropuerto de
Isla Grande

MIRAMAR

CONDADO

C. Loíza

Bahía de
San Juan

Expreso Luis Muñoz Rivera

Av. R.H. Todd

SANTURCE

SEE CONDADO, SANTURCE,
AND OCEAN PARK MAP, PAGE 106

CATAÑO

Bahía de
Puerto Nuevo

Av. del Caño

Av. J. F. Kennedy

Canal Puerto Nuevo

HATO REY

Expreso de Diego

Expreso de las Américas

Av. F. D. Roosevelt

Museo de
Caparra

Q. Margarita

Av. Jesus T. Piñero

SEE HATO REY AND
RÍO PIEDRAS MAP, PAGE 120

Expreso Martínez Nadal

GUAYNABO

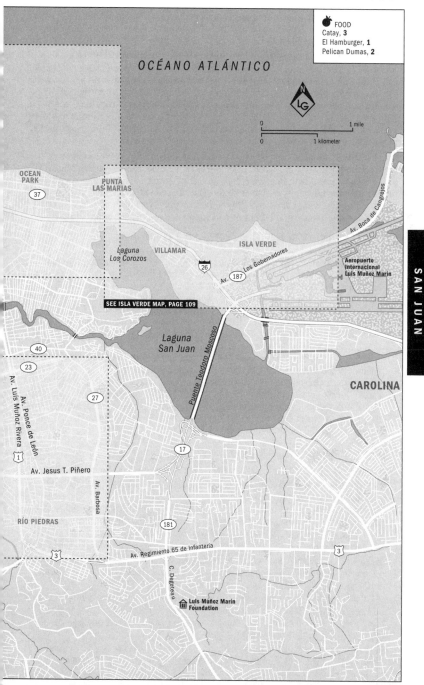

FOOD
Catay, **3**
El Hamburger, **1**
Pelican Dumas, **2**

OCÉANO ATLÁNTICO

SAN JUAN

OCEAN PARK
37

PUNTA LAS MARIAS

Laguna Los Corozos

VILLAMAR

ISLA VERDE

Av. Boca de Cangrejos

Aeropuerto Internacional Luis Muñoz Marín

26

Av. 187 Los Gobernadores

SEE ISLA VERDE MAP, PAGE 109

Laguna San Juan

CAROLINA

40
23

Av. Ponce de León
Av. Luis Muñoz Rivera
1

27

Puente Teodoro Moscoso

Av. Jesus T. Piñero

Av. Barbosa

17

RÍO PIEDRAS

181

3

Av. Regimiento 65 de Infantería

3

C. Degetau

Luis Muñoz Marín Foundation

of **Villamar** consists of seven numbered streets. **Punta las Marías** is the small peninsula dividing Ocean Park from Isla Verde. Many surfers have set up camp in this area, and it's a good place to find water sports equipment. In this chapter, establishments in Punta las Marías are listed under the Isla Verde header.

HATO REY. This is San Juan's business district; almost all of San Juan's major banks call Hato Rey home. **Avenida Ponce de León** and **Avenida Luis Muñoz Rivera** (Hwy. 1), the two major north-south thoroughfares, hold most of the skyscrapers, while smaller businesses radiate outward. **Avenida Franklin D. Roosevelt** (not to be confused with Ave. Eleanor Roosevelt), a busy street with lots of restaurants, connects Ave. Ponce de León to **Expreso de las Américas** and **Plaza las Américas.** Hato Rey is difficult to navigate on foot, as many of the roads do not have sidewalks.

RÍO PIEDRAS. Avenida Jesus Piñero (Rte. 17) divides Hato Rey from Río Piedras, the most recent addition to San Juan. Río Piedras sometimes feels like a different world as it is much more Latin American than the rest of the city. Most visitors spend their time around the university and the market. This area can be a bit confusing, so use a map and be careful after dark. Ave. Ponce de León and Ave. Luis Muñoz Rivera (Hwy. 1) continue south through Río Piedras and connect to east-west running Hwy. 3.

⌐ LOCAL TRANSPORTATION

Buses: Metropolitan Bus Authority (☎250-6064) runs a comprehensive system throughout San Juan. The helpful **A5** line leaves from Covadonga station in Old San Juan, follows Ave. Ponce de León through Miramar, turns left on Ave. José de Domingo, continues along C. Loíza and Ave. Isla Verde, and finally ends in Carolina (last bus 8:45pm). Route **B21** leaves from Old San Juan, crosses Puerta de Tierra, follows Ave. Ashford through Condado and continues south to Hato Rey and Plaza Las Américas (last bus M-Sa 9pm, Su 7:45pm). **Metrobús M1** leaves from Old San Juan and passes through Santurce and Hato Rey en route to Río Piedras (last bus 11:15pm). There are 2 main bus stations: one in **Old San Juan,** near Pier 4, and another in **Río Piedras,** 2 blocks north of Paseo de Diego. Metrobuses come every 10min., routes beginning with an "A" come every 15min., routes beginning with a "B" come every 20min., and routes beginning with a "C" come every 30min, but only Metrobuses regularly run on schedule. All buses run much less frequently on Sundays. When a bus passes, make sure the driver sees you or he may not stop. Metrobuses costs $0.50; all other buses cost $0.25. Exact change is required.

PATIENCE IS A VIRTUE Anyone who has spent significant time driving around the San Juan may describe it as a mind-numbing, death-defying experience that they don't ever want to repeat. *Let's Go* offers five easy tips to prevent insanity while driving in San Juan.

1. Don't drive in Old San Juan. Especially on weekend nights. The city is easily walkable and there are several parking garages conveniently located on the eastern edge.

2. NEVER drive in Hato Rey during rush hour. In the morning, avoid driving from Bayamón or Caguas into the city, and in the evening avoid driving out to these suburbs

3. Whenever possible, take Hwy. 26 to get between Old San Juan and Isla Verde, thus avoiding the slow traffic in Condado, Santurce, and Ocean Park. Heck, just take Hwy. 26 whenever possible—it's one of the most convenient roads in the city.

4. It would be nice to avoid Hwy. 3, but that's almost impossible if you want to explore eastern Puerto Rico. However, always take Hwy. 26 to Carolina, avoiding Hwy. 3's slow crawl through Río Piedras, and if you're going east of Luquillo, try taking Hwy. 52 to Caguas, then Hwy. 30 east to Humacao, then Hwy. 53 north.

5. Bring some good music, good company, or a large dose of patience. No matter how many times you honk your horn, it's impossible to completely escape traffic jams.

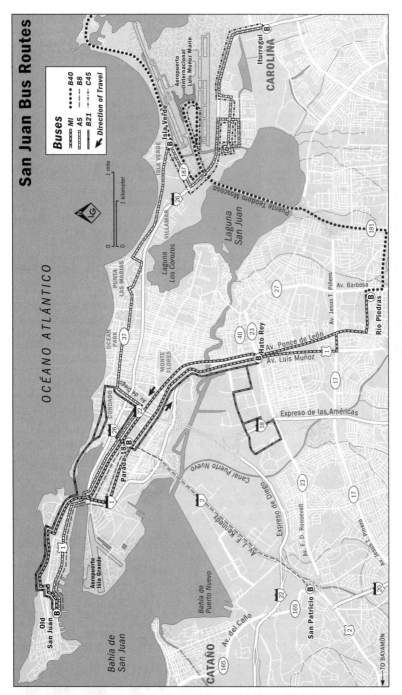

San Juan Bus Routes

Buses
- MI
- A5
- B21
- •••• B40
- --- B8
- •-•-• C45
- → Direction of Travel

OCÉANO ATLÁNTICO

CAROLINA

Iturregui

Aeropuerto
Internacional
Luis Muñoz Marín

Isla Verde

PUNTA
LAS MARÍAS

OCEAN
PARK

VILLAMAR

Laguna
Los Corozos

Laguna
San Juan

Puente Teodoro Moscoso

CONDADO

MONTE
FLORES

Hato Rey

Av. Ponce de León

Av. Luis Muñoz

Río Piedras

Av. Jesús T. Piñero

Av. Barbosa

Av. de Diego

Parada 18

Canal Puerto Nuevo

Expreso de las Américas

Expreso de Diego

Av. J. F. Kennedy

Canal Puerto Nuevo

Av. del Caño

Bahía de
Puerto Nuevo

N. F. D. Roosevelt

San Patricio

Av. Jesús T. Piñero

TO BAYAMÓN

Old
San Juan

Aeropuerto
Isla Grande

Bahía de San Juan

CATAÑO

Bahía de
San Juan

Taxis: Licensed taxis in San Juan are called **taxis turísticas** and identifiable by the yellow lighthouse logo on the side. Fixed rates include: Airport to Isla Verde $8, Airport to Condado or Miramar $12, Airport to Old San Juan $16, within Old San Juan $6, Old San Juan to Condado or Mirarmar $10, and Old San Juan to Isla Verde $16. Outside of these areas, all taxis should use a meter. In **Old San Juan** taxis congregate around the Plaza de Armas, outside the Windham Hotel near the pier, and behind the Teatro Tapia. Late at night try the latter two options. In **Condado** try one of the big hotels or just flag down a taxi along Ave. Ashford. In **Isla Verde** taxis sometimes wait in front of the Hotel InterContinental. In **Santurce, Miramar, Ocean Park, Hato Rey,** and **Río Piedras,** you can attempt to hail a taxi along one of the major thoroughfares, but it may be best to call. Try: **Cooperativa Major Taxi Cabs** (☎ 723-2460), **Metro-Taxi Cab** (☎ 725-2870), and **Rochdale Radio Taxi** (☎ 721-1900).

Trolleys: A **free** trolley passing all the major sites in **Old San Juan** departs regularly from the Covadonga bus terminal (daily 8am-10pm). Wait at any one of the marked trolley stops throughout the city. The **north route** passes both forts and the museums along C. Norzagaray. The **south route** passes the Plaza de Armas and the piers.

Ferries: AcuaExpreso (☎ 729-8714) sends a ferry from Pier 2 in Old San Juan to **Cataño** (10min.; 40-46 per day 6am-10pm; $0.50, ages 60-74 $0.25, over 74 free).

Bike Rental: Adrenalina (☎ 727-1233), next to Ave. Isla Verde 125, Isla Verde, rents bikes ($20 per 24hr., $10 per hr.). Helmet and lock included. Reservations recommended. Open M-F 10am-7pm, Sa 9am-6pm. **Local Riders,** Ave. Ashford 1106 (☎ 403-8055), Condado, rents bikes ($10 per hr., $20 per day, $25 per 24hr.). A 40min. urban ride from the Piñones bike path. Open daily 10am-5pm. MC/V. **Hot Dog Cycling,** Ave. Isla Verde 5916 (☎ 982-5344), Isla Verde, rents brand new bikes ($25 per day, $15 per ½ day). Open M-Sa 9am-6pm. MC/V.

Scooter Rental: Scooters Rental, C. O'Donnell 204 (☎ 721-0851), Old San Juan, rents automatic Korean scooters to experienced riders ($25 for the 1st hr., $20 for each additional). $500 credit card deposit required. 21+. Open daily 10am-6pm. MC/V.

▣ PRACTICAL INFORMATION

TOURIST AND FINANCIAL SERVICES

Tourist Offices: Puerto Rican Tourism Company (☎ 722-1709 or 724-4788), in the yellow house at C. Comercio and Plaza de la Darsena, near Pier 1, Old San Juan. Free pamphlets and info. English spoken. Open M-W 9am-8pm, Th-F 8:30am-5pm, Sa-Su 9am-8pm. The **municipal tourist information center,** C. Recinto Sur 99 (☎ 977-4845 or 977-4825), Old San Juan, offers **free walking tours of Old San Juan.** Advanced booking required. Most tours in Spanish. Usually open M-F 8am-4pm. Another **municipal tourist office,** C. Tetuan 250 (☎ 449-9174). Open M-Sa 8am-4pm. The only tourist office outside of Old San Juan is a small booth at the western edge of **Condado** (☎ 644-7519). Open M-Sa 10am-6pm.

Tours: Many big resort hotels open their overpriced tours to non-guests. Before booking, check to see if transportation and meals are included.

Castillo Tours, C. Brumbaugh 100 (☎ 791-6195 or 726-5752; wyndham@castillotours.com), in the Wyndham Hotel, Old San Juan. One of the most comprehensive tour operators in San Juan; several trips leave every day. To: El Yunque (½-day $40, full-day $60); El Yunque and Luquillo Beach (full-day $60); Ponce (full-day $60); Río Camuy and the Arecibo Observatory (full-day $70); and Old San Juan and the Bacardi factory (½-day $35). They also offer a catamaran trip from Fajardo with picnic and snorkeling ($69), a horseback ride on Luquillo beach ($65), kayaking in Fajardo's bioluminescent bay (night trip $70), golf packages (from $85), deep-sea fishing (½-day $150), and diving (2 tanks ½-day $80, full-day $95). Only the catamaran trip includes lunch. Open daily 7:30am-7:30pm. AmEx/MC/V.

Eco Action Tours (☎791-7509 or 640-7385; ecoactiontours@yahoo.com). This 2-person company offers most of the tours found at larger companies, but much less formalized service. To El Yunque (½-day $37), El Yunque and Luquillo Beach (full-day $50), Ponce ($50; 5 person min.), and Old San Juan and the Bacardi Factory ($35). Also offers kayaking in Fajardo's bioluminescent bay ($40), 2hr. beach horseback rides ($35-45), snorkeling trips ($69, to Culebra $89), 2-tank dives ($55-85), rappelling in the Camuy caves ($90-125), and power or sailboat rental ($179 for ½-day). Admissions not included. Transportation available at additional cost. MC/V.

Las Tortugas Adventures, 4 C. la Puntilla D-1-12 (☎725-5169; www.kayak-pr.com) offers kayak/snorkeling trips to: Río Espiritu Santo ($50); Laguna de Piñones ($50); Lago Mareullas ($70); Isla Cardona (1 day $65, 2-day camping $150); Cayo Santiago ($50); islands around Fajardo ($65); Las Cabezas de San Juan (½-day $55, full-day $65). Cash only.

Legends of Puerto Rico (☎531-9060; www.legendsofpr.com) offers 2hr. walking tours of Old San Juan ($25; doesn't include forts), a 3hr. San Juan nights tour that visits 3 local restaurants with live music or performances ($30; drinks and appetizers not included), and a full-day tour to countryside coffee plantations ($75; includes transportation). AmEx/MC/V.

Madrid Tours (☎791-8777 ext. 1023), at the Hampton Inn, Isla Verde, offers tours to the following locations: Old San Juan and the Bacardi Factory (4hr., M-F, $35); El Yunque and Luquillo Beach (7hr., Th-F, $55); El Yunque (4½hr., daily, $40); Ponce (8hr., Th, $61); and the Camuy Caves (8hr., W and F, $61). Prices do not include lunch or admission fees. They will pick you up from the closest major hotel. Tours only leave when enough people sign up. Reservations required. Open daily 8am-noon. MC/V.

Consulates: Britain, Ave. Chardón 350 (☎758-9828), Hato Rey. Open M-F 9am-1pm and 2-5pm. **Canada,** Ave. Ponce de León 268 (☎759-6629), Hato Rey. Open by appointment. **Dominican Republic** (☎725-9550), on Ave. Ponce de León in the Edificio Cobian's Plaza, Parada 22. Open M-F 8am-4pm.

Camping Permits: Departamento de Recursos Naturales y Ambientales (☎724-3724), Parada 8, Miramar. Coming from Old San Juan on Ave. Fernández Juncos, enter the parking lot directly before the Club Naútico and turn right. Provides camping permits and reservations for 9 designated camping areas (see **p. 58**). $4 per person. Open M-F 7:30am-4pm.

Banks and Currency Exchange: Banco Popular cashes AmEx Traveler's Cheques, exchanges currency (1% commission), and gives MC/V cash advances (no commission). In **Old San Juan,** C. Tetuan 206 (☎725-2636). ATM out back. The 3rd floor houses a gallery with changing exhibits about Puerto Rican culture. English and Spanish captions. Open M-F 8am-4pm, Sa 9am-1pm. In **Condado,** Ave. Ashford 1060 (☎725-4197). ATM. Open M-F 8am-4pm. In **Santurce** (☎725-5100), at Ave. Ponce de León and de Diego. ATM. Open M-F 8am-4pm. In **Isla Verde,** Ave. Isla Verde 4790 (☎726-5600). ATM. Open M-F 8am-6pm, Sa 9am-1pm. **BBVA Banco,** C. Arzuaga 112 (☎756-4643), at C. M. Torres, **Río Piedras.** ATM. Open M-F 8:15am-4pm, Sa 8:30am-12:30pm.

Western Union: All **Pueblo** supermarkets (see **Supermarkets,** p. 98) have Western Union offices. Money sent to "San Juan" can be picked up at any location.

American Express: Bithorn Travel, Ave. Ashford 1035 (☎723-9320), Condado, serves as an AmEx office but does not hold mail. Open M-F 9am-5pm, Sa 9-11am.

Work Opportunities: The Caleta Guest House, Old San Juan (see p. 100), sometimes hires 1-2 student guests to clean. Spanish-speakers seeking long-term employment can try the **Departamento del Trabajo y Recursos Humanos,** Ave. Luis Muñoz Rivera 50 (☎754-5751), 15th fl., at C. Domenech, Hato Rey. Has some office job listings. Open M-F 7:30am-4pm.

LOCAL SERVICES

English-Language Bookstores: Bookshop, C. Cruz 201B (☎721-0863), near the Plaza de Armas, Old San Juan, has a wide variety of Spanish and English novels, as well as a section by Puerto Rican authors. Cafe sells sandwiches ($3-5) and cappuccino ($2-3). Open M-F 9am-7pm, Sa 10am-7pm, Su 11am-5pm. AmEx/D/MC/V.
Bookworm, Ave. Ashford 1129 (☎722-3344), is a gay-friendly bookstore. Open M-

Sa 10am-9pm, Su 1-9pm. D/MC/V. **Bell, Book, and Candle,** Ave. de Diego 102 (☎728-5000), Condado, has the largest selection of English-language titles in Condado. Open M-F 8am-7pm, Sa 8am-6pm, Su 8am-5pm.

Language Classes: Berlitz, Ave. Jesus Piñero 282 (☎753-2585 or 753-2586; centro.hato_rey@berlitz.com.mx), 2nd fl., Río Piedras, will give you private Spanish lessons and all you have to give them is an arm and a leg ($39 per 45min. lesson). Call ahead for an introductory interview and evaluation. Payment required for 10 lessons in advance. Open M-Th 8am-9pm, F 8am-6pm, Sa 8am-noon. AmEx/D/DC/MC/V.

Library: Biblioteca Carnegie, Ave. Ponce de León 7 (☎722-4739 or 722-4753), Puerta de Tierra, in the large pink building, has a full library and free Internet (1hr. per day max.). Open M 9am-5:15pm, Tu-Th 9am-8:45pm, F-Sa 9am-4:45pm. **Biblioteca José M. Lázaro,** at the Universidad de Puerto Rico (see p. 128), is also open to the public.

Ticket Agencies: Ticket Center (☎759-5000; www.ticketcenterpr.com), on the 2nd floor of Plaza las Américas (see p. 139), near the food court. Sells tickets for most concerts and performances. Open M-W 9am-9pm, Th-Sa 9am-10pm, Su 11am-9pm. MC/V. **Ticketpop** (☎294-0001 or 866-994-0001; www.ticketpop.com), sells tickets for shows at the Centro de Bellas Artes (see p. 137) as well as other venues. Pick up tickets at the store Casa de los Tapes, at select movie theaters, or have them mailed to you on the island.

Markets: Plaza del Mercado (see p. 117), Santurce, has a lively fruit and vegetable market. The Plaza del Mercado in **Río Piedras** (see p. 127), is even bigger.

Supermarkets: Pueblo has locations across San Juan. In **Old San Juan,** C. Cruz 201 (☎725-4839), on the Plaza de Armas. Open M-Sa 6:30am-midnight, Su 8am-6pm. In **Condado** (☎725-1095), at the corner of C. de Diego and Wilson. Open 24hr. In **Santurce,** Ave. Ponce de León 670 (☎725-4479). Open M-Sa 6am-9pm, Su 11am-5pm. In **Isla Verde** (☎791-3366), on Ave. Gobernadores near Embassy Suites. Open 24hr. All accept AmEx/MC/V.

Laundromats: La Lavandería, C. Sol 201 (☎717-8585), at C. Cruz, is the coolest laundromat in Puerto Rico. Friendly staff, modern art, soothing music, and current magazines laundry a much more pleasant experience. Change available. Snacks $1-1.50. Wash $1.50; dry $0.25 per 5min. Open M-Th 7am-9pm, F-Sa 7am-8pm, Su 8am-8pm. **Laundry Condado Cleaners,** C. Condado 63 (☎721-9254) will wash your clothes for you in 24hr. $2 per lb. Open M-F 7am-7pm, Sa 8am-5pm. **Coin Laundry,** Ave. McLeary 1950 (☎726-5955), Ocean Park. Wash $1.75; dry $0.25 per 5min. Open M-Sa 6am-9pm, Su 6am-10pm. **Isla Verde Laundromat** (☎728-5990), at C. Emma and C. Rodriguez. Wash $1.50; dry $0.25 per 5min. Open M-Sa 7am-8pm, Su 8am-5pm.

Weather Conditions: ☎253-4586

Publications: The San Juan Star, available at most newsstands, has been providing English-language news to the capital city for over 50 years ($0.45). The half-English, half-Spanish monthly publication **Mangrove** (www.mangrovepr.com), available in most higher-end restaurants and hotels, includes book reviews, entertainment news, classified ads, and a calendar of events (free). **Agenda Noctambulo** (www.agendanoctambulo.com), a small color brochure, has information about the hottest nightlife on the island, but it's all in Spanish.

EMERGENCY AND COMMUNICATIONS

Emergency: ☎911. **Fire:** ☎722-1120.

Police: Tourist police (☎726-7020). English spoken. Open 24hr. **State Police** (☎977-8310), on Fernández Juncos, Puerta de Tierra. Open 24hr. **Municipal Police** (☎724-5170), in the Covadonga bus station, on C. Harding, Old San Juan. Open 24hr. In **Isla Verde,** Ave. Isla Verde 5980 (☎449-9320). Open 24hr. In **Río Piedras,** C. Georgetti 50 (☎765-6439 or 274-1612), on the plaza. Open 24hr.

Rape Crisis Line: ☎877-641-2004

Late-night Pharmacies: Puerto Rico Drug, C. San Francisco 157 (☎ 725-2202), on the Plaza de Armas, Old San Juan. Open M-Tu 7am-10pm, W-F 7am-9:30pm, Sa 8am-9:30pm, Su 8am-8:30pm. AmEx/D/DC/MC/V. **Walgreen's,** Ave. Ashford 1130 (☎ 725-1510), Condado. Open 24hr. AmEx/D/MC/V. **Walgreen's,** Ave. Isla Verde 5984 (☎ 982-0222), Isla Verde. Open 24hr. AmEx/D/MC/V. **Farmacía El Amal,** Ave. Jesus Piñero 282 (☎ 763-2095), Río Piedras. Open 24hr. AmEx/MC/V.

Hospital: Ashford Medical Center, Ave. Ashford 1451 (☎ 721-2160), is the largest hospital in the tourist area. Ambulance service. Clinic open M-F 7am-7pm, Sa 7am-noon. Emergency room open 24hr. In an emergency, dial ☎ 911.

Fax Office: See **Internet Access,** below.

Internet Access:

Diner's Restaurant, C. Tetuan 311 (☎ 724-6276). This restaurant (see p. 114) has the cheapest Internet in **Old San Juan** ($3 per 30min., $5 per hr.). Moneygram service and phone stations. Open Sa-W 11am-10pm. AmEx/D/MC/V.

Crew Discount Internet Cafe, C. Gilberto Concepcion de Gracis 111 (☎ 289-0344), **Old San Juan.** Enter on C. la Marina, between Piers 2 and 3. Internet $4 for 15min., $6 for 50min., $20 for 4hr. Fax service available. Open M-Tu 9:30am-12:30am, W 9:30am-11pm, Th-F 9:30am-5pm, Sa 10am-8:30pm, Su 10am-9pm. Hours vary with the cruise ship schedule. MC/V.

Ben & Jerry's (☎ 977-6882), at C. del Cristo and C. Sol, **Old San Juan,** has 1 computer. $3 for 15min. 1 scoop of ice-cream $3. Open M-Th noon-10pm, F-Su noon-11pm.

Cybernet Café, Ave. Ashford 1128 (☎ 724-4033), **Condado.** This new age cyber cafe charges $3 for 15min., $9 for 1hr., $36 for 5hr., $99 for 20hr. Fax service available. Coffee $1-3. Open M-Th 9am-10pm, F-Sa 9am-midnight, Su 10am-9pm. AmEx/MC/V. Another location at Ave. Isla Verde 5980 (☎ 728-4195), **Isla Verde,** only charges $3 for 20min. All other prices are the same. Open M-Sa 10am-10pm, Su 11am-9pm.

UPS Store, Ave. Ponce de León 1507 (☎ 723-0613), **Santurce.** Internet $3.50 for 20min., $10 for 1hr. Open M-F 8am-6pm, Sa 9am-1pm. AmEx/MC/V.

PostNet, C. Loíza 1750 (☎ 726-5458), Santurce, near **Ocean Park.** $3 for 15min., $5 for 30min., $9 for 1hr., $12 for 1½hr. Open M-F 9am-6pm, Sa 9am-5pm. AmEx/MC/V.

eMilio's, Ave. Universidad 107 (☎ 759-5130), **Río Piedras.** $4 for 30min., $8 for 1hr., $10 for 2½hr. Open M-Sa 9am-9pm, Su noon-9pm. MC/V.

Post Offices: In **Old San Juan,** C. Fortaleza 153 (☎ 723-1277). Address General Delivery to: John DOE, General Delivery Section, Old San Juan, Puerto Rico, 00902. Open M-F 7:30am-4:30pm, Sa 8am-noon. In **Condado,** C. Magadelna 1108 (☎ 723-8204). No General Delivery. Open M-F 8:30am-4pm, Sa 8:30am-noon. San Juan's largest post office is in **Hato Rey,** 585 Ave. F.D. Roosevelt (☎ 622-1758 or 622-1759). Address General Delivery to: Jane DOE, General Delivery, 585 F.D. Roosevelt Ave., San Juan, PR 00936. General Delivery open M-F 5:30am-6pm, Sa 6am-2pm. Lobby open M-F 6am-10pm, Sa 8am-4pm. Bring ID to pick up mail. All post offices: AmEx/D/DC/MC/V.

Zip Codes: Old San Juan: 00901. **Puerta de Tierra:** 00902 or 00906. **Santurce:** 00907 or 00908. **C. Fernández Juncos:** 00909 or 00910. **Calle Loíza:** 00911 or 00914. **Hato Rey:** 00917 or 00919. **Río Piedras:** 00917 or 00919. P.O. Box zip codes vary.

⌐ ACCOMMODATIONS

Accommodations in San Juan are quite expensive, but there are a few small, affordable guest houses. In terms of ambiance, safety, and proximity to cultural attractions, **Old San Juan** can't be beat. But the area does not have a beach. Travelers looking for days of fun in the sun should head to Condado, Ocean Park, or Isla Verde. **Condado** is a very tourist-friendly beach area, with lots of restaurants and a beautiful promenade, but it does not have the nicest beach in town. Most accommodations in **Ocean Park** are on residential streets that offer peace and quiet, but little excitement. Watch out for hidden service charges in this area. **Isla Verde** has the best beaches in the city, but accommodations generally offer less value and

SAN JUAN

THE BIG SPLURGE

A NUN'S LIFE

In Old San Juan there are two ways to sleep in a convent. One is to become a nun. Those not quite ready to devote their lives to a higher deity can spend a night at the **Hotel El Convento.**

Located in the heart of the old city, Hotel El Convento is one of the city's few non-chain luxury hotels. The building was first erected in 1651 when widow Doña Ana de Lansos y Menéndez de Valdez inherited a chunk of money almost as long as her name and decided that she wanted to build a convent. The Monastery our Lady Carmen of San José (or the Carmelite Convent), conveniently constructed next to the cathedral, housed nuns until 1903 when the Archbishop of San Juan decided that it was too expensive to maintain. For 50 years the hotel slowly deteriorated, functioning temporarily as a store, a dance hall, and eventually a parking lot. Just when it was about to be demolished the Institute of Puerto Rican Culture decided to renovate the building as a hotel. After a few false starts, and many extensive renovations, the hotel opened for good in January 1997.

El Convento continues to be one of the island's premier hotels and serves as the official government guest house for visiting foreign dignitaries. Anyone can enjoy a classy meal in one of the three restaurants, or a stroll through the spacious, plant-filled courtyard.

are sandwiched between huge resorts and condominiums. Furthermore, the entire neighborhood rests along a busy thoroughfare. Real budget travelers who don't mind walking a few blocks to the beach may choose to stay in **Santurce** or **Miramar,** two neighborhoods inland from Condado where the accommodations offer a much more bang for your buck. During the day Miramar is slightly more attractive than Santurce, but at night Santurce bounces with a hot nightlife scene while Miramar becomes silent. Remember that frequent buses connect all neighborhoods and the longest commute (between Old San Juan and Isla Verde) takes less than an hour. Unless otherwise stated, all rooms below have private bathrooms. **Unless otherwise indicated, prices do not include the 9% Puerto Rico accommodations tax.**

RENTAL AGENCIES

Several rental agencies offer short-term contracts specifically designed for travelers. Most of these are located in furnished condominiums along the beach, but make sure that you understand exactly what you are getting before you hand over your credit card number. Almost all have minimum stays of three days to one week. **The Caleta** (see below) specializes in short-term rentals in Old San Juan.

ReMax (☎ 268-1241; www.remax-islaverde.com), on Ave. Isla Verde, in the Marbella del Caribe building, specializes in Isla Verde rentals. Check the web site for photos. Utilities not included in monthly rates. Nov.-Apr. studios $1000-1500 per month; 1 bedroom $1200-2000; 2 bedroom $1500-2600. May-Oct. $750-1100/$1100-2600/$1500-2300. Weekly rates available. Open M-F 9am-6pm, Sa 9am-1pm. MC/V.

San Juan Vacations (☎ 727-1591 or 726-0973; fax 268-3604; www.sanjuanvacations.com), next to ReMax, Isla Verde, rents units in Isla Verde and Condado. Dec. 16-Apr. 15 ocean-view studios and 1-bedroom apartments $665-910 per week, $1500-1850 per month. Apr. 16-Dec. 15 $525-1600/$1150-1200 per month. Open M-F 8:30am-6pm, Sa 8:30am-1pm. Money order or certified check required for reservation.

OLD SAN JUAN

🏨 **The Caleta,** Caleta de las Monjas 11 (☎ 725-5347; www.thecaleta.com), ideally located on a quiet, picturesque street near the ocean. By far Old San Juan's best deal for budget travelers. Smallest rooms have concrete floors, few decorations, and sometimes no windows. The penthouse "sunshine apartment" has bright orange walls and a balcony overlooking the water. Most rooms have cable TV and a portable A/C unit; all rooms have phone and kitchenette. Also rents 35 units around Old San Juan.

Owner Michael Giessler helps newcomers find employment and sometimes employs 1-2 students to help clean. Coin laundry. 3-night min. Reception open M-F 10am-6pm, Sa-Su 11am-3pm. Check-out noon. Doubles and quads $210-700 per week. Rentals $450-800 per week; $475-750 per month. MC/V. ❷

The Gallery Inn, C. Norzagaray 204-206 (☎722-1808; fax 724-7360; www.thegalleryinn.com). Ring the bell at the unmarked gate. Fifty percent working art gallery, fifty percent hotel, The Gallery Inn defies any classification. Owner and artist Jan D'Esopo decorated each room with her own artwork and the result is incredible. Sleep on a tempor-pedic mattress in an 18th century building, sweep aside the canopy surrounding your bed, turn on the hand-sculpted lamp, and have breakfast on the rooftop patio with one of the best views in Old San Juan. All rooms $145-350; low season discounts available. AmEx/MC/V. ❺

Hotel Plaza de Armas, C. San José 202 (☎722-9191; fax 725-1919; www.ihphoteles.com). Location is everything, and when this hotel opened in early 2003 it became the most centrally located accommodation in Old San Juan. Though new and modern, the hotel has been stuffed into an old building; rooms tend to be small and not all have windows. Cable TV, phone, A/C, and hair dryer. Continental breakfast included. Dec. 16-Apr. 14 singles $85; doubles $105; 2-person suites $150; 3-person suites with balcony $175. Apr. 15-Dec. 15 $75/$95/$125/$150. AmEx/D/MC/V. ❹

Guest House, C. Tanca 205 (☎722-5436). You get what you pay for at this inexpensive guest house. Larger rooms include a table and sometimes a balcony, but smaller rooms are more like glorified closets. Avoid the cheapest rooms. Common baths are less than desirable. A few rooms have A/C; all have fans. No English spoken. Singles $15-30; doubles $40. Weekly $70-175/$140-210. Tax included. Cash only. ❶

El Jibarito, C. Sol 280 (☎725-8375). The owners of this popular restaurant (see p. 111) also rent out a few guest rooms upstairs. 2 large rooms come with a double bed, A/C, and a living area. 2 smaller rooms come with, well, a single bed. All rooms have the feel of a spare bedroom. Maybe because that's what they are. Singles $60 per week; doubles $60 per day. AmEx/D/MC/V. Tax included. ❶

Hotel Milano, C. Fortaleza 307 (☎729-9050 or 877-729-9050; fax 722-3379; http://home.coqui.net/hmilano). This traditional hotel might as well be an American chain. Rooms come with all the amenities—cable TV, telephone, A/C, small fridge—but little of the city's charm. Steps from restaurant row. Rooftop restaurant. 4 rooms have Internet connections. Breakfast included. Check-out 3pm. Check-out noon. Nov. 20-May 31 singles $85-115; doubles $115-145. June 1-Nov. 19 $75-95/$95-125. AmEx/MC/V. ❹

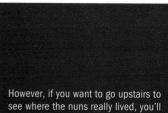

However, if you want to go upstairs to see where the nuns really lived, you'll have to cough up the moolah—access to the top three floors is restricted to guests only.

The rooms themselves are attractive but unexceptional, with a traditional bed, dresser, and private bath set-up. However, the perks are nice. All rooms come with a VCR, cable TV, A/C, breakfast, an iron, a refrigerator, an in-room safe, and complimentary bottles of water. Smart guests don't miss the daily wine and cheese reception, when they can help themselves to gourmet food then relax on the rooftop patio or sit by the (tiny) pool where small frog statues spit out water from the corners. Afterward, guests can work off their indulgence with a trip to the modern, though small, gym. All in all, Hotel El Convento provides a welcome change to the generic chain hotels—and really, where else can you sleep in a 16th-century convent? (C. del Cristo 100. ☎723-9020, from San Juan ☎800-468-2779; fax 721-2877; www.elconvento.com. Check-in 3pm. Check-out noon. Reservations recommended. May-Nov. all rooms $160-250; Dec.-Apr. $285-385. AmEx/D/DC/MC/V. ❺)

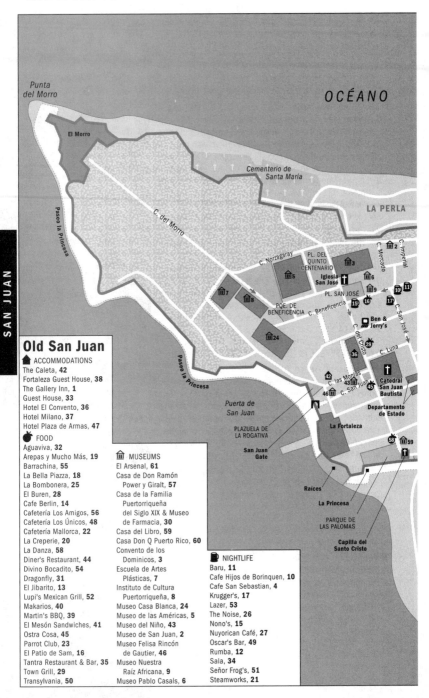

SAN JUAN

OCÉANO

Punta del Morro

El Morro

Cementerio de Santa María

LA PERLA

Paseo la Princesa

C. del Morro

C. Norzagaray

C. Imperial

C. Mercado

PL. DEL QUINTO CENTENARIO

Iglesia San José

PL. SAN JOSÉ

PQE. DE BENEFICENCIA

C. Beneficencia

C. San José

C. del Cristo

Ben & Jerry's

C. Luna

Paseo la Princesa

C. las Monjas

C. San Juan

Catedral San Juan Bautista

Departamento de Estado

Puerta de San Juan

PLAZUELA DE LA ROGATIVA

San Juan Gate

La Fortaleza

Raíces

La Princesa

PARQUE DE LAS PALOMAS

Capilla del Santo Cristo

Old San Juan

🏠 ACCOMMODATIONS
The Caleta, **42**
Fortaleza Guest House, **38**
The Gallery Inn, **1**
Guest House, **33**
Hotel El Convento, **36**
Hotel Milano, **37**
Hotel Plaza de Armas, **47**

🍴 FOOD
Aguaviva, **32**
Arepas y Mucho Más, **19**
Barrachina, **55**
La Bella Piazza, **18**
La Bombonera, **25**
El Burén, **28**
Cafe Berlin, **14**
Cafetería Los Amigos, **56**
Cafetería Los Únicos, **48**
Cafetería Mallorca, **22**
La Creperie, **20**
La Danza, **58**
Diner's Restaurant, **44**
Divino Bocadito, **54**
Dragonfly, **31**
El Jibarito, **13**
Lupi's Mexican Grill, **52**
Makarios, **40**
Martin's BBQ, **39**
El Mesón Sandwiches, **41**
Ostra Cosa, **45**
Parrot Club, **23**
El Patio de Sam, **16**
Tantra Restaurant & Bar, **35**
Town Grill, **29**
Transylvania, **50**

🏛 MUSEUMS
El Arsenal, **61**
Casa de Don Ramón
  Power y Giralt, **57**
Casa de la Familia
  Puertorriqueña
  del Siglo XIX & Museo
  de Farmacia, **30**
Casa del Libro, **59**
Casa Don Q Puerto Rico, **60**
Convento de los
  Dominicos, **3**
Escuela de Artes
  Plásticas, **7**
Instituto de Cultura
  Puertorriqueña, **8**
Museo Casa Blanca, **24**
Museo de las Américas, **5**
Museo del Niño, **43**
Museo de San Juan, **2**
Museo Felisa Rincón
  de Gautier, **46**
Museo Nuestra
  Raíz Africana, **9**
Museo Pablo Casals, **6**

🍸 NIGHTLIFE
Baru, **11**
Cafe Hijos de Borinquen, **10**
Cafe San Sebastian, **4**
Krugger's, **17**
Lazer, **53**
The Noise, **26**
Nono's, **15**
Nuyorican Café, **27**
Oscar's Bar, **49**
Rumba, **12**
Sala, **34**
Señor Frog's, **51**
Steamworks, **21**

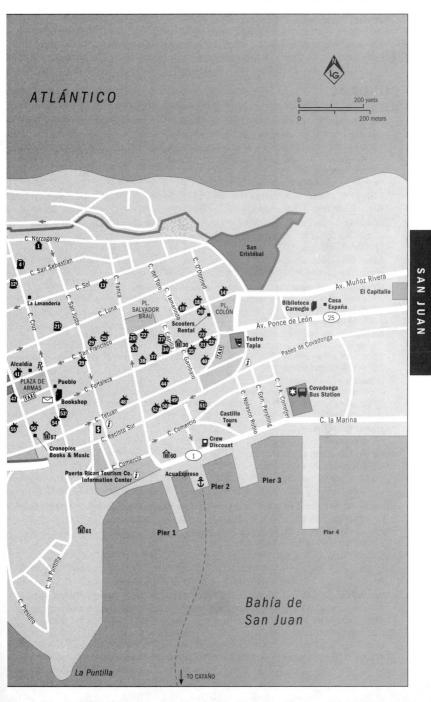

ATLÁNTICO

San Cristóbal

Av. Muñoz Rivera

El Capitolio

C. Norzagaray

C. San Sebastian

C. Sol

C. Tanca

C. del Toro

C. O'Donnell

C. Tamarindo

C. Capilla

PL. COLÓN

Biblioteca Carnegie

Casa España

La Lavandería

C. San Justo

C. Luna

PL. SALVADOR BRAU

Scooters Rental

Av. Ponce de León

C. Cruz

C. San Francisco

Teatro Tapia

Paseo de Covadonga

Alcaldía

PLAZA DE ARMAS

Pueblo

Bookshop

C. Fortaleza

C. Gen. Pershing

C. Nolasco Rubio

C. J.A. Corretjer

Covadonga Bus Station

C. la Marina

Castillo Tours

C. Tetuan

C. Recinto Sur

C. Comercio

Crew Discount

Cronopios Books & Music

C. Comercio

Puerto Rican Tourism Co. Information Center

AcuaExpreso

Pier 2

Pier 3

Pier 1

Pier 4

C. la Puntilla

C. Presidio

Bahía de San Juan

La Puntilla

TO CATAÑO

0   200 yards
0   200 meters

Fortaleza Guest House, C. Fortaleza 303 (☎ 721-7112). Look for the tiny sign next to the door. This guest house is more like a boarding house, as many guests stay for months. Tiny ants have been known to invade, and the rooms are very small, but the weekly rates are quite a bargain. Common balcony. Shared bath with electric hot water. No English. Singles $25-30; doubles $40-50. Weekly $55-80/$90. Tax included. ❶

CONDADO

🏠 **At Windchimes Inn,** C. Taft 63 (☎ 727-4153, toll-free 800-946-3244; fax 728-0671; www.atwindchi mesinn.com), at C. McLeary 1750. This restored Spanish villa has the amenities of a resort with none of the pretension. Wicker furniture and glass tables grace bright rooms. Singles are small and some rooms are in the basement, but the charming decor compensates for minor deficiencies. Friendly staff. All rooms have cable TV. Internet $15 per day. Limited room service. Small pool with a jacuzzi bench. Parking $5 per night. Check in 2-10pm. Dec. 1-May 30 singles $80-95; doubles $99-110; extra person $15. June 1-Nov. 30 $65/$65-85/$10. Possible surcharge for stays of less than 3 days. AmEx/D/MC/V. ❸

El Canario Hotels (☎ 800-533-2649; www.canariohotels.com) has expanded to 3 locations in the Condado area (see below). All have clean, bright, modern rooms with cable TV, telephones, and A/C. Continental breakfast included. Check-in 2pm. Check-out 11am. For all 3 locations extra person May 1-Dec. 15 $10, Dec. 16-April 29 $15. A $3 energy charge is added to all room prices. AmEx/D/DC/MC/V. ❸

El Canario Inn, Ave. Ashford 1317 (☎ 722-3861; fax 722-0391). This self-dubbed bed and breakfast, in a little yellow house with a tiny fountain out front, certainly has a homey feel. With a friendly staff, a central location, and a pleasant courtyard, the Inn is the most charming of the Canarios. Dec. 16-April 30 singles $99; doubles $114. May 1-Dec. 15 $75/$85.

El Canario by the Sea, Ave. Condado 4 (☎ 722-8640; fax 725-4921) has fewer rooms than the other Canarios, but they tend to be larger. It is also the only Canario located literally 10 steps from the beach. The yellow bathrooms look like flashbacks to the 1970s, but there are plans to renovate. Dec. 16-April 30 singles $99; doubles $114. May 1-Dec. 15 $75/$85.

El Canario by the Lagoon, C. Clemenceau 4 (☎ 722-5058; fax 723-8590). The largest and most institutional of the 3 locations, and the only one with an elevator, balconies, and free parking. 2 blocks from the ocean, but many rooms have views of the lagoon. Dec. 16-April 30 singles $105-145; doubles $115-145. May 1-Dec. 15 $70-80/$75-90.

Embassy Guest House, C. Sea View 1126 (☎ 725-8284 or 724-7440; fax 725-2400; embas-syguesthouse@worldnet.att.net). With low prices and an oceanfront location, it's easy to ignore the slight mustiness at Embassy Guest House; just splurge on a front room and spend all day looking out over the water. When you've had enough sand, retreat to the small pool and tiny jacuzzi. All rooms have cable TV, fridge, and A/C. Continental breakfast included. Dec.1-Apr. 30 doubles $65-125; extra person $15. May 1-Nov. 30 $45-95/$10. AmEx/D/MC/V. ❸

Alelí by the Sea Guest House, C. Sea View 1125 (☎ 725-5313; fax 721-4744). Years of wear near the salty ocean air have definitely affected Alelí aesthetics. However, the staff works hard to keep up the hotel—glass tables and mirrors surrounded by seashells create a charming seaside atmosphere. Less expensive rooms are depressingly small and dark. Common balcony overlooks the ocean. Dingy hallway illuminated by 1 bare bulb. Cable TV and A/C. Common kitchen. Laundry $4. Parking. Dec.15-Apr. 15 doubles $65-100; Apr. 16-Dec. 14 $55-90. Extra person $10. AmEx/D/MC/V. ❸

Casa del Caribe, C. Caribe 57 (☎ 722 7139, toll-free 877-722-7139; fax 725-3995 ext. 114; www.casadelcaribe.com). From the owners of At the Windchimes Inn comes this slightly more budget option. The 13 rooms are clean and friendly, but the tiles are decaying and the paint is beginning to chip off the walls. A/C, cable TV, and phone. 1½ blocks from the beach. Continental breakfast included. Parking $5. Dec. 15-May 15 doubles $75-125; extra person $15. May 15-Dec. 14 $55-99/$10. AmEx/D/MC/V. ❸

Hotel El Portal, Ave. Condado 76 (☎ 721-9010; fax 724-3714; www.hotelelportal.com). From Magdalena walk down C. Condado; El Portal is on the right directly before the small plaza. For over 42 years El Portal has been providing clean, standard rooms with superb A/C. The only drawback is the location, about 3 blocks from the beach. The hotel compensates with a rooftop terrace that boasts terrific views of the ocean and the city. Rooms are all the same size, so those with more beds can get a bit squished. All rooms have refrigerator, phone, and cable TV. Dec. 16-Apr. 30 singles $85; doubles $95; triples $105. May 1-Dec. 15 $75/$85/$95. AmEx/MC/V. ❸

Hotel El Consulado, Ave. Ashford 1110 (☎ 289-9191; fax 723-8665), boasts a subtle medieval theme, with a Spanish-tiled facade and artistic suits-of-armor in the lobby. The hotel is maintained, but its age is beginning to show. Some rooms have balconies; all have A/C and cable TV. Continental breakfast included. Check-in noon. Check-out 3pm. Dec. 15-Apr. 15 1 queen bed $105; 2 beds $115. Apr. 16-Nov. 30 $86/$95. AmEx/D/DC/MC/V. ❹

El Prado Inn, C. Luchetti 1350 (☎ 728-5925; fax 725-6978), in a large white house at Ave. Cervantes. El Prado lacks the refinement of other hotels, as there are scuffs on the walls and many rooms have views of a concrete wall. However, the 1 renovated room hints at better things to come. Small pool. Phone, cable TV, A/C, and ceiling fan in every room. Some rooms have kitchenettes. Continental breakfast included. Parking. Dec. 15-Apr. 30 doubles $99-129; quads $119-139. May 1-Dec. 14 $79-99/$89-109. AmEx/MC/V. ❹

SANTURCE AND MIRAMAR

Hotel Las Américas, Ave. Ponce de León 604 (☎ 977-0159; fax 268-7131), Miramar. While the ornate lobby of this 4-story hotel creates a regal ambiance, the prices prove that this hotel was not made for kings. Rooms vary greatly; some have glistening white bathrooms and a microwave and fridge, while others look a bit worn and only have a bare light bulb. Watch out for the rickety old elevator. A/C, cable TV, and phone. Parking. Check-out noon. 1 full bed $55; 2 full beds $65. Discounts for stays over 2 nights. AmEx/MC/V. ❷

Hotel Metropol, Ave. Ponce de León 1661 (☎ 725-0525), at C. Bolívar, Santurce. Well off the beaten path, this hotel does not cater to the whim of the tourist. Some rooms don't have A/C, some rooms don't include anything but a bed, and the management doesn't speak English. But the rooms are clean and if you're willing to put up with an old building and a walk to the beach, this is a great bargain. Some shared baths. Doubles $30-40. Monthly $275-400. ❷

Hotel Olimpio Court, Ave. Miramar 603 (☎ 724-0600; fax 977-0655; hotelolimpiocourt@hotmail.com), Miramar. From Ave. Ponce de León turn south on Ave. Miramar (away from the ocean); the hotel will be on your left. This hotel has all of the amenities, but they are a bit worn. Overlook this slight defect (and the drab exterior) and Olimpio Court is not a bad deal, especially during high season. Some rooms have a tiny kitchenette. All rooms have phone, cable TV, and A/C. Check-out noon. Singles $58-92; doubles $72; triples $82; quads $92. Monthly 50% off. AmEx/MC/V. ❷

OCEAN PARK

Hostería del Mar, C. Tapia 1 (☎ 727-3302, toll-free 877-727-3302; fax 268-0772; hosteria@caribe.net). Take one step into the spacious lobby with its oriental carpets and ocean views, and you may never leave. Hostería lacks the refinement of other guest houses, but compensates with ample charm. Rooms have bright floral bedspreads, wicker furniture, and aquatic-themed shower curtains, in addition to the standard A/C, phones, and cable TV. Service charge $7 per person. Check-in 4pm. Check-out noon. Nov. 15-May 15 doubles $90-140; extra person $25. May 16-Nov. 14 $55-130/$15. Up to 2 children free. AmEx/D/MC/V. ❹

Beach Buoy Inn, C. McLeary 1853 (☎ 728-8119; fax 268-0037). This aging hotel brings back the glory days (the 1970s) with ancient TVs and cracked linoleum floors. One of the cheapest options in Ocean Park. A/C, cable TV, and small fridge. Continental breakfast. Reception 8am-8pm. Dec. 16-Apr. 30 singles $60; doubles $70; extra person $15. May 1-Dec. 15 $50/$60/$10. AmEx/MC/V. ❷

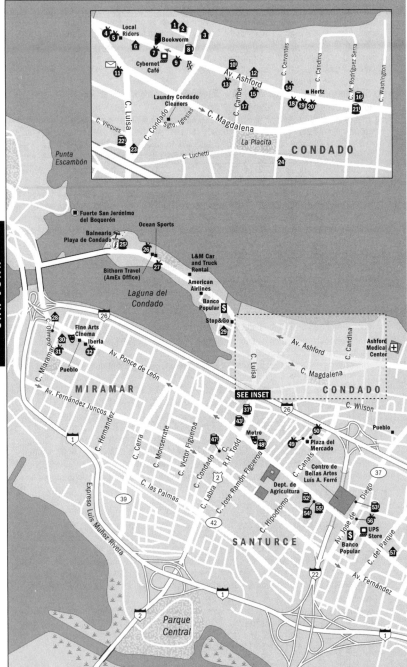

Local Riders
Bookworm
Cybernet Café
Rx
Av. Ashford
C. Cervantes
C. Candina
C. M. Rodríguez Serra
C. Washington
Hertz
C. Caribe
C. Luisa
Laundry Condado Cleaners
Sgto. Iglesias
C. Magdalena
C. Vieques
C. Condado
C. Luchetti
La Placita
CONDADO
Punta Escambón

Fuerte San Jerónimo del Boquerón
Ocean Sports
Balneario Playa de Condado
Bithorn Travel (AmEx Office)
L&M Car and Truck Rental
American Airlines
Banco Popular
Stop&Go
Laguna del Condado
Av. Ashford
C. Candina
Ashford Medical Center
C. Luisa
C. Magdalena
SEE INSET
CONDADO
C. Wilson

C. Miramar
C. Olimpio
Fine Arts Cinema
Iberia
Pueblo
Av. Ponce de León
MIRAMAR
Av. Fernández Juncos
C. Hernández
C. Cerra
C. Monserrate
C. Victor Figueroa
C. Condado
C. Labra
C. R.H. Todd
C. Jose Ramón Figueroa
Metro
Plaza del Mercado
Pueblo
UPS Store
Centro de Bellas Artes Luís A. Ferré
C. Canals
Av. Jose de Diego
Dept. de Agricultura
C. las Palmas
Expreso Luis Muñoz Rivera
C. Hipodromo
SANTURCE
Banco Popular
C. del Parque
Av. Fernández

Parque Central

SAN JUAN

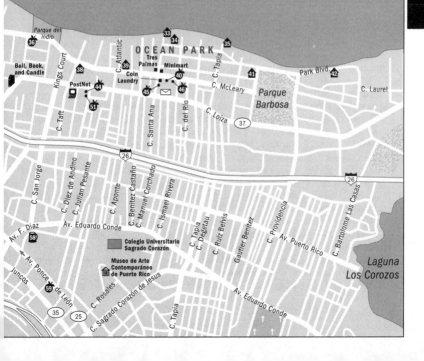

Condado, Ocean Park, Santurce, and Miramar

ACCOMMODATIONS

Alelí by the Sea Guest House, **1**
At Windchimes Inn, **38**
Beach Buoy Inn, **39**
El Canario by the Lagoon, **29**
El Canario by the Sea, **3**
El Canario Inn, **12**
Casa del Caribe, **17**
Embassy Guest House, **2**
Hostería del Mar, **35**
Hotel El Consulado, **6**
Hotel El Portal, **23**
Hotel Las Américas, **28**
Hotel Metropol, **57**
Hotel Olimpio Court, **30**
L'Habitation Beach
   Guest House, **34**
Numero Uno Guest House, **33**
El Prado Inn, **24**
Tres Palmas Guest House, **42**
Tu Casa Boutique Hotel, **41**

FOOD

Ajili-mójili, **27**
Bla Bla Coffeehouse, **56**
Café del Ángel, **5**
Cielito Lindo, **11**
Condado BBQ, **4**
Da Luigi, **51**
Danny's International, **14**
Dunbar's, **40**
The Greenhouse, **13**
Kasalta Bakery, **46**
Latin Star Restaurant, **9**
Nueva Hacienda Don José, **26**
La Patisserie de France, **36**
Pinky's, **45**
Piu Bello Gelato, **15**
Pura Vida, **59**
The Red Snapper Marisquería, **7**
Restaurant D'Arco, **31**
Restaurant Don Tello, **49**
Restaurant El Popular, **50**

Salud!, **18**
Taqueria Mexicana Pico
   de Gallo, **44**
Tepe a Tepe, **32**
Via Appia's, **19**
Wasabi, **20**

NIGHTLIFE

Bliss, **22**
Cups, **58**
Eros, **48**
La Fiesta Lounge, **25**
Habana Club, **43**
Junior's, **47**
Kali's, **16**
Nuestro Ambiente, **54**
Olé Olé Bar and Grill, **52**
Río Bar & Club, **10**
Stargate/Pleasure, **37**
El Teatro, **55**
La Terraza del Condado, **21**
Tía Maria Liquor Store, **53**
Upstairs Sports Bar & Grill, **8**

SAN JUAN

OCÉANO ATLÁNTICO

0   400 yards

0   400 meters

Parque del
Indio
36

Bell, Book,
and Candle

Kings Court

PostNet

C. Taft

C. Atlantic

33
34
OCEAN PARK
Tres
Palmas   Minimart
38   39
Coin
Laundry
44
45
51

C. Santa Ana

C. del Río

35

C. Tapia

40
41

C. McLeary

46

C. Loíza
37

Park Blvd.
42

C. Laurel

Parque
Barbosa

26

C. San Jorge

C. Díez de Andino

C. Julián Pesante

C. Aponte

C. Benítez Castaño

C. Manuel Corchado

C. Ismael Rivera

Av. F. Díaz

58

Av. Eduardo Conde

Colegio Universitario
Sagrado Corazón

Museo de Arte
Contemporáneo
de Puerto Rico

Av. Ponce de León

Juncos

59

35   25

C. Rosales

C. Sagrado Corazón de Jesús

C. Tapia

C. Tapia

C. Dogetau

C. Ruiz Belvis

Gauther Benítez

C. Providencia

Av. Puerto Rico

Av. Eduardo Conde

C. Bartolomé Las Casas

26

Laguna
Los Corozos

L'Habitation Beach Guest House, C. Italia 1957 (☎ 727-2499; fax 727-2599; www.habitationbeach.com). From the individually decorated pastel rooms to the rainbow flags at the counter to the welcoming staff, this gay-friendly hotel makes everyone feel at home. All rooms have A/C and cable TV. Pets welcome. Coin laundry. Continental breakfast included. Check-in 1pm. Check-out 11am. Dec. 15-Apr. 15 doubles $75-96; quads $96. Apr. 16-Dec. 14 $60-83/$83. Extra person $15. AmEx/D/MC/V. ❸

Tres Palmas Guest House, Park Boulevard 2212 (☎ 727-4617, toll-free 888-290-2076; fax 727-5434; www.trespalmasinn.com). Although it's a bit of a walk from Ocean Park, Tres Palmas compensates with a picturesque location across the street from the ocean. The view is especially good from the 2 rooftop jacuzzis. Rooms are slightly dark, but otherwise well-equipped with cable TV, fridge, and safe. Large swimming pool with tiny waterfall. Continental breakfast included. Check-in 1pm. Check-out noon. Dec. 15-May 1 doubles $75-112; quads $117-134. May 1-Dec. 15 $73-100/$100-115. Extra person $15. AmEx/MC/V. ❸

Numero Uno Guest House, C. Santa Ana 1 (☎ 726-5010; fax 727-5482). This is as close to the ocean as it gets; waves come within 5 ft. of the restaurant. Yet the immaculate white hotel manages to avoid the decay normally associated with an oceanside location. Spotless rooms include cable TV, A/C, private baths, and Internet ($15 per 24hr.). A 15% service charge pays for continental breakfast, beach towels, chairs, and umbrellas. Check-in 3pm. Check-out 11am. Dec.-Apr. singles $115-235; doubles $135-255. May-Nov. $60-145/$80-165. Extra person $20. AmEx/MC/V. ❹

Tu Casa Boutique Hotel, C. Cacique 2071 (☎ 727-5100; fax 982-3349). Someone clearly put a lot of care into the decoration of this boutique hotel. Each room has its own style; check out the gorgeous romantic suite, with dark blue walls, white bedspread, and gauzy canopy. Even the patio has carefully coordinated plants surrounding the pristine pool. 2 blocks from the beach. Bike rental $20 per 5hr. Check-in 3pm. Check-out noon. High season 1 double bed $124-149; 2 double beds $195. Low season $99-175/$175. AmEx/D/MC/V. ❺

ISLA VERDE

Hotel La Playa, C. Amapola 6 (☎ 791-1115 or 791-7298; fax 791-4650; www.hotellaplaya.com). Driving from Ave. Isla Verde turn north on C. Rosa, then left on Gardenia, then right at the blue hotel sign, then left again on Amapola. Walking, turn north on C. Rosa, then right on C. Iris and left on Amapola. Tucked away on a small peninsula, this family-run beach hotel offers clean rooms and a great location for surprisingly low prices. Both sides of the hotel have ocean views, although some rooms only look out on the courtyard. All rooms have cable TV and A/C. Continental breakfast. Key deposit required. Check-in 2pm. Check-out noon. Dec.14-Apr. 15 singles $90-105; doubles $100-115. Apr. 16-Dec. 13 $75-90/$85-100. Extra person $15. AmEx/MC/V. ❹

Hotel Villa del Sol, C. Rosa 4 (☎ 791-2600 or 791-4120; fax 791-5666; www.villadelsolpr.com), on a quiet road off the main street This beautiful 2-story white villa charms at first sight with a great pool area and a lobby decorated in medieval swords and suits of armor. However, the rooms are a bit of a gamble—some have clean, white walls and photos of San Juan, but others are in desperate need of retiling. All rooms have A/C and cable TV. Dec. 1-spring (dates vary) singles $80; doubles $90; suites $95-115. Spring-Nov. 30 $65/$70/$75-90. AmEx/D/MC/V. ❸

Hotel Casa de Playa, Ave. Isla Verde 4851 (☎ 728-9779, toll-free 800-916-2272; fax 809-727-1334). Good news first: Casa de Playa is cheap and it sits right next to the beach. The bad news? Linoleum floors, aging furniture, and a bit of dirt on the walls make rooms feel a bit dingy. Still a bargain. Cable TV, phones, and A/C. Oceanfront bar open daily 3pm-last person leaves. Dec.15-Apr. 15 singles $80; doubles $90. Apr. 16-Dec. 14 $70/$80. Extra person $10. AmEx/D/MC/V. ❸

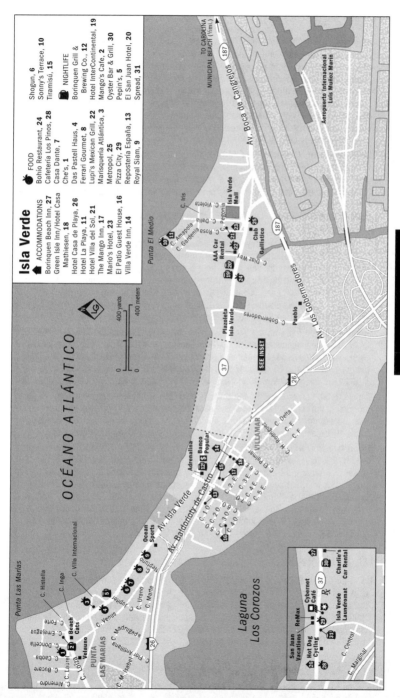

SAN JUAN

Isla Verde

ACCOMMODATIONS
Borinquen Beach Inn, **27**
Green Isle Inn/Hotel Casa
Mathiesen, **18**
Hotel Casa de Playa, **26**
Hotel La Playa, **11**
Hotel Villa del Sol, **21**
The Mango Inn, **17**
Mario's Hotel, **23**
El Patio Guest House, **16**
Villa Verde Inn, **14**

FOOD
Bohío Restaurant, **24**
Cafetería Los Pinos, **28**
Casa Dante, **7**
Che's, **1**
Das Pastell Haus, **4**
Ferrari Gourmet, **8**
Lupi's Mexican Grill, **22**
Marisquería Atlántica, **3**
Metropol, **25**
Pizza City, **29**
Repostería España, **13**
Royal Siam, **9**
Shogun, **6**
Sonny's Terrace, **10**
Tiramisú, **15**

NIGHTLIFE
Borinquen Grill &
Brewing Co., **12**
Hotel InterContinental, **19**
Mango's Café, **2**
Oyster Bar & Grill, **30**
Pepin's, **5**
El San Juan Hotel, **20**
Spread, **31**

El Patio Guest House, C. Tres 87 (☎726-6952 or 726-6298), in Villamar. From Ave. Isla Verde, cross the bridge over the freeway near Texaco, then walk along Ave. Baldorioty De Castro to the end of the cemetery. Turn left on C. Seis Oeste and walk 3 blocks, then turn right on C. Tres. El Patio is on the left. This family-run hotel consists of converted rooms in a house on a quiet residential street about 12min. from the beach. Those in search of peace and quiet should look no further, as El Patio has clean rooms with cable TV, A/C, and a fridge, a clean pool, laundry facilities, and friendly management. But those looking for a party should move on, as drunken debauchery does not jive well with the children's toys in the courtyard. High season singles $65; doubles $69; suites $90. Low season $60/$65/$75. Possible discount for longer stays. MC/V. ❸

The Mango Inn, C. Uno 20 (☎726-4230, toll-free 800-777-1946; fax 728-2882; www.themangoinn.com), in Villamar. From Villa Verde Inn continue straight and take your first right on C. Uno. Oh, to be across the freeway. With an open lobby livened up by plants and a fountain, clean rooms, and a small pool area, The Mango Inn lacks little but a good location. Check-in 1pm. Check-out noon. Nov. 9-Apr. 23 singles $70-75; doubles $80-85. Apr. 24-Nov. 8 $50-55/$60-65. Extra person $15. AmEx/D/MC/V. ❸

Villa Verde Inn (☎727-9457 or 728-5912; www.villaverdeinn.com), in Villamar. From Ave. Isla Verde cross the freeway bridge that lies between Cafetería Los Pinos (see p. 118) and Banco Popular (see p. 97). Your stereotypical roadside inn. The bright orange and green exterior lies somewhere between tacky and vibrant. However, if you can get over the kitsch, the linoleum floors, and the distance from the beach, this hotel is a great deal. Every room has a kitchenette with microwave and fridge, A/C, a tiny cable TV, and a balcony. Dec. 15-Apr. 14 singles $52; doubles $62. Apr. 15-Dec. 14 $48/$57. Extra person $10. Discounts for stays over 2 days. AmEx/D/MC/V. ❷

Borinquen Beach Inn, Ave. Isla Verde 5451 (☎728-8400, toll-free 866-728-8400; fax 268-2411; www.borinquenbeachinn.com). Nicely located near the beach, Borinquen looks the same inside and outside—decent, but slightly dated. Cable TV and A/C. Check-in 2pm. Check-out noon. Dec. 1-Apr. 15 and June 15-Labor Day singles $70-95; doubles $85-95. Apr. 16-June 14 and Labor Day-Nov. 30 $56-76/ $68-76. Extra person $10. AmEx/D/DC/MC/V. ❹

Mario's Hotel, C. Rosa 2 (☎791-6868; fax 791-1672). The old, wood-paneled lobby is a good indicator of the entire hotel. Rooms have cable TV, phone, and A/C, but lack any decor. Bathrooms are clean, if a bit small. Nov. 16-Apr. 30 and July 1-Aug. 31 doubles $70; quads $80; suites $90. May 1-June 30 and Sept. 1-Nov. 15 $60/$80/$90. AmEx/D/MC/V. ❸

Green Isle Inn/Hotel Casa Mathiesen, C. Uno 14 or 36 (☎726-4330, from the US 800-677-8860; fax 268-2415; greeninn@prtc.net), just past Villa Verde Inn, in Villamar. 2 identical adjacent hotels owned by the same person. The price is right, but there's not much space to move around the cramped rooms. All rooms include A/C and cable TV—the "kitchenette" actually consists of a sink and a tiny portable stovetop. 2 small, less-than-clean pools. Check-in 3pm. Check-out noon. Dec. 15-Apr. 30 doubles $70, with kitchenette $79; quads with kitchenette $84. May 1-Dec. 14 $58/$73/$82. Extra person $10. AmEx/D/MC/V. ❸

RÍO PIEDRAS

Hotel de Diego, Paseo de Diego 207 (☎753-6008), at the end of the market, between C. William Jones and C. Padre Capachino. This little white hotel doesn't quite fit in with the surroundings. A good option if you're planning to leave on an early-morning *público*. Hallways are narrow and dark, but rooms sport all the amenities, including TV and a cramped private bathroom. Be careful walking in this area after dark. Check-out noon. 1 double bed $40, with TV and fridge $60; 2 beds $70. MC/V. ❷

⧉ FOOD

It's safe to assume that most restaurants have English menus, although some small *cafeterías* may cater exclusively to Spanish-speakers.

OLD SAN JUAN

Finding a good meal in Old San Juan is not difficult; it's finding an affordable meal that may prove problematic. Trendy restaurants along C. Recinto Sur and C. Fortaleza serve food from almost every nationality, eagerly competing for cruise passengers' dollars. Most restaurants near the docks theoretically close around midnight, but actually morph into hopping bars and stay open until the last customer leaves. The southern end of C. del Cristo, near the water, becomes a pedestrian walkway with a series of outdoor restaurants serving traditional Puerto Rican food during the day (entrees $8-18). For the penny-pinchers, cheaper food lies just off the beaten path, including a few *cafeterías*. During the day several vendors, including an excellent fresh fruit vendor, set up around Plaza de la Darsena, near the tourist office.

▨ **El Jibarito,** C. Sol 280 (☎ 725-8375). Over the last 27 years El Jibarito has become one of Old San Juan's most popular eateries. This cleverly decorated restaurant keeps busy with a steady stream of locals and foreigners who come to enjoy the tasty Puerto Rican food. Appetizers $1.50-4. Entrees $8-14. Open daily 10am-9pm. AmEx/D/MC/V. ❸

▨ **Arepas y Mucho Más,** C. San Francisco 351 (☎ 724-7776). As the name suggests, this small Venezuelan restaurant specializes in *arepas*, grilled corn dough patties served with your choice meat, cheese, and veggies ($3-4). *Arepas* are small, so it's best to combine one with a delicious *cachapa*, sweet corn dough filled with cheese or meat ($3-5). Venezuelan paraphernalia covers the bright restaurant. *Batidas* $3. Open M-Sa 8am-8pm, Su 8am-6pm. MC/V. ❷

Ostra Cosa, C. del Cristo 154 (☎ 722-3672). Welcome to the most intimate restaurant in the world. Set in a historic building, this sophisticated but unpretentious restaurant offers more of a multi-sensory experience than a normal meal. Listen to the romantic sounds of the tree frogs, stare into the eyes of your companion over candlelight, feel the cool breeze sweep through the courtyard, and taste the scrumptious cuisine. All entrees (mostly seafood with some veggie and meat options) are rated on an aphrodisiac scale from one star (Oh!) to three stars (Ay Ay Ay!!!). Be careful what you wish for at the infamous hugging tree—the menu warns "We are not responsible for increments in passion. Please direct your claims to your partner." Ay ay ay!!! Appetizers $6-9. Entrees $12-18. Open Su-Th noon-10pm, F-Sa noon-11pm. AmEx/D/MC/V. ❹

La Bombonera, C. San Francisco 259 (☎ 722-0658). In this classically decorated restaurant photos of Old San Juan in 1900 and waiters dressed in smart red jackets revive turn-of-the-century life. For over 100 years, this friendly soda fountain and restaurant has been serving the self-proclaimed "best coffee in town." Those not interested in history can just enjoy the tasty, inexpensive Puerto Rican food or skip straight to the pastry case ($0.80). Entrees $6-17. Open daily 7:30am-8:30pm. D/MC/V. ❸

Transylvania, C. Recinto Sur 317 (☎ 977-2328). American and Romanian owners bring a taste of Transylvania to the enchanted isle. A portrait of Vlad Tepes, the original vampire, and other figures from Romanian folklore enhance the spooky ambiance. The brave try Dracula's Feast ($18) and Vampire Wine ($20). The not-so-brave stick to more traditional pasta entrees ($12-19). We won't tell you what comes in "Dracula's Orgasm." Lunch specials M-F 11:30am-2:30pm $5-8. Live music F-Sa 10pm. Open daily 11:30am-3pm and 6-10pm. AmEx/D/MC/V. ❹

La Creperie, C. San Francisco 366 (☎723-5086). Salty or sweet is your main choice at this tiny fluorescent green restaurant. Grab the house specialty, a salmon crepe with alfalfa, black pepper, onion, and tomato, and climb the small steps to the 2nd floor alcove. Sweet crepes $3-5, salty crepes $4-5. Open daily 10:30am-10pm. D/MC/V. ❶

El Mesón Sandwiches (☎721-5286), at C. San José and C. San Francisco. Locals have figured out that this local sandwich chain dishes up some of the best food in Old San Juan. Save on a combo meal (sandwich, fries, and a drink; $3-5) or choose from over 25 sandwiches ($2-5). Open M-Sa 6am-10pm, Su 7am-10pm. AmEx/MC/V. ❶

Martin's BBQ, C. San Francisco 210 (☎977-7619). Glorified fast food it may be, but Martin's BBQ serves up cheap and tasty barbecue to locals and foreigners alike. Enjoy the spotless, spacious restaurant while you wolf down ½ BBQ chicken, a side dish, and a drink ($5.25). Or play it healthy and stick with the chicken caesar wrapper ($5.50). All meals $4-8. Open M-Sa 11am-7pm, Su 11am-5pm. MC/V. ❷

Lupi's Mexican Grill, C. Recinto Sur 313 (☎722-1874). Autographed photos of athletes and numerous TVs give Lupi's the feel of an American sports bar. Sit on an elevated seat against the wall and watch the game or crowd around an intimate booth and slurp "Island Famous Margaritas" ($7-15). Entrees $9-20; lunch $6-9. Happy Hour daily 6-10pm. Karaoke F-Sa 10pm. Open M-Th 11am-10pm, F-Su 11am-2am. AmEx/MC/V. ❸

Makarios, C. Tetuan 361 (☎723-8653), allows even the most wary traveler to join San Juan's chic jet set crowd. Fine dining prevails at the elegant restaurant upstairs, which serves a large menu of Middle Eastern cuisine ($15-25). But even the plebeians are invited to sit at one of the silver outdoor tables and select from a limited menu consisting primarily of creative Mediterranean-style pizzas (entrees $6-13). Don't forget your cell phone and Prada bag. Bar inside. Lunch $8-13. Beer $3.50-5. Sa 9:30pm live belly dancing show. Open M 6pm-midnight, Tu-Su 11am-midnight. AmEx/MC/V. ❹

Cafetería Mallorca, C. San Francisco 300 (☎724-4607), on Plaza Brau, has been serving up quality Puerto Rican food for 41 years. A good location, clean interior, and pictures of entrees on the walls draw a largely local crowd. Menu varies daily. Breakfast (until 11am) $2-6; entrees $5-16. Open daily 7am-7pm. D/MC/V. ❸

Tantra Restaurant and Bar, C. Fortaleza 356 (☎977-8141), is one of the few Indian restaurants in Puerto Rico. Those who really like the swanky South Asian decor can take it home—one large Thai Buddha statue costs $1350. Traditional Indian entrees $18-24. F-Sa 9pm belly dancing show. Open daily noon-11pm. AmEx/D/MC/V. ❺

El Buren, C. del Cristo 103 (☎977-5023). This hip new restaurant seems straight out of New York City. With lights shining through the tabletops, American pop music blasting out of the speakers, and modern photography lining the walls, El Buren screams urban chic. Even the "cocina creativa international" food defies the rules and some claim that this is the best pizza in town. But coolness does come at a price. Italian entrees $14-19. 12" pizzas $9-16. Open Su-W 11am-midnight, Th-Sa 11am-2am. AmEx/MC/V. ❹

Barrachina, C. Fortaleza 104 (☎721-5852). Why splurge on yet another tourist-oriented Puerto Rican restaurant? Is it the charming, plant-filled courtyard? The fun-loving staff that occasionally breaks into salsa? The scrumptious *mofongo?* Of course not. It's the famous piña colada ($6), which supposedly originated here. Free samples. Entrees $14-23; lunch $7-11. Open Th-T 9:30am-11pm, W 9:30am-6pm. AmEx/D/MC/V. ❹

La Bella Piazza, C. San Francisco 355 (☎721-0396). Save up your pennies and revel in the decadence of one of San Juan's finest Italian restaurants. Dress to impress and prepare to loosen your belt after indulging in this classic Italian food. There are wine holders at every table, but check the price before you order—good bottles run $30-140. Pastas $17-26. Open Th-T noon-2:30pm and 6:30-10:30pm. AmEx/D/MC/V. ❺

Cafetería Los Únicos, C. Tetuan 255 (☎977-0386). No frills, just good, cheap Puerto Rican food. Sit at a small table and watch TV while you scarf down a quick lunch. Many office workers come here for breakfast or lunch. Breakfast $2-3; sandwiches $2-4; specials $5-7; entrees $5-7. Open M-F 5:30am-4pm. ❶

FOOD BY TYPE

AMERICAN AND BURGERS
El Hamburger (115)   PT ❶
El Hambergón (122)   RP ❶
Danny's International (116)   CO ❷
The Greenhouse (116)   CO ❸
Dunbar's (117)   OP ❹
Ciao Mediterranean Café (119)   IV ❹
El Patio de Sam (114)   OSJ ❺

INDIAN, JAPANESE, AND THAI
Shogun (118)   IV ❷
Wasabi (116)   CO ❸
DragonFly (114)   OSJ ❺
Royal Siam Thai Restaurant (118)   IV ❺
Tantra (112)   OSJ ❺

BAKERIES
Golden Bagel Bakery (119)   IV ❶
Repostería España (119)   IV ❶
Kasalta Bakery (117)   OP ❷
Das Pastell House (118)   IV ❷

BBQ
Condado BBQ (115)   CO ❶
Martin's BBQ (112)   OSJ ❷

CAFETERÍAS
Cafetería Los Únicos (112)   OSJ ❶
Cafetería Los Amigos (114)   OSJ ❶
Cafetería Los Pinos (118)   IV ❷
Cafetería Las Rosas (122)   RP ❷
Cafetería Mallorca (112)   OSJ ❸

CHINESE
China Express (119)   IV ❸
China Buffet (122)   HR ❸
Catay (114)   PT ❷

PUERTO RICAN
Café del Ángel (116)   CO ❷
Bohío Restaurant (119)   IV ❷
Plaza del Mercado (117)   SA ❷
Sonny's Terrace (119)   IV ❸
Latin Star Restaurant (116)   CO ❸
Restaurant D'Arco (117)   MI ❸
Diner's Restaurant (114)   OSJ ❸
El Jibarito (111)   OSJ ❸
La Bombonera (111)   OSJ ❸
Barrachina (112)   OSJ ❹
Casa Dante (119)   IV ❹
Parrot Club (114)   OSJ ❺
Ajili-mójili (116)   CO ❺

FRENCH
La Creperie (112)   OSJ ❶
La Patisserie de France (115)   CO ❷

INTERNATIONAL
Metropol (118)   IV ❸
Transylvania (111)   OSJ ❹

ITALIAN
Via Appia's (115)   CO ❷
Danny's International (116)   CO ❷
Da Luigi (118)   OP ❸
Tiramisú (118)   IV ❸
El Buren (112)   OSJ ❹
La Bella Piazza (112)   OSJ ❺

MEXICAN
Los Mexicanos (122)   RP ❶
Cielito Lindo (115)   CO ❷
Taqueria Mexicana (117)   SA ❷
Margaritaville/Burritos (122)   HR ❸/❷
Lupi's (112)&(119)   OSJ ❸ & IV ❸
Nueva Hacienda Don José (116)   CO ❸

MIDDLE EASTERN
Al Salam (122)   HR ❸
Makarios (112)   OSJ ❹

PIZZA
Town Grill (114)   OSJ ❶
Via Appia's (115)   CO ❷
Das Pastell House (118)   IV ❷
Ferrari Gourmet (118)   IV ❷
Pizza City (119)   IV ❷

SANDWICHES AND CAFES
El Mesón Sandwiches (112)   OSJ ❶
Guajanas Arte Cafe (122)   RP ❶
Piu Bello Gelato (116)   CO ❷
Tepe a Tepe (117)   MI ❷
Pinky's (117)   OP ❷
Bla Bla Coffeehouse (117)   SA ❷

SEAFOOD
Pelican Dumas(115)   PT ❸
Ostra Cosa (111)   OSJ ❹
The Red Snapper Marisquería (116)   CO ❹
Marisquería Atlántica (119)   IV ❹
Aguaviva (114)   OSJ ❺

SOUTH AMERICAN
Arepas Y Mucho Más (111)   OSJ ❷
Che's (118)   IV ❹

SPANISH
La Danza (114)   OSJ ❸
Divino Bocadito (114)   OSJ ❹

VEGETARIAN
Country Health Food (122)   RP ❶
Salud! (116)   CO ❷
Pura Vida (116)   SA ❷
Hostería del Mar (118)   OP ❸
Cafe Berlin (114)   OSJ ❹

LEGEND
CO=Condado   OSJ=Old San Juan
HR=Hato Rey   PT=Puerta de Tierra
IV=Isla Verde   RP=Río Piedras
MI=Miramar   SA=Santurce
OP=Ocean Park

SAN JUAN

HE BIG SPLURGE

THREE'S COMPANY

If you are trying to find the hippest restaurants in Old San Juan,
ook no farther than the corner of
C. Fortaleza and C. O'Donnell.
Chef Robert Treviño has created
hree trendy restaurants that are
he place to be for chic urbanites.
t all started with the notorious
Parrot Club, C. Fortaleza 353,
where the decor embodies Puerto
Rico's fun-loving tropical atmosphere. Here trendy Puerto Ricans
and tourists unite to sip elegant
cocktails and await scrumptious
entrees. After the Parrot Club
became somewhat of a tourist
nstitution, with its famous Nuevo
Latino cuisine (entrees $17–30;
unch $13-18) and scrumptious
Parrot Passions ($6), Treviño
expanded across the street and
entered the realm of Asian cuisine
with **Dragonfly**, C. Fortaleza 364.
This slightly more intimate restau-
ant holds only 45 people, but it
was also a resounding success.
People flocked to try the Latin
Asian cuisine amidst red lights,
Asian lanterns, and a subtle
echno beat (entrees $12-18;
wine $7-9). Three years later, a
hird restaurant opened next door.
Aguaviva, C. Fortaleza 364, cen-
ers on an underwater theme with
blue tables, large blue oyster
amps hanging from the ceiling,
and a waitstaff dressed in blue.
This innovative seafood restaurant
offers guests the opportunity to
watch the chefs prepare their oys-
ers ($2 each) and ceviche ($14
or a sampling).

Diner's Restaurant, C. Tetuan 311 (☎724-6276).
Tucked away on a quiet side street, Diner's is more of a
communication hub than a restaurant. Patrons sit alone
and chat on the phone while eating. Brick walls, tall ceilings, modern lighting, and several Internet terminals
contribute to the trendy atmosphere. Puerto Rican/inter-
national food $10-17. Internet $3 per 30min., $5 per
hr. Open Sa-W 11am-10pm. AmEx/D/MC/V. ❸

La Danza, C. Fortaleza 56 (☎723-1642), at C. del
Cristo. This pleasant Puerto Rican restaurant is uninspiring, except for its specials. At $20, the paella for 2,
with 2 glasses of wine, fried plantains, garlic bread,
and coffee, is a bargain. Or just sit outside and sip a
Planter's Punch ($2). Entrees $8-17. Open F-W
11:30am-8pm. AmEx/MC/V. ❸

Divino Bocadito, C. Cruz 252 (☎977-0042). Even the disco
balls look classy in this impeccably decorated restaurant
specializing in Spanish tapas ($4-12). Can't decide? Try
one of the "menu degustaciones," which include a variety
of tapas and house wine or sangria ($55-71 for 2 people).
Open W-Sa 6pm-1am, Su 6-11pm. AmEx/MC/V. ❹

El Patio de Sam, C. San Sebastian 102 (☎723-1149 or
723-8802). Yet another tourist-oriented restaurant that is
overpriced at dinner but reasonable for lunch, Sam's is
more notable for its location than its value. Many a tourist
has stopped here for a burger ($9) after visiting El Morro.
The glass-covered courtyard allows you to simultaneously
enjoy the sun and the A/C. A semi-popular bar on weekend nights. Puerto Rican entrees $13-33. Cocktails $4.50-
6. Open daily 11:30am-midnight. AmEx/MC/V. ❺

Cafe Berlin, C. San Francisco 407 (☎722-5205). This
bright cafe is the cleanest place this side of Germany. You
definitely pay for the view overlooking Plaza Colón, but Berlin does offer a nice range of vegetarian options ($12-14),
organic foods, and pastries ($2-3). Entrees $12-20; breakfast $2-10. Wine $5. Open M-F 11am-10pm, Sa-Su 9am-
10pm. AmEx/MC/V. ❹

Town Grill, C. San Francisco 157 (☎451-0934) is Old
San Juan's requisite fast food pizza joint. Grab a slice
of pizza ($1.65-2.25) or indulge on burgers and subs
($2.75-4.65). Permanent Happy Hour Medalla $1.
Open M-W 10:30am-7pm, Th-Sa 10:30am-3am, Su
10:30am-5pm. MC/V. ❶

Cafetería Los Amigos, C. San José 253. The facade is
dingy, the black and white tiles are falling apart, and
the only menu is on the wall, but this *cafetería* serves
up some of the best sandwiches in town ($1.50-3).
Nothing over $3. Open M-Sa 6:30am-6pm. ❶

PUERTA DE TIERRA

Catay, Ave Ponce de León 410 (☎722-6695), at C.
Martín Fernández. Old San Juan suffers from a deficit of
good Asian food, but this elegant Chinese restaurant

may merit a trip into Puerta de Tierra. The dark ornate interior matches the fancy decor outside. Chinese entrees $7-12. Weekday lunch menu $6-9. Open daily 11:30am-10:30pm. AmEx/MC/V. ❷

Pelican Dumas, Ave. Muñoz Rivera 401 (☎721-3550 or 721-1574), in the Reserve Officer's Beach Club near Parque del Tercer Milenio (see p. 134). This "restaurant by the sea" utilizes its superb location with a covered wooden patio overlooking the ocean. Munch on a whole fried red snapper ($24) while you gaze out over its former home. Entrees $7-20. Beer $3.25; wine $6. Open daily noon-10pm. AmEx/MC/V. ❸

El Hamburger, Ave. Muñoz Rivera 402 (☎721-4269). It's good, it's cheap, and it's fast. This popular shack serves up small, thick burgers ($2-4) to hungry beach-goers. Watch them grill, then add your own choice of fixings. Open Su-Th 11:30am-12:30am, F-Sa noon-3:30am. ❶

CONDADO

Condado has restaurants that will satisfy almost every culinary craving. For those midnight munchies, **Stop & Go,** C. Magdalena 1102 (☎724-3106), a small convenience store, serves sandwiches ($3.50) 24hr. a day.

▨ **Via Appia's,** Ave. Ashford 1350 (☎725-8711). The walls are lined with liquor but it's the pizza, some of the best in Puerto Rico, that draws crowds. A small patio allows patrons to avoid the dark, alcoholic interior. Medium pizza $9-13. Italian entrees $8-16. Homemade sangria $4. Open Su-Th 11am-11pm, F-Sa 11am-midnight. AmEx/MC/V. ❷

Cielito Lindo, C. Magdalena 1108 (☎723-5597). At this friendly restaurant mariachi music and creative decor just beg you to try a margarita ($4.50-5) and mentally transport yourself to Mexico. The restaurant is small, but an annex opens on weekend nights. Tasty Mexican enchiladas, burritos, and quesadillas $9-11. Lunch $4.50-11. Open M-Th 11am-10pm, F 11am-midnight, Sa 5-11pm, Su 5-10pm. AmEx/MC/V. ❷

Condado BBQ, Ave. Ashford 1104 (☎723-1292). It tends to get hot in this informal 4-table restaurant, so if you can't stand the heat, stay out of the kitchen. But that means you'll miss the tasty barbecue. Get ¼ BBQ chicken, a side, and a drink for $3.50. Gyros $3.50. *Mofongo* $7-8. Everything else $3-6. Open M-Sa 10:30am-10pm. ❶

La Patisserie de France, Ave. Ashford 1504 (☎728-5508). Stray from the tourist track and head to this charming corner bakery and deli. It fills up at lunch when trendy *sanjuaneros* bring their cell phones and come for sandwiches ($6-8) and pasta ($9-11). If you can't make it past the tempting pastry counter ($1.50-2.50), you may want to stick to the "Slim Fit" menu ($6-8). Open M-F 7am-7pm, Sa-Su 9am-6pm. AmEx/MC/V. ❷

On any given weekend night, all three restaurants are usually packed, as both locals and foreigners try to battle their way in. With such resounding success, Old San Juan is eagerly waiting to see what Treviño has up his sleeve next, and there are rumors that a fourth restaurant may be under way. Until then, the trio of trendiness merits a visit, despite prices that would make even New Yorkers cringe. But it's best to make a reservation, or you may join the legions that stand outside, waiting to get in. And waiting outside is just so uncool. *(The Parrot Club:* ☎724-7370; www.parrotclub.com. Live Puerto Rican, Cuban, or rumba music Tu, Th, and Sa. Open M 11:30am-3pm and 6-10pm, Tu-W 11:30am-3pm and 6-11pm, Th-F 11:30am-3pm and 6pm-midnight, Sa noon-4pm and 6pm-midnight, Su noon-4pm and 6-10pm. AmEx/MC/V. **Dragonfly:** ☎977-3886. Open M-W 6-11pm, Th-Sa 6pm-midnight. AmEx/MC/V. **Aguaviva:** ☎722-0665. Open Tu-W 6pm-11pm, Th-Sa 6pm-midnight. AmEx/MC/V. ❹)*

Danny's International, Ave. Ashford 1351 (☎ 724-0501),dishes out a variety of international dishes ($8-10), but their specialty is pizza (personal pizzas $7-13). Try the Puertorriqueña, a pizza with cheese, ground beef, and plantains. Very popular. Outdoor and indoor seating. Beer $3-3.25. Open M-Th 7am-1am, F-Sa 7am-2am. AmEx/D/MC/V. ❷

Ajili-mójili, Ave. Ashford 1006 (☎ 725-9195). Arguably the best Puerto Rican restaurant in the city, Ajili-mojili receives rave reviews from everyone who tries the delectable cuisine. This elegant restaurant spares no details—candlelit tables, views of the lagoon, and waiters dressed as fashionable *jíbaros* complete the ambiance. No shorts or T-shirts. Entrees $10-30. Open M-Th 11:45am-3pm and 6-10pm, F 11:45am-3pm and 6-11pm, Sa 6-11pm, Su 12:30am-4pm and 6-10pm. AmEx/MC/V. ❺

Piu Bello Gelato, Ave. Ashford 1302 (☎ 977-2121). Yes it's a chain, but this immaculate, modern cafe serves yummy gelato ($2.50-4) and scrumptious sandwiches ($4-8). Hip college students and tired tourists enjoy relaxing at the tables overlooking Ave. Ashford. Vegetarian options. Open M-Th 8am-1am, F-Su 8am-2am. AmEx/D/MC/V. ❷

Café del Ángel, Ave. Ashford 1106 (☎ 643-7594). This bright no-frills restaurant and fruit bar skipped out on the decorating bill (note the plastic furniture) and instead opted to serve cheap, hearty Puerto Rican food. A traditional island menu. Breakfast $4-4.50; sandwiches $3-5; dinner $7-13. Open M and W-Su 10am-10pm. MC/V. ❷

Wasabi, Ave. Ashford 1372 (☎ 724-6411). With metallic furniture, bright red accessories, and a full sushi bar, modern Wasabi is classic urban chic. Offers traditional sushi ($4-5) and maki roll ($4.50-15) options, as well as surprising Spanish tapas ($6-15). Take a look at the fish pond out front, then think again about what you're eating. Open M-F 11:30am-2:30pm and 6pm-1am, Sa 6pm-1am. AmEx/MC/V. ❸

The Red Snapper Marisquería, Ave. Ashford 1120 (☎ 722-3699). If a day at the beach puts you in the mood for good seafood, head to The Red Snapper. This long, narrow restaurant serves up a variety of fresh seafood ($17-24), including lobster ($30) and, of course, red snapper ($17-18). Landlubber entrees $11-19. High season open daily noon-10:30pm; low season Th-T noon-10:30pm, W 5-10:30pm. AmEx/D/MC/V. ❹

Salud!, Ave. Ashford 1350 (☎ 722-0911), is actually just a few tables in the back of health food store, but it's one of the few vegetarian restaurants in town. Indulge with a blended fruit drink or just buy some yogurt wheat germ on your way out. Here's to your health! Breakfast $3.50-4; lunch entrees $4-7. Open M-Sa 8:30am-5pm. ❷

Nueva Hacienda Don José, Ave. Ashford 1025 (☎ 723-5959). This unabashed tourist trap is one of Condado's only oceanfront restaurants. Breakfast $3.50-6. Puerto Rican and Mexican entrees $10-20. Margaritas $3.75-5. Open daily 7am-11pm. MC/V. ❸

The Greenhouse, Ave. Ashford 1200 (☎ 725-4036), in the lobby of the Diamond Palace Hotel. Overcome any negative preconceptions about hotel restaurants and enjoy this neighborhood favorite. Serves typical diner food, including daily specials ($6-11), caesar salad ($6), and the omnipresent hamburger ($6.50-8). Seafood is a bit more expensive ($22-26). Free parking. Open daily 11:30am-4am. AmEx/D/MC/V. ❸

Latin Star Restaurant, Ave. Ashford 1128 (☎ 724-8141) serves Puerto Rican food and spaghetti all day long. After a long night at the disco, nothing looks better than a big *mofongo* filled with crab ($16). Savor the A/C, or chill on a large outdoor patio covered with sports pictures. Entrees $8-23; specials $6-12. Open 24hr. D/MC/V. ❸

SANTURCE AND MIRAMAR

Countless indistinguishable restaurants along Ave. Ponce de León serve inexpensive Puerto Rican food to office workers. The few stand-outs are listed below.

🔲 **Pura Vida,** Ave. Ponce de León 1764 (☎ 726-4168), Santurce, near the Museo de Arte Contemporaneo. Although it's a bit out of the way, this immaculate vegetarian restaurant shines among the monotony of Santurce cuisine. Menu changes daily, but always contains healthy vegetarian entrees prepared without oil or animal products. Spanish only menu. Salads $2-5; entrees $5.50-11. F-Sa 6pm live Bohemian music. Open M-Th 7am-7pm, F 7am-9pm, Sa 8am-9pm, Su 8am-5pm. MC/V. ❷

Tepe a Tepe, Ave. Ponce de León 762 (☎977-8373), Miramar. Benecio del Toro is among the elites known to frequent this hip Miramar restaurant. Set in an old mansion and its spacious gardens, Tepe a Tepe serves up exquisite sandwiches to trendy *sanjuaneros* who check their palm pilots while they wait (and wait, and wait) for the food. Try the "Black Forest Dream," a Kaiser role with black forest ham, gouda cheese, and asparagus ($6.15). Sandwiches $5.50-7. Salads $3.50-6.50. Open M 10am-4pm, Tu-W 10am-5pm, Th 10am-10pm, F 10am-midnight, Sa 11am-6pm. MC/V. ❷

Bla Bla Coffeehouse, Ave. de Diego 353 (☎724-8321; www.blablacoffeehouse.com), is more than just a stylish coffeehouse with a fun name. The bright yellow dining area serves a small variety of entrees, including lasagna, wraps, and salads. Breakfast $2-3.50; lunch $6-7.50. Open M-F 7:30am-4pm, Sa 8am-2pm. AmEx/MC/V. ❷

Restaurant D'Arco, C. Miramar 605 (☎724-7813), Miramar. This clean but unexceptional restaurant is a good place to get a Puerto Rican meal in Miramar. Try the specials written on notecards at every table ($7-16). Breakfast $2-3. Open M-Sa 7am-9pm. AmEx/MC/V. ❸

Plaza del Mercado, 2 blocks north of Ave. Ponce de León between C. Canals and C. Dos Hermanos. A quaint **fruit and vegetable market** surrounded by clean restaurants serving traditional Puerto Rican food (entrees $6-11, seafood slightly more expensive; beer $1.25-2). Market open M-Sa 5am-5pm, Su 5:30am-noon. Some of the best are:

Restaurant Don Tello, C. Dos Hermanos 180 (☎724-5752). Open M 11am-5pm, Tu-W 11am-9pm, Th 11am-10pm, F 11am-11pm, Sa 11am-9pm. MC/V. ❷

Restaurant El Popular, C. Capitol 205 (☎722-4653). Open M 8am-4pm, W 8am-5pm, Th and Su 8am-6pm, F 8am-11pm, Sa 8am-8pm. MC/V. ❷

OCEAN PARK

A few good restaurants around Ocean Park cater to the beach crowd, but many only serve lunch. Dozens of *cafeterías* line C. Loíza, but that's not a good place to wander at night. What is the poor budget traveler to do for dinner? One solution is to head to Isla Verde or Condado, where good restaurants abound. Another solution is to just stock up on chips and drinks at the **Minimart** at the corner of C. McLeary and C. Santa Ana and wait until morning. (Open daily 8am-8pm. MC/V.)

Pinky's, C. Maria Moczo 51 (☎727-3347), at C. McLeary. When California meets San Juan you get Pinky's, a healthy sandwich shop full of funk. Tucked into a small crevice and directed toward an Anglophone crowd, Pinky's is, of course, characterized by its bright pink walls. The friendly staff will bring you a sandwich at the small metal tables, or they will deliver—even to the beach (free). Try the house specialty, the "Surfer" ($6), then hit the waves, dude. Wraps and sandwiches $5-8. Breakfast $4.50-8. Limited free parking. Open Tu-Th 7am-4pm, F 7am-8pm, Sa 11am-8pm, Su 11am-4pm. MC/V. ❷

Dunbar's, C. McLeary 1954 (☎728-2920). Photos of satisfied customers line the walls of this über popular English pub and restaurant. For over 20 years Dunbar's has been catering to a surprisingly local crowd (with lots of foreigners mixed in). Offers a wide selection of American food, including Dunbar's famous potato skins ($6-9). By night, the restaurant transforms into a lively pub. Entrees $15-24; sandwiches $9-15. Beer $3-4. Happy Hour daily 5-7pm. Open M-Th 11:30am-midnight, F 11:30am-1am, Sa 5pm-1am, Su 10am-midnight. AmEx/MC/V. ❹

Kasalta Bakery, C. McLeary 1966 (☎723-7340). People have been known to come to Kasalta for lunch, but they never leave without dessert. This incredible bakery boasts a counter filled with a huge variety of sweets, from flan to cheesecake to *dulce de leche*—and most only cost $1.25. Sandwiches $4-8. Open daily 5am-10pm. AmEx/MC/V. ❷

Taqueria Mexicana Pico de Gallo, C. Loíza 1762 (☎727-1603), actually in Santurce, but pretty close to Ocean Park. Amidst the drab, mediocre dining options of C. Loíza, this taqueria shines. Literally. The bright yellow walls still glow from their recent paint job. Mexican food $3-13. Open daily 11:30am-10pm. AmEx/D/DC/MC/V. ❷

Hostería del Mar, C. Tapia 1 (☎727-3302 or 727-0631), in the guest house of the same name (see p. 105). This restaurant sits on a breezy wooden patio less than 15 ft. from the water. Even locals come to sample the appetizing cuisine and enjoy the lovely view. The hostería specializes in fresh, healthy food and offers at least 1-2 vegetarian options. Entrees $12-14; sandwiches $6-9. Open daily 8am-10pm. AmEx/D/MC/V. ❸

Da Luigi, C. Diez de Andino 104 (☎977-0134), at C. Loíza. This classy little restaurant offers a taste of Italy at a fraction of the price found in Old San Juan. Come for lunch and revel in the pasta primavera for only $7. Lunch $7-9; dinner $14-17. Wine $4.25. Open M-Sa 11:30am-3pm and 6-10pm, Su noon-5pm. AmEx/MC/V. ❸

ISLA VERDE

Most of the restaurants listed below provide at least a few parking spaces as well as free or inexpensive delivery within the Isla Verde area.

Ferrari Gourmet, Ave. Isla Verde 51 (☎982-3115). Since 2002 this simple pizzeria has been tempting *sanjuaneros* and foreigners with its amazing concoctions. Take one sniff and you'll be hooked. The extensive menu includes traditional pizzas, special pizzas, and "specially for you" pizzas. Small pizzas $6-10. Wine $5-6. Free delivery. Open Su-W 11:30am-10pm, Th-Sa 11:30am-11pm. AmEx/MC/V. ❷

Che's (☎726-7202 or 268-7505), at C. Caoba and C. Laurel, is widely acknowledged as the best Argentinean restaurant in town. Blue-and-white checkered tablecloths make you feel right at home—if home serves tasty breaded veal cutlet à la Argentina ($17). Entrees $9-20. Wine $6.50. Open daily 11am-11pm. AmEx/D/DC/MC/V. ❹

Das Pastell House, C. Loíza 2482 (☎728-7106 or 728-7107). This modern and affordable cafe/bakery/pizzeria offers nourishment for all occasions. Start the day with a homemade pastry ($1-2.50), then come back for lunch and sample one of the international sandwiches ($6). Finally, make one last stop for dinner and one of the specialty pizzas, served with a white cream sauce and the toppings mixed together ($6-10). Then just try to bypass the incredible desserts. Open daily 7am-11pm. AmEx/MC/V. ❷

Cafetería Los Pinos (☎268-1259), on Ave. Isla Verde between Banco Santander and 7-11. For some tasty, inexpensive local food head to Los Pinos, one of Isla Verde's only *cafeterías.* Most patrons just pull up a seat at the long counter and watch TV while they eat. Puerto Rican entrees $6-13. Delicious sandwiches $2.75-5. Open 24hr. ❷

Tiramisú, C. Marginal Ave. Baldorioty de Castro 19 (☎268-5002), in Villamar. Take the bridge heading to Villa Verde (see p. 110), and immediately turn right. It's amazing how crossing one little bridge can decrease prices so much, but this is one of San Juan's most affordable Italian joints. Still the cozy restaurant doesn't skip out on any finishing touches; dried flowers decorate the interior and the Sardinian cuisine is first rate. Entrees $8-17. Wine $4.25. Open Tu-Su 11am-4pm and 6-10pm. AmEx/MC/V. ❸

Metropol (☎791-5585 or 791-4046), on the eastern edge of Ave. Isla Verde, at the intersection with Ave. Gobernadores. Locals recommend the quality Cuban food at this slightly upscale restaurant with its perfectly aligned tables. Despite the low prices, you still get waiters in bow ties and wine glasses on the tables. Try the cornish hen, if you can ignore the fact that the restaurant is next to the cockfight arena. Specials $9-14; seafood $12-22. Open daily 11:30am-10:45pm. AmEx/D/DC/MC/V. ❸

Royal Siam Thai Restaurant, Ave. Isla Verde 65 (☎726-1167 or 726-1173). San Juan has few Asian restaurants, but Royal Siam proudly represents Thailand. After recently relocating from Old San Juan, this restaurant has created ambiance in a hurry, with huge bronze statues, wall murals, and candlelit tables. Relatively upscale. Entrees $16-25. Wine $6. Free delivery. Open Tu-Su 11am-11pm. AmEx/MC/V. ❺

Shogun, Ave. Isla Verde 35 (☎268-4622). Of the many Japanese restaurants in Isla Verde, Shogun provides the best sushi at reasonable prices. Stick with the standard options of tuna and California rolls, or experiment with designer rolls, such as the Boston (salmon, lettuce, cucumber, and avocado; $8). The decor is less than exceptional, but there are some Japanese lanterns and swords in the back. Sushi and maki rolls $5-7. Open M-F 11:30am-2pm and 5-11pm, Sa 5-11pm, Su 4-10pm. AmEx/MC/V. ❷

Casa Dante, Ave. Isla Verde 39 (☎726-7310). This Puerto Rican restaurant may have the most extensive selection of *mofongos* this side of Cuba. Try crushed plantains filled with chicken soup...or fajitas...or filet mignon. The list goes on and on. Also has options for those who don't live on *mofongos* alone. Entrees $11-20. ½ jar of sangria $13. Delivery $3. Open M-Sa 11:30am-11pm, Su 11:30am-10pm. AmEx/MC/V. ❹

Lupi's Mexican Grill (☎253-1664), at Ave. Isla Verde and Diaz Way. The Isla Verde version of this Old San Juan restaurant (see p. 112) sports a larger space, more hopping nightlife, and basketballs signed by Shaquille O'Neal and Kareem Abdul-Jabbar. Many choose to sit outside and sip a post-beach beer ($3.75). Entrees $9-20; lunch specials $6-9. Live rock music F-Sa 11pm. Open daily 11am-4am. AmEx/MC/V. ❸

Bohío Restaurant (☎253-2992), across from Hotel InterContinental, is a Puerto Rican restaurant repackaged and cleaned up to appease fickle tourist tastes. Serves affordable Puerto Rican and Italian food in a pleasant, modern setting. Cappuccino and iced coffee $2.50. Entrees $5-15. Open M-F 3-11pm, Sa-Su 11am-11pm. AmEx/MC/V. ❷

Ciao Mediterranean Café, Ave. Isla Verde 5961 (☎797-6100 ext. 280), in the Inter-Continental Hotel. Walk across the lobby, leave through the back door, and continue past the pool to the beach. Or, preferably, find the restaurant on the beach. Surprisingly affordable given its location, the Mediterranean Café provides the budget traveler a look at the life of luxury. This glamorous cafe sits on a large patio on the beach and serves a motley collection of anything rich hotel guests may want. Lunch wraps, burgers, and pizzas $8-17. Dinner $12-25. Open daily 11am-11pm. AmEx/MC/V. ❹

Sonny's Terrace, C. Anapola 2 (☎791-3083), in Hotel Empress, just past Hotel La Playa (see p. 108). Visible from almost anywhere on the beach, Sonny's Terrace actually sits on a dock over the water at the end of a peninsula. Besides the superb location, Sonny's also boasts live music and great views of Isla Verde. Serves *comida criolla*, hamburgers, and a lot of ribs. Breakfast $6-8; lunch $4-15; dinner $14-17. Live jazz Th 10pm, live merengue and salsa F-Sa 10pm. Open daily 8am-11pm; bar open later. ❸

Golden Bagel Bakery (☎791-2575), in Plazoleta Isla Verde. This small strip mall store is one of the few bagel stores on the island. Bagels $0.60; bagel sandwiches $4-6. Open M-F 6:30am-7pm, Sa 7am-7pm, Su 7am-2pm. MC/V. ❶

Marisquería Atlántica, C. Loíza 2475 (☎728-5444 or 728-5662). Change out of your beach clothes—after 6pm shorts and T-shirts are not allowed in this elegant seafood restaurant. So put on some fancy duds and come sample the baked marinated red snapper ($17) with a glass of wine ($4.50-7). Entrees $16-24. Or just head to the seafood store on the side and buy your own ingredients to cook at home. Open M-Th noon-10pm, F-Sa noon-11pm. Store open M-Sa 9am-8pm, Su 10am-3pm. AmEx/MC/V. ❹

Repostería España (☎727-3860 or 727-4517), on C. Marginal Ave. Baldorioty de Castro, in Villamar. Cross the bridge heading to El Patio Guest House (p. 110), and turn immediately left. This Spanish bakery is not quite as elaborate as Ocean Park's Kasalta (see p. 117), but it still manages to supply Isla Verde with an abundant source of goodies. A huge counter contains cakes, pies, cheesecakes, pastries, and other temptations ($1-2). Sandwiches $4-6. Open daily 6am-10pm. AmEx/MC/V. ❶

Pizza City (☎726-0356), at. Ave. Isla Verde and C. Diaz May, with the huge Medalla Light sign on the roof. Sometimes you just need a slice of pizza at 3am, and Pizza City exists to fulfill that urge. This large, informal, open-air pizzeria is nothing special during the day, but it's a good place to satiate post-clubbing munchies. Slice of pizza $1.75-3. Puerto Rican entrees $7-17. Sandwiches $3-5. Beer $2.50. Open 24hr. ❷

China Express Restaurant (☎491-4680), in the Plazoleta Isla Verde. Large fans on the walls are a meager attempt at decoration, but there's not a lot you can do in a strip mall. China Express does serve a nice selection of Chinese food with lots of seafood options. Entrees $7-26. Open Su-Th 10am-10pm, F-Sa 10am-11pm. MC/V. ❸

SAN JUAN

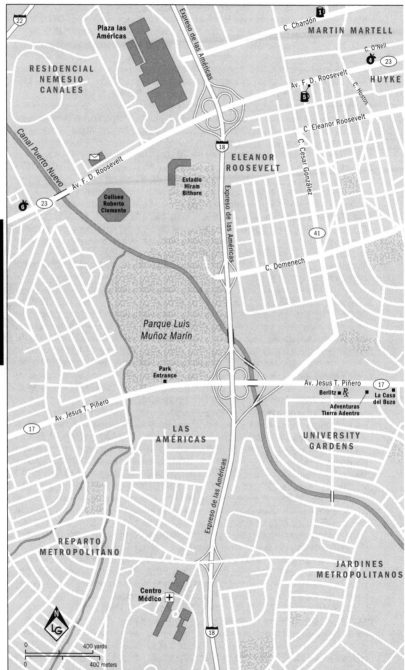

Hato Rey and Río Piedras

ACCOMMODATIONS
Hotel de Diego, **12**

FOOD
Al Salam, **4**
Cafetería Las Rosas, **13**
China Buffet, **2**
Country Health Food, **11**
Guajanas Arte Cafe, **10**
El Hambergón, **7**
Margaritaville/Burritos, **6**
Los Mexicanos, **9**

NIGHTLIFE
El 8 de Blanco, **8**
Coaches Sports Restaurant, **3**
El Meson y Algo Más, **5**
San Juan Reggae, **1**

SAN JUAN

HATO REY

It's a bit of a trek, but Hato Rey boasts an impressive assortment of restaurants, both in terms of quality and diversity of selection. It may be worth the journey just to escape the monotonous beachside routine.

Al Salam, Ave. F.D. Roosevelt 239 (☎751-6296). With over 50 options, it should be easy to find a tasty entree at this reasonably priced restaurant. Menu includes lots of kebabs, yogurt, and other Middle Eastern favorites. The photos lining the walls provide an interesting glimpse at the diversity of the Middle East, from a packed mosque in Saudi Arabia to the old city streets of Jerusalem. Entrees $9-17. Wine $5. F 8:30pm belly dancing. Open Sa-Th 11:30am-10pm, F 11:30am-11pm. AmEx/MC/V. ❸

China Buffet, Ave. F.D. Roosevelt 124 (☎754-7407), is one of the few Chinese buffets that actually looks appetizing. With sushi, dumplings, egg rolls, soup, shrimp, and all the traditional Chinese favorites, this extensive buffet is quite a bargain. For an extra $7, get lobster as well. Lunch $9. Dinner after 5pm $12. Children $4.50. Open M-Th 11am-10pm, F 11am-11pm, Sa noon-11pm, Su noon-9:30pm. AmEx/MC/V. ❸

Margaritaville/Burritos, Ave. F.D. Roosevelt 1013 (☎781-8452; www.restaurantmargaritas.com), 1 block past the Coliseo Roberto Clemente. 2 quality Mexican restaurants in 1. Margaritaville is the sit-down, upscale version, complete with classic Mexican decorations and a cactus girl on the front door. Take the time to savor the sizzling fajitas prepared in passion fruit sauce ($16). Entrees $10-17. Margaritas $5-5.50. Open M-W 11:30am-10pm, Th-Sa 11:30am-11pm, Su 11:30am-10:30pm. Or skip out on the tip and head to **Burritos,** the fast, inexpensive, *cafetería*-style annex catering primarily to Puerto Ricans on their lunch breaks. Serves daily combos that include an entree, a drink, and a dessert for $5-7. Open daily 10:45am-10:30pm. AmEx/MC/V. ❸/❷

RÍO PIEDRAS

Ave. Universidad, leading up to UPR, has a number of small, cheap restaurants catering to students. Real bargains await at the back of Plaza del Mercado, where countless *cafeterías* dish out local fare.

▨ Guajanas Arte Cafe, C. Amalia Marín 4 (☎766-0497) puts some funky flavor in the Río Piedras culinary scene. Located at the SW corner of UPR, this brand new restaurant/ cafe provides an artsy venue for students to grab lunch. Student artwork lines the cafe's brightly colored walls and the sandwiches are named after famous artists. Try the Francisco Oller—otherwise known as ham and cheese. Puerto Rican combos with some vegetarian options $5. Sandwiches $2-3. Open M-Sa 7am-4pm. MC/V. ❶

El Hambergón, Ave. Universidad 153 (☎250-3487). The classic college hamburger joint. El Hambergón dishes out cheap and tasty combos to poor and hungry undergrads. Sports posters, electronic slot machines, and a friendly staff welcome everyone. Combos $4-6. Happy Hour daily 3-7pm beer $1-2. Open M-Sa 11am-10pm. ❶

Country Health Food, C. Robles 53 (☎763-7056), between the market and the University. Head all the way to the back to find a metal counter filled with the daily selection of tasty vegetarian cuisine. A refreshing option after walking through the meat-filled market. Entrees $4-6. Delicious *batidas* $2. Open M-Sa 9am-3pm. AmEx/MC/V. ❶

Cafetería Las Rosas, C. Monseñor Torres 112 (☎274-1261), is one of the cleanest cafeterías in the market area, but you pay a bit more for that luxury. Get your food buffet-style, then settle down at a quaint wooden table. Puerto Rican combos $5-8. Sandwiches $2-4.50; burgers $2-3. Open M-Sa 6:30am-3pm. ❷

Los Mexicanos, Ave. Universidad 52 (☎282-8007). Yellow-and-white checkered table cloths liven up this small Mexican joint. UPR students gather here at lunchtime for inexpensive south-of-the-border specials ($2-5). Burritos $3.45. Open M-F 11am-3pm. ❶

◉ SIGHTS

OLD SAN JUAN

▨**CASTILLO SAN FELIPE DEL MORRO (EL MORRO).** Most of San Juan has changed considerably over the last 500 years. However, when you walk up to the walls of El Morro, it's easy to transport yourself back to a time when Puerto Rico was largely uninhabited and pirates still posed a threat. The awe-inspiring six-level fortress, named after the patron saint of Spain's King Philip II, draws over two million visitors per year and became a **UNESCO World Heritage Site** in 1983.

Construction of El Morro began in 1539, when the Spaniards realized that La Fortaleza was located too far inland to effectively prevent ships from entering the bay. El Morro originally consisted of one small tower, but as foreigners and pirates continued to besiege the island, the fortress continued to expand. El Morro's day of glory came in 1625 when Dutch soldiers attacked the fort by land and by sea. (By then 10% of the fortress was designed to prevent land attacks, while the other 90% was designed for sea attacks.) Stationed inside El Morro, Spaniard Don Juan de Haro and his army refused to surrender. Rumor has it that even the released prisoners chose to stay and help fight. Finally, over a month after their arrival, the Dutch left, burning the rest of San Juan on their way. Encouraged by their success, the Spaniards continued renovating the fort, and it wasn't officially "finished" until the 1780s. In 1876 they added a lighthouse to the sixth floor, which is now the oldest on the island and still in use. El Morro was put to the test once again in 1898 when the Americans bombarded the fort for 2½ hours, leaving 100 men dead. Then, during both World Wars, the US Army (now working from inside the fort) used it as a look-out post to protect the island. Finally in 1961 the military abandoned El Morro and donated it to the government. Today it is one of Puerto Rico's two US National Park protected areas (the other is **San Cristóbal,** down the road).

Visitors enter on the fourth floor, the Plaza Principal, which contained the prison, the chapel, and several cannon rooms. Today the prison room shows a 15min. video about the fort and several of the cannon rooms have become a museum with captions in English and Spanish. Look up and you will see three flags—the Puerto Rican flag, the US flag, and the old Spanish military flag. The original first floor is closed, but don't miss the second floor where a piece of wood still sticks out of the ceiling—this shell is a gift from the US Army, left over from the 1898 American attack on San Juan. It's quite incredible that the shell managed to penetrate the walls, which are 12 ft. thick here. *(C. Norzagaray 501. ☎ 729-6777; www.nps.gov/saju. Open daily 9am-5pm. Free tours 10am and 2pm in Spanish, 11am and 3pm in English, depending on staff available. $3, over 65 $2, ages 13-17 $1, 12 and under free.)*

CASTILLO DE SAN CRISTÓBAL. Frequently overlooked by tourists who visit El Morro and decide that one fort is enough, San Cristóbal is actually the larger of the two forts, although less area is open to the public. While the two forts have many similar architectural aspects, San Cristóbal offers some unique features, such as a fully decorated replica of troops' quarters—complete with beds, shirts on the walls, and an interrupted game of dominos—as well as a new set of historical trivia. However, San Cristóbal does have the same basic structure as El Morro, including cannon openings, historical exhibits, and splendid views of the city.

After the Spaniards built El Morro to protect the bay, attacks by the British in 1598 and the Dutch in 1625 soon demonstrated that the city was still susceptible to land attacks. Thus in 1634 they began constructing San Cristóbal about half a mile down the road. The fort was not tested until 1797 when the British again tried, unsuccessfully, to take the city. Then, in 1898, Puerto Rico's involvement in the Spanish-American War was announced with a bang as a shot was fired from San

FROM THE ROAD

A MATCH MADE IN SAN JUAN

It was the event of the year and I was there to see it. Pop sensation Marc Anthony was going to remarry Miss Universe 1994 Dayanara Torres. *Sanjuaneros* prepared well in advance. Banners lined the streets and the city government, coincidentally, freshened up the ugly scaffolding near the San Juan gate with a paint job, just in case the couple happened to walk by. This was important.

Unaccustomed to both celebrity weddings and Puerto Rican levels of celebration, I paid no attention to the commotion until I walked down the street on the day of the wedding. The plaza in front of the cathedral was filled with people—at noon. The wedding didn't start until 4pm, but women had come early to set up lawn chairs and wait. Rumors flew through the crowd like wildfire—they're going to have seven limos, they're going to have the reception at El Morro. In a culture that idolizes beautiful women, catching a glimpse of Miss Universe is a big deal.

Attempting to eschew the hype, I continued on with my day. However, I must admit that it was not a coincidence that I happened to be walking past the church when the wedding started. The crowd had grown immense and I could barely see. But I did—I saw the shoulders and the back of the head of Miss Universe. I quickly got over the excitement and went back to work, but the crowds kept waiting—maybe she would come back...I gave up, deciding that maybe this was one aspect of Puerto Rican culture that I just wouldn't understand.

Cristóbal. After the US won the war it took control of the fort, and in 1942 San Cristóbal was used as a WWII observation post. Today much of the fort is open to visitors, who upon entering are given directions for a self-guided tour. *(C. Norzagaray 501. ☎729-6777; www.nps.gov/saju. Open daily 9am-5pm. Free tours 11am and 3pm in Spanish, 10am and 2pm in English, depending on staff availability. $3, over 65 $2, ages 13-17 $1, 12 and under free.)*

LA FORTALEZA. Reigning over the southwest corner of Old San Juan like a castle, La Fortaleza is the oldest **governor's residence** in the western hemisphere still used today. The Spanish originally began constructing the edifice in 1533 as a fort to protect San Juan, but after five years of work (and only one year shy of completion), they realized that the position of La Fortaleza would not allow them to actually see attackers entering the bay. Thus construction began on another fort, soon to be known as **El Morro,** and La Fortaleza became the official residence and office of the governor. Over the years, the Neoclassical building has housed 124 governors appointed by the Spanish crown, 20 appointed by the US government, and seven elected by the people of Puerto Rico. The governor lives on the third floor of the mansion and works on the second. The flag out front waves only when the governor is on the island and flies at half-mast when he is away.

A free tour is the only way to see the mansion, but these are limited to the courtyard and never actually enter the house. If you lack time or interest, Plazuela de la Rogativa offers beautiful views of the facade. *(C. Fortaleza 1. Use the entrance at the end of C. Fortaleza. ☎721-7000 ext. 2211, 2323, or 2358; www.fortaleza.gobierno.pr. Tours (30min., 6 per day M-F 9am-3:30pm, free) offered in English on the hr. and in Spanish on the ½ hr. Check the poster outside the gate for the day's schedule.)*

PASEO LA PRINCESA. Extending from the San Juan gate to the piers, this wide promenade lined with trees, benches, and flowers provides one of the nicest places in the city for an evening stroll or a midday run. The 1290 ft. path was originally constructed in 1843, but it deteriorated over the years and was only recently renovated at a cost of $2.8 million. Start your walk on the westernmost edge of the old city at the **San Juan Gate,** the symbolic entrance to the city. Governor Don Enríque Enriquez de Sotomayor commissioned construction of the gate in 1635 as one of six entrances into the city, but during the 18th and 19th centuries it served as the primary entrance. New Spanish governors were welcomed here before they entered the city. After you pass through the gate, follow Paseo de la Princesa to the left, where the path continues between the water and **La Muralla,** the original walls fortifying the city that took the Spaniards almost 150 years to build. Take a look at the thickness of the wall as you pass through the gate to fully comprehend the magnitude of its size. As the path turns away from the sea it approaches **Raíces,** a statue surrounded by water. Possibly the most photographed sight in Old San Juan, the statue, constructed in 1992 by Spanish sculptor Luis Antonio Sanguino, symbolizes Puerto Rico's cultural heritage. In front, a young man stands admiring the beauty around him, while in the back a young woman flanked by two friendly dolphins welcomes visitors to the island. Images of a family and a traditional *jíbaro* complete the sculpture. The ensuing broad prome-nade provides benches and a welcome respite from the sun. **La Princesa,** on the left, was constructed in 1837 as a prison. Today it is the central office of the Puerto Rico Tourism Company. Visitors may be more interested in the small gallery inside that hosts a series of temporary exhibits by local artists. There are no descriptions, but the front desk provides an English/Spanish information booklet. *(Open M-F 8am-4:30pm.)* Continue past the enclosed botanical gardens on your left to reach Plaza la Princesa, a brick rotunda centered on **Al Inmigrante,** a sculpture by Prat Ventos.

CATEDRAL SAN JUAN BAUTISTA. Situated in the heart of the old city, the gorgeous San Juan Bautista is important for more than the fact that it houses **the tomb of Juan Ponce de León** (though this is what draws most visitors). Construction began in 1521 under the direction of Bishop Alonso Manso, but the cathedral came tumbling down in 1526 when a hurricane demonstrated that island buildings should not be made of wood. The cathedral was reconstructed in 1529 and that same year hosted the **first ordi-nation of a bishop in North America.** When Spanish settlers first came to the island, they would visit the church immediately upon arrival to thank God for a safe journey. Over time the building suffered attacks by indigenous tribes, pirates, and foreigners, but the stone remained intact. In 1977 San Juan Bautista became the only Puerto Rican church to be granted the status of a **Minor Basilica.** Not surprisingly, images of San Juan Bau-tista dominate the church—he appears in figurines on the outside facade, in the nave on the left-hand side of the interior, and in a stained glass window overlooking the main entrance. *(C. del Cristo 151-153. ☎/fax 722-0861; www.catedralsanjuan.com. Open M-F 8am-5pm, Sa 8am-3pm, Su 7am-2pm. Mass held M-F 12:15pm, Sa 7pm, Su 9 and 11am. Free.)*

PARQUE DE LAS PALOMAS AND CAPILLA DEL SANTO CRISTO. A pigeon-hater's worst nightmare and many a child's greatest dream, Parque de las Palomas **(Pigeon Park)** is crawling with this urban bird. If you're into that sort of thing, buy some bird food from the vendor in the corner ($0.50) and soon birds will be crawling all over you. If you've seen Alfred Hitchcock's movie *The Birds* a few too many times, skip directly to the **Capilla del Santo Cristo,** the tiny chapel next to the park. Legend has it that the silver altar inside, dedicated to the Holy Christ of Miracles, was con-structed in honor of Baltazar Montañez, who barely survived a horse-racing acci-dent in the 1750s. History, however, has it that he was actually killed in the race. Regardless, the altar is beautiful. Come on Tuesdays when the gate is open to get a closer look. *(At the south end of C. del Cristo. Chapel open Tu 11am-4pm. Other times the people at the pigeon food stand may be able to open the outer door. Free.)*

CEMENTERIO DE SANTA MARÍA MAGDALENA DE PAZZIS. Known simply as "the cemetery," this small plot of land hovering precipitously between the old town walls and the sea may have the best views of any cemetery in the world. Con-structed in 1863, the cemetery has been the resting place for many of San Juan's most prominent citizens and is still used today. *(On the north side of the city between El Morro and Las Peñas. Walk down the street tunnel from C. Norzagaray. Avoid the cemetery and neighboring La Perla after dark. Open daily 8am-3pm.)*

EL TEATRO ALEJANDRO TAPIA Y RIVERA. One of the largest theaters in Puerto Rico, the Tapia Theater serves as a monument of historical, architectural, and artistic interest. Governor Don Miguel de la Torre commissioned the building in 1824 to serve as the first theater in San Juan and the Tuscan-style Romantic building officially opened in 1836 as the Teatro Municipal (Municipal Theater). In 1937 the government renamed the theater after Alejandro Tapia y Rivera, one of Puerto Rico's most famous playwrights. The facade is beautiful, but it is the interior that really shines. Although it is not officially open to the public, people working at the ticket booth sometimes let visitors peek inside. The theater has 642 seats, but the third balcony and all of the booths are reserved for the governor and members of the municipal government—if they decide not to come, the seats remain empty. For ticket information see **Entertainment, p. 136.** *(On the south side of Plaza Colón. Tickets ☎ 721-0180 or 723-2079, administration 721-0169. Office hours vary by performance.)*

PLAZA DE ARMAS. On most days Old San Juan's Plaza de Armas is just a large slab of concrete with a fountain, some benches, and a popular cafe. However, during holidays and special events (which tend to happen about once a week), the plaza fills with vendors hawking souvenirs, musicians playing traditional music, and hordes of people. Moreover, two important buildings lie on the plaza. The **Alcaldía** (Mayor's Office), on C. San Francisco, is a Neoclassical building originally constructed in 1604 and restored in 1966-68 under the fashionable Mayor Felisa Rincón. The mayor still works here, but visitors are free to visit the pleasant courtyard and **sala San Juan Bautista,** which holds a small gallery of local artwork A small tourist desk on the left-hand side of the lobby can answer some questions. *(☎ 724-7171. Open M-F 8am-5pm.)* On C. San José, the **Departmento de Estado** (State Department) also merits a quick visit. This Neoclassical building has housed government offices since the 18th century and today the Secretary of State, the second-in-command of the Puerto Rican executive branch, works here. Just inside the entrance a semi-functional computer terminal explains the tourism, economy, and government of Puerto Rico, but visitors may be more interested in the courtyard, which houses a modern art gallery. *(☎ 722-3890. Open M-F 8am-noon and 1-4:30pm.)*

IGLESIA SAN JOSÉ. Constructed in 1523, this beautiful building is the second-oldest church in the Western Hemisphere. Iglesia San José was closed for repairs in early 2003, but is expected to reopen by 2004. *(On Plaza San José, at C. San Sebastian and C. del Cristo. Open M-F 7am-3pm. Mass Su noon.)*

PLAZAS. At the intersection of Caleta de las Monjas and Calle Recinto Oeste, picturesque **Plazuela de la Rogativa** is a great place to rest in the shade and take a few photos. The statue in the middle of the plaza, La Rogativa, depicts the women and the bishop of San Juan tricking the English into believing that reinforcements were coming to protect the island and thus saving the city from the invaders. A huge statue of Eugenio María de Hostos dominates **Parque de Beneficencia,** behind the Museo de las Américas on Norazagaray. Otherwise, Beneficia is just your standard mix of benches, lanterns, and concrete. **Plaza San José** seems to have a split personality. By day it's the typical plaza with a small outdoor dining area; at night it transforms into the hottest gathering point in town. On weekend nights and festivals Puerto Ricans flock to San José to meet, greet, wine, and dine. Things have gotten so out of control in the past that police have had to come in to break up the party, thus the ban on the public consumption of alcohol. Nearby, **Plaza del Quinto Centenario** was constructed in 1992 to commemorate the 500 year anniversary of the discovery of America. The large totem pole in the middle, "Totem Telurico," stands as a monument to the earth and plenitude of America. The top level supposedly represents the present while the lower level represents the past and the stairs represent the connection between the two. Drivers may be more interested in the **parking lot** underneath the plaza. Back in lower San Juan, off C. San Francisco, **Plaza Salvador Brau** was constructed in 2000 next to the huge mental health clinic. The plaza centers on a statue of—you guessed it—Salvador Brau (1842-1912), noted journalist, historian, and politician. In addition to pigeons and skate-boarders, the plaza is a popular venue for people playing dominos.

PUERTA DE TIERRA

EL CAPITALIO. San Juan's enormous capital building is the home of the legislative branch of the government, with the Senate on the left (facing the building) and the House of Representatives on the right. It is easy to identify which branch anyone in the building works for based on their clothing—employees associated with the House wear green while Senate employees wear red. **Luis Muñoz Rivera** first proposed the building in 1907 when he realized that the legislature could not fit in its old edifice, but construction did not begin until 1924 and the building was not inaugurated until 1929, after Muñoz Rivera had already died. Architect Rafael Carmoega designed the building in an Italian Renaissance Neoclassical style, modeled after the US capitol in Washington, D.C. An interesting (and free!) tour leads through the entire building, including both the Senate and the House chambers. Even if one of the branches is in session, tours frequently enter the gallery and observe the proceedings. Enormous piles of paper on various legislators' desks reveal the excessive bureaucracy involved. Even if you don't have time for a tour, it's worthwhile to enter the building and wander around. The main rotunda contains an original copy of **Puerto Rico's constitution** and an engraved mural (look at the top of the walls) depicts the history of the island from the Taínos to the present. (On Ave. Muñoz Rivera, about ½ mi. from Old San Juan. ☎ 724-8979. Open M-F 8am-5pm. Free tours in English, Spanish, and French. Call ahead.)

CASA DE ESPAÑA. Currently housing the Spanish cultural center and a Spanish restaurant, the aptly named Casa de España merits a stop for its beautiful Iberian architecture alone. The building was originally constructed in 1935 as a gentleman's club for the Spanish expat community, but today anyone is free to enter. (Ave. Ponce de León 9, between Carnegie Library and the Capital. Open daily 9am-10pm.)

FUERTE SAN JERONIMO DEL BOQUERÓN. Hidden behind the Hilton, this small 15th-century fort looks like a miniature version of San Cristóbal and played a similar role in protecting San Juan from foreign attacks. The fort has been closed since 1995, but the Puerto Rican Institute of Culture hopes to reopen the structure soon. Until then, it is possible to view the fort from outside. (Enter the Hilton Caribe and follow signs to the San Cristóbal ballroom, then exit the glass doors behind the ballroom.)

HATO REY AND RÍO PIEDRAS

■ **PLAZA DEL MERCADO AND PASEO DE DIEGO.** If endless fast food restaurants and American chains have convinced you that Puerto Rico really is the 51st state, head to Paseo de Diego. This five-block pedestrian street is a truly Latin American experience that will leave your senses swirling as vendors call out their sales and blast salsa music, crowds of shoppers bustle past, and the smell of fresh fruit and trash wafts through the air. Every type of store lines Paseo de Diego, from disco clothes vendors to McDonalds, but even people with no consumer interest can enjoy a stroll through this lively thoroughfare. When you think you've seen it all, head to the intersection of C. de Domingo and C. Monseñor Tores to visit the **Plaza del Mercado.** This is San Juan's largest food market, and if you can survive the overwhelming scent of cilantro and the sight of large chunks of fresh meat, a visit to the market can be a fascinating glimpse of true Puerto Rican culture. In back countless *cafeterías* serve up good, cheap *comida criolla*. (Along Paseo José de Domingo between Ave. Ponce de León and C. Padre Capuchinos. It's best to visit during daylight hours. Plaza del Mercado open daily 6am-5:30pm.)

■ **JARDÍN BOTÁNICO DE PUERTO RICO.** Of San Juan's many attractive parks, the botanical gardens in southern Río Piedras easily stand out as the best. Managed by the University of Puerto Rico, the 75-acre Botanical Gardens contain two small lakes, a sculpture garden, an orchid garden, a herbarium, countless paths and most importantly, a place to escape the noise and commotion of the city. The visitors

SAN JUAN

office provides a map of the premises, but it's equally enjoyable to just wander the well-marked paths and see what you stumble upon. Despite optimistic titles such as "Laguna Grande" (Big Lake), the park is relatively small and it's easy to walk across the grounds in well under an hour. The info center provides tours to large groups and individuals are welcome to join, but most are in Spanish. The University also welcomes volunteers who are interested in working in the gardens. Call ahead for more information. *(Located directly south of the intersection of Hwy. 1 and Hwy. 3. From San Juan drive south on Ave. Ponce de León to the end and follow signs. If you miss the sign (which can be hard to see) make a U-turn and look for the sign heading north on Hwy. 1. To reach the tourist office enter the park and veer uphill to the left just before the "Jardín Botánico" fountain sign. ☎767-1710 or 250-0000 ext. 6578. Gardens open daily 6am-6pm. Info center open M-F 8am-4pm. Tours M-F 8, 10am, 1pm; $25 for a group of up to 30. Admission free.)*

UNIVERSIDAD DE PUERTO RICO. The largest university in Puerto Rico occupies an attractive campus in the heart of Río Piedras. Anyone who has chosen to wander the streets of Río Piedras will appreciate the serenity of this tree-filled area, but the campus holds a number of interesting attractions in addition to its landscape. The **Museo de Arte, Historia, y Antropología** (Museum of Art, History, and Anthropology) was under construction at the time of publication, but it still managed to squeeze a sampling of its collection into two small temporary rooms. The anthropology component has been reduced to a few Egyptian mummies, but the art section still has room for Francisco Oller's large painting, *El Velorio*. *(Enter the University's main entrance, go to the top of the circular driveway, and turn left. ☎764-0000 ext. 5852 or 2452. Open M-F 9am-4:30pm, Sa-Su 9am-3pm. Free.)* UPR's largest theater is also under construction, but the drama department has relocated many performances to the small **Teatro Julia de Borgos.** During the school year (Sept.-May), this theater hosts faculty performances and fourth-year pre-graduation productions, both of which are open to the public. Call for more information about current shows. *(From the entrance, pass through the main building, then continue through the quadrangle patio, and look for the theater building on the right. ☎764-0000 ext. 2085 or 2089. Department of Cultural Activities ☎764-0000 ext. 2563 or 5608. Shows free-$35.)* Most of the University buildings are open for the public to wander around. The building directly opposite the main entrance on Ave. Ponce de León has a handsome seal dedicated to the American Republics for the Advancement of Learning. Facing the museum, turn right and head up the slight hill to **Biblioteca José M. Lázaro.** Anyone is welcome to explore the two floors and check out the books from the various collections. *(Entrance in back. Bring ID to check out books. Open M-Th 7am-8pm, F 7am-5pm, Sa 8am-6pm.)* Continue along the same road to the **Centro Universitario** (the student center) where students gather to eat and hang out. A food court in the basement serves several varieties of fast food. On the first floor, to the right, through the sliding glass door, the **Office of Cultural Activities** provides information about concerts, movies, and cultural events on campus. *(At the intersection of Ave. Ponce de León and C. Universidad. Buses A3, A52, B4, B28, B29, C18, C31, and M1 pass in front. ☎764-1000.)*

LUIS MUÑOZ MARÍN FOUNDATION. If one figure stands out in Puerto Rican history, it has to be Luis Muñoz Marín, the island's first elected governor and the founder of the Partido Popular Democrático (p. 19). Thus it's not surprising that there's an entire foundation dedicated to studying Muñoz Marín and preserving the great man's legacy. In addition to providing ample fodder for academics, the Foundation also maintains the grounds and contents of the ex-governor's house and opens them to the public. Today visitors are welcome to come and explore; the house is closed, but anyone can peek through the windows at the furniture, decorations, and documents that remain intact within. Muñoz Marín occupied the house with his second wife, Inés Muñoz Marín, from 1946-48 and 1964-80 (from 1948 to 1964 he lived in La Fortaleza). Two buildings out front hold Muñoz Marín's preserved office and a small gift shop. Car lovers will enjoy the garage, which contains

Muñoz Marín's personal 1942 Packard, originally owned by US president Franklin D. Roosevelt. For true Muñoz Marín fanatics, this foundation also shows a 35min. video (in Spanish) about the man's life. *(Rte. 877 km 0.4. From San Juan take Hwy. 3 east, turn right onto Rte. 181, take the first left at the light, then a quick right; the house is on the left.* ☎ *755-4506; www.munoz-marin.org. All info is in Spanish. Open M-F 8:30am-4:30pm. Free Spanish tours if you come when no group is visiting. $2, under 12 and over 60 $1.)*

PARQUE LUIS MUÑOZ MARÍN. Situated on the border between Hato Rey and Río Piedras, Parque Luis Muñoz Marín offers an oasis of green amidst the sea of concrete. This sizable park has fallen into a bit of disrepair over the last few years, but it's still a great place to take a bike ride on a weekend afternoon. In addition to the large grassy fields, the park has playground equipment, picnic tables, concrete **bike paths,** and bike rental service. On weekends and holidays, or whenever the park is sufficiently crowded, a **train** and a **funicular** tour the grassy expanse. *(Located south of Estadio Hiram Bithorn and west of Expreso las Américas. Enter on Ave. Jesus Piñero. It is difficult to get to the park on foot—be prepared to walk along the edge of a busy 10-lane road. Bus B28 passes in front.* ☎ *721-6121 or 763-0613 ext. 2247 or 2274. Funicular $2, ages 3-10 $1, over 75 free. Train $1. Bike rental $2.50 per hr., depending on model. Parking $2. Open W-Su 8am-5pm. Free.)*

🏛 MUSEUMS

OLD SAN JUAN

Old San Juan is easily the cultural capital of Puerto Rico. In addition to the numerous museums listed below, many streets, especially C. del Cristo, are teeming with local art galleries. Your best bet is to wander around and explore, especially during the Gallery Nights Festival (see p. 138). Most museums close on Mondays.

■ MUSEO DE LAS AMÉRICAS. Unlike most Old San Juan exhibits, this well-maintained museum extends beyond Puerto Rico and focuses on arts throughout the Americas in its two permanent and several temporary exhibits. The highlight of the 40,000 sq. ft. museum is a permanent exhibit on folk arts and handicrafts in the western hemisphere, including tools, clothes, musical instruments, and masks. A model of a Puerto Rican country home, a full Mexican Day of the Dead altar, and a video presentation enhance the display. The hodgepodge of items exemplifies the similarities and differences between the countries grouped together as Latin America. A second permanent exhibit on the western hemisphere's African heritage has captions only in Spanish, but the handcuffs and photos speak for themselves. The building itself is a display, as it was built in the 19th century and over the years has served as military barracks and hospitals. *(On Cuartel Ballajá, off C. Norazaray, in the large green and yellow building. Enter the large courtyard and take any staircase to the 2nd fl.* ☎ *724-5052; www.prtc.net/~musame. Open Tu-Su 10am-4pm. Free.)*

■ MUSEO NUESTRA RAÍZ AFRICANA. In a noticeable effort to recognize Puerto Rico's diverse cultural heritage, the government recently open the Museum of Our African Race to commemorate the history of Africans on the island. Starting with a description of African tribes, the museum progresses through the history of blacks with a series of photos and artifacts, including real handcuffs and collars. Peak inside the green swinging doors for an eerily realistic presentation of life on a slave ship. But the display transcends the oppressive history of slavery to commemorate African contributions to Puerto Rican culture through displays on masks and music. *(On Plaza San José.* ☎ *724-4294 or 724-4184; http://icp.gobierno.pr. Spanish signs only. Open Tu-Sa 9am-5pm. $2, ages 4-12 or 60 and over $1, under 3 free.*

MUSEO DEL NIÑO. If the child inside of you is still alive and well, then you're sure to enjoy San Juan's fabulous, newly remodeled children's museum. The carefully thought-out museum has been designed to simultaneously educate and entertain the young and the young at heart. Friendly, informative tour guides lead groups or individuals through the eclectic assortment of displays, ranging from a giant ear in the health room (teaching children how to clean their ears) to a replica of a Puerto Rican town center (educating about Puerto Rican heritage) to a fully intact front half of a car (teaching about car safety and wearing a seat belt). More interactive rooms allow children to make crafts out of recycled materials, draw self-portraits, and do wood construction. During weekday mornings the staff is frequently busy with large school groups, so it is best to visit in the afternoon or on weekends. The museum also hosts special events on weekend afternoons; stop by for a three month calendar. *(C. del Cristo 150. ☎ 722-3791; www.museodelninopr.org. Open Tu-Th 9am-3:30pm, F 9am-5pm, Sa-Su 12:30-5pm. $1 additional cost to use recycled products construction room. Free English/Spanish guided tours. $4, under 15 $5. AmEx/MC/V.)*

MUSEO DE SAN JUAN. Everything you ever wanted to know about San Juan is explained in this museum of immense proportions. Formerly known as the Museo de Arte e Historia de San Juan, the name was shortened in 2000 when the museum reopened with the first permanent exhibition devoted exclusively to the city. The main room presents the history of San Juan through floor-to-ceiling displays, interactive computer monitors, and videos. The display in the second room changes regularly, but always focuses on some aspect of the capital. There are no English captions, but this is a worthy stop for Spanish-speakers interested in San Juan's history. *(C. Norzagaray 150. ☎ 723-4317 or 724-1875. Open Tu-F 9am-4pm, Sa-Su 10am-4pm. Free. Suggested donation $1, foreigners $1.50, students and seniors $0.75, children $0.50.)*

MUSEO CASA BLANCA. The White House Museum was originally constructed in 1521 as the home of the first Spanish governor of Puerto Rico, **Juan Ponce de León.** Unfortunately, a hurricane soon leveled the wooden edifice. Thus in 1523 the Spaniards reconstructed the house as the first building made of stone on the island. Ironically, Ponce de León never actually lived here, as he was off searching for the Fountain of Youth, but the house remained in his family's possession for the next 250 years. Casa Blanca also served as one of the few safe havens when invaders attacked the city, and in 1898 it became the home of the Commander of the US Army in Puerto Rico. Today the house has been redecorated in 16th-century style in honor of Ponce de León. The interior only holds some old furniture, but the gardens out back are a beautiful place to rest on a hot day. *(C. San Sebastian 1. From C. Norzagaray, turn down C. del Morro, pass Parque Beneficio, and enter the small gate on your right. ☎ 725-1454. Open Tu-Sa 9am-noon and 1-4pm. $2, under 12 and over 65 $1.)*

CASA DON Q PUERTO RICO. Although not quite as famous internationally as Bacardi, Don Q rum still has quite a presence in Puerto Rico; it is the best-selling rum on the island. This small museum explains the history of the rum, from its creation in 1865 by Don Juan Serrallés to the current distilling process. While the historical information is nicely displayed with photos and English/Spanish captions, the highlight of the museum undoubtedly comes at the end with the **free sample** of a Don Q rum drink. *(On C. la Marina, across from Pier One. ☎ 977-1721. Open Oct. 25-April 30 F-Su 9am-6pm, M-W 11am-8pm; May 1-Oct. 24 M-F 9am-6pm. Free.)*

CASA DE DON RAMÓN POWER Y GIRALT. In the 18th century this building housed Don Ramón Power y Giralt (1775-1813), an important Puerto Rican social reformer who served as Puerto Rico's representative to the Spanish Courts. Today, this museum has absolutely nothing to do with Don Ramón and instead contains the office and museum of the **Conservation Trust of Puerto Rico,** an organization dedicated to preserving the island's natural resources. Their permanent exhibition, **Ojo Isla,** uses a variety of media and interactive exhibits to explain Puerto Rico's current environmental situation. Watch out for the live colony of honeybees. *(C. Tetuan 155. ☎ 722-5834. Open Tu-Sa 9am-5pm. Free.)*

CASA DE LA FAMILIA PUERTORRIQUÑA DEL SIGLO XIX AND MUSEO DE FARMACIA. This two-story museum illuminates various aspects of life in historic San Juan through two relatively small displays. Downstairs, the Pharmacy Museum contains a pharmacy counter and various artifacts from the first pharmacy in the nearby town of Cayey. The tour guide may remind you that the first pharmacy in the Americas was built in Puerto Rico in 1512 (this is not it). Upstairs, the Museum of the 19th-Century Puerto Rican family contains furniture from the 1870s. The rooms are purposely connected to replicate the tradition of that era—old wives' tales state that mothers liked to have connected rooms so that they could always keep an eye on their children. Check out the chair with the hole in it—this served as the bathroom on nights when the outhouse was just too far away. The museum merits a quick visit, although there are few captions and the rooms are sparsely decorated. *(C. Fortaleza 319. ☎ 977-2700. Open Tu-Sa 9am-noon and 1-4pm. Spanish tour sometimes included. Free.)*

ANTIGUO ARSENAL DE LA MARINA ESPAÑOLA (EL ARSENAL). This surprisingly spacious modern art museum has three rooms of rotating displays. Exhibits vary, but generally focus on contemporary art in any media. Every two years El Arsenal hosts the Bienal International De Fotografía de Puerto Rico, a Caribbean-wide photography competition. The next competition will be displayed in 2004. *(On C. la Puntilla. At the end of Paseo la Princesa turn right on C. Puntilla, then turn left immediately after the pink customs house. Walk to the center courtyard and enter on the right. ☎ 724-5932 or 723-3068. Open Tu-F 10am-1pm and 2-5pm, Sa-Su noon-5pm.)*

MUSEO FELISA RINCÓN DE GAUTIER. This small museum is dedicated entirely to preserving the memory of an extraordinary woman who devoted her life to establishing the rights of Puerto Rican women and improving the lives of the poor. Felisa Rincón de Gautier (1897-1994) entered politics early and after helping to found the Partido Popular Democrático (PPD) in 1938, she served as the mayor of San Juan from 1946 to 1969. Rincón was the first female mayor of a major city in the Western Hemisphere. The museum celebrates Rincón's accomplishments by displaying many of her honors and medals, including 11 honorary degrees from Puerto Rican and American universities and a Certificate of Appreciation from the US Army. Rincón's personal life is portrayed through dresses, fans, and photos with countless foreign dignitaries, including Lyndon B. Johnson and Eleanor Roosevelt. *(Caleta de San Juan 51. ☎ 723-1897. Open M-F 9am-4pm. Free.)*

MUSEO PABLO CASALS. Music lovers will appreciate this tiny museum devoted to Pablo Casals (1876-1973), one of Puerto Rico's most famous musicians (see p. 28). Casals was born in Spain, but he moved to his mother's home of Puerto Rico at an early age. Here he played a role in the founding of the Puerto Rico Symphony Orchestra, the Casals Music Festival, and the Conservatory of Music. However, one step into the museum will remind you where Casals's musical interests began—with his cello. The museum doesn't contain much more than some photos and Casals's numerous diplomas, but the music room upstairs playing recordings of Casals's performances is a pleasant place to relax. *(C. San Sebastian 101. On Plaza San José. ☎ 723-9185. Open Tu-Sa 9:30am-5pm. $1, under 12 and over 60 $0.50.)*

THE BUTTERFLY PEOPLE. For the last 32 years The Butterfly People have been accumulating butterflies from around the world and artistically assembling them into display cases designed to prevent oxidation. Now in its second generation, this small gallery/shop displays these unique creations in a cheerful setting. *(C. Cruz 257. ☎ 723-2432. Open M-Sa 10am-6pm. Free.)*

CASA DEL LIBRO. This small museum holds a collection of about 5000 historical books, mostly about the graphic arts. The management boasts that the collection includes over 200 Spanish books written before 1501, the fourth largest collection of books of this type in the western hemisphere. If that doesn't excite you, then this museum probably won't be of much interest. A small gift shop helps support the museum. *(C. del Cristo 255. On the left through the unmarked door. ☎ 723-0354; www.lacasadellibro.org. Open Tu-Sa 11am-4:30pm. Free.)*

INSTITUTO DE CULTURA PUERTORRIQUEÑA. In addition to sponsoring almost every museum in Old San Juan, the Puerto Rican Institute of Culture also houses a small gallery of work by local artists in its central courtyard. Located in the Casa de Beneficencia, which opened in 1848 as a poorhouse, the Institute also provides information about cultural events, art shows, plays, and concerts. *(On Paseo del Morro, near the intersection with C. Norzagaray. ☎ 724-0700; http://icp.gobierno.pr. Open Tu-Su 9am-4pm; sometimes closes for lunch. Exhibit and most events free.)*

CONVENTO DE LOS DOMINICOS. First constructed in 1523 as a convent by Fray Antonio de Montesinos, this building has seen a wide range of inhabitants. From the 16th to the early 19th century, the convent functioned as a nucleus of university studies for many wealthy Puerto Rican families. In 1835 it was converted into a military quarters, housing first the Spanish and then the American armies. Then in 1968 the building was donated to the Puerto Rican government and became an annex of the Puerto Rican Institute of Culture. Depending upon the time of year, the convent may have a few exhibits open to the public. The **Lucy Boscana Theater** puts on a variety of shows, some of which are free, and an exhibition room hosts temporary art shows. *(C. Norzagaray 98. ☎ 721-6866. Open M-F 9am-5pm, Sa 9am-noon and 1-5pm. Free. Theater prices vary.)*

ESCUELA DE ARTES PLÁSTICAS. The large white building across from El Morro houses one of the largest fine arts schools in Puerto Rico. Originally constructed as a mental hospital in 1861, the building was used to shelter soldiers wounded in the 1863 war in the Dominican Republic before construction had even finished. In 1898 it became the US army headquarters in San Juan until 1976 when the Americans finally allowed it to be used as a school. Today visitors can wander in the courtyard and watch students work or head back to the small gallery of student art. A small food kiosk in the courtyard serves sandwiches ($2-3) and Puerto Rican entrees. *(On C. Norzagaray, across from El Morro. ☎ 725-8120. Open M-Sa 8am-5pm. Free.)*

PUERTA DE TIERRA

MUSEO MILITAR GUARDIA NACIONAL DE PUERTO RICO. Hidden amidst the government buildings on Puerta de Tierra, the Puerto Rico National Guard Museum presents a surprisingly interesting history of 20th-century American wars. Upstairs a large room focuses on American participation in WWII. Another room highlights the participation of the Puerto Rican Air National Guard in the various wars. Even those who have no military interest may enjoy comparing the uniforms of different armies (German, Japanese, and American World War Two uniforms look remarkably similar) or looking at newspaper clippings announcing the various conflicts. All captions are in English and Spanish except, interestingly enough, the explanations of the Spanish-American war. *(On C. General Esteves. From Old San Juan walk down Ave. Luis Muñoz Rivera; the museum is on your right about 5min. after the capital building. ☎ 289-1675. Open Tu-Sa 8:30am-noon and 1-3:30pm. Free.)*

SANTURCE

■**MUSEO DE ARTE DE PUERTO RICO.** It may be an exaggeration to say that Puerto Rico's newest and largest art museum is comparable with the great European museums, but in terms of quality of display, presentation, and facilities, it certainly does not lag far behind. The 13,000 sq. ft. Museum of Art, which stages a comprehensive display of Puerto Rican art from pre-colonial times to the present, is a must-see for anyone interested in the island's culture, and fortunately all exhibits are described in English and Spanish.

Government leaders first conceptualized the museum in 1995 when they saw that San Juan lacked one central location to display major artwork and decided to do something about it. With a $55.2 million donation from the Government Development Bank, the plan became a reality and construction began in 1997. Museum designers received enough support from both the private and public sector that they were able to create a comprehensive facility for the largest collection of Puerto Rican art in the world.

The third floor contains the bulk of the permanent collection, a chronological display of Puerto Rican art. The North Wing starts with a display of pre-colonial and colonial art from throughout Latin America, then later becomes exclusively Puerto Rican. A large section devoted to **José Campeche** contains his famous work *Las Hijas del Gobernador don Ramón de Castro* (The Children of the Governor don Ramón de Castro). Just past a collection of santos, the museum houses a few works by **Francisco Oller,** one of the first major artists to focus explicitly on Puerto Rican images. The South Wing moves into 20th-century art and introduces a few different media. One of the first exhibits explains the Puerto Rican poster art of the mid-20th century and displays several works by **Irene Delano** and **Rafael Tufiño.** The fourth floor houses a display of Puerto Rican art since 1970, including photography, ceramics, installation art, and works in a variety of other media that are arranged thematically rather than chronologically. An interesting exhibit at the end is devoted to limited edition xylography that was created for the museum.

The structure that houses the museum is itself a piece of art. The building on Ave. Ponce de León was originally constructed as the Santurce surgical hospital, but by 1995 it had long been abandoned. Developers renovated the Neoclassical facade of the two story structure, then creatively added a five story extension in back to hold temporary exhibits and administrative offices. In an effort to broaden the museum's appeal, creators added a number of distinguishing features. Behind the museum a five acre **sculpture garden** houses countless sculptures, beautiful flora, and a large screen for special events. The first floor **education center** provides child and adult classes and holds a rotating exhibit of local student work. Any child will love the **Family Gallery,** a large room that contains computer programs, a painting station, and games for visitors to create their own artwork. Finally, the museum's **400-seat theater** hosts regular events, including orchestra concerts, dance performances, and plays. The theater curtain is created out of the world's largest piece of **mundillo** lace, commissioned exclusively for the museum. Check the museum calendar or the web site for more information. *(Ave. de Diego 299. Buses A5 and B21 stop. From Ave. Ashford, walk or drive down C. del Parque which turns into de Diego. ☎ 977-6777 ext. 2230; www.mapr.org. Open Tu and Th-Sa 10am-5pm, W 10am-8pm, Su 11am-6pm. $5, students and under 12 $3, ages 60-74 $2.50, over 75 free.)*

MUSEO DE ARTE CONTEMPORÁNEO DE PUERTO RICO. Before the Museo de Arte was built down the street, the Contemporary Art Museum was San Juan's premier gallery for contemporary art. Although the museum pales in comparison to its larger neighbor, it still holds an impressive collection in top-of-the-line facilities. The captions are in Spanish, but it is not difficult to grasp the meanings of the works, many of which make strong political statements. Most of the pieces are by local Puerto Rican artists, but artists from other Latin American countries are mixed in as well. The back of the museum hosts a series of rotating exhibits. *(In the Edificio Barat on the campus of the Universidad del Sagrada Corazón. From Ave. Ponce de León, turn north on C. Rosale and enter the university campus at the end of the street. The museum is on the second floor of the large blue building on the left. ☎ 727-5249; www.museocontemporane-opr.org. Open M-F 8am-noon and 1-5pm, Sa 9am-noon and 1-5pm. Free.)*

🏖 BEACHES

As a general rule, the beaches get better as you go farther east. Few beaches in the San Juan area have amenities or public bathrooms. **Do not swim near Old San Juan**—although small sandy beaches do appear during low tide, the bay is quite polluted.

PUERTA DE TIERRA

Encompassing Parque Escobar, Estadio Sixto Escobar, and Balneario Escombron, the extensive **Parque del Tercer Milenio** has something for everyone, including the closest beach to Old San Juan—several roped-off swimming areas with calm shallow water. When the waves are right, surfers are drawn to the offshore reefs in this area. A reef about 15 ft. offshore makes for some easy **snorkeling,** especially in the morning before crowds arrive. The eastern beaches tend to be nicer than the western beaches, which progressively have less and less sand area. Parque del Tercer Milenio has many amenities, including **lifeguards, restrooms, snack bars, trash cans and signs identifying the current water quality.** The park also includes several picnic tables, a well-lit walkway, a bit of grass, a playground, and a large parking lot. (At the western end of Puerta de Tierra, near Ave. Muñoz Rivera. Parking $3.)

CONDADO

Almost every perpendicular street in Condado ends at the beach, which is fairly empty on weekdays and crowded on weekends. While this is far from being the nicest beach on the island, it is clean and the location is unbeatable. Because this is the city's gay district, many gay men frequent the beaches around the end of C. Condado. The official public beach, **Balneario Playa de Condado,** is located at the far western edge of Condado near the bridge to Puerta de Tierra. A line of rocks protects the bay here, creating a lagoon of shallow, wave-free water. The beach also has lifeguards (daily 8:30am-5pm), outdoor showers, and beach chairs (Th-Tu $4 per day). Be forewarned—there are few public bathrooms in the area and many restaurants along Ave. Ashford only let customers use their facilities.

OCEAN PARK

Condado may have the reputation, but Ocean Park can deliver. The shores of this posh suburb boast nicer sand, less trash, and better waves for swimming. The downside is that many people have already discovered Ocean Park's great beaches, and thus they can get quite crowded on weekends and holidays, especially with Puerto Rican teenagers who like to play loud music.

ISLA VERDE

Isla Verde has the best beaches in San Juan. Although it is hard to access the western beaches, a few tiny paths squeeze between the row of condominiums. The eastern side of Isla Verde has long, beautiful beaches occupied mostly by older hotel guests. Near the San Juan Hotel, **Edwin's Easy Chairs** rents to the plebeians for $3 a day. Directly in front of the hotel, **Archie Jet Ski Rental** rents jet skis (singles $50 for 30min., doubles $60). The far eastern edge, in front of the airport and the Ritz Carlton, is farther away from the amenities and shops, but consequently has fewer people, smoother sand, and a more picturesque landscape.

BALNEARIO DE CAROLINA

San Juan's best public beach actually lies beyond Isla Verde in the city of Carolina. On weekends this enormous *balneario* is packed with Puerto Ricans who want to enjoy the long stretch of white sand and crashing waves. But come on a weekday, and the beach is one of the least crowded in the metro area. Facilities include covered benches, a playground, bathrooms, fire pits, vendors, trash cans, and life guards. (Rte. 187, about 1 mi. past Isla Verde. ☎791-2410. May-Sept. open daily 8am-6pm. Oct.-Apr. open Tu-Su 8:30am-5pm. Cars $3, vans $4.)

⚓ OUTDOOR ACTIVITIES

WATER SPORTS
DIVING AND SNORKELING

Ocean Sports, Ave. Ashford 1035 (☎ 723-8513 or 268-2329; www.osdivers.com), Condado, specializes in advanced diving but handles all sorts of water sports equipment rental and lessons. Snorkeling gear rental half-day $20, full-day $30. Kayak rental $20/$40. Boogie boards $10/$15. Half-day diving trips in San Juan $75-95; full-day trips to the Fajardo area $95-110; half-day shore dives $65-75. Once a month they lead trips to more exotic dive sites, such as Isla Mona, La Parguera, or St. Thomas (2-tank dive $100, equipment $25). 4-day NAUI/SSI certification course $350. Ocean Sports also offers rebreather dives, Nitrox and advanced Nitrox drives, and Normoxic Trimix diver training. Open M-Sa 10am-7pm. D/MC/V. Additional locations include Ave. Isla Verde 77 (☎ 268-2331). Open M-Sa 9am-6pm. Isla Verde Mall, Suite 219 (☎ 791-3483). Open Tu-F 11am-6pm, Sa 11am-4pm.

La Casa del Buzo, Ave. Jesus Piñero 293 (☎ 758-2710; fax 753-3528; www.lacasadelbuzo.com), Río Piedras. Possibly the cheapest PADI certification courses in San Juan. 4-week course includes evening classroom instruction twice a week, and 4 weekend dives ($150 per person). Open M-Sa 9am-6pm. AmEx/MC/V.

Scuba Dogs, C. 5 #D-4, Prado Alto (☎ 783-6377 or 399-5755; scubadogs@yunque.net), Guaynabo, offers open-water certification (group course $250 including equipment, advanced certification $300) and all specialties. Excursions go to dive sites around the island ($150-200 including lunch and equipment). In Sept. they organize a huge beach clean-up. Call ahead. Cash only.

Caribe Aquatic Adventures, Ave. Muñoz Rivera 499 (☎ 281-8858; www.diveguide.com/p2046.htm), in the Radisson Normandie, Puerta de Tierra, leads shore dives from the beaches behind the hotel that go to a max. depth of 30 ft. ($50). More advanced divers make the full-day trip to Isla Palominita, off Fajardo (1 dive $115, 2 dives $135; snorkelers $85). 40hr. certification course $465. Open W-Su 9am-5pm. MC/V.

SURFING, SAILING, AND WINDSURFING

Reefs lining the coast of San Juan create several good surfing spots, and any surfboard rental company listed below can provide the full scoop. Many people surf off Parque del Tercer Milenio, in Puerta de Tierra, but local surf shops recommend that beginners head to Pine Grove, near the Ritz Carlton in Isla Verde.

Wave Rider, Ave. Muñoz Rivera 51 (☎ 722-7103), Puerta de Tierra, near the Hilton, rents long boards ($30 per 24hr.) and short boards ($25). Open M-Sa 10am-6pm, Su 10am-3pm.

Tres Palmas, C. McLeary 1911 (☎ 728-3377), Ocean Park, rents long boards ($35 per 24hr.) and foam boards ($25). Open M-F 10am-6pm, Sa 10am-7pm, Su 11am-5pm. AmEx/D/MC/V.

Beach Cats, C. Loíza 2434 (☎ 727-0883), Punta Las Marías, teaches catamaran sailing lessons ($450 per 8hr., including all equipment). They also sell kayaks, windsurfers, Hobie Cats, sunfish, and surfboards, as well as repair surfboards. Open M-Sa 10am-6pm. During high season also open Su.

Velauno, C. Loíza 2430 (☎ 728-8716), Punta Las Marías, rents surfboards ($35 for the first day, $25 per additional day; $120 per week) and windsurfers ($75 per day, $225 per week). They also teach classes in windsurfing ($150 for a 4hr. beginning class), kite surfing ($100 per class for a series of three 2hr. classes), and surfing ($50 per hr.). Open M noon-7pm, Tu-Sa 11am-7pm. On Su they operate on the beach. MC/V.

SAN JUAN

FISHING

Mike Benítez Marine Services, Ave. Fernández Juncos 480 (☎ 723-2292 or 724-6265; fax 725-4344), in the Club Naútico, sends a 45" air conditioned boat on daily deep-sea fishing trips. In winter fish for mahi mahi, sailfish, and tuna; in summer, blue marlin. Half-day $150 per person. Private charter for up to 6 people, half-day $490, full-day $850. All equipment and sodas included. Open daily 7:30am-6pm. AmEx/MC/V.

DRY LAND ADVENTURES

Adventuras Tierra Adentro, Ave. Jesus Piñero 268A (☎ 766-0470), Río Piedras, specializes in rock climbing and repelling in the Río Camuy caves (see p. 166). Experienced guides lead full-day trips to Río Tanamá and Angeles Cave, and a child-friendly trip to Yuyu Cave. No experience necessary—all expeditions begin with a short lesson. $150 per person includes all supplies except food. Open Tu-Sa 10am-6pm. AmEx/MC/V.

🎭 ENTERTAINMENT

CASINOS

Gambling is a popular activity in San Juan, but unless you stick to the five cent slot machines it can quickly eat up your budget. Almost all of the large chain hotels have sizable casinos. For a night of betting, hit up the glamorous row in **Isla Verde**—the Wyndhman El San Juan, the InterContinental, the Embassy Suites, and the Ritz Carlton all have impressive casinos. On Ave. Ashford in **Condado** the Radisson Ambassador Plaza and the San Juan Marriott provide places to bet. The Condado Plaza Hotel casino has nightly live music. Old San Juan's only place to gamble is the **Wyndham Old San Juan,** by the piers. Remember to dress the part (rich, elegant tourist) or bouncers may stop you at the door.

CINEMA

Most of the movie theaters are located away from the primary tourist districts. **Metro,** Ave. Ponce de León 1255, Santurce, runs three American films. (☎ 721-5903. $5, under 10 $3.50.) Plaza las Américas (see **Shopping,** p. 139) has two large movie theaters. On the third floor, **Plaza Theaters** is the cheaper of the two. (☎ 758-3929. Nine movies with Spanish subtitles. $5.50, children and seniors $3.50. MC/V.) One floor down, **Caribbean Cinemas** has a slightly larger selection. (☎ 767-4775. 11 movies with Spanish subtitles. $6, ages 2-10 $3.50, seniors $4.) The **Fine Arts Cinema,** Ave. Ponce de León 654, shows three foreign films in English or with English subtitles. (☎ 721-4288. $5, children $3.50, ages 60 and over $4, student discount with ID.)

PARTICIPATORY SPORTS

San Juan's premier outdoor sports area, **Parque Central,** has exceptional sports facilities. The large well-manicured park holds 22 **tennis courts,** four **racquetball** courts, a **playground,** several large fields, **basketball hoops,** a well-lit **stadium,** a series of **jogging** paths, a **track,** a cafeteria, public restrooms, and telephones. Covered benches provide a shady place for parents to sit while their children play. Parque Central is open to the public, but it is almost impossible to reach without a car. It can also be quite busy on evenings and weekends when San Juan families head out after work, so if you want to play tennis during these peak hours it's best to stop by in the morning and reserve a court (in person; telephone reservations not accepted). The tennis shop sometimes offers free beginning tennis lessons—all you need to bring is a new set of tennis balls. Call ahead for more information. (☎ 722-1646. In Santurce. Drive south on C. Roberto H. Todd until it turns into a freeway, then look for signs. Or from Puerta de Tierra take Hwy. 1 south to the Parque Central exit. Open M-Th 6am-10pm, F 6am-9pm, Sa-Su and holidays 6am-7pm. Parking $1. Tennis courts $3, after 6pm $4. Racquetball courts $8 per hr.)

Parque Barbosa, next to Ocean Park, also offers a plethora of athletic facilities. Named after notable politician José Celso Barbosa (1857-1921), the park includes basketball courts, soccer fields, a large track, baseball fields, a swing set, and several tennis courts. A 24hr. police station on the premises promises a safe experience. (Directly east of Ocean Park, next to the ocean. Police ☎726-7020. Free parking. Track lights on until 10pm.)

There are a few good areas for **running** in San Juan, if you can bear the heat. **Paseo de la Princesa,** along the western edge of Old San Juan (see p. 124) hosts several joggers around dusk when it finally cools down a bit. A nice track passes through Parque del Tercer Milenio (see p. 134).

SPECTATOR SPORTS

BASEBALL. Puerto Rico has an active professional baseball league, and most of the action takes place in San Juan. From the end of October until the beginning of January, the Santurce Cangrejeros play about three times per week at **Estadio Hiram Bithorn.** Tickets and schedules are available at the stadium box office on game days. (South of Ave. F.D. Roosevelt and west of Expreso Las Américas, across from Plaza las Américas. Enter from Ave. F.D. Roosevelt. ☎294-1480. Box office open from 9am on the day of the game. Most games 8pm, Su 4pm. $5-7, children $2.50. MC/V.)

BASKETBALL. During the month of May, professional basketball descends upon San Juan. For information and a schedule, contact the Coliseo Roberto Clemente (see **Theater and Music,** p. 137)

COCKFIGHTS. The **Club Gallistío,** at the intersection of Ave. Isla Verde and Ave. Los Gobernadores in Isla Verde, is the only touristic **cockfighting arena** in Puerto Rico. While this is a tourist attraction, it is also a working arena, complete with gambling and cocktail lounge. Before the fight, it is possible to go upstairs and check out the cocks, then bet by ribbon color. Each fight lasts 15min. and one session can include up to 40 fights. Come on Saturday for a truly rambunctious experience. Women are welcome, but they should wear pants and be prepared for a predominately male crowd. (Ave. Isla Verde 6600. ☎791-6005. $10, tourists $5, women free. Fights Tu 4pm, Sa 2:30pm, sometimes Th 2:30pm. Buy tickets at the door. Office open M-F 8:30am-3pm.)

THEATER AND MUSIC

San Juan's premier fine arts center, the **Centro de Bellas Artes Luis A. Ferré** in Santurce, created in 1981, holds a variety of different performances, from dance shows to symphony orchestra concerts to theater to stand-up comedy. The center has three theaters: the Antonio Paoli seats 2000 people, the Carlos Mavichal seats 240, and the René Marques seats 1000. Twice a month the Puerto Rican symphony orchestra performs here, and in January the majority of the **Casals Festival** (see **Festivals,** p. 138) is held here. For tickets, check **Ticketpop** online (see p. 98) or visit the box office. (On Ave. Ponce de León, west of the intersection with C. de Diego. ☎620-4444; www.cba.com.pr. Shows F-Su; $20-60, ages 60-74 50% off, ages 75 and over free. Wheelchair accessible. Ticket office open M-Th 10am-6pm, F-Su 10am-the show begins. MC/V.)

Teatro Tapia (see p. 125), on Plaza Colón in Old San Juan, has theater performances or musicals every weekend. Shows rotate every 2-3 weeks, but most are in Spanish. (☎721-0180 or 723-2079. Shows F-Su; $25-30. Ticket office hours vary. MC/V.) The small **Corralón de San Juan,** C. San José 109, Old San Juan, occasionally hosts student performances. The **Lucy Boscana Theater,** C. Norzagaray 98, in the Convento de los Dominicos, Old San Juan, also hosts performances. For information on both, contact the Instituto de Cultura (see p. 132).

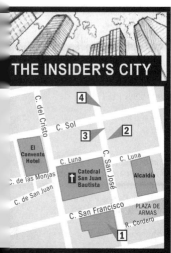

C. del Cristo
C. Sol
4
3   2
El Convento Hotel
C. Luna   C. Luna
C. de las Monjas   Catedral San Juan Bautista   C. San José   Alcaldía
C. de San Juan
C. San Francisco   PLAZA DE ARMAS
R. Cordero
1

GALLERY DAYS

On the first Tu of almost every month (see p. 138) Old San Juan hosts Gallery nights. Thousands come to check out the newest exhibits from 7-9pm, then head to C. San Sebastian for some post-premier partying. The walk below can be done either during the festival or during the day.

1 **Departamento de Estado,** on the Plaza de Armas. During Gallery Nights the Secretary of State himself makes a showing. (Open M-F 8am-noon and 1-4:30pm.)

2 **L'Enfant Galeria,** C. San José 107. Washington D.C. Native Anne Lane displays her San Juan-inspired paintings in this hip gallery. (Open Tu-Sa 10am-6pm, Su noon-5-pm.)

3 **Galeria Coabey,** C. San José 101. The modern art at this 2-floor gallery includes San Juan street scenes, as well as work by artists from around Latin America. (Open M-Sa 11:30am-4:30pm.)

4 **Mark Stuart Fine Art,** C. San José 57. For a change from Latin American art, check out this gallery that has mostly antique European art. (Open most days 11am-5pm.)

Many of the biggest acts touring the US also make a stop at San Juan's **Coliseo Roberto Clemente.** Over the last few years, the 10,000 seat theater has seen performances by Jennifer Lopez, the Backstreet Boys, and Luis Miguel, as well as events such as the Miss Universe Pageant, National Salsa Day, and Disney on Ice. To buy tickets or find information about coming events, check Ticket Center (see **Ticket Agencies,** p. 98), in Plaza las Américas or online. (Located in Hato Rey, south of Ave. F.D. Roosevelt, west of Expreso Las Américas. ☎754-7422. Parking $1, during events $2.) The **Universidad de Puerto Rico** (see p. 128), Río Piedras, hosts regular performances in its two theaters during the school year.

◘ FESTIVALS

San Juan hosts more festivals, and more outlandish festivals, than any other city on the island. Most are held in Old San Juan and the hordes of visitors can create horrendous traffic jams; take the bus or park on the eastern edge of town. Some of the largest events are listed below. For more information about any festival, or exact dates, contact the Puerto Rican Tourism Company (☎722-1709 or 724-4788).

GALLERY NIGHTS. Haute culture and hot culture mix at this monthly festival. The premise is that galleries stay open late to show new exhibitions and host special events. However, many young people skip the galleries and head straight to C. San Sebastian, which becomes an enormous street party lasting until the wee hours of the morning. Although the entire area is abuzz with energy, the Plaza de Armas, C. del Cristo, and Plaza San Sebastian tend to be the centers of activity. Many public buildings, including El Arsenal (p. 131) and the Museo de las Américas (p. 129), also host special exhibits for this event. See Gallery Days (p. 138) and Gallery Nights (p. 139) for itinerary suggestions. *(First Tu of the month Feb.-May and Aug.-Dec. Exhibitions 7-9pm. Old San Juan.)*

FESTIVAL DE LA CALLE SAN SEBASTIAN. By day this is one of the biggest *artesanía* festivals on the island, as hundreds of artisans exhibit their wares in the Cuartel de la Ballajá (the same building as the Museo de las Américas). As dark falls the government shuts down C. San Sebastian for an incredible party packing in thousands of drunken revelers. *(A full week in mid-Jan., though the party gets going on the weekend. Old San Juan.)*

FESTIVAL SAN JUAN BAUTISTA. San Juan's patron saint festival is the island's largest party, hands down. In addition to the traditional art, music, and food, this unusual festival includes bonfires and parties on the beach. To bring luck for the following year hundreds of *sanjuaneros* walk backwards into the ocean. *(The week preceding June 24. Old San Juan and Isla Verde.)*

BACARDI FERIA DE ARTESANÍA. The Bacardi Corporation hosts yet another enormous artisans festival. Every Dec. over 100,000 people venture out to Cataño to check out local arts and crafts, dance to live salsa and merengue, and, of course, sample their favorite rum. The drinks aren't free, but all proceeds go to charity. *(First two weekends in Dec. Bacardi Factory (p. 145), Cataño.)*

CINEMAFEST DE PUERTO RICO. This internationally renowned film festival draws producers, directors, and actors from around the world; however, only films relating to the Caribbean are allowed to compete for prizes. Over 100 films are shown. *(Held over one week in Nov. Screenings at various locations around the island, but primarily in San Juan.)*

HEINEKEN JAZZ FESTIVAL. Heineken hosts Puerto Rico's largest jazz festival, which draws acts such as Manhattan Transfer and Eddie Palmieri. The event focuses on Latin jazz, but includes musicians from all over the world to play under the Caribbean stars. *(Th-Su in May or June. www.prheinekenjazz.com. 1-day ticket $23, 4-day tickets $65; available from Ticketpop (p. 98). Parque Sixto Escobar (p. 134), Puerta de Tierra.)*

CASALS FESTIVAL. Created by Spanish composer Pablo Casals (see p. 28), this two-week festival consists of a series of classical music performances by the Puerto Rican Symphony Orchestra and visiting musicians. *(Dates vary: in 2004 the festival was held Feb. 28-March 13. ☎721-7727; www.festcasalspr.gobierno.pr. In the Centro de Bellas Artes Luis A. Ferré (see p. 137), Santurce.)*

LELOLAI FESTIVAL. This continual event is less of a festival and more of a series of shows and performances, including salsa lessons, tropical music, and rumba performances, designed by the Puerto Rican Tourism Company to highlight Puerto Rico's multicultural heritage. Some of the events are free, but others require the "Puerto Rico is Fun" card, available for purchase at over 50 island hotels. *(6 nights per week. ☎800-866-7827 or 723-3136; lelolai@prtourism.com. Primarily in San Juan, but shows held throughout the island.)*

❒ SHOPPING

For a truly Latin American shopping experience, head to **Paseo de Diego** in Río Piedras (see p. 127). The stores lining the street sell everything from women's clothes to stationery to vegetables, typically at very reasonable prices.

Old San Juan is a great place to shop for hokey Puerto Rican souvenirs, some quality artwork, and expensive jewelry. It's also a great place to wander,

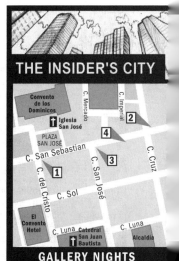

THE INSIDER'S CITY

GALLERY NIGHTS

Perusing fine art is just fine, but when it comes right down to it, many *sanjuaneros* come to Gallery Nights just for the pub crawl along C. San Sebastian. Although the party is especially hopping on Gallery Nights, this "walk" (re: stumble) can be done any night of the week. For complete information see Nightlife, p. 140.

1 **Nono's,** C. San Sebastian 107. The bartender here brags about his heavy hitting mixed drinks; always a good way to start out the night. (Open daily noon-4am.)

2 **Cafe San Sebastian,** San Sebastian 153. Live music and friendly staff provide excellent background to enjoy a nice cool one. (Open Th-Sa 8pm-people leave.)

3 **Cafe Hijos de Borinquen,** C. San José 51. Brave the crowds and find a dance partner for the next stop. (Open Th-Sa 8pm-last person leaves.)

4 **Rumba,** C. San Sebastian 109. There's no better place to end the night than Old San Juan's most popular bar. Salsa the night away. (Open Tu-Su 8pm-3am.)

and purchases frequently ensue. C. Fortaleza has an abundance of souvenir and clothing shops, while C. San Francisco has many jewelry shops. C. del Cristo is the best place to find original (and expensive) Puerto Rican modern art. In **Condado,** Puerto Rican Handmade Crafts and Masks Center, Ave. Ashford 1035, has a large collection of *vejigante* masks ($25-125), as well as other souvenirs made by the shop owners. (☎724-3840. Open M-Sa 9:30am-9pm, Su 9:30am-6pm. AmEx/MC/V.)

More generic shopping awaits in Hato Rey, home of **Plaza las Américas,** the largest shopping mall in the Caribbean. This three-story consumer extravaganza has over 300 stores, two movie theaters, a food court, a ticket center, a fountain, and everything else you could want in a mall. (Ave. F.D. Roosevelt 525. ☎767-5202. In Hato Rey. Take Las Américas Expressway to the Roosevelt Ave. exit. Bus B21 circumnavigates the mall. Open M-Sa 9am-9pm, Su 11am-5pm.)

NIGHTLIFE

Check out local publications Agenda (www.agendanoctambulo.com) and Mangrove (www.mangrovepr.com) for more information on the latest nightlife happenings (see **Publications,** p. 98).

NIGHTCLUB SECURITY Many San Juan nightclubs have tighter security than the airport. To save time and hassles, do not bring pocket knives, pens, or any potentially hazardous object when you go out, and prepare to be frisked.

OLD SAN JUAN

In terms of bars and restaurants, Old San Juan has the trendiest nightlife scene in the capital. There are a few bars and clubs scattered throughout the southern half of the city, but C. San Sebastian is consistently the nucleus of activity. On weekend nights Paseo de la Princesa is crowded with vendors and young couples. A more mature crowd chooses to relax in the botanical gardens near La Princesa, which open up on Sa and Su nights with a bar and some live light jazz music. Finally, two companies send out weekend cruises from the dock in front of Plaza de la Darsena that quickly become lively dance parties on weekend nights ($12 per person).

Rumba, C. San Sebastian 130 (☎725-4407), is the Latin club you've always been looking for. Rumba packs in a crowd of all ages, races, and nationalities to dance the night away. Sip a drink up front or push your way to the back where live bands play charanga, salsa, and rumba (W-Su 11pm). Beer $3.50. Open Tu-Su 8pm-3am. AmEx/MC/V.

Nuyorican Cafe (☎977-1276), on Callejón de la Capilla, off C. Fortaleza. This popular little club has something for everyone. On Sa a play is followed by live salsa music; on Su a poetry slam is followed by live jazz—check the schedule out front for complete details. Dinner served 7pm-1am; entrees $12 and under. Beer $3; mixed drinks $4-6. Cover $2-10 depending on performer. Open Tu-Su 7pm-last person leaves. MC/V.

Señor Frog's (☎977-4142), on C. Comercio. Every night is a party at this flashy Mexican chain where drinks are sold in yard-long bottles. Señor Frog arrived in San Juan in early 2003 and instantly became the hottest venue in town. On weekends arrive by 10pm to join the line of trendy *sanjuaneros* who heed the restaurant's informative sign: "If the music is too loud...you're too old." Beer $3-3.50; mixed drinks $6; yards $7.50-20. W-M live rock and pop 9pm. Open daily 11am-2am or people leave. AmEx/D/MC/V.

The Noise, C. Tanca 203 (☎724-3426), proves that Puerto Rican clubs don't have to play salsa music to be hot. Pumping out 100% rap music, all the time, The Noise packs in crowds of hip college-aged Puerto Ricans who disappear into the depths of this long, narrow club. Beer $5; mixed drinks $6. 18+. F is ladies night; ladies free, men cover $15. Sa cover $5 before midnight, $15 after. Open F-Sa 10pm-last person leaves.

Lazer, C. Cruz 251 (☎725-7581; www.clublazer.com). From the makers of Santurce's El Teatro comes San Juan's oldest disco. Young Puerto Ricans come to boogie on one of 2 dance floors or lounge on the rooftop patio. On M-Tu (cruise nights) the crowd becomes predominantly foreign. Th is "Level Three" with electronic music. F is "Dance Hall" with R&B and hip-hop music. Sa is "Ladies Night"—ladies get free entrance and free wine before midnight, when there is a male strip show downstairs. Mixed drinks $5-7. Cover $10-15. Open M-Tu at 8pm, Th at 9pm, F at 9:30pm, Sa at 10pm.

Cafe Hijos de Borinquen, C. San José 51 (☎723-8126), at C. San Sebastian. Crowds of tipsy Puerto Ricans pack into this bar on weekends. Push your way in, grab a beer ($2-3.50) and just try to make conversation over the shouts and the jukebox. Mixed drinks $3.50-6. Happy Hour 10pm-1am. Open Th-Sa 8pm-last person leaves. MC/V.

Cafe San Sebastian, C. San Sebastian 153 (☎725-3998), at Plaza del Mercado. Every night a slightly more laid-back crowd heads to San Sebastian to relax on wicker furniture and enjoy the breeze coming through the large open windows while listening to live Novatrova music. Beer $2.50-3; mixed drinks $3.50-7.50. Open W-Su 8pm-3am.

Sala, C. Fortaleza 317 (☎724-4797). On some nights, enter through the unmarked door on Callejón de La Capilla. This classy restaurant/lounge hosts a more upscale crowd than other discos in the old town; women wear dresses and men button up their shirts. The scene varies from lounge parties with house music to boisterous dancing with live salsa music. Beer $3-4; mixed drinks $4-8. Th live jazz 10pm. F live salsa 10pm. Sa DJ with house music. Open Tu-W 6-10pm, Th-F 6pm-1:30am, Sa 6pm-5am. MC/V.

Nono's, C. San Sebastian 109 (☎725-7819), at C. Fortaleza, is a good place to drink. And drink. And drink. A relatively sedate crowd settles down at the bar with a drink in hand to listen to the Latin music. The bartender claims that after 2 Perfect Storms ($7), a signature drink with 8 liquors, you'll be set for the night. Beer $3.50-4; mixed drinks $4-8. Open daily noon-4am. AmEx/MC/V.

Krugger's, San José 52 (☎723-2475), ½ block down from C. San Sebastian. Because everybody needs a karaoke fix from time to time. Normally Krugger's hosts a relatively small crowd for drinks and pop music, but on Th-F nights it hops as one of Old San Juan's only karaoke bars. Beer $1-3; mixed drinks $4-8. Open M and Th-F 10am-3pm and 8pm-people leave, Tu-W 10am-3pm, Sa-Su 8pm-people leave. AmEx/D/MC/V.

Oscar's Bar, C. Recinto Sur 321 (☎724-7255). Walk past the giant fish and enter this cavernous bar filled with red Budweiser lamps. With 4 pool tables, mirrors on the walls, and countless TVs, this hole-in-the-wall doesn't seem to fit in with its trendy neighbors, but it's that local quality that makes it a great place to relax with some friends over a beer ($3.25). Open daily noon-last person leaves. AmEx/MC/V.

Baru, C. San Sebastian 150 (☎977-7107), is the place to go if you're feeling upscale and wealthy. An older crowd sips martinis under elegant yellow and purple lights. Dress to impress; dresses for women and button-up shirts for men. Wine $7; mixed drinks $6-10. Open M-F 5pm-midnight, Sa-Su 5pm-1am. AmEx/D/MC/V.

CONDADO

Condado has a relatively mellow nightlife scene, primarily limited to a few low-key bars. Of course compared to Santurce's debaucherous discos, anything seems mellow. A relatively hard-core punk crowd gathers at **Café del Angel** (see p. 116) on weekend nights to hear the live Spanish rock. (F-Sa 10pm. Cover $5-6.)

Río Bar & Club, Ave. Ashford 1309 (☎723-8680). Classy 30-something professionals pack into this hip bar to unwind after a long week at work. The glowing white stairs fit in perfectly with the over-the-top beach scene. Beer $3.50-4.50; mixed drinks $4.50-7. W life salsa/merengue 5pm. 18+/23+. Open W-Sa 5pm-5am, Su 5pm-3am. AmEx/MC/V.

La Terraza del Condado (☎723-2770), at the eastern intersection of Ave. Ashford and C. Magdalena. The high school crowd comes out in full force for F night Happy Hour at this large, open-air bar. Otherwise a pleasant place to drink a cheap beer (3 for $4.50) or a classy margarita ($5) while you enjoy the breeze. Puerto Rican entrees $9-16. Open Su-Th 5pm-midnight, F-Sa 5pm-2am. AmEx/D/MC/V.

Upstairs Sports Bar & Grill (☎725-3210), on Ave. Ashford at C. Vendig. You'll never get bored at this smoky 2nd-story sports bar filled with pool tables, video games, air hockey tables, and huge windows overlooking Ave. Ashford. Predominantly young, local crowd. Beer $3.50; mixed drinks $5-6. F live rock music 11:30pm. 21+. Open daily 5pm-8am.

Kalí's, Ave. Ashford 1407 (☎721-5104). Named after the Hindu god of destruction, this trendy new bar is fully decked out in a South Asian theme. *Sanjuaneros* in their 30s sweep aside the gauzy curtain to find candlelit tables, dark maroon walls, and thoughtful Indian decor. Appetizers $11-18. Beer $3-4; mixed drinks $5-7. Open W-Th 6pm-midnight, F-Sa 6pm-last person leaves (kitchen closes at 1am). AmEx/D/MC/V.

La Fiesta Lounge (☎721-1000), in the Condado Plaza Hotel, on the western end of Ave. Ashford. While the children head to Santurce, their parents come to this elegant locale to salsa with style. Even those who aren't quite yet lords of the dance can still enjoy the beautiful hotel. Beer $6-7; mixed drinks $7-9. Th-Sa live Latin music 7:30pm. Su live big band music 3-7:30pm. Open daily 5pm-last person leaves. AmEx/D/MC/V.

SANTURCE

Santurce is the home to most of San Juan's most outlandish and popular discos. Don't wander too far east into the C. Loíza area, as it becomes dangerous at night.

■ **Stargate/Pleasure,** Ave. Roberto H. Todd 1 (☎725-6446), north of Ave. Ponce de León, across from Pizza Hut. The enormous line outside betrays the fact that this is San Juan's most popular disco. Pass through the mock cave to Stargate, a truly out-of-this-world experience. The main club plays reggaeton in a large, dark room stuffed with stylish dancers. On the other side, Pleasure plays hip-hop and R&B for a college crowd. Beer $5; mixed drinks $6. 18+. Th open bar, cover $25 for men, free for women. F-Su cover $15. Stargate open Th-Su 8pm-whenever. Pleasure open sporadically.

Habana Club, C. Condado 303 (☎722-1919). Enter from C. Todd next to Stargate, across the street from Burger King. The Habana Club claims to be the home of the true salsa dancer and on weekend nights it seems like everyone in San Juan gets dressed up in their finest duds and comes here to dance. Come early; it's packed by 11pm. Beer $3; mixed drinks $4-7. Once a month the club hosts alcohol-free childrens salsa night. W-Th 8pm 1½ hr. salsa class; W basic, Th advanced; $20. Th rumba. F-Sa live salsa. 23+. Cover $5. Open W-Su 10pm-6am. D/MC/V.

Olé Olé Bar and Grill, Ave. Ponce de León 1402 (☎721-5925), between Ave. de Diego and C. Canals. The young and hip come here to drink the night away. Beer $2-3.50; mixed drinks $3.50-5; Happy Hour specials every night. Th $5 open bar 9-11pm. Karaoke all night. F women enter free and get complimentary wine until 11pm. Live music. Sa live rock. Su hip-hop and R&B. 21+. Cover $3-5. Open Th-Su 9pm-3am. AmEx/D/MC/V.

Plaza del Mercado (see p. 117). Want to get far off the tourist path? Head to Plaza del Mercado on a weekend night when the small bars host live **salsa bands.** This is a very local scene—older Puerto Ricans sit on folding chairs in the street, sipping a beer, and listening to the music. While **Café Tonita** and **Carnecería y Restaurant Velázquez** have been known to host a boisterous crowd, the exact location of the live music varies; your best bet is to head to the Plaza and listen for the sounds of salsa.

Bliss, C. Luisa 66 (☎722-6042; www.bliss-pr.com), at C. Vieques. Sweep aside the gauzy curtain to mingle with Puerto Rico's upscale, elegant 20-somethings. A young professional crowd drinks early and dances late. Mostly dance, house, and trance music with some salsa and merengue. Beer $2.50-5. 21+. Cover $5. Open W-Sa 6pm-2am.

El Teatro, C. Ponce de León 1420 (☎722-1130; www.elteatropuertorico.com). This popular club is a bit of a chameleon. On Th nights the club welcomes one and all with an open bar and pumpin' disco music. On F-Sa the club may or may not be open for special events, from heavy metal concerts to college nights. On Su El Teatro goes gay and prominent drag queens frequently put on a show. Beer $3-4; mixed drinks $3-6. 18+, depending on the activity. Cover $7-26. Usually open Th-Su 9pm-3am.

ISLA VERDE

The rich and famous (and the wannabe rich and famous) flock to Isla Verde after dark to party with the best of them. The dress codes is slightly more elegant in this area—T-shirts, sandals, and other beachware are generally not allowed. **Lupi's** (see p. 119) becomes a popular nightlife venue; a predominantly male crowd congregates by the bar and couples sip drinks on the outdoor terrace. **Sonny's Terrace** (see p. 119) has all the makings of a successful bar (live music, ample space, good location), but nobody seems to be catching on. This is a good place to relax and have some personal space.

Club Babylon, Ave. Isla Verde 6063 (☎791-2781 or 791-1000 ext. 1657; www.babylonpr.com), in the El San Juan Hotel. It's not unusual to see a celebrity at this chic disco located at the fanciest hotel in town. Opulent Babylon manages to make even green walls with white polka dots look classy. On a busy night the 2-story club holds over 1000 people. Tourists descend on F nights when the club plays "party" music. But Sa is the big night as the 2nd floor becomes a VIP lounge and the DJ plays everything from salsa to trance. Beer $4; mixed drinks $4-7. Th college night. Happy Hour 10pm-midnight beer $3. Th 19+, F-Sa 23+. Cover $10. Open Th-Sa 10pm-4am. AmEx/MC/V.

Shots Sports Bar & Grill (☎253-1443), in Isla Verde Mall. Defying all of Isla Verde's glamour and pretension, Shots opened up a sports bar less than a mile away from El San Juan Hotel with resounding success. A predominantly young, male Puerto Rican crowd lines up to rock the night away at this dark Irish pub. Beer $3.50-4. Happy Hour daily 5-8pm beer 2 for $5. F R&B and hip-hop. Th-Sa live music 11pm. 21+. Cover $5. Open daily 9:30pm-4:30am. D/MC/V.

El Chico Lounge, Ave. Isla Verde 6063 (☎791-1000), in the El San Juan Hotel. While the disco-hoppers head to Club Babylon, the die-hard salsa fans head to El Chico, a glamorous bar where a full band decked out in sequins and suits stands on an elevated stage, leading guests into a tropical frenzy. Casual elegance encouraged. Mixed drinks $6-11. Live music W 9pm, Th-Sa 10pm. 18+. No cover, but 2 drink min. Open W 8pm-1am, Th 10pm-2am, F-Sa 10pm-3am. AmEx/D/DC/MC/V.

Pepin's, Ave. Isla Verde 2479 (☎728-6280 or 726-4462), near Punta Las Marías. Classy Puerto Ricans flood this sophisticated bar/restaurant combo on W and F nights to sip cocktails and bounce to the live music. Get creative with the Absolut Pepin's, a mixture of Absolut Mandarin, lemon juice, and simple syrup ($6). W karaoke. Th live Latin jazz. F live blues. Su live rock. Beer $4. Entrees $15-26. Open Tu-F 5pm-2am, Sa 8pm-2am, Su 6pm-1am. AmEx/MC/V.

Oyster Bar & Grill (☎726-2161), on Ave. Isla Verde, across from the Marbella Caribe building. This highly publicized restaurant hit pay dirt with the after-hours crowd. On weekend nights the bar is packed with young foreigners and locals grinding to the sounds of Nelly and J. Lo. For better or worse, this tends to be one of the most intoxicated venues in Isla Verde. Music varies. Beer $4; mixed drinks $4-6. 21+. F-Sa cover $3. Open M-W 11am-1:30am, Th-Sa 11am-6am, Su 11am-4am.

Mango's Cafe, C. Laurel 2421 (☎727-9328). After work, countless 20-somethings head to Mango's Cafe, where they are greeted by new age club music and a large "Absolut Mango's" sign. Some like to grab a bite to eat (sandwiches and entrees $6-16). Others skip straight to the drinks (beer $3-6). Open Tu 5-10pm, W-Sa 11am-2am. MC/V.

Spread, Ave. Isla Verde 5940 (☎ 727-3422), at C. Emma, 2nd fl. Look for the burly bouncer. After the party there's Spread, Isla Verde's best after-hours martini lounge. The decor is quintessential Isla Verde nouveau riche, with gauzy curtains, metallic furniture, and white couches. Crowds really come after 3am. On F the club becomes Oxxide, and DJ Luigi spins trance and progressive music while patrons sip martinis and sample the free sushi and chocolate covered strawberries. Happy Hour 11pm-1am. 18+. Cover free-$5. Open Tu-Su 11pm-whenever. MC/V.

Borinquen Grill & Brewing Co., Ave. Isla Verde 4800 (☎ 268-1900 or 268-1910). Beer is the drink of choice at this authentic brewery, which makes 4 house brews and uses them to throw quite a party. During the day, the grill serves burgers ($6.50-8.50) and generic pub food (ribs, chicken; $9-20). Homemade beer $2.50. Happy Hour 4-7pm beer $2. Th college nights, live rock music and bikini contest at 10pm (cover $5, students with ID $4). F live jazz. Sa live oldies music. Cover $3 after 9pm. Open Tu-Su 11:30am-midnight. Kitchen closes at 10pm. AmEx/MC/V.

HATO REY AND RÍO PIEDRAS

■ **San Juan Reggae,** C. Chardón 9, Hato Rey. Drive south on Hwy. 1, then turn right on C. Chardon; the club is on your right. Fashionable college students line up 2hr. before opening to maximize their time at San Juan Reggae, one of the city's hottest discos. The underground club typically plays Spanish rap music F-Sa. On Su, gay night, the club adds some salsa and merengue to the mix. Beer $5; mixed drinks $5. F high school night; all ages welcome. Sa 18+. Cover varies; usually $10. Open F-Su 10:30pm-5am.

El 8 de Blanco (☎ 751-5208), at Ave. Universidad and C. Consuelo Carbo. Located 2 blocks from UPR, El 8 de Blanco is the classic student bar, with cheap beer, loud music, video games, and pool tables. The only reason to trek all the way out to Río Piedras is to party with the college crowd. Beer $1; mixed drinks $2-3. 18+. Tu-Th and Su live DJ. Open M-Sa 2pm-4am, Su 5pm-last person leaves. MC/V.

Coaches Sports Restaurant, Ave. F.D. Roosevelt 137 (☎ 758-3598), Hato Rey. Take an American sports bar, put it in San Juan, snazz it up, and you have Coaches. Customers can choose between pool tables, a plethora of televisions showing different sporting events, and a large bar. Also serves dinner (entrees $8-10). Beer $2-3. Mixed drinks $4-6. Happy Hour daily 5pm-midnight. Live music W-Th and Sa 10:30pm Spanglish rock, F 7pm English 80s music, 10:30pm Spanish rock. Open M-Th 4pm-1:30am, F 3pm-1:30am, Sa 7pm-3am, Su noon-4am. AmEx/D/DC/MC/V.

El Mesón y Algo Mas, Ave. F.D. Roosevelt 300 (☎ 767-3721), Hato Rey. There's always something going on at El Mesón. During the day the restaurant serves a wide selection of sandwiches ($3-7) and the bar is dead. After 11pm the bar is hoppin' and the restaurant is degraded to overflow seating. Tinted windows allow the post-college crowd to drink anonymously. Beer $2.50-3.25; mixed drinks $3-6. Open 24hr. AmEx/D/MC/V.

GAY AND LESBIAN NIGHTLIFE

When the sun goes down, San Juan's gay and lesbian population migrates from the streets of Condado to the dark, polished clubs of Santurce. Sunday is gay night at **El Teatro** (see p. 143), and famed drag queen Nina Flowers frequently makes an appearance. **San Juan Reggae** (see above), in Hato Rey, also turns gay on Sunday nights. For the latest information and events, check out **Puerto Rico Breeze,** the capital's gay and lesbian newspaper, available at stores in Condado's gay district or online at www.puertoricobreeze.com. In addition to the clubs listed below **Steamworks,** C. Luna 205, Old San Juan, is a popular destination for San Juan's gay population. As Puerto Rico's only male spa, Steamworks offers a gym, a sauna, a pool, and a steam room. All men over 21 welcome, but they must first become a member and agree to the club rules. (In an unmarked building. ☎ 725-4993; www.steamworksonline.com. 6-month membership $6. Lockers $10 per visit. AmEx/D/MC/V.)

Eros, Ave. Ponce de León 1247 (☎721-1131; www.erostheclub.com), Santurce. Eros is the venue of choice for well-dressed gay men and lesbians who like to dance. This 2-level club plays house, progressive, and techno music, with some hip-hop thrown in. Be fashionably late or you may be dancing alone. Beer $3-4. Th drag show and college night; college students get in free. F Back to the 90s. Sa Sex in the Sea Sábado has a mixed crowd. Th-F 18+, Sa 21+. Cover $8-10. Open Th-Sa 10pm-6am. AmEx/D/MC/V.

Cups, C. San Mateo 1708, Santurce, 1 block off Ave. Ponce de León on the street parallel to C. Diaz. San Juan's only lesbian bar attracts a friendly crowd on weekend nights to dance, drink, and chat. Predominantly women, with a smattering of men as well. Intoxicating wall decor includes everything from half-naked women to children's posters. The bar is not in the best neighborhood, so do not walk here at night. Beer $4; mixed drinks $6. W and F live Latin music. 18+. Open W-Sa 5pm-3am.

Nuestro Ambiente, C. Ponce de León 1412 (☎724-9093), Santurce. Both gay men and lesbians enjoy the 2 bars at this steamy club. Despite the glow-in-the-dark spider web, the party doesn't get started until after 11pm. Plays a mix of house, techno, salsa, and merengue. Beer $3; mixed drinks $4.50. F-Sa live music. 21+. Open Th-Sa 8pm-everyone leaves. AmEx/D/DC/MC/V.

Junior's, C. Condado 615 (☎723-9477), is one of San Juan's less pretentious gay discos—if you can make it past the bouncers outside. The small, dark club feels like a cozy private party playing an unremarkable mix of salsa, reggae, and pop. Sa night women are welcome as well; otherwise it's a strictly male crowd. Beer $3; mixed drinks $5. 18+. Open daily 8pm-5am or people leave. AmEx/MC/V.

Tía Maria Liquor Store, C. de Diego 326 (☎724-4011), Santurce. Cheap beer and 3 pool tables are the main draws at this seedy liquor store. A popular gathering point for gay men before they hit the town. Beer $1.25-2; mixed drinks $2.50-10. Open Su-W 10am-midnight, Th-Su 10am-2am. Cash only.

◪ DAYTRIPS FROM SAN JUAN

CATAÑO

Public Transportation: From Pier Two in Old San Juan take the AquaExpreso ferry (10min.; 40-46 per day 6am-10pm; $0.50, ages 60-74 $0.25, over 75 free) to Cataño. To get to the Bacardi factory, walk outside, turn right, and walk to the large pink building and the waiting públicos ($2 per person for 4 or more people or $6 alone). Driving: Take Rte. 165 from San Juan and turn right after the John Deere factory (on the left); if you see the huge Bacardi sign, you've gone too far.

Rum's the word that most visitors have in mind as they head across the bay to Cataño, home of the **Bacardi Rum Factory.** Although Bacardi originated in Cuba, and now has factories in Mexico and the Bahamas, the Cataño factory is the world's largest producer of Bacardi rum and one of the largest companies on the island, paying over $250 million in taxes annually. All of this combines to make the Bacardi Factory one hot tourist attraction.

Upon arrival, visitors receive one ticket for the tour and **two free drink tickets.** Many *sanjuaneros* have been known to come for the ferry ride and the two free drinks, then leave before the tour. However, Bacardi fanatics may find that the tour provides an interesting explanation of the rum-making process and the company's history. It all begins with a tram ride to the distillery, where visitors see a display of all the different Bacardi products and hear about how rum is made. At a small museum illustrating the history of Bacardi an enormous family tree emphasizes that the company is still controlled by the descendents of Don Facundo Bacardi Masó himself. Check out the display of Bacardi Millennium, the limited edition rum that now runs for $750-1000. Finally, a walk through the operating bottling room provides an illuminating glimpse at how rum goes from a barrel in Puerto Rico to a neighborhood liquor store. In early 2003 the Bacardi Company was in the process of designing a new visitors center which could significantly alter the tour.

Few visitors make it past the Bacardi Factory, but believe it or not, Cataño has more to it than rum. Just down the road, **Isla de Cabras** used to be an island with its own leper colony, but it has long since been converted into a grassy peninsula with a few picnic tables and some superb views of Old San Juan. And unlike Old San Juan, Isla de Cabras is quite peaceful, making it an ideal spot to get away from all the commotion and have a picnic. The island also houses **El Cañuelo**, a Spanish fort built in the 1500s to create crossfire with El Morro. The fort looks like a mini version of El Morro, and no one is allowed to enter, so there's really not much more than what you see from across the bay. Unfortunately, public transportation to Isla de Cabras is difficult. A taxi from the Bacardi factory costs at least $6 each way, so the island is really only worth a visit if you have a car. From Rte. 165, drive past the Bacardi factory, turn right on Rte. 870, and continue to the end. (Open daily 8:30am-5:30pm. Theoretically it costs $2 per car to enter, but the guard station is frequently unattended.)

BOSQUE ESTATAL DE PIÑONES

Public Transportation: San Juan city bus B40 travels from the Isla Verde bus stop, in front of the Cockfight Arena, along Ave. Boca de Cangrejos to the eastern edge of Piñones. *Driving:* From Isla Verde, Rte. 187 runs though the forest. *Biking:* By far the best way to experience Piñones is by bicycle. Bike path open daily 6am-6pm.

 CAR BREAK-INS There have been numerous reports of car break-ins in the Piñones Forest. If you choose to drive, try to park your car within eyesight and make sure that nothing is visible which could provoke a theft.

Although they are physically separated by less than 1 mi., wild and rugged Piñones State Forest and ritzy Isla Verde could not be more different. Where Isla Verde has condominiums, Piñones has untamed tropical forest. Where Isla Verde has fast food joints, Piñones has rustic food stands with open flames frying African-influenced Puerto Rican foods. Where Isla Verde has a population of wealthy Puerto Ricans and expats, Piñones has a relatively poor community of Puerto Ricans. Where Isla Verde's beaches are full of sunburnt tourists, Piñones's beaches are deserted. In other words, travelers who have become disillusioned with the American-influenced, English-speaking, overly developed beaches of San Juan should head immediately to Piñones for a truly Caribbean experience.

Coming from San Juan along Rte. 187 visitors will first pass **Boca de Cangrejos**, a small peninsula filled with restaurants and food shacks. An offshore reef makes this a bad area to swim, but a great place to stop for a snack. About 1 mi. down the road a second cluster of restaurants has a couple of more refined dining experiences. But keep going, because it's not until around Km 9 that you will find the pristine, deserted **beaches** with white sand and rows of palm trees. Pull off on any one of the sandy roads leading to the ocean and relax. Piñones is also a popular **surfing** spot; any local surf shops can point out the best breaks.

Lying on the beach is nice, but the best way to experience Piñones is by riding along the ⬛**Paseo Piñones bike path.** With a combination of paved trails and wooden bridges, the path weaves through the forest providing incomparable views of the flora, the small communities of houses, and the beach. A fabulous daytrip from San Juan can be spent riding along the path, swimming for an hour or two at a deserted beach, then stopping for a snack at a food kiosk on the way home. It is possible to rent a bicycle at any shop in the city (see p. 96), then ride

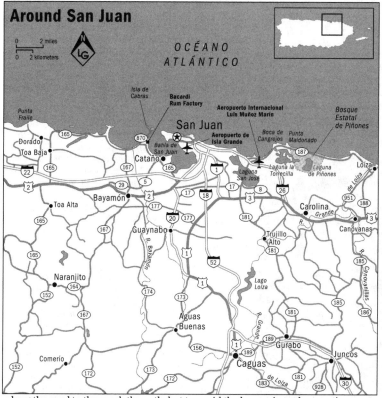

along the road to the reach the path, but to avoid the harrowing urban section, rent a bike at **El Pulpo Loco,** located in the second cluster of restaurants, right on the bike path. (☎791-8382. Look for the bright yellow building. Bikes $10 per hr., $20 per day. Open daily 10am-6pm.)

Farther inland, the forest also encompasses **Laguna de Piñones** and **Laguna la Torrecilla.** These two lakes are quite swampy and can emit a powerful smell, but it is possible to **kayak** around on them. To reach the lake, drive to Km 9 and turn right at the sign pointing toward Bosque Estatal de Piñones. Continue all the way down the road to the parking lot and the kayak launch. Tortuga Kayak in San Juan (see p. 97) leads 3hr. tours for $50 per person.

Piñones has so many small food vendors that it's hard to believe that they can all make a profit. The best, and cheapest, option is to head to one of the small shacks. grab an *empanadilla*, and sit on the beach. However, visitors who have not yet acclimated to the greasy Puerto Rican food may want to stick to more hygienic cuisine. In addition to renting bikes, **El Pulpo Loco ❸** (see above) doubles as a clean restaurant with palm-covered picnic tables and tasty Puerto Rican seafood. Specialties include red snapper, crab, and octopus, but the menu offers less adventuresome options as well. (Entrees $8-17. Open Su-Th 10am-11pm, F-Sa 10am-2am. AmEx/MC/V.) **The Reef Bar and Grill ❹,** in the first inlet of restaurants directly after the bridge coming from San Juan,

O WORK, ALL PLAY

ESTIVAL DE SANTIAGO APOSTAL OR THE CARNAVAL DE LOÍZA

Nowhere on the island is Puerto Rico's rich African heritage more evident than the small northeastern town of Loíza during its annual carnaval festival, celebrated every year over five days at the end of July. This lively party combines Catholic and African traditions with a religious ceremony, parades, food, and detailed costumes. After dark the entire town settles down to participate in the traditionally interactive *bomba* song and dance (see p. 29). The carnaval festival originated in 15th century Spain, as the Spaniards reenacted the defeat of the Moors, and it has remained faithful to its roots. In Loíza participants dress up either as finely dressed *caballeros* (Spanish gentleman) or brightly colored *vejigantes* (representations of the Spanish Moors). Though they are supposedly the villains, *vejigantes* have become much more renowned because they wear the beautiful *vejigante* masks (see **Arts and Crafts,** p. 26). The distinct Loíza-style masks are made out of painted coconut shells with several thin circular horns protruding. In recent years the Loíza carnaval has attracted a fair number of tourists, but it retains its original fidelity to preserving yet another component of Puerto Rico's rich and varied heritage. For more information and exact dates contact the Loíza municipal government at ☎876-3570.

undoubtedly has the best view in Piñones. Sit on a balcony with crystal clear water breaking underneath you and ponder the dichotomy between the palm trees in the foreground and the condos in the background. The menu includes typical seafood-based entrees and some Argentinean steak options. (☎791-1374. Entrees $14-18. Beer $2.75-3. Open W-M noon-10pm. MC/V.) Piñones also has a surprisingly impressive **nightlife scene.** Both of the restaurants above double as bars, but the hotspot is **Soleil Beach Club ❹.** Located next to El Pulpo Loco in the second inlet, the two story restaurant has live music five nights per week and serves spendy seafood named after various Puerto Rican sights. (☎253-1033 or 791-2299. Entrees $8-21. Live music W jazz 7-10pm, Th 70s and 80s music 10pm-1am, F salsa 7-10pm, Sa blues 10pm-1am, Su *bomba y plena* 2-5pm. Open Su-Th 11am-11pm, F-Sa 11am-2am. AmEx/D/MC/V.)

LOÍZA

Public Transportation: Públicos *go from Río Piedras (p. 90) to Loíza (30-75min., M-Sa 5am-3pm, $1.75). From the público terminal in Loíza face the grass area, turn left, and walk 3 blocks to the plaza.* **Driving:** *Take Rte. 187 east through the Piñones Forest. After you cross the large bridge over Río Grande de Loíza follow signs into the town center.*

With the most concentrated black population in Puerto Rico, the small town of Loíza has a fascinating culture, but unfortunately a very underdeveloped tourism infrastructure. However, all faults disappear during the last week in July during the town's annual carnaval festival (see p. 148). This is really the only motivation to visit Loíza; during the rest of the year, it is a sleepy town with only a few small attractions. Three miles south of town on Rte. 187, the **Estudio de Arte Samuel Lind** is one of the best working art galleries in the metro area. The studio/gallery/home of Loíza's premier artist includes a collection of paintings and sculptures, both finished and in-progress. Lind's beautiful work is largely inspired by the people and culture of Loíza and over the last few years he has created a poster for every town festival. Some small reproductions go for as little as $15. However, Lind also welcomes people who just come to look. (☎876-1494. Drive toward Río Grande and look for the small sign pointing to the studio, then turn left onto the small road; it's the third house on the left. Or take a *público* to Río Grande and ask to be let off at the studio. Open daily 10am-6pm, when Lind is home. MC/V.) Across

Worry Free Travel is Just a Click Away

Trip Cancellation
International Medical Insurance
Emergency Evacuation
All Nationalities

Personalize your travel insurance needs
with our online Policy Picker®

USA / Canada: 1 800 234 1862
International: +1 703 299 6001

ww.Letsgo.WorldTravelCenter.com   Travel Insurance Experts

blue for a better airline?

nonstop service from nyc to san juan

With new planes, big leather seats and super low fares, JetBlue isn't the only way to fly - but it should be. Check out jetblue.com for information about TrueBlue, our customer loyalty program.

jetblue.com

1.800.jetblue

trueBlue
FLIGHTGRATITUDE

©2003 JetBlue Airways.

the street, the **Ayala Souvenir Shop** displays *vejigante* masks crafted by Raúl Ayala, a second-generation Loíza mask artist. Both the masks ($20-200) and the small wooden dancer figurines ($20) are for sale. (☎876-1130. Open daily 9am-6pm.)

Loíza's only sight is the large orange church on the plaza. Registered as a **National Historic Sight,** the attractive church is unfortunately closed most of the time. Across the street a small visitors center theoretically provides information about the town, but it is also almost always closed. **Yawa's Café ❶,** C. Espiritu Santo 20, on the plaza, is the only restaurant in the town center—if you can call it that. Go up to the counter and ask what they have available, because that's what you're eating. (☎886-6084. Entrees $2-3.50. Open M-F 7am-2pm.)

CAGUAS

Public Transportation: Públicos *make the trip from Río Piedras to Caguas (35min., $1). From Caguas públicos travel to Cayey (30min., $1.25), Gurabo (20min., $0.70), and Río Piedras (35min., $1).* **Driving:** *Take Hwy. 1 south out of San Juan, then exit onto Hwy. 52 (toll $0.50). Just before Caguas, merge back onto Hwy. 1, which leads straight into town past the main plaza (30min., depending on traffic).*

Caguas

⬤ FOOD
Kam Ying, **1**
RexCream, **6**

🏛 MUSEUMS
Casa del Trovador, **2**

Casa Rosada Abelardo Díaz Alfaro, **3**
Centro Musical Criollo José Ignacio Quintón, **5**
Museo de Arte de Caguas, **4**
Museo del Tobaco, **7**

Caguas (pop. 144,000) seems to be Puerto Rico's forgotten destination. For years this city has been wallowing in the center of the island, ignored by visitors and neglected by the tourism industry. But no longer. Over the last few years Caguas has opened five carefully planned museums highlighting the island's culture. Unfortunately all exhibits are in Spanish, but the city still makes an attractive daytrip.

All five museums focus on one distinct aspect of the city's cultural heritage. From the plaza, walk one block down C. Betances to the **Museo del Tobaco,** C. Betances 187. The bulk of the museum contains several display boards about the history of tobacco and its importance in Caguas, which was a major tobacco producer throughout the 19th century. Today there are no tobacco farms near the city, but the art of cigar-making is preserved in the second half of the museum, where several elderly *cagüeños* spend four hours per day making cigars by hand. Many of these people worked in the tobacco industry when they were younger, and working in the museum allows them to preserve their *artesanía* while earning some extra cash. Visitors can watch them work and even buy the finished products afterward. (☎744-2960. Cigars $4 for 25. Open Tu-F 8:30am-noon and 1-4pm, Sa 8:30am-noon and 1-3pm. Free.) At the corner of C. Ruiz Belvis and C. Padial the **Museo de Arte de Caguas** upholds Puerto Rico's tradition of impressive art collections with an exhibit of primarily local work in attractive facilities. Upstairs, the **Departamento de Desarrollo Cultural** (Department of Cultural Development) displays the work by Argentinean Alberto Williams, as well as several Ponce *vejigante* masks. (☎744-8833 ext. 1804 or 1836. Open Tu-Sa 9am-noon and 1-4pm, Sa 8:30am-noon and 1-3pm. Free.) **Casa del Trovador,** C. Tapia 18, is the city's newest museum. **Trovadores** are traditional island musicians, found primarily in the central mountains, who sing a popular rhythm called the *décima.* The museum explains the *trovador* through photos, musical instruments, and a full *trovador* costume, while *trovador* music plays in the background. (☎744-8833 ext. 1843. Open Tu-Sa 9am-noon and 1-4pm. Free.)

Continue down C. Ruiz Belvis to reach the **Centro Musical Criollo José Ignacio Quintón**, at the corner of C. Intendente Ramírez. The most interesting aspect of this museum may be the building that it's housed in, a church temple remodeled in 1908 in a combination of Roman and Gothic architectural styles. Inside, a few display boards explain Puerto Rican music and the various musical groups in Caguas. The museum becomes more engaging when local groups perform inside; call ahead or ask at the tourist office for more information. (☎744-4110 or 744-4075. Open Tu-F 8:30am-noon and 1-4pm, Sa 8am-3pm. Free.) Finally, head half a block down Intendente Ramírez to **Casa Rosada Abelardo Díaz Alfaro,** C. Intendente Ramírez 12, former home of **Carlos Manuel Rodríguez,** a native *cagüeño* who was beatified by the Pope and continues to be Puerto Rico's highest ranking Catholic. Technically he remains one miracle short of becoming a saint, but still the people of Caguas come close to worshiping him. The first floor contains a collection of late 19th century furniture, but the second floor is devoted exclusively to Manuel Rodríguez, with an explanation of his life, pictures of his beatification, and some of his personal belongings. Strangely, the house is named not after Manuel Rodríguez, but after a famous Puerto Rican writer. The house was originally designed to serve as a center for literary activity in Caguas, but with the renovation of the second floor there was no room for meetings, which are now held in the Centro Musical. (☎286-7640. Open Tu-F 8:30am-4pm, Sa 8am-3pm. Free.) The helpful tourist office plans to open additional museums in the near future. For the latest information, and to pick up the city's tourism magazine, *Caguas,* head to the large **Oficina de Turismo,** on Plaza Palmer across from the cathedral. (☎744-8833 ext. 2906. Open M-F 8am-noon and 1-5pm.)

Most of the upper-end restaurants are located outside of the city center proper, but budget travelers can find several good, affordable eateries within walking distance. **Kam Ying ❶,** C. Acosta 22, serves surprisingly good Chinese food with a Puerto Rican twist—everything comes with french fries and most patrons order fried chicken. (☎743-3838. Combos $4-7. Open daily 10:30am-11pm. MC/V.) Those with a sweet tooth should not miss a trip to **RexCream ❶,** C. Muñoz Rivera 45, which serves the best ice cream in town. (Ice cream $1-2. Open daily 9am-10pm.)

GUAYNABO

Public Transportation: Take Metrobús II from Parada 18 in Santurce. ***Driving:*** *Take Rte. 2 south; after the intersection with Rte. 20 look for the museum on the right.*

The only real attraction of this suburban town is the **Museo de Caparra,** located at the sight of Ponce de León's first home and the island's original capital. In 1935 archaeologists excavating the area found artifacts from the time of Ponce de León's inhabitation, but there was no venue to display them. Consequently the government opened this one-room museum to hold the old spears and broken shreds of pottery. In front of the museum, the ruins of Ponce de León's home have disintegrated beyond recognition. Most visitors will be able to get their Ponce de León fix with a stop by Museo Casa Blanca in Old San Juan (see p. 130)—only diehard de León buffs need to make the trek out to Guaynabo. (☎781-4795. All displays in Spanish only. Open Tu-Sa 8am-noon and 1-4pm. Free.)

BAYAMÓN

Public Transportation: By the end of 2003, the new commuter train will provide easy, clean, efficient transportation to Bayamón from Hato Rey. Until then Metrobús II goes from Parada 18 in Santurce to Bayamón (30min., $0.50). ***Driving:*** *From San*

Juan take Rte. 2 (J.F.K. Expressway) all the way into Bayamón. When you see the immense city hall hanging over the center of the road, turn right and park in a garage near C. Degetau.

The suburb of Bayamón, located 4 mi. southwest of San Juan, claims such dubious honors as being one of the most densely populated cities on the island, and having the most shopping malls of any city outside of San Juan. For some reason, this just doesn't seem to be drawing the crowds of tourists. One sight that does consistently draw crowds (mostly Puerto Rican schoolchildren) is the **Luís A. Ferré Parque de las Ciencias** (Science Park). This educational theme park contains over 10 museums, a trolley, a planetarium, a 500-seat theater, a panoramic elevator, a zoo, an artificial tropical jungle, and a miniature river with paddle boats. Though definitely geared toward a pre-adolescent audience, the museums are surprisingly interesting for visitors of all ages. The **Museo de Transportación** contains a collection of historical cars from as early as 1907. The **Museo de Arqueología** holds dioramas of the Taínos and explanations of their cultures. The **Museo de Reproducciones Artísticas** contains reproductions of famous artwork from around the world. With the largest concentration of museums outside Old San Juan, Parque de las Ciencias merits a visit. (On Rte. 167, about ½ mi. from central Bayamón. The freeway is a difficult place to walk; instead, drive or take a taxi from in front of the *público* station. ☎ 740-6868, or 740-6871. Open W-F 9am-4pm, Sa-Su 10am-6pm. Parking $1. Admission $5, ages 2-12 and over 65 $3. Trolley $1. Planetarium $3, children $2. Paddle boats $2, children $1.50.)

Although Bayamón is largely composed of highways, malls, and residential areas, the government has restored a historical downtown area and opened three interesting museums. The most unique is undoubtedly the two-story, excessively pink **Museo de Muñecas** (Doll Museum), C. Degetau 45, which contains an incredible variety of dolls of all shapes, sizes, races, and colors displayed in several fully decorated bedrooms. Visitors will find old favorites (Barbie, Cabbage Patch Kids, a Menudo doll) as well as some more artistic porcelain dolls. Ask the employees to show you the "smallest doll in the world." (☎ 787-8620 or 785-6010. Open M-F 8:30am-4pm. Free.) Down the street, the **Museo Francisco Oller** has a slightly misleading name, as only one room out of about six contains works by Oller, but it nonetheless houses a respectable collection of artwork by artists such as Tomás Batista and Juan Santos. The museum honors Oller because he was born in Bayamón. Upstairs, the museum crams a substantial body of work by contemporary Puerto Rican artists into a relatively small space. (C. Degetau 12, at C. Maseo. ☎ 787-0620. Open M-F 8:30am-4pm. Free.) Next door, the **Museo Archivo Bayamón** is neatly divided into two sections. The first floor details the history of the city, and its astounding growth, through pictures, city models, and maps. The second floor contains memorabilia related to the former mayor, Ramón Luis Rivera, who controlled Bayamón from 1976 until 2000, when his son was elected mayor. The historian who works at the museum is usually willing to explain anything you ever wanted to know about Bayamón. (C. Degetau 14. ☎ 785-6010. If the door is locked at either museum, go to the other one and ask them to open it. Open M-F 8:30am-4pm. Free.)

The rustic wooden sign at **Nino's Café ❶** beckons passersby to come enjoy steaming plates of *comida criolla*. (On Rte. 167. From C. Degetau, walk uphill past the plaza, turn left on C. Dr. Veves, and continue all the way down to Rte. 167. Turn right and walk 5min.—Nino's is just after the Universidad Metropolitano on the left. Lunch combos $5.25-6.25. Open M-Tu 9am-5pm, W-Sa 9am-2pm.)

Countless visitors come to San Juan, lie on the beach for a week, and never see the majority of the island. For people who want to experience just a little bit more, but are short on time, the Central Mountain Scenic Drive offers a glimpse of Puerto Rico's incredible natural diversity. From the towering office buildings of Hato Rey to the towering peaks of the Cordillera, from the traditional devotion of Trujillo Alto to the traditional roadside snacks of Piñones, the following roadtrip highlights the island's variety in a great one-day excursion from the capital.

TIME: 5-7hr.

DISTANCE: 50 mi.

SEASON: Dec.-Mar., or when no rain is expected.

Travelers should take note that the times given are highly variable estimates, dependent on traffic and weather conditions. The trip travels along narrow winding mountain roads with steep cliffs on one side and heavy traffic on the other. This affords incredible views, but passengers will enjoy the trip much more than drivers, who need to focus their attention on the road. Finally, leave early as the winding roads can become perilous after dark.

The expedition originates in San Juan. Take Hwy. 1 south through the business district of Hato Rey. After passing through the city, take Hwy. 3 heading east toward Carolina. This is far from the most picturesque aspect of the journey, but it does provide insight into San Juan's massive suburban area. Stay on Hwy. 3 for about 1 mi., then turn right and head south on Rte. 181, a pleasant tree-lined street that leads to the suburb of Trujillo Alto.

1 LA GRUTA DE LOURDES. After passing the intersection with Rte. 850, take the next exit to the right and head up the hill on the middle street; then turn right at the sign for La Gruta de Lourdes. This small place of worship was created in 1925 as a replica of the sanctuary in Lourdes, France where three girls supposedly saw the apparition of the Virgin Mary in 1858. Continue to the top of the hill to visit a 12-pew chapel with a small but attractive altar. A path out back passes a large church and several beautiful statues depicting various biblical scenes. In addition to its unusual religious significance, this church also boasts lush grounds that are a nice escape from the road. (Church open daily 7am-10pm.) When you've gotten you're daily dose of piety, continue on Rte. 181, even as it turns into a small road without lane lines. You will cross **Río Grande de Loíza**, one of the largest rivers in Puerto Rico, before turning onto Rte. 851.

2 EMBALSE RÍO GRANDE DE LOÍZA. Tiny Rte. 851 continues to ascend through the mountains providing some of the most spectacular views on the island before it eventually descends into more tropical vegetation. When you reach a small village, turn onto Rte. 941 for excellent views of the 422 hectare **Lago Loíza,** constructed by the government in 1954 to provide water for the metropolitan area. It is difficult to actually reach the lake, as most side roads lead to private, gated residences, but the main road provides adequate views. And finally, you've escaped the traffic of San Juan. The village of Jaguas has a couple of small mini-markets if you need to make a stop. Soon the surroundings flatten out and the road passes through idyllic arches of trees and vegetation. Continue past the end of the lake.

3 GURABO. Rte. 941 leads straight into the village of Gurabo. Gurabo is known as the city of the stairs and it's easy to see why—streets leading toward the mountain end in steep steps heading up the hill. Hike all the way up for a great view of the city and the surrounding valley. There's not much else to Gurabo, but the city is currently remodeling the central Plaza de Recreo and the plans look promising. The **Departamento de Arte y Cultura,** on C. Santiago, across from the church, supposedly has a small gallery of local artwork on the second floor, but opening hours are sporadic. (☎737-8416. Theoretically open M-F 8am-4pm.) If you're starving, or looking for a dirt cheap meal, there are a few inexpensive *comida criolla* and pizza joints along C. Santiago. If you're looking for a more sophisticated meal, hop back in the car and drive east toward Juncos.

4 EL TENEDOR. To leave Gurabo, head east on the street perpendicular to C. Santiago next to the plaza, follow it to the end, then turn right and hop on Hwy. 30 east. Those in a hurry can skip to Sight 5. Otherwise, take the first exit at **Juncos,** and follow the road toward the building with the tall brick chimney, **El Tenedor 5.** Formerly a rum distillery, the stately edifice now holds one of the best restaurants on the island, where well-dressed waiters bring every cus-

OCÉANO ATLÁNTICO

San Juan

6

Laguna
la Torrecilla

Bosque Estatal
de Piñones

Laguna
de Piñones

Loíza

Bahía de
San Juan

Canal Blasina

Carolina

Trujillo Alto **1**

Guaynabo

2

Embalse
Río Grande
de Loíza

Canóvanas **5**

Río
Grande

El
Yunque

Aguas
Buenas

Gurabo **3**

Juncos **4**

Caguas

---

mer wine glasses full of water, buttered bread, and steak or seafood entrees. *Sanjuaneros* ave been known to drive all the way out here for a meal. The entrees are a bit heavy for nch, but after such a long drive you deserve a hearty 8 oz. steak, and at only $16, it's quite deal. (C. Emelia Principe 1. ☎734-6573. Entrees $9-19. Open Su-Th 11am-9pm, F-Sa 1am-10pm. AmEx/MC/V.) To leave El Tenedor, go to the intersection with Hwy. 30, but take te. 952, then turn right on Rte. 185.

FINAL DESCENT. To continue the scenic route, head north on the small, winding Rte. 185, hich leads through more verdant mountains, humble villages, and grassy fields. (If you want the uick route home, take Hwy. 30 west to Hwy. 52, which will lead right back to San Juan.) After about 5 mi., head east on the large Hwy. 3 for about 1 mi., then exit onto Rte. 188 north. Now you're back a lower elevation, and the vegetation is much more wild and tropical. If you're up for another stop, e. 951 leads to the small town of Loíza, with its historical church and fascinating African culture ee p. 148). Otherwise, continue on Rte. 188 then take a left onto Rte. 187 west.

BOSQUE ESTATAL DE PIÑONES. Rte. 187 leads through the incredible wilderness of ñones State Forest (see p. 146). Wrapping along the Atlantic Coast, the scenery here is stunning as the mountain regions you just left, but in a completely different way. If your omach has any room left, grab a snack at a roadside kiosk and eat while watching waves ash over the reefs. Or, if it's not too late, stop at one of the deserted beaches for a quick vim. Then it's back onto Rte. 187, which leads straight into San Juan.

153

SCENIC DRIVE

NORTHWEST

Welcome to the wild, wild west. As you head past Dorado, the terrain becomes more rugged, the locals more laid back, and you begin the transition into western Puerto Rico. The geographical landscape of Puerto Rico's north coast is consistently stunning. The Atlantic Ocean pounds the coast with the heaviest waves on the island, creating ideal surfing territory and wild, picturesque landscapes. Farther inland the geography is defined by the phenomenon known as karst, limestone cliffs and sinkholes that create a rugged, other-worldly atmosphere. When these two features meet, you find long bays of crashing white-capped waves surrounded on either side by steep limestone embankments and long rows of palm trees, a sight unequalled along Puerto Rico's coasts. Though these are some of the island's most beautiful beaches, strong waves make it difficult to swim in places.

The attractions in the northwest rival the landscape for drawing power. Just north of Arecibo, the Camuy Caves and Arecibo Observatory (the world's largest radio telescope) are two of the most impressive sights on the island and make an excellent daytrip from San Juan. Farther west, Isabela and Rincón have some of the best surfing in the Caribbean, but even non-surfers will be enamored with the beautiful terrain, the friendly atmosphere, and the comfortable accommodations. Driving from sight to sight provides a taste of northwest Puerto Rico, but to really explore the region try bypassing the main highways and take small one-lane roads along the northern coast or through inland karst country.

Lamentably, this region is also one of the most developed on the island. Many of the factories created during Operation Bootstrap landed along Hwy. 2, and overpopulation, huge factories, and heavy traffic mar much of the natural landscape. Indeed, most urban areas on the north coast—Manatí, Arecibo, Isabela, Aguadilla—should be avoided entirely if possible. Even Puerto Ricans realize that these town centers have declined and most of the hotels are outside the city centers. Fortunately, Hwy. 22 skirts most of the heavy traffic and deposits travelers in Arecibo within an hour and a half. Most travelers leave San Juan and head east, but those who buck the trend and try the northwest may be surprised to find a beautiful region waiting to be explored.

HIGHLIGHTS OF NORTHWEST PUERTO RICO

HANG TEN, OR JUST HANG OUT in Rincón, Puerto Rico's favorite expat haunt and home of some of the world's best surfing (see p. 178).

TRAVEL TO ANOTHER PLANET by exploring the underground world at the Camuy Caves or the spatial world at Arecibo Observatory (see p. 163).

GET UP CLOSE AND PERSONAL with the geographic landscape of karst country by hiking through Bosque Estatal de Guajataca (see p. 173).

START THE WEEKEND EARLY at Isabela's super-relaxed surfer beach with a six-pack and a bass-pumpin' truck (see p. 170).

DORADO

Dorado's coastal location allows for unsoiled beaches, great surfing, and ocean-fresh seafood. Two enormous Hyatt resorts dominate the city's tourist scene and occupy a huge area of prime real estate in the middle of the town, but there's a reason why Hyatt chose to build here. Contrary to popular opinion, the budget traveler can enjoy the area's natural resources without breaking the bank. The public beach in nearby Cerro

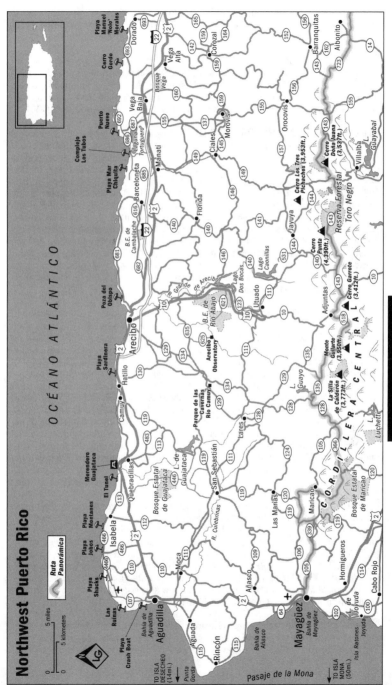

Northwest Puerto Rico

Ruta Panorámica

0 5 miles
0 5 kilometers

OCÉANO ATLÁNTICO

NORTHWEST

TO ISLA DESECHEO (14mi.)

Punta Gorda

Bahía de Aguadilla

Playa Crash Boat

Aguadilla

Las Ruinas

Playa Shacks

Playa Jobos

Playa Montanes

Isabela

Rincón

Aguada

Moca

Añasco

Bahía de Añasco

Bahía de Mayagüez

Mayagüez

Pasaje de la Mona

TO ISLA MONA (50mi.)

Isla Ratones

Joyuda

Bahía de Joyuda

Cabo Rojo

Hormigueros

Bosque Estatal de Maricao

Maricao

Las Marías

R. Culebrinas

San Sebastián

L. de Guajataca

Bosque Estatal de Guajataca

Quebradillas

Merendero Guajataca

El Tunel

Playa Montanes

Parque de las Cavernas Río Camuy

Camuy

Hatillo

Playa Sardinera

Arecibo

Poza del Obispo

B.E. de Cambalache

Barceloneta

Playa Mar Chiquita

Complejo Los Tubos

Puerto Nuevo

Manatí

Vega Baja

Laguna Tortuguero

Bosque Vega

Vega Alta

Vega

Cerro Gordo

Playa Manuel 'Mole' Morales

Dorado

Florida

Ciales

Morovis

Orocovis

Corozal

Barranquitas

Aibonito

Guayabal

L. Guayabal

Villalba

Cerro Doña Juana (3,537ft.)

Reserva Forestal Toro Negro

Cerro Los Tres Pichachos (3,953ft.)

Jayuya

Cerro Punta (4,390ft.)

Cerro Garrote (3,412ft.)

C O R D I L L E R A   C E N T R A L

Adjuntas

Monte Guilarte (3,950ft.)

La Silla de Calderón (3,773ft.)

L. Luchetti

Utuado

B.E. de Río Abajo

Arecibo Observatory

Lago Dos Bocas

Lago Caonillas

R. Grande de Arecibo

Lago Guayo

L. Guayo

Lares

Gordo receives little attention, but rivals Luquillo in terms of aesthetics and amenities, and the attractive town center is a pleasant place to spend an afternoon. Best of all, Dorado is only 30min. from San Juan on a road with relatively little traffic.

⊏ TRANSPORTATION. From Hwy. 22 exit at Rte. 693, drive to the end, then turn left onto Rte. 165, which runs past the city center. **Públicos** from Bayamón ($1.20) leave passengers in front of the Dorado Community Library, C. Méndez Vigo 331. **Vias Car Rental,** on the Rte. 693 marginal road, charges $26-36 for a compact car. (☎796-6404. Insurance $13 per day. 25+. Open daily 8am-5pm. AmEx/D/MC/V.)

◼ ☑ ORIENTATION AND PRACTICAL INFORMATION. As Rte. 165 passes the plaza it becomes **C. Méndez Vigo,** Dorado's main road. After the big shopping center, the road again becomes Rte. 693, and the marginal road holds several classy restaurants and some services. Immediately after the marginal road, taking a right on Rte. 697 leads to a residential neighborhood and the public beach. Continuing on Rte. 693 leads to the two Hyatt resorts and Cerro Gordo. The **Banco Popular** inside Grande supermarket on C. Méndez Vigo has an ATM. (☎278-1171. Open M-F 10am-6pm, Sa 10am-3pm, Su 11am-3pm.) **Grande,** on C. Méndez Vigo, sells groceries. (☎278-2400. Open M-Sa 6am-11pm, Su 6am-10pm.) The **police station** is located near the beginning of C. Méndez Vigo, at the corner of Ave. Albizu Campos. (☎278-0541. Open daily 7am-1am.) **Walgreen's,** Rte. 693 #4210 (☎278-5800), remains open 24hr. **Dorado Medical Hospital** (☎796-6050), on Rte. 698, just off C. Méndez Vigo, has a 24hr. emergency room. The **post office,** Rte. 698 #100, offers General Delivery service. (☎796-1052. Open M-F 8am-4:30pm, Sa 8am-noon.) **Zip Code:** 00646.

⋔ ACCOMMODATIONS. There is only one somewhat budget accommodation in Dorado, so fortunately it's a good one. Tucked away in a quiet residential area **Costa de Oro Guest House ❸,** C. H #B28, is within walking distance of Dorado's public beach and has sparkling clean rooms comparable to any spendy chain. Leave some time to hang out at this friendly establishment, be that lounging by the pristine pool, dining at the restaurant, or hitting the green at the 3-hole putting range. (Drive toward the beach on Rte. 697, then turn left on C. H. Transportation from the airport $70 per car; call ahead. ☎278-7888; fax 278-7892. Cable TV, A/C, and phone. 1 full bed $75; 1 queen bed $90; 1 queen and 1 full $110. 9% tax not included. AmEx/MC/V.) About 15min. east of Dorado in Levittown, **Hotel Campomar ❷,** on Rte. 165, has dark rooms with small bathrooms and all the standard amenities. The office is located across the street from the parking area, through the jungle-esque walkway. (☎784-7295 or 795-8323. Check-in 2pm. Check-out noon. Reservations necessary. Doubles M-Th $49, F-Su $69; extra person $10. AmEx/D/MC/V.) Balneario Cerro Gordo, about 5min. away, has an attractive **campground** (see p. 157).

❏ FOOD. Dorado's dining options vary significantly with location. By the public beach, the best choice is **Restaurante Rancho Mar,** C. G146, across the street with a red roof. The open-air restaurant hires three fisherman to go out every morning and catch fresh seafood—the menu varies daily depending on what they catch. (☎796-3347. Entrees $13-24. Wine $3.50-4. Open M-Th 11:30am-10pm, F-Sa 11:30am-midnight. MC/V. ❹) When you've had enough seafood, try **Los Pioneros ❷,** Ave. Méndez Vigo 412. The festive restaurant decorated as a traditional hacienda serves typical Mexican entrees ($2-7) with a few surprises thrown in. (☎278-3351. Happy Hour M-F 3-7pm. Open Su-Th 11am-10pm, F-Sa 11am-11pm. MC/V.)

◧ SIGHTS. Like so many Puerto Rican cities, Dorado has attempted to develop cultural venues with limited success. **Museo Historico del Dorado,** on C. Méndez Vigo, behind the church, displays a mishmash of petroglyphs, modern art, and architectural artifacts. The only noteworthy exhibit is the skeleton of a 15-year-old girl recovered from the area 1000-1500 years ago. (☎796-5740. Open M-Sa 7:30am-4pm. Free.) On the plaza, to the left if you're facing the church, **Museo y Escuela de Arte Marcos J. Alegría,** C. Norte 192, is even smaller than its rival. In front, a museum exhibits local art and some antique furniture, while in back the art school teaches local students. (☎796-1433. Open M-Sa 8am-4:30pm. Free.)

◪ **BEACHES AND SURFING.** The best public beach in the Dorado area is actually located in nearby Cerro Gordo, but the town does have its own patch of sand. Despite the huge rocky peninsula, **Balneario Manuel "Nolo" Morales** still has a designated swimming area and ample space to lie in the sun. Unfortunately the beach is not particularly well maintained and there is some trash near the picnic tables. (Coming from Dorado on Rte. 693, turn right on Rte. 697 at the Gulf Station, and continue to the beach. ☎796-2830. Open Tu-Su 8:30am-5pm.) In nearby Toa Alta, **Balneario Punta Salinas** is one of the more unique public beaches in that it is located on an isthmus, set off from the road by a small forested area. On one side of the isthmus a long, narrow beach has small waves and a designated swimming area. On the other side, picnic tables line the rocky shore. When you get overly sunsoaked, a few short trails crisscross the forest. (20min. east of Dorado on Rte. 165. ☎795-3325. Food kiosks, lifeguards, basketball courts, trash cans, and bathrooms. Parking $2. Open daily 8:30am-5pm.)

Dorado also has several popular **surf** breaks in front of the Hyatt hotels. **Kalichee Surf Shop,** in the Grande shopping center, rents shorts boards ($25 per day) and long boards ($30 per day) with a credit card and ID. They also provide a map of good surfing spots and info about lessons. (☎796-3852. Open M-Sa 9:30am-6:30pm, Su 11am-5pm. AmEx/D/MC/V.) Antonio Solla Bueno teaches 2hr. **surfing lessons** and guarantees that beginners will stand by the end. (☎209-4878. $60 per person.)

🎝 **ENTERTAINMENT.** Dorado does not have a thriving nightlife scene. **La Terraza Restaurant,** C. Marginal C-1, off Rte. 693, near Rte. 697, has a nice second floor bar with views of the ocean far, far away. (☎796-1242. Beer $3.25. 21+. Open M-Th 5pm-1am, F 5pm-2am, Sa 7pm-3am, Su 5pm-midnight. AmEx/MC/V.) **Restaurante Rancho Mar** (see **Food,** above) is open late and provides a good venue to enjoy a beer to the sounds of the ocean. In a weak imitation of the Old San Juan spectacle, Dorado has started celebrating **Gallery Nights** on the first Thursday of every month. On this evening the town's two museums change their exhibits and the plaza fills with vendors, musicians, and partygoers.

NEAR DORADO: CERRO GORDO

Some beaches have all the luck. While Luquillo basks in the glory of receiving the unofficial title of "the most beautiful beach in Puerto Rico," Balneario Cerro Gordo has been consistently neglected by travelers who either bypass Dorado or head directly to the resorts. But no longer. The Puerto Rican government is investing $3.4 million into remodeling this **public beach,** thus creating first-rate facilities in an already first-rate environment. The area currently boasts tiny waves of crystal clear water, a palm tree-lined beach, and views of the picturesque village of Cerro Gordo. And so far, Cerro Gordo lacks the commercialism that is beginning to destroy Luquillo, thus creating an ideal daytrip from San Juan or a requisite stop on any tour of the island. (☎883-2730. Lifeguards, picnic tables, food stands, and public showers. Parking $2. Open daily 8:30am-6pm.)

Cerro Gordo has a nice **campground ❶** in the woodsy area up the hill on the eastern edge of the beach. Some sites have ocean views, but there is little privacy. Call the beach for reservations, especially from June to August. ($13 per person.) The cheapest **food** in the area comes from the beach kiosk, but those in search of a real meal should try **El Batey del Indio ❸,** on Rte. 690, one block up the road away from the ocean. The small, casually refined restaurant specializes in *mofongos* and sea-food. (☎883-7312 or 319-1575. Entrees $7.50-22. Open Th-Su noon-10pm. MC/V.)

To reach Cerro Gordo from Dorado, head west on Rte. 693 past the two Hyatts, then turn right onto Rte. 6690 at the sign pointing toward the beach. Follow this road all the way to the end, then turn right; the beach entrance is on your right. Occasional **públicos** traveling to Cerro Gordo from Vega Baja will let you off at the beach entrance (M-Sa, $0.75). You should be able to catch a passing *público* back to Vega Baja, where additional connections can be made.

MANATÍ

From Dorado to Arecibo, Hwy. 2 stretches through northern Puerto Rico connect-ing a series of homogenous towns created by, and heavily dependent upon, the industrial boom of Operation Bootstrap. Large factories, fast food restaurants, and the occasional urban center lining the road create a decidedly unattractive land-scape. But farther afield some interesting natural attractions, including rugged surfing beaches and lakes full of crocodiles provide some reasons for venturing out to this area. Manatí itself holds little of interest to the traveler, but it is one of the largest cities east of Arecibo, and a good place to find all of those practical items necessary for exploring the wilds of the northern coast.

▣ **TRANSPORTATION.** Manatí centers on Hwy. 2, but it is much faster to travel via Hwy. 22, despite the intermittent tolls ($0.50-0.70), then exit onto Rte. 149, and turn right a0t the intersection with Hwy. 2. **Públicos** traveling between Parada 18 in Santurce and Arecibo will stop in Manatí, or anywhere along Hwy. 2. To catch a *público*, sit at a green bench along Hwy. 2 and flag one down. However, it is almost impossible to reach most sights via public transportation, and there really is nothing to do in Manatí proper.

▣ **ORIENTATION.** Notwithstanding the lack of addresses, Manatí is very easy to navigate. Just drive along Hwy. 2 and eventually you'll find everything. Barcelon-eta lies to the west and Vega Baja lies to the east. Most sights are located to the north, between Hwy. 2 and the ocean. Traveling west to east along the ocean, Rte. 686, Rte. 692, and Rte. 691 provide superb views and access to numerous beaches.

▣ **PRACTICAL INFORMATION. Banco Popular,** at Hwy. 2 and C. Vendig, has an **ATM.** (☎854-2030. Open M-F 8am-4pm, Sa 8am-noon.) **Grande,** on Hwy. 2 across from Banco Popular, is a good place to stock up on groceries. (☎884-7273. Open M-Sa 7am-9pm, Su 11am-5pm. AmEx/MC/V.) They also have **Moneygram** money transfer service. The **police station** (☎854-2020 or 854-2011), just up the road from the intersection of Hwy. 2 and Rte. 149, is open 24hr. **Walgreen's,** at the intersection of Hwy. 2 and Rte. 149, in Manatí Plaza, parcels out pharmaceuticals 24hr. a day. (☎854-0545. AmEx/D/MC/V.) The enormous sign at **Hospital Alejandro Otero Lopez** is visible from Hwy. 2, but the building is set back from the road one block along Rte. 668. (☎721-3700. 24hr. emergency room.) In Barceloneta, **www.vkcafe.com** has two touch screen computers with **free Internet** (see **Nightlife,** below). The **post office,** C. Eliot Velez 29, across from Burger King, set back from Hwy. 2, does not have Gen-eral Delivery. (☎854-2296. Open M-F 8am-4:30pm, Sa 8am-noon.) **Zip Code:** 00674.

▣ **ACCOMMODATIONS & CAMPING.** Not many people choose to stay in the Manatí area, and as such the accommodations are less than ideal. **Motel La Roca ❷,** just off Hwy. 2 near Barceloneta, rents some rooms by the night and others by the hour (see **The Luv Nest,** p. 159). The former come with TV, A/C, and luv music dials on the walls. Not all rooms have windows. (From Hwy. 2, turn south on

THE LUV NEST An outlandish sign points toward a hotel. The weary traveler searching for accommodations breathes a sigh of relief and turns into the gated driveway, only to find a surreal community. There is no reception desk, just a dark office with a telephone operator. All of the rooms have private garages, ensuring complete anonymity. And the rates are charged by the hour. Wait a minute...

Welcome to the Puerto Rican luv nest, a common phenomenon on the northern half of the island. Yes, these motels are used for exactly what you think they are. Many charge per hour, but also have 8hr. or 24hr. rates. The rooms tend to be a bit unusual—small, with mirrors lining all four walls and jacuzzis in the bathrooms—but they are functional. Unlike similar establishments in other countries, these hotels are usually well-maintained, friendly, and surprisingly legitimate. And you can get a clean room for as little as $25 for 8hr. Just don't let your significant other know where you spent the night.

Rte. 663. ☎ 881-0483. 1 double bed $40; 2 double beds $50. Cash only.) With such lackluster hotel choices, the best option is to camp at **Bosque Estatal de Cambalache ❶** (see **Sights,** p. 159). The large La Rosa area holds up to 30 people and has covered picnic tables, trash cans, showers, and toilets (when the water is turned on). You must have a DRN permit ($4 per person) and a reservation to camp here (see p. 58). Upon entering the forest, look for someone to unlock the inner gate; otherwise it's a ½ mi. walk down to the camping area.

▯ FOOD. Most Puerto Ricans dine at the fast-food restaurants lining Hwy. 2. Never fear—more authentic options await. **▧Capulinas Tacos Place ❷**, Rte 686 Km 9.1, convenient to Laguna Torgtuguera and the beaches, provides welcome refuge from the ramshackle food joints lining the beach roads. The menu at this festively decorated restaurant includes everything from vegetarian burritos to fajitas to, of course, tacos. Come for dinner, but the friendly owners may convince you to stay for a margarita or two. (☎858-6281. Entrees $2-13. Beer $2. Open Th-Su 10am-10pm. MC/V.) A few classy restaurants hide along the Hwy. 2 marginal road in Manatí. **Nuestra Cocina ❸**, just west of the intersection with Rte. 668, goes by the oh-so-hip nickname of "NC Restaurant." The decor looks Italian, but the food is pure Puerto Rican. (☎884-5527. Entrees $7-15. Open M-Tu 10am-3pm, W-F 10am-10pm, Sa 5-10pm. AmEx/MC/V.)

◎ SIGHTS. Bosque Estatal de Cambalache provides a welcome retreat from the endless commercialism of Hwy. 2. At slightly over 1000 acres, this humid subtropical forest is large enough to provide a full day of activity, but small enough to tackle in one day; for visitors staying in San Juan, this is a convenient day-long introduction to karst country. Over 4 mi. of well-marked hiking trails wind through the forest, including an interpretive trail with signs, a **wheelchair accessible trail,** and a **mountain biking path.** Unfortunately, San Juan (see p. 96) is the closest place to rent bikes. The picnic area contains covered tables and playground equipment. From Hwy. 22, take the exit immediately after the Arecibo tollbooth, then go north on Rte. 683. Turn right on Rte. 682 and look for the large sign on the right. To get to the forest office, take a right as soon as you enter the premises, directly before the welcome sign. (☎881-1004. Open M-F 8am-4:30pm.)

The Department of Natural Resources has classified **Laguna Tortugero** as the only natural lake in Puerto Rico. And it's full of crocodiles. Don't be confused—crocodiles, or to be more precise, caimans, are not native to Puerto Rico. In the mid-1970s many Puerto Ricans began purchasing the South American animal as pets; however, they soon discovered that caimans are cranky little critters and ditched their new reptile friends in the lake. Unfortunately, the introduction of a new species inevitably disrupted the existing ecosystem. The Department of Natural Resources attempted an eradication program in the early 1980s, but to no avail.

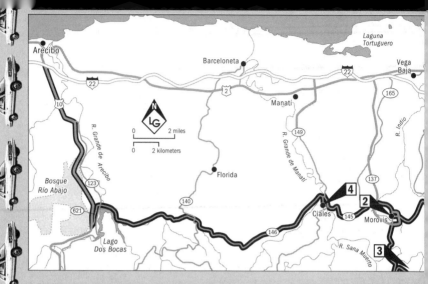

Driving to Arecibo's principal sights (the observatory and the caves) leads past the steep limestone sinkholes of karst country (see p. 163). However, the fastest route from San Juan also entails a substantial drive along depressing freeways, speeding past the beautiful countryside. For a more leisurely route, try this series of backroads that twists and turns through the spectacular scenery of northern Puerto Rico, from verdant farmlands to the

Time: 3-4 hr.

Distance: 55 mi.

Season: Dec.-June, or when it's not raining.

heart of karst country. With the exception of Corozal's Centro Histórico Turístico, the sights along this scenic drive are nothing special, but they do serve as good breaks during the long drive. Because the route runs parallel to Hwy. 2 and Hwy. 22, it is easy to detour north at any time and zip on to Arecibo. Otherwise, sit back and enjoy the ride through some of Puerto Rico's most dramatic countryside.

The drive begins just past Manatí. From San Juan, take Hwy. 22 west, then take Exit 22 north onto Rte. 165. Turn onto Hwy. 2 and drive west to take Rte. 142 toward Corozal. Drive south past the bright orange trees, then turn right (west) on Rte. 818 and continue past the residential neighborhood to Km 2.5.

1 CENTRO HISTÓRICO TURÍSTICO DEL CIBUCO (HISTORICAL TOURIST CENTER). No people do not just come for the view, though it is incredible. Settled in the foothills of Corozal, surrounded by steep karstic cliffs, this tourist center offers a sampling of various Puerto Rican cultural attractions all united on the 80 acre grounds of an old sugar plantation. The guided visit begins at the plantation's old home, **Casa Museo Aurora.** Although it was built in the 1930s, the house museum has been redecorated with 19th century furniture and a mishmash of historical artifacts. Next stop is the small **Museo de la Caña de Azucar** (Museum of Sugar Cane), which explains the history of sugar cane (in Spanish). Tours then go back about 500 years in history as visitors hop on a tram to see **Taíno petroglyphs.** A wooden walkway leads about 3 ft. away from the original petroglyphs, but the museum has constructed a replica that visitors can inspect up close. Then visitors return to the tram and ride to a small mock sugar mill where they can sample the sickeningly sweet sugar milk. Last stop is the **Artificial Lake.** With a maximum depth of 30 ft., the lake is large enough to support wildlife and visitors can borrow a paddle boat or just stand at the edge and watch the turtles swim below. In mid-July the center hosts an **artisans festival.** The complex is designed for groups (primarily Puerto Rican schoolchildren) and visits require a guided tour. However, when it's not busy guides are happy to accommodate individual visitors.

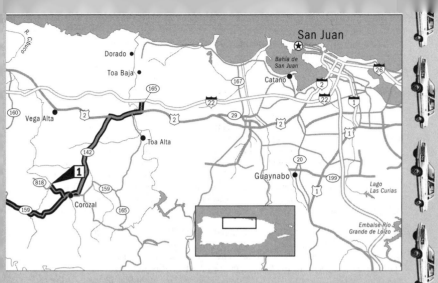

Only one guide speaks English and the center may be boring for non-Spanish speakers. (Rte. 818 Km 2.5. ☎859-8079 or 859-0213. Open Th-Su and most holidays 9am-5pm. $5, ages 1-12 $3, ages 60-74 $2.50, over 75 free.) If you plan to visit during the last weekend of October, don't miss Corozal's **Festival del Plátano,** which features artisans, music, and lots of plantain-based foods in the city plaza. After leaving the complex, turn left and backtrack on Rte. 818 to Rte. 159, then head west toward Morovis.

2 MOROVIS. Upon reaching Morovis, turn left onto Rte. 137, then turn right at Rte. 155 which leads right into town. Despite the fact that Morovis serves as the production center for much of Puerto Rico's *artesanía*, including traditional *cuatros* and *tiples* (see p. 29), there is almost no tourist infrastructure. The **Alcaldía** public relations office on the plaza provides a list of the names, phone numbers, and specialties of current artisans.

3 CASA BAVARIA. The Dutch may have been turned back at the walls of Old San Juan, but the Germans seem to have left their mark on the island at this charming Bavarian beer garden. The drive up to **Casa Bavaria ❸** is stunning; as you enter Morovis turn left onto Rte. 137, then left again onto Rte. 155, and continue for about 20min. to Km 38.3. Around Km 41 look left to see a waterfall cascading down the mountain across the valley. Once you reach the restaurant, let the atmosphere envelop you. Long wooden tables overlooking the valley provide the perfect location to enjoy schnitzel, bratwurst, and Lowenbräu. During the third weekend of October Casa Bavaria springs to life with its own Puerto Rican version of **Oktoberfest.** (Rte. 155 Km 38.3. ☎862-7818. Puerto Rican and German entrees $7-15. German beer $2.50. Sa live jazz *criollo* music. Open Th and Su noon-9pm, F-Sa noon-10pm; bar open until 1am. MC/V.) Take Rte. 155 back to Rte. 137, then turn right onto Rte. 137, then right again onto Rte. 155 (avoiding town) then turn onto Rte. 145, which leads to Ciales.

4 CIALES. From Morovis it's a straight shoot to Hwy. 10 and the speedy return to Arecibo. However, if you're looking for a break, try the picturesque mountain town of Ciales, which offers beautiful views and a miniscule coffee museum. (At C. Santiago Palmer and C. Hernández Usera, on Rte. 149 one block past the plaza. ☎871-3439. Open sporadically. Free.) From Ciales, continue west on Rte. 146 as it winds around sinkholes to reach **Lago Dos Bocas** (see p. 167). Be careful, as the road has a couple of sharp turns that aren't particularly well marked. From Dos Bocas it's a quick 20min. drive down to the town of Arecibo and Hwy. 2.

Now both parties have accepted mutual coexistence. The caimans only come out at night, so most visitors remain peacefully oblivious to their presence. The curious, or masochistic, can obtain a special permit from the office in Manatí to visit after nightfall and attempt to see one of the animals. The management reports that nobody has been attacked—so far. During the day the peaceful lake is a great place to fish, kayak, or just sit with a picnic and enjoy the scenery. A 5min. trail leads uphill to great views of the lake and the ocean. From Hwy. 22 take Exit 41, turn right on Hwy. 2, then left on Rte. 687, and look for the second big sign on the left. Manatí office (☎ 884-2587. Open W-F 8am-4pm, Sa-Su 6am-6pm.)

North of Manatí, **Reserva Natural Hacienda la Esperanza** has the potential to be a monumental attraction. This 19th-century sugar cane plantation occupies over 2300 acres with six different ecosystems, from mangroves to coral reefs, much of it preserved as it was 100 years ago. The Conservation Trust of Puerto Rico has big plans to renovate the house and open the area to the public; unfortunately, they're not done yet. For now the area just offers a bit of solitude and a nice view. From Manatí head north on Rte. 685, then turn left on Rte. 616, continue past the town, and pass through the empty fields, until you see the reserve sign on the left.

◪ **BEACHES.** The rugged beaches lining the northern coast rival Piñones in terms of solitude, surfing potential, and sheer beauty. The best way to find your own private spot is to drive along the oceanside highway and pull off on any dirt road. Unfortunately the beach is rocky in places, creating superb vistas, but not the best swimming conditions. The westernmost beach in the Manatí area, **Playa Mar Chiquita**, at the end of Rte. 648, is also one of the more popular—several cars can usually be found watching the waves crash through a small rock isthmus. From Rte. 686, turn north at Manatí Office Supply and drive over the hill. (No facilities.) Just down the going east, **Complejo Los Tubos** has a more developed beach area with a gated parking lot, lifeguards, covered picnic tables, bathrooms, and several large animal statues. Big waves and an offshore reef create decent **surfing** conditions, although most surfers choose to bypass this complex and head farther east. (Open W-F 8am-4pm, Sa-Su 9am-5pm.)

◪ **NIGHTLIFE.** Surprise! Manatí doesn't have a robust nightlife scene. However, in nearby Barceloneta, the bar/restaurant/Internet cafe **www.vkcafe.com,** Hwy. 2 Km 56.4, has become popular with the young professional crowd. After work, hordes of 20-somethings head to this trendy yellow bar for appetizers ($4-10), a drink, and good rock music. (☎ 846-0404; www.vkcafe.com. Beer $2-3; mixed drinks $5. Th live one-man band 6pm. F live Spanish rock 8pm. Sa live 80s music 10pm. Open M-Tu 11am-4pm, W-Sa 11am-midnight. AmEx/MC/V.)

DAYTRIP FROM MANATÍ: VEGA BAJA

Driving: From Manatí drive east to the intersection of Rte. 686 and Rte. 692.

Forget Dorado: Vega Baja is the real beginning of the west. Leave your pretension in San Juan, pack up the surfboard, grab a six pack, and head to **Balneario Puerto Nuevo,** the most party-friendly beach this side of Arecibo. This is an area where Bob Marley blasts from all stereos and laid-back Puerto Ricans of all ages park their cars on the sand and watch the waves with a couple of beers. In the background food kiosks serve replenishments throughout the night. As a public *balneario*, Vega Baja has a small recreation area with covered picnic tables, showers, and bathrooms, but it is set back from the ocean, thus leaving plenty of room to party after dark. Despite strong rip tides, the ocean is a full of **surfers, snorkelers, swimmers,** and **jetskiers.** For great views and even better surfing, continue east to the end of Rte. 691. (At the intersection of Rte. 686 and 692. ☎ 855-4744. Lifeguards during the day. Recreation area open M-F 8am-5pm, Sa-Su 8am-6pm.)

WHAT THE *%#@! IS KARST?

Geologists aside, most people are not very familiar with karst; however, this natural formation covers almost all of northern Puerto Rico from Dorado to Hatillo. Simply put, karst occurs when carbon dioxide-filled rain erodes a system of carbonate rocks (in Puerto Rico this is primarily limestone) for millions of years, eventually creating a rugged landscape of caves, sinkholes, subterranean rivers, valleys, and mogotes. Mogotes may be the most easily identifiable formation, as these vegetation-covered mounds of limestone protruding from mountains look like haystacks. Karst is named after a region in the former Yugoslavia, but now applies to several temperate and tropical locations around the world. Over 20% of Puerto Rico's land can be defined as karst, including the north coast and parts of Vieques, Isla Mona, and Cabo Rojo. In addition to being a fascinating tourist destination, karst also forms an important part of Puerto Rico's ecosystem—the region is a major source of fresh water and contains a unique array of flora and fauna, including the largest number of tree species per square mile on the island. Driving along the northern coast provides some exposure to karst, but the best places to see it up close are the **Camuy Caves** (p. 166), **Bosque Estatal de Guajataca** (p. 173), and the **Karst Region Scenic Drive** (p. 160).

ARECIBO

Arecibo is a municipality of superlatives. The area contains the world's largest radio telescope, the world's third largest underground cave system, the island's largest municipality, and possibly Puerto Rico's least attractive town. Luckily, it is easy to explore Arecibo's sights without ever stepping foot in the decaying town center. Arecibo Observatory and the Camuy Caves easily rank among the island's most impressive and tourist-friendly destinations. Traveling to these two parks will lead through Arecibo's stunning karstic landscape, and the views may entice you to spend more time exploring nearby lakes and natural reserves. Arecibo has the potential to please for days, but only for those who can overlook the jarring blemish of a city. To avoid the traffic and endless commercialism of Hwy. 2, consider taking the Karst Country Scenic Drive (see p. 160) to reach Arecibo's backcountry attractions.

▐ TRANSPORTATION

Driving to Arecibo is the only way to see the sights without battling irregular *públicos* and spending extensive amounts of time in the city. From San Juan, take Hwy. 22 west, then exit onto Rte. 129 and go north to reach the town and the lighthouse or south to reach the other attractions. It is possible, albeit difficult, to explore Arecibo without a car. From the **Terminal Sur** *públicos* go to: **Manatí** (1hr., $2); **San Juan** (2-3hr., $6-7); and **Utuado** (30min., $2). However, most vans leave before 8am and locals recommend that if you want to go to San Juan after 9am, you should hail down a passing van on Hwy. 2. The **Terminal Norte** sends *públicos* to: **Camuy** (10-25min., $1.25); **Hatillo** (15-25min., $1.25); and **Quebradillas** (30-45min., $3.50). Vans from this terminal also head to the neighborhood of Esperanza, which is somewhat near the observatory; negotiate with a *público* driver to see if he will drop you off and come pick you up later. Even better, head down C. José de Diego to **Arecibo Taxi Cab,** on the plaza, where taxis can take you to the observatory ($15) or the Camuy Caves ($20-25) and pick you up later. (☎878-2929. Open M-Sa 4am-midnight, Su 6am-10pm.) Another option is **Diego Taxi Cab** (☎878-1050).

NORTHWEST

ORIENTATION AND PRACTICAL INFORMATION

Arecibo's city center sits between Hwy. 2 and the Atlantic Ocean. However, most action takes place along Hwy. 2 and in the various suburbs. The major sights lie about 15-20 mi. south of Arecibo proper just off Rte. 129. Ave. Rotario holds most of the government offices and connects Hwy. 2 to Rte. 129.

Bank: Banco Popular, Ave. Gonzalez Marín 65 (☎878-8500), on the plaza. ATM. Open M-F 8am-4pm. Numerous other banks line Hwy. 2.

Camping Permits: The **DRN** office (☎878-9048) is in Centro Govermental building A, behind the police headquarters on Ave. Rotario. Reserve 2 weeks in advance. Open M-F 7:30am-noon and 1-4pm.

Supermarket: Pueblo (☎878-1975), in the shopping center at Hwy. 2 and Ave. Rotario. **Western Union**. Open M-Sa 6am-midnight, Su 11am-5pm. AmEx/D/DC/MC/V.

Police: Ave. Hostos 300 (☎878-2020). Open 24hr.

24-Hour Pharmacy: Walgreen's, Hwy. 2 Km 81.8 (☎880-0290), across from Plaza del Norte mall, in Hatillo. AmEx/D/MC/V.

Hospital: Hospital Dr. Cayetano Coll y Toste (☎878-7272 or 650-7272), at the intersection of Rte. 129 and Ave. Rotario. Open 24hr.

Internet Access: PostNet (☎817-9089), in the shopping center at Hwy. 2 and Ave. Rotario. $4 per 30min., $8 per hr. Open M-F 8am-6pm, Sa 8:30am-5pm. Cash only.

Post Office: Hwy. 2 Km 75.8 (☎878-1246). Address General Delivery mail to: Megan MONAGHAN, General Delivery, Ave. Llorens Torres, Arecibo, PR, 00612. Open M-F 7:30am-4:30pm, Sa 7:30am-noon.
Zip Code: 00612.

ACCOMMODATIONS & CAMPING

Arecibo has very few accommodations. There are some camping options farther south, but if you're looking for an actual hotel, try nearby Hatillo (see p. 168) or Utuado (see p. 275).

Hotel Villa Real, Hwy. 2 Km 67.2 (☎881-4134 or 881-8277; fax 881-1992), about 4 mi. east of Arecibo. Designed for businessmen on the go, this roadside hotel has all the necessities but few perks. Stark rooms with A/C, fridge, phone, and TV. Pool. Coin laundry. $25 key deposit. Check-in 3pm. Check-out noon. 1 queen bed $66; 2 queen beds $77; suites $87-98. Tax included. AmEx/MC/V. ❸

Parque de las Cavernas del Río Camuy (☎898-3100), 20min. south of Arecibo (see p. 166). The CPN allows visitors to camp at this tourist attraction. You set up a tent in the picnic area, but the site does have bathrooms, showers, and a 24hr. guard. Reservations required. $5 per person. AmEx/MC/V. ❶

Bosque Estatal de Río Abajo (☎880-6557), on Rte. 621. From Hwy. 2 take Hwy. 10 south, then turn right onto Rte. 6612, which soon intersects Rte. 621. A beautiful creek-side camping area in the middle of karst country. Includes trash cans, water spigots, bathrooms, rustic showers, fire pits, and picnic tables. 1 marked trail. Must have a permit ($4) and a reservation from the DRN (see p. 58). ❶

FOOD

When asked to recommend a good restaurant most *arecibeños* are stumped and eventually start mentioning the chain restaurants in Plaza del Norte, on Hwy. 2 in Hatillo. There are dining options near every attraction, but nothing outstanding.

Restaurante El Observatorio, Rte. 625 Km 1.1 (☎880-3813), near the observatory. One of the few Arecibo restaurants to receive mention in *Que Pasa*. With a souvenir shop, pictures of the observatory, and signed pictures from SETI on the walls, the restaurant is clearly geared toward passing tourists. Serves generic seafood and *comida criolla*. Medalla $2.50. Entrees $7-16. Open W-Su 11am-5pm. AmEx/MC/V. ❸

Tony's BBQ, Hwy. 2 Km 75.8, (☎881-2871), across from the post office, is very popular. Though it looks like a generic fast-food joint, this sparkling restaurant serves up some of the town's best *comida criolla*. Combos $3-6. Open daily 9:30am-10pm. Cash only. ❶

Criollo, Rte. 129 Km 19.6 (☎897-6463), just past the Camuy caves. After you work up an appetite exploring Puerto Rico's famous caverns, forego the overpriced cafeteria and try this *comida criolla* buffet. The food is good when hot, but gets cold quickly. Buffet $8; drinks $1.69. Open W-Su 11am-3:30pm. AmEx/MC/V. ❷

SIGHTS

◙ OBSERVATRIO DE ARECIBO. You can't really understand the enormity of Arecibo Observatory, the world's largest radio telescope, until you drive over the final mountain and see the gigantic structure protruding from the landscape. Even non-scientists will be awed by the complex structure and the adjacent museum. The observatory was built in the late 1960s about 6 mi. south of Arecibo because the site fits two specific requirements; it was close to the equator and the karstic geography provided a natural sinkhole for the reflector. Since then the observatory has served as a work station for countless scientists from around the world, including the 1993 Nobel Prize winners. One of the more exciting projects at Arecibo involves SETI, the

Search for Extra Terrestrial Intelligence. The telescope can detect a signal from over 1500 light years away and the ongoing Project Phoenix seeks out other radio signals sent our way, either on purpose or accidentally. So far the project has been fruitless, but scientists promise to keep the world updated. Recently the observatory served as the site of several more frivolous projects, including the filming of four movies (*Contact, Goldeneye 007, Survivor, Dream Team*) and an episode of the *X Files*. The observatory is run by Cornell University with assistance from the National Science Foundation and all signs are in both English and Spanish.

Visits begins at the two-story **museum.** The lower level has several interactive displays designed to make astrophysics accessible to everyone from scientists to children, and provide a thorough introduction to astronomy. Upstairs, signs describe the different projects undertaken at the observatory. When it's playing, a 20min. movie explains how the telescope operates. Finally, head out back to the viewing platform and see the main attraction, the telescope itself. On the ground the enormous fixed reflector, 1000 ft. in diameter, is made out of over 40,000 perforated aluminum platforms. Hanging 450 ft. above the reflector, the 700 ton platform looks like an enormous golf ball. The sight is especially impressive when the entire platform rotates. *(From Arecibo take Rte. 129 south, turn left on Rte. 134, continue east on Rte. 635, and finally turn right onto Rte. 625. You can take a público from Terminal del Norte in Arecibo headed to the barrio of Esperanza, but there will be a surcharge. Or take a taxi from Arecibo ($15). ☎878-2612; www.naic.edu. Open W-F noon-4pm, Sa-Su and holidays 9am-4pm. $4, ages 5-12 and over 65 $2, ages 0-4 free. AmEx/D/MC/V.)*

PARQUE DE LAS CAVERNAS DEL RÍO CAMUY. The Camuy Cave Park is one of Puerto Rico's most extraordinary and accessible natural attractions. For millions of years Río Camuy has been slowly eroding away the soft karstic limestone to create the third-largest underground cave system in the world. In 1950 scientists discovered this unique phenomenon, and in the 1980s the site opened to the public. Today Puerto Rico's National Parks Company operates 250 acres of the incredible terrain as a tourist attraction where visitors can walk through one of the enormous caves amidst slowly dripping water and hundreds of sleeping bats. Most visitors come to Camuy in the morning, then continue to the observatory in the afternoon. Consequently, the park is quite crowded before noon. Arrive at the park in the early afternoon to avoid a long wait for the tour.

The tour starts with a 20min. film covering the safety features of the visit and a brief history of the park. Afterward, tour groups of up to 50 people board trolleys that lead to the main attraction, **Cueva Clara.** At 170 ft. in height, Clara truly astounds. Groups follow a winding path through the artistically lit cave past a series of stalactites and stalagmites, including the largest known stalagmite in Puerto Rico, as the mist rises eerily around them. At the Palma sinkhole visitors can look down at the river rushing 150 ft. below. Groups then reboard the trolley to head to **Tres Pueblos Sinkhole,** an enormous 400 ft. hole located at the intersection of Lares, Camuy, and Hatillo. Unfortunately, it is not allowed to descend into the sinkhole. The last stop, **Spiral Sinkhole,** is most recent addition to the park. A 205-step wooden staircase leads to a platform looking into a huge ravine. Finally, it's back on the trolley for a stop by the cafeteria, the gift shop, and the picnic area.

Most visitors will be satisfied with a tour through the park, but the truly adventurous may try a guided expedition into the caves. **Tanamá Expediciones,** in nearby Utuado, leads intense kayaking/hiking trips into the caves but does not offer rappelling (see p. 275). In San Juan **Adventuras Tierra Adentro** specializes in 1-day rappelling trips (see p. 136). In the future, the CPN also looks to offer additional attractions, including the opportunity to rappel 80-120 ft. down into **Cathedral Cavern** for only $50. *(Rte. 129 Km 18.9. 20min. from Arecibo. ☎898-3100; www.geocities.com/espeleodatos. Open W-Su and holidays 8am-3:45pm, but the last tours skip the sinkholes. $10, ages 4-12 $7, ages 60-74 $5, ages 0-3 and over 75 free. AmEx/MC/V.)*

ARECIBO LIGHTHOUSE HISTORICAL PARK. Arecibo's attractive lighthouse is one of the few in Puerto Rico that has been developed and opened to the public. Unfortunately, administrators have also added a cheesy historical park and implemented a hefty price tag, marring what could be an appealing destination. The historical park around the lighthouse contains a playground and models of a Taíno village, Christopher Columbus's three ships, a pirate ship, and a slave hut, complete with recorded African music. The entire assortment is just as tacky as it sounds, but two wooden platforms afford great ocean views that almost compensate for the rest. The lighthouse has a small nautical museum with assorted maritime artifacts and absolutely no explanations. You can climb up the stairs, but the US Coast Guard still uses the top of the lighthouse. *(Take Hwy. 2 to Rte. 681, then turn left on Rte. 655. ☎880-7250. Parking $2. Open Tu-F 9am-6pm, Sa-Su 10am-7pm. $5. MC/V.)*

LA CUEVA DEL INDIO (INDIAN'S CAVE). This attraction is less of cave and more of a wild limestone cavern that the ocean has carved out over the years. Leave your car in the dirt parking area, then climb out over the lunar-like landscape to the rock steps that lead down into the cave. The petroglyphs on the wall were supposedly created by the Taínos over 500 years ago, but the crashing ocean may be more impressive. Wear good shoes and watch your step, as holes in the limestone lead down to the ocean over 20 ft. below. *(2 mi. past the lighthouse on Rte. 681, just past the Esso station. Parking $1. Admission $0.50 when one of the local kids is around to collect it.)*

◢ BEACHES AND WATER SPORTS

Arecibo's most popular **beach** for both surfers and swimmers is Poza del Obispo, just east of the lighthouse. On the western edge of the beach a small protected inlet provides a good place to swim. **Surfers** head east, where the surf gets progressively more impressive. There is no shade and few facilities. (From Hwy. 2 turn north on Rte. 681 and continue past the lighthouse.) If you continue down Rte. 681, several turn-offs mark additional popular surf breaks. To reach the public Balneario Morillo, follow directions to the Arecibo Lighthouse (see Sights, above); the beach is on the left, across from the parking lot.

Arecibo Dive Shop, Ave. Miramar 868, at Hwy. 2 Km 78, leads excursions to local destinations, such as a sunken barge, underwater mountains, and Cueva del Indio, as well as more distant destinations, such as Isla Desecheo and Isla Mona. They also offer PADI certification courses. (☎/fax 880-3483. 2-tank dive $45-215. Equipment rental $30. You must have your own snorkel gear. Group open-water certification $150. 8 person min. Open M-Sa 10am-6:30pm. Cash only.)

NEAR ARECIBO

LAGO DOS BOCAS

After a long day of driving around Arecibo, visitors may welcome the tranquility of Lago Dos Bocas. Surrounded by steep limestone cliffs and lush mountain vegetation, this calm lake in the hills of karst country has several activities. Dos Bocas is a popular fishing lake if you bring your own equipment. **Locura Arecibeña** rents **kayaks** from the main ferry dock. (☎878-1809. Call ahead. Single $15 per hr., double $25.) But perhaps the most relaxing way to explore is by riding the **free government ferry** that circumnavigates the lake every hour. The ferry brings visitors to several restaurants, or you can just enjoy the 40min. loop. (☎879-1838. Ferries leave M-F every hr. 6:30am-5pm; Sa-Su 8 per day 6:30am-3pm. Office open M-F 7:30am-3pm.)

Located on 132 acres of land, the relatively new **Rancho Marina Restaurant ❸ and camping ❶** stands out as one of the lake's superior food and accommodation combos. Large wooden platforms over the water provide a picturesque setting from which to enjoy delicious morsels of *comida criolla*. The friendly owners also allow travelers to camp on the manicured grounds, or stay in one of the renovated cabins. The rustic cabins can accommodate up to six people and have ceiling fans, some sort of kitchen, and cold water. The ranch also rents kayaks ($10 per hr.) and plans to build one trail. (Ask the ferry to drop you off here. Also accessible by car from Rte. 146 Km 7.6, but you must have 4WD and call for directions. ☎894-8034 or 630-2880; ranchomarina@centennialpr.net. Entrees $8-13. Camping $25 per tent. Cabana prices not established at time of publication; call ahead. Open Sa-Su 10am-7pm. MC/V.) Anyone can use the clean **pool** next door at **Los Salcedo** ($3). To get to Lago Dos Bocas, drive south on Rte. 10, then turn left at the sign and take Rte. 621 east to Rte. 123 south. You can't miss the dock at Km 67.1.

HATILLO

At first Hatillo (pop. 39,000), a small dairy-producing town just west of Arecibo, seems like another generic settlement along Hwy. 2. And it is. However, the area also has a popular festival, some attractive beaches, and accommodations that make a convenient base from which to explore the sights around Arecibo. Hatillo's annual ▓**Festival de las Máscaras** (Mask Festival), held on December 28, is the island's third-largest mask exhibition. Inspired by a traditional festival in the Canary Islands, this popular celebration includes parades, music, and colorful costumes, as participants dress up to reenact the Catholic tale of King Herod. The rest of the year, Hatillo is a quiet town with two attractive beaches. **Playa Sardinera,** Hwy. 2 Km 84.6, at Centro Vacacional Luis Muñoz Marín, is one of the best north coast beaches for young children. Several large boulders shelter a calm, shallow wading area perfect for the young 'uns. Older visitors can head past the boulders where big waves pound the beach, though the entire area is a bit rocky. Just west, in the actual town of Hatillo, wild **Playa Marina** makes an ideal destination for sunbathing or long beach walks. As you continue west the sand gets smoother and the big waves make for perfect boogie boarding. (From Hwy. 2 turn north onto Rte. 119 and continue to downtown Hatillo. Turn north again at Rte. 130. No facilities.)

As the island's only municipal-run vacation center, **Centro Vacacional Luis Muñoz Marín ❸**, Hwy. 2 Km 84.6, better known as Punta Maracayo camping, offers a bit more entertainment than typical government-run beach cabanas. The complex contains two pools, a waterslide, a romantic wooden walkway, and a large playground complete with huge concrete animals. Best of all, the entire complex sits in front of Playa Sardinera (see above). The six-person cabanas far outshine other vacation centers; newly constructed clean buildings have bright yellow walls, A/C, cable TV, full kitchens, and balconies. Don't forget to request an ocean view; it's the same price. Eight-person villas are a bit older and don't have A/C. The grassy **camping/RV area ❶** offers water spigots, indoor bathrooms, and cold-water showers. (Turn north at Casa Borincanas. ☎820-0274; fax 820-8404. Cafeteria and picnic tables. Office open M-F 8am-4:30pm, Sa-Su 8:30am-5pm. Non-guest entrance $3, with waterslide $5. Check-in 3pm. Check-out 2pm. Camping $50 per tent for a 3-day weekend; $70 for a 4-day holiday weekend; $20 for an additional night. 6-person cabins $195/$225/$40. 8-person villas $250/$290/$60. Tax included. MC/V.) There is little to complain about at **Parador El Buen Cafe ❹**, Hwy. 2 Km 84, just west of Arecibo. The roadside *parador* feels institutional, but the big, clean rooms contain cable TV, fridge, A/C, and phone. The friendly staff adds a touch of life to the hotel. (☎898-3484; fax 898-7738; www.elbuencafe.com. Pool. Check-in 3pm. Check-out noon. Doubles $91-97; extra person $15. Tax included. AmEx/MC/V.)

Ignore the ugly facade; the waterfront **Baja Beach Restaurant ❺**, Rte. 119 Km 1.9 has the best views in town. Unsurprisingly, Baja Beach serves the usual combo of burgers, sandwiches, Puerto Rican food, and seafood with a few pasta dishes thrown in for variety. (☎820-8773. Beer $2.50-3. Entrees $5-20. Open W-Th 11:30am-10pm, F-Sa 11:30am-11pm, Su 11:30am-9pm. AmEx/MC/V.) For quick eats head to **Cafetería El Buen Cafe ❸**. Locals flock to the large diner for inexpensive Puerto Rican breakfasts and lunches. For more elegant dining, the *mesón gastronómico* next door opens at 11am. (☎898-3495. Breakfast $2.50-5; sandwiches $1.75-3.50; entrees $5-26. Open daily 5:30am-10pm. AmEx/MC/V.)

QUEBRADILLAS

Quebradillas will never be anyone's final destination, but with a small zoo, several beaches, and Puerto Rico's only Barbie museum, it does provide enough entertainment to make an appealing stop along a north coast drive. Furthermore the small coastal city contains two attractive *paradores* that rank among the best accommodations options along the north coast. Nostalgic adults, children, and anyone interested in dolls should start at Quebradillas's unique **Museo de Muñecas** (doll museum), Rte. 482 Km 0.9. Don't let this cryptic name fool you; originally named after Barbie herself, this small museum had to change its name when Mattel learned about its existence. Nomenclature aside, the museum contains over 800 Barbies, from the first Barbie, issued in 1959, to the (debatably) gay Ken doll. The accommodating owner happily points out landmarks such as the first overweight Barbie, the handicapped Barbie, Barbie's pregnant friend, paleontologist Barbie, and Barbie's entire, unnaturally blond family. (☎356-4360. Open Sa-Su and holidays noon-5pm. $3, ages 0-10 $2.) Travelers may have mixed reactions to **El Arca de Noé**, Rte. 482 Km 1. This **privately run zoo** has an impressive assortment of animals, including caimans, zebras, deer, ostriches, goats, monkeys, and an enormous variety of birds from around the world. Unfortunately, many of the animals inhabit very small cages and only about half have an identification sign. Nonetheless, this continues to be a very popular attraction for children. A small miniature golf course across the road completes the afternoon of family fun. (☎895-0377. Open W-F 9am-3pm, Sa-Su 9am-5pm. $4, children $3.)

In addition to its more unique attractions, Quebradillas also contains several of those big, beautiful, northern **beaches**. One mile west of Quebradillas, **El Tunel** is an old railroad tunnel running through a cliff on the side of the beach that now makes an excellent seaside path. The tunnel was last used in September 1953 and serves as one of the last remainders of Puerto Rico's railroad network. The picturesque beach is a bit rough for swimming, but a popular surfing area and a great place to catch some rays. Beware: there are almost no facilities and little shade. Just to the east, **Merendero Guajataca**, Hwy. 2 Km 103.8, is a pleasant **picnic area** with covered tables, trash cans, and bathrooms. It's hard to see the beach through the vegetation, but a barely defined trail leads down to the water. (Parking closes at 5:30pm.)

Two *paradores* face off in Quebradillas from opposite sides of Hwy. 2. **Parador El Guajataca ❸**, Hwy. 2 Km 103.8, is slightly less expensive and has direct beach access. However, the hotel is 70 years old and the facade has not aged well. Rooms look slightly decayed, but they all have an ocean view, a private balcony, A/C, and cable TV. (☎895-3070, toll-free 800-964-3065; fax 895-2204; www.elguajataca.com. Restaurant and pool. Doubles $70-90; extra person $12. 12% tax not included. AmEx/D/DC/MC/V.) Across the street **Parador Vistamar ❸**, Rte. 113 #6205, at Hwy. 2 Km 103.8, sits on a hill, removed from the commotion below. Several big yellow buildings surround a sparkling pool in the style of an elevated seaside resort. More expensive rooms have balconies and ocean views; all have A/C, cable TV, and phones. (☎895-2065, Puerto Rico toll-free 888-918-0606, USA toll-free 888-391-0606; fax 895-2294; www.paradorvistamar.com. Continental breakfast included. Check-in 3pm. Check-out noon. Doubles $71-105; extra person $20, 2 children under 12 free. 7% tax not included. AmEx/D/MC/V.)

Both *paradores* have *mesones gastronómicos* with similar menus at similar prices, but only **Restaurant & Lounge Vistamar ❷**, in the hotel of the same name, has a terrific panoramic view. Sit on top of the world and enjoy the traditional island food. (☎895-2065. Sandwiches $5-8; entrees $9-16. Open M-Th 1-9pm, F 1-10pm, Sa 7am-10pm, Su 7am-9pm. AmEx/D/MC/V.) For fresh seafood, try one of the three indistinguishable seafood restaurants near Merendero Guajataca.

ISABELA

If Rincón reigns as the king of surfing destinations, then Isabela's Playa Jobos is the duke; slightly more in touch with reality, almost as impressive, and constantly standing just in the shadow of his more famous brother. When the surf is poor in Rincón, surfers in the know head to Isabela, where northern winds frequently make Playa Jobos a good second choice. But Isabela's shoreline deserves more than second-class status. With steep karstic cliffs in the background, tall palm trees and tropical vegetation along the coast, and continuous fierce Atlantic waves pounding the beach, this is one of the island's most picturesque shorelines. The Jobos area attracts a sizable surfing crowd, but the presence of several resorts and upscale hotels proves that the region is popular among landlubbers as well. And unlike Rincón, Isabela has not yet become overwhelmed by expats, leaving a beautiful, relatively undiscovered, fully equipped ocean getaway.

▐ TRANSPORTATION

To reach the town of Isabela from Hwy. 2, turn north at Rte. 112. If you want to go straight to Jobos (and you do) continue through town onto Rte. 466, which leads to the beach. If you're coming from the west, take Rte. 110 north, then turn right onto Rte. 4466 and the road will eventually become Rte. 466. From Aguadilla, drive north through Base Ramey, exit Gate 5, and continue on Rte. 110 to Rte. 4466, one of the most beautiful roads in Puerto Rico. Isabela has a **público** station just off the plaza, but it only sends cars to nearby *barrios*. *Públicos* to **Aguadilla** leave from Ave. Augustín Ramos Calero at the intersection of Rte. 113 and Rte. 112 (30-45min.; $1.75). *Públicos* to the Jobos area leave from the small concrete pavilion two blocks east of the plaza, across from Econo supermarket (15min., $1).

▗▌ ▐ ORIENTATION AND PRACTICAL INFORMATION

All of Isabela's tourist activity takes place along the coast. Technically, several distinct beaches have their own names, but most locals refer to the entire coastline as **Jobos.** Most of the hotels and restaurants are located at the intersection of Rte. 466 and Rte. 4466, near Playa Jobos proper. Bosque Estatal de Guajataca, also part of Isabela's jurisdiction, lies another 7 mi. inland, south of Hwy. 2. Once you get to Playa Jobos it is easy to walk between beaches, restaurants, and most accommodations. Unless otherwise stated, all of the practical services are located in Isabela, 5 mi. east of Jobos.

   Bank: Banco Popular, Ave. Culera 73 (☎872-2945). ATM. Open M-F 8am-4pm.

   Equipment Rental: Hang Loose Surf Shop, Rte. 4466 Km 1.2 (☎872-2490). Rents all types of surf and boogie boards ($25 per day), sells gear, and offers lessons ($45 per hr. including board). Upstairs, surf legend Werner Vega makes and repairs long boards. Open Tu-Sa 10am-4pm, Su 11am-4pm. AmEx/MC/V.

   Supermarket: Supermercado Econo, C. Barbosa 4, a few blocks west of the plaza. Open M-Sa 6:30am-9:30pm, Su 11am-5pm. AmEx/MC/V.

   Laundromat: Laundromat El Familiar, Ave. Juan Hernández Ortiz 474, past the police station, behind Plaza del Mercado. Wash $1. Dry $1. No change available. Open daily 7am-6pm.

   Police: Ave. Hernández Ortiz 3201 (☎872-2020 or 872-3001). From the plaza, go south on Rte. 112, take the first left, and continue for about ¼ mi. Open 24hr.

Late-Night Pharmacy: Super Farmacia Rebecca, C. Noel Estrada 51 (☎872-2410), east of the plaza. Open M-Sa 8am-9pm, Su 9am-9pm. AmEx/D/DC/MC/V.

Hospital: Centro Isabelino de Medicina Avanzada (☎830-2705), 1½ mi. south on Rte. 112. Clinic open M-F 7am-3pm. Emergency room open 24hr.

Post Office: C. Jesus Piñero 5 (☎872-2284), behind the *público* station. No General Delivery. Open M-F 8am-4:30pm, Sa 8am-noon.

Zip Code: 00662.

ACCOMMODATIONS

All of the following accommodations are located in the Jobos area.

Ocean Front Hotel, Rte. 4466 Km 0.1 (☎872-0444; www.oceanfrontpr.com). Someone should tell the owners of Ocean Front Hotel that bright ocean view rooms with TV, coffee maker, A/C, and (tiny) private balconies are supposed to be expensive. Or maybe not. In spite of its roadside location, this small hotel maintains an aura of professionalism and refinement. A great deal during the week. Restaurant. Check-out noon. Doubles Su-Th $60-65, F-Sa $90-100; extra person $20. 9% tax not included. AmEx/MC/V. ❸

Costa Dorada Beach Resort, Rte. 466 Km 0.1 (☎872-7255, US toll-free 800-981-5693; fax 872-7595; www.costadoradabeach.com), is a slightly budget version of the standard beach resort. Several 3-story buildings surround a dry grassy courtyard filled with palm trees, a bar, and a big pool. The exceptional part of this resort is the price; rooms get as cheap as $65. Modern rooms include telephone, TV, fridge, and a small courtyard balcony. Direct beach access. Doubles $65-250; villas with kitchen $125-400; extra person $20. 9% tax not included. AmEx/D/MC/V. ❸

Happy Belly's (☎398-9452), at Rte. 4466 and C. Pedro Albizu Campus. This popular restaurant also rents out the cheapest rooms in town in an unmarked guest house 2 mi. west of Rte. 466. The big lime green building won't win any beauty contests, and rooms are a bit worn, but overall this hotel is a great deal. All rooms include 1 double bed, TV, A/C, and fridge. Inquire at the restaurant. Doubles $40. Tax included. AmEx/MC/V. ❷

La Torre Guest House, Rte. 466 Km 7.2 (☎872-7439), 1 mi. from the beach. This friendly guest house/pizzeria is located on the first floor of the owner's home. Popular surfer hang-out, despite the distance form the beach. Small, unexceptional rooms have few decorations, but are clean and include TV and A/C. Doubles $55, with kitchen (no dishes) $65; quads $70/$75. Prices rise on weekends. Tax included. Cash only. ❷

Pelican Reef Apartments (☎872-6518 or 895-0876), at the intersection of Rte. 466 and Rte. 4466, is actually a small apartment complex with a few nightly rentals. The concrete hotel-style building was not built with aesthetics in mind, but it does overlook the ocean. Clean, no-frills rooms include TV, A/C, stove, and fridge. Doubles $80; quads with pull-out futon $100; 2-bedroom quads $125. Tax included. No credit cards. ❸

FOOD

Happy Belly's (☎872-6566), on Rte. 466, just east of Rte. 4466, is your stereotypical ocean-front tourist bar. The wooden patio overlooking the water is a perfect place to enjoy shrimp *mofongo* ($15) with a lively crowd. Sandwiches guaranteed to make your belly happy. Sandwiches $6-7; entrees $10-19. Open M-Tu 11am-10:30pm, W-Su 11am-2am. AmEx/MC/V. ❸

Ocean Front Restaurant, Rte. 4466 Km 0.1 (☎872-3339), in the hotel of the same name, is Jobos's premier seafood restaurant. Over 13 years, this restaurant has perfected its recipe for the best salmon on this side of the island. Decorated with tiny lights and lush plants, the interior dining room is one of the classier areas of Jobos. Relaxed outdoor patio. Entrees $12-20. Wine $4. Live guitar music every night. Open W-Th and Su 11:30am-10pm, F-Sa 11:30am-midnight. AmEx/MC/V. ❸

NORTHWEST

FROM THE ROAD

CLOSE ENCOUNTERS OF A TROPICAL KIND

You haven't really lived until you've had a large jungle rat hanging over your head. I sort of missed my big moment, as I didn't realize it was happening at the time. I was sitting on a porch in Rincón, having a pleasant conversation, and I didn't even glance back when I heard the rustling. "Ah, just another lizard," I thought to myself. It wasn't until later that night when my friend asked: "Hey, did you see that big rat today?" He gestured toward the Corona bottle sitting on the table. "It was about that size and dangling above your head." No, I'm quite happy that I did not see the rat.

Puerto Rico may not have the big animals of other tropical destinations, but don't confuse size with might. One of the island's most dangerous animals is the killer biting ant. They're tiny, but present everywhere. Frequently I'll be sitting at an outdoor table when I imagine that I feel something crawling on my leg. "Aw, it's nothing," I think to myself. Seconds later I'm trying to find the nearest place to submerge the ants that are eating me alive. And then there are always the monstrous bugs. One night I opened my hotel room door for half an instant and a huge bug flew in. And when I say "monstrous," I mean 4" long with two twitching 4" antennae. Huge. I resisted the urge to scream and panic. Instead, I was on my way to go find a small bucket (to capture the creature) when the bug politely flew out the front door. And who ever said that Puerto Rico had no wildlife?

Cano's Trattoria Italiana, Hwy. 2 Km 111 (☎830-9154), about 5 mi. from the beach. Cano serves up large portions Italian food made the way it was meant to be, with recipes straight from Italy. The huge menu includes pizzas, foccacias, pastas, calzones, meats, and pretty much anything else you could wish for. Blue checked table cloths liven up the friendly interior. Outdoor seating available. Wine list. Entrees $6-19. Open M-W 11am-10pm, Th and Su 11am-11pm, F-Sa 11am-1am. AmEx/MC/V. ❸

Sonia Rican Restaurant (☎872-0808), on Rte. 466, at the Playa Jobos parking lot, benefits greatly from its beachfront location. Essentially just a very long bar, Sonia Rican serves up affordable seafood and well-prepared Puerto Rican cuisine. Sit inside for great views of the surf. After dark a quiet crowd comes to enjoy drinks at the bar. Beer $1.50-2. Entrees $6-26. Open daily 11am-8pm. AmEx/MC/V. ❸

🏖 BEACHES AND SURFING

Sitting at the intersection of Rte. 4466 and Rte. 466, the large **Playa Jobos** bay is Isabela's surfing mecca and the site of the **1989 world surfing championship.** Waves almost always pound the coast, especially when there is a north shore wind. On the eastern edge of the beach, in front of the sand parking area, a protected bay provides a calm, shallow area for swimmers. Because surfers paddle out here and sunbathers park here, the eastern edge of Playa Jobos can get crowded and filled with trash at times. The next bay to the west is known as **Playa Shacks.** This bay looks similar to Jobos, but has a few more rocks and no parking area, thus it remains significantly less crowded. Shacks is known as the best **snorkeling and diving area** near Isabela. The consistent waves make Shacks one of the best wind- and kite-surfing beaches on the island. Even without all the diversions, Shacks provides a nice place to lie on the beach. (Follow directions to Tropical Trail Rides, Rte. 4466 Km 1.8. Park just past the bridge and continue to the end of the road on foot. No facilities.)

If Jobos is too wild for your swimming and sunning needs, drive east on Rte. 466 to Km 10.2, then turn left toward Villas del Mar Hau and continue to the end of the road to reach **Playa Montanes,** a much calmer beach. There are no facilities, but there is a long bay and lots of grainy sand. The water is deep, but gets shallower as you head east.

🚣 WATER SPORTS AND OUTDOOR ACTIVITIES

Playa Shacks is Isabela's best **snorkeling** beach and one of the few places on the island where **shore diving** is feasible and worthwhile. The only dive shop in the area, **La Cueva Submarina**, Rte. 466 Km 6.3, leads two shore dives every day (9:30am and 1:30pm; 1-tank dive $45 including equipment; extra tank $20). They also offer Nitrox dives ($65), guided snorkeling trips ($25), Discover Scuba packages ($45), and 4-day open-water certification courses ($250, including equipment) through NAUI and SSI. (☎/fax 872-1390; lacuevasubmarina.net. Open M-Sa 9:30am-5:30pm, Su 9am-4pm. AmEx/MC/V.)

Some claim that **Tropical Trail Rides,** Rte. 4466 Km 1.8, offers the best **horseback rides** in Puerto Rico. This professional, American-run operation leads 2hr. rides along the beach, through the almond forests, and then back along the cliff caves. (☎872-9256; http://home.coqui.net/barker. Daily 9am and 4pm. $35 per person. Reservations required. Open daily 7:30am-6:30pm. AmEx/D/MC/V.)

◙ NIGHTLIFE

Happy Belly's Sports Bar & Grill (☎872-6566), on Rte. 466, just east of Rte. 4466. As the night goes on this popular restaurant morphs into a relaxed beach bar. By the time karaoke starts on Th nights, everyone's ready to sing. Primarily foreign crowd. Balcony over the beach. Beer $2.50; mixed drinks $4-5. W, F, Sa live Spanish rock, salsa, merengue. Th and Su live DJ. Open W-Su 11am-2am, M-Tu 11am-10:30pm. AmEx/MC/V.

Escape (☎830-5814), on Rte. 4466, 1½ mi. east of Rte. 466. With flashing lights, a huge dance floor, 2 bars, and an outdoor patio, this nightlife extravaganza couldn't be more of an escape. The DJ plays whatever dancers request—usually reggaeton. Most people show up after other bars close. Beer $2.50; mixed drinks from $3. 18+. Cover $0-5, women usually free. Open daily 6pm-people leave. Cash only.

Mi Casita Tropical (☎872-5510), attracts the spillover crowd from Happy Belly's. On busy nights young visitors chill on the oceanfront balcony. On slow nights, a local crowd congregates around the bar. Beer $1.50-3; mixed drinks $2.50-5. W karaoke night. Th live Spanish rock 9pm. Open W-M noon-midnight, or people leave. AmEx/MC/V.

NEAR ISABELA

BOSQUE ESTATAL DE GUAJATACA

As if having some of the island's most beautiful shoreline wasn't enough, the municipality of Isabela also contains the 2357 acres of Bosque Estatal de Guajataca, one of the island's prime examples of karst country. Despite its diminutive size, this subtropical forest is one of the more clearly organized on the island, with a cave, several picnic areas, and a camping area. Twenty-seven well-marked trails provide the best means to explore the forest. Unlike almost all other trails in Puerto Rico, these narrow dirt paths were originally constructed as trails (not access roads) and they have not yet been paved over, providing a much more natural hiking experience. First stop by the **visitors center,** 5 mi. down Rte. 446 in the middle of the forest, where rangers distribute maps and info about which trails are open. (☎872-1045. Open daily 8am-5pm.) One perennial favorite is the 1½ mi. **interpretative trail,** which starts at the visitors center and loops past 14 marked points of interest, including an observation tower. The popular **trail number one** (2.55km) starts on the interpretative trail, then breaks off to lead to **Cueva del Viento,** where wooden stairs lead down into a dark cave filled with stalactites and stalagmites. Bring a flashlight to explore the 180 ft. cave, but make sure the rangers know you're inside. The Department of Resources also maintains several small **picnic areas** along Rte. 446 in the vicinity of the visitors center. The first area has a bathroom, but continue south for more serene and spacious eating areas. The Guajataca **camping area** was under construction at the time of publication, but should be open by 2004. Contact any office of the Department of Natural Resources for reservations and a permit (see p. 58; $4 per person). To reach Guajataca from Hwy. 2 drive east to Rte. 446, then follow Rte. 446 south all the way into the forest.

NORTHWEST

LAGO DE GUAJATACA

The 3.6 sq. mi. Lago de Guajataca has some of Puerto Rico's best fishing. Located in the heart of karst country, but less than 30min. from Hwy. 2, Guajataca is also a pleasant place to experience Puerto Rico's serene countryside. The best destination for day trippers is the **Department of Natural Resources visitors center,** Rte. 119 Km 22. This office lends out bamboo fishing poles (bring your own bait) and provides a dock, full bathrooms with shower, and a grassy picnic area. During holidays the area gets crowded, but on weekdays it is the perfect place to relax with a fishing pole and a cool drink. Swimming is prohibited; kayaking is allowed, but nobody near the lake rents kayaks. (☎896-7640. Open Tu-Su 6am-6pm.)

If the serenity of the lake entraps you, check out **Nino's Camping ❶,** Rte. 119 Km 22.1. Nino's offers a lakeside camping area, three small cabins, and a clean pool. The pleasant tent area includes water spigots, a bathroom, a cold-water shower and an electric light bulb. The cabins look like *centro vacacional cabanas* (see p. 58), with linoleum floors and rooms stuffed with lots of beds. All cabins have a balcony with a hammock, a full kitchen, a TV, and fans, but only one has A/C. Bring your own sheets and utensils. (☎896-9016 or 349-5074. $25 per tent per night. 4- to 7-person cabin Su-Th $50, F-Sa $175-200, long weekends (F-Su) $225-$250; 12-person cabin $75/$300. Cash only.)

AGUADILLA

Bustling Aguadilla holds all of the practical necessities that nobody wants to deal with, but nobody wants to live without. If you need an airport, a mall, or if you miss traffic, Aguadilla can help. The commercial town holds few attractions, but it does have a nice beach, an oceanside golf club, and an interesting history. In 1939 the US Air Force established a base just north of Aguadilla, and for the next 30 years the area served as US headquarters for protecting the Caribbean and the Panama Canal. Ramey Base, as it was renamed after WWII, closed in 1973, leaving behind the only international airport outside of San Juan and an eerie collection of indistinguishable houses and deserted buildings. But unless you're dying for quirky historical trivia, a game of a golf, or a new beach, Aguadilla should be one of those towns you pinpoint on the map while speeding past on Hwy. 2.

▐ TRANSPORTATION. Aguadilla's airport is the only direct link from the US to the west coast of Puerto Rico. **Aeropuerto Rafael Hernández** (☎891-2286), is located on Ramey Base. Continue north on Rte. 107, then turn right after entering the base. **Continental Airlines** (☎800-525-0280) flies direct to **Newark, US** (4hr.; daily 9:15am; $155, round-trip $313). Not to be confused with American Airlines, **North American Airlines** (☎800-371-6297 or 890-5805) flies to **Orlando, US** (4hr.; 2 per week; $224, round-trip $314) and JFK airport in **New York City, US** (4hr., 2 per week, one-way $174-254). **Prinair** (☎890-0698 or 890-1630) flies to **Santo Domingo, Dominican Republic** (M, W, F 10:45am; $249). Numerous car rental agencies operate out of the airport; the most affordable are generally **Budget** (☎890-1110; $32-42 per day, insurance $15; ages 21-22 surcharge $10 per day, ages 23-24 surcharge $6; open daily 9am-6pm; AmEx/D/MC/V) and **L&M** (☎890-3010; $31-42 per day, insurance $14.50; 25+; open daily 8am-5pm; AmEx/D/DC/MC/V). Aguadilla has regular *público* service from the terminal in town to: **Isabela** (25-30min., $1.75); **Mayagüez** (30-45min., $3); **Moca** (15min., $1.25); **Ramey Base** (30min., $1.10). **Choferes Unidos** (☎891-5653 or 751-7622) and **Blue Line** (☎891-4550) travel to **Río Piedras, San Juan** (2-3hr., 7 per day, $10).

▐ ORIENTATION AND PRACTICAL INFORMATION. Aguadilla's city center is located on a narrow strip of land between Hwy. 2 and the ocean. All of the city's accommodations and sights lie north of the center. **Route 111** runs north-south through the city, then connects to Rte. 107, which continues north to Ramey Base.

Take the first right after the airport, then turn left, then right on Coast Guard Rd., then left again at the end of the road, then take the first right to get on Rte. 110, which leads to Isabela's Playa Jobos. Aguadilla's branch of the **Puerto Rican Tourism Company,** in the airport, provides issues of *Que Pasa* and information about the area. (☎819-1030. Open M-Sa 8am-4:30pm.) **Western Bank** is conveniently located on Rte. 107 just south of the turn-off to Playa Crash Boat. (☎891-5005. ATM. Open M-F 7:30am-5pm, Sa 8:30-11:30am.) For **camping permits,** head to the Aguadilla DRN office, Hwy. 2 Km 120.5. This office requires 15 days advance notice. (☎882-5893 or 882-5752. $4 per night, children $2. Open M-F 7:30am-4pm.) To stock up on **groceries,** stop by **SuperCoop,** Rte. 107 Km 3. (☎882-1425. Open M-Sa 7am-9pm, Su 11am-5pm. MC/V.) **Mr. Laundromat,** Rte. 110 Km 9, has self-serve washers ($1.25) and dryers ($0.25 per 5min.), as well as detergent and a change machine. (☎882-2397. Open M-Sa 9am-9:30pm, Su 10am-8pm.) The **police station,** Ave. Victoria 463, is south of town along Rte. 111. (☎891-2020. Open 24hr.) **Walgreen's,** Hwy. 2 Km 129.3, at Ave. Juan Santos, is open 24hr. (☎882-8005. AmEx/D/MC/V.) To reach **Hospital Communitario Buen Samaritano,** Ave. Kennedy 18, take Rte. 107 south toward Hwy. 2, then turn right at the last stoplight before the highway. (☎658-000. Clinic open daily 8am-5pm. Emergency room open 24hr.) **Post Net,** Rte. 107 Km 2.8, has **Internet** service. (☎997-4190. $4.50 for 30min. or $8 per hr. Open M-Sa 8am-6pm. MC/V.) The **post office,** Rte. 459 #50, Ste. 1, is in the Aguadilla Shopping Center, just north of the intersection of Rte. 107 and Hwy. 2. (☎882-2240. No General Delivery. Open M-F 7:30am-4:30pm, Sa 8am-noon.) **Zip Code:** 00603.

⌐ ACCOMMODATIONS. One of the few reasons to stop in Aguadilla is the city's profundity of attractive accommodations. **Hotel Cielo Mar ❸,** Ave. Montemar 84, sits high up on a hill over-

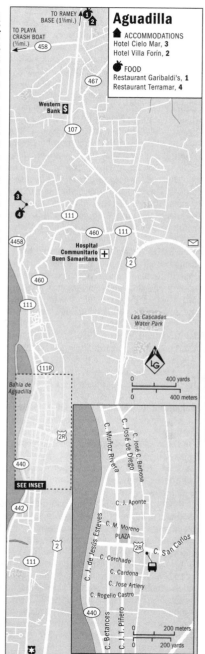

Aguadilla

▲ ACCOMMODATIONS
Hotel Cielo Mar, **3**
Hotel Villa Forín, **2**

🍴 FOOD
Restaurant Garibaldi's, **1**
Restaurant Terramar, **4**

TO RAMEY BASE (1½mi.)
TO PLAYA CRASH BOAT (½mi.)

Western Bank

Hospital Communitario Buen Samaritano

Las Cascadas Water Park

Bahía de Aguadilla

SEE INSET

0   400 yards
0   400 meters

NORTHWEST

C. Muñoz Rivera
C. José de Diego
C. José C. Barbosa
C. J. Aponte
C. M. Moreno
PLAZA
C. J. de Jesús Esteves
C. Corchado
C. Cardona
C. José Artiery
C. Rogelio Castro
C. San Carlos
C. Betances
C. J. T. Piñero

0   200 meters
0   200 yards

looking the ocean. Turn uphill at Rte. 111 Km 1.3, then follow signs. Almost every room boasts views of the water and the spectacular sunset from a small private balcony. The lobby feels like a resort, and the rooms almost maintain this excellence, with carpeted floors, A/C, TV, VCR, and phone. (☎882-5959 or 882-5960; fax 882-5577; www.cielomar.com. Pool. All-inclusive packages available. Doubles $62-$93; extra person $15; up to 2 children free. Tax included. AmEx/MC/V.) **Hotel Villa Forín ❸**, Rte. 107 Km 2.1, is one of the town's most economical options, but still maintains the aura of a professional hotel. Some rooms have been nicely renovated, while others still have linoleum floors and electric showers. Quads have two rooms and a kitchenette lacking only dishes; doubles have a microwave and a fridge. (☎882-8341; www.villa-forin.com. Small pool. Check-in 2pm. Check-out noon. Doubles $64; quads $70. Tax included. AmEx/MC/V.) To satiate that burning desire to know what it feels like to live on an Air Force Base, try **Ramey Guest House ❸**, Loop 102 #16-17. Enter the base from Rte. 107, take the first left after the golf course and follow the street as it veers to the left. These four full houses contain all of the conveniences of home, from a laundromat to a coffee maker. Three of the homes still have much of the original Air Force decor, including fortified doors and tiles in questionable colors. (☎890-4208 or 431-2939; www.rameyguesthouse.com. All houses include A/C and TV. 3-person studio $65-75; 1- to 4-bedroom houses $110-150. Tax included. No credit cards.)

🄲 **FOOD.** Aguadilla is the original home of **El Mesón Sandwiches ❶**, and several branches lie along Rte. 107. While *Let's Go* does not normally endorse fast food, this Puerto Rican chain serves inexpensive sandwiches comparable to almost any *cafetería*, and the speed and service is generally far superior (almost everything under $6). The new kid on the block is **Restaurant Garibaldi's ❸**, Rte. 107 Km 2.2, an authentic Mexican restaurant serving huge burritos, enchiladas, and tostadas that will fill you up for days. Choose between the cozy candlelit interior and the balcony over the street. (☎997-4730. Entrees $10-16. M-F 11:30am-2pm lunch specials $6. Tu 50% off margaritas. Open M-F 11:30am-10pm, Sa-Su noon-10pm. AmEx/MC/V.) Many restaurants in Aguadilla have fresh seafood but only **Restaurant Terramar ❹**, in the CieloMar Hotel (see **Accommodations**, p. 175), has a circular patio overlooking the ocean. The limited menu serves almost exclusively seafood and *mofongos*. But really, what else could you ask for? (Entrees $10-22. Open Su-Th 7am-10pm, F-Sa 7am-1am. AmEx/MC/V.) **Paradise Health Food ❶**, Rte. 110 Km 10.8, is Aguadilla's contribution to the world of vegetarianism. Smooshed into the back of a health food store, Paradise offers a daily menu with rice, vegetables, and tofu, as well as an interesting selection of *batidas*. (☎890-2043. *Batidas* $1.75-2.50. Entrees $4.50-6. Open M-F 8:30am-5:30pm. MC/V.)

🄱 **BEACHES.** Aguadillans boast about **Playa Crash Boat** (Crash Boat Beach) as if it's the highlight of the city, and it very well may be. This small palm tree-lined beach has medium-sized waves, good swimming, and lots of shaded picnic tables. Unfortunately, it also attracts quite a large crowd, especially on weekends and during the summer, when traffic backs up en route to the beach. Furthermore, a large cement structure (conveniently excluded from most postcards) mars the pristine coastline. If you're in the area, Crash Boat is a wonderful place to spend the day, but if you have time head to Rincón or Isabela. The beach has bathrooms, but only the most desperate would consider using them. (From Hwy. 2 turn west onto Rte. 107, then follow Rte. 458 to the turn-off for the beach.) To explore more uncharted territory, head to **Las Ruínas**, a wild beach area named after the ruins of several old Air Force buildings. The first turn-off leads to a rarely visited white sand beach at the edge of a picturesque white cliff. Continue along the bumpy dirt road to find big waves popular wtih **surfers,** and beautiful vistas popular with young couples. (Drive north on Rte. 107 into Base Ramey, turn left on the road that goes through the golf course, and continue to the end. No facilities.)

◙ SIGHTS. Eighteen-hole **Punta Borinquen Golf Club,** inside Base Ramey, boasts palm trees, distant ocean views, and reasonable prices. (Enter Base Ramey on Rte. 107 and turn left at the golf club entrance. ☎890-2987. Green fees M-F $18, Sa-Su $20; golf cart $20, required on weekends. Equipment $10. Open M-F 7am-dusk, Sa-Su 6:30am-dusk. AmEx/MC/V.) In 2001 Aguadilla opened **Las Cacadas Water Park,** Hwy. 2 Km 126.5. The park has been built into the side of the hill and contains several waterslides and a large wave pool. (☎819-1030. Open late March-Sept. daily 10am-6pm. $10, ages 4-12 $8, ages 55-74 $5, under 3 and over 75 free. MC/V.)

Aguadilla is not particularly known for its diving, but **Aquatica Adventures,** Rte. 110 Km 10, still manages to find some good spots, including shore dives in the Isabela and Aguadilla area ($45, equipment $10) and two-tank dives off a 28' boat in Cabo Rojo ($65, equipment $10). A full day of snorkeling off the boat runs about $45. They offer private PADI and SSI certification courses for $350. (☎890-6071; aquatica@caribe.net. Open M-Sa 9am-5pm, Su 9am-3pm. MC/V.)

▨ NIGHTLIFE. Like most west coast Puerto Ricans, Aguadillans head to the beach for their nightlife. If you decide to stay in town, try **J.D.'s Pub,** Rte. 110 Km 10.8, a popular Americanized bar conveniently located near the Coast Guard station. The interior looks a bit seedy at first glance, but this sports bar can hop on weekend nights, especially when the club throws one of its legendary parties. With two pool tables, a dance floor, and a long bar, everyone has a rip-roarin' good time. (☎890-2433. Beer $2-3; mixed drinks $4-5. W open bar 8pm-midnight. F-Sa live DJ. Cover $5 when there is live music. Open M-Th 3pm-midnight, F-Sa 3pm-2am. AmEx/MC/V.) If J.D.'s is a bit too raucous, head for the elegant **Moonlight Lounge** at Hotel Cielo Mar (see **Accommodations,** p. 175). On Fridays the establishment remains true to its Latin roots with salsa, merengue, and Spanish ballads at 5pm. However, Saturday is 80s night from 5 to 9pm, then live tropical music starts at 9pm. This may be the only disco in Puerto Rico where you can dance with an ocean view. (Beer $3. 21+. Open Su-Th 7am-10pm, F-Sa 7am-1am. AmEx/MC/V.)

DAYTRIP FROM AGUADILLA: MOCA

Public Transportation: Públicos make the short trip from Aguadilla to Moca (15min., $1.25). *Driving:* From Aguadilla, continue south on Rte. 111 past Hwy. 2, and follow the road as it turns east. Turn right at the town center just before the pedestrian bridge.

The small town of Moca is the island's center for the production of *mundillo,* an intricate type of lace originally imported from Spain and now famous in Puerto Rico. Many *mocanos,* especially women, spend hours hand-weaving the fine lace that adorns shirts, towels, and, most frequently, beautiful baby clothes. *Mundillo* is considered to be one of Puerto Rico's premier handicrafts (see p. 26). Just walking through town demonstrates the importance of the art, as several houses advertise *mundillo* where women weave and sell from the comfort of their own living rooms. **Artesanía Leonides,** C. Blanco E. Chico 185, the only real *mundillo* store in town sells a variety of products, but focuses primarily on elaborate baby dresses. (☎877-4092. Open M-Sa 10am-6pm, Su 10am-5:30pm. MC/V.) For the scoop on the *mundillo* scene, stop for a chat with **Ada Hernández,** who seems to know every *mundillo* artisan in town. She is more than happy to give visitors a grand tour, or take them to individual artisans' houses to buy the lace. (Facing the *Alcaldía,* turn left and walk down the side street known as C. Miranda. Ada lives at number 126. ☎877-3800.)

The town is currently in the process of constructing a museum dedicated exclusively to *mundillo,* but organizers are stuck in typical bureaucratic confusion. Until it opens, visit *mocano* Sr. Augusto Hernández (not related to Ada), who wrote a several hundred-page book called *Historia y Desarrollo del Mundillo Mocano* (History and Development of Moca Mundillo; $17) that he sells from his school supply shop, C. Blanco Chico 176. (☎877-5086. Open M-Sa 8am-4:30pm.)

The best time to visit Moca is at the end of June during the annual 3-day **Festival de Mundillo,** when the town's artisans gather on the main plaza to display and sell their wares. For more information contact Sra. Hernández.

RINCÓN

Most surfers already know about Rincón. The city leaped into the spotlight in 1968 as the host of the world surfing championships and it hasn't looked back since. Waves here can get as high as 25 ft., and at least 15 breaks lie within close proximity to town, making this the best surfing area in Puerto Rico, and the Caribbean. But Rincón is a lot more than a big wave. The beautiful jungle-like area remains largely undeveloped, with a series of tiny roads winding through tropical forest down to pristine beaches. A sort of cult following has developed around this natural playground, symbolized by the "University of Rincón" and "Rincón 413: Road to Paradise" bumper stickers placed on cars throughout the island, and the robust expat community welcomes visitors with open arms. Life in Rincón is essentially one relaxed party and even non-surfers find it easy, and appealing, to join right in. With first-rate diving, snorkeling, and whale-watching conditions, there's no lack of activities to keep busy. Life in Rincón is simple and inviting. The only real worry is that you'll never want to leave.

▐▀ TRANSPORTATION

Take Hwy. 2 to Rte. 115, which eventually leads through the town of Rincón. To reach Puntas, and most of the beaches and guest houses, turn off on Rte. 413, a small road that follows the arc of the coastline. Very few **públicos** come to Rincón from other cities, but you can occasionally find transport to **Aguadilla** (20min., $2) and **Mayagüez** (20min., $1.75). More frequent *públicos* follow Rte. 413 to **Puntas** (15min., $0.50). Most long-distance *públicos* leave by 7am. A **free trolley** travels between the post office north of town on Rte. 115 and the factories south of town (daily 8am-2pm). Wait at any of the marked stops. **Angelo's Car Rental,** Rte. 115 Km 10.9, rents cars to anyone with a valid driver's license and will pick up customers from the Aguadilla and Mayagüez airports, or any guest house. (☎823-3438 or 479-8304. Cash rentals $40 for the first day, $35 for each additional day; $250 deposit. Credit card rentals $43/$38. Open M-Sa 8am-5pm. MC/V.)

◢◪ ▟ ORIENTATION AND PRACTICAL INFORMATION

Even veteran Puerto Rican travelers may initially find themselves a bit lost in Rincón. With only about 10 streets, the town itself is reasonably straightforward, but most of the action takes place in the surrounding hills. From the town center continue north on Rte. 115 to the intersection with **Route 413,** which follows the coastline. After about ½ mi. you'll reach a turn-off to the Black Eagle Marina, marked by a huge sign for Taíno Divers. Another ½ mi. down the road, a sign points to **"the lighthouse road."** North of the lighthouse you are officially in **Puntas.** Five steep roads lead downhill to the beach, but only three intersect with Rte. 413. The southernmost road, at Km 3.3, passes Nuclear Vista Rd. and leads to the flat road lining the beaches, known as **"Beach Rd."** The next road to the north sometimes has a sign labeling it as Vista Linda Rd. The northernmost road is referred to as **"Bummer Hill,"** because if you have to walk up it, that's a bummer. Bummer Hill runs between a Shell station on Rte. 413 and The Landing. The **Estella** neighborhood, about 14 numbered streets south of town near the intersection with Rte. 429, contains several condos on Playa Corcéga.

Tourist Information: Rincón Municipal Tourist Office (☎823-5024), at the end of C. Nueva, behind the police station, has limited literature. The English-speaking staff can answer questions. Open M-F 8am-4:30pm.

Bank: Banco Popular, C. Comercio 2 (☎823-2260), at C. Muñoz Rivera. ATM. Open M-F 8am-4pm, Sa 9am-noon.

Rincón

🏠 ACCOMMODATIONS

Amirage Apartments, **33**
Beside the Pointe Guest House, **2**
Casa Isleña, **5**
Casa Verde Vacation Rentals, **11**
Coconut Palms Guest House, **31**
Dos Angeles del Mar Guest House, **13**
Joey O's Bummer Hills Room Rental, **17**
Parador Villa Cofresí, **29**
Pipons Resort, **15**
Rincón Surf and Board, **14**
Sandy Beach Inn, **10**

🍴 FOOD

Broadway's Deli and Bagels, **32**
Calypso Cafe, **20**
Golden City Restaurant, **34**
The Landing, **6**
El Nuevo Flamboyan, **9**
Punta Mar Bakery, **22**
Restaurante Bambino's, **30**
Rincón Tropical, **35**
The Spot, **28**
Tamboo Bar & Seaside Grill, **3**

🍸 NIGHTLIFE

Machu Picchu Cafe, **21**

〰️ SURF BREAKS

Antonio's Beach, **1**
Dead Man's, **16**
Dogman's, **25**
Domes, **12**
Indicators, **18**
Maria's, **23**
The Pistons, **24**
The Point, **19**
Pools Beach, **7**
Sandy Beach, **4**
Spanish Wall, **8**
Tres Palmas, **27**
Toilet Bowl, **26**

NORTHWEST

Equipment Rental: Coconut Watersports & Bicycle Rental (☎309-9328 or 823-2450), at Parador Villa Cofresí (see p. 181) rents kayaks (singles $10 per hr., doubles $15), 3-person pedal boats ($20 per hr.), inflatable tubes ($5 per day), boogie boards ($5 per day), beach umbrellas ($5 per day), snorkel gear ($10 per day), and bikes ($5 per hr.). They also offer banana boat rides (20min., $10). Open Sa-Su during daylights hours, M-F by phone only.

Publications: The Rincón Cultural Center (see **Sights,** p. 183) publishes the bi-monthly newsletter *Juntos,* available at the cultural center. This seemingly random collection of articles, poems, and photos perfectly exemplifies Rincón's quirky charm.

English-Language Bookstore: See **Internet Access,** below.

Supermarket: Econo, Rte. 115 Km 12.8 (☎823-2470), south of town. Open M-Sa 7am-9pm, Su 11am-5pm. AmEx/MC/V.

Laundromat: #1 Laundromat, C. Comercio 18 (☎823-6614), in town. Wash $1.25. Dry $1.75. Change available. Open M-Sa 7am-6pm.

Police: At the end of C. Nueva (☎823-2020 or 823-2021), in town. Open 24hr.

Late-Night Pharmacy: Farmacia del Pueblo, C. Muñoz Rivera 33 (☎823-2540), has a relatively large selection. Open M-Sa 8am-9pm, Su 8am-6pm. AmEx/D/MC/V.

Medical Services: Rincón Health Center, C. Muñoz Rivera 29 (☎823-5555). Clinic open M-F 8am-4:30pm. Urgent care open M-F 8am-8pm, Sa-Su 8am-4pm.

Internet Access: Cowabunga's Ice Cream and Internet Cafe, Rte. 115 Km 11.6 (☎823-5225). Offers Internet service ($1 per 15min.) and sells used English books. Open Tu-Su 1-9pm. **Rincón Public Library** (☎823-9075), on C. Nueva, has 1 computer with free Internet access. 30min. limit. Open M-F 8am-5:30pm and 6:30-9pm.

Post Office: Rte. 115 #100 (☎823-2625) has General Delivery. Open M-F 8am-4:30pm, Sa 8am-noon.

Zip Code: 00677.

ACCOMMODATIONS

Excluding San Juan, Rincón has the best selections of accommodations on the island. A number of American- (and American/Puerto Rican-) run guest houses cater to both surfers and plain ol' vacationers. If you want to jump right into the surfer scene, hang out with Americans all day, and drink lots of beer, head straight to Puntas. For more Puerto Rican accommodations, try the area south of town, where a few nice hotels hide in quiet residential neighborhoods.

REALTOR

Island West Properties, Rte. 413 Km 0.7 (☎823-2323; fax 823-3254; www.islandwest.com), rents condos, beach houses, and villas throughout Rincón for $105-$350. 3 night min. 50% deposit required. Open M-Sa 9am-3pm. MC/V. ❹

PUNTAS

🏖 **Rincón Surf and Board** (☎823-0610; fax 823-6440; www.surfandboard.com), in Puntas. With inexpensive dorm rooms and an on-site surf school (p. 183), it's no wonder that this has become the prime surfer hangout. This guest house sits on stilts 70 ft. above a jungle canopy, creating a unique tropical atmosphere. The facade is decaying, but attractive private rooms have handmade mosaics, a private library, and cable TV. Dorms have a common room with cable TV. Quiet time starts at 10pm. Small pool. 20min. walk from the beach. Private rooms include continental breakfast. Internet $5 per hr. or $3 for 30min. 4-bed coed dorms $20. Doubles $55-65; 2-person suites with kitchen $85-95; extra person $10. 3-bedroom house $175. Apr. to mid-Nov. $5-10 low season discount. 9% tax not included. MC/V. ❶

Sandy Beach Inn (☎823-1146), on the 2nd road from the south, offers Rincón's most affordable private accommodations. Clean, well-equipped rooms contain TV, A/C, and fridge. However, some mattresses are a bit past their prime. 4min. walk to the beach. Great view from the 3rd floor restaurant. Singles $40-60; doubles $50-80; 4-person apartment with kitchen $100; 8-person apartment $275. Tax included. AmEx/MC/V. ❷

Dos Angeles del Mar Guest House (☎431-6057; www.dosangelesdelmar.8k.com), up the street from Casa Verde. One of the newest players in the Puntas vacation scene offers an aesthetic charm unavailable at most other guest houses. The beautiful 2-story house has 4 spotless rooms with microwave, fridge, TV, A/C, wicker beds, daily maid service, and ocean views. Friendly owners. Doubles $69-89; quads $109. MC/V. ❸

Casa Verde Vacation Rentals (☎605-5351; www.enricon.com) on Beach Rd., has become one of the most hopping surfer hang-outs, primarily due to its ideal location (1min. from Sandy Beach) and its well-stocked bar. Unlike the fading green facade, the rooms are quite modern. All include a kitchen, A/C in 1 room, and a TV. Doubles $60; 2-bedroom apartment $129; 3-bedroom house $200. 9% tax not included. MC/V. ❸

Joey O's Bummer Hills Room Rental (☎943-0706), on Bummer Hill, offers hard-core surfers the cheapest place to sleep in Puntas. 2 small coed dorms have rickety bunks beds with thin mattresses, overhead fans, and lockers under the bed. Very rustic private rooms in a cabin have wooden walls and bare light bulbs. Cable TV to come. Common area with full kitchen. No office; call ahead. Open Nov.-March. Dorms $15 per night, $300 per month; private doubles $25/$400. No credit cards. ❶

Casa Isleña (☎823-1525, toll-free 888-289-7750; www.casa-islena.com), just off Beach Rd. For luxurious accommodations in Puntas, look no farther than Casa Isleña, a gorgeous 6-room hacienda right on the beach. Big, spacious rooms with Mexican tiles offer incomparable ocean views; it actually feels like you're on the water. All rooms have A/C, cable TV, and daily maid service; most have fridges, and 2 have private balconies. Big patio, swimming pool, direct beach access, and restaurant (see p. 182). Doubles $115-145; extra person $15. 9% tax not included. AmEx/MC/V. ❹

Beside the Pointe Guest House (☎/fax 823-8550, toll-free 888-823-8550; www.besidethepointe.com), on Beach Rd. This guest house boasts a great location right on Sandy Beach, and a popular restaurant/bar (see Tamboo Bar, p. 182). 8 brightly painted rooms with murals on the wall have lots of character, but the building itself is not as pristine as you may expect. Cable TV, fridge, and A/C. Dec. 15-Apr. 24 doubles $90-150; quads $120; 2- to 6-person apartments with kitchen $125-180. Apr. 25-Dec. 14 $70-120/$100/$110-150. 9% tax not included. MC/V. ❹

Pipons Resort (☎/fax 823-7154 or 823-5106; www.piponsresort.com), on Bummer Hill, has 6 spacious luxury apartments in a huge white house overlooking Antonio's Beach. Every room has a private balcony, an ocean view, A/C, kitchen, TV, and wicker furniture. The 5th and 6th guests have to sleep on couches. ¼ mi. from beach. Nightly: doubles $115; quads $150; 6-person $165. Weekly: $750/$925/$1000. MC/V. ❹

SOUTH OF TOWN

Amirage Apartments, Rte. 429 Km 4 (☎/fax 823-6454; www.proceanfront.com), is the ultimate word in tranquility. An expat couple has constructed their dream home, a beautiful white villa overlooking the water, and luckily they've opted to share it. Three gorgeous rooms with tasteful murals feel just like home, down to the bathrobe waiting in the closet. Common courtyard contains a lush garden and a jacuzzi. Want more? All rooms have cable TV, VCR, A/C, ocean-view balcony, kitchen, and dishwasher. Free kayak and snorkel equipment use. The one fault is the rocky beach, but it's a short kayak trip to sandier seas. 2-person suite $125; 4- to 6- person suites $150. No credit cards. ❹

Parador Villa Cofresí, Rte. 115 Km 12 (☎823-2450; fax 823-1770; www.villacofresi.com), feels like a beachside resort, but at a fraction of the price. As soon as you enter the spacious lobby, your vacation may start to look like it needs an extension. Big pool area, bar, and 3 pool tables right on the beach. Cable TV, A/C, and fridge. Check-in 3pm. Check-out noon. Doubles $95-135; 2-bedroom apartments $140-155; extra person $15; 2 children under 15 free. 9% tax not included. AmEx/D/MC/V. ❹

Coconut Palms Guest House, C. 8 #2734 (☎823-0147; fax 823-5431; www.coconut-palmsinn.com). A low-key beach villa in a quiet residential neighborhood. This white house centers on a wild courtyard garden filled with birds and a jacuzzi. Board games, used book libraries, kitchenette, and cable TV. Right on Playa Corcéga. Studios $75-100; apartments $100-125; extra person $10. MC/V. ❸

⬛ FOOD

Rincón offers a smorgasbord of dining options designed to satiate the healthy surfer appetite. Most of the food options are heavily American influenced and almost all Puntas restaurants have a vegetarian option.

THE SURF BREAK (PUNTAS, LIGHTHOUSE AREA, THE MARINA)

The Spot (☎823-3510), at Black Eagle Marina. When you tire of burgers, sandwiches, and beach grub, head to The Spot for a satisfying gourmet meal. The owner brings in a rotating series of chefs from the US to cook up elegant fusion cuisine found nowhere else in Rincón. His plain white house has been converted into a relaxed, welcoming, tropical restaurant; try the back patio at sunset. Entrees $6-24. Happy Hour 4-6pm. Open winter W-M 5-10pm; summer Th-Su 5-10pm. MC/V. ❹

El Nuevo Flamboyan, on the southernmost road, manages to serve Puerto Rican cuisine and still be a foreign favorite. This simple eatery offers candlelit dinner in a small house hanging over the cliff in prime sunset-viewing position. Brush up on your Puerto Rican history with the patriotic posters on the wall. Entrees $8-15. Happy Hour daily 5-7pm Open daily 5-9pm. Bar open later. Cash only. ❸

Tamboo Bar & Seaside Grill (☎823-8550), at Beside the Point Guest House (see p. 181). In addition to being a popular bar (all day long), Tamboo serves a variety of moderately priced grill items, including fish, burgers, chicken, and wraps, on the big patio. Good lunch spot. Entrees $9-18; sandwiches $6-9. Open Th-Tu noon-9pm. MC/V. ❸

The Landing (☎823-4779), on Beach Rd. It's not cheap to be trendy, and The Landing is certainly the coolest place in town. Before the large wooden restaurant transforms into nightlife central, foreigners gather on the back patio to munch on Americanized island specials. Food is tasty, but nothing extraordinary. Sandwiches $7-10; entrees $13-20. Open Su-Th 11:30am-10pm, F-Sa 11:30am-11pm. AmEx/MC/V. ❹

Casa Isleña (see p. 181), on Beach Rd., serves up an elegant breakfast and lunch on its poolside courtyard. This is one of the only places in Puntas to eat breakfast, and even if it wasn't, it would still be one of the best. Don't miss the walnut pineapple chicken salad ($7.25). Breakfast $4-6.25; lunch $5-13. Open W-Su 7am-3pm. AmEx/MC/V. ❷

Punta Mar Bakery, Rte. 413 Km 4.1 (☎823-2455). This generic *panadería* is one of the cheapest eateries in Puntas. Grab a quick breakfast or sandwich on the go. Very limited indoor and outdoor seating. Also sells some toiletries and groceries. No written menu. Everything under $5. Open daily 6am-10pm. MC/V. ❶

Calypso Cafe (☎823-2616 or 823-1616), on the road to the lighthouse, stands out for its prime location. Use the outdoor patio to watch either the sunset or the surfers below at Maria's Beach. Popular lunch break spot for surfers. Generic sandwiches and expat-friendly dishes $3.50-10. Open daily 1-6:30pm. MC/V. ❷

THE REAL WORLD (TOWN, SOUTH OF TOWN)

Rincón Tropical, Rte. 115 Km 12.4 (☎823-2017), south of town. To experience real Puerto Rican culture, forego the American-run places in Puntas and try out a more tropical Rincón. Reasonably priced seafood and *comida criolla* at a clean outdoor restaurant. M-F $4 lunch special. Entrees $6-19. Open daily 11am-9:30pm. ❸

Broadway's Deli and Bagels, Rte. 115 Km 11.3 (☎823-7641), south of town, won't quite take you back to the Big Apple, but this is one of Puerto Rico's few bagel places. Not surprisingly, a largely foreign crowd comes for the gourmet lunch sandwiches and fresh salads. Entrees $3.75-5. Open W-Sa 7am-5pm, Su 8am-2pm. Cash only.❶

Restaurante Bambino's, Rte. 115 Km 12 (☎823-3744). A friendly Italian restaurant that offers reasonably priced sit-down meals. Italian and *comida criolla* entrees $11-19. Lunch buffet M and W-F $5. Open F-W 11am-10pm. AmEx/MC/V. ❸

Golden City Restaurant, C. Muñoz Rivera 57/Rte. 115 (☎823-5829). Good, cheap Chinese food. The generic City serves Hunan Beef ($6.50), *comida criolla* ($3-4.50), and everything in between. Entrees $4-7.25. Open daily 11am-10pm. Cash only. ❶

◉ SIGHTS

Nobody comes to Rincón for its sights, but there are a couple of attractions.

PUNTA HIGÜERA LIGHTHOUSE. Rincón's lighthouse is both newer and less dramatic than others on the island. The original 1892 lighthouse was destroyed in 1918 and rebuilt in 1921 (then again in 1922). A fire severely damaged the structure in the 1930s but, undeterred, officials rebuilt the lighthouse once again in 1993 to commemorate the 500th anniversary of Columbus's landing on the island. You cannot enter the lighthouse, but the manicured park, with benches, grass, and trees, is a popular and pleasant place to walk and watch the surfers below. Sometimes a Puerto Rican couple offers horse and carriage rides around the lighthouse and over to Maria's Beach, a particularly romantic trip at sunset. *(At the end of lighthouse road. Carriage rides F-Su and holidays 11am-6pm. Adults $3, children $2.)*

B.O.N.U.S. NUCLEAR REACTOR. Of all the contraptions the US has bestowed upon Puerto Rico, this may be worst. The large green dome just past the lighthouse was built in 1964 as the first nuclear energy plant in Latin America, but quickly closed in the 1970. There have been plans to turn the plant into a nuclear museum, but locals are apprehensive about the hazards of reopening the plant; the deteriorating sign out front doesn't look promising. *(Just past the lighthouse.)*

CENTRO CULTURAL RINCONEÑO. This eclectic museum seems to house everything that nobody could find a home for elsewhere in Rincón. The two rooms contain local artwork, Taíno artifacts, *vejigante* masks, and assorted antiques. *(Rte. 413 Km 0.3. ☎823-5120. Open Tu and Th 9:30am-2:30pm, Sa-Su 9am-2pm. Free.)*

◢ RIDING THE WAVES

Rincón is the premier surfing spot in the Caribbean, and one of the top surfing destinations in the world. Below is a list of the various surfing spots and services, but this is just a brief summary of a rapidly changing industry. Conditions change daily, surfing instructors come and go, and many surfers threaten bodily harm if their favorite spots are listed in a travel guide. To get the scoop, head to Happy Hour at Calypso, make some new friends, and find out what's really happening in Rincón.

SURF SHOPS AND LESSONS

Rincón Surf and Board (www.surfandboard.com; see p. 180), is the only surf school in town. Full-day lessons for all levels (9am-4pm $89, 2 days $169) include transportation and equipment. The shop also rents surfboards ($20 per day), boogie boards ($13 per day), snorkel gear ($9 per day), and beach supplies. Discounts for guests. MC/V.

West Coast Surf Shop, C. Muñoz Rivera 2E (☎823-3935; www.westcoastsurf.com), in town. Rents surfboards ($20 for 24hr.), boogie boards ($10 for 24hr.), and snorkel gear ($15 for 24hr.). They also arrange surfing lessons ($20 per hr. per student) and sell a wide selection of surf gear. Open M-Sa 9am-6pm, Su 10am-5pm. AmEx/MC/V.

NORTHWEST

THE LOCAL STORY

DAVID STILES, SURF GURU

New Jersey-native David Stiles has lived in Rincón for the last 18 years. He repairs and builds surfboards to fund his life as a professional surfer.

LG: Why Rincón?

A: When I was in 8th grade, rich kids got money to come surfing here. This place got popular in '68 with the World Amateur Contest. I have always seen the photo albums and read the articles, but I've never been able to come here. Then I bought a new truck and I had two tickets with American Airlines anywhere they fly good for a year. I was on my way to Disney World with my wife and my kids and I thought "Nah, I'm going to go surf Puerto Rico." I didn't do it when I was 17, so I did it when I was 35.

LG: Why surfing? What's appealing about it?

A: The adrenaline thing, the thrill. I like the water and boating and all that stuff. But when I started surfing I stopped doing everything else. I saw a surfer dragging a board down the beach at Malibu, California in *Life* magazine in 7th grade and I just went "Yup, that's what I want to do."

LG: So what do you think of the people who come down here for just a week or two and try out the waves?

A: They're just like me. It's like I say, doctor, lawyer, Indian chief, it's interesting as hell. You don't know who's going to walk in the shop. Paul McCartney comes and surfs in Australia, in Barbados. So it's pretty interesting. About the time I can't stomach it anymore the surf season stops and it's just the Puerto Ricans and me.

Closeout, C. Muñoz Rivera 40 (☎823-2515), in town, sells surfboards and surf gear. The friendly staff answers questions about the area. Open daily 9am-5pm. AmEx/MC/V.

Hotwayz Surf Shop (☎823-3942), on the lighthouse road below El Calypso (see p. 182), rents fun boards and boogie boards ($8 for the 1st hr., $2 for each additional hr.; $15 per day; $20 per 24hr.). They also provide info about surfing lessons and sell gear. Open daily 11am-6pm. MC/V.

Desecheo Dive Shop (☎823-2672 or 823-0390), on the lighthouse road, rents surfboards, boogie boards and snorkeling equipment ($10 per ½ day, $15 per day). They also sell beachware and arrange boating trips through other companies. Open winter daily 10am-6pm; summer M-F 11am-5:30pm, Sa-Su 10am-6pm. AmEx/MC/V.

SURFBOARD REPAIRS

David Stiles (☎823-2364), on Bummer Hill, has built over 11,000 surfboards and currently repairs boards and builds upper-end custom surfboards. He also sells some used boards. Open during the surf season only (Dec.-Apr.). Call ahead. No credit cards.

Dr. Ding (☎823-8018), on Nuclear Vista Rd., repairs boards and makes new boards. Open daily; call ahead for an appointment.

SURF BEACHES

From south to north, the principal surfing beaches in Rincón are listed below.

Tres Palmas. The best surfing spot in the Caribbean. Waves up to 25 ft. and beyond break about ¾ mi. out. Experienced surfers only.

Toilet Bowl. The surf here will pull you under like a toilet bowl would.

Dogman's. A shallow beach with fast, well-formed waves. Better for more advanced surfers. A local favorite (see **Surf Guru,** p. 184).

The Pistons. Named after the WWII engine pistons that remain lodged in the water. The pistons can be dangerous if you get caught up in them; experienced surfers only.

Maria's. A popular break right underneath Calypso Cafe (see p. 182). The waves break relatively close to the shore here, so you won't have to paddle out much.

Indicators. Located under the lighthouse.

Dead Man's. No it's not folklore, this beach was actually named after the dead bodies that have washed up here. This is an advanced break right against a perilous cliff.

Domes. One of the most popular and consistent breaks in the Rincón area. Can get quite crowded. Located in front of the nuclear reactor.

Sandy Beach. Come early in the morning to beat the crowds. A sandy bottom makes this a good place for beginners.

Antonio's Beach. Located in front of The Landing (see p. 182).

🏔 OUTDOOR ACTIVITIES

BEACHES

In spite of the ample coastline, many of the beaches near Rincón are too rough or inaccessible for swimming. However, a few patches of white sand and calmer waters invite more tame recreation. A couple of miles south of town **Playa Corcéga** has the best swimming beaches near Rincón and during the winter months Corcéga remains refreshingly empty. Drive south on Rte. 429 to the area around Km 1, then turn west, park near the condos, and walk between buildings to the beach. The *balneario municipal* **(public beach)** has both gentle Caribbean waves and larger Atlantic waves. Half of the beach has almost eroded away, but the other half is still a nice place for swimming. Facilities include trash cans, a playground, parking, and bathrooms that occasionally work. To reach the beach, take the road marked *balneario* just south of town, past Closeout surf shop (see p. 184).

FISHING

Captain José Alfonso of **Makaira Fishing Charters** leads fishing charters on his 32' boat (½-day $450, full-day $640). He also charters whale watching and sunset cruises upon request. (☎823-4391 or 299-7374; makaira@caribe.net. Price includes refreshments, gear, and tackle. 25% deposit required. MC/V.)

HORSEBACK RIDING

It is illegal to ride horses on beaches in Rincón. However, **Pintos "R" Us,** next to Casa Verde (see p. 181), leads rides along the Domes trail through fields and woods during the day (1hr., $25; 2hr., $40) and beach rides (2hr., $50) after dark. (☎598-8614. Cash only.)

SNORKELING AND DIVING

Some of Puerto Rico's best diving and snorkeling waits just 14 mi. from Rincón around rocky, deserted **Isla Desecheo.** With thriving reefs, visibility consistently over 100 ft. and ample fish species, this ranks among the best diving spots in Puerto Rico. The DRN prohibits visitors from coming on the island, but Rincón's two superb dive shops take visitors out to dive and snorkel near the shore. Both of the first-rate dive operators below are extremely qualified. If you don't want to head out on a boat, **Playa Shacks** is the best snorkeling beach on land.

🏊 **Oceans Unlimited,** Rte. 115 Km 11.9 (☎823-2340; fax 823-2370; www.oceans-unlimited.com), takes their 46' boat on regular trips to Desecheo and the Cabo Rojo wall (8am-3:30pm; 2-tank dive $95, snorkeling $45, swimming $25, 2-tank Discover Scuba package $150). Shorter trips go to the Mayagüez reefs (8am-12:30pm; 2-tank dive $65, snorkeling $40). Full-day expeditions include snorkel-

LG: What were you saying earlier about the competition that springs here? Is that unique to this area?
A: No, that's part of surfing. There's a pecking order and when you go to a surf spot and are a visitor you invade the locals' pecking order. And it's how you present yourself and it has to be done with respect or you'll get thrown out, beat up, shut down, whatever it takes to get you outta there, they're going to push you out. When you stay local, stay at your own break, then they have to bust into your pecking order.
LG: And what's your favorite spot here, that's not secret?
A: Dogman's.
LG: Why Dogman's?
A: It's shallow, it's fast, and it's thrilling even when it's small. It has great form. It can be good waist high and it can be good four times your body height there. Offshore winds are perfect. A lot of people stay at the safer breaks. It's not radical compared to worldwide surfing, but it is for this corner of the world.
LG: So how does this compare to worldwide surfing?
A: It's not consistently as big. But it has consistent waves enough that you can appease your surfing appetite. It's very warm all the time. Warmer than Hawaii. And it's one of the few places where you can cat around and play to win. You can still get up in the morning and go surfing with two guys out. And you get up the next day and there's 62 guys out. But it's those days that you get 2, 3, 6, 10, or 12 that really make it worthwhile. That's hard to do anywhere in the world. You'll never do that in California or Hawaii. Never.

ing equipment and lunch; scuba equipment rental $20. Half-day expeditions include a snack. Also offers 2hr. BYOB sunset cruises ($25), whale watching cruises (Jan.-Mar.; $25), and PADI dive certification (3 day open-water diver course $400). Also goes to Isla Mona and offers Nitrox diving. Boat leaves from Puerto Real. Open daily 9am-6pm. MC/V.

■ **Taíno Divers**, Rte. 413 Km 1 (☎823-6429; www.tainodivers.com), in Black Eagle Marina. Their 34' boat goes to Desecheo almost daily (2-tank dive $95, snorkeling $40). Shorter trips go to reefs around Rincón (2-tank dive $65, snorkeling $25). All trips include lunch and beverages. Scuba equipment rental $20. Deep-sea fishing charters $500, including all equipment. 2hr. whale watching and sunset cruises $25. 1-tank Discover Scuba package $125. Open-water certification $400. Goes to Isla Mona. Open daily 10am-6pm. MC/V.

WHALE WATCHING

As if there wasn't already enough to do, Rincón also has a prime location to watch the humpback whales migrate through the deep waters of the Mona passage every winter. From January to April, it is quite common to see the massive creatures spurting water, or even jumping, from most area businesses. The lighthouse park is prime observation area, and both **Oceans Unlimited** and **Taíno Divers** (see **Snorkeling and Scuba Diving,** p. 185) offer excursions to head out for a closer look.

▌ NIGHTLIFE

It's tough to surf at night, and as a result of this technical difficulty, Rincón has a hopping nightlife scene. Because most partiers are on vacation, weeknights can be almost as exciting as weekends. Even nightlife is a bit of a misnomer, as it's quite common to find people relaxing with a Medalla at 11am. Cheers to the surfing life.

The Landing (☎823-4779), on Beach Rd., is Rincón's most popular bar in Rincón, and can feel like an alternative frat party. M is the biggest night, closely followed by every other night. The fleet of bartenders stands in the middle, tossing bottles in the air like pros. M open jam 11pm. Th college night. F karaoke 11pm. Sa live rock 11pm. Su live jazz 2pm. Beer $3.25-3.50; mixed drinks $5.50-6.50. Open daily 11:30am-last person leaves. AmEx/MC/V.

Calypso Cafe (see **Restaurants,** p. 182), on the road to the lighthouse. This tropical outdoor bar is *the* Happy Hour destination. Every day from 5 to 7pm surfers, locals, and wanderers gather here to watch the sun drop down over Maria's Beach and enjoy the Happy Hour specials (rum punch $2). Sa live tropical music 10pm. Su live jazz 6-9pm. Beer and mixed rum drinks $2.75-3. Open daily 11am-last person leaves. MC/V.

Machu Picchu Cafe, Rte. 413 Km 2.8 (☎823-2787), provides one of the few places to get your groove on in Puntas. The night starts off slow, with a few people playing pool downstairs or sipping drinks at the bar, then crescendos to a 2-story dance party with fluorescent lights and loud rock/pop/reggae music. Puerto Rican and foreign crowd. F-Su live music 11pm. Open Tu-Th and Su 8pm-3am, F-Sa 2pm-5am. AmEx/MC/V.

Tamboo Bar & Seaside Grill (☎823-8550), at Beside the Pointe Guest House. Don't worry, be happy; everyone's just chillin' at Tamboo. Surfers and surf-lovers sit on the large wooden patio watching people try their luck at Sandy Beach. Happy Hour daily 7-9pm. Beer $2-2.50; mixed drinks $3.50-4. Open Th-Tu 11am-last person leaves. MC/V.

SOUTHWEST

Don't miss southwest Puerto Rico. It may seem like a long drive from the capital, but the stunning landscape in this corner of the island holds a wealth of unique natural attractions. Forget those images of lush palm tree-lined beaches; that's the north. Here the landscape is dramatic and dry, and the coastline alternates between striking cliffs, stretches of uninterrupted sand, and rocky ports. Just offshore, hundreds of mangrove-filled islands are great for exploring. Meanwhile, back on land, the dry, rolling plains look like they're out of an old Western movie. Those who come ready for adventure will be amazed by the incredible nature here.

The high point of southwest Puerto Rico is Guánica's dry forest, almost 10,000 acres of cacti and dry scrub set against the background of the tumultuous Caribbean. This area has great hiking and water sport opportunities, but most Puerto Ricans forego these active pursuits and head straight to the beach. The gentle waves of the Caribbean coast seem more like a large lake than an ocean, creating an ideal family beach. These conquerable waters, along with long bays of white sand, make southwest Puerto Rico, and La Parguera and Boquerón in particular, one of the island's most popular domestic travel destinations.

But southwest Puerto Rico may be most notable for what it doesn't have—people. This is one of the least populated areas of the main island, and it can be a refreshing experience for those daunted by crowds, factories, and traffic. Most of the prime vacation spots hide in small *barrios*, far from even the relative hustle of a municipal center, and not much happens here until weekends and holidays when Puerto Ricans flock south for their own vacations. This is a place to forget the worries of real life and dive into the vacation spirit, be that relaxing on a calm Caribbean beach, windsurfing in a protected bay, or hiking through unique dry forest. Southwest Puerto Rico offers it all in one easily accessible package.

HIGHLIGHTS OF SOUTHWEST PUERTO RICO

REVEL in the many delights of Guánica's superb dry forest (p. 214).

GET IN TOUCH WITH YOUR WILD SIDE and venture to Isla Mona, land of enormous iguanas, gorgeous beaches, and the best diving in Puerto Rico (p. 195).

HEAD TO THE ENDS OF THE EARTH at the Cabo Rojo Lighthouse, where you'll find some of Puerto Rico's most incredible scenery (p. 204).

JOIN THE PARTY in Boquerón, home of the mainland's best public beach and local vacation hot spot (p. 199).

MAYAGÜEZ

The self-proclaimed capital of the west coast has few attractions, but ample spirit. With over 100,000 inhabitants, Mayagüez is one of the island's major metropolis areas, yet unlike other cities it has not yet developed its natural assets for tourist consumption. Like Ponce, Mayagüez has some beautiful turn-of-the-century houses, but most have fallen into a state of decay. Like Fajardo, Mayagüez has a deep port, but this one is used primarily for industrial purposes, and no tropical islands await just off shore. Like *sanjuaneros*, *mayagüezanos* have a special pride for their city, but it may be difficult to see where this pride originates. There are really only two reasons to visit Mayagüez: you're passing through on the way to or from the Dominican Republic,

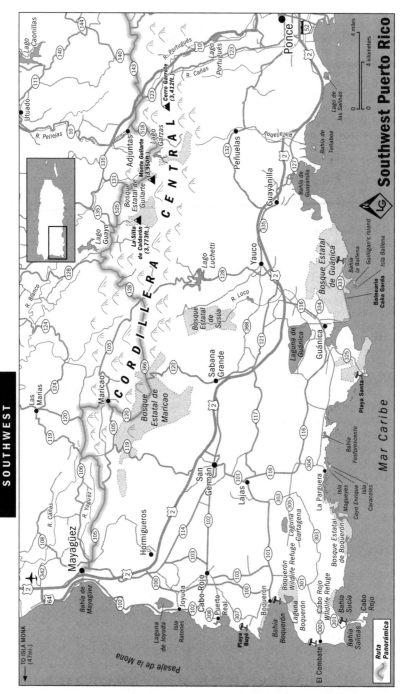

Southwest Puerto Rico

Ponce

Lago Caonillas

Lago Portugués

Utuado

Cerro Garrote (3,412ft.)

R. Portugués

R. Cañas

Lago de las Salinas

R. Pellejas

Adjuntas

Lago Garzas

Monte Guilarte (3,950ft.)

Bosque Estatal de Guilarte

La Silla de Calderón (3,773ft.)

Peñuelas

Bahía de Tallaboa

Guayanilla

Bahía de Guayanilla

Lago Guayo

Lago Luchetti

Yauco

Bosque Estatal de Guánica

Bahía la Ballena

Guilligan's Island

Isla Ballena

R. Blanco

Bosque Estatal de Susúa

R. Loco

Balneario Caña Gorda

Las Marías

Maricao

Laguna de Guánica

Guánica

Bosque Estatal de Maricao

Sabana Grande

Playa Santa

Mar Caribe

R. Cañas

R. Yagüez

San Germán

Hormigueros

Lajas

Bahía Fosforescente

La Parguera

Isla Magueyes

Mayagüez

Cayo Enrique

Isla Caracoles

Bahía de Mayagüez

Laguna Cartagena

Laguna de Joyuda

Isla Ratones

Joyuda

Cabo Rojo

Puerto Real

Boquerón

Boquerón Wildlife Refuge

Laguna Guánica

Bosque Estatal de Boquerón

Cabo Rojo Wildlife Refuge

Bahía Sucia

Cabo Rojo

Playa Buyé

Bahía Boquerón

Laguna Boquerón

Bahía Salinas

El Combate

TO ISLA MONA (4.7mi.)

Pasaje de la Mona

Ruta Panorámica

CORDILLERA CENTRAL

SOUTHWEST

or you're passing through on a tour of the west coast. And the city does provide ample entertainment for an afternoon visit, with the island's large zoo and an active university district. Furthermore, the renovated plaza indicates that Mayagüez does have potential for a more attractive future.

TRANSPORTATION

Flights: Aeropuerto Eugenio Maria de Hostos (☎832-3390), 4 mi. north of town on Rte. 342, just off Hwy. 2, has 1 airline: **American Eagle** (☎791-5050, reservations 800-981-4757) sends flights to **San Juan** (2 per day, one-way $135). A taxi into Mayagüez costs about $7 (plus luggage), though you may have to call.

Públicos: The *público* terminal is located at the end of C. Pablo Maiz, near Parque de los Proceros. *Públicos* head to: **Aguadilla** (30-60min., $3); **Añasco** (10-15min., $2); **Cabo Rojo** (15-20min., $2); **Ponce** (80-90min., $5-6); **Rincón** (20min., $1.75). **Linea Sultana** (☎832-1041 or 832-2502) sends vans to **Río Piedras, San Juan** (3-3½hr.; 6, 7, 9, 11am, 1, 3, 5pm; $12). Call ahead and they'll pick you up from your hotel.

Ferries: Ferries del Caribe (☎832-4800 or 832-4905), north of town. From Hwy. 2 turn left at Km 152.2 on Rte. 102 and follow signs. A taxi costs about $6. An enormous 1000-passenger ferry travels between **Santo Domingo, Dominican Republic** (12hr.; M, W, F 8pm) and Puerto Rico (Tu, Th, Sa 8pm). Prices vary depending on cabin size: general ticket (no cabin) $109, round-trip $153; suites (shared 4-person rooms) round-trip $193; single cabins (essentially a hotel room) $162, round-trip $239-259; double cabins round-trip $189-199 per person. The boat has airplane-like seats for those who do not purchase a bed. To purchase a one-way ticket you must have an airplane ticket or some other proof of departure from the Dominican Republic. Cars round-trip $146; vans, mini vans, and pick-ups $176; motorcycles $96; bikes $20. You must reserve at least 1 day in advance or there is a $10 fee. The ferry terminal does not have parking, but a local man named Willy allows people to park at his house for $5 per day (☎831-0835). Arrive 2hr. early. Terminal office open Tu, Th, Sa 8am-5pm; M, W, F 8am-8pm; Su noon-4pm. MC/V.

Cars: The car rental companies below operate out of the airport. All prices are for the smallest compact cars available. Rates rise during Christmas, Easter, and summer.

> **Avis** (☎833-7070). $40-61 per day. 25+. Open daily 7am-9:30pm. AmEx/D/DC/MC/V.
>
> **Budget** (☎832-4570). $33-42 per day, with insurance $48-57. 21+. Under 25 surcharge $10 per day. Open daily 7:30am-1pm, 2-6 and 7-9:30pm. AmEx/D/MC/V.
>
> **Thrifty** (☎834-1590). $30-37 per day. Insurance $15 per day. 21+. Under 25 surcharge $10 per day. Open daily 8am-noon and 1-5pm. AmEx/D/DC/MC/V.

Taxis: White Taxi Cab, C. de Diego 18 (☎832-1154), at C. Peral. Open daily 6:30am-midnight. **City Taxi** (☎265-1992) leaves from the *público* station. Open daily 6:30am-11pm. **Western Taxi** (☎832-0562), at C. del Río and C. McKinley. Open daily 6am-midnight.

ORIENTATION

Mayagüez has a relatively small, walkable city center on the eastern side of Hwy. 2. To reach the city center from Hwy. 2, exit toward C. McKinley or C. Post. This is one of the few cities in Puerto Rico where most hotels and restaurants do congregate around the plaza. **Calle Post,** also called Hwy. 2R, leads north from Plaza Colón to the university area. **Mayagüez Town Center,** located at the intersection of C. Post and Hwy. 2, just north of the center, holds some convenient services and a food court.

After dark stick to the well-lit streets on and around Plaza Colón, or the university area at the northern end of C. Post.

SOUTHWEST

🗚 PRACTICAL INFORMATION

Tours: AdvenTours (☎831-6447; www.adventours.tk) offers walking tours of downtown Mayagüez (3hr., M-Tu, $30). 2 person min. Cash only.

Camping Permits: The **Departmento de Recursos Naturales** (DRNA; ☎833-3700 or 833-4703), north on Hwy. 2. Exit toward the east at Km 150.2, then follow signs; the office is at the end of Alturas de Mayagüez shopping center. Issues permits to camp ($4 per person) and visit Isla Mona ($25 per person), but you must first call the San Juan office to check availability and make a reservation. Open M-F 7:30am-noon and 1-4pm.

Banks: Banco Popular, C. Méndez Vigo 9 (☎832-0475). ATM. Open M-F 8am-4pm.

American Express: Bithorn Travel, C. Méndez Vigo 8 (☎834-3300; fax 832-1442; www.bithorntravel.com). Open M-F 8:30am-5pm.

Supermarket: Pueblo (☎834-8720), on the 1st floor of the Mayagüez Town Center. **Western Union.** Open M-Sa 6am-midnight, Su 11am-5pm. AmEx/MC/V.

Laundromat: Radio Centro Laundromat (☎640-4839), at C. Bosque and C. Post. Wash $1.25-2.25. Dry $0.25 per 5min. Change available. Open daily 8am-6pm.

Police: The **municipal police station,** C. Santiago R. Palmer 17 (☎834-0378 or 833-1848) is convenient to downtown. Open daily 8am-noon and 1-4:30pm. **Policía de Puerto Rico** (☎832-9699) is about 2 mi. south of town on Ave. Corazones. Turn left at Denny's. Open 24hr.

Pharmacies: Farmacia Yaguez, C. Ramos Antonini 5 (☎832-5060), at C. Basora, near the plaza, has a mediocre selection. Open M-Sa 8am-10pm, Su 9am-10pm. AmEx/MC/V. **Walgreen's,** Ave. Hostos 2097 (☎805-4005), just north of town at Hwy. 2 Km 152.7, is open 24hr. AmEx/D/DC/MC/V.

Hospital: Hospital San Antonio, C. Post 18 Norte (☎834-0056). 24hr. emergency room.

Internet Access: eMilios (☎986-0929), on the 2nd floor of Mayagüez Town Center, has lots of computers with fast connections. $4 for 20min., $5 for 30min., or $10 per hr. Open M-Sa 9am-9pm, Su noon-5pm. MC/V.

Post Office: C. McKinley 60 Oeste (☎265-3133). General Delivery available. Open M-F 7am-5pm, Sa 7am-2pm.

Zip Code: 00680.

🗚 ACCOMMODATIONS

This is one of the most affordable places to stay in Puerto Rico, and you can expect to get quite a bang for your buck. Still, it's rare to find the following hotels even close to full capacity. Most hotels include continental breakfast.

Hotel Colonial, C. Iglesia 14 Sur (☎/fax 833-2150; www.hotel-colonial.com), offers one of the best values on the island. This colonial building has most of the traditional amenities—A/C, TV, parking—and throws in tall ceilings and 24hr. front desk. Of course the rooms redefine the term "small" and there's a bit of dirt in the corners. Nonetheless a bargain. Continental breakfast. Parking. Check-in 1pm. Check-out noon. Singles M-Th $32, F-Sa $43; doubles $43-54/$54-65; quads $97/$108; extra person $11. Tax included. MC/V. ❷

Hotel Mayagüez Plaza, C. Méndez Vigo 70 Este (☎832-9191), is the nicest hotel downtown. Tropical bedspreads brighten up clean, airy rooms with glistening bathrooms. Ideally located right behind the church. Only the small pool suffers from the Mayagüez size deficit. Cable TV, A/C, phone. Continental breakfast included. Parking. Check-in 3pm. 1 king bed $82; 2 full beds $93. Tax included. AmEx/D/DC/MC/V. ❸

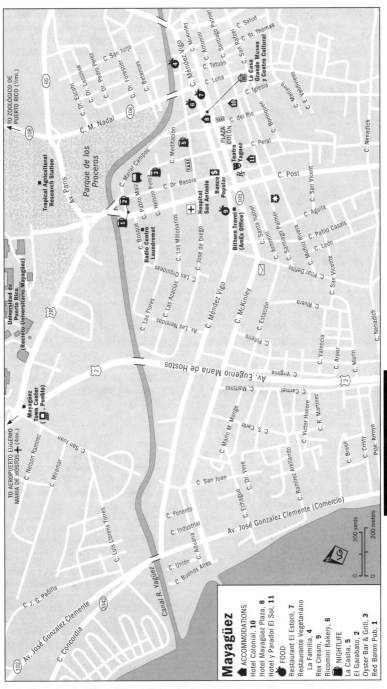

Mayagüez

▲ ACCOMMODATIONS
Hotel Colonial, **10**
Hotel Mayagüez Plaza, **8**
Hotel y Parador El Sol, **11**

🍴 FOOD
Restaurant El Estoril, **7**
Restaurante Vegetariano
  La Familia, **4**
Rex Cream, **9**
Ricomini Bakery, **6**

🍸 NIGHTLIFE
La Casita, **5**
El Garabato, **2**
Oyster Bar & Grill, **3**
Red Baron Pub, **1**

TO ZOOLÓGICO DE
PUERTO RICO (½mi.)

TO AEROPUERTO EUGENIO
MARIA DE HOSTOS ✈ (4mi.)

Tropical Agricultural
Research Station

Parque de los
Proceros

Universidad de
Puerto Rico
(Recinto Universitario Mayagüez)

Mayagüez
Town Center
(☐ ● Pueblo)

La Casa
Grande Museo
y Centro Cultural

Radio Centro
Laundromat

Hospital
San Antonio

Banco
Popular

PLAZA
COLÓN

Teatro
Yaguez

Bithorn Travel
(AmEx Office)

SOUTHWEST

C. Salud
C. McKinley
C. Antonini
C. Santiago Palmer
C. St. Thomas
C. San Rafael
C. Méndez Vigo
C. Tetuan
C. Luna
C. Iglesia
C. Mariquero
C. E. Valdivieso
C. Nenadich
C. del Rio
C. Bonriquen
C. Peral
C. Post
C. San Vicent
C. Aguila
C. Santa Isabel
C. Santiago Palmer
C. Muñoz Rivera
C. Pablo Casals
C. León
C. Pilar Defillo
C. San Vicente
C. Araez
C. Marin
C. Nenadich
C. Rivera
C. Estación
C. Piñero
C. Valencia
C. Virginia
Av. Eugenio Maria de Hostos
C. Martinez
C. Carmel
C. Brasil
C. Cristy
Psje. Arroyo
C. R. Martinez
C. Victor Honore
C. Ramirez Arellando
C. Dr. Veve
C. Echague
C. San Juan
C. Marin M. Monge
C. S. Carló
C. Salud
C. San Jurjo
C. Dr. Escabi
C. Dr. Lassise
C. Dr. Pedro Perez
C. Dr. Foresier
C. Betances
C. M. Nadal
Av. Paris
C. Mariel Campos
C. Bosque
C. Pablo Maiz
C. Nelson Perea
C. Meditación
C. Dr. Basora
C. Los Millonarios
C. Jose de Diego
C. Las Orquideas
C. Las Acacias
C. Las Flores
C. Las Nereidas
Av. Las Nereidas
C. Méndez Vigo
C. McKinley
C. Nelson Ramirez
C. Miramar
C. San Juan
C. Luis Lloréns Torres
C. J. G. Padilla
C. Concordia
Canal R. Yaguez
Av. José Gonzalez Clemente
C. Fonento
C. Industrial
Av. José Gonzalez Clemente (Comercio)
C. Unión
C. Aduana
C. Buenos Aires

102
65
108
108
2
2
105
3342

200 yards
200 meters

TAXI

Hotel y Parador El Sol, C. Santiago Palmer 9 Este (☎834-0303), suffers from a lack of space, despite the fact that this 5-story building is one of Mayagüez's tallest. Tiny rooms still manage to fit in a phone, A/C, a tiny cable TV, and a small fridge. Clean and well-maintained. A small pool is tucked into the courtyard. Restaurant. Continental breakfast. Parking. Singles $70-86; doubles $70-96; extra person $11. Tax included. AmEx/MC/V. ❸

🎨 FOOD

Mayagüez has a surprising number of attractive dining options around the plaza. Of course, most students opt for the fast food and cheap fare near campus.

Ricomini Bakery/Brazo Gitano, C. Méndez Vigo 101 (☎832-0565), takes the cake (and the flan, and the *quesito,* and the *arroz con dulce*) as the best bakery/cafe/eatery in town. This European-style cafe bustles with activity during the lunch hour when it seems like everyone in Mayagüez stops by. Delicious food, efficient service, immaculate setting. Hot *comida criolla* $4.50 per lb. Breakfast $2.50-3. Sandwiches $3.50-5. Pastries $0.30-1.50. Open daily 6am-midnight. AmEx/MC/V. ❶

Restaurant El Estoril, C. Méndez Vigo 100 Este (☎834-2288). The owners claim this is "The Best in the West" and they're not far off. First-rate Portuguese food in a first-class setting, with fountains in the corner, porcelain plates decorating the wall, and a huge wine rack. Try the fillet medallions in sherry wine sauce ($20). Lunch buffet $10. Entrees $12-30. Open Tu-Sa 11:30am-10:30pm. AmEx/MC/V. ❹

Rex Cream, C. Méndez Vigo 7 (☎832-2121). It's no secret: people come to Rex Cream for the scrumptious ice cream. But while they're there, some also stop for the inexpensive Chinese and Puerto Rican food ($2-6). A popular lunch place. Open M-Th 10am-10pm, F-Sa 10am-11pm, Su 11am-11pm. MC/V. **Another location** at C. McKinley 17 drops the pretense and just serves ice cream. Open daily 9am-11pm. ❶

Restaurante Vegetariano La Familia, C. de Diego 151 Este (☎833-7571). Clean, spacious, and super friendly; these are rare attributes in a Puerto Rican vegetarian restaurant, but La Familia defies the expectations. A full buffet serves a variety of vegetarian entrees, usually including several kinds of rice, a tofu dish, and a fresh salad. Mix and match your favorites ($1.40-4). Open M-F 11am-3pm. Cash only. ❶

📷 SIGHTS

ZOOLÓGICO DE PUERTO RICO. If you're still lamenting the fact that Puerto Rico is tropical island without any large mammals, you may enjoy a visit to Puerto Rico's largest zoo. Managed by the Compañia de Parques Nacionales, the zoo contains a wide selection of animals divided into "African Forest" and "African Savannah" groups, which boils down to a typical selection of monkeys, zebras, lions, camels, caimans, and hippopotami. All things considered, this is a laudable effort by the CPN and by far the most interesting attraction in Mayagüez. *(Take Rte. 108 north past the university, then turn right at the sign for the zoo. Don't attempt to walk as the road is narrow and cars drive fast. A taxi costs about $4. ☎834-8110. Open W-Su 8:30am-4pm. Parking $2, vans $3. Admission $6, ages 11-17 and 60-74 $3, ages 0-10 and 75+ free. MC/V.)*

RECINTO UNIVERSITARIO MAYAGÜEZ (RUM). Any university with the acronym RUM has to be something interesting, and Mayagüez's branch of the University of Puerto Rico does not disappoint. NASA and other government agencies have been known to recruit engineering students from this primarily science-focused division of UPR. The attractive palm-filled campus is one of the more picturesque in Puerto Rico. Enter the gate across from Mayagüez Town Center and follow the broad Ave. Palmeras to reach the main university plaza, the general library, and the student center. *(North of the city at the intersection of C. Post and Hwy. 2.)*

TROPICAL AGRICULTURE RESEARCH STATION. Ecologists and botanists may drool over this 127 acre agricultural center where the US Department of Agriculture (USDA) breeds plant species suitable to the South Atlantic area. Currently the USDA is focusing on two projects: one to genetically adapt the dry bean to temperate regions, and another to develop tropical crops for the interior US. For less ecologically-inclined visitors, the research station is a nice place to walk and identify many of the plants you've seen around the island. A pleasant self-guided tour leads past over 70 labeled plant species, all native to the island. *(Between Rte. 108 and Rte. 2R. ☎ 831-3435. Open M-F 7am-noon and 1-4pm. Free.)*

TEATRO YAGUEZ. Mayagüez has one of the most attractive public theaters in Puerto Rico. In 1976 the municipal government bought a historic church and converted it into the city's grandiose theater, complete with enormous chandeliers and two balconies. The 900-seat theater was under renovation in 2003, but should be up and running by 2004. *(Behind the Alcaldía between C. McKinley and C. Antonini.)*

LA CASA GRANDE MUSEO Y CENTRO CULTURAL. Built in 1890, this renovated house-museum has an attractive facade, but the decorations inside are quite spartan; the city supplemented period furniture with portraits of former mayors and other local celebrities. Don't miss the kitchen, which incongruously combines 19th-century kitchenware and a newfangled cappuccino machine. *(C. Méndez Vigo 104 Este. ☎ 832-7435. Open M-F 8am-4pm. Free.)*

NIGHTLIFE

The university students dominate Mayagüez's nightlife scene, which hops on Wednesday and Thursday, then dies down over the weekend when everyone heads to the beach. If drinking with college kids is not your cup of tea, **Cine Vista** (☎ 265-2121), on the second floor of the Mayagüez Town Center, plays six Hollywood films every night. ($5, children and seniors $3.50. AmEx/MC/V.)

El Garabato, C. Post 102 Norte (☎ 834-2524), is the requisite university pub. Students gather here throughout the day and night to grab a beer, play some dominos, and chat. Daily Happy Hour specials with various $1 beers. Open M-Sa 1pm-1am. MC/V.

Red Baron Pub, C. Post 102 Norte (☎ 805-1580), upstairs from El Garabato. Once they've gotten good and toasted downstairs, RUM students head up to this dark and steamy pub to dance the night away. From W to Sa a live DJ plays reggaeton, rock, and hip hop. Beer $1-2. Occasional live Spanish rock. W-Sa cover $6, includes open bar. Open Tu-Sa 7pm-last person leaves. Cash only.

La Casita, C. de Diego 65 (☎ 805-1505), is, remarkably enough, located in a little house. The homey well-loved pub is filled with ample fans to keep things cool. Beer $2.25-2.50; mixed drinks $2.25-4. Daily Happy Hour specials $1.25-1.50. Th-Sa 11pm cover bands. Open M-F at 5pm, Sa-Su 8pm; closes whenever people leave. MC/V.

Oyster Bar & Grill, C. Peral 36 (☎ 831-3727). This touristy American chain restaurant spends big bucks on advertising, and it seems to pay off. On weekend nights the place is packed with mayagüezanos young enough to enjoy F night karaoke, but old enough to afford the pricey drinks. A dance floor with mirrors and flashing colored lights practically begs to be danced on. Appetizers $6-20. Beer $2.75-3.25; mixed drinks $3.75-6. W 7-11pm cover $10 includes limited open bar. 21+. Open Su-Tu 11am-11pm, W 11am-1am, Th 11am-2am, F-Sa 11am-3am. AmEx/MC/V.

Mayagüez Resort & Casino (☎ 832-3030), north of town off Hwy. 2 at Km 152.6, has 2 bars at this fancy hotel cater to a wealthy, older crowd. **Paradise Island Casino** attracts a much, much older crowd; many social security checks have been gambled away here. (Open 24hr.) The **sports bar** across the hall has live merengue and salsa music (F-Sa

8pm), although you would never guess it from the scant decor and slightly seedy feel. Tu-Th 8pm live ballads. Open daily 2pm-1am. **Veranda Terrace Bar** has the classy atmosphere you'd expect at a resort, with white couches overlooking the pool and, in the distance, the ocean. F 8pm live guitar music and ballads. Open daily 11am-midnight. Both bars: 18+. Beer $3-4.25; mixed drinks $5. AmEx/D/DC/MC/V.

NEAR MAYAGÜEZ: JOYUDA

Seafood-lovers take note: Joyuda may be your dream come true. This 3 mi. strip of coastal road contains more seafood restaurants than any other place in Puerto Rican, and *mayagüezanos* regularly drive down to sample the fresh delicacies and watch the sunset. Scattered amidst these culinary temptations, several small hotels and guest houses offer remarkable value and a good home base for explorations of the southwest. The town has few beaches, but **Isla Ratones,** about ½ mi. offshore, has a small sandy beach. A regular ferry runs out to the island from Rte. 102 Km 13.7, next to Island View Restaurant. (☎851-7708. Open Tu-Su 9am-5pm. $3 round-trip.) For a much longer trip out to sea, check in with **Tourmarine Adventures,** Rte. 102 Km 14.1. Captain Elick Hernández charters his 34 foot boat for the 3hr. trip to Isla Mona ($135 per person; min. 10 people) or for more local sightseeing. He is very flexible, but you must either have a preformed group or pay for the entire boat. Common trips include: a 2-tank dive at the offshore cliffs ($40 without equipment), a 5-6hr. whale watching trip in the Mona Passage (Feb.-Mar.; $40 per person), or local snorkeling. Call ahead to see if you can join a prearranged group. (☎851-9259 or 375-2625; tourmarine@yahoo.com. AmEx/MC/V.)

Joyuda has an extraordinary number of hotels considering the area's limited attractions. Little **Hotel Costa de Oro Inn ❷,** Rte. 102 Km 14.7 is a modern building with a friendly, guest house feel and immaculate rooms that live up to the standards you would expect at a much larger hotel. A tiny pool fills the cramped courtyard. (☎851-5010. A/C and cable TV. Check-in 2pm. Check-out noon. low season, roughly Sept.-May, doubles Su-Th $44, F-Sa $50; quads $50/$66. High season doubles $60; quads $83. Extra person $15. MC/V.) After the endless rows of modern, commercial hotels, **Punta Arenas Guest House ❸,** Rte. 102 Km 9.8, is a nice return to small Puerto Rican guest houses. This beachside hotel has a large wooden deck, lots of palm trees, and a patriotic swimming pool. The rooms are a bit dingy, but this is a quiet place to relax close to the water and away from the crowds. (☎851-2202. Rooms have A/C and TV. Doubles $60; quads $82; 8-person cabins with kitchen $125. Tax included. MC/V.) Finally, the owner of **Tourmarine Adventures ❷** (see above) also rents out 5-person apartments (M-Th $50, F-Su $75) and allows people to **camp ❶** in the backyard ($10).

Choosing a restaurant in Joyuda is like picking a bar in San Juan; there are just too many good options. Most of the seafood is fresh and almost all restaurants serve the standard crab, mahi mahi, red snapper, lobster, shrimp, conch, trunk fish, and octopus options. The only real variance is in location and atmosphere. **Island View Restaurant ❸,** Rte. 102 Km 13.7, stands out for just that—its island view. The balcony of this family restaurant sits over the water with incomparable views of Isla Ratones. All the standard seafood options ($13-21) as well as some meats ($7-14) appear on the long menu. (☎851-9264. Open Th-Tu 11am-10pm. AmEx/MC/V.) The Puerto Rican Tourism Company selected **Tino's Restaurant ❹,** Rte. 102 Km 13.6 as the only Joyuda *mesón gastronómico*. Although it does not look out over the water, Tino's offers a touch of class and specialty seafood-filled *mofongos*. (☎851-2976. Entrees $8-26. Open W-Sa 11am-11pm, Su 11am-10pm. AmEx/MC/V.)

ISLA MONA

Disclaimers who believe that Puerto Rico is too developed for adventure have clearly never heard of Isla Mona. Touted as "the Caribbean's best kept secret" and "the Galapagos of the Caribbean," Isla Mona offers one of the best natural excursions in the Caribbean. At almost 14,000 acres, the island is twice as large as Culebra, but remains completely uninhabited except for a few researchers. Nature still reigns on this protected nature reserve, as enormous iguanas, thousands of hermit crabs, and invasive goats and pigs roam the island. Arriving on Mona can be a surreal experience. Visitors who have not seen photos are surprised by the flatness of the island, which looks like a large pancake sitting on the water. As you get closer, it becomes apparent that the sheer edges of the island are actually cavernous limestone cliffs. Even closer and strips of bright white sand emerge, and the water turns an incredible clear blue. About this time, visitors usually start congratulating themselves for choosing to visit Mona. Despite the fact that there are no telephones, TVs, or commercial buildings, it is nearly impossible to get bored here. You could spend days exploring the extensive cave network, hiking through the dry scrub forest, diving and snorkeling at the flourishing reefs, or lounging on the exquisite beaches. In addition to the adventure, Mona also offers almost absolute tranquility. It is not uncommon for the only sounds to be the waves crashing on the beach and the quiet rustling of the hermit crabs. Most charters head to the island for three or four days and this taste of Mona provides just enough time for visitors to get hooked and begin planning the next trip.

AT A GLANCE

AREA: 12,800 acres.

CLIMATE: Semi-arid subtropical. Year-round temperatures 80-90° F.

HIGHLIGHTS: Wildlife, caves, Taíno petroglyphs, spectacular beaches, untainted coral reefs, lighthouse.

FEATURES: Where to start? Climbing through caves, diving in 120 ft. visibility, swimming through aquamarine water, hiking with endemic animals.

GATEWAYS: Boquerón (p. 199), Joyuda (p. 194), Rincón (p. 178), San Juan (p. 88).

CAMPING: Permitted at Playa Sardinera and Playa Pájaro with a DRN permit ($1 per person).

FEES: Boat passage alone costs $115-400. Most groups charge more for food, equipment, tour services, and snorkeling or diving.

🔲 FLORA AND FAUNA

Isla Mona's wildlife is simply incredible. The small island houses 700 species of animals, 58 of which are endemic to the island and 75 of which have never been found on the Puerto Rican mainland. By far the most famous is the **Mona Iguana,** a gargantuan 4 ft. reptile found nowhere else in the world. These stunning creatures frequently emerge from their burrowed nests to observe new campers. Visitors will also be greeted by piles of crawling **hermit crabs,** crustaceans that migrate to the sea during early August to breed. The only amphibian on Mona is the unique **Mona coquí,** which has a song slightly different from its Puerto Rican relative. Unlike Puerto Rico, Mona also has a significant number of creepy crawlies. Watch out for the 52 species of spiders and the three species of scorpions. Luckily the 3 ft. **Isla Mona Boa,** yet another endemic species, generally only comes out at night and is not harmful to humans. This curious creature is one of the only snakes that gives birth to developed offspring and does not lay eggs. **Bird-watchers** will enjoy looking for the 100 species of birds found on Mona. Only two, the yellow-shoul-

SOUTHWEST

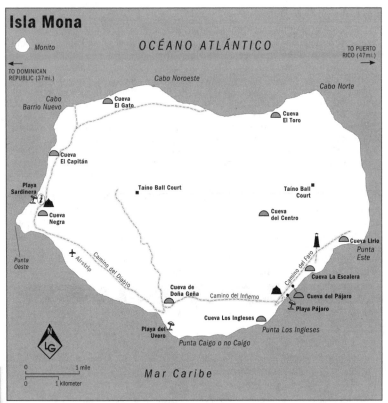

SOUTHWEST

dered blackbird and the ground dove, are native to the island. Finally, the goats
and pigs that were left behind after earlier attempts to farm the island are similar
to B-movie stars—abundant, but not too impressive. There **are** over 270 species of
fish around Mona, including dolphins, silky sharks, nurse sharks, barracudas, flying fish, moray eels, and, during the winter months, humpback whales. From May
to October the endangered hawksbill turtle nests on the shores of Mona. The log-
gerhead sea turtle also swims in the waters around Mona; if you see a turtle, leave
it alone, as human interference is one large cause of the species' decline.

Mona's flora cannot match the diversity of its fauna, but the island does contain
four endemic plant species. The vegetation is a combination of eastern Hispaniola
and southwestern Puerto Rico, and most of the island consists of **dry plateau forest**
filled with white cedar, cactus, and posionwood. Most of the coastal forest consists of princewood and oysterwood, although there are three acres of mangroves.

▐▄ TRANSPORTATION

It takes a bit of tenacity to reach Isla Mona. The small airstrip is currently closed,
so anyone who doesn't have a private boat will have to find passage on a Puerto
Rican charter. If you have a group of at least eight people, or a lot of money, the
easiest option is to arrange a trip with one of the operators below. However, the

ordinary traveler will have to join a pre-existing group that is still accepting additional passengers. Dive shops travel to Mona most regularly, but many accept non-divers and snorkelers at a reduced cost. Individuals or small groups attempting to go to Mona should first call the two chartered boats to inquire about expeditions planned during the time period they're interested in going. If that is unsuccessful, then contact the two dive shops in Rincón that make frequent trips to Mona on their own boats. Finally, try calling the various dive shops that make one or two trips to Mona per year. All prices listed below are round-trip.

 A ROUGH JOURNEY Getting to Mona requires taking a relatively small boat 50 mi. across open seas; if you have ever been **seasick**, or even worried about seasickness, it's wise to plan ahead. Some boat captains recommend that potentially queasy travelers take **Dramamine** the night before the boat ride. For a more natural cure, **ginger** has been known to ease the pain of seasickness.

CHARTERED BOATS

Tourmarine Adventures, Rte. 102 Km 14.1 (☎851-9259 or 375-2625; tourmarine@yahoo.com), Joyuda (p. 194). Captain Elick Hernández has a 34' boat. One-day passage $135 per person; 10 person min. AmEx/MC/V.

Mona Aquatics, C. de Diego 59 (☎851-2185; fax 254-0604), Boquerón (p. 199), has a 42' boat. Passage to Mona $115 per person; 15 person min. The PADI- and YMCA-certified owner leads dives (1 day $70; 2 days $95), but does not rent equipment. $150 surcharge per group for spending the night. Can arrange DRN permits. MC/V.

DIVE SHOPS WITH BOATS

Oceans Unlimited, Rte. 115 Km 11.9 (☎823-2340; fax 823-2370; www.oceans-unlimited.com), Rincón (p. 185), has a 46' boat. 3-day, 6-dive trip $375; 1-day, 2-dive trip $150. Equipment and permits included. 8 person min. Open daily 9am-6pm. MC/V.

Taíno Divers (☎823-6429; www.tainodivers.com), Rte. 413 Km 1, in the Black Eagle Marina, Rincón (p. 178), has a 34' boat. 3-day trip $400, divers $475. Equipment and permits included. Open daily 10am-6pm. MC/V.

DIVE SHOPS WITHOUT BOATS

Scuba Dogs, C. 5 #D4, Pardo Alto (☎/fax 783-6377 or 399-5755; scubadogs@yunque.net), Guaynabo. 3-day, 4-dive trip $275; BCD and regulator rental $20. Includes transport, food, and all permits. PADI certified. No credit cards.

Ocean Sports, Ave. Ashford 1035 (☎723-8513 or 268-2329; www.osdivers.com), San Juan (p. 135). 2-tank dive $100, equipment rental $25. NAUI certified. Open M-Sa 10am-7pm. D/MC/V.

Arecibo Dive Shop, Ave. Miramar 868/Hwy. 2 Km 78 (☎/fax 880-3483), Arecibo (p. 167). 3-day, 4-dive trip $215. Includes food and DRN permit. You must have your own snorkeling gear. 8 person min. Spanish only. Open M-Sa 10am-6:30pm. Cash only.

ORIENTATION AND PRACTICAL INFORMATION

Located 47 mi. west of Puerto Rico and 37 mi. east of the Dominican Republic, Isla Mona sits roughly in the middle of nowhere. Most visitors arrive at Playa Sardinera, home of the main dock, the DRN offices, and one Mona's most beautiful beaches. From Sardinera marked trails lead to Playa Pájaro (the other camping area), the lighthouse, the airport, and several caves. Little **Monito,** 3 mi. northwest of Mona, is an inaccessible 160-acre limestone rock.

SOUTHWEST

WHEN TO GO The DRN prohibits camping on weekdays during goat- and pig-hunting season (Dec.-Apr. M-Th). During school vacations Puerto Ricans with private boats significantly decrease the serenity of Mona.

Visitors Center: The **DRN** office next to Playa Sardinera is almost always open.

Maps: Theoretically the DRN provides a map of hiking trails, but it frequently runs out of copies.

Supplies: There are **absolutely no supplies on Mona.** You must bring everything that you might want on the island, including **drinking water** and **toilet paper.** In addition to the typical supplies don't forget mosquito repellent, long pants, sneakers if you plan to do any hiking, any food you may want (snacks if your tour operator is bringing food), trash bags (to take your trash out when you leave), and a flashlight.

CAMPING AND FOOD

If you're looking for the Ritz, head back to San Juan. On Mona the only option is to camp at the two official beachfront camping areas. **Playa Sardinera ❶,** on the west coast, is the larger of the two and has two rustic cold-water showers and two flush toilets. For more seclusion head to **Playa Pájaro ❶,** on the southeast coast. This beautiful beach has a dock and room for 30 campers, but no facilities. Visitors looking for isolation and the "real" Mona tend to head here.

Isla Mona also has no food apart from fresh fish (bring your own pole). Many tour groups provide food and a cook, but if not, travelers must be entirely self-sufficient. Furthermore, the DRN does not allow open flame fires.

OUTDOOR ACTIVITIES

It is a good idea to decide what activities you're interested in before heading to Mona in order to procure the necessary supplies. Obviously divers should invest in a dive trip, but everyone should bring snorkeling equipment. Visitors interested in exploring the caves need a good flashlight, and those seeking more intense exploration should look for a tour group with a knowledgeable guide.

BEACHES

Isla Mona has over 5 mi. of beautiful beaches and the most popular activity may be lying in the sand. **Playa Sardinera** is a long white beach with relatively calm water protected by an offshore reef. The pine trees lining the sand drop some needles, and there are occasionally bothersome sand flies, but these two small inconveniences do not hamper Sardinera's beauty. This is also the only beach with facilities, including bathrooms, picnic tables, and showers. The other camping area, **Playa Pájaro,** looks similar, but has more palm trees, rocks, and seaweed. Although these are the two most frequented beaches, all of the sand on Mona is a bright white color that far outshines the mainland beaches, and yes, the water maintains that incredible blue color all the way around the island. Other beaches include: **Playa Mujeres, Playa del Uvero,** and **Playa Brava.**

DIVING AND SNORKELING

Isla Mona has the best diving in Puerto Rico, with visibility regularly reaching 150-180 ft. Reefs nearly surround the island and many organisms grow on the island's steep cliffs, creating almost limitless dive opportunities. Because of the distance from any larger body of land, the reefs around Isla Mona are remarkably healthy and receive very little outside pollution. More advanced divers head to one of

Mona's most spectacular sights, a sea wall that starts at 50-60 ft., descends to 150 ft., then drops again. Due to potentially strong currents and deep sites, Mona divers should choose their sites carefully according to experience.

CAVE EXPLORATION

Mona has over 150 acres of limestone caves that vary greatly in terms of size (heights range 3-30ft.) and accessibility. Only experienced spelunkers should attempt to navigate the caves without a guide. DRN employees occasionally accompany interested visitors to various caves, but don't count on this. Some tour groups and boat captains also lead visitors through the caves; check before departing to see if your trip includes any cave exploration. **Cueva Negra** and **Cueva Carita,** near Playa Sardinera, are some of the most easily approachable caves. There are more spectacular caves on the southeastern shore, near Playa Pájaro, but these can be difficult to find. Visitors with a guide should not miss **Cueva del Agua,** where you crawl through a tiny passage to reach a pitch-black pool of water.

HIKING

> **!** **Take caution** when hiking on Isla Mona. The flat terrain makes it very easy to get lost, and recently a Boy Scout died on Mona after losing his way. Also, watch out for deep limestone holes. Finally, there are several dangerous plants on Mona. Wear long pants and don't touch anything that you cannot identify.

Over 10 trails wind through Isla Mona, but not all are regularly maintained. The most frequented path is a dirt access road traveling south from Playa Sardinera to: **Cueva Negra** (33 ft., 2min.); **Playa Mujeres** (1 mi., 20min.); **Cueva Carita** (½ mi., 15min.); the **airport** (¾ mi., 20min.); **Playa Carabinero** (2 mi., 40min.); **Playa del Uvero** (3¼ mi., 1¼hr.); **Playa Pájaro** (6mi., 3hr.); and **the lighthouse** (8mi., 4hr.). A second, more rustic path leaves Playa Sardinera and heads east straight up the cliff where it breaks off into two paths; one continues east across the island and the other continues north along the cliff. Before undertaking any hikes, check in with the DRN to ensure that they are still open to the public.

BOQUERÓN

Forget Luquillo; Boquerón has the most attractive public *balneario* on the island, with clear, gentle, shallow water, and a long beach of white sand lined by sporadic palm trees. For this reason the small town is probably the most popular domestic vacation destination. At night the party moves into the tiny, two-road town, where streets close down so that people can roam freely, Medalla in hand. Unlike some other premier beach areas, Boquerón is geared more toward Puerto Ricans than foreigners. Yes, the entire town feels a bit prepackaged for tourist consumption, and it can get a bit crazy on school holidays. But if you're up for a town that lives for family vacation, Boquerón is a great place to just chill, Puerto Rican style.

SOUTHWEST

⬛ TRANSPORTATION

Coming from the east (Ponce, San Germán, Lajas, and La Parguera), take Rte. 101 west straight into town. From Mayagüez and San Juan, take Hwy. 2 to Rte. 100, which travels south and intersects with Rte. 101 just outside Boquerón. **Públicos** come from Cabo Rojo (the city) and drive through Boquerón on weekdays and some Saturdays, but have no designated stops (5min., $1.50). From Cabo Rojo, *públicos* continue to **Mayagüez** (15-20min., $2).

ORIENTATION AND PRACTICAL INFORMATION

Boquerón is a *barrio* in the Cabo Rojo district on the island's west coast. The main street, **Route 101,** becomes Calle Muñoz Rivera as it enters town, then turns north along the coast and changes names again, to Calle José de Diego. **Route 307** splits off Rte. 101 to become the town's other road, Calle Estación, then heads north toward Joyuda. Boquerón is tiny, and if you want to find most practical necessities you'll have to head into Cabo Rojo, or even better, Mayagüez.

Tourist Office: Puerto Rican Tourism Company, Rte. 100 Km 13.7 (☎851-7070), 1 mi. north of town. Open daily 8am-noon and 1-4:30pm.

ATM: Boquerón has 1 ATM, located at the liquor store on the left as you enter town from the intersection of Rte. 100 and Rte. 101. Nearby Cabo Rojo has several banks.

Equipment Rental: Boquerón Kayak Rental, C. de Diego 15 (☎255-1849), rents single kayaks ($10 per hr., $40 per day), double kayaks ($15/$65), 5-person pedal boats ($15 for the first 2 people, $5 for each additional person), and surfbikes, a combination surfboard and bike ($15 per hr.). They also give 15min. banana boat rides ($5 per person). Call when the office is closed. Summer open daily 10am-5pm; Labor Day-*semana santa* open F-Sa 10am-5pm. Cash only.

Supermarket: Super Colmado Rodriguez, C. Muñoz Rivera 46 (☎851-2100), has limited groceries. Open M-Sa 6am-6:30pm, Su 6am-12:30pm. MC/V.

Laundromat: At **Adamaris Apartments,** on C. de Diego. Wash $1. Dry $0.25 per 7min. Open daily 7am-7pm.

Police: Rte. 101 Km 18.6 (☎851-4040). Open 24hr.

Internet Access: Boquerón Travel Agency, C. Muñoz Rivera 60 (☎851-4751; fax 254-2144) offers 1 computer with Internet access ($6 per hr.) and fax service. Open M-F 8:30am-5pm, Sa 9am-noon.

Post Office: Rte. 101 Km 18.3 (☎851-3848). Open M-F 7:30am-4pm, Sa 8am-noon.

Zip Code: 00622.

ACCOMMODATIONS

Boquerón is flush with accommodations, offering something to satisfy every budget, group size, and whim. Many of the rooms are actually 1-2 bedroom apartments designed to accommodate large Puerto Rican families (see p. 58). Prices go up considerably during the summer, which generally begins during *Semana Santa* and ends on Labor Day, in the beginning of September.

Boquerón Beach Hotel (☎851-7110; fax 851-7110; www.boqueronbeachhotel.com), at the turn-off to the *balneario.* This industrial sized hotel is one of Boquerón's more professional and popular accommodations. The recently remodeled front rooms charm with wrought-iron beds, but cost a bit more. Back rooms have been around for a few years, but they're still clean and well-kept. All rooms have TV, A/C, and fridge. Near the beach. Large pool area. Parking. Check-in 1pm. Check-out noon. Mar. to mid-Sept. doubles $88-109; quads $120-148. Mid Sept.-Feb. $60-77/$89-99. Tax included. MC/V. ❸

El Muelle Guest House (☎254-2801; fax 802-609-9105; www.elmuelleguesthouse.com), in the middle of town, is a budget friendly option during low season. All rooms have been individually decorated with such care that it's easy to overlook the little bits of dirt left in the corners. The administration is hard to reach; call ahead. Cable TV. Parking. Mar.-Sept. 1-bedroom apartment with kitchen and dishware $120; standard hotel rooms with A/C $130-140; rooms with kitchen and A/C $150. Sept.-Feb. $40/$50/$60. All prices for 2 people; extra person $10. Tax included. MC/V. ❹

Restaurant & Hotel El Pescador, Rte. 307 Km 9.3 (☎255-2490; hotelelpescador@hotmail.com). For clean rooms at an affordable price (even during summer) look no farther than El Pescador. The modern rooms in this mid-sized hotel contain A/C, cable TV, and sometimes even a VCR or a balcony. Parking. Checkout noon. Summer doubles $85; quads $95. Winter $55/$65. Tax included. AmEx/MC/V. ❸

Wildflowers, C. Muñoz Rivera 13 (☎851-1793). This white Victorian houses oozes charm rarely found in Puerto Rico. Rooms have been carefully decorated with dark wood furniture and coordinated linens, but also include practical benefits like TV, A/C, and fridge. All rooms fit 4 people; smaller rooms have 1 full and 1 bunk bed, larger rooms have 2 full beds. Call ahead. Parking. Check-in 1pm. Check-out noon. June-Aug. small rooms $100; large rooms $125. Sept.-May $75/$95. MC/V. ❹

Centro Vacacional de Boquerón (☎851-1900). Coming into town on Rte. 101, turn left at the sign for the

Boquerón

▲ ACCOMMODATIONS
Boquerón Beach Hotel, **14**
Centro Vacacional
de Boquerón, **16**

Hotel Tropical Inn, **15**
El Muelle Guest House, **2**
Parador Boquemar, **6**
Restaurant &
  Hotel El Pescador, **12**
Wildflowers, **11**

🍴 FOOD
The Fish Net, **7**
Galloway's, **5**
Pika-Pika, **13**
Pizzeria Lyken, **3**
Roberto's Villa Playera, **10**

🌙 NIGHTLIFE
Rincón del Olvido, **1**
El Shamar, **8**
Sunset Sunrise, **9**

balneario and continue to the end. This enormous government vacation complex resembles most other *centros vacacionales* (see p. 58), except for the fact that it is remarkably well maintained, and cabanas have an ideal beachfront location. If you go for the villa, request one of the brand new units at the south end of the beach. Check-out 1pm. Cabanas $66; villas $109. Tax included. MC/V. ❸

Hotel Tropical Inn, Rte. 101 Km 18.7 (☎851-0284), is one of the cheapest places in town year-round. Located across the street from the road to the *balneario,* this fading building houses crowded rooms with few windows. Despite the slightly overwhelming floor tiles, this is overall a good bargain. Rooms have TV and A/C. May-Sept. 15 doubles $55; quads $75. Sept. 16-Apr. $45/$55. 9% tax not included. AmEx/MC/V. ❸

Parador Boquemar (☎851-2158, toll-free 888-634-4343; fax 851-7600; www.boquemar.com), just off C. de Diego. You can't miss this ostentatious pink building rising above town. This hotel lacks the elegance of other *paradores* and feels somewhat cramped; even the pool is squashed into a concrete courtyard. Modern rooms come with a phone, A/C, and a small TV. Check-in 4pm. Check-out noon. Doubles $70-97; quads $123-129; extra person $16, 2 children under 12 free. Tax included. AmEx/MC/V. ❸

🗋 FOOD

Boquerón is the only place in Puerto Rico where you'll find multiple vendors selling fresh oysters (*ostiones;* about $3-4 per dozen) and clams (*almejas;* about $8 per dozen). Don't leave town without stopping by a cart, peeling apart the shells, and dumping hot sauce onto the succulent centers. For some inexplicable reason, Boquerón also has a disproportionate number of good Mexican restaurants.

SOUTHWEST

■ **Pika-Pika,** C. Estación 224 (☎851-2440), is expensive, plain and simple. But once you take a bite of the scrumptious Mexican entrees, prices seem like superfluous details. A variety of meat options are served with rice, beans, and tortillas. Don't miss the incredible *tres leches* for dessert ($4). Entrees $13-21. Margaritas $5.50. Open M and W-Th 5-10pm, F 5-11pm, Sa 3-11pm, Su 1-10pm. AmEx/MC/V. ❹

The Fish Net (☎851-6009) and **Roberto's Villa Playera** (☎254-3163), both on C. de Diego. Roberto had such success with his first seafood restaurant that he opened another one right across the street. These 2 restaurants share the same menu, the undisputed title of best seafood in town, and similar nautical decor, although only Villa Playera has a view of the canal out back. Entrees $5-18. Fish Net open W-Th and Su 11am-9pm, F-Sa 11am-9:30pm. Villa Playera open F-Tu 11am-8pm. AmEx/MC/V. ❸

Galloway's (☎254-3302), next to Club Náutico. Americans, come on down, this is your home away from home. Galloway's caters to the foreign crowd with an English menu, US TV, and rows of license plates lining the ceiling. The oceanfront dining room is a great place to watch the sunset. *Comida criolla* with a few American faves $6-26; lunch special starts at $4. Open Th-Tu 11am-10pm. AmEx/MC/V. ❸

Pizzeria Lyken (☎851-6335), on C. de Diego, offers an exciting alternative to the endless seafood—pizza! But never fear, they also serve a full spread of seafood entrees, as well as seafood pizza. Windchimes and fake flowers brighten up the informal outdoor seating area. Entrees $10-20; small pizza $7-10. Open Th and Su 11am-8:30pm, F-Sa 11am-9:30pm; bar open until midnight. AmEx/MC/V. ❸

⚑ OUTDOOR ACTIVITIES

BOSQUE ESTATAL DE BOQUERÓN. This 4773 acre reserve encompasses the mangroves west of La Parguera (p. 209), the salt flats in Cabo Rojo (p. 204), the Boquerón Wildlife Refuge near the intersection of Rte. 101 and 301, and Joyuda's Isla Ratones (p. 194) and protects over 120 species of birds. The best place to utilize the protected area's resources is the **Boquerón Wildlife Refuge,** which has two marked trails (old access roads) leading through the mangroves. During dry season the biting flies get quite annoying, but this is one of the best places on the island to see mangroves. The 2 mi. trail starts with a wooden walkway over the lagoon, then continues past a nice picnic area and several docks. Keep an eye out for the crabs crawling in the shallow waters. *(Rte. 101 Km 1.1. ☎851-4795. Open daily 7:30am-4pm.)* Back in town, the forest's main office, just past Club Náutico, has an information office and a 700 ft. wooden walkway leading into the mangroves. *(☎851-7260. Open M-F 7:30am-3:30pm.)*

🌊 BEACHES AND WATER SPORTS

The **public balneario** is the only show in town, and it's stunning. Like most beaches run by the Compañia de Parques Nacionales, this *balneario* contains picnic tables, showers, bathrooms, a cafeteria, and life guards. The beach attracts crowds, but there's more than enough sand to go around. (Rte. 101 Km. 18.8. Open daily 7:30am-7pm. Parking $2. Showers $1, children $0.50.) **Mona Aquatics,** C. de Diego 59 (☎851-2185; fax 254-0604), next to the Club Náutico, has a 42' boat. The PADI- and YMCA-certified owner leads diving expeditions to Isla Mona (see p. 195) and local sights ($50), but does not rent equipment. MC/V.

📷 NIGHTLIFE

Boquerón attracts large crowds on weekend nights. The plaza in front of El Shamar closes down to traffic after 6pm and people gather around tables to play dominoes, beers in hand. Students and younger adults gather farther north, near the Club Naútico. The entire town resembles a street party and it's almost impossible to miss the hot spots. **It is illegal to drink out of a bottle on the streets in Boquerón, so make sure that you get a plastic cup or a can from any bar.**

Rincón del Olvido, across from Club Naútico. This corner kiosk proves that you don't need fancy decor and gimmicks to draw in the crowds. Students and young people park their cars around the bar, then use it as a refueling point and meeting place. Beer $1-1.25; mixed drinks $1.25-3.75. Open W-Th 2-10pm, F-Su 9am-1am. Cash only.

El Shamar, C. de Deigo 1 (☎851-0542), has 3 main factors going for it: 1. It has a plaza overlooking the ocean. 2. It serves tasty *empanadillas*. 3. It's located right in the center of town. Add a pool table and $1 Medalla, and it's no wonder that this place is consistently packed. Beer $1-2; mixed drinks $2-6. Open daily 11am-midnight. Cash only.

Sunset Sunrise, C. Barbosa 65 (☎255-1478), on the main square. (Look for the sign that says Sunset Bar & Grill.) This little hole-in-the-wall is a popular gathering spot for the demure crowd that grabs a drink then sits on the tables out front playing dominos. Beer $1-2; mixed drinks $2-4. Open Su-Th 10am-midnight, F-Sa 10am-1am.

Galloway's (☎254-3302), on C. de Diego (see **Food,** above). The countdown to St. Patrick's Day starts early at this popular Irish pub. The bar provides a relatively quiet place to relax and make some new friends. Parking. Beer $2.50; mixed drinks $3.75-5. Appetizers $3-7. Open Su-Tu and Th 11am-midnight, F-Sa 11am-1am. AmEx/MC/V.

EL COMBATE

If the diminutive nature of many of Puerto Rican's beaches has gotten you down, perk up and try El Combate on for size. El Combate's beach is one of the longest on the island, as the white sand extends for miles in either direction, and locals claim that it is also one of Puerto Rico's cleanest. During weekdays this tiny *barrio* feels like a ghost town, but during holidays and summer vacations it becomes your typical southwest beach town, without the attractions of La Parguera or the touch of class in Boquerón. There's not much to do here but lay on the beach and drink beer, but luckily that's exactly what most people come to do.

El Combate sits at the end of Rte. 3301. Turn left at the Combate Hotel sign to reach the enormous beach parking lot, and the better, southern half of the beach. Or continue straight on Rte. 3301 to enter town, which extends north on four parallel streets; C. 1 is closest to the water, C. 2 is the next inland, etc. *Públicos* occasionally journey out from Cabo Rojo, but service is sporadic. Almost every house in town becomes some sort of vacation rental, and countless signs advertise a room for rent. However, this is difficult to negotiate because few owners live near their properties. For more traditional accommodations, try **Combate Beach Hotel ❸**, Rte. 3301 Km 2.7, a real hotel that retains the familiar feeling of a guest house. Clean, spacious rooms have TV, fridge, and A/C, but the hotel's real draws are the pool, jacuzzi, and direct beach access. Locals place the hotel's seafood restaurant among the best in town. (☎254-2358; fax 851-2134. June-Aug. doubles $88; quads $109, with kitchen $137. Sept.-May $45-64/$75-100. MC/V.) On the northern edge of town, concrete-friendly **Apartamentos Kenny ❸** is El Combate's best value for groups. The small, no-frills, one-bedroom apartments manage to fit in a double bed, a set of bunkbeds, a satellite TV, a kitchen area with stove and fridge, a small kitchen table, bedroom A/C, and supposedly up to six people. The last two people better be easygoing, because they'll be sleeping on a small fold-out couch. (☎254-0002 or 509-8833. Check-in 4pm. Check-out 3pm. *Semana Santa*-Labor Day $100; Labor Day-*Semana Santa* $90. No credit cards.)

El Combate has a number of seafood restaurants, but nobody can beat the location and rave reviews at **Annie's Place ❸**, auspiciously located at the turn in the road. This is the place to sit over the ocean enjoying *mofongo* filled with fresh seafood, and watch the sunset. After the sunset, the front half of the restaurant comes to life as a bar and *empanadilla* stand. (☎254-2553. Entrees $7-23. Beer $1.50-2. Open M and W-Th 10:30am-7pm, F-Sa 10:30am-11pm, Su 10:30am-8pm. MC/V.)

SOUTHWEST

If you don't like suspense, stop reading now and skip down to Sight Three, because the Cabo Rojo lighthouse and its spectacular surroundings are the undisputed highlight of this roadtrip. However, if you have a bit more time on your hands, meandering down Rte. 301 to the tip of Punta Jagüey, through the flat plains and dry vegetation, is a pleasant way to see the region's fascinating topography en route to the most southwestern point on the island.

1 **REFUGIO DE VIDA SILVESTRE CABO ROJO.** First stop: the well-maintained Cabo Rojo Wildlife Refuge (Km 5.1), 587 acres of subtropical dry forest managed by the US Fish & Wildlife Service. A small museum in the headquarters explains the area's flora and fauna (English/Spanish captions) and a decent 1½ mi. interpretive trail provides a real life introduction to the nature you just read about. (☎851-7258 ext. 35. Open M-F 7:30am-4pm.)

2 **CABO ROJO SALT FLATS.** The landscape becomes progressively flatter as you continue south to Puerto Rico's largest salt production facilities. The scenery is impressive alone, but this area also serves as the Caribbean's most important meeting point for migratory shore birds, with over 125 species of birds stopping here. The

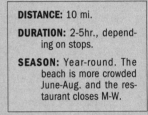

DISTANCE: 10 mi.

DURATION: 2-5hr., depending on stops.

SEASON: Year-round. The beach is more crowded June-Aug. and the restaurant closes M-W.

new observation tower (Km 11.1) affords terrific panoramic views, and the opportunity to spot Cape May Warblers, Prairie Warblers, and Common Yellowthroat Merlin.

3 **CABO ROJO LIGHTHOUSE.** From the salt flats, continue south on Rte. 301 all the way to the end—after it becomes a bumpy dirt road, after you're sure that you've gone too far, and after you feel like you're in the middle of nowhere. Then the Cabo Rojo Lighthouse will appear like a beacon. Park and continue on foot up the hill to this Neoclassical structure, built by the Spanish in 1881. The lighthouse is impressive, but really just an addendum to the truly incredible views. Standing on a limestone cliff 200 ft. over the crystal waters of the Caribbean crashing below is one of the most amazing experiences in Puerto Rico.

4 **PLAYA BAHÍA SUCIA.** Anyone who explores the lighthouse area will eventually stumble upon Playa Bahía Sucia, the beautiful beach just east of the point. This long white sand bay has some of the best swimming in Puerto Rico, as the clear, turquoise water hits the beach in a gentle downward slope. There are no facilities, but the remote location also means that there are fewer people than you will find at other nearby beaches.

5 **PARADOR BAHÍA SALINAS BEACH HOTEL.** If you're up for a splurge there's no better place to stop for lunch than **Agua al Cuello Restaurant** ❹, Rte. 301 Km 11.5, at the Bahía Salinas Beach Hotel, back at Km 11.2. This *mesón gastronómico* scores big points for its elegant wooden balcony over the calm water. In addition to the typical seafood entrees, the chef tests your taste buds with the creative, but spendy, "exotic menu." Choose from such rarities as char-grilled kangagroo kabobs ($28) and other unexpected specialties. (☎254-1212. Entrees $14-28. Open Th-Su 11am-9pm, sometimes M-W 5-9pm. AmEx/MC/V.) If the region has you sufficiently bewitched, this is also a good place to spend the night. **Bahía Salinas** ❹ is one of the island's premier *paradores*, with 2 pools, an oceanside location, an all-natural mineral water jacuzzi, and a relaxed, tropical atmosphere. (☎254-1212; fax 254-1215; www.bahiasalinas.net. Continental breakfast included. Check-in 3pm. Check-out noon. Doubles Su-W $85-125; Th-Sa $145 with breakfast and dinner. Extra person $10. Tax included. AmEx/MC/V.) The hotel also offers information about **kayak rental** ($20 per hr.).

SAN GERMÁN

Apart from physical location, San Germán (pop. 37,100) has nothing in common with its southwestern neighbors. This mountain town happens to be easily accessible from Hwy. 2, and for most travelers, this may be the best reason to come out here; San Germán makes an attractive daytrip after too much partying on the beach. The city is one of the oldest settlements on the island and still contains the island's oldest chapel. In 1514 when the Spanish crown divided Puerto Rico in half San Juan served as the capital of the east, governed by Juan Ponce de León, and San Germán reigned in the west, with Aurelio Tió as governor. In spite of this illustrious history, most of the current buildings were constructed in the early 20th century and look remarkably similar to Old San Juan or Ponce. The intricate, though decaying, architecture makes San Germán a pleasant place to wander, and the presence of the Universidad Interamericana lends a youthful feel to the city.

⌐ TRANSPORTATION

From Hwy. 2 exit onto Rte. 122, then turn right onto C. Luna. Coming from Boquerón, La Parguera, or anywhere southwest of the city, just follow Rte. 101 all the way into town. *Públicos* connect San Germán to **Cabo Rojo** (20min., $1.75); **Lajas** (20min., $1); **Mayagüez** (30min., $2.25); and **Sabana Grande** (15min., $1.30). The *público* station is near the intersection of C. Luna and Rte. 122; turn right and walk up C. Luna to reach the historical center.

◢ ▸ ORIENTATION AND PRACTICAL INFORMATION

San Germán's busy main street used to be called **Calle Luna,** but the government recently changed the name to Ave. Universidad Interamericana. Like most sangermeños, *Let's Go* still refers to the street as C. Luna. The two plazas sit a couple of short blocks north of C. Luna, but almost no residents venture to this historic area. Instead, they congregate around the western end of C. Luna, with the fast food restaurants and the university, or the eastern end of C. Luna, where Rte. 122 leads to a shopping plaza, a pharmaceutical factory, and Hwy. 2.

Bank: Western Bank, Rte. 102 Km 32.3 (☎892-1207), exchanges traveler's checks, but not foreign currency. Drive-thru ATM. Open M-F 7:30am-5pm, Sa 8:30-11:30am.

Supermarket: Mr. Special Supermercado, Rte. 102 Km 32.9 (☎892-1098), sells super special groceries. Open daily M-Sa 6:30am-9pm, Su 11am-5pm. AmEx/MC/V.

Laundromat: Emmsue Wash & Dry, Rte. 102 Km 34 (☎892-5252), behind Panadería La Marqueta, 1½ mi. east of town. Wash $1.50. Dry $0.25 per 4min. Change available. Open daily 5am-10pm.

Police: On C. Casto Perez, behind the *público* terminal (☎892-2020). Open 24hr.

Late-Night Pharmacy: Walgreens (☎892-1170), at the corner of C. Luna and C. Carro. Open M-Sa 7am-10pm, Su 9am-6pm. AmEx/D/MC/V.

Hospital: Hospital de la Concepción, Rte. 102 Km 31.2 (☎892-1860). Open daily 6:30am-10:30pm. Emergency room open 24hr.

Internet Access: Biblioteca Pública, C. Acosta 11 (☎892-6820), on Plaza Quiñones, offers free Internet access. Open M-Th 8am-8:30pm, F 8am-6pm, Sa 8am-1pm and 2-4:30pm. **Password Internet Cafe,** C. Ruiz Belvis 9 (☎892-7945), at C. Carro, charges $3 per 30min. Open M and F 9am-5pm, Tu-Th 9am-6pm, Sa 8:30am-1pm.

Post Office: C. Luna 181 (☎892-1313), near the intersection with Rte. 122. No General Delivery. Open M-F 7:30am-4pm, Sa 8am-noon.

Zip Code: 00683.

SOUTHWEST

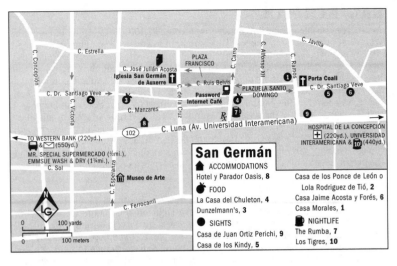

San Germán

🏠 ACCOMMODATIONS

Hotel y Parador Oasis, **8**

🍴 FOOD

La Casa del Chuleton, **4**
Dunzelmann's, **3**

● SIGHTS

Casa de Juan Ortiz Perichi, **9**
Casa de los Kindy, **5**

Casa de los Ponce de León o
  Lola Rodriguez de Tió, **2**
Casa Jaime Acosta y Forés, **6**
Casa Morales, **1**

🎵 NIGHTLIFE

The Rumba, **7**
Los Tigres, **10**

🏠 ACCOMMODATIONS

San Germán's only two accommodations are both relatively budget friendly, but don't come looking for first-class rooms.

Residencia Hostelería (☎264-1912 ext. 7300 or 7301). Continue on C. Luna to the university's 2nd entrance, then enter the blue building to the left of the track field. This option may be your dream come true or your worst nightmare, depending on how you feel about living in an all-male dorm. The university rents several clean rooms with a small living room in the front, a bedroom in the back, and 2 dorm-style showers in the middle. You must reserve in advance M-F 8am-noon and 1-5pm, although you can check in anytime. Rooms without sheets: singles $22; doubles $27; triples $33; quads $38. With sheets: $27/$33/$38/$49. TV, A/C, and sheets: $49/$59/$65/$75. Larger rooms available. Tax included. AmEx/MC/V if you check in M-F 8am-5pm. ❶

Hotel y Parador Oasis, C. Luna 72 (☎892-1175), is much more budget than other *paradores*, both in terms of price and quality. All the amenities are here—pool, cable TV, A/C—but the entire hotel is a bit run down. Nonetheless, a friendly staff and a prime location makes this a good base for exploring downtown. Check-out noon. Singles $61-63; doubles $68-70; extra person $10. Tax included. MC/V. ❸

🍴 FOOD

La Casa del Chuleton, C. Carro 13 (☎264-2430), at C. Dr. Veve, is one of the best eateries in town. Workers on their lunch break come for the clean interior, friendly stuff, and heaping piles of *comida criolla* (lunch $5). Entrees $9-13. Open M-W 11am-3pm, Th-Sa 11am-10pm. MC/V. ❷

Chaparritas, C. Luna 171 (☎892-1078), successfully combines classy decor, quality food, and affordable prices. This brightly colored restaurant serves a variety of meat-heavy Mexican entrees ($11-15). Beer $2.50-2.75. Open W-Su 11:30am-3pm and 6-9pm, F 11:30am-3pm and 6-10pm, Sa 6-10pm, Su 1-9pm. MC/V. ❸

Dunzelmann's, C. Dr. Veve 19b (☎ 425-8708), brings a touch of university life to downtown San Germán. Students relax in this charming European-style cafe and enjoy a variety of coffees and baked goods. Also serves 1 lunch item, usually a ham and cheese croissant with chips and a drink ($3-3.50). Open M-Sa 8am-11pm, Su 5-11pm. ❶

🔾 SIGHTS

Apart from the two exceptional churches, most of San Germán's "sights" are actually private residences with exquisite architecture. Most sights are close to the main plazas—**Plaza Francisco Quiñones,** a quiet tree-lined plaza overshadowed by the enormous modern church, and **Plazuela Santo Domingo,** a slightly more active plaza just to the east. The most interesting way to sightsee may be to just wander the streets, where a pleasant surprise awaits around every corner. Some of the more historically significant houses are described below.

PORTA COALI CHAPEL AND MUSEUM OF RELIGIOUS ART. This modest structure on the southern edge of Plazuela Santo Domingo, known as "The Gate to Heaven," is the oldest chapel in Puerto Rico, the second-oldest religious building (Iglesia San José in Old San Juan takes the prize), and San Germán's star attraction. The building was constructed in 1606 when Friar Antonio Mejia decided that the western half of the island needed a convent, but over time the building slowly deteriorated and by 1866 only the chapel remained. Finally in 1949 the Puerto Rican Institute of Culture took control of the building and restored it to a recognizable shape, though only the columns, walls, and stairwell are original. The 17th-century altar originally resided in the Iglesia San José, but was transferred to Porta Coali in 1930. The chapel is no longer used for services, but it now houses a small museum of religious art. This collection of paintings and large *santos* will probably only interest die-hard religious historians, especially as the few captions are in Spanish, but entering the chapel is one of the best ways to experience San Germán's extensive history. (*At C. Ramos and C. Dr. Veve. ☎ 892-5845. Open W-Su 8:30am-noon and 1-4:30pm. $1, under 12 free.*)

IGLESIA SAN GERMÁN DE AUXERRE. Porta Coali may have the historical value, and the town's esteem, but San Germán's largest religious structure is by far the more attractive of the two. The original 1737 church was reconstructed in 1842 and decorators pulled out all the stops on the Neoclassical building. The church closes for most of the day, but it's worthwhile to stop by just before mass (or attend mass) in order to see the elegant interior, with its tall ceilings, numerous chandeliers, and creative paint job. (*☎ 892-1027. Office open M-F 8-11am and 1-3pm, Sa 8-11am. Church open for mass M-Sa 7am and 7:30pm; Su 7, 8:30, 10am, 7:30pm.*)

HISTORIC HOUSES. San Germán is plumb full of 'em (although you can't enter any of them). Start your tour just north of the church at **Casa de los Ponce de León o Lola Rodriguez de Tió (1870),** C. Dr. Veve 13. The unremarkable, Neoclassical brown house is included on the list of National Historical Places, and once served as a visiting place for famous poet and political protestor Lola Rodriguez de Tió. Continue down C. Dr. Veve, past both plazas, then turn left on C. Ramos. Across from Porta Coali, the well-maintained **Casa Morales** was built in Queen Anne Victorian style in 1915 and continues to be one of the city's most aesthetically pleasing houses. Just past the chapel you'll see **Casa de los Kindy,** C. Dr. Veve 64, on your right. This beautiful 19th-century house stands out for its exceptional polychrome stained glass windows. Farther down the street, the bright yellow Art Nouveau house on the right, **Casa Jaime Acosta y Forés,** C. Dr. Veve 70, was built between 1917 and 1918, and continues to shine today. Finally turn right and loop back onto C. Luna to find the **Casa de Juan Ortiz Perichi,** C. Luna 94. The big, two-story house has seen better days since its construction in 1920, but still exemplifies ornamental Puerto Rican architecture.

MUSEO DE ARTE Y CASA DE ESTUDIO ALFREDO RAMÍREZ DE ARELLANO Y ROSELL. On the way back from a walking tour through San Germán's historic district, you may want to stop by this turn-of-the-century home that now holds a small art museum. The unexciting collection contains primarily stenographs from the 1960s and 70s, but this is a rare opportunity to actually enter one of San Germán's historic homes. *(C. Esperanza 7. ☎892-8870. Open W-Su 10am-3pm. Free.)*

UNIVERSIDAD INTERAMERICANA. You can't miss the presence of the Interamerican University in San Germán. Founded in 1912 as the Instituto Politécnico de San Germán, this is now the largest private university in Puerto Rico. The attractive campus on the western edge of town, off C. Luna, is a pleasant place to wander and absorb the hustle of student activity. The campus grounds include a primary forest and the only round chapel in Puerto Rico.

📻 NIGHTLIFE

Considering the size of the university, San Germán has a remarkably tame nightlife scene, as most students head to Mayagüez or La Parguera for their nights out.

▨ **Los Tigres,** C. Luna 6 (☎264-5504), at the main university entrance, is *the* student hangout. All day long, college kids shoot pool in the small wooden house or chill on the porch with a beer, taking advantage of daily Happy Hour specials. This is the place to bond with the younger crowd. Happy Hour daily generally 8pm-midnight beer $1-1.50. Th live music. Open M-W 11am-1am, Th-Sa 11am-2am. MC/V.

The Rumba (☎922-3340), on C. Carro, opened in early 2003 and has all the ingredients for success, including antique brick doorways, intimate corner tables, and a large dance floor. Plays salsa, Spanish rock, and merengue. Beer $1.50-2; mixed drinks $2-4.50. 18+. Open W 7pm-1am, Th-Sa 7pm-2am. AmEx/MC/V.

NEAR SAN GERMÁN: BOSQUE ESTATAL DE SOSÚA

Just 40min. east of San Germán, the 3341 acre Bosque Estatal de Sosúa provides an excellent taste of the Puerto Rican countryside for those vacationing on the southwest coast, and a refreshing return to nature for anyone overwhelmed by city life. Sosúa is the only state forest with both dry and humid forest, in addition to over 150 species of trees. Though it's nothing extraordinary, anyone who has not seen superstars like Guánica or Toro Negro should enjoy Sosúa.

This is one of the island's more isolated forest reserves on the island, and unlike most of the forests along the Rúta Panoramica, Sosúa does not have a thoroughfare bisecting the forest. Instead, visitors must drive east on Rte. 10 through Sabana Grande, then follow Rte. 368 to Km 2.1, where they'll turn left and continue on the small road for 15-20min. to reach the forest center. The DRN office is located in a valley in the middle of the forest next to a large and attractive picnic area. (☎721-5495. Open M-F 7am-3:30pm, Sa-Su 9am-5pm.) There are lots of covered **picnic tables** (although many don't have benches), fire pits, bathrooms, and even a snack machine. A few **hiking trails** leave from the recreation area, but they are not well marked and you'll probably need a ranger to find the trailhead. More compelling is the rigorous **mountain bike trail,** which narrows to a small path throughout its 3 mi. loop. You must bring your own bike.

In 2003 the Department of Natural Resources was in the process of renovating the three **camping areas** ❶ at Sosúa, adding cabins to the first, and expanding water and bathroom facilities at the other two. The camping areas are not Puerto Rico's best, but the new additions look promising. By the end of 2003 facilities at all three sites should include bathrooms, fire pits, and cement showers. For more info about the cabins, contact the DRN. (See **Camping**, p. 58. Tents $4 per person.)

LA PARGUERA

Most foreigners come to La Parguera to see the phosphorescent bay, frequently touted as the best Puerto Rico. Don't be confused—this is not La Parguera's principal attraction and although it is the cheapest place to see the glowing water, both Fajardo and Vieques have better bioluminescent bays. However, Puerto Ricans know that the other diversions in this small *barrio* make for an excellent long weekend. Just offshore, several mangrove islands, calm shallow water, and lots of docks create a paradise for boaters and water lovers. Farther afield, The Wall, a 20 mi. long coral reef cliff, attracts serious scuba divers from around the island. On weekends and holidays the small neighborhood takes on the feel of an oceanside carnival, with crowds of people wandering the streets, munching on *pinchos*, and looking for a cheap Medalla. Yet on a quiet weekday during the low season, not much has really changed in La Parguera, where few cars transverse the one main street and roosters still crow with the sunrise.

▐ TRANSPORTATION

Coming from the east, drive west on Hwy. 2, then turn toward Guánica on Rte. 116 and continue west to the intersection with Rte. 304, which leads south into town. From the west, take Rte. 2 to Rte. 100, then turn left on Rte. 101. Continue on Rte. 303, then Rte. 305, and finally take a right onto Rte. 116, which leads to Rte. 304, which leads to La Parguera. (It's much easier than it sounds.) Occasional **públicos** pick up travelers from the brightly painted bench just north of town on Rte. 304 and take them to Lajas ($1.50), but this service is very sporadic. From Lajas *públicos* continue to San Germán.

◀✴ 🛈 ORIENTATION AND PRACTICAL INFORMATION

After about 15min. of wandering you'll feel like you've always known your way around tiny La Parguera, where everything is easy to find despite the lack of addresses. Rte. 304 leads straight into town and becomes the main thoroughfare. After the church turn right on Ave. los Pescadores to find Centro Comercial **El Muelle**, a small shopping center filled with traveler-friendly amenities.

> **ATMs:** La Parguera has no banks, but there are ATMs in the **supermarket** (see below) and in front of **Panadería Lucerna Bakery** (see p. 211).

> **Equipment Rental: Ventoera** (☎808-0396 or 505-4148), in El Muelle, rent 12-17' sailboats ($125 per day) and kayaks (singles $10 per hr., double $15). Also offers lessons in sailing ($35 per hr.; 8hr. to complete course), windsurfing (8hr. course $275) and kite surfing ($55 per hr.). All equipment included. Open Tu-Sa 9am-8pm, Su 9am-5pm. Summers also open M 9am-8pm. AmEx/MC/V.

> **English-Language Books:** A **free book exchange** in the corner of El Muelle next to the post office has a large selection of English-language books.

> **Supermarket: Supermercados Selectos** (☎899-6065), in El Muelle, carries several English-language magazines. Open M-Sa 7am-10pm, Su 7am-8pm. AmEx/MC/V.

> **Laundromat: Lavamatico** (☎899-6065), on the left side of El Muelle. Wash $1; dry $1. No soap. Change available in the supermarket. Open M-Sa 7am-8pm, Su 7am-6pm.

> **Pharmacy: Farmacia San Pedro** (☎899-8719), in El Muelle. Open M-Sa 8am-8pm, Su 8am-5pm. AmEx/MC/V.

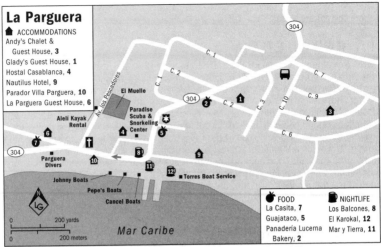

La Parguera

🏠 ACCOMMODATIONS
Andy's Chalet &
  Guest House, **3**
Glady's Guest House, **1**
Hostal Casablanca, **4**
Nautilus Hotel, **9**
Parador Villa Parguera, **10**
La Parguera Guest House, **6**

El Muelle
Paradise Scuba & Snorkeling Center
Aleli Kayak Rental
Parguera Divers
Johnny Boats
Pepe's Boats
Cancel Boats
Torres Boat Service

Mar Caribe

🍎 FOOD
La Casita, **7**
Guajataco, **5**
Panadería Lucerna
Bakery, **2**

🍺 NIGHTLIFE
Los Balcones, **8**
El Karokal, **12**
Mar y Tierra, **11**

Police: (☎ 899-2020). On Rte. 304, just east of downtown. Open 24hr.

Post Office: The small postal service in El Muelle (☎ 899-6075) does not offer General Delivery. Open M-F 8am-noon and 1-3:30pm.

Zip Code: 00667.

🏠 ACCOMMODATIONS

La Parguera offers a pick of relatively affordable accommodations, from quasi-oceanside resorts to rustic guest houses.

🔖**Andy's Chalet & Guest House,** C. 8 #133 (☎ 899-0000). Entering the town from Rte. 304, turn left on C. 7, then right on C. 8. The residential location is the only fault of this pleasant accommodation, which manages to combine the professionalism of a hotel with the friendly feel of a guest house. Modern rooms include A/C, TV, and sometimes a tiny fridge. Common patio with microwave. Singles $45; doubles $55; triples $65; quads $71. 2-room apartments with kitchen $80-95. Tax included. AmEx/MC/V. ❷

Nautilus Hotel (☎ 899-4565 or 899-1708; fax 899-5337), near the boat parking lot. This stylish hotel is one of the best deals in town. Glistening rooms with TV and A/C are just as nice as the *paradores* at a fraction of the price. Private balconies look out at the parking lot. Pool. Jacuzzi. Doubles Sept. 16-June 14 M-Th $50, F-Sa $70; June 15-Sept. 15 $70/$80. 8- to 12-person apartments $85-125. Tax included. AmEx/MC/V. ❸

La Parguera Guest House (☎ 899-3993), at the western end of Rte. 304, looks quite snazzy with its fresh coat of bright blue paint. On weekends this seems just like a hotel, complete with reception area and a parking lot, but during weekdays the place is deserted; call ahead. Small rooms are functional but not outstanding, with linoleum floors, fridge, TV, and A/C. Check-out noon. Doubles $60; triples $70; quads $80; 6-person apartments $125. 9% tax not included. AmEx/MC/V. ❸

Parador Villa Parguera (☎ 899-7777 or 899-3975; www.elshop.com), on Rte. 304, has competitive rates for some of the most deluxe rooms in town. Excessive nautical kitsch only minimally mars the exceptional oceanside setting. Beautiful poolside grass patio. Pristine rooms. A/C, phone, TV, and private balcony. Check-in 3pm. Check-out noon. Doubles Su-F $90-100, Sa $100-112. 7% tax not included. AmEx/D/MC/V. ❹

Glady's Guest House, C. 2 #42B (☎899-4678), near the intersection with Rte. 304, exudes a slightly more professional air than most La Parguera guest houses. Still, rooms are on the second floor of a residence and could use a bit more decorative touch—the bare light bulbs and linoleum floor just lack a bit of charm. All rooms have A/C and TV. Doubles $60; triples $65; 4-person apartment $75. Tax included. AmEx/MC/V. ❷

Hostal Casablanca (☎899-4250), on Rte. 304, is certainly in the middle of the action. You can see the best part of the hotel from out front—a beautiful swimming pool and a large, breezy patio. Unfortunately the rooms are in need of a face lift. Hopefully renovation plans will come through soon. A/C but no TV. Check-out noon. Doubles F-Sa $85, Su-Th $65; quads $118/$97; extra person $17. Tax included. AmEx/MC/V. ❸

📛 FOOD

La Parguera's tourist influx has prompted the development of several tasty, inexpensive restaurants serving a smorgasbord of delectable foods.

La Casita (☎899-1681), on Rte. 304 at the western edge of town. This big family-friendly restaurants fills up on weekend nights with Puerto Ricans who know that they don't have to go to one of the fancy 5-star restaurants to get the freshest seafood in town. Entrees $8-22 including lobster. House wine $4.50. Open Tu-Th 11am-9:30pm, F-Sa 11am-10pm, Su 11am-9pm. AmEx/MC/V. ❸

Dave's Deli (☎899-6065), in El Muelle. This utterly American diner serves hamburgers, sandwiches, and ice cream to a largely foreign crowd. Take that for what you may, but all of the food is fast and well-prepared. Pleasant outdoor patio. Entrees $2-5. Sa-Su breakfast buffet $8. Open M-Sa 7am-10pm, Su 7am-8pm. ❶

Guajataco, Rte. 304 Km 3.2 (☎808-0303), has cute tiled tables on an outdoor patio. Choose from over 30 varieties of simple and flavorful burritos, quesadillas, and tacos. Wheat and spinach tortillas. Entrees $2-6, but it may take more than 1 to fill up. Open M and W-Th 11am-9pm, F-Sa 11am-11pm, Su 11am-10pm. MC/V. ❶

Panadería Lucerna Bakery (☎899-7637), at the intersection of Rte. 304 and C. 2, provides a dose of Puerto Rican reality amidst the otherwise international culinary scene. This tiny, 2-booth bakery is a good place to go for a hearty island breakfast, or a big, tasty muffin. No menu, but the friendly staff will whip up just about any breakfast food. Also serves sandwiches. Everything under $5. Open daily 7am-10pm. MC/V. ❶

Golden City Restaurant (☎899-5644), in El Muelle, lacks any ambiance except the oh-so-charming feel of a shopping center restaurant. Nevertheless, Golden City serves up tasty Chinese favorites at an affordable price. Combos $3.50-7. Open M-W 11am-10pm, Th 11am-10:30pm, F-Sa 11am-11pm, Su 11am-10:30pm. Cash only. ❶

El Blues Pizzeria & Sports Bar (☎899-4742), in El Muelle. A spartan menu offers several varieties of thin-crust pizza and some random American-based entrees (ribs and fajitas). The big plant-filled patio could only be nicer if you took it out of the parking lot. Also becomes a popular nightlife venue. Entrees $5-14. Beer $2.50-3; mixed drinks $3-4. Happy Hour daily 5-9pm Medalla $1.25. Sa 10pm live Spanish rock and tropical music. Open M-Th 5-10pm, F-Sa 5pm-12:30am, Su 3:30pm-midnight. AmEx/MC/V. ❷

🎏 OUTDOOR ACTIVITIES

La Parguera is possibly the most popular harbor for Puerto Rican small boat owners and during school vacations, the area is packed. Several boat rental companies (see **Boating,** below) take visitors out to tour the mangrove channels, daytrip on nearby mangrove islands, and visit the phosphorescent bay. The protected bay also provides an excellent area for

FROM THE ROAD

GREEN SEAS

This is it, I thought as I woke up in the morning. The big day. I'm going to see The Wall. After fraternizing with the Puerto Rican dive scene for awhile, you start to hear stories about how great it is and I was excited about the trip.

I swaggered into the dive shop, flush with confidence. This was the day for me to prove myself as a diver. So when the dive master asked if I got seasick, of course I said no. I had never been sick before, why would I get sick now? "Do people frequently get sick?" I asked. "Well yesterday the first woman to get sick was the one who said that she never got seasick." We all laughed and headed to the boat.

It's not hard to see where this story is headed. Fast-forward two hours and I'm leaning over the side, puking up everything I've eaten for the last 2 days. The dive masters were very nice and didn't even laugh as I ate my words and quietly paid the price for my overconfidence. Yet not even a few hours of feeling green could make me regret the trip. The Wall was everything I expected and more. In addition to some amazing memories, I took home a few important life lessons. 1. There's a first time for everything. 2. The divemasters always know what they're talking about—listen. 3. Always use sunscreen before diving, because you never know when you'll spend most of the trip hanging over the side of the boat.

beginners to try their hand at windsurfing, sailing, or kayaking (see p. 215), while the huge reefs farther out create some superb snorkeling and diving opportunities (see p. 213).

BOATING

The numerous islands around La Parguera offer a variety of experiences to fulfill any mariner's desires. Most Puerto Rican boaters head to **the mangrove canals** (*los canales manglares*) just west of the main docks, where they anchor their boats and jump in the shallow water. There is no public dock, so don't come this direction unless you really like your boat. To the east of the main docks, **Caracoles Island** provides a similar experience—3 ft. water around an impenetrable mangrove island that lacks a dock. On busy days, a floating store sells *pinchos* and other Puerto Rican snacks. Just to the north, **Caracoles Tierra** looks identical to Caracoles, but has a bit of land in the middle where people have been known to **camp.** Farther north, **Isla Mata de Gatas** is the most distant island accessible by small motorboat, the only island with a dock, and supposedly the best area for snorkeling (if you have a guide who can show you around). The small island has bathrooms, picnic tables, and trash cans, but as a result it's quite over-visited; you might be happier parking your boat offshore and exploring the shallow waters. (Open June-Sept. Tu-Su 9am-5pm; Oct.-May Th-Su 9am-5pm. If M is a holiday, open M and closed Tu. $1 per person.) **Cayo Enrique,** west of Mata de Gatas, looks similar to Caracoles, but receives fewer visitors. On the way out to any of the eastern islands you'll pass **Isla Magueyes,** an island managed by the University of Puerto Rico marine sciences department. You have to get special permission from the Mayagüez campus to visit the island, but if you take one of the smaller boat tours, the guide may hop out and open the gate so that the huge iguanas (used for research) can come out on the dock. Then there is the **Bahía Fosforescente (Phosphorescent Bay),** the amazing all-natural water light show (see **Swimming Through The Stars,** p. 258). The nighttime trip to the bay takes about 25min., and most companies only stay for 5-10min. Smaller boats allow a more personalized trip.

Theoretically, most of the boat companies at La Parguera's main dock are open every day. On busy weekends in the summer this may be true, but on slower weekdays it is difficult to find anyone at all. At least one company opens every night for trips to the phosphorescent bay from 7:30pm until people stop showing up. All companies charge $5 per person for the 1hr. trip, but there are slight variations in the service provided. Trips only leave if and when customers come.

Cancel Boats (☎899-5891 or 899-2972). Their 150-passenger glass-bottomed takes daytrips through the mangrove channels to see Isla Mata de Gata and the coral reefs (Sa 3:30pm, Su 2 and 5pm) and night trips to the phosphorescent bay (Sept.-Dec. and late Jan.-Mar. Sa-Su 7:30pm; Mar.-Sept. and late Dec.-early Jan. daily 7:30pm) for only $5 per person. Smaller motorboats lead private tours throughout the day ($25 for 1-5 people or $5 per person with up to 10 people). MC/V.

Johnny Boats (☎299-2212), is the only company that lets you swim in the phosphorescent bay. Daytime tours of the mangroves in small motorboats $5 per person with at least 5 people. Motorboat rental $20 for the first hr., $15 for the 2nd hr.

Alelí Kayak Rental (☎899-6086), has a spot at the main dock, as well as a repair shop across the street from El Muelle. They rent kayaks (single $10 per hr., $30 for ½ day, $50 for full day; doubles $15/$40/$60) and lead 2-4hr. guided ecotours through the mangrove channels ($50 per person). Open Th-Su 10am-5pm.

Torres Boat Service (☎899-5136), rents small motor boats ($15 per hr. for 4 people, $20 for 5, $25 for 7) and offers 40min. guided tours of the bay on a larger boat ($5 per person). June-Aug. open daily 8:30am-midnight; Sept.-May open Sa-Su only.

DIVING AND SNORKELING

Many of the dive operators in San Juan actually head to La Parguera when they want to do some serious diving—that's how good it is here. The big attraction is **The Wall** *(La Pared)*, a 20 mi. coral reef cliff that starts at 60 ft. and drops down to over 150 ft.. Visibility tends to be 60-100 ft. and divers have reported seeing sea turtles, manatees, and even dolphins. But beware; The Wall is 6 mi. offshore in open sea, and the voyage tends to be rough. Even those who don't normally get seasick may consider taking anti-nausea medications (see **Green Seas,** p. 212).

Paradise Scuba & Snorkeling Center (☎899-7611; paradisescubapuertorico@hotmail.com), next to Hostal Casa Blanca, offers several water opportunities, including: a daytime snorkeling trip to 3 different areas (3hr., 10am, $35), a sunset snorkeling trip that includes a swim in the phosphorescent bay (5hr., 4pm, $50), a 2-tank dive to The Wall ($70, with equipment rental $80), a 1-tank night dive ($50), and a Discover Scuba package with 1 pool lesson and 1 open-water dive ($125). Private PADI certification course $400, 3-week group course $200. Snorkeling trips include all equipment and a snack. Open daily 9am-9pm. AmEx/MC/V.

Parguera Divers (☎899-4171; www.pargueradivers.com), in Parador Posada Porlamar, also offers daily trips to The Wall on their new 30' Island Hopper. 2-tank dive $70, equipment rental $15; wet suit not included. 1-tank night dive $45, equipment $10. 4-day PADI & NAUI open-water certification course $275. 3hr. snorkeling trip to 2 sights $25. Open most days 9:30am-5pm. AmEx/MC/V.

FISHING

The ocean around La Parguera is considered to be one of the most productive fishing areas in Puerto Rico. The two outfits below provide opportunities to head out to open waters, at least 6 mi. offshore, and catch more exotic fish such as barracuda, mahi mahi, blue marlin, dorado, and tuna.

Parguera Fishing Charters (☎899-4698 or 382-4698; http://hometown.aol.com/mareja), uses a 31' Bertram Sportfisherman. Snorkeling available. Equipment included. 1-4 people ½-day $400, full-day $700. Additional person (up to 6 total) $25/$50. MC/V.

Mahi-Mahi Tours & Fishing Charters (☎642-2587), has 2 vessels. The 28' boat takes out up to 4 people for ½-day (8am-noon, $350) or full-day ($500) trips. The 21' boat holds only 2 people (½-day $225, full-day $375). All trips include fishing and snorkeling gear. Snorkeling and sightseeing trips for up to 6 people $225. Cash only.

SOUTHWEST

NIGHTLIFE

La Parguera knows how to party—quickly. On weekends and holidays the many bars along main street are packed until midnight, when the local law requires that they shut down. On Saturday nights the restaurant at Parador Villa Parguera (see p. 210) hosts an elaborate live music/dance/Spanish comedy show that attracts a fair number of older visitors ($35 includes dinner and show).

Los Balcones (☎899-2145), across from the plaza, attracts a rambunctious college crowd, especially on Sa nights when live music packs the place. Ironically, the balcony is closed, but pool tables still draw a loyal crowd. Beer $2-2.50. Happy Hour Sa 7-10pm. Sa 10pm live Spanish rock. 18+. Open Th-Su 4pm-midnight. Cash only.

Mar y Tierra (☎899-4627), on Rte. 304. Young male Puerto Ricans practice their game at the 4 pool tables at this popular sports bar. In back, the cafeteria attracts an entirely different crowd of families who enjoy hot *empanadillas* with their beer ($1-2.25). Piña colada $4. Open M-Th 5pm-midnight, F 4pm-midnight, Sa-Su noon-midnight. MC/V.

El Karokal (☎899-5582), in front of the docks. For over 36 years this classy bar has been serving up the house specialty—Coño Sangria in a signature cup ($4.50). Many people stop by while they're waiting for a boat, and $1 refills keeps 'em coming back all night long. Open Su-Th 11am-11pm, F-Sa 11am-midnight. Cash only.

BOSQUE ESTATAL DE GUÁNICA

Few sights live up to their glossy brochures, but Bosque Estatal de Guánica far surpasses the pamphlet handed out in tourist offices. The incredible scenery in this area cannot be captured in photos or words; you have to stand on a cactus-covered cliff overlooking the tumultuous Caribbean to really understand the wild land. Guánica State Forest contains such a unique diversity of plant and animal life, including the largest variety of bird species on the island, that it has been distinguished as a United Nations Biosphere Reserve. This is Puerto Rico's paradise for active visitors, as it has some of the best hiking and water sports on the island. With over 20 miles of trails, two islands, and wild Caribbean beaches, this reserve easily keeps guests entertained for a week and still aching to come back for more.

AT A GLANCE

AREA: 9876 acres.

CLIMATE: Hot and dry. Average temperature 79°F. Little variation.

HIGHLIGHTS: Rare dry limestone scrub, incredible Caribbean landscapes.

FEATURES: Hiking through some of the island's most dramatic landscape, water sports, bird-watching.

GATEWAYS: Guánica, Ponce (see p. 220).

CAMPING: Unfortunately, nobody offers camping in or near Guánica. However, there are several attractive accommodations.

FEES: None, except equipment rental and ferry fare.

TRANSPORTATION

From Hwy. 2, turn south onto Rte. 116. The first important left will be Rte. 334, which leads to the forest info center. The next left, onto Rte. 333, leads to most of the beaches, the accommodations, and the ferry dock. The next intersection, at Rte. 116R, leads to Guánica's center. In Guánica, **carros públicos** leave from the corner of C. 25 de Julio and S.S. Rodriguez, across from Banco Santander, for Yauco (15-30min., 6am-6pm, $1.10), where connections can be made to Ponce. Guánica has no taxis, but most *público* drivers will take you to the hotels.

🔳 ORIENTATION

Bosque Estatal de Guánica is divided into two sections. The larger eastern half contains the hiking trails, the two most popular beaches, and the two off-shore islands. Playa Santa and the surrounding sights lie directly in front of the western section. In between, the small one-road town of Guánica is a good place to stock up on supplies. Rte. 116R deposits drivers on **C. 25 de Julio,** which passes the plaza and veers left past the *malecón* before intersecting with Rte. 333. C. 39 de Marzo intersects 25 de Julio just past the plaza and holds most government services.

🔲 PRACTICAL INFORMATION

Visitors Center: The **DRN** info center (☎821-5706), at the end of Rte. 334, provides extensive info about the trails (in Spanish). Open daily 8:30am-4:30pm.

Hours: The DRN parking area, and thus most trails, is open daily 8:30am-4:30pm.

Supplies: Sunscreen and water are the most important items you will need in Guánica; many paths don't have shade. Bring at least 35 oz. of water per person per hr. of hiking.

Equipment Rental: Caribbean Vacation Villa (see p. 215) rents kayaks, windsurfers, snorkeling and scuba equipment, mountain bikes, surfboards, boogie boards, and caving equipment (all equipment free for those staying at the villa, $25 per day for those in nearby hotels, $35 for those from other cities). He also rents a Hobie Cat ($25 per hr.), offers windsurfing lessons ($35 per hr.), and provides info about area attractions. **Dive Copamarina,** in Copamarina Beach Resort (see **Scuba Diving,** p. 219), rents tennis rackets ($5 per hr.), kayaks (singles $12 for 1st hr., doubles $20), snorkel gear ($10 for 3hr.), a Hobie Cat ($40 per hr.), and a Craig Cat ($25 per hr.).

Bank: Banco Santander, C. S.S. Rodriguez 63 (☎821-2700 or 821-2283), at the corner of C. 25 de Julio. ATM. Open M-F 8:30am-4pm.

Supermarket: Econo (☎821-2789), at the intersection of Rte. 116 and 116R. Open M-Sa 7am-8pm, Su 11am-5pm. AmEx/D/DC/MC/V.

Police: C. 13 de Marzo 57 (☎821-2020). Open 24hr.

Hospital: From Rte. 116 drive down C. 25 de Julio and turn right after the plaza, turn right at the end of the street, then take the first left. The **emergency room** (☎821-1481) is open 24hr.

Post Office: C. 13 de Marzo 39 (☎821-2645). General Delivery available. Open M-F 8am-4:30pm, Sa 8am-noon.

Zip Code: 00653.

🔲 ACCOMMODATIONS

Bosque Estatal de Guánica has no camping options and most guest houses are fairly expensive (though ultimately worth their cost). Nearby Ponce or La Parguera have more affordable accommodations.

🔲 **Caribbean Vacation Villa,** C. San Jacinto 15 (☎821-5364; www.caribbeanvacation-villa.com), is a sports-lover's paradise. Former competitive windsurfer and kayaker Paul Julien has combined endless knowledge about water-related sports, a huge stock of equipment, and a love for the area to create one of the most fun-filled guest houses on the island. Julien manages about 5 different houses on C. San Jacinto, ranging from a 1-bedroom studio to a 5-bedroom house. Decor varies, but most have a modern ambiance and all include a full kitchen, A/C, ocean-view deck, and best of all, complimentary access to all of Julien's equipment (see p. 215). On-site massages $60 per hr. Doubles $115-200; extra person $25. 10% tax not included. No credit cards. ●

Mary Lee's By The Sea, C. San Jacinto 25 (☎821-3600; fax 821-0744; www.maryleesbythesea.com). It's difficult to surpass the cuteness of the name, but this lovely guest house manages to do just that. US expat Mary Lee has put extensive care into the decorations of each room. Haitian grass rugs, brightly colored curtains, and lots of small white lights create a charming and utterly tropical effect. All rooms include a kitchen, A/C in the bedroom, and access to a deck with a BBQ. TV/microwave $5 per day. Trips to Guilligan's island $5 per person. Kayak rental single $10 per hr., double $15. Laundry room. Check-in 3pm. Check-out noon. Studios $80-100; doubles $120; quads $130-140; 6-person rooms $140-250; extra person $10. 10% tax not included. MC/V. ●

Guayanilla Guest House, Rte. 127 Km 8 (☎835-3382), about 8 mi. east of Guánica in Guayanilla, on the 1st floor of a *panadería*. From Hwy. 2 take Exit 207, then go east on Rte. 127. This small guest house is a budget option close to the forest. Excluding the sounds of the freeway, this is one of the nicer guest houses near Ponce. Cable TV, A/C, fridge, and microwave. Breakfast included. Doubles $45; quads $65. MC/V. ●

⚑ FOOD

Most visitors will have a full kitchen, so the most affordable option is clearly to stock up on groceries and cook.

San Jacinto Boats & Restaurant (☎821-4941), on C. San Jacinto about ½ mi. past Rte. 333; look for the large parking lot on the right. This bayside restaurant wears many hats; by day it sells ferry tickets and serves inexpensive *comida criolla* lunches ($4-5), but by night it opens up as one of Guánica's best seafood restaurants (entrees $15-20). The midday dining area consists of a few worn, kid-size picnic tables, but the nighttime atmosphere is much better, as the intimate interior has been designed to resemble a ship's hull. They also deliver lunches to Islas Guilligan and Ballena ($5). Outside open daily 9:30am-6pm; inside open M-F 3-10pm, Sa-Su noon-10pm. MC/V. ●/●

Danny & Gaby Bakery (☎821-5307), on the right side of Rte. 334, has a pastry cabinet, a small convenience store, and a few tables. This small bakery is a good place to stock up on picnic supplies, snacks, or water. Sandwiches ($1.25-3) are a bit lackluster, but the bread is tasty. Cheese pizza $5. Open daily 6am-10pm. MC/V. ●

⚐ HIKING

Unlike most reserves, Guánica's trails are long and frequently loop between sights, making it easy to spend a whole day (or longer) hiking through the forest. However, because of the somewhat monotonous vegetation, many of the trails look similar. The DRN Information Center can provide personalized trail information. Some of the more popular hikes are listed below.

CAMINO BALLENA. This 1 mi. gravel trail is possibly the best path in Guánica. Not only does it pass through some of the most wild desert scenery, but it also conveniently leads from the information center down to the beautiful beach. Along the way you'll pass **Guayacán Centenario,** a 100-year-old tree that rises proudly above the lowland vegetation. The 30min. downhill hike becomes part of a loop by continuing east on Rte. 333 for 30min., then heading up Camino Cueva. The marked, northern trailhead is next to the info center. The southern trailhead is not marked, but is easily identifiable by the large blue gate on Rte. 333.

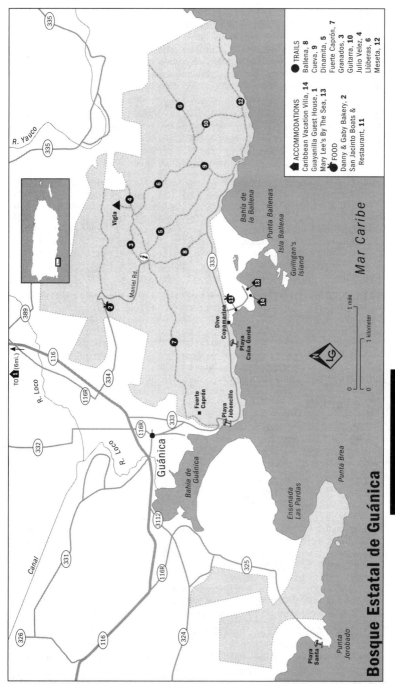

Bosque Estatal de Guánica

TRAILS
Ballena, **8**
Cueva, **9**
Dinamita, **5**
Fuente Caprón, **7**
Granados, **3**
Guitarra, **10**
Julio Velez, **4**
Llúberas, **6**
Meseta, **12**

ACCOMMODATIONS
Caribbean Vacation Villa, **14**
Guayanilla Guest House, **1**
Mary Lee's By The Sea, **13**

FOOD
Danny & Gaby Bakery, **2**
San Jacinto Boats & Restaurant, **11**

Mar Caribe

Bahía de la Ballena
Punta Ballenas
Isla Ballena
Guilligan's Island

Dive Copamarina
Playa Caña Gorda

Fuerte Caprón
Playa Jaboncillo

Guánica
Bahía de Guánica
Ensenada Las Pardas
Punta Brea

Punta Jorobado
Playa Santa

Maniel Rd.
Vigía

R. Yauco
R. Loco
Canal

SOUTHWEST

VEREDA MESETA. Meseta is the only trail in Guánica that borders the ocean. The path departs from the Puerto Ballena parking lot, then continues west along the coastline, and the view remains consistently incredible. At the beginning there are several good beaches just off the path, but farther west sand gives way to steep oceanside cliffs. The flat trail also makes a good mountain biking path. There is not much shade, so bring sunscreen and water. The trail continues for over 2 mi. and is one of the most isolated paths in the forest; bring a friend or a cell phone.

CAMINO JULIO VELEZ/CAMINO LOS GRANADOS. This 2 mi. circular route leaves from the information center and provides a nice introduction to the forest. Reserve workers recommend this path because it is well-marked, relatively short (only 1½ hr. round-trip) and a great place to see many of the forest's birds; over 40 bird species have been identified in this area. A detour at the eastern edge of the circle leads to La Vigia, a look-out with incredible views of the forest.

FUERTE CAPRÓN. One of the forest's longer trails leads southwest from the info center along a gravel path toward a small fort. Don't be misled by the word "fort"—this is a tiny observation tower built by the Civilian Conservation Corps in the 1930s. The path does not pass through particularly dramatic vegetation, but it does have great views of the city of Guánica and the bay. The 2½ mi. trail undulates up and down small hills and eventually intersects Rte. 333 at Km 3.2. Coming from the south, park in the small turn-off at Km 3.2 and take the narrow path headed toward the old water tower. The trail takes 1½ hr., but you can reach the fort in about 1hr., and there's not much reason to continue all the way to the end.

CAMINO CUEVA. This unmarked path leads uphill from the Punta Ballena swimming area parking lot to the intersection with Camino Llúberas. The trail is clear, but lacks adequate signage. To enter from the south, step over the short wire gate next to the turquoise gate at the parking lot entrance, then continue uphill. No sign marks the intersection with Camino Llúberas, but keep veering to the left and eventually you'll reach Julio Velez. Supposedly there are caves off this trail, but they're nearly impossible to find without a guide. Otherwise, the 1 mi. trail offers little apart from a connection between the beach and the info center.

◪ BEACHES

Guánica's heterogeneous coastline alternates between steep cliffs and sandy beaches, and the water can be everything from large, rough waves to tiny, shallow pools. There are several nice public beaches, but the most rewarding experience may be to explore until you find that perfect stretch of sand.

THE ISLANDS. If you've ever wanted to visit Guilligan's Island, here's your change. A 10min. ferry ride takes you to the tiny mangrove-covered island where a few small beaches hide amidst the trees. There's not much sand, so arrive by 11am on weekends to get a spot. The water here is shallow and clear, making for some nice **snorkeling.** Nobody's going to get stranded on Guilligan's Island, which has an outhouse, a DRN office, and covered picnic tables, but nearby **Isla Ballena** is a different story. The ferry only stops at Ballena on request and because of this, the island tends to be much less crowded. Ballena has a long sandy isthmus good for lounging, but no facilities—double-check to make sure the ferry is really returning to pick you up. *(Ferries travel from Restaurant San Jacinto (see Food, p. 216) to Guilligan's Island (Tu-F every hr., Sa-Su every 30min. 9am-5pm; $4 round-trip). Open Tu-Su 9am-5pm. To get to Ballena, you must sweet-talk the ferry captain and pay an additional $2.)*

BALNEARIO CAÑA GORDA. Situated right next door to the Copamarina Beach Resort, this long, white sand beach lined with dry forest trees has some excellent sunning areas. The big advantage of this popular beach is that it has all the amenities of a *balneario*, including lifeguards, showers, bathrooms, chair rental ($4 per day with ID), covered picnic tables, a cafe, and a mini market. Seaweed litters the western side of the beach, but the eastern edge is ideal for swimming. *(Rte. 333 Km 6. ☎821-5676. Open daily Sept.-May 8am-5pm; June-Aug. 7am-6pm.)*

BAHÍA LA BALLENA. This long patch of sand provides ample space for sunbathing, and the water is deep enough that people can swim. However, the only facilities are trash cans, and the area can get relatively crowded. *(At the end of Rte. 333.)*

PLAYA JOBONCILLO. For true privacy, head down the steep dirt road to this beautiful sandy bay surrounded by rocky cliffs on either side. A few picnic tables and some very old outhouses reveal that people have actually found this beach, but during weekdays it can provide an oasis of picturesque solitude. *(Rte. 333 Km 3.1.)*

⚓ SCUBA DIVING

Dive Copamarina, in the **Copamarina Beach Resort,** Rte. 333 Km 6.5 (☎821-0505, toll-free 800-981-4676; www.copamarina.com), offers 2-tank dives to The Wall, the famous drop-off near La Parguera (see p. 209), and prices are fairly reasonable. (2-tank dive $75, equipment $20. 3-day certification course $300; advance registration required. Discover Scuba package $100. Open daily 9am-5pm. AmEx/MC/V.)

DAYTRIPS FROM GUÁNICA: PLAYA SANTA

Driving: *From Guánica, follow Rte. 116 west, turn off onto Rte. 3112, turn south onto Rte. 325, continue to the end, turn left at the T, and take the first right to the parking area.*

Playa Santa is a long, white strip of fine sand that far outshines Guánica's beaches, even if the sand becomes somewhat littered with trash and the water filled with seaweed as you progress farther west. Playa Santa does not have public facilities but **Pino's Boats and Water Fun** (☎821-6864 or 484-8083), a stand on the beach, rents jet skis ($40-45 per 30min.), kayaks (single $12 per hr., doubles $18), pedal boats (2-person $12 per hr., 4-person $18), beach umbrellas ($6 per day) and lounge chairs ($5 per day). The owner also offers 40min. motorboat ecotours through the mangroves ($5 per person), 20min. Banana Boat rides ($6), and jet ski tours ($45) of the mangroves. (Open most weekdays and always Sa-Su 11am-5pm. MC/V.)

SOUTHWEST

SOUTHEAST

In southeast Puerto Rico, the mountains abruptly give way to miles of flat land reaching to the ocean; this was sugar country, and a few stalks still grow today. Almost every town played some role in the production process, and the entire landscape has been transformed from dry forest to empty plains in memory of the acres of crops. After sugar stopped being profitable the region had to find to other means of revenue and you'll see the replacement industry, in the form of large factories, along Rte. 3. Yet the influence of the mighty plant cannot be completely dismissed as history; Castillo Serraillés in Ponce serves as a reminder that sugar still forms the backbone of Puerto Rico's powerful rum industry. This is also, officially, the Caribbean. But forget the stereotypes; beaches are generally better on the northern, Atlantic coast. West of Patillas, palm tree-lined beaches with tiny waves make for postcard perfect sunsets, but are not great for swimming or sunning. The one exception may be the *balneario* in Arroyo, but even here shallow water appeals more to cautious families than adventurous travelers. For a really good beach you'll have to take the make to Isla Caja de Muertos, off Ponce, or travel farther west. Ponce is the undisputed capital—and star—of southern Puerto Rico. With its diverse architecture and myriad museums, it's worth a trip over the mountains for this city alone. However, apart from this pearl, southeast Puerto Rico is not filled with sights, and very few foreigners make it to this corner of the island. But maybe that's just the reason to come. Since the fall of King Sugar not much has happened in this languid area, so locals just sit back and relax, enjoy the beautiful scenery, and welcome anyone who makes their way out to visit.

HIGHLIGHTS OF SOUTHEAST PUERTO RICO

BECOME A BEACH BUM at any one of the many idyllic accommodations along Route 901 (see p. 240).

TRY OUT TURN-OF-THE-CENTURY LIFE at the spectacular museums, houses, and sights in dignified Ponce (see below).

HITCH A RIDE on a boat at the active port in Salinas (p. 235).

PONCE

Elegant, proud, and steeped in tradition, Ponce is one of the most pleasant and attractive cities in Puerto Rico. In many ways the city still lives in the 19th century—ornate turn-of-the-century buildings line the streets and locals seem to have a sense of hospitality from a different era. *Ponceños* are proud of their beautiful city and eagerly welcome visitors, knowing that they're sharing something truly special.

Ponce first found its way into the spotlight in 1511 when the city's namesake, Juan Ponce de León, finally defeated the Taínos here. Left to make its own way on the south coast far from the activity of San Juan, Ponce thrived as the base port for contraband goods. But in the early 1700s *ponceños* transferred their resources into more legitimate businesses and the city became one of the largest exporters of tobacco, coffee, and rum. Everything was going just fine until 1820 when a fire destroyed much of the city. Still, by the mid-19th century the city had the largest concentration of sugar cane on the island. When sugar diminished in importance the city began producing other goods, including metal, iron, plastic piping, and textiles. Throughout the 19th century the city remained fiercely independent—when the Americans took over in 1898, Ponce still had its own currency.

But Ponce hit its prime at the turn of the century and by 1950 the city began to decay. Most of the big factories created by Operation Bootstrap landed in the north, and Ponce continued to subsist on cement and textiles—not exactly quick money makers. Just a few blocks away from the plaza you can see how the entire city would look if government officials had not invested big bucks into renovating the center. This is Old San Juan minus the tourist kitsch, plus a dose of reality and a couple of suburban comforts. The municipal government and the Institute of Culture maintain several good museums, and nearby Hacienda Buena Vista and Tibes Indigenous Ceremonial Center are among the best sights on the island. However, the heart of Ponce continues to be the charming plaza, filled with historic buildings and admiring visitors. Standing on a balcony overlooking the bustling city center can transport anyone back to Ponce's glory days.

◪ INTERCITY TRANSPORTATION

Flights: Aeropuerto Mercedita (☎848-2822), 4 mi. east of town. From the plaza take Rte. 1 (C. Cristina) east to Rte. 5506. Hwy. 52 also passes by the airport. A taxi from the city center should run $6-7. Only one airline flies out of Ponce: **Cape Air** (☎844-2020 or 253-1121) goes to Aeropuerto Luis Muñoz Marín in **San Juan** (20min.; 5 per day; $87, round-trip $102). Open daily 6am-7pm.

Públicos: Ponce's *público* terminal is located 3 blocks north of the plaza at C. Unión and C. Vives. More popular routes run 6am-5pm, or whenever people stop showing up. *Públicos* head to: **Adjuntas** (45min., $2.25); **Coamo** (30min., $2.50); **Guayama** (1hr., $5); **Jayuya** (1½hr., $3.25); **Mayagüez** (1hr., $6); **Playa Ponce** (5min., $0.75); **Salinas** (45min., $3); **San Germán** (45min., $5); **Utuado** (90min., noon, $5); **Villalba** (25min., $2); **Yauco** (25min., $2.75). Three companies go to **Río Piedras, San Juan** (45min.-2hr., $10) including: **Linea Atlas** (☎842-4375 or 765-3302); **Linea DonQ** (☎842-1222 or 764-0540); and **Linea Universitaria** (☎844-6010 or 765-1634). *Públicos* to **Tibes Indigenous Ceremonial Center** leave from the Texaco behind Nuevo Plaza del Mercado (15min., $6).

Cars: Most car rental companies operate out of the airport. All prices are for the smallest compact cars available. Some of the cheapest are listed below.

Dollar Rent-A-Car, Rte. 1 Km 124.7 (☎843-6970 or 843-6940). $31 per day, with insurance $37. Ages 21-24 $3 per day surcharge. AmEx/D/DC/MC/V. Open M-Sa 8am-5pm.

L&M Car Rental (☎841-2482), in the airport. $27 per day, with insurance $36. Ages 21-24 $4 per day surcharge and insurance required. AmEx/D/DC/MC/V.

Payless Car Rental, Ave. Hostos 1124 (☎842-9393 or 1-800-PAYLESS), on Rte. 10 between Ave. las Américas and Rte. 2, near the city center. $35-39 per day, with insurance $37-44. Ages 21-24 $5 per day surcharge. Open M-F 7am-6pm, Sa 9am-5pm. AmEx/D/DC/MC/V.

Thrifty (☎290-2525), in the airport. $35 per day, with insurance $43. Ages 21-24 $6 per day surcharge. AmEx/D/DC/MC/V.

◪ ORIENTATION

Don't be intimidated by Ponce's size; the city is quite easy to navigate. The vast majority of sights cluster around the compact city center and **Plaza las Delicias,** making it feasible to get around by public transportation. Routes 10, 1, and 14 lead toward the city center. Just south of the center, **Route 163 (Avenida las Américas)** is a large tree-lined street that serves as a convenient landmark. **Highway 2,** also referred to as the **Ponce By Pass,** originates just east of the city, skirts around the edges, and continues toward the western half of the island. If you are just passing through, Highway 52 avoids the center entirely and deposits travelers on Route 2 west of the city. Route 12 connects the city center to the **port** area, the boardwalk, and the beach. *Ponceños* do their shopping at the malls along Routes 1 and 2.

SOUTHEAST

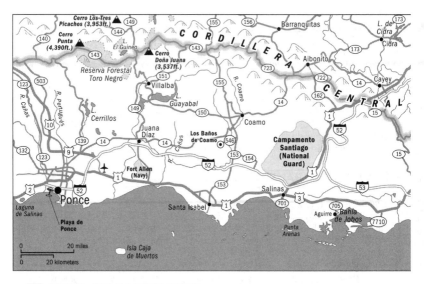

▐ LOCAL TRANSPORTATION

> **!** **Plaza Delicias** is fine during the day, but a bit worrisome at night. Police patrol the plaza, but to be safe, don't wander far from the plaza alone after dark.

Taxis: Ponce Taxi (☎842-3370), on C. Méndez Vigo, just south of C. Villa. Open daily 4am-midnight. **Cooperativa Taxi,** C. Concordia 22 (☎848-8248 or 848-8249), has cabs at their office and at the intersection of C. Estrella and C. Salud. Open daily 4am-midnight. **Victory Taxi** waits on C. Vives at the intersection with C. Atocha. Open daily 6am-6pm. Most taxis charge $1 plus $0.10 for each tenth of a mile.

Trolleys: The city of Ponce operates 4 **free tourist trolley routes** that take visitors from the plaza to various sites around the city. Each complete route takes about 1½-2¼hr. depending on demand and traffic. The north, east, and west routes depart from in front of the cathedral (daily 8:30am-7pm). The **north route** goes to the Cruceta del Vigia and the Castillo Serallés. The **east route** passes Hotel Melia, Ponce High School, and Museo "Pancho" Coímbre. The **west route** passes the Museo de la Música, the Museo de la Historia, Casa Weichers Villaronga, and Panteón Nacional Román Baldorioty de Castro. The **south route** (daily 9am-6pm) is actually a fake train that leaves from the Alcaldía and passes the university en route to **La Gauncha.**

▐ PRACTICAL INFORMATION

Tourist Offices: The **municipal tourist desk** (☎284-3338; www.ponceweb.org), in the Parque de Bombas, on Plaza las Delicias, has a helpful, English-speaking staff that distributes maps and brochures, answers questions, and provides trolley schedules. Open daily 9am-5:30pm. The **Puerto Rican Tourism Company** office, Paseo del Sur Plaza 291 (☎284-4913), is at Rte. 1 Km 124.2. The staff distributes copies of *Que Pasa* and answers questions, but focuses more on the island as a whole than Ponce specifically. Open M-F 8am-5pm, Sa-Su 8:30am-noon and 1-5pm.

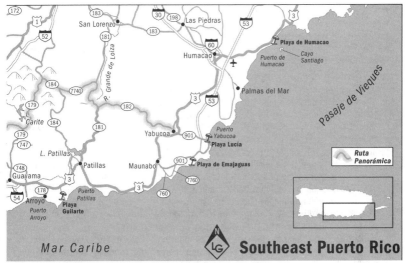

Mar Caribe

Southeast Puerto Rico

Tours: The horse and buggy in front of the *Alcaldía* provides **free 30min. rides** around the historic plaza area (F-Su 11am-6pm). See also **Trolleys,** p. 222.

Consulate: The **Dominican Republic,** C. Marina 9113 (☎984-2068), near Ave. las Américas. Open M-F 8am-4pm.

Camping Permits: DRN (☎844-4660 or 844-4051), on the 2nd floor of the poorly labeled building across from Pier 5, near the turn-off to La Gaand the Amer-ican and Puerto Rican flags; the building is poorly labeled. Provides camping permits ($4, children $2). Open M-F 7:30am-4pm.

Banks: Numerous banks line Plaza las Delicias. **Banco Popular,** C. Marina 9205 (☎843-8000), has an ATM in the alley to the left of the bank. Open M-F 8am-4pm.

English-Language Bookstore: Isabel II Books & Magazines, C. Isabel 66, sells US magazines, and a few used English-language paperbacks. Open daily 7am-6pm.

Supermarket: Pueblo (☎844-7488), in Centro Comercial Santa Maria, on C. Ferrocarril. **Western Union.** Open M-Sa 6am-midnight, Su 11am-5pm. AmEx/MC/V.

Laundromat: León Lavandería, C. Villa 149 (☎841-7883). Wash $1; dry $1.50. Change available. Open M-Sa 8:30am-5:30pm.

Publications: La Perla del Sur, Ponce's largest newspaper, comes out every W (free).

Police: Ave. Hostos 1242 (☎284-4040), at Rte. 10 and Ave. las Américas. Open 24hr.

24-Hour Pharmacy: Walgreen's, Rte. 2 Km 225 (☎812-5960 or 812-5961), west of Ponce, just past the intersection with Rte. 585. AmEx/D/DC/MC/V.

Hospital: Hospital Dr. Pila (☎848-5600, emergency room ext. 127 or 124), on Ave. las Américas, across from the police station. Emergency room open 24hr.

Internet Access: Candy & Magazine Store, C. Isabel 72, has 1 computer. $4 per 30min. or $5 per hr. Open M-F 7am-6pm, Sa 8am-6pm, Su 8am-1pm. **Universidad Interamericana,** on the 1st floor of Plaza del Caribe (see p. 231 below), near Sears Home Store, offers Internet access. $4 per hr. Open M-Sa 9am-9pm, Su 11am-5pm.

Post Office: C. Atocha 93 (☎842-2997). General Delivery. Open M-F 7:15am-4:45pm, Sa 7:30am-noon.

Zip Code: 00717.

▐ ACCOMMODATIONS

Ponce has a wide variety of accommodations, but only two are conveniently located for sightseeing. There are several guest houses, but you should only bypass the attractive hotels on the plaza if you *really* want to save money.

Hotel Melia, C. Cristina 75 (☎842-0260 or 800-742-4276; fax 841-3602; http://home.coqui.net/melia). With tall ceilings, elegant decor, and balconies overlooking Plaza las Delicias, colonial Hotel Melia harkens back to the golden age in true Ponce style. Most rooms on the top 2 floors have balconies overlooking the Parque de Bombas. Cable TV, A/C, telephone. Continental breakfast included. Doubles $88-120; quads $115-131. Tax included. AmEx/MC/V. ❸

Hotel Belgica, C. Villa 122C (☎844-3255; fax 844-6149; http://hotelbelgica.somewhere.net), is one of the best bargains on the island. The clean, high-ceiling rooms with A/C, TV, and sparkling bathroom let even budget travelers enjoy the dignity of Ponce. An ideal location just off Plaza Delicias and a friendly staff top off the package. Request a front room with a balcony if you can handle noisy weekend nights. Check-out noon. Small double with no TV $50; doubles $65; quads $75. Tax included. MC/V. ❷

Ponce Inn, Rte. 1 Km 123.5 (☎841-1000 or 866-668-4577; ponceinn@coqui.net; www.hidpr.com), near the airport. This 120-room hotel used to be a Days Inn, and it shows. The professional lobby, coordinated rooms, and sparkling central pool all scream of a chain hotel. Request a room facing the courtyard or you'll end up with a great balcony overlooking the parking lot. Rooms have cable TV, A/C, coffee maker, and phone. Restaurant. In-room Internet $0.85. Check-out noon. All rooms (up to 4 people) $86.33-108. Tax included. Discounts for stays over 5 days. AmEx/D/DC/MC/V. ❸

Hotel El Tuque, Ponce By Pass 3330 (☎290-0000; www.eltuque.com), at Rte. 2 Km 220.1, about 4 mi. west of town. This chain-style hotel is part of the family-oriented El Tuque entertainment complex (see **Sights,** below). During the winter this is a peaceful option away from the city, but during the summer the place fills up with families headed to the water park. Cable TV, A/C, free Internet connection, and telephone. Tiny bathrooms. Pleasant courtyard with pool, jacuzzi, and hammock pavilion. Continental breakfast included. Doubles $85-105; extra person $10. AmEx/MC/V. ❸

Las Cucharas Hotel, Rte. 2 Km 218.7 (☎841-0620), 5½ mi. west of town, is the best of Ponce's inexpensive guest houses. The rooms at Las Cucharas feel like somebody's spare bedrooms, but the hotel exudes a rare hint of professionalism. The ocean-view balcony provides a nice escape from the dark rooms with linoleum floors and unpleasant smells. All rooms have A/C, some have TVs. Doubles $45; triples $60. Cash only. ❷

▐ FOOD

El Bohío (☎844-7825), at Spur 2 and A-2. This restaurant sets the bar high by serving outstanding *comida criolla* at reasonable prices. Locals have been keeping El Bohío busy since it was founded in 1960. Try the intricate house specialties. Entrees $6-20. Open daily 11am-9pm. AmEx/D/DC/MC/V. ❸

Pizza's Heaven, C. Concordia 8023 (☎844-0448 or 717-1512; www.pizzasheaven.com), is one of the best Italian eateries in town. The facade has seen better days, but inside checkered tablecloths and an atrium-like addition create a friendly ambiance. In addition to pizza, the restaurant serves Puerto Rican, and Italian entrees. Vegetarian lasagna $9. Entrees $8-18. Open daily 11am-10pm. AmEx/MC/V. ❸

Tompy's (☎840-1965), at C. Isabel and C. Mayor, is one of those *cafeterías* that everyone raves about. The staff is friendly, and the generic buffet-style *comida criolla* is above average. A great place to come for local lunch. Breakfast $1-3. Lunch $4.50-5.50. Open M-Sa 8am-10pm. AmEx/MC/V. ❶

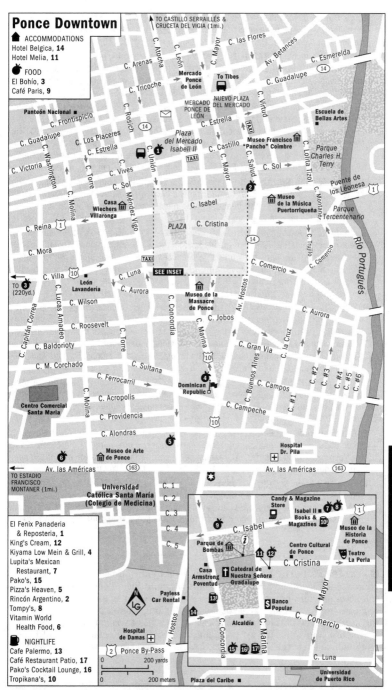

Ponce Downtown

ACCOMMODATIONS
Hotel Belgica, 14
Hotel Melia, 11

FOOD
El Bohío, 3
Café Paris, 9

El Fenix Panaderia
& Reposteria, 1
King's Cream, 12
Kiyama Low Mein & Grill, 4
Lupita's Mexican
Restaurant, 7
Pako's, 15
Pizza's Heaven, 5
Rincón Argentino, 2
Tompy's, 8
Vitamin World
Health Food, 6

NIGHTLIFE
Cafe Palermo, 13
Café Restaurant Patio, 17
Pako's Cocktail Lounge, 16
Tropikana's, 10

SOUTHEAST

King's Cream, C. Marina 9322 (☎843-8520), may be the best ice cream shop in Puerto Rico. The staff slaps huge scoops of delicious ice cream into a dish for refreshingly low prices. Ice cream $1-2. *Batidas* $1.50-2. Open daily 9am-11:45pm. ●

Café Paris, C. Isabel (☎840-1010), on the plaza, is remarkably hip considering that it's technically half of a jewelry store. Sit at a small table overlooking the plaza and indulge on cakes and chocolate drinks ($1-3) designed to make you drool. The best gourmet coffee in town. Sandwiches $2.50-5. Open M-Sa 8am-6pm, Su 9am-5:30pm. ●

Rincón Argentino, C. Isabel 34 (☎284-1762), at C. Salud, somehow manages to be both a local favorite and a tourist-pleaser. This is one of the most romantic restaurants in Ponce, with hanging plants and Christmas lights decorating an elegant courtyard. The food doesn't disappoint either—the carefully prepared meat, seafood, and pasta options are delicious. Entrees $10-20. Wine $4. Th-Sa live piano music 8pm. Open M-W noon-10pm, Th noon-11pm, F-Sa noon-midnight, Su noon-9pm. MC/V. ❸

Lupita's Mexcian Restaurant, C. Isabel 60 (☎848-8808), is open late, close to the center, and reasonably priced. Come for these conveniences, not the generic Mexican entrees ($9-16). Despite the beautiful patio most people sit inside by the blaring TV. Margaritas $6. Open M-W 11am-midnight, Th-Su 11am-midnight. AmEx/D/MC/V. ❸

Restaurante El Ancla, Ave. Hostos 805 (☎840-2450 or 840-2454), at the end of the street overlooking the water. For quality seafood, look no farther than El Ancla. This elegant *mesón gastronómico* unsurprisingly focuses on a nautical theme with seashell tablecloths, sea-inspired artwork, and a long menu of seafood options. But quality doesn't come cheap. Entrees $9-30. Wine $5. Live Bohemian music F 7:30pm, Su noon. Open Su-Th 11am-10pm, F-Sa 11am-midnight. AmEx/D/DC/MC/V. ❹

Pako's, C. Luna 70 (☎290-4602), at C. Concordia. When the endless beans, rice, and seafood get a bit old, head to Pako's, one of the few truly innovative restaurants in Ponce. This relative newcomer to the culinary scene introduces a fusion of flavors from Asia to Africa to Puerto Rico to create award-winning entrees. The spacious, brightly colored art gallery/dining room completes the dining experience. Entrees $17-28. Open M-F 11am-4pm and 6-11pm, Sa 6-11pm, Su noon-8pm. AmEx/DC/MC/V. ❺

Vitamin World Health Food, Ave. las Américas 2223 (☎284-1300), in a health food store. The menu at this vegetarian restaurant changes daily but usually includes rice, a few entrees, and a salad. Fake flowers and wooden tables brighten up an otherwise simple setting. Lunch $5.50. Drinks $1.50-2. Open M-F 10:30am-2:30pm. AmEx/MC/V. ●

El Fenix Panadería & Repostería, C. Unión 110, across from the *público* station. The scrumptious smell emanating from this simple bakery draws people from blocks away for fresh bread and pastries. A great place to escape the tourists for a cheap lunch. Sandwiches $1-3. Corn flakes with milk $1.25. Open M-F 6am-4pm, Sa 7am-3pm. ●

Kiyama Low Mein & Grill, C Marina 9113 (☎284-5331), north of Ave. las Américas, provides 2 items that are hard to find in Ponce: Asian food and inexpensive food open late. The decor is as nice as you can get in a shopping center. Menu includes lots of low mein ($5.50-6.50) and grilled *comida criolla*. Open M-Sa 11am-9pm, Su 1-9pm. ●

🔍 SIGHTS

🏛 **PLAZAS LAS DELICIAS.** As the home to an enormous fountain, a stately church, and one of the funkiest museums in Puerto Rico, Ponce's legendary central plaza provides hours of entertainment and a charming place to wander. The requisite first stop is the **Parque de Bombas,** the bright red-and-black structure on the northern side of the plaza. Featured on dozens of postcards, calendars, and tourist brochures, this unique museum serves as the unofficial symbol of Ponce and a monument to the city's long history. Three years after a fire nearly destroyed the city in 1820, Ponce officials created Puerto Rico's first firefighter corps. In 1883 the fire department moved to an Arabic Pavilion that had been constructed on the main plaza for the 1882 Exposition Fair. Fast-forward over 100 years and the city government transformed the same building into a monument to honor the many fire officials who have protected the city from countless disasters. Today the small museum contains old fire equipment, a timeline of firefighting, and an old fire engine, but the monument is really most valuable for the photo opportunities in front. (☎ 284-3338. Open daily 9am-5:30pm. Free.) You can't miss the enormous **Catedral de Nuestra Señora de Guadalupe,** behind the Parque de Bombas. The largest cathedral in Ponce was built in 1836 on the sight of the city's first church, built in 1670, and still rises as one of the tallest and most awe-inspiring buildings in town. There aren't many surprises inside, but be sure to look up and take note of the impressive stained glass windows. This is a functioning Catholic church, so do not enter if you're wearing shorts. (☎ 842-0134. Open M-F 6am-1pm, Sa-Su 6am-12:30pm and 3-8pm.) Across the street, the exquisite **Casa Armstrong Poventud** was built in 1899 as a residence and most recently housed the offices of the Institute of Puerto Rican Culture. The house is currently under construction and it may eventually become another museum. On the southern border of the plaza, the **Alcaldía** was also under construction in 2003, although that project seems to be progressing much more rapidly. When open, the beautiful city hall, built in 1490, contains a few temporary art exhibitions. Call ahead for a free guided tour. (☎ 284-4141. Open M-F 8am-4:30pm.)

CASTILLO SERRAILLÉS. It may have been over a century since Puerto Rico was ruled by a monarch, but the island definitely has its own royalty. One such dynasty is the Serraillés family, the original producers of DonQ rum (see p. 23), and their house reigns over Ponce like the castle it was designed to be. The family immigrated to Puerto Rico from Spain in the mid-18th century and by 1890 their Hacienda Mercedita produced over 4000 acres of rum-making sugar cane. In 1930 the family initiated construction on a Spanish Revival house overlooking Ponce, but the elaborate structure took over four years to complete. This is truly one of the most beautiful homes on the island that is open to the public, and fortunately almost all of the original furniture has been preserved. The only way to visit the interior is with a 45min. guided tour, which starts with a melodramatic 15min. film, continues through the elegant family rooms, passes through a display on the rum production process, and ends with an exhibition of the house's crowning achievement—the original, still functioning 1933 elevator, the second residential elevator on the island. After the tour take some time to wander through the castle's beautifully manicured gardens. (El Vigil 17. Located just downhill from the Cruceta del Vigia (see p. 228). ☎ 259-1774 or 259-1775. Open Tu-Th 9:30am-5pm, F-Su 9:30am-5:30pm. Free English/Spanish tours. $3, ages 3-15 and students with ID $1.50, over 60 $2. AmEx/D/DC/MC/V.)

LA GAUNCHA. Ponce utilizes its coastal location with La Gauncha, an elaborate boardwalk filled with food kiosks. By day this is a pleasant, quiet place to walk (on weekdays it can be absolutely empty), but come weekend nights the boardwalk overlooking the harbor is packed. *Ponceños* of all ages come out of the woodwork to enjoy a cool drink and sway to the sounds of live salsa. An observation tower at the end of the boardwalk affords great city views, although hours are sporadic. (From the plaza head south on Ave. Hostos, turn left on Rte. 2, then turn right onto Rte. 12 and follow signs. Kiosk hours vary, although at least a couple are usually open during the day and everything is open on weekend nights.)

TEATRO LA PERLA. It's only fitting that Ponce's theater should be a regal Neoclassical building. Designed in 1941 in imitation of the original 1864 theater that was destroyed in an earthquake, La Perla has a large balcony and 1047 vel-

SOUTHEAST

vet seats, all of which boast views of the stage. The beautiful building is regularly open to the public, but the best way to experience the theater is by attending one of the many musical and theatrical performances. *(Corner of C. Mayor and C. Cristina. ☎843-4322, box office. ☎843-4080. Open M-F 8am-noon and 1-4:30pm. Performances late Aug.-early July F-Su. Tickets $20-35. Student discounts available occasionally.)*

PANTEÓN NACIONAL ROMÁN BALDORIOTY DE CASTRO. In 1843 the city of Ponce constructed a Catholic cemetery at what was then the edge of the city. For over 70 years Ponce's most prominent citizens were buried here, including Román Baldorioty de Castro, an instrumental figure in securing emancipation for Puerto Rico's slaves, and members of the Serraillés family (see **Castillo Serraillés,** above). Of course you had to be rich, white, and Catholic to merit such a coveted space, so over the years the city added sections for Protestants, cholera victims, and the poor, just outside the gates or in the corner. The cemetery closed in 1918 for health reasons, and has been severely vandalized over the years, but in 1991 the government reopened the area, began renovations, and even buried famous tenor **Antonio Paoli** and former governor **Roberto Sanchez Vilella** here. This sight is rarely visited, but it is a nice place to escape the city and the guided tours are surprisingly interesting. *(At C. Simón de la Torre and C. Frontispicio. The west trolley route stops here for 30min. ☎841-8347. Open W-Su 8:30am-5pm. Free 15-20min. English/Spanish tour. Free.)*

CRUCETA DEL VIGIA. Despite what it may look like, the huge cross on the hill overlooking the city is not an alien spacecraft, but a monument and a popular tourist attraction. The original Vigia cross was built on this spot (233 ft. above sea level) in 1801 to mark the spot where guards sat to watch ships entering the harbor. If the ship was an enemy to the Spanish crown or full of pirates, they would alert the authorities. If it was an ally, they would alert local traders to come fetch their goods. The current cross was built in 1984 to honor these faithful guards. An elevator leads to the observation tower, which has the best views in the city and an interactive English/Spanish directory describing points of interest. *(On Vigia Hill. From the plaza drive down C. Cristina, turn left on C. Salud, turn left on C. Guadalupe, and turn right on C. Bertoly, which leads all the way up the hill. The north trolley takes visitors up the hill. ☎259-3816. Open Tu-Su 9:30am-5pm. 1st F-Sa of every month open 9:30am-10pm. $1.)*

MARKETS. Ponce has two traditional markets within walking distance of the plaza. The smaller of the two, **Mercado Juan Ponce de León,** is much more interesting. At this row of kiosks you can get your sewing done, buy homegrown coffee, watch a cobbler at work, or sample a tasty piña colada. *(Between C. León, C. Mayor, C. Estrella, and C. Guadalupe. Open M-Sa 6am-6pm.)* Next door the enormous **Nuevo Plaza del Mercado** building screams 1970s but inside it's just like any other market, with *cafeterías,* lottery stands, and lots vegetables. *(Open M-Sa 6am-6pm, Su 6am-noon.)*

COMPLEJO TURISTICO RECREATIVA EL TUQUE. Sometimes kids just want to have fun, and there's no better place to do just that than at this family fun complex 4 mi. west of Ponce. The main attraction is Speed and Splash Water Park, which has several water slides, a wave pool, and an endless river. *(At the El Tuque Hotel (see Accommodations, p. 224.) Open Apr.-May and Sept.- Dec. F-Sa 10am-6pm; June-Aug. daily 10am-6pm. $11, ages 0-12 $8. AmEx/MC/V.)* In the same complex the Ponce International Speedway Park offers an entirely different type of entertainment. The ¼ mi. drag strip and 1½ mi. raceway open up to any group that wants to race; call ahead for information about upcoming races. *(☎744-0717. Open mid-Jan. to Nov. Races usually W and F-Su. $6-10, children and hotel guests free. Cash only.)*

SOUTHEAST

🏛 MUSEUMS

🖼 MUSEO DE ARTE DE PONCE. While San Juan's new art museum consists primarily of Latin American and Puerto Rican works, the Ponce museum focuses almost exclusively on European art and continues to be the premier European art museum in the Caribbean. The two-story building includes rooms for the Spanish School, the Dutch School, the Flemish School, and several Italian schools. Some of the more famous artists include El Greco, Peter Paul Rubens, Charles Le Brun, and Edward Coely Burne-Jones. Of course, the museum also has a room dedicated to Latin American artists, including Francisco Oller, José Campeche, and Tomás Batista, as well as two rooms reserved for temporary exhibitions of modern work. From outside, the building, designed by Edward Durell Stone, a student of Frank Lloyd Wright, looks quite unexceptional, but the interior is exquisitely designed to display art. *(Ave. las Américas 2325. ☎848-0505 or 848-1510; www.museoarteponce.org. Open daily 10am-5pm. $4, students with ID $1, ages 3-12, over 65, and handicapped $2.)*

MUSEO DE LA HISTORIA DE PONCE. It is only appropriate that a city with so much local pride should also have a museum dedicated exclusively to city history. The Ponce History Museum uses a combination of artifacts, descriptive signs, and photos to describe Ponce's evolution from illegal port to prospering sugar town to tourist attraction. All captions are in Spanish, but employees offer impromptu tours for groups or lucky individuals. With a tour, this is one of the best historical museums on the island. Without a tour, the eclectic collection of materials can be overwhelming. *(C. Isabel 51/53, at C. Mayor. ☎844-7071. Open M and W-F 10am-5pm, Sa-Su 10am-6pm. $3, students $2.50, over 65 $1.50, ages 5-12 $1, under 5 free.)*

CASA WIECHERS VILLARONGA. This museum recreates the early 20th century with original furniture and decor. The house was designed in 1911 by architect Alfredo Wiechers, who lived here for seven years before selling it to the Villaronga family. As one of Ponce's richest families the Villarongas were among the first to have electricity and much of their furniture was imported from Europe. Although not particularly original, the museum is worth a visit, if only for two oddities: the convoluted turn-of-the-century shower and the terrific view from the rooftop pergola, known as the wedding cake for its strange white appearance. *(C. Reina 106, at Méndez Vigo. ☎984-5582. Open W-Su 8:30am-4:30pm. Free.)*

MUSEO DE LA MÚSICA PUERTORRIQUEÑA. Using mostly musical instruments and artwork, the Institute of Culture created this museum dedicated exclusively to Puerto Rican music, from the Taínos to salsa. An entire room is dedicated to *bomba y plena*, (see p. 29), and the helpful guides will inform you that *bomba* originates from Ponce and continues to play an important role in the city's culture. All captions are in Spanish but guides speak English. *(C. Salud 45, at C. Isabel. ☎848-7016 or 848-7018. Open W-Su 8:30am-noon and 1-4:30pm. Free English/Spanish tour. Free.)*

MUSEO DE LA MASSACRE DE PONCE. In 1937 nineteen Puerto Rican Nationalist demonstrators were killed by police forces in Ponce. For a long time afterwards the government denied any responsibility and schools neglected to teach students about the controversial event. In an effort to remedy this situation, the city of Ponce opened a small museum to create awareness about the tragedy and prevent something similar from happening again. Unfortunately, the museum is quite small, all of the displays are in Spanish, and the only artifacts include a blood-stained flag and Pedro Albizu Campos's posthumous honorary doctorate.

SOUTHEAST

O WORK, ALL PLAY

PONCE CARNAVAL

Ponce's elaborate carnaval allows or one last party in the days prior to the sacrifices of Lent. With a combination of African, Spanish, and Native American cultures, Puerto Ricans celebrate Lent by having masqueraders (referred to as *vejigantes*) dress up in brightly colored overalls and ornate handmade masks. The "good" characters, as represented by the *vejigante* masks (see Arts & Crafts, p. 26), are supposed to scare away the evil ones by doing a *bomba* and *plena* dance to the tune of old folk songs *(estribillos)*. In Ponce the primary character is the **King Momo,** a local who dresses up in an enormous doll costume. Throughout the week people try to guess the identity of the *Rey Momo,* and the winner receives a monetary reward. Though it by no means rivals the crazy parties of Río de Janeiro or New Orleans, Ponce's carnaval festival provides seven days of fun for everyone involved. Every day has its own unique activity. Unless otherwise stated, all events take place in the plaza at 7:30pm.

Day 1 (W): Masquerade Dance. Everyone shows off their costumes.

Day 2 (Th): Entrance of the King Momo. Celebrated with a parade.

Day 3 (F): Crowning of the Infant Queen. Celebrated with a parade.

Day 4 (Sa): Crowning of the Queen. Celebrated with a parade.

Day 5 (Su): Grand Carnaval Parade. Starts at 1pm.

Day 6 (M): Carnival Grand Dance. A big party with life music.

Day 7 (Tu): Burial of the Sardine. A parade and a party.

However, the English-speaking guides eagerly explain the full history of the massacre and their interest in the subject is contagious. *(C. Marina at C. Aurora. ☎844-9722; massacredeponce@hotmail.com. Open Tu-Su 8:30am-4:30pm. Free.)*

MUSEO FRANCISCO "PANHCO" COIMBRE. Named after one of Ponce's all-time greatest baseball players, this one-room museum honors Puerto Rican athletes in all sports. Endless rows of portraits may not be the most interesting way to present information, but there are also a couple of pieces of memorabilia, including an exhibit on Ponce's short-lived female baseball team. This museum is really only worthwhile for devoted sports fans. *(On C. Lolita Tizol, near C. Castillo. ☎843-6553. Open W-M 8:30am-4:30pm. Free.)*

CENTRO CULTURAL DE PONCE. This Neoclassical building houses one of Ponce's only modern art galleries. Most artists are *ponceños*, although there have been displays by artists from the rest of the island as well. *(C. Cristina 70. ☎844-2540. Open M-F 8am-1pm. Free.)*

🎵 ENTERTAINMENT

BEACHES
Beaches are clearly not Ponce's strong point, but the city has created one acceptable beach area just east of La Gaucha. The imported sand barely covers a concrete surface and the water doesn't get much more than two feet deep, yet *ponceños* fill the beach on hot weekend days. Umbrellas, lifeguards, bathrooms, playground equipment, and parking appease the masses, and food kiosks are just steps away. For a better beach, catch the boat to **Isla Caja de Muertos** (see p. 233).

CINEMA
Caribbean Cinemas has two locations in Ponce. The first, in **Ponce Towne Center** (☎843-2601), Rte. 2 Km 225, behind Wal-Mart, has 10 theaters. The location in **Plaza del Caribe Mall** (☎844-6704), at the intersection of Rte. 2 and Rte. 123, has only six theaters. Both play current Hollywood films. ($5, ages 2-10 $3, over 65 $3.50.)

CONCERTS
Founded in 1883 as the Firefighter's Corps Band, the **Municipal Band of Ponce** has been entertaining locals for well over a century. Today the band performs every Sunday at Parque Dora Colon (8pm).

FESTIVALS
Ponce's big shebang is undoubtedly carnaval (see sidebar). However, all of the following festivals are known to bring out the crowds. The city's **patron saint festival,** held on the six days around December 12 around La Gaucha, includes mariachi-filled proces-

sions, traditional music, *artesanía*, and carnival rides. On December 12 a huge public breakfast is served on the boardwalk around 3am to celebrate the end of a long night out on the town. During a three-day weekend in mid-March the city hosts a **Fería Artesanía.** Over 100 artists set up booths on the south side of the plaza for this enormous artisan festival. Music and parties complete the festivities.

SHOPPING
Ponce's best shopping awaits on the pedestrian **C. Atocha,** just north of Plaza las Delicias. This three-block market spills onto the streets and both American chains and independent Puerto Rican stores offer great deals on clothes, shoes, and other miscellanea. This busy shopping experience is most active on weekdays.

For more stereotypical American shopping try **Plaza del Caribe,** the largest mall in the Ponce area. Here you can stock up on favorites from the Gap, Sears, and Foot Locker. There is also a carousel and a food court. (At the intersection of Rte. 2 and Rte. 123. ☎840-8989. Open M-Sa 9am-9pm, Su 11am-5pm.)

SPORTS
The **Leones de Ponce** (Ponce Lions), Ponce's professional baseball team, play from November to January at **Estadio Francisco Montaner,** near the intersection of Ave. las Américas and the Rte. 2 spur. Games are held approximately three times per week in the evening or on Sunday afternoon. Purchase tickets at the stadium box office. (☎848-0050. $5, children and seniors $2.50.)

THEATER
La Perla (see **Sights,** p. 227), is the city's primary venue for theatrical performances. Ponce's **Escuela de Bellas Artes,** on C. Lolita Tizol at C. Castillo, holds occasional student ballet and theater performances. Contact the school or check *La Perla del Sur* for more information. (☎848-9156. Admission $3.)

NIGHTLIFE

Ponce is not a great place to find discos, but the bar scene is alive and well. The best place to enjoy a drink, live music, and even livelier Puerto Rican company, is **La Gauncha,** the seaside boardwalk south of town. On Friday and Saturday nights kiosks blast music and couples, families, and teenagers turn out to wander the street. Mixed drinks run $3-6, beer $1-2. To test your luck, head to one of the city's two **casinos,** at the Ponce Hilton, just off Rte. 14 (see **La Bohemia,** below; open daily 10am-3:30am), or the **Holiday Inn,** Ponce By Pass 3315 (☎844-1200; open daily 10am-6am).

PLAZA LAS DELICIAS

Café Restaurant Patio, C. Luna 35 (☎848-3178), at C. Marina, claims to be one of the oldest bars in the city and it is certainly one of the most popular. Young professionals are attracted to the long bar, great backyard patio, and killer Happy Hour specials (Th-Sa 10pm-1am Medalla $1; all day Sa Cuba Libre $1). During the day, the cafe serves traditional Puerto Rican breakfast and lunch. Beer $2-3. Occasional live Spanish rock music. 18+ after 10pm. Open M 7:30am-3pm, Tu-Su 7:30am-3am. AmEx/D/MC/V.

Pako's Cocktail Lounge, C. Luna 70 (☎290-4602), at C. Concordia, adds a metropolitan edge to Ponce's nightlife scene. Bold colors and vibrant modern art give this hip bar a New York feel but the large courtyard out back is pure Ponce. The attached restaurant serves sizzling tapas until 2am. Beer $1-3; mixed drinks $3-7. Th-Sa live rock or 80s music 10pm. Open M-Tu 4-11pm, W-Sa 4pm-2am, Su noon-8pm. AmEx/DC/MC/V.

Cafe Palermo, C. Unión 3 (☎812-3873), on the plaza, is popular with tourists who enjoy the convenient location and the pleasant outdoor tables. However, photos on the wall reveal that Puerto Ricans have also had some crazy nights here. Beers $2-3; mixed drinks $3-5. Live pop F-Sa 11pm. Open Tu-Su 6pm-3am. MC/V.

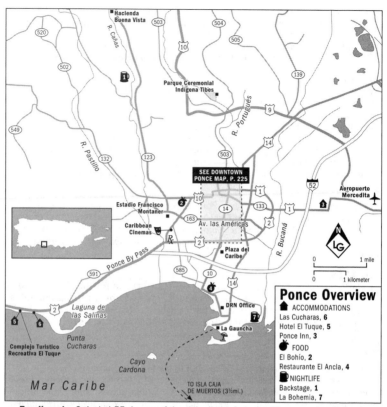

Ponce Overview

🏠 ACCOMMODATIONS
Las Cucharas, **6**
Hotel El Tuque, **5**
Ponce Inn, **3**
🍎 FOOD
El Bohío, **2**
Restaurante El Ancla, **4**
◼ NIGHTLIFE
Backstage, **1**
La Bohemia, **7**

Tropikana's, C. Isabel 55, is one of the only discos in town. All rap music, all the time, tends to attract a younger, rougher crowd. The interior courtyard has the potential to be an attractive bar area, if renovation plans actually come through. Beer $2-3; mixed drinks $4-5. Cover $3-10, women usually free. Open Th-Sa 9pm-3am.

OUTSIDE THE PLAZA

◼ **Backstage** (☎448-8112), off Rte. 123, north of the city. Follow directions to Hacienda Buena Vista (see p. 234), but after you pass the huge Puerto Rico Cement Factory. Turn left at the Esso station and drive up the hill about 1 mi.; Backstage is up a hill on the left. So this is where all the hip *ponceños* are hiding. With flashing lights, disco balls, smoke machines, and a room packed with gyrating young things, Backstage is everything a disco should be, and more. This is a gay club, and many fashionable young men do strut their stuff, but everyone is welcome. F-Sa drag shows. F 1am stripper. Mixed drinks $3-6. 18+. Cover $5. Open F-Sa 10pm-last person leaves. AmEx/MC/V.

Hollywood Café, Rte. 1 Km 125.5 (☎843-6703). Welcome to Hollywood, folks, land of the rich and famous. Here bartenders cater to your every whim, serving up mixed drinks ($2.50-6) or beer ($2.50-3) at your beck and call. You can sit on the outside patio, you can dance to the live Spanish rock music (F-Sa), or you can challenge the competition at the pool table—because this is Hollywood, where all your dreams come true. 21+. Open W-M 6pm-people leave. AmEx/D/MC/V.

SOUTHEAST

La Bohemia (☎2259-7676 ext. 5121), in the Ponce Hilton. Take Rte. 14 toward La Ga22ncha, then turn left after the Texaco station. This luxurious retreat opens its doors to the masses on weekend nights. What starts as drinking soon progresses to festive salsa dancing as the live band gets going. Beers $4.50-6; mixed drinks $6-8. Th 8:30-9:30pm salsa lessons $5. Th-Sa live salsa music 10pm. 18+. Open Th-Sa 8:30pm-last person leaves.

🔒 DAYTRIPS FROM PONCE

ISLA CAJA DE MUERTOS

Island Ventures (*☎842-8546) sends a boat to Isla Caja de Muertos for daytrips almost every weekend (Sa-Su 8:30am-4:30pm) to scuba dive ($60), snorkel ($40), or just enjoy a day at the beach ($20). The price includes equipment, a picnic lunch, and refreshments. The people at Island Ventures rarely answers their phone, so leave a message and they should call you back. The only other means of accessing the island is to ask fishermen around the docks for a ride.*

Isla Caja de Muertos (Coffin Island), a 500-acre island with subtropical dry forest surrounded by a few nice beaches, provides one of those relaxing escapes that you imagine before traveling to the Caribbean. The secret behind Caja de Muertos's magic is the limited means of transportation—in an attempt to minimize human influence and protect the island's rare animal population, the DRN mandates that only private boats carrying fewer than 150 people can visit the island. Consequently, from May to December hawksbill turtles are able to lay their eggs on the eastern side of the island without human interference. And nobody is allowed on the southern tip of the island, which serves as a protected bird sanctuary.

Caja de Muertos's main attractions are the quiet beaches, small strips of sand that stay relatively empty, and gentle, clear waters that make for excellent **snorkeling**. **Scuba divers** can explore a 40 ft. wall just offshore, and on a good day the visibility can be as good as 100 ft. Back on land, the DRN maintains bathrooms and covered picnic tables. Caja de Muertos is large enough that it also offers activities beyond the beach. An easy **30min. hike** leads through the shrubs and cacti and up the hill to a 19th-century **lighthouse**. The US Coast Guard operates the lighthouse today, so visitors cannot enter, but they can enjoy the astounding view from the top. A small cave on the island has **Taíno petroglyphs** inside, but there is no trail. The resident DRN employee sometimes offers guided tours.

THE LOCAL LEGEND

PIRATE TALES

With a name like Isla Caja de Muertos (Coffin Island), it seems inevitable that this small piece of land should have an exceptional history. Over the years the island has served as the hideout for several pirates, including notables such as Sir Frances Drake and the more local menace Roberto Cofresí. Originating from the Cabo Rojo area, Cofresí supposedly traveled the southern shores on a 60 foot schooner, burning ships and stealing the treasure. And what better place to bury a treasure than an isolated island off the coast of one of the most corrupt cities in Puerto Rico? Legend has it that Cofresí divided his treasure in two and buried half on the north side of the island and the other half in the cave to the south. In 1954 one of these caves collapsed and excavators discovered a human skeleton inside, still chained to the wall. Of course people have searched for the treasure but to no avail. Then again, many locals have stories about cousins or friends who mysteriously disappeared during an expedition to Caja de Muertos. Maybe they got a little bit too close to the pile of gold? Who knows, but an aura of mystery continues to shroud the island today. And as for the name, well, that's no mystery at all. An 18th-century French writer called the island "Coffre A'morr" (Coffin Island) because from a distance the island looks like a large coffin. Sometimes wonders do cease.

HACIENDA BUENA VISTA

*No **public transportation** goes to Buena Vista. It may be possible to have a público heading to Adjuntas drop you off, but you'll have to hitch a ride back. **Driving:** Drive west on Ave. las Américas (Rte. 163) past the Museo de Arte, then turn right on Rte. 585. Turn left at the first light, and continue on Rte. 123 until Km 16.8. Alternatively, from the city center, take C. Isabel Reina west to the intersection with Rte. 123, then turn right (30min.).*

This restored coffee plantation is one of the best-preserved farm houses on the island and one of Ponce's must-see attractions. Back in 1821 Salvador de Vives arrived in Ponce and began looking for land to buy. Unfortunately, he couldn't afford the prime real estate by the sea, which was used to grow sugar cane, so instead in 1833 he purchased 500 acres in the mountains just north of the city. Initially the land was used as a fruit farm, then it became a corn flour factory; however, by 1872, when the third generation of the Vives family took over, the plantation was used almost exclusively to grow Arabic coffee. The frequent changes mean that a variety of equipment exists on the plantation today. Most interesting is the 1121 ft. canal system that the Vives family used to extract water from Río Canas, power the machinery, and return the water to the river without polluting or damaging the ecosystem. The farm continued to be used until the 1950s when it was divided between local farmers.

Since 1984 the sight has been managed by the Conservation Trust of Puerto Rico, a private organization that strives to preserve the island's natural resources while educating the public, and both goals are well accomplished here. The only way to visit the plantation is through a 1½hr. guided tour that includes a visit to the redecorated house, a beautiful walk through the surrounding subtropical forest, and fascinating demonstrations of the plantation's still functioning machinery. (Rte. 123 Km 16.8. ☎722-5882, weekends 284-7020. **Reservations required.** Call at least one week in advance. Tours F-Su Spanish 8:30, 10:30am, 1:30pm, 3:30pm; English 1:30pm. $7, ages 5-11 and over 65 $4, under 5 free.)

PARQUE CEREMONIAL INDÍGENA TIBES

*Public Transportation: Públicos to Tibes leave from the Texaco behind Nuevo Plaza del Mercado (15min., $6). **Driving:** From central Ponce, drive down C. Cristina, turn left on C. Salud, then turn left on C. Guadalupe and right on C. Mayor, which turns into Rte. 503. The sign is quite small; look for a large beige fence. Alternatively, drive north on Hwy. 10, then exit at the Tibes sign onto Rte. 503.*

Tibes is the largest known indigenous anthropological center on the island. Given the island's vocal Taíno pride, it is quite ironic that technically this is not a Taíno site, as it was constructed between 600 and 1200 AD, during the reign of the pre-Taínos and Igneris. Regardless, many of the customs were the same and Tibes is the best place on the island to learn about the area's indigenous peoples. The sight was uncovered in 1975 when Hurricane Eloise flooded the banks of the Río Portugués, allowing a surprised Puerto Rican farmer to discover several Taíno artifacts. The city expropriated the land and upon excavation unearthed 12 structures, including seven *batey* courts, lots of pottery, and almost 180 human remains (see **Taíno Terminology,** p. 276). The presence of multiple structures leads archaeologists to believe that this was one of the largest ceremonial sites in the Caribbean.

Most visits to Tibes begin with a stop at the small museum, which explains various aspects of the Taíno and pre-Taíno cultures and displays most of the pottery found on the site. Next a 10min. film describes the history of this particular site and the excavation process. Finally, during the 45min. tour, guides lead visitors through the forest, past a replica of a Taíno village, and finally to several *batey* courts. The sight is not overwhelming in the quantity of artifacts, but together the complex provides a thorough introduction to Puerto Rico's indigenous culture. On several days during the year (usually Oct. 12, Nov. 19, and Apr. 30) employees don indigenous dress and recreate Taíno ceremonies; call ahead for more information. (Rte. 503 Km 2.3. ☎840-2255 or 840-5685; http://ponce.inter.edu/tibes/tibes.html. Open Tu-Su 9am-4pm. Visits with guided tours only; free English/Spanish guided tours every hr., usually on the hr. $2, ages 5-12 and over 60 $1, under 5 free.)

SALINAS

This unremarkable town is just about the last place you would expect to find an enclave of international mariners, but wonders never cease; just south of the town center Playa Salinas has one of the largest ports on the island. This is the place for wandering island-hoppers to find passage on vessels traveling throughout the western hemisphere. The activity centers around Marina de Salinas & Posada El Náutico, a hotel complex with a bulletin board that travelers use to coordinate rides. The town itself has little, but Playa Salinas offers scrumptious seafood, some boating opportunities, and a funky international charm rarely found in small Puerto Rico towns.

TRANSPORTATION. Two of Puerto Rico's major thoroughfares, Rte. 1 and Rte. 3, meet in downtown Salinas. From San Juan take Hwy. 52 south to the final intersection with Rte. 1; this road becomes C. Muñoz Rivera. **Públicos** travel to **Guayama** (30min., $1.55) and **Playa Salinas** (5min., $0.50). To reach the plaza from the *público* station turn left onto C. Unión, and walk one block.

ORIENTATION AND PRACTICAL INFORMATION. Salinas is easy to navigate. Rte. 1/3 is the main street; to the west Rte. 1 is called C. Unión and to the east Rte. 3 becomes C. Barbosa. C. Muñoz Rivera runs perpendicular to this street along the plaza. To reach **Playa Salinas** drive west on **Rte. 1,** then turn south on **Rte. 701,** which follows the bay. All of the services are located near the town center, about 1 mi. north of Playa Salinas. **Banco Popular,** C. Muñoz Rivera 1, on the plaza, has two ATMs. (☎824-3075. Open M-F 8am-4pm.) **Grande supermarket,** on Rte. 701 across from the post office, has **Moneygram** service. (☎824-1400. Open M-Sa 7am-8pm, Su 11am-5pm. AmEx/MC/V.) The police station, C. Muñoz Rivera 500, is a quarter mile north of the plaza. (☎824-2020. Open 24hr.) **Sur Med Medical Center,** C. Colón Pacheco 8, lies east of town off Rte. 3, behind the Esso Station. (☎824-1100 or 824-1199. 24hr. emergency room. Open M-F 7am-3pm.) The **post office,** Rte. 701 #100, near the intersection with Rte. 1, has General Delivery. (☎824-2485. Open M-F 8am-4:30pm, Sa 8am-noon.) Zip Code: 00751.

ACCOMMODATIONS. More than just a sailor's port, **Marina de Salinas & Posada El Náutico ❸,** C. Chapin G-8, on Rte. 701, also runs a pretty darn good hotel. Cheerful yellow and blue rooms with A/C, cable TV, and wicker furniture may tempt the wary seafarer to stay a few days. Spacious suites come with a full kitchenette. The hotel also offers laundry facilities, a restaurant, a book exchange, a small pool, a waterfront snack bar, a playground area, and on the weekends (F-Su), complimentary boat trips around the bay. (On Rte. 701 past the seafood restaurants. ☎752-8484 or 824-3185. Check-in 2pm. Check-out 1pm. Doubles $84; quads $96-108; suites $120; extra person $15, 2 children under 15 free. Tax included. AmEx/D/DC/MC/V.) Across the bay, **Puerta La Bahía ❸,** has a similar design, but lacks the facilities and the aesthetic touch. Plain white rooms with scant decorations and aluminum doors don't aim to charm, but they do come with TV, A/C, and private baths. The hotel plans to add an adjacent **camping area.** (From Rte. 701 drive to Marina de Salinas, turn left at the gate, then continue around the bay, always veering right. ☎824-7117. Pool. 1 double bed $75; 2 beds $150. Tax included. AmEx/MC/V.)

SOUTHEAST

◘ **FOOD.** Food options tend to clump together in Salinas. C. Muñoz Rivera, north of the plaza, has several inexpensive *comida criolla* lunch options. The seafood restaurants in the Playa Salinas area, along Rte. 701, are slightly more expensive, but offer fresh morsels on patios overlooking the water. Both of the hotels have nice restaurants, but they can't beat **El Balcón del Capitan** ❸, C. A 54, on Rte. 701. The restaurant's bright blue balcony sits directly over the water, providing incomparable views and a cool sea breeze. El Balcón specializes in seafood flavored with the local favorite, *mojo isleño*, a tomato-based sauce. (☎824-6210. Entrees $7-24. Wine $3-4.50. Open daily 11am-10:30pm. AmEx/MC/V.)

▓ **OUTDOOR ACTIVITIES.** The numerous off-shore islands provide ample opportunity for nautical exploration. **Marina de Salinas & Posada El Náutico** rents **kayaks** ($15 per hr. or $50 per day) and bikes ($20 per hr. or $50 per day). For less independent explorers, **Maravillas del Sur Ecotours** (☎313-3194) leads 3hr. **kayak tours** around Salinas Bay that sometimes include stops for snorkeling ($40 per person). Or just forget the kayak and hop on **La Paseadora**, a fun-filled, music-blasting boat that takes groups out for a tour of the bay ($3, children $2) or drops people off at a nearby island ($5, children $3). The boat leaves every weekend; for more information contact Ity Jimenez (☎824-2649) or wait on the dock next to El Balcón del Capitan (see **Food**, above) in the morning. Playa Salinas's only swimming area is at **Polita's Beach,** Rte. 701 Km 2.1. Sadly, there is no sand, just a large wooden platform. (☎824-4184. Open Sa-Su and holidays 9am-dusk.)

NEAR SALINAS

COAMO

Puerto Rico has plenty of opportunities to de-stress, but few compare to the **hot springs** just outside of Coamo. With temperatures reaching 109°F, the baths are like all-natural, communal jacuzzis—without the bubbles. As early as 1847 a hotel at the baths allowed rich Puerto Ricans to access the baths. Today **Hotel Baños de Coamo** ❸, at the end of Rte. 546, is a restored version of the earlier classic, still based on the idea of providing a relaxing experience in the soothing hot water. The attractive *parador* looks and feels like a ski lodge plopped down in the middle of a tropical forest. Coordinated rooms have cable TV, phone, and A/C. (☎825-2186 or 825-2239; www.banosdecoamo.com. Pool and restaurant. Check-in 2pm. Check-out 1pm. Singles $86; doubles $91; extra person $10; 2 children under 12 free. Tax included. AmEx/D/MC/V.) If you choose to come for the day, two **public baths** just behind the hotel are free to the public. Park at the end of Rte. 546, then walk past the gate to the rock-lined pools. To satiate the post-bath munchies, try **La Cava Grill House** ❹, Rte. 153 Km 11.2, where golf murals and golf course views leave no questions about the anticipated clientele. Steak and seafood prices are a bit high, but isn't this the place to indulge? (☎825-4843. Entrees $9-28. Open M-Th 11am-11pm, F-Sa 11am-2am. MC/V.)

To get to Coamo from Salinas take Hwy. 52 west to Exit 76, then drive north on Rte. 153 to Rte. 546. The baths are at the end. *Públicos* between Ponce and Coamo will drop passengers off at the intersection of Rte. 546 and Rte. 153, 1 mi. from the baths ($2.50). They may go all the way to the end if arranged in advance ($5).

BAHÍA DE JOBOS

Just between Salinas and Guayama, the 2883-acre Bahía de Jobos reserve protects the diverse ecosystem created by the confluence of the ocean and the Ríos Nigua and Guamani, including wetlands, mangrove forests, sea grass beds, coral reefs, and salt flats. Within these various environments you'll find Puerto Rico's largest population of manatees, as well as brown pelicans, peregrine falcons, and sea turtles. Birdwatchers will especially appreciate the 88 species of birds in the reserve, and anyone will appreciate the serene sight of a field full of elegant egrets. In 1981 the National Oceanic and Atmospheric Administration chose to preserve the area and continues to administer the reserve in conjunction with the Department of Natural Resources and the National Estuary Research Reserve System. This bureaucratic combination has created a first-rate info center. Unfortunately most of the area remains inaccessible to the public, but there is one superb hike. The 30min. ◪**Jagüeyes Forest Interpretative Trail** winds through mangroves, dry forest, and salt flats with informative signs in English and Spanish pointing out plants and animals along the way. To reach the path from the visitors center, drive west on Rte. 3, then turn left at Km 154.6. Signs mark the 7min. drive down dirt roads to the trailhead. A 1½hr. interpretive **kayak path** leaves from central Aguirre. The reserve does not provide kayaks, but **Maravillas del Sur Ecotours** (☎313-3194), in Salinas, rents double kayaks for $15 per hour and can drop them off at the dock in Aguirre.

Through English and Spanish interactive displays, the visitors center explains the various plants and animals in the reserve, the research being done here, and the fascinating history of the ghost town of Aguirre. Glass windows in the back allow visitors to glimpse the researchers who collect data on the reserve conditions every 15min. as part of the water quality control process. Reserve officials are currently creating a **camping area.** Call ☎864-0105 to check the status of the project or make reservations. (From Salinas, take Rte. 3 west to Rte. 705. Follow signs to Km 2.3. Open M-F 7:30am-noon and 1-4pm, Sa-Su 9am-noon and 1-3pm.)

GUAYAMA

The remains of two sugar mills serve as a reminder of Guayama's (pop. 43,600) more glamorous history as one of the major players in Puerto Rico's sugar industry. Today the city makes its living from pharmaceutical companies and serves as an important transportation hub. In addition to having all the requisite services, and traffic, that such a title entails, Guayama also houses several interesting museums and an attractive plaza that elevate the city beyond its utilitarian status.

THE HIDDEN DEAL

AGUIRRE GOLF COURS

On the majority of the island, gol is a sport reserved for the wealthy and green fees can get as high as $200. But all of this changes in littl Aguirre, where the local golf club seems to be frozen in time. This 18 hole course was built back wher Aguirre was a bustling sugar towr and the rich Yankee executives needed some way to amuse them selves while the profits rolled in.

Over time sugar stopped makin a profit, the mainlanders disap peared, and Aguirre entered a slow state of decay. However, the gol club continues to be alive and wel one of the few lively areas in thi quasi-ghost town. Best of all, the prices also seem frozen in time—yo can get a green fee as low as $10. A this price, even amateurs may be tempted to pass a few hours on the neatly cut grass with the local Puertc Ricans who continue to utilize the course on a regular basis.

Green fees are $10 from Tues day through Friday and $18 or weekends and holidays. Golf cart are an additional $12 per nin holes, though this cost can be divided between two people shar ing one cart. The pro shop also rents equipment for $10 per per son per day. On weekends, a small restaurant in the pro sho serves *comida criolla*. So take a step back in time and visit the most affordable golf course on the island. (*Rte. 705 Km 1.6. From Rte 3 turn south onto Rte. 705 and vee right when the road splits. ☎853 4052. Open Tu-Su 7am-6pm. AmEx D/MC/V. Credit card required.*)

⊫ TRANSPORTATION

Rte. 3 leads directly into downtown Guayama. **Públicos** leave from the station at the corner of C. Ashford and Enrique Gonzalez for: **Patillas** (30min., $0.80) via **Arroyo** (10min., $0.60); **Ponce** (45min., $4.35); **Río Piedras/San Juan** (1½hr., $7) via **Caguas** (45min., $7); and **Salinas** (30min., $1.40). Most *públicos* leave before 2pm. From the *público* station exit onto C. Ashford, turn left, walk two blocks, and turn left again to reach the plaza. **Hertz,** in Hotel Molino (see **Accommodations,** below), rents compact cars for $34-42 per day without insurance. (☎866-6417. 21+. Under 25 surcharge $10 per day. Open M-Sa 8am-5pm. AmEx/MC/V.)

◼️ 🛈 ORIENTATION AND PRACTICAL INFORMATION

The commercial areas of Guayama is near the intersection of Rte. 3 and Hwy. 54. **Route 3** leads past the **plaza,** but it can get a bit confusing and road signs are sporadic. The tall church steeple on the plaza is visible from far away and serves as a handy landmark if you get lost. Coming from the east, Rte. 3 becomes **Calle Ashford,** a major thoroughfare that runs parallel to C. Santiago Palmer, which passes the plaza. Drive past the church, then turn left on C. Vicente Pales, then left again on C. Martinez, going around the plaza, to stay on Rte. 3. **Plaza Guayama Mall,** Rte. 3 Km 135.2, east of town, has many shops and services.

Banks: Banco Popular (☎866-0288), in front of Plaza Guayama Mall, has an ATM. Open M-F 8am-4pm, Sa 8:30am-1pm.

Camping Permits: The **DRN** office, Rte. 3 Km 144.5 (☎864-5353 or 864-8903; fax 864-1147), west of town, issues camping permits ($4). Allow 3-4 days for processing. Open M-F 7:30am-noon and 1-4pm.

Supermarkets: Pueblo Xtra (☎866-1225), in Plaza Guayama Mall. **Western Union.** Open M-Sa 6am-midnight, Su 11am-5pm. AmEx/MC/V.

Police: ☎866-2020. Located on Ave. José Torre, behind the hospital. Open 24hr.

Hospital: Hospital Episcopal Cristo Redentor, Hwy. 54 Km 2.7 (☎864-4300). Clinic open M-F 8am-4pm. Emergency room open 24hr.

Internet Access: Ofi-Centro, C. Ashford 107 (☎864-0747), has 1 computer. Internet $5 per hr. Open M-F 8am-5pm, Sa 9am-2pm.

Post Office: C. Ashford 151 (☎864-1150), several blocks east of the plaza. General Delivery available. Open M-F 7:30am-4:30pm, Sa 7:30am-noon.

Zip Code: 00784.

⊫ ACCOMMODATIONS

Hotel Brandemar (☎864-5124), at the end of Rte. 748. From Guayama drive east on Hwy. 54 to Km 5.7, then turn right on Rte. 748; the reception is in the restaurant. Located in a quiet neighborhood near the water, this affordable hotel has everything travelers need, including private bath, cable TV, A/C, and a large swimming pool. Unfortunately mattress quality varies greatly and the linoleum floors get a bit dreary. Doubles $54-64; triples $75; quad with kitchenette $95. Tax included. AmEx/D/MC/V. ❷

Hotel Molino, Hwy. 54 Km 2.1 (☎866-1515; fax 866-5510), is the only hotel within city limits and guests soon acclimate to the sweet sound of traffic. Sterile chain hotel-style rooms include A/C, phone, cable TV, and a balcony overlooking the courtyard and the large, narrow pool. Check-in 3pm. Check-out noon. In-room Internet $4.50 for the first 15min. Nov. 15-Feb. 14 and May 15-Aug. 14 doubles Su-Th $101, F-Sa and holidays $106. Feb. 15-May 14 and Aug. 15-Nov. 14 $95/$101. Tax included. AmEx/MC/V. ❹

SOUTHEAST

🍴 FOOD

Fine dining is sparse in Guayama; however, a few restaurants do surprise with intriguing decor and good food. Several restaurants in the *barrio* of **Pozuelo,** at the end of Rte. 7710, off Rte. 3, west of town serve fresh seafood near the water.

> **La Casa de Los Pastelillos,** Rte. 7710 Km 3.8, in Pozuelo, serves over 75 different types of *pastelillos* (long, fried dough), filled with everything form pizza to crocodile. The highlight of this creative restaurant is the laid-back atmosphere; chow down on the large deck or lay in a hammock overlooking the beach. The restaurant does not serve alcohol, but encourages diners to bring their own cooler. *Pastelillos* $2-5, but you may need more than 1 to fill up. Open daily 11am-8pm. ❶

> **El Suarito** (☎864-1820), at C. Derkes and C. Hostos. This tastefully restored brick building is a local favorite and the best place to come for lunch downtown. Choose from the 4 daily specials written on a chalkboard, then enjoy the old pictures of Guayama on the walls. Open M-Sa 8am-3pm. Cash only. ❶

> **Cafetería Vegetariana,** C. Hostos 46 (☎864-5471), at C. Enrique Gonzalez, in the back of a health food store. This small cafeteria serves vegetarian sandwiches ($1.50-3.25) and a daily *comida criolla* lunch special ($5). Open M-F 11am-2pm. MC/V. ❶

👁 SIGHTS

MUSEUMS. The cultural tour of Guayama begins on the plaza at **Museo Casa Cautiño.** Built in 1887 by a *guayamés* architect, this magnificent house has been restored to its former glory and decorated with much of the original artwork and furniture. A walk inside provides insight into the life of Guayama's wealthy sugar families. *(C. Vicente Pales 1, on the plaza. ☎864-9083. Open Tu-Su 9am-4pm. $1, under 10 and over 65 $0.50.)* Housed in a Classical 1927 Superior Tribunal building, Guayama's **Centro de Bellas Artes** displays a variety of paintings, sculptures, and prints by professional Puerto Rican artists and incredibly talented art students. One room holds Taíno artifacts, but all the explanatory signs are in Spanish. *(Rte. 3 Km 138, west of the plaza. ☎864-7765. Open Tu-Su 10am-4:30pm. Free.)* The quirky **Pabellón de la Fama Deporte Guayama** (Pavillion of Guayama Sports Fame) details all of the local sports accomplishments through photos, newspaper clippings, and memorabilia. Who knew that a *guayamés* played for the Yankees? *(C. Ashford 22, at C. Derkes. ☎866-0676. Open M-F 8am-noon and 1-4:30pm, Sa 9am-noon and 1-4:30pm.)*

RESERVA NATURAL MARIPOSARIO LAS LIMAS. The first butterfly farm in Puerto Rico hides about 5 mi. north of Guayama. Created by a Puerto Rican couple to protect the environment, the 198-acre reserve has received support from several government facilities, including the Department of Natural Resources, but still retains the personal feel of a private enterprise. A 1¼hr. guided walk leads visitors from a small museum detailing the development of a butterfly, past ponds filled with shrimp, turtles, and fish, and into the woods, where guides point out the various species of plants and animals. Of course, there is time for a stop at the small butterfly cage, and a cafeteria and gift shop await at the end. *(From Guayama take Rte. 15 north to Rte. 179. After about 2 mi., turn onto Rte. 747 and make a right at Km 0.7 where signs lead to the forest. ☎864-6037 or 866-6756. Open Th-Su 10am-3pm. Mostly Spanish, but guides speak some English. Mandatory tour $3. Reservations recommended.)*

NEAR GUAYAMA: ARROYO

When the sugar boom came to an end and Guayama moved ahead toward industry, little Arroyo lagged behind, leaving a much smaller, and much more charming, oceanside town that still seems to reminisce about the good old days. Arroyo's main draw is the nearby beach (see **Centro Vacacional Guilarte,** below), but there are also some interesting attractions near the town center. Arroyo's **Tren del Sur,** Rte. 3 Km 130.9, the only operating train left in Puerto Rico, rekindles the atmosphere of the sugar era on a 1hr. ride leads through sugar fields and past plantation ruins. (Open Sa-Su and some holidays 9am-4pm. $3, under 12 $2.) Employees at Arroyo's **tourist office,** in the same parking lot as Tren del Sur, distribute a pamphlet about the town and can answer questions. (☎271-1574. Open M-F 8am-4:30pm.) Arroyo's old customs house has been converted into the **Museo de la Antigua Aduana,** C. Morse 65, a two-room museum that contains photos of Arroyo and a rotating exhibit of local artwork. (South of the plaza. ☎839-8096. Open W-Su 9am-4pm.) The charming **boardwalk** at the end of C. Morse was under construction in 2003; however, the government invested half a million dollars in the project, and when finished this should be a beautiful place to walk along the water.

Arroyo may attempt to flaunt its rich history, but most visitors are more interested in **Centro Vacacional Guilarte,** the best beach between Yabucoa and Guánica. This enormous government-run vacation center (see p. 58) has a rugged, distinctly Caribbean feeling, with scattered palm trees, lush vegetation, and incredible sunsets. The long, narrow beach does not have much sand, but the shallow water provides a good area for small children to play. Facilities include outdoor showers, bathrooms, trash cans, and lifeguards during daylight hours. The accommodations options at this large complex fit any budget. An enormous grassy **camping area** ❶ at the far eastern edge of the complex has trash cans and a bathroom that may or may not be open (otherwise you'll have to walk down to the public beach bathrooms). The tiny cement **cabanas** ❸ provide a roof over your head, in addition to two cramped bedrooms that hold up to six people. The rooms are less than comfortable, but *cabana* guests also have access to the large, clean **pool.** For a more relaxed sleeping experience, head straight to the **villas** ❹, which are similar to the cabanas but have been newly renovated and include A/C and hot water. (Off Rte. 3, east of Arroyo. The western entrance leads to the villas; the eastern entrance leads to the cabanas, the camping area, and the office. ☎839-3565. Office open Sa-Th 8am-4:30pm, F 10am-6:30pm. Beach $2 per car. Camping $10 per tent. Cabanas $66; villas $109. Tax included. AmEx/D/DC/MV/V.) Arroyo does not have great restaurants. When the boardwalk reopens, seafood restaurants lining the water should provide more picturesque and appetizing dining experiences. Until then, visitors will have to be satisfied with the nondescript **Panedería and Repostería La Familia** ❶, on C. Morse, two blocks south of the plaza, which serves pizza (slice $1-1.50), sandwiches ($1-4), a daily lunch special ($3), and pastries. (☎271-5162. Open daily 7am-9pm. MC/V.)

Públicos between Patillas and Guayama stop in Arroyo along C. Morse; flag down a van and ask which direction it's going (15min., $0.50). If you're going to Centro Vacacional Guilarte, ask the driver to drop you off at the intersection, then walk 1 mi. down to the beach. It's about a 2 mi. walk back into town.

ROUTE 901

Following the southeast corner of the island through the heart of sugar country, Rte. 901 is the tail end of Puerto Rico's scenic route, and the road's lush vegetation and superb ocean vistas certainly merit the title. Several enterprising Puerto Ricans have capitalized on the road's ideal location by building attractive accommodations and appetizing seafood restaurants. There is not really much to do, but foreigners and Puerto Ricans alike make the trek out to this corner of the world to relax on a hammock with a book, bake in the sun, or just watch the waves. Yabucoa, at the northern end of the road, serves as the starting point for the scenic Rúta Panoramica (see p. 261), and anyone embarking upon this journey should take one last glance at the ocean from Rte. 901 before heading into the mountains.

▐ **TRANSPORTATION.** From San Juan take Hwy. 52 south to Caguas, get on Rte. 1 temporarily to catch the exit for Hwy. 30 east, then exit onto Hwy. 53 south. At the end of Hwy. 53 turn right to reach Yabucoa or turn left for Rte. 901. Rte. 901 is easiest to navigate by car; however, **públicos** do go from Yabucoa to **Humacao** (20min., $1.20) and **Maunabo** (20-25min., $1). From Yabucoa's *público* station, walk uphill and turn right on C. Cristóbal Colón to reach the plaza and the taxi stand. **Taxis** travel to **Playa Lucía** ($6), **Maunabo** ($15), and everywhere in-between. (☎266-4047. Open 6am-6pm.) If you do plan to reach a hotel by public transportation, bring your own food or head to an all-inclusive—this is not a walking area.

▆▐ **ORIENTATION AND PRACTICAL INFORMATION.** Rte. 901 follows the southeast coast of the island between Yabucoa and Maunabo; however, the scenic route continues south past Maunabo along Rte. 3 all the way to Patillas. If you get lost just follow the numerous signs to the *parador*. Coming into Yabucoa, when you reach the concrete island, turn right onto **C. Cristóbal Colón** (also called Rte. 9901) to reach the plaza, or continue straight onto C. Catalina Morales (also called Rte. 182) for most government buildings and the beginning of the Rúta Panoramica. All of the services listed below are in Yabucoa. **Banco Popular,** C. Cristóbal Colón 50, has two ATMs. (☎893-2620. Open M-F 8am-4pm.) **Yabucoa Municipal Library,** on C. Catalina Morales, past the post office, houses the city's small **Casa de la Cultura** and its collection of antique tools, musical instruments, and Taíno artifacts. (☎893-5520 or 893-3385. Open M-Th 8am-7pm, F 8am-4:30pm when school is in session.) **Supermercado del Este,** on Rte. 901, just outside of Yabucoa in the Centro Comercial Jardínes de Yabucoa, has all the food you could need. (☎893-4340. Open M-W 6am-8pm, Th-Sa 6am-9pm, Su 11am-5pm. MC/V.) **Minutos Cleaners,** C. Cristóbal Colón 67, has self-serve washers ($1.25) and dryers ($0.50), but tends to be crowded. (☎893-2855. Open M-Sa 7am-5pm, Su 8am-2pm.) The **police station,** C. Catalina Morales 102 (☎893-2020), is open 24hr. **Farmacia Feliciano** sits next to Supermercado del Este. (☎893-6709. Open M-F 7:30am-9pm, Sa 8am-9pm. AmEx/D/MC/V.) Yabucoa's small **hospital** is across from the supermarket. (☎893-7100. 24hr. emergency room.) **PostNet,** on Rte. 901, about half a mile south of town, across from the stadium, has **Internet access.** (☎893-0180. $5 per hr. Open M-Sa 8am-5:30pm.) There is no General Delivery at the **post office,** C. Catalina Morales 100. (☎893-2135. Open M-F 7:30am-4:30pm, Sa 8am-noon.) **Zip Code:** 00767.

▐ **ACCOMMODATIONS.** The inviting accommodations along this scenic route are one of the region's major draws. Most are designed for families and will frown upon groups of drunk teenagers. The combination of welcoming hosts, an ideal location, and reasonable prices makes ▨**Playa Emajaguas Guest House ❷,** Rte. 901 Km 2.5, a great deal for budget travelers. Located behind a field off the road, this two-story guest house comes with pool tables, makeshift tennis courts, a clean pool, picnic tables, and a path down to Playa Emajaguas (see **Beaches,** below). Rooms are functional but a bit worn. (1½ mi. north of Maunabo. ☎861-6023. TV, A/C, and fridge. Fall-spring small rooms $50; apartments $70. Summer $60/$80. Cash only.) Those with money to burn should look no farther than **Caribe Playa Beach Resort ❸,** Rte. 3 Km 112.1, south of Maunabo. Located directly on the beach, this relaxing hotel enhances the striking location with numerous hammocks, BBQs, a pool, a whirlpool, and balconies in almost every room. Smaller rooms barely have enough room to walk; larger rooms come with fridge, telephone, A/C, cable TV, and sometimes a kitchenette. (☎839-6339; www.caribeplaya.com. Dec.-Apr. small doubles $79; large doubles $104. May-Nov. $72/$100. 9% tax not included. AmEx/MC/V.) A parrot greets guests at **Parador Palmas de Lucía ❹**, at Rte. 901 and Rte. 9911, about 5 mi. southeast of Yabucoa. As one of the island's premier *paradores*, this elegant hotel surrounds a large pool area. Large carpeted rooms resemble any chain motel. Best of all, the hotel is just steps away from the pleasant Playa Lucía. (☎893-4423 or 893-0291; www.palmasdelucia.com. Cable TV, A/C, and phone. 2 double beds $90; 2 kings $110; extra person $18. All inclusive 2 nights $280 for 2 people. Tax included. AmEx/MC/V.) Surfers might check out **Lunny Mar Guest House ❸**, Rte. 901 Km 8.4, just minutes from El Cocal beach. This rustic guest house has small rooms with the shower actually in the room (the toilet is in the bathroom). Larger rooms have a stove. The yard area has a common BBQ and a miniscule above-ground pool. (☎893-8996 or 379-8464. A/C, TV, and fridge. Check-in 3pm. Check-out 1pm. Doubles $65-$90. Tax included. MC/V.)

❐ FOOD. Several restaurants along Rte. 901 offer spectacular views and comparable seafood entrees. If you happen to be near Yabucoa, **Doredemar Restaurant ❸**, on Rte. 3 just south of the intersection with Rte. 901, is one of the few standouts. A small back patio surrounded by vegetation is a great location to enjoy fresh steak and seafood. (☎893-3837. Entrees $5-25. Open daily 11am-midnight. MC/V.) The decor at **Restaurant Irimar ❸**, on Hwy. 901, half a mile past Playa Emajaguas is one of the only restaurants open every day. Young Puerto Ricans like to lounge on the porch with a beer; more refined dining awaits inside. (☎861-1042. Entrees $6-24. Beer $1.50-2. Open Su-Th 11am-10:30pm, F-Sa 11am-midnight. AmEx/MC/V.)

◪ BEACHES. Rte. 901 is lined with beaches, but many are rocky and have small shore area. Just below the guest house of the same name, palm-lined **Playa de Emajaguas** has lots of sand, medium-sized waves, and remarkably small crowds. Unfortunately, there are no facilities, but this is still one of the best sites for lounging and swimming. **El Cocal**, past Lunny Mar Guest House (see **Accommodations**, above), is famous for its **surfing**, but the broad, clean beach is great for any activity. Another attractive beach is **Playa Lucía**, located just past Parador Palmas de Lucía (see **Accommodations,** above). The long beach lined with palm trees receives crowds from many hotels. A few food kiosks open when the beach is crowded.

The only sight in this area is actually located on a beach; the **Punta Tuna Lighthouse,** just outside of Maunabo, is visible from both Playa Maunabo and Playa Larga. Built by the Spanish in the late 1800s, the lighthouse is now operated by the US coast guard and closed to the public. For the best views, head down to the secluded **Playa Larga.** Coming south on Rte. 9011 turn toward the ocean on Rte. 7760, pass Villa del Faro, and take the first left going downhill at the mailboxes. When you get to the closed gate, walk down the short path to the beach. There can be a lot of seaweed on the sand, but it is a small price to pay for this rare sense of solitude. Traveling south, the next beach area is **Playa Maunabo,** which has a bit more sand. However, signs warn that the shore break can be dangerous. To reach the beach, continue down Rte. 760 and follow signs to Restaurant Los Bohíos.

NORTHEAST

Northeast Puerto Rico is essentially one big daytrip from San Juan, if you don't mind traffic. The region has been graced with several extraordinary natural attractions within a relatively small area, making it easy for visitors to come for one day to explore the forests of El Yunque, lie on the beach at Luquillo, or snorkel on an expedition out of Fajardo. This is also the most stereotypically tropical area of Puerto Rico, filled with lush forest and turquoise waters. Playa Luquillo and Balneario Seven Seas are beautiful palm tree-lined crescents of sand good for both swimming and sunbathing. La Cordillera, an archipelago of islands off Fajardo, looks like a series of deserted oases in the midst of the deep blue Caribbean. However, the highlight of the area lies not by the sea, but farther inland. El Yunque tropical rainforest, the largest protected area on the island, inspires pride in residents and awe in visitors. You can "see" El Yunque in one day, but several affordable ecolodges offer the opportunity for more quality R&R time within the confines of a tropical rainforest.

Of course northeast Puerto Rico is not just one natural playground. Like so many areas near San Juan, the region's population ballooned following Operation Bootstrap, resulting in several unattractive metropolitan areas. Fajardo, the unofficial capital of northeast Puerto Rico, exemplifies this urban sprawl with feeble attempts at culture amidst a city of pharmaceutical factories, highways, and fast-food joints. But avoid the cities, erase ugly Hwy. 3 from your memory, and enjoy northeast Puerto Rico for the unique natural riches that the area offers.

HIGHLIGHTS OF NORTHEAST PUERTO RICO

DISCOVER the 27 miles of hiking trails, two waterfalls, and countless peaks of the only tropical forest in the United States at El Yunque (p. 243).

SNORKEL, DIVE, SWIM, OR TAN on an excursion to La Cordillera, the archipelago of islands off Fajardo (p. 257).

MONKEY-WATCH from the deck of a boat near the infamous Cayo Santiago (p. 260).

EL YUNQUE

Occupying over 28,000 acres of land Puerto Rico, the Caribbean National Forest, commonly referred to as "El Yunque," is one of the island's greatest treasures. El Yunque is the only tropical rainforest in the US and the largest protected land area in Puerto Rico. With four different types of forest, over 200 native species of trees, several species of mammals, and countless insects, El Yunque provides a venue to experience the real nature of Puerto Rico, uninfiltrated by factories, pollution, and cars. Well, maybe not cars. Rte. 191 cuts through the forest, providing a means of accessing the forest, but also welcoming over 1 million people per year. Unfortunately, on a busy day it can seem like a good portion of them are right behind you on the path. However, quieter trails and a bit of exploration allow anyone to get away from it all and see what Puerto Rico is really made of.

TRANSPORTATION

There is no public transportation to El Yunque. Most visitors come either with a tour group or by car. It's easy to arrange a **tour** from San Juan (see p. 96), but the park is easily navigable without a guide. It only takes a little over an hour to **drive**

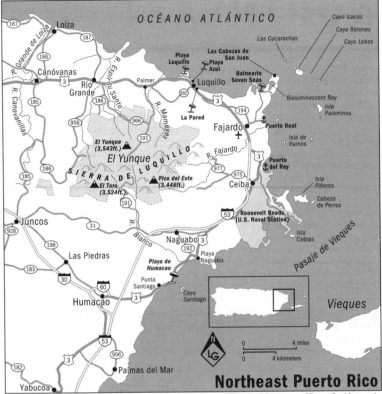

Northeast Puerto Rico

to the park from the capital. From San Juan take Hwy. 26 east to Hwy. 3. About 4
mi. past Río Grande turn right on the small Rte. 191 and follow signs up the hill.
Alternatively, from Isla Verde take Rte. 187 east through Piñones until it intersects
Hwy. 3. This small road takes about 10min. longer (depending on traffic), but
offers scenic ocean views. It may be possible to take a *público* from Fajardo to the
small village of Palmer ($1.60), at the base of the park, then hitchhike up Rte. 191.
If you choose this route start early, because you will have to get back down the
mountain with enough time to catch the last *público* back to Fajardo (as early as
2pm). Also remember that hitchhiking in this area is both difficult and dangerous,
and there are no hotels around Palmer if you get stuck overnight.

AT A GLANCE

AREA: 28,000 acres.

CLIMATE: Tropical. Rainy season is May-
June and Oct.-Nov., but showers occur
year-round.

HIGHLIGHTS: Tropical forest, diverse
flora, 2 waterfalls, Yokahú Tower.

FEATURES: Hiking over 27 mi. of trails,
swimming in pristine waterfalls.

GATEWAYS: Luquillo (see p. 250), San
Juan (see p. 88).

CAMPING: Free at select areas throughout the park. Must obtain a permit from
the park office (see p. 245).

FEES: $3 to enter El Portal Visitors Cen-
ter.

NORTHEAST

⚑ 🄽 ORIENTATION AND PRACTICAL INFORMATION

Although El Yunque occupies almost 25% of the land area of northeast Puerto Rico, most tourist activities occur around **Route 191,** which leads past the tourist centers and the trailheads. The southern half of the road is closed due to landslides.

Visitors Centers: El Portal Visitors Center (☎ 888-188), Rte. 191 Km 4.3, is the first stop for most visitors. The well-maintained, attractive center offers a 12min. English/Spanish movie, a gift shop, and a small museum with interactive exhibits. The friendly staff distributes brochures with rudimentary maps and lots of information. Worth the nominal admission fee. Bathrooms, pay phones, and snack machines. Entrance $3, ages 5-12 and seniors $1.50, ages 0-4 free. Open daily 9am-5pm. **Palo Colorado Information Center,** Rte. 191 Km 11.8, has a souvenir shop and a park ranger who can answer questions. Park tours (see below) also leave from here. On Sa-Su, this information center distributes camping permits. Open daily 9am-5pm.

Maps: Campers and serious hikers should definitely purchase the National Geographic map available at both visitors centers ($10); day visitors should be able to navigate with the visitors center brochure and the map in this book.

Hours: The gate at Coca Falls is open daily 7:30am-6pm.

Supplies: All visitors should bring mosquito repellent, water, food, and a swimsuit.

Tours: Many companies in **San Juan** offer excursions to El Yunque (see p. 96). A National Forest Service ranger leads 1hr. English/Spanish tours from the Palo Colorado Information Center along the Caimitillo and Baño de Oro trails (every hr. 11:30am-3:30pm; $5, children 0-12 and seniors $3). Tours are offered regularly Dec. 15-May 15 and sporadically the rest of the year—call ahead.

> **! WARNINGS** The National Park Service warns that all visitors should watch out for **flash floods,** especially during the rainy season. If it starts to rain heavily, immediately head to higher ground. Visitors should also be aware of **mongoose attacks.** Most mongooses who approach humans are infected with **rabies**—avoid any contact.

🏕 ACCOMMODATIONS & CAMPING

To camp ❶ in El Yunque you must first get a **free permit,** available in the park. From Monday to Friday pick up a permit at the **Catalina Work Center,** Rte. 191 Km 4.4, directly after El Portal Visitors Center. (Open M-F 8am-4:30pm.) On weekends and holidays, pick up a permit at the **Palo Colorado Information Center** (see p. 245). Permits are good only for the day they are distributed. With the permit, park rangers also hand out a map designating permissible camping areas. There are no facilities in the park, so campers should remember to pack out everything that they bring in (including trash). There are no hotels along the northern section of Rte. 191, but more refined options await near Naguabo (see p. 259) and on the western edge of the park, near Río Grande (see **Welcome to Paradise,** p. 249).

🄵 FOOD

There are no food facilities along the hiking paths, but many families come with picnics. **Covered picnic tables** at Palmas de Sierra, Caimitillo, Palo Colorado, and Quebrada Grande have running water and grills. Palo Colorado, at the head of La Mina trail, is the most popular area. For those who don't want to cook their own food, **El Bosque Encantado ❶,** Rte. 191 Km 7.2, serves up delicious *batidas* ($3), freshly fried *empanadillas* ($1-3), and other snacks. (Usually open 9am-6pm.)

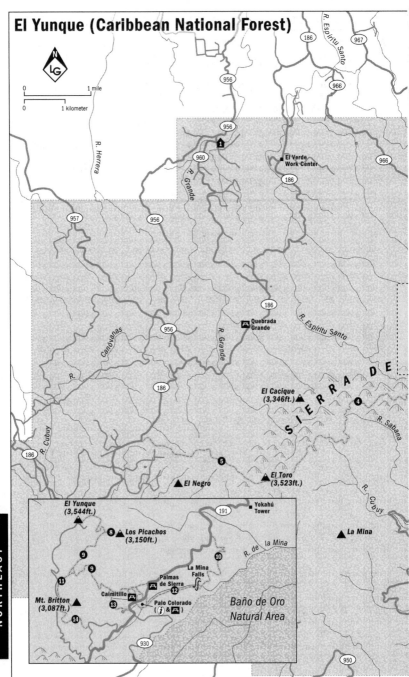

El Yunque (Caribbean National Forest)

N

0   1 mile
0   1 kilometer

R. Espíritu Santo

186
967

956

966

956

960

1

El Verde
Work Center

186

966

957

956

R. Herrera

R. Grande

Canóvanas
R.

956

186

Quebrada
Grande

R. Grande

R. Espíritu Santo

S I E R R A   D E

El Cacique
(3,346ft.)

4

R. Sabana

186

R. Cubuy

186

5

El Negro

El Toro
(3,523ft.)

R. Cubuy

El Yunque
(3,544ft.)

Yokahú
Tower

191

La Mina

8 Los Picachos
(3,150ft.)

9

9

R. de la Mina

10

La Mina
Falls

11

Palmas
de Sierra

12

Caimitillo

13

Palo Colorado

Baño de Oro
Natural Area

Mt. Britton
(3,087ft.)

14

930

950

NORTHEAST

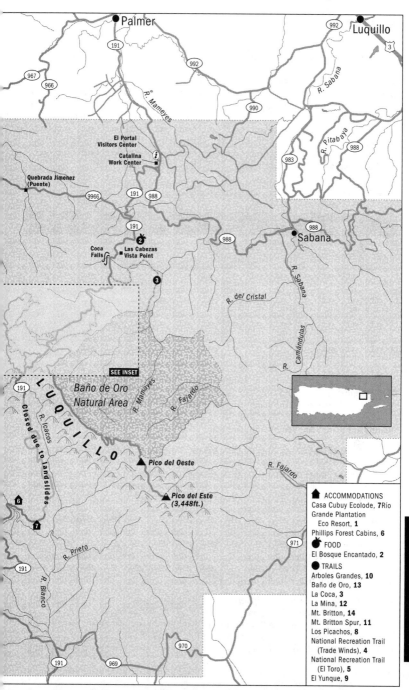

ACCOMMODATIONS
Casa Cubuy Ecolode, **7** Río
Grande Plantation
  Eco Resort, **1**
Phillips Forest Cabins, **6**

FOOD
El Bosque Encantado, **2**

TRAILS
Arboles Grandes, **10**
Baño de Oro, **13**
La Coca, **3**
La Mina, **12**
Mt. Britton, **14**
Mt. Britton Spur, **11**
Los Picachos, **8**
National Recreation Trail
  (Trade Winds), **4**
National Recreation Trail
  (El Toro), **5**
El Yunque, **9**

NORTHEAST

👁 SIGHTS

Heading up Rte. 191 the first major sight is **Coca Falls,** Km 8.4. There is not much more to see than the view of the waterfall from the road (and Mina Falls, farther up, is more impressive). **Yokahú Tower** appears on the left at Km 8.9. Built in the 1930s as a Civilian Conservation Corps (CCC) project, the tower provides spectacular views of El Yunque, Luquillo, and far-off Fajardo. **La Mina Falls,** accessible via a 30-40min. walk along Arboles Grandes Trail or La Mina Trail, is undoubtedly the most popular destination in El Yunque. On weekend afternoons it can seem like every family in San Juan journeyed out to the falls to picnic on the rocks and swim in the small lagoon. Nonetheless, the sight merits its popularity. Bring a swimsuit and join in the merriment. Continuing up the highway, the **Palo Colorado Visitors Centers** has a gift shop and a park ranger.

🥾 HIKING

TRAILS	DURATION (ONE-WAY)	DIFFICULTY	LENGTH	ALTITUDE
La Coca	1½hr.	Difficult	1¾ mi.	1476-820 ft.
Arboles Grandes	40min.	Moderate	¾ mi.	1833-1667 ft.
La Mina	30min.	Easy-Moderate	¾ mi.	2132-1640 ft.
Baño de Oro	20min.	Easy	¼ mi.	2132-2362 ft.
El Yunque	2hr.	Moderate	2½ mi.	2067-3445 ft.
Los Picachos	5min.	Easy	¼ mi.	2952-3051 ft.
Spur Mt. Britton	10min.	Easy	¼ mi.	2788-2952 ft.
Mt. Britton	40min.	Moderate-Difficult	½ mi.	2493-3087 ft.
National Recreation Trail	7hr.	Difficult	6¼ mi.	2533-3578 ft.

LA COCA. Most visitors ignore the first trail on the way up Rte. 191, which makes it the ideal path to experience the forest in blissful solitude. Unfortunately, the hike is quite arduous and descends in altitude, so there are no amazing views at the end. This is one of the more rugged paths, with dirt trails and small streams that you must cross without the aid of a bridge. The steep inclines get quite muddy, so do not try this hike in the rain.

ARBOLES GRANDES. As one of two hikes that lead to Mina Falls, Arboles Grandes, or "Big Trees," is one of the most popular hikes in El Yunque. Almost the entire path is paved and steep inclines have stairs, making the trail easily accessible for hikers (or walkers) of all abilities. Informative signs along the path provide educational facts about the surrounding tarabuco forest.

LA MINA. This hike is essentially the second half of the Arboles Grandes Trail, and an alternative route to Mina Falls. La Mina receives comparable crowds and has comparable quantities of concrete, but this trail runs alongside Río de la Mina, allowing hikers to take a quick dip along the way down. La Mina is slightly easier, and more attractive, than Arboles Grandes. It is possible to walk down one trail and up the other, but you will have to walk along busy Rte. 191 to return.

BAÑO DE ORO. This short trail across from Palo Colorado is one of the park's hidden treasures. Baño de Oro is easy enough to be accessible by all visitors, but it is not ruined by solid concrete. Furthermore, this hike doesn't get nearly as crowded as La Mina or Arboles Grandes. With long flat stretches and a stream toward the end, little Baño de Oro is the ideal trail to wind down on after a long day of hiking.

EL YUNQUE. The Big Daddy of El Yunque trails, this aptly named path travels from Rte. 191 all the way to the peak of El Yunque mountain. Along the way the trail consists of a little bit of everything, from pavement to pebbles. Many foreigners do this hike, but it is long enough that you can still feel isolated. Several turn-offs (Mt. Britton Spur, Los Picachos) allow tired hikers to choose an alternative ending along the way, but those who continue all the way up with be rewarded with a feeling of accomplishment and amazing views. When you reach the road at the end of the trail, turn left and go all the way up to the El Yunque tower for the best views. From the top on a clear day you can see all the way out to St. Thomas.

LOS PICACHOS. A small turn-off about 30min. from the peak of El Yunque, Los Picachos provides an alternate ending for hikers who just can't make it to the top of the mountain. The short, rocky trail has a steep cliff on one side and the 59 steps are a tough finale. However, the trail recompenses with terrific views.

MT. BRITTON SPUR. Mt. Britton Spur is an easy pebble path connecting El Yunque to Mt. Britton. To make a full loop, head up El Yunque, cross over on Mt. Britton Spur, then head down Mt. Britton. However, at the end you will have to hike several miles to get back to your car. Mt. Britton has a steep incline, so it is easier to ascend El Yunque, then descend Mt. Britton, rather than vice versa. If you're coming off Mt. Britton Spur, walk downhill on the road to reach Mt. Britton.

MT. BRITTON. Rugged hikers may be disappointed that the entire Mt. Britton trail is paved, and it ends with a short walk along the road. However, the trail is shorter than El Yunque and provides a relatively quick route to yet another observation tower with views of Fajardo, Luquillo, San Juan, and the Spanish Virgin Islands. For this reason, Mt. Britton is quite popular with foreign tourists. The steep path gets extremely slippery when wet—proceed with caution.

NATIONAL RECREATION TRAIL. Consisting of El Toro Trail and Trade Winds, the National Recreation Trail, the longest trail in El Yunque, follows the mountain peaks from Rte. 191 to Rte. 186. The highlight of the path is the summit of El Toro, the tallest mountain in El Yunque. Only experienced hikers should attempt this hike, as they must battle mud, overgrown plants, steep hills, and isolation.

THE BIG SPLURGE

WELCOME TO PARADISE

Puerto Rico can be a difficult place to get away from it all (a common problem when you stuff 4 million people on an island the size of Connecticut). Even El Yunque seems overpopulated and prepackaged at times. So if you really want to experience Puerto Rico's natural beauty, with a few of those amenities that make life comfortable, don't look back, and head immediately for **Río Grande Plantation Eco Resort.**

Located in the foothills of the forest, Río Grande boasts 40 acres of forest with 63 species of trees, a river, and countless birds, including occasional visits by the rare Puerto Rican parrot. Guests enjoy the nature from the comfort of an impeccable two-story villa in the plantation's hotel. The large rooms contain 4 double beds, 2 cable TVs, a kitchen with fridge, microwave, and sink, 2 baths, 1 jacuzzi bathtub, and a balcony overlooking a spotless swimming pool. Although the rooms are ideal for groups, this is not the place to party—instead, come to enjoy nature in an ideal location minutes from El Yunque and Luquillo Beach. Smaller rooms have the same natural location, but fewer amenities. Río Grande is primarily used for conventions and events, so call ahead or your isolated vacation could become part of a Puerto Rican wedding. *(Rte. 956 Km 4.2, Río Grande, off Hwy. 3. ☎887-2779 or 887-5822; fax 888-3239. Singles $125-175; 2-person lanais $200-225; 4-bed villas $250-350. AmEx/MC/V.* ❺

LUQUILLO

Many visitors to Luquillo (pop. 19,817) never actually see the town—they come for the beach, spend a day lounging in the sun, then return to San Juan. For years Luquillo's beach has been touted as the best public beach on the island, and in comparison to San Juan, Luquillo Beach is undoubtedly paradise—it is lined with palm trees, it has ample amenities, and during weekdays in the winter it offers solitude that people in Isla Verde only dream about. Don't be misled—Luquillo does not have the best beach on the island, just the best developed swimming beach close to San Juan. Those with only a short time on the island may find this small town, with its picturesque beaches, to be the perfect escape.

TRANSPORTATION. **Públicos** traveling between Río Piedras and Fajardo will let passengers off at Luquillo (45min., $3). To get back, sit at the green benches on Hwy. 3 and flag down a passing *público*. If you choose this option, remember that *públicos* primarily run M-Sa 6:30am-3pm. Driving from San Juan (45min.-1¼hr., depending on traffic), you'll first see the food kiosks to your left—continue another ½ mi. to reach the intersection with Rte. 193 and the exit to the city center.

ORIENTATION AND PRACTICAL INFORMATION. Most of the city is located along **Route 193,** which becomes **C. Fernández Garcia** as it passes by the main plaza. The parallel street C. 14 de Julio holds most of the city government buildings. It is easy to orient yourself by the large condominium towers. Facing the ocean, the group of towers to the left are called Playa Azul and they sit directly in front of Playa Azul. To the right, the two Sandy Hills condominiums mark the eastern edge of the city center. The central Plaza de Recreo is sandwiched between the two groups of condominiums. Playa Luquillo is just west of town, about 1 mi. from the plaza.

Banco Popular, on Hwy. 193, is right at the main town entrance. (☎889-2610. ATM. Open M-F 8am-4pm, Sa 8:30am-noon.) **La Selva,** C. Fernández Garcia 250, 2 blocks off the plaza away from the beach, **rents surfboards** ($20 per day), **boogie boards** ($10 per day), and **snorkels** ($10 per day) to travelers. (☎889-6205. Surfing lessons $25 per hr. Open M-Sa 9am-5pm, Su 9am-3pm. AmEx/MC/V.) **Amigo,** across Hwy. 3 in Brisas del Mar, sells groceries and offers Moneygram service. (☎889-1919. Open M-Sa 7am-10pm, Su 11am-5pm. MC/V.) **Economía Laundromat,** in the Luquillo Complejo Touristic, near Playa Azul will wash ($1) and dry ($0.25 per 5min.) your clothes. (☎405-0237. Open M-Tu and Th-F 8am-6pm, W 8am-noon, Sa 7am-4pm.) The **police station,** C. 14 de Julio 158, is one block south of the plaza. (☎889-2020. Open 24hr.) **Luquillo Community Health Center,** at the end of C. 14 de Julio, provides medical assistance, but Fajardo has much better facilities. (☎889-2771. Open M-F 8am-noon.) For **Internet access** ($10 per hr.) head to **Optimum,** C. H #JJ17, in Brisa del Mar. From Luquillo center, cross Hwy. 3 and take the street behind McDonald's to the left and up the hill. (1 computer. Open M-F 8am-5pm.) The **post office,** C. 14 de Julio 160, is easy to find. (☎889-3170. Open M-F 8am-4:30pm, Sa 8am-noon.) **Zip Code:** 00773

ACCOMMODATIONS. Considering its popularity, Luquillo has surprisingly few accommodations options. **Playa Azul Apartment Realty ❹,** in the huge beachfront condos, rents vacation homes in the Playa Azul condominiums, the Sandy Hills condominiums, and the Solimar townhouse complex. Playa Azul is the most affordable, and offers direct beach access, swimming pools, and tennis courts. All apartments are decorated according to the whims of the permanent tenants. (☎889-3425 or 889-3939. Parking at Playa Azul $20. 3 night min. Office open M-F 8:30am-6pm, Sa 9am-5pm. $100 deposit required. In Playa Azul for 3 nights: studio (1-2 people) $325; 1 bedroom (up to 4 people) $375; 2 bedroom (up to 6 people) $475; 3 bedroom (up to 8 people) $575. MC/V.) To get to **La Posada del Tinglao ❷**, C. Veve Calazada 25, start with your back to the church, then walk to the upper right-hand corner of the plaza, continue down the street to the ocean, then turn left. This recently painted house overlooks La Pared. Two full apartments on the first floor come with kitchen and living room. The second floor has been divided into three very different rooms that can be rented separately or together. Only some rooms have private bath in some rooms. (☎ 888-8947 or 399-9534; manny2@yahoo.com. Fans, but no A/C. Rooms $45-65; apartments $110; 2nd floor $165. AmEx/MC/V.) **Playa La Monserrate ❶** has a large grass **camping** area with concrete picnic tables and grills scattered throughout. (☎ 889-5871. Call ahead. $13, with electricity $17.)

◻ FOOD. Most of the food in Luquillo comes straight from the sea. Beach-goers should not skip a trip to the famous **food kiosks** that line Hwy. 3 at the western edge of Playa Luquillo. Over 80 kiosks, ranging from full restaurants to small shacks, serve traditional food (full lunches $3-5) and all of your favorite fried feasts (*empanadillas* $1-2). Hours vary with the size of the crowd but there are always a few kiosks open. In town, **Erik's Gyros & Deli ❷**, C. Fernández Garcia 352, three blocks south of the plaza. provides a tasty alternative to the traditional lunch choices. (☎ 889-0615. Greek and Puerto Rican combos $5-8.50. Open M-Sa 7am-4pm. MC/V.) For a slightly fancier meal, try **The Brass Cactus ❸**, on Rte. 193 just west of Playa Azul. With a wooden floor, US license plates lining the walls, and sizzling steaks, the Brass Cactus provides Americans with a little taste of home. (☎ 889-5735. Sandwiches $7-8.25; entrees $14-18. Open Su-Th 11am-midnight, F-Sa 11am-1am. Kitchen closes 1hr. earlier. AmEx/MC/V.) The utilitarian **La Exquisita Bakery ❶**, Ave. Jesus Piñero 1, on the plaza, serves up big sandwiches to hungry schoolchildren and the occasional beachgoer. (☎ 633-5554. Sandwiches $1-4. Open M-Sa 6am-9pm, Su 8am-8pm. MC/V $10min.) Next door, **Victor's Place Seafood ❹**, Ave. Jesus T. Piñero 2, has been selected as one of the 10 best restaurants in Puerto Rico. Bypass the hot outdoor patio to peruse the wood-paneled dining room decorated with fish nets. (☎ 889-5705. Entrees $10-25; lobster $25-26. Open Tu-Su 11am-10pm. MC/V.)

◧▨ BEACHES AND OUTDOOR ACTIVITIES. The crescent-shaped **Playa Luquillo**, or more properly **Playa Monserrate**, is the city's primary attraction and one of the most beautiful public beaches on the island. As a public *balneario*, Playa Luquillo has lifeguards, picnic tables, souvenir shops, bathrooms, showers, food kiosks, and lawn chair ($4 per day) and umbrella rental ($8 per day). However, Playa Luquillo has almost become too popular for its own good, as the beach is crowded in the summer and the sand is combed regularly, giving it a somewhat artificial look. Still, anyone who comes to Luquillo with realistic expectations should enjoy this picturesque setting. To reach the beach, take Rte. 193 all the way to the west. (☎ 889-5871. Parking $2. Open daily 8:30am-5:30pm.)

Playa Luquillo also contains the remarkable **Sea Without Barriers, the island's only handicapped-accessible beach** (☎ 889-4329). The idea originated when 14-year-old Rosimar Hernández wrote a letter to then-governor Pedro Roselló, pointing out that people in wheelchairs, including herself, could not enjoy the natural attractions of Puerto Rico. Today Hernández's dream has become a reality. Sea Without Barriers has a ramp and ample facilities specifically designed to let handicapped people and elderly citizens with mobility limitations enter the water.

Located east of Playa Monserrate, **Playa Azul** has better sand, slightly larger waves, and usually much smaller crowds. However, it is not a public beach and thus lacks the facilities of Monserrate. Luquillo is also a popular destination for **surfers.** The next beach to the east, **La Pared,** in front of the central plaza, has good waves and a sandy

NORTHEAST

bottom ideal for beginners. The surfing extends for about 2 mi. to the east and just gets better. Try **La Selva,** another surfer favorite farther to the east with both sand and reef bottom, or just walk along the beach until you find a break that suits your fancy.

Just outside of town, Hacienda Carabalí offers **horseback rides** through the forest. One route traverses the foothills of El Yunque along the Río Mameyes; the other follows Luquillo Beach (2hr.; daily 10am, noon, 2pm; $40, ages 3-12 $25). Call ahead for reservations and specify which route you prefer. Carabalí also offers short, impromptu rides on the ranch (1hr.; $20, children $10) to anyone who shows up at the gate. (☎889-5820. From Luquillo take Hwy. 3 west, turn left on Rte. 992, take the first right up the hill, and go through the second gate. Am/Ex/MC/V.)

⑥☐ SIGHTS AND FESTIVALS. Luquillo's government recently constructed a **Centro de Arte y Cultura** (Center for Art and Culture), Hwy. 3 Km 38.4 on the south side of town. The complex has great facilities, with an exhibition hall, a 550-seat theater, and an open-air amphitheater, but not much to put inside. The most remarkable exhibits usually come from *luquillense* Tomás Batista. (☎633-1096 or 447-5233. Open M-F 9am-noon and 1-3pm. Free. Concerts and performances $20-25, children $8-10.)

In addition to the Luquillo's patron saint festival (held on the week preceding March 19), the city also celebrates an annual **Festival de Platos Típicos** (the last weekend in Nov.). The festival brings music, *artesanía,* and feasts of delicious Puerto Rican food to the Plaza de Recreo. In 2002, Dawn dishwashing soap sponsored the event, and the city government broke the Guiness Book of World Records for the most dishes washed. To help out, all 80+ food kiosks used real dishware on that day. The municipality has not decided how to top that spectacle.

📓 NIGHTLIFE. Luquillo's nightlife scene is meager to say the least. Most expats and foreigners down a couple of beers at **The Brass Cactus** (see **Food,** p. 251). Down the street **El Flamboyan** hosts a much more local crowd attracted to the pool tables, cheap beer (Medalla $1.25-1.50), and semi-outdoor tables. (On Rte. 193. ☎889-2928. Happy Hour Sa 10pm-1am. Open daily 8am-last person leaves.) The bars at the food kiosks (see p. 251) also attract a fair number of locals in the evening.

FAJARDO

Despite what it says on the map, there are actually several different Fajardos (pop. 40,000) in northeast Puerto Rico. Fajardo proper is the unexceptional city with heavy traffic. However, most visitors will never even make it to this area, as they head directly to Puerto Real and hop on the next ferry to the Spanish Virgin Islands. For wealthy yachtsmen and daytrippers from San Juan, Fajardo is the developed area around Villa Marina, with its masses of catamarans and seafood restaurants. Regardless of where you go, the attraction of Fajardo is not the city, but the surrounding nature. Las Cabezas de San Juan has some of the best mangroves in Puerto Rico and La Cordillera, a beautiful archipelago off the east coast, is ideal for snorkeling and boating expeditions. The reserve's Laguna Grande bay is one of the best place's on the island to see the incredible phenomenon of bioluminescence. If you look in the right places, Fajardo actually does have a lot to offer.

📑 TRANSPORTATION

It is almost impossible to get around Fajardo without a car. Getting to one sight should be no problem, but visiting multiple destinations on public transportation will be frustrating and time-consuming.

Flights: Fajardo's tiny airport (☎863-1011) sends even tinier planes to Culebra, San Juan, St. Croix, St. Thomas, and Vieques. Most airlines sell tickets by phone or at the airport. Reserve in advance or the flight may not leave. To reach the airport, take the main entrance to central Fajardo, then follow signs. Parking $8.50 per 24hr.

Airlines:

Air Flamenco (☎801-8256) flies to **Culebra** (7am, noon, 5:45pm; $25, round-trip $45). If someone wants to fly to San Juan the 3:30pm flight from Culebra will stop in Fajardo ($40). MC/V.

Isla Nena (☎863-4000, toll-free 877-812-5144) flies on demand to: **Vieques** (8min.; $20, round-trip $35) and **Culebra** (15min.; 1-2 per day; $25, round-trip $45). Open daily 6am-6pm. MC/V.

Vieques Air Link (☎863-3020 or 860-2290) sends flights on demand 6am-6pm. To: **Culebra** (6 per day, $40 round-trip); **St. Croix** (2 per day; $75, $145 round-trip); and **Vieques** (10 per day, $36 round-trip). AmEx/MC/V.

Públicos: From Fajardo's terminal *públicos* go to: **Ceiba** (10min., $0.85); **Humacao** (45min., $2.45); **Las Croabas** (5min., $0.65-75); **Luquillo** (15min., $0.70); **Palmer** (25min., $1.60); **Río Piedras** (1hr., $3.50). If you take a *público* from San Juan to the ferry terminal, ask the driver to go all the way to the port.

Taxis: Theoretically there's a taxi stand on the plaza along Rte. 195, but it is frequently empty. *Públicos* go to almost all major sights—just ask around at the station.

Ferries: The **Puerto Rican Port Authority** (☎863-0705 or 863-4560) runs ferries from Puerto Real to the Spanish Virgin Islands. To get to Puerto Real from central Fajardo take C. Aguilera (parallel to C. Muñoz Rivera) away from the plaza, then turn right on Rte. 195 (1 mi.). To avoid the traffic downtown, from Hwy. 3 take the 2nd Fajardo exit onto Ave. Conquistadores, then turn right onto Rte. 194 (after the Church's Chicken), then turn left on Rte. 195. Long-term **parking** $5 per day. *Públicos* from Fajardo go to the port ($1) and are usually waiting when a boat comes in. **Travel With Padin taxi service** takes passengers from the San Juan airport to the ferry terminal ($55 for 2 people, $60 for 4 people). Call for reservations (in English call after 6pm ☎889-6202, in Spanish 8am-6pm ☎644-3091). **Passenger ferries** go to **Culebra** (70min.; M-F 9:30am and 3pm, Sa-Su 9am, 2:30, 6:30pm; $2.25, ages 3-11 $1) and **Vieques** (1hr.; M-F 9:30am, 1, 4:30pm, Sa-Su 9am, 3, 6pm; $2, ages 3-11 $1). **Cargo ferries** take cars to **Culebra** (M-Tu and Th 3:30am and 4pm, W and F 3:30am, 10, 4pm; $26.50) and **Vieques** (M-F 4, 9:30am, 4:30pm; $26). Reservations required for cars. Show up at least 1hr. in advance. Reservation office open 8-11am and 1-3pm.

Car Rental: L&M Car Rental, Hwy. 3 Km 43.7 (☎860-6868). Compact cars for $35-49. Collision insurance $11.50. 25+. Open M-F 7am-6pm, Sa-Su 8am-5pm. AmEx/D/DC/MC/V. If you're desperate, there are a few small independent car rental companies near the ferry terminal. The least suspicious is **Best Way Car Rental** (☎860-1750 or 860-1705), C. Unión 474. Compact cars $40 per day. 18+ with ID and a credit card. Open M-F 8am-11am and noon-5pm, Sa-Su 8am-noon and 2-6pm. MC/V.

IN RECENT NEWS

BE CAREFUL WHAT YOU ASK FOR

For years the Puerto Rican government has been demanding that the US Navy leave their training grounds on Vieques (see p. 286). Finally, on April 1, 2003 the US complied, removing all Navy presence from Vieques. However, an unexpected consequence of the departure from Vieques was that the Navy also took steps to significantly downsize the Roosevelt Roads base, just south of Fajardo. Rosie Roads, as it is commonly known, served primarily as a staging ground for the Vieques training operations. Therefore, on April 11, 2003 the US announced that it would eliminate 2772 jobs at the base (one of the island's largest employers). The base would remain open, but indefinitely—in 2005, when the Navy was scheduled to review military facilities across the US, it will consider closing Rosie Roads completely.

Governor Sila Calderón and most Puerto Ricans protested this move, which had a significant negative impact on the economy. Ceiba's mayor, Gerardo Cruz, was quoted in the *San Juan Star* as saying that the base closure would create "economic, social, and even political chaos." On the other hand, many *independentistas* applauded the move, claiming that it was one step closer to getting the US out of Puerto Rico's affairs and off the island. The official position of the Puerto Rican government could change with the new administration, but Calderón promised in April 2003 to continue protesting the base closure.

Fajardo

🏠 ACCOMMODATIONS
Anchor's Inn, **4**
Ceiba Country Inn, **9**
Fajardo Inn/Scenic Inn, **6**
Hotel La Familia, **1**
Puerto Real Guest House, **10**

🍎 FOOD
Friends Restaurant, **11**
Golden Bagel Bakery, **8**
Lolita's, **5**
Restaurant La Conquista, **2**
Rosa's Seafood, **7**

🍸 NIGHTLIFE
Racar Seafood, **3**

▣ 🔢 ORIENTATION AND PRACTICAL INFORMATION

Fajardo is spread out and difficult to navigate without a car. Congested **Highway 3** divides the city, but most attractions are located on the eastern side of the road. The first exit goes to **Route 194,** which travels roughly parallel to Hwy. 3 and passes the center before intersecting Hwy. 3 again. The second major exit leads to Ave. Conquistador, which goes to the Wyndham hotel (watch out for a sharp right turn). The third and most prominent exit deposits visitors on **Route 195,** which passes the plaza then continues to the **ferry dock. Route 987** originates from Rte. 195, passes **Villa Marina** (a major port with a shopping center), intersects Ave. Consquistador, and eventually leads to the beach, the nature reserve, and Las Croabas.

Banks: Banco Popular (☎863-0101), on C. Garlinda Morales. ATM. Open M-F 8am-4pm, Sa 8:30am-noon.

Laundromat: Wash n' Post, C. 2 #100 (☎863-1995), in Villa Marina Shopping Center. Wash $1.50; dry $0.25 per 5min. Change available. Also has **Western Union,** FedEx, and UPS service. Open M-Sa 8am-8pm, Su 10am-5pm. MC/V.

Supermarkets: Grande (☎863-3420), on Hwy. 3, just east of the intersection with Rte. 195. Open M-Sa 8am-10pm, Su 11am-5pm. AmEx/MC/V.

NORTHEAST

Police: ☎863-2020 or 863-2042. Across from the *público* station. Open 24hr.

Hospital: Hospital San Pablo del Este (☎863-0505), on Rte. 194 just off Ave. Conquistador. The largest hospital in eastern Puerto Rico. 24hr. emergency room.

Internet Access: Pizz@ Net (☎860-4230), in Villa Marina. Internet $3 for 30min., $5 per hr. Small pizza $4-7. Open daily 11am-11pm. MC/V.

Post Office: In Puerto Real, C. Unión 477 (☎863-1827). General Delivery available. Open M-F 8am-4:30pm, Sa 8am-noon.

Zip Code: In Central Fajardo: 00738. In Puerto Real: 00740.

ACCOMMODATIONS & CAMPING

Fajardo has several budget-friendly options, but they vary greatly in terms of quality. Spending a few extra dollars here can result in a huge jump in room quality.

Ceiba Country Inn, Rte. 977 Km 1.2 (☎885-0471; prinn@juno.com), 5 mi. from Fajardo in Ceiba. On a clear day you can see St. Thomas from this quiet mountain lodge. The patio/library is a great place to curl up with a book or grill some fresh seafood. Sparkling rooms include phone, A/C, and fridge. Continental breakfast included. Singles $60; doubles $69; triples $74; quads $78. 9% tax not included. AmEx/D/MC/V. ❸

Anchor's Inn, Rte. 987 Km 2.6 (☎863-7200; frenchman@libertypr.net). Providing a happy medium between the rustic guest houses and the expensive hotels, this nautically themed inn offers rooms with clean bathrooms, comfy beds, cable TV, and A/C at reasonable prices. The reception is at the back of the lively restaurant. 1 queen bed $61; 2 queens $72; 3 queens $95. Tax included. AmEx/MC/V. ❸

Fajardo Inn, Parcelas Beltrán 52 (☎860-6000; fax 860-5063; www.fajardoinn.com), off Rte. 195; look for signs pointing uphill to the Inn. This beautiful *parador* is the place to stay if you plan to spend extensive time in the city. Spotless pool. A/C and cable TV. Doubles $90-125; extra person $10. 9% tax not included. AmEx/MC/V. ❹ On the same property, the inn also manages the **Scenic Inn,** which has smaller rooms and lacks the splendour of the Fajardo Inn. Doubles $66; extra person $10. 9% tax not included. ❸

Puerto Real Guest House, C. Cometa 476 (☎863-0018). Homey is an understatement for this small guest house—the lobby is actually someone's living room. The front desk is rarely attended. Sleek black furniture is reminiscent of Las Vegas. Cable TV and small fridge. 1 double bed $40; 2 double beds $60. Tax included. Cash only. ❷

Hotel La Familia, Rte. 987 Km 4.1 (☎863-1193; fax 860-5345; www.hotellafamilia.com). One step up on the budget hotel food chain, La Familia exudes an aura of professionalism not found elsewhere on Rte. 987. Polished rooms surround a clean above-ground pool with views of the El Conquistador golf course. A/C and cable TV. Check-in 3pm. Check-out 11am. Doubles M-Th $78, F-Sa $86; extra person $11. Up to 2 children under 12 free. Tax included. AmEx/D/DC/MC/V. ❸

Balneario Seven Seas (☎863-8180), off Rte. 987 (see **Beaches,** p. 256) has an RV park and a large field for tents. The beach and the tent area are close together, so be prepared for neighboring beachgoers during the day. Call ahead. $10 per tent. ❶

FOOD

Fajardo has good seafood restaurants in Las Croabas and along Rte. 978, but they are expensive. Apart from that, don't expect anything memorable.

Rosa's Seafood, C. Tablazo 536 (☎809-863-0213), near Puerto Real. Widely acknowledged as the best seafood restaurant in Puerto Real, Rosa's seems like an oasis of class. Enjoy fresh seafood on white tableclothes in this big, 2-story house. Entrees $14-25. Open Th-Tu 11am-10pm. AmEx/MC/V. ❹

NORTHEAST

Lolita's, Hwy. 3 Km 41.3 (☎889-0250), is technically in Luquillo, but it's closer to Fajardo and an excellent change from endless seafood. The popular Mexican restaurant serves up all the favorites, from tacos to enchiladas to fajitas. Come early to grab one of the attractive tiled tables by the window. Entrees $6-15. Margaritas $5-6. Open Su-M and W-Th 11am-10pm, F-Sa 11am-midnight. AmEx/MC/V. ❸

Golden Bagel Bakery, C. Unión 171 (☎860-8987), is a little out of place in Fajardo. The cheerful, modern interior provides one of the nicest places in the city to enjoy a casual lunch. Even the food seems more east coast US than east coast Puerto Rico, with a variety of bagels, sandwiches served on several types of rolls, and specialties such as tomato quiche. Entrees $2-7. Open M-Sa 6:30am-6pm, Su 7:30am-1pm. Cash only. ❶

Restaurant La Conquista, Rte. 987 Km 4.8 (☎863-3722), a short walk up from the beach. This is one of the best seafood restaurants along Rte. 987, and the refreshing A/C feels great on a hot day. As usual, quality seafood is not cheap, but the lunch special ($5-6) is a great deal. Entrees $12-25. Open daily 11am-midnight. AmEx/MC/V. ❹

Friends Restaurant, C. Muñoz Rivera 203 (☎860-0497), is unexceptional, except for the fact that it serves Arabic food and always has a vegetarian entree. Veggie burger $4. Daily combos $4-5. Open M-F 7:30am-2pm. MC/V. ❶

🟠 SIGHTS

LAS CABEZAS DE SAN JUAN NATURE RESERVE. This 316-acre nature reserve is by far the most interesting land attraction in Fajardo. The reserve contains **seven different ecological zones**—coral reef, Thalassia bed, sandy beach, rocky beach, mangrove forest, lagoon, and dry forest—in addition to over 40 species of fish, 84 species of birds, and several species of mammals. Most visitors will at the very least see tiny fiddler crabs, huge iguanas, and countless termites. Although Hurricanes Hugo (1989) and George (1998) destroyed over 80% of the reserve, it has recovered quickly and seems to be thriving again.

The privately run Conservation Trust of Puerto Rico maintains the reserve and offers 2hr. guided tours that pass all seven ecosystems, including a tram ride through the dry forest, a leisurely 30min. stroll along a wooden boardwalk over the mangroves, a stop at a rocky point overlooking the ocean, and a visit to the small lighthouse museum. Upstairs the **lighthouse** affords great views of La Cordillera, Culebra, and St. Thomas. The only other way to see the reserve is by taking a **kayak trip** through the bioluminescent bay that occupies over 100 acres of the park. The Conservation Trust does not offer kayak tours; for more information see **Kayaking,** p. 258. *(Off Rte. 987 just past Seven Seas beach (see p. 256). M-F ☎722-5882, Sa-Su ☎860-2560.* **Reservations required**—*call at least a week in advance. Tours W-Su Spanish 9:30, 10, 10:30am, 2pm; English 2pm. $7, ages 5-11 and over 65 $4. AmEx/MC/V; $25 min.)*

BAHÍA DE LAS CROABAS. Unlike the rest of Fajardo, Las Croabas bay has not been commercialized. Here local fishermen still head out every morning to catch the sea creatures that fuel the restaurants along Rte. 987. All of the action takes place in the morning, but in the afternoon the bay becomes a serene place to walk along the boardwalk or relax at one of the seafood restaurants. If you come early, it may be possible to negotiate with one of the fishermen for an inexpensive trip to the islands. Freddy and Raymundo have been known to take visitors sailing on old-fashioned wooden boats for as little as $100 per boat per day. *(At the end of Rte. 987. Públicos from central Fajardo (5min.) cost $0.65-0.75.)*

🟠 BEACHES

BALNEARIO SEVEN SEAS. On a sunny day Fajardo's public beach glistens as one of the best on the mainland, and the water really does look like it has seven different colors. However, when the climate is less cooperative, Seven

Seas looks dreary and the pine needles and trash become much more obvious. There is good **snorkeling** on the far right side of the beach. *(Rte. 987 Km 5. ☎863-8180. Lifeguards daily 9am-5pm. Parking $3. Open 24hr.)*

WATER SPORTS

The land is fine and dandy, but most visitors to Fajardo head straight toward the sea and the archipelago that extends from the eastern tip of Puerto Rico to the Spanish Virgin Islands. These beautiful tropical islands, and their surrounding coral reefs, provide opportunities for snorkeling, diving, fishing, swimming, or just relaxing. The most popular islands are Cayo Icacos, Cayo Lobos, and Isla Palominos, although the latter is owned by the Wyndham Resort and theoretically closed to outside visitors. Charters usually have their own favorite spots and they will take you wherever the weather looks good and the crowds are relatively small.

BOATING
Fajardo has two enormous marinas, Villa Marina and Puerto del Rey (about 5 mi. to the south). Many of the boats anchored here offer charter expeditions to La Cordillera with snorkeling, swimming, and sunbathing. Some boats are listed below; check a recent issue of *Que Pasa* (see p. 78) for the most current offerings. Most boat owners operate out of their homes—call in advance to make a reservation.

Caribbean School of Aquatics (☎728-6606 or 383-5700). Captain Greg Korwek offers snorkeling trips on the Fun Cat (includes all supplies, lunch, and transportation from San Juan; $79) and diving trips on the Island Safari (includes 2 dives, transportation from San Juan, and picnic lunch ;$135). Prices lower with cash payment in advance of if you provide your own transportation. AmEx/D/MC/V.

Club Naútico (☎413-1147), in Villa Marina, rents 22' power boats ($300 per day, with captain $400). Drivers must have 2 years experience. Call ahead. MC/V.

Erin Go Bragh (☎860-4401; www.egbc.net), a 50' sailboat in Puerto del Rey, travels to the 2 islands. Trips include BBQ lunch, snacks, open bar, and snorkel gear. 6 person max., 2 person min. Trips (10am-4:30pm) $75 per person. Sunset cruises $55, 4 person min. Dinner cruises $75. Also offers overnight charters to Vieques and Culebra ($250 for the first 2 days, $175 for each additional day).

Getaway (☎860-7327), a 32' catamaran in Villa Marina. Trips (10am-3:30pm) include soda, lunch, and a piña colada for $55. Sunset cruise $45.

Traveler (☎863-2821; www.fajardotourspr.com) a 50' catamaran (with a waterslide) operating out of Villa Marina. Trips (10am-3:30pm) include snorkeling equipment, lunch, and an all-you-can-eat salad bar. $55, ages 5-12 $35. Also offers a sunset cruise.

Ventajero 3 (☎645-9129; www.sailpuertorico.com), a 43' sailboat docked at Puerto del Rey, holds up to 6 people. Trips (7am-5pm) include beer, snorkeling equipment, and a full Puerto Rican lunch. 4 person min. $85 per person. MC/V.

DIVING

Puerto Rico Diver Supply, A-E6 Santa Isidra III (☎863-4300; www.prdiversupply.com), in front of Villa Marina, sends their 36' boat that does regular expeditions to La Cordillera (2-tank dive $75, 1-tank dive $50, snorkeling $50) and the Spanish Virgin Islands (2-tank dive $95). All equipment included. PADI certification course $175 for large groups, $350 for small groups. Open daily 8am-5pm. AmEx/D/MC/V.

Sea Ventures Pro-Dive Center (☎863-3483; www.divepuertorico.com), at Puerto del Rey, goes to Palomino (M-Sa; 2-tank dive $80) and the Spanish Virgin Islands (Su; 2-tank dive $95, snorkeling $60). Discover Scuba package $150. Transportation from San Juan $20 per person. 1-week PADI certification course $290-350. Open daily 8:30am-6pm. AmEx/D/MC/V.

NORTHEAST

SWIMMING THROUGH THE STARS If there is one thing that every visitor to Puerto Rico should experience, it is kayaking on, swimming through, or boating across a **bioluminescent bay.** In a bioluminescent bay tiny single-celled organisms called dinoflagellates light up like stars as a defense mechanism to warn away predators. The result is that whenever anything moves the water (human being, kayak paddle, boat), it glows. No special effects, no funky nuclear pollution. This all-natural light show only occurs in about seven places around the world (the number varies according to different reports), but Puerto Rico is lucky enough to have three bioluminescent bays (also called phosphorescent bays). The brightest is Mosquito Bay, in **Vieques** (see p. 292), which has possibly the best bioluminescence in the world. **Fajardo's** Laguna Grande (see **Kayaking**, p. 258) is almost as good, and much more accessible. **La Parguera's** bay (see **Boating**, p. 212) is the cheapest place to see bioluminescence, but it has been severely damaged by pollution. Most bays offer both large boat trips and kayaking expeditions. With kayaking you are close to the water and easily able to swim. However, you also (obviously) have to paddle, so travelers who tire easily may want to consider a boat tour. You can only see bioluminescence at night, and the light appears even brighter when the moon is small or non-existent.

Bioluminscence is a delicate phenomenon that only occurs under a few specific conditions. All of Puerto Rico's bio bays are surrounded by **mangroves,** which leave deposits of vitamin B-12, a common nutrient for dinoflagellates. However, this only works in a shallow bay with a narrow outlet to the ocean, or else all of the nutrients will wash out to sea. Furthermore, any minor pollutant can severely damage the delicate ecosystem (as in La Parguera, and many other bio bays throughout the world). A couple of organizations in Vieques work to preserve and protect the bays (see p. 290), but they are still threatened by development and increasing pollution. Visiting a bioluminescent bay is a win-win situation; ecotourism is one of the few ways to protect these bays, and swimming through glowing water is one of Puerto Rico's most amazing experiences.

KAYAKING
Fajardo has one of Puerto Rico's most amazing **bioluminescent bays** (see **Swimming Through The Stars,** above). All tours are done through private companies.

Yókahu Kayak (☎604-7375). 1½-2hr. Tours $35 per person. AmEx/MC/V.

Eco Action Tours (☎791-7509 or 640-7385), takes kayaks ($40 per person) and motorboats ($20 per person) into the bioluminescent bay. Large snack at the end. Transportation from San Juan available. MC/V.

FESTIVALS
Every January, Puerto del Rey hosts the Caribbean's largest in-water **boat exhibition,** with local music and an incredible display of boats. For more information or exact dates, call ☎860-1000 ext. 4232 or 4214.

NIGHTLIFE
Despite its size, Fajardo has no real nightlife scene. A few restaurants along Rte. 987 double as bars and stay open late on weekend nights. **Racar Seafood,** Rte. 987 Km 6.7, next to Las Croabas, has live music from 7pm to midnight on Saturday nights (beer $1.50-2). For a more lively scene, head to the surprisingly active **Marina Liquor Store,** in Villa Marina. A motley collection of yachters and Puerto

Rican men gather at this liquor/convenience/cigar store to sit at outdoor tables and drink their purchases. Come on Friday night for live Latin music. (☎ 860-8112. Beers $1 and up; mixed drinks $2-4. Open daily 8am-last person leaves.)

NAGUABO

Life passes a little bit slower in Naguabo. The tourist trail screeches to a halt in Fajardo. and farther south, residents sit on their porches watching the traffic go by. The town itself has no real attractions, but the vistas from Playa Naguabo, trips to the mystical monkey island, and several attractive accommodations in the nearby mountains make this sleepy little town a good place to relax.

Naguabo is located just off Hwy. 53, along Rte. 31. From Rte. 31, turn down C. Gazot, across from the post office, to reach the town plaza. C. Muñoz Rivera runs perpendicular to C. Gazot along the plaza; C. Goyco is on the other side of the plaza. **Públicos** leave from the terminal next to the plaza across C. Gazot for: **Fajardo** (20min., $1.65); **Humacao** (20min., $1.40); and **Playa Naguabo** (15min., $0.70). **Banco Popular,** C. Gazot 19, on the plaza, has an ATM in back. (☎ 874-2880. Open M-F 8am-4pm, Sa 8:30am-noon.) **Econo,** on Rte. 31 across the street from the post office, sells groceries. (☎ 874-3720. Open M-Th 7am-8pm, F-Sa 7am-9pm, Su 11am-5pm. MC/V.) To reach the **police station** from Rte. 31, head down C. Gazot, turn right on C. Muñoz Rivera, and continue three blocks to the end of the street. (☎ 874-2020. Open 24hr.) The **hospital,** Rte. 31 Km 4, just west of the city at the intersection with Rte. 192, has a 24hr. emergency room. (☎ 874-2837, emergency room ☎ 874-3152. Open M-F 7:30am-4pm.) The **post office,** Rte. 31 #100, lies across from C. Gazot. (☎ 874-3115. Open M-F 8am-4:30pm, Sa 8am-noon.) **Zip Code:** 00718.

For many, ◪**Casa Cubuy Ecolodge ❸** is the only reason to venture out to Naguabo. This American-run B&B perches on the edge of Rte. 191, 1500 ft. above sea level in the middle of El Yunque. With a small library, trails surrounding the property, and spectacular forest views from every room, the tranquil lodge is the ideal spot to get away from it all. Beautiful rooms are tastefully decorated with wooden furniture and comfy mattresses. (From Naguabo, go west on Rte. 31, then turn right on Rte. 191 and head all the way up to the end of the road; about 20min. ☎ 874-6221; www.casacubuy.com. No phones or TVs. Dinner $20. Doubles $80-100; extra person $25. 9% tax not included. AmEx/MC/V.) **Phillips Forest Cabins ❷**, Rte. 191 Km 24.2, actually has just one operating cabin about ¼ mi. off the road, deep in the forest, with cold water and a double bed. A small house is slightly more refined with a queen-sized bed and hot water. (☎ 874-2138; www.rainforestsafari.com. Cabin $35 for the 1st night, $25 for each additional night; extra cot $5. House $35; extra person $15.) The best restaurants serve fresh seafood in Playa Naguabo or Punta Santiago. Within city limits, busy **Joe's Pizza Place ❶**, C. Muñoz Rivera, on the plaza, offers big slices of mouth-watering pizza. (☎ 874-1519. Large pizza $9-15. Open daily 8am-midnight. Cash only.)

DAYTRIPS FROM NAGUABO

PLAYA NAGUABO

Public Transportation: A público runs from Naguabo to the beach ($0.50). Públicos between Humacao and Fajardo also stop at Playa Naguabo ($2 to either city). Driving: From Hwy. 53, take Exit 18 onto Rte. 31. Turn left, then go south on Hwy. 3 to Playa Naguabo (Km 66).

The serene bay at Playa Naguabo provides a terrific setting to escape the hustle and bustle of life for a few hours. Technically called **Playa Húcares,** this bay doesn't have a beach, but an attractive boardwalk overlooks the water, Cayo Santiago, and in the distance, Vieques. At the southern end of the bay, two large

HE LOCAL STORY

RANK LOPEZ, MASTER CAPTAIN

Frank Lopez has been running trips o Cayo Santiago, or "Monkey sland" for the last six years. On a rip back to Naguabo he shared his ove for the area with Let's Go.

_G: Why do you go to Monkey sland?

A: Those monkeys have been there ever since 1938 and I was born right across the way from this island. I knew about the project ever since hey started. At the beginning there used to be a couple that used to stay on the island—a Russian couple— hose were the ones that started out. This is such a marvelous place in the Caribbean Sea. And it helps out as ar as the research, for the science.

_G: Have you seen any big storms?

A: Well, I've seen Hugo, Frederico, David, George, just about every one of hem. They usually come through the eastern part of the island, so they come right through here. But after a certain number of years, you start getting ready for the first one, then the next year if you get another one, you start building up your supplies for the hurricane, so it gets better. This is such a beautiful place. You can see El Yunque, the rain forest. And there's Monkey Island—this is unique in the western hemisphere.

_G: Do you see other animals?

A: Oh yes. We see the dolphins. We see manatee. This is an outstanding place. And the water is so warm. In December, right before Christmas, we can still snorkel in the islands. I guess you an't do that in Canada.

pink turn-of-the-century houses, both registered on the list of National Historic Sights, provide an interesting lesson in development. One house has been kept up and is now the most attractive residence in the area. The other, **El Castillo Villa del Mar,** was built at the same time by the same person, but it has fallen into such a state of decay that it now looks like fodder for a horror movie. Playa Naguabo has several similar restaurants with a good view and equally good food. Locals like the $4 lunch special at **Restaurante Vinny ❶,** at the northern end of the beach. (☎874-7664. Beer $1.25-2. Open daily 8am-10pm. MC/V.) If you're looking for something a bit classier, the air conditioned **Restaurante Griselle Seafood ❸,** at the bend in Hwy. 3, serves live lobsters right out of the tank for $20-23. (☎874-1533. Entrees $7-23. Open Su-Tu and Th 11am-8pm, F-Sa 11am-midnight. AmEx/MC/V.)

CAYO SANTIAGO

*The island is only accessible via private tour. Contact **Frank Lopez** (see below) or **Tortuga Kayak** in San Juan (see p. 96).*

A cross between Jurassic Park and Gilligan's Island, Cayo Santiago is one of the most truly unique attractions in Puerto Rico. In 1938 the University of Puerto Rico and Columbia University in New York City teamed up to create a new research area—they took 500 Indian rhesus monkeys, isolated them on Cayo Santiago, and **Monkey Island** was born. The monkeys thrived in their new environment and today over 1200 primates frolic on the tropical shores. Only scientists and researchers are allowed on the island, but visitors can take a boat close to the island and watch the monkeys from afar. An abandoned 1944 boat wreck just off the shore makes this a great place for snorkeling, and unlike other islands near Fajardo, Cayo Santiago is usually isolated. Amiable Captain Frank Lopez leads 3hr. excursions from Playa Naguabo to Monkey Island on his boat, **La Paseadora.** For only $25 per person, Lopez offers the opportunity to fish, kayak, snorkel, and swim. This is a very different experience than the Fajardo boat trips— come with expectations of a friendly face, lively music, and personal attention, and you'll have a great time. (Look for Lopez's boat at the northern end of Playa Naguabo on Sa-Su, or call ahead ☎316-0441 or 850-7881. Limited equipment provided. Cash only.)

LA RUTA PANORÁMICA

A vast majority of visitors to Puerto Rico come for the beaches and leave knowing only the beaches, painfully unaware of the amazing topography on the island's interior. But you cannot really know the island without experiencing the central mountains. Puerto Rico's *jíbaro*, a mythical countryman and popular folklore character, specifically comes from the central mountains—it is this incredible area that serves as the heartland of the island, both geographically and culturally. The best way to see this area is by undertaking the windy, multi-day journey along La Ruta Panorámica (The Panoramic Route). For over 100 miles this series of roads twists through the forest, cresting peaks, descending into valleys, and crossing some of Puerto Rico's prettiest countryside. Driving through a tunnel of flowering flamboyán trees overlooking acres of lush farmland may not be the typical Puerto Rican experience, but it is undeniably one of the most awe-inspiring.

Despite its splendor, the Ruta Panorámica is far from perfect. Trash, including an incomprehensibly large number of abandoned cars, litters many roads. Many mountain towns still suffer from traffic jams. Perhaps most importantly, this is no calm drive through the woods. Roads range from narrow to miniscule, and Puerto Ricans feel no need to slow down. Go slow and honk your horn around blind curves. If you have concerns about your car, get it checked by a mechanic before heading to the mountains. Bring a cell phone, even though you will not get service along most of the route. Finally, never drive on the Ruta Panorámica at night or during a rainstorm. For those who can master the roads and accept the faults, a drive through Puerto Rico's mountains is an incomparable experience. Many knowledgeable travelers vacation exclusively in the mountains, where welcoming inns and well-equipped campgrounds provide an ideal base from which to explore the surrounding attractions. This is also one of the few areas on the island where you can go miles without seeing a fast food restaurant, the stars are actually visible at night, and locals may actually respond to you in Spanish, not English. As the home of the *jíbaro* and the last home of the Taínos, the central mountains hold the roots of Puerto Rican culture—do not miss the true heart of the island.

HIGHLIGHTS OF LA RUTA PANORÁMICA

DESCEND into the depths of the Cañón de San Cristóbal near Aibonito (see p. 265).

ASCEND the island's highest peak at Reserva Forestal Toro Negro (see p. 269).

UNCOVER the secrets of Taíno culture amidst the numerous *batey* fields at Utuado's Parque Indigena Caguana (see p. 275).

JUST DO IT! Drive. The whole route or one section, but the true highlight of La Ruta Panorámica is not a destination but the journey itself.

BOSQUE ESTATAL DE CARITE

Carite's proximity to the capital makes it one of the most frequently visited nature reserves on the island. During summer months hundreds of *sanjuaneros* trek over the hills to picnic in the humid subtropical forest or feast on the tasty *lechon* (roast pig) at one of the area's famous *lechoneras* (see p. 21). However, the reserve's location also has its downfalls; in 1998 Hurricane George bulldozed the area, destroying most of the trails and severely damaging the infrastructure. Due to the typical lack of funding, many of the trails remain in disrepair and don't look to be usable any time soon. Still, one gorgeous, albeit short path leading to a small pool provides a nice break from the road. From September to May the reserve sees few visitors and makes an excellent place to camp on the way across the island

TRANSPORTATION

The only way to reach Bosque Estatal Carite is by car. The most picturesque means of entering the forest is the Ruta Panorámica. If you're driving from San Juan take Hwy. 52 south to Exit 32, then hop on Rte. 184. From Ponce, head north on Hwy. 52, then exit at Cayey and take Rte. 1 to the intersection with Rte. 184.

AT A GLANCE	
AREA: 6680 acres.	**GATEWAYS:** Cayey, San Juan (see p. 88).
CLIMATE: Humid and cool. Average temp. 72°F. Dry months Jan.-Mar.; wet May-Oct.	**CAMPING:** The park has camping areas at Charco Azul and Guavate. Campers must obtain a DRN permit ($4) in advance (see p. 58).
HIGHLIGHTS: Charco Azul area.	
FEATURES: Wading in streams, dining on *lechón*, driving through lush forest.	**FEES:** None

ORIENTATION AND PRACTICAL INFORMATION

Rte. 184 runs directly through the forest and contains most of the park's sights. The DRN office is located in the northwest corner of the park near Cayey. To reach the popular Charco Azul recreation area, follow Rte. 184 southeast to Km 15.9. Rte. 179 leads the Ruta Panorámica out of the forest toward Lago Carite, which is located near a separate section of forest southwest of the main reserve.

Visitors Center: The **DRN** office, Rte. 184 Km 27.5 (☎ 747-4545 or 747-4510), at the northwest corner of the park. Open M-F 7am-3:30pm.

Hours: Charco Azul Recreation Area open daily 9am-6pm. **Guavate Recreation Area** open M-F 9am-4:30pm, Sa-Su 8am-5pm.

Supplies: All visitors should bring mosquito repellent, bottled water, and any food they may want. There are no supplies in the park.

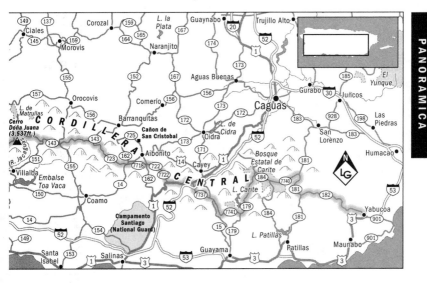

ACCOMMODATIONS & CAMPING

The unique lodging options in and around Bosque Estatal Carite are designed as a destination, not as a place to crash for the night.

Jájome Terrace, Rte. 15 Km 18.6 (☎738-4016), just after Rte. 741, near the town of Cayey. This gorgeous mountain retreat was destroyed by Hurricane George and reopened with a bang in 2002 by inviting the entire Miss Universe pageant up for dinner. All of the 10 beautiful rooms have views of the mountains, the town of Salinas, and on a clear day, the Caribbean Sea. There are no TVs and no phones, just ample room for relaxation. Larger rooms upstairs have private balconies with wicker furniture. Beautiful restaurant open W-Th 11am-8pm, F-Sa 11am-10pm, Su 11am-9pm. Doubles $90; quads $125. Tax included. AmEx/MC/V. ❸

Las Casas de la Selva, Rte. 184 Km 17.6 (☎839-7318), 1 mi. past Charco Azul. This 1000-acre private reserve opened over 20 years ago in an effort to protect, reforest, and maintain the surrounding forest. They rent out one rustic room with a private bath, a curtain for a door, and a mosquito net over the bed. Campers can set up tents either under a shelter near the lodge or out in the middle of the forest. If you rent a tent you get access to the kitchen and bathroom. An incomparable opportunity to spend the night in the forest. Most guests are volunteers (see p. 83). Guided tours (5 person min.), hiking trails, and meals available. Possible Internet connection. Reservations required or the gate will be closed. Tent space $10; dome tent rental with 2 air mattresses $40. Room with private bath $50. Tax included. Cash only. ❶

Carite Lake Village, Rte. 742 Km 2 (☎763-4003 or 763-4004). From San Juan follow directions to Carite, then take Rte. 184 to Rte. 179 to Rte. 742. The huge Carite Lake Village looks a bit like a Alpine retreat, with over 50 peach-and-white villas surrounding Lago Carite. The large, barren 2-story villas are designed in the style of a *centro vacacional* (see p. 57), with 2 bathrooms, a full kitchen, a living room full of plastic furniture, and 3 bedrooms. Restaurant, basketball court, playground, and boat ramp. Reservations required. Villas Su-Th $75, F-Sa $82. MC/V. ❸

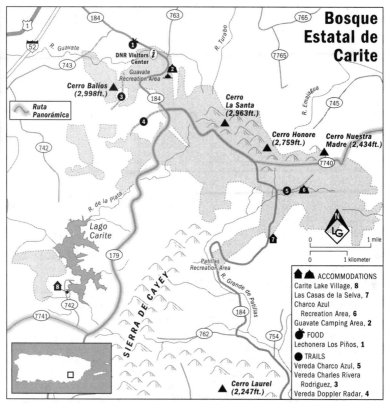

Bosque Estatal de Carite

DNR Visitors Center

Guavate Recreation Area

Cerro Balíos (2,998ft.)

Ruta Panorámica

Cerro La Santa (2,963ft.)

Cerro Honore (2,759ft.)

Cerro Nuestra Madre (2,434ft.)

R. Guavate

R. Turabo

R. Emajagua

R. de la Plata

Lago Carite

Patillas Recreation Area

R. Grande de Patillas

SIERRA DE CAYEY

Cerro Laurel (2,247ft.)

0   1 mile

0   1 kilometer

■▲ ACCOMMODATIONS
Carite Lake Village, **8**
Las Casas de la Selva, **7**
Charco Azul
  Recreation Area, **6**
Guavate Camping Area, **2**
🍴 FOOD
Lechonera Los Piños, **1**
● TRAILS
Vereda Charco Azul, **5**
Vereda Charles Rivera
  Rodriguez, **3**
Vereda Doppler Radar, **4**

Charco Azul Camping Area, Rte. 184 Km 15.9, is the prettier of the two DRN camping areas. The large grassy area next to a stream can get a bit muddy. Facilities include bathrooms, trash cans, and fire pits. Additional campsites at the end of the trail lack bathrooms and plumbing. Reservations and a DRN permit ($4) required (see p. 58). ❶

Guavate Camping Area, Rte. 184 Km 27.2, just south of the visitors center. This hillside camping area is divided into two sections; sites on the top are a slight walk from the parking area, but sites on the bottom can get a bit muddy. The road is visible regardless of where you choose to plant your tent. Better for solo campers or those wanting to be closer to civilization. Bathrooms, covered picnic tables, and an outdoor shower. Reservations and a DRN permit ($4) required (see p. 58). ❶

◗ FOOD

What could make *sanjuaneros* leave their homes days before Christmas and brave rainstorms and potholes to drive halfway across the island? Roast pig, of course. *Lechon,* as it's called in Spanish, is a holiday staple in Puerto Rico and Rte. 184 just north of the visitors center is the best place to get it. Curious visitors can choose from a long row of *lechoneras,* where whole pigs roast in the windows. Most of the open-air cafeterias only open on weekends, but local favorite **Lechonera Los Piños ❶**, Rte. 184 Km 27.7, opens daily. Get a full meal with *lechon,* rice, side, and drink for $5. A pool table and bar in back provide more raucous entertainment after dark. (☎286-1917 or 703-0122. Sa live traditional music 3pm. Su live merengue 2pm. Open daily 6am-8pm, bar open until 10pm. MC/V.)

The DRN maintains several **picnic areas** throughout the park. The best are at **Charco Azul**, across the road from the campground, where a dozen covered picnic tables are spread throughout a large area surrounded by the river. (Facilities include latrines and picnic tables.) The largest picnic area, **Area Recreativa Guavate**, on Rte. 184 about 1 mi. south of the visitors center, has countless picnic tables, although it is not as lush as Charco Azul. (Facilities include fire pits, trash cans, water, and bathrooms.)

🔲 HIKING

Since Hurricane George wiped out many of the longer trails, the DRN has only been able to maintain three short paths. (Inquire at the visitors center to see if El Seis, Doña Jovita, or El Relámpago have been repaired.) Serious hikers should head to **Las Casas de la Selva** (see p. 263) where the managers can provide information about, or guides for, several longer treks, including the harrowing 6hr. journey through the Hero Valley. Only experienced hikers should attempt this trek, as 60 ft. precipices lead down to a boulder-filled river. More subdued (read: sane) hikers can try some of the trails below.

VEREDA CHARCO AZUL. (8min.) The short, paved Charco Azul path follows a creek through some of the most beautiful forest in the reserve before arriving at a little lagoon good for wading. In the summer the path can become overcrowded with vacationing families, but during the winter it's pure bliss.

VEREDA CHARLES RIVERA RODRIGUEZ. (35min.) Named after a boy scout who died on a trip to Isla Mona, the Charles Rivera Rodriguez trail leads up a steep hill near the Guavate Recreation Area. In 2003 the path was extremely muddy and overgrown; check with the visitors center for current conditions. To reach the trailhead, enter the main gate to Guavate Recration Area and continue down the road past the picnic tables.

VEREDA DOPPLER RADAR. (30min.) Desperate for trails after Hurricane George, the DRN put a sign at the beginning of the road up to the Doppler Radar station and called it the newest trail. The mile-long path is still just a road, but cars rarely drive up and there is a great view from the top. Watch out for malicious guard dogs on the way. The clearly marked trailhead is at the intersection of Rte. 184 and Rte. 179. Park in a clearing on the side of the road about 100 ft. up the hill.

AIBONITO

Oh, pretty *(Ay, bonito)*, exclaimed the Spaniard upon seeing this mountain hamlet. Or so the legend goes. More likely the town's name came from a Taíno word, but the Spanish expression is still applicable today. It's no wonder that Aibonito (pop. 28,000) has been the vacation home for many *sanjuaneros*. This is the coldest town on the island, which in Puerto Rico signifies an eternal spring-like temperature, but it's more than a cool breeze that brings visitors over the mountains. Every June the town celebrates the Flower Festival, one of the largest such festivals in the world. Aibonito also serves as the point of origin for hikes into the enormous Cañyón de San Cristóbal.

🚍 TRANSPORTATION. From the Ruta Panorámica turn right on Rte. 722, which leads directly into town. Alternatively (or if you're coming from the west), continue on Rte. 722 and turn north on Rte. 162. From San Juan take Hwy. 52 to Cayey, then take Rte. 1 south to Rte. 7722. **Públicos** (☎735-1375) from Aibonito go to: **Barranquitas** (25min., $2); **Cayey** (30min., $2); and **Coamo** (30min., $2). Supposedly **taxis** (☎735-7144) gather across from the *Alcaldía*, but it might be faster to call.

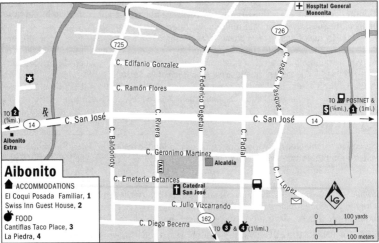

Aibonito

▲ ACCOMMODATIONS
El Coqui Posada Familiar, **1**
Swiss Inn Guest House, **2**

● FOOD
Cantiflas Taco Place, **3**
La Piedra, **4**

ORIENTATION AND PRACTICAL INFORMATION. Almost all streets in Aibonito are clearly labeled by their route number and commonly referred to by their name. The main street, **Route 14 (C. San José)** runs one block north of the plaza and is usually clogged with traffic. From the Ruta Panorámica, Rte. 162 goes directly into the city center, passes the plaza, then intersects Rte. 14. Rte. 725 and Rte. 726 originate at Rte. 14 then head north into the mountains. Rte. 722 intersects with Rte. 14 just east of the city center. The city center is walkable, but most sights lie outside of town. **Banco Popular** is at the intersection of Rte. 14 and Rte. 722. (☎735-3681 or 735-6191. ATM. Open M-F 8am-4pm, Sa 8:30am-1pm.) For groceries try **Aibonito Extra,** C. San José 96 (Rte. 14 Km 50.3. ☎735-7979. Open M-Sa 7am-9pm, Su 11am-5pm. MC/V.) The **police station** (☎735-2020 or 735-2111), C. San José 53 (Rte. 14 Km 50.2) is open 24hr. Next door **Farmacia Unity**, C. San José 51, sells pharmaceuticals. (☎735-4747 or 735-2241. Open daily 8am-9pm. AmEx/MC/V.) The largest medical center in the area is **Hospital General Mononita,** Rte. 726 Km 0.5. (☎735-8001 or 735-8002. 24hr. emergency room. Open daily 10am-8pm.) Surprisingly Aibonito has public **Internet** service at **PostNet,** C. Mercedita Serrallés 8, off Rte. 14 east of the plaza, across from McDonald's. (☎991-1125. $2 for 15min., $3 for 30min., $5 per hr. Open M-F 8am-5:30pm, Sa 9am-1pm. MC/V.) The **post office,** C. Ignacio Lopez 20, does not have General Delivery. (☎735-4071. Open M-F 8am-4:30pm, Sa 8am-noon.) **Zip Code:** 00705.

ACCOMMODATIONS. Aibonito is one of the few mountain towns that has accommodations options within walking distance of the plaza. If it's chain motel-style sterility you're looking for, try **El Coqui Posada Familiar ❸**, Rte. 722 Km 7.3. All rooms include private bath, cable TV, telephone, kitchenette with microwave, and a balcony overlooking a parking lot. Lamentably, the hotel is located on the second floor of a shopping center. If nobody is at the second-floor reception, ask at the first floor pharmacy. (Check-in 1pm. Check-out 11am. 1 double bed $70; 2 double beds $81. Tax included. AmEx/MC/V.) The highlight of the **Swiss Inn Guest House ❷**, Rte. 14 Km 49.3, ¾ mi. west of the plaza, is the friendly host, who offers discounts for groups, long stays, solo travelers, and generally nice people. The linoleum floors are beginning to show their age, and the thin walls conceal few night sounds, but this is still a great bargain. (☎735-8500. Common fridge, TV, and microwave. Doubles $50, during the Flower Festival $75 for 1 night or $40 per night for the week. 7% tax not included. AmEx/MC/V.)

FOOD. A journey through the mountains can try anyone's patience with *comida criolla*, the only option for miles on end. **Cantiflas Taco Place ❷**, at Rte. 722 and Rte. 162, on the Ruta Panorámica, provides a welcome change. Their specialty is fajitas, but everything on the menu is fast, tasty, and less than $11. (☎738-8870. Sa-Su live merengue, salsa, and ballads 3pm. Open M-W 11am-9:30pm, Th 11am-midnight, F-Sa 11am-1:30am, Su 11am-10pm.) Ask anyone in Aibonito about the best restaurant in town and they'll immediately answer **La Piedra ❹**, Rte. 7718 Km 0.7. Located next to Mirador Piedra Degetau, this restaurant uses only the freshest of ingredients to make its seafood and *comida criolla* entrees. The friendly owner (see **The Bionic Man,** p. 272) also coordinates tours of Cañón de San Cristóbal. (☎735-1034. Entrees $7-25. Su buffet $14. F live harmonica and accordion music 6pm, Su live 1-man-band 2pm. Open W-Th 11am-6pm, F-Sa 11am-10pm, Su 11am-8pm. D/DC/MC/V.)

SIGHTS. The crème de la crème of Aibonito's attractions is the **Cañyón de San Cristóbal,** located on the route to Barranquitas. For years this 5½ mi. canyon, created primarily by the Usabón River, was used as the local garbage dump. Then in the early 1970s a group of local citizens protested the destruction of such a treasure and in 1974 the Association of Environmental Control ordered that the canyon be protected. Later the private **Conservation Trust of Puerto Rico** acquired control of the canyon, and ever since they have been reforesting the area and using it for research purposes. Apart from the sheer depth, the canyon also boasts impressive waterfalls, several ecological zones, and about 50% of the species endemic to Puerto Rico. The best way to experience the canyon is by hiking into the basin. However, locals strongly recommend that **nobody should attempt the descent into the canyon without a guide,** as several visitors have been killed hiking into the canyon alone. For information about local guides contact Joe at Las Piedras restaurant (see **Food,** above). At least one trek usually leaves every weekend, unless it rains, in which case it is too dangerous to enter the canyon. (½-day tours $10 per person. All proceeds go to the local Bell Choir.)

Private property surrounds most of the canyon, but non-hikers can still catch a glimpse. From Aibonito take Rte. 725 to approximately Km 5.5, then turn right down any of the roads leading downhill. Tell locals that you're interested in seeing the canyon and most should be able to point out the best viewing spot; some will even let you stand on their roof. If your Spanish is rusty, the best view of the canyon is from the Conservation Trust office in Barranquitas (see p. 269).

Anyone driving along the Ruta Panorámica should take a break to enjoy the **Mirador Piedra Degetau,** Rte. 7718 Km 0.7. It's just a big look-out tower with great views of the island, but the government has added enough infrastructure and hype to turn some rocks into a major tourist site. On a clear day you can see San Juan, El Yunque, the Caribbean, and the Atlantic. (Covered picnic tables and bathrooms. Open W-Su 9am-6pm. When M is a public holiday open Th-M 9am-6pm. Free.)

FESTIVALS. Aibonito blossoms during the biggest event of the year, the annual **Festival de las Flores (Flower Festival),** held over the last 10 days of June. Locals display their home-grown flowers, farmers compete for the prizes of best garden and best plant, vendors hawk mountain-style foodstuffs, and musicians perform traditional mountain tunes. (For more info contact the mayor's office, ☎735-8181. Admission $1, under 10 $0.50.)

BARRANQUITAS

Inauspicious Barranquitas has been inspiring greatness for the last century. The town's claim to fame is that it was the birthplace of Luís Muñoz Rivera, politician, journalist, and ostensibly the most important man in island history (see **History,** p. 10). Several sights in the city are dedicated to this luminary, but only the most dedicated historians will find enough of interest to merit the detour. The real attrac-

Barranquitas

♠ ACCOMMODATIONS
Hacienda Margarita, **2**
🍴 FOOD
Café Sandoval's, **1**

tion of Barranquitas is what it has become today—an archetypal mountain town perched on the edge of a steep hill in the middle of the forest. With 25,600 residents, Barranquitas is smaller than Aibonito but large enough to have attractions, character, and, of course, traffic. This makes a nice stop off the Ruta Panorámica, but be careful or the small town charm might just entice you to stay longer.

⌗ TRANSPORTATION. From the west continue on Rte. 143 after it leaves the Ruta Panorámica then turn left on Rte. 162. Coming from Aibonito skip the Ruta Panorámica altogether and take Rte. 14 to Rte. 162. Alternatively, coming from the east on the Ruta Panorámica, turn right on Rte. 143, then take a left onto Rte. 162, which leads into town. **Taxis** (☎857-0508) and the occasional **público** congregate around the plaza, especially in front of the *Alcaldía*, but there is no regular public transportation to surrounding towns. A taxi to Aibonito, which has regular *públicos*, costs about $15.

🔲🔳 ORIENTATION AND PRACTICAL INFORMATION. Coming into town Rte. 162 becomes **Calle Muñoz Rivera,** the main street, which passes the *Alcaldía* and the plaza before intersecting Rte. 156, which leads east. The town is easy to navigate even though streets are poorly marked and locals don't know many of the street names (except, incidentally, C. Muñoz Rivera). Remember that going downhill will always lead east. Continue east along Rte. 156 to find a large supermarket, fast food, and suburbs. **Casa Museo Joaquín de Rojas,** on C. Ubaldino Font, behind the church, does double duty as a **tourist office** and a small museum. The English-speaking staff answers questions and distributes maps. (☎857-2065. Open M-F 8am-4:30pm.) **Banco Santander,** Rte. 156 Km 16 (C. Barceló 60), 1½ blocks downhill from the plaza, exchanges AmEx Traveler's Cheques and has an ATM. (☎857-2355. Open M-F 8:30am-4pm.) The **police station,** Ave. Villa Universitaria 2 (☎857-2020 or 857-4400), down the hill at the intersection of Rte. 156 and Rte. 719, is open 24hr. **Farmacia del Pueblo,** C. Muñoz Rivera 27, is next door to the *Alcaldía.* (☎857-3065. Open M-Sa 7:30am-5:30pm. MC/V.) The **Centro de Medicina Primaria de Barranquitas,** Rte. 156 Km 16.4, about ¼ mi. downhill from the police station, is the main hospital. (☎857-5923. Open M-F 6am-4:30pm. Emergency room open 24hr.) Head uphill to find the **post office,** C. Muñoz Rivera 41. (☎857-3020. General Delivery. Open M-F 8am-4:30pm, Sa 8am-2pm.) **Zip Code:** 00794.

🔳🔲 ACCOMMODATIONS AND FOOD. Barranquitas is a small town with few options for eating and sleeping. Even if they had a choice of hotels, savvy travelers would still head to recently renovated ▨**Hacienda Margarita ❸,** in the suburb of Quebrada Grande, about 15min. from town. The peaceful mountain retreat sits on the side of a hill with incredible views of the valley. Rooms vary greatly—some are wood paneled cabins, others are carpeted hotel-style rooms, one has a whirlpool, another has rock walls—but all come with the standard amenities, and all are sparkling clean. (Head east on Rte. 156 past the Shell Station, then turn left on Rte. 152. Drive all the way up the hill, then at Km 1.7, turn right directly before the wooden restaurant. Passing all the driveways, take your first left, then take another left. Continue to the end of the residential road. ☎857-8116. Check-in noon. Check-out noon. Restaurant and pool. Sa-Su live music. 1 double bed $79; 2 double beds $89. Tax included. MC/V.) Locals swear by the inexpensive *cafeterías* surrounding the plaza. The cleanest and most welcoming, **Café Sandoval's ❶**, C. Muñoz Rivera 34 (labeled Cafe Sandwich), serves a variety of lunch foods, from burritos to sandwiches to pizza to ice cream. The latter two options make this a popular after-school destination. (☎857-3475. Entrees $1-6. Breakfast $1-3. Open M-Sa 6:30am-4pm.)

◎ SIGHTS. This is Muñoz Rivera country, and most sights are related to the great man. First stop is the **Mausoleo Familia Muñoz,** on C. El Parque, where Luis Muñoz Rivera, his son Luis Muñoz Marín, and their wives are buried. The quiet courtyard provides a calm place to relax and ponder the Muñoz family greatness. Inside, a small exhibit contains biographical information about both men, as well as an impressive mural depicting Muñoz Rivera's life. If the building is closed, ask someone in the office on the left side of the building to open it. (Open M-F 8am-3:30pm. Free.) For a second helping of Muñoz trivia, head back down C. Muñoz Rivera to the **Casa Museo Luis Muñoz Rivera.** Before he was the town's hero, Luis Muñoz Rivera was born in this small wooden house. The structure has been reconstructed with much of the original furniture, including Muñoz Rivera's 1912 Pierce Arrow. The most interesting item in the house is Muñoz Rivera's book of poetry, which receives little attention in comparison to his political work. (☎857-0230. Open Tu-Sa 8:30am-4:30pm. $1.)

Tours of the immense **Cañón de San Cristóbal** leave from neighboring Aibonito (see p. 267), but the best views are actually found in Barranquitas at the office of the Conservation Trust (Fideicomiso de Conservation). Although the office does not have much information about the canyon or tours, you can stop by to enjoy the vistas. (Head east on Rte. 156, then turn right at Km 17.7. Continue to the end of the street, turn left on Calle A, and drive to the end. The office is on the right after the road becomes a narrow one-lane path. ☎857-3511. Open M-F 1-3:45pm.)

Just outside of Barranquitas another government-constructed viewpoint rivals Mirador Degetau in terms of stellar views and sheer quantities of concrete used. Inaugurated in November 2000, **Mirador Villalba-Orocovis**, Rte. 143 Km 39.3, makes a nice stop for those driving the Ruta Panorámica. The viewpoint has covered picnic tables, bathrooms, a play area, a basketball court, a small restaurant, and of course the panoramic view—on a clear day it is possible to see the Caribbean, the Atlantic, Ponce, Embalse Toa Vaca, and the islands off the southern coast. (☎867-6111. Open W-Su 9am-6pm, when M is a holiday open Th-M 9am-6pm. Free.)

RESERVA FORESTAL TORO NEGRO

Toro Negro is the high point of the island—literally. The reserve contains the peak of Cerro Punta (4930 ft.), the highest mountain in Puerto Rico. But most visitors don't even make it that far west, as this former coffee-producing area offers a number of more accessible attractions within the popular Area Recreativa Doña Juana, including almost 10 short trails, a large swimming area, and acres of sierra palm forest. Of the three largest protected forests in Puerto Rico (the others being El Yunque and Carite), Toro Negro receives the fewest visitors, is the least accessible, and is the most difficult to navigate, making it a rewarding destination for more rugged travelers.

AT A GLANCE

AREA: 6945 acres.

CLIMATE: Cool and moist. Averages 67-75°F. Rainy season Apr.-Dec.

HIGHLIGHTS: Waterfalls, panoramic views, highest mountain in Puerto Rico.

FEATURES: Bathing in cascading waterfalls, summitting Cerro Punta, reveling in views of the distant Caribbean.

GATEWAYS: The Ruta Panorámica, Adjuntas, Ponce (p. 220).

CAMPING: The park has room for 30 tents at Los Viveros camping area. Campers must obtain a DRN permit ($4) in advance (see p. 58).

FEES: $1 to enter Area Recreativa Doña Juana, under 10 free.

TRANSPORTATION

You must drive if you want to visit Reserva Forestal Toro Negro. The most scenic way to enter the park is along the Ruta Panorámica, which runs through the reserve between Barranquitas and Adjuntas. From San Juan take Hwy. 22 to Barceloneta, then take Rte. 140 south past Florida to Rte. 141. Turn left on Rte. 144 which will run into Rte. 143. From Ponce, take Hwy. 23 north then exit onto Rte. 143 and drive east.

ORIENTATION AND PRACTICAL INFORMATION

Almost all sights lie along **Route 143,** which runs directly through the forest as the Ruta Panorámica. The only other important road, **Route 149,** bisects Rte. 143 just west of the Doña Juana recreation area and runs north-south between Manatí and Juana Díaz. Toro Negro is Puerto Rico's most remote reserve. Come prepared, as the nearest town, Barranquitas, is an hour away and doesn't have much to offer.

Visitors Center: The **DRN** office, Rte. 143 Km 32.5 (☎867-3040), west of Area Recreativa Doña Juana, distributes written info and a hand-drawn trail map. Theoretically open daily 8am-4pm. Guards at the park's police office next door can help when nobody is at the DRN office.

Hours: Area Recreativa Doña Juana is open daily 9am-5pm. The pool is only open Apr.-Sept. Sa-Su 9am-5pm.

Supplies: All visitors should bring mosquito repellent, bottled water, and food. There are no supplies in the park and the only "restaurant" open regularly doubles as a gas station.

ACCOMMODATIONS & CAMPING

There are no hotels around Toro Negro, but several locals along Rte. 149 advertise guesthouses. These are usually rustic, two-bedroom cabins with enough room for large families. Most include a kitchen, a bathroom, and several beds, but no sheets or dishes. **Terraza y Gasolinera Divisoria ❷,** at Rte. 143 and Rte. 149 (see **Food,** below), rents a large house about 10min. off Rte. 149. The house has seen better days, and the lack of insulation and tin roof results in cold nights, but there is a large yard and a tiny, rustic pool. (☎847-1073. $75 deposit required for weekend reservations. Su-Th $40 per night, F-Sa $150 for the weekend. MC/V.) The most economical and idyllic accommodation in Toro Negro is a campground. The DRN maintains **Los Viveros camping area ❶,** Rte. 143 Km 32.5, just east of the office down a short paved road. This large field surrounded by Doña Juana Creek has covered picnic tables, fire pits, trash cans, and bathrooms. Several trails start here. You must get a DRN permit ($4) in advance (see p. 58).

FOOD

The best option in Toro Negro is to bring your own food and picnic. Almost all of the rental cabins have kitchens and **Area Recreativa Doña Juana** has an attractive picnic area with fire pits, running water, and 10 covered tables. There are also a

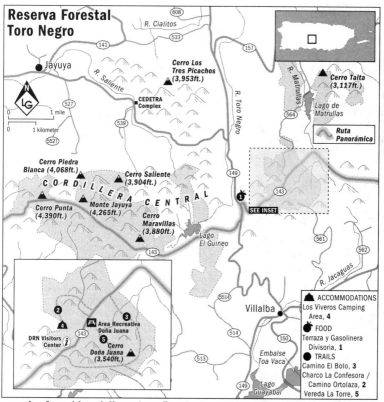

Reserva Forestal Toro Negro

Jayuya

R. Saliente

R. Cialitos

Cerro Los Tres Picachos (3,953ft.)

CEDETRA Complex

Cerro Talta (3,117ft.)

R. Matrullas

Lago de Matrullas

Ruta Panorámica

Cerro Piedra Blanca (4,068ft.)

C O R D I L L E R A

Cerro Saliente (3,904ft.)

C E N T R A L

Cerro Punta (4,390ft.)

Monte Jayuya (4,265ft.)

Cerro Maravillas (3,880ft.)

Lago El Guineo

SEE INSET

Villalba

R. Jacaguas

Area Recreativa Doña Juana

DRN Visitors Center

Cerro Doña Juana (3,540ft.)

Embalse Toa Vaca

Lago Guayabal

ACCOMMODATIONS
Los Viveros Camping Area, 4
FOOD
Terraza y Gasolinera Divisoria, 1
TRAILS
Camino El Bolo, 3
Charco La Confesora / Camino Ortolaza, 2
Vereda La Torre, 5

couple of *comida criolla* options. Despite its name, **Las Cabañas de Doña Juana ❶,** Rte. 143 Km 30.5, is actually a restaurant specializing in charcoal grilled meats. The "cabañas" are covered concrete picnic tables that allow guests to be one with the surrounding mountains. (☎897-3981. Everything on the menu under $6. Open Sa-Su 8am-6pm, summer also open F.) If Las Cabañas is closed, try **Tarraza y Gasolinera Divisoria ❶,** at the intersection of Rte. 143 and Rte. 149. The foods hibernating in glass cases will probably not make your mouth water, but we all have to eat. (☎847-1073. Meals under $5. Open daily 7am-8pm. MC/V.)

🔆 SIGHTS

Stunning waterfalls, panoramic views, and incredible trails seem to pale in comparison to the popularity of **the pool** at Area Recreativa Doña Juana, Rte. 143 Km 33. During the summer months this concrete structure is more popular than a Shakira concert. (Changing rooms, showers, lifeguards, and bathrooms. Open Apr.-Sept. Sa-Su 9am-5pm. $1, under 10 free.) About 20min. down the road, **Doña Juana Waterfall,** Rte. 149 Km 39.5, cascades 120 ft. over a rocky cliff just off the road. This is a great photo spot and one of the most impressive waterfalls on the island.

The western portion of Toro Negro has not been developed for tourism, but that is absolutely no reason to ignore this half of the forest. West of the intersection with Rte. 149, Rte. 143 continues ascending until it follows the ridge of Puerto Rico's tallest peaks. Almost all of the mountains have radio towers, which means that they also have

HE LOCAL STORY

THE BIONIC MAN

oe Esterás, proprietor of La Piedra restaurant and faithful Aibonito resident, is known throughout the island as the voice of WOSO .030AM's Garden Program, broadcast every Saturday at 9am. In his chat with Let's Go he discussed his affection for his hometown and some of the highlights, and pitfalls, of his high-flying restaurant.

.G: How long have you been living in Aibonito?

A: Since June 17, 1967.

.G: What's keeping you here?

A: The weather. Background. My mother's from here.

.G: And what do you do besides unning this restaurant?

A: I'm a farmer. Probably the oldest farmer in town. I have a radio program about gardening. And I do some consultant work about gardening. I used to teach, but now I just do the garden program, he restaurant, and I have half an acre of herbs.

.G: And that's all? (Laughs.) What would you say are the main attractions of Aibonito?

A: Well first is the weather. Aibonito has the lowest average temperature n Puerto Rico; 72 degrees. It has some unusual agriculture. We have he largest flower-growing area in the Caribbean here in Aibonito. We are he biggest chicken raisers on the sland. We have the biggest processing plant on the island. And we also have the egg growing industry. So we have plenty of work.

.G: How would you say the culture is different in the mountains versus in an Juan and the other big cities?

roads leading to the top. Traveling east to west you first past Cerro Maravillas (3880 ft.) at the intersection of Rte. 143 and Rte. 577. Although it is by no means the tallest, this peak is well-known as the site of one of the most influential murders in Puerto Rican history (see **The Watergate of Puerto Rico,** p. 16). Two small white crosses still mark the gravesite. Continue 1 mi. past Maravillas to reach the road up to **Cerro Punta, the tallest mountain in Puerto Rico.** The mountain is distinguishable by the huge gravel area at the base and the steep paved road winding up the side. From the observation platform at the summit you really do feel like you're on top of the world. Go early before the clouds roll in and you'll be rewarded with the best view on the island.

⚑ HIKING

The DRN claims to maintain 10 trails around the Doña Juana area, but many are actually ¼ mi. roads going to the campground or the pool. Some of the longer and more popular trails are listed below; for a complete list, visit the DRN office.

CAMINO EL BOLO. At 2¾ mi., this is the longest trail in Toro Negro, but it's still an easy path accessible to hikers of all abilities. The trail begins across the street from the visitors center; walk through the parking lot and continue on the rocky road leading uphill. After about 15min. you reach a flat grassy path along the ridge of the mountain with great views to the south. When you come to the paved road, turn left to continue along the path. Vereda La Torre crosses this trail and leads uphill to a great viewpoint. El Bolo ends farther east on Rte. 143. It is possible to make a circle by coming back along the road, but given the blind turns and narrow roads, it is safer to return via the same path.

VEREDA LA TORRE. Because the trailhead is located at the Doña Juana Recreation Area, and because it leads up to an observation tower with stellar views, Vereda La Torre is the most frequented trail in Toro Negro. From the picnic tables follow the grass path uphill past valleys full of ferns and palm trees. The 2 mi. trail gets slightly more rugged as you progress, but the path is always easy to follow. After 20min. the trail comes to what looks like an old service road; it is actually Camino El Bolo. Turn left and walk about 5min. past the short stretch of concrete to reach the second half of La Torre, which leads to the observation tower.

CHARCO LA CONFESORA/CAMINO ORTOLAZA.
Two paths lead south from Los Viveros camping area, but the DRN office only acknowledges one of them. From Los Viveros, continue along the paved Charco La Confesora (½ mi.) all the way to the end. When you reach a bridge, turn left and follow the red mud trail

through lush, tropical vegetation and rows of orange trees. Eventually Camino Ortolaza (1 mi.) leads back to Rte. 143, though it's quite a walk back along the road.

JAYUYA

Located at the foothills of Cerro Punta, 45min. off the Ruta Panorámica, this town merits a visit for its collection of Taíno sights, from impressive petroglyphs to a small museum designed as a *cemí*. Jayuya (pop. 15,500) holds an important role in island history as the site of the only true revolution against American control. In 1950 Blanca Ciales and 20 male *nacionalistas* led a minor rebellion that resulted in the independent republic of Jayuya—for three days. Today the town is less distinguished and offers nothing more than a quiet place to spend the night.

TRANSPORTATION. Coming from the Ruta Panorámica, detour north on Rte. 140 between Toro Negro and Adjuntas, then take Rte. 144 straight into town. From San Juan, take Rte. 123/Hwy. 10 to Utuado, then follow Rte. 111 to Rte. 144. **Públicos** in Jayuya leave from the parking lot next to Mueblería Doris between C. Figueros and C. Guillermo, just off the plaza. They head to **Ponce** ($4) and **Utuado** ($2) very early in the morning—ask locals the night before for scheduled times. No public transportation goes to the major sights outside of town.

ORIENTATION AND PRACTICAL INFORMATION. Coming into town Rte. 144 deposits you on C. Figueros, then you will have to veer right onto C. Guillermo. **Calle Guillermo, Calle Figueros, and Calle Barceló,** the three main streets in town, run parallel to each other and the latter two border the plaza. Most of the major sights are on Rte. 144 as it continues west out of town. **Banco Popular,** C. Guillermo Esteves 84, has an ATM. (☎828-4120. Open M-F 8am-4pm.) To reach the **police station,** C. Cementerio 1 (☎828-2020 or 828-3600) from the plaza, walk down C. Barceló, turn right after the *Alcaldía,* and walk uphill. (Open 24hr.) Across the street, the **hospital,** C. Cementerio 2, has a 24hr. emergency room. (☎828-3290 or 828-0905. Open M-F 8am-4:30pm.) The **post office,** C. Barceló 15, has General Delivery. (☎828-3010. Open M-F 7:30am-4:30pm, Sa 7:30am-11:30pm.) **Zip Code:** 00664.

ACCOMMODATIONS AND FOOD. Parador Hacienda Gripiñas ❹, on Rte. 527, was originally a 19th-century coffee plantation and still retains the charm of an old country house, with high-ceilinged rooms and wooden porches overlooking an incredible mountain landscape. Carpeted rooms include modern amenities

A: Well the culture is definitely different because we are what you would call a "family-oriented culture." In a small town nobody goes hungry. A cousin always feeds you. It's a style of living where if somebody needs you in the family you're there. It makes you feel like you're always welcome somewhere.

LG: Do you have any good stories from the restaurant?

A: Well this is probably the only restaurant that has helicopter service so we have people that come up here, like the gentleman who was a boxer, Oscar de la Hoya. Chayanne visited. We never know who's going to come here. We tell them not to tell us. The governess has been here. The helicopter gives us a touch that most people don't have because you can imagine everyone is sitting here eating and the helicopter comes down and the first lady walks in. The last ones who came down were Dayanara Torres and her husband, what's his name?

LG: Marc Anthony?

A: That's right. (Laughter.) Yeah they were here about two days after the wedding. Everyone thought they were on an island somewhere, no they were up here. Have you heard about the hijacking at the prison? At the prison in Ponce two weeks ago. Well they hijacked a helicopter and they took something like five prisoners out of the prison. That is the guy who brought all of the celebrities to our place. So that was one of the sadder occurrences of course. We had another one prior to that who was hijacked as well. So it's some unusual stories we get up here.

such as cable TV and A/C. The hotel provides information about a 4hr. **guided tour to Cerro Punta** on jeep, horse, or foot ($20-40 per person). Room prices include dinner and breakfast at the hotel restaurant. (Take Rte. 144 east to Rte. 527, then continue up the hill for 5min., and turn right at the green sign. ☎828-1717 or 828-1718; www.haciendagripinas.com. 2 swimming pools. Check-out 11am. Singles $93; doubles $63 per person; triples $53 per person; quads $48 per person. 7% tax and $3 daily gratuity not included. AmEx/MC/V.) Those who want to stay in town have one choice—**Hotel Posada Jayuya ❸**, C. Guillermo Esteves 49. The hotel looks a bit rugged from the front, and you must walk through a tunnel to enter from the main street, but the back entrance reveals Posada's modern charm. Textured murals decorate the walls. (☎828-7250. Small pool. Fridge, TV, and A/C. Doubles $69; 1 full bed and 3 twins $100; 2 full beds $125; extra person $10. AmEx/MC/V.)

The restaurant at **Parador Hacienda Gripiñas ❸** is the best in town. This *mesón gastronómico* utilizes its historic setting to create an exceptionally attractive dining experience—try the central room with its glass ceiling and tree in the middle. Entrees include the traditional seafood and steak options. (Entrees $11-19. Open daily 8am-10pm.) Apart from the *parador*, Jayuya is not a good place to be hungry. **Kafeé de la Tierra Alta ❶**, Rte. 144 Km 5.4, a clean, bright cafe on the way out of town, is popular with factory workers who enjoy the outdoor seating. (☎898-9236. Burgers, fried chicken, and *comida criolla* $2-7. Open daily 7:30am-9pm.)

⬛📷 SIGHTS AND FESTIVALS. The only reason to come to Jayuya is to visit the **CEDETRA (Development and Labor Center)** complex, Rte. 144 Km 9.2, which has a variety of Taíno and antique artifacts. Coming up the road, visitors will first notice the odd-shaped **Museo El Cemí.** Constructed in 1989, the structure was designed to look like a *cemí*, a Taíno idol carved in stone. Don't worry if the building just looks like an amorphous blob—there are at least 20 different theories about what the *cemí* was designed to look like. The museum contains Taíno artifacts and replicas, including an *espatula vomita*, a spatula that the Indians used to induce vomiting before they took hallucinogenic drugs. (☎828-0900 ext. 242. or 818-1241. Open M-F 8am-4:30pm, Sa-Su 10am-3pm. Free.) Completely unrelated, but just next door, **Casa Canales** has housed some of Jayuya's most important families. Built in the late 19th century by Don Rosario Canales Quintero, the town's first mayor and one of the founding members, the house has also served as residence for Nemesio Canales Rivera, a legislator who aided in the legal emancipation of women, and Blanca Canales, one of the leaders of the revolution of October 30, 1950. The house was destroyed after the 1950s, but in the early 1990s CEDETRA painstakingly renovated it to its original form. (☎828-4094. Open Sa-Su 10am-5pm. $1, under 12 $0.50.) The nondescript building in back holds the **CEDETRA exhibition hall** and a small *artesanía* souvenir shop. The kiosks across the path theoretically provide a venue for **local artisans** to sell their work, but the kiosks are frequently empty. Finally, near the kiosks, the **Museo de Cafe** is nothing more than a display of coffee-related antiques. Despite the extensive work put into the CEDETRA complex, the most impressive sight lies about 1 mi. down the road. **La Piedra Escrita,** Rte. 144 Km 7.7, is a huge rock in the middle of the creek covered with Taíno petroglyphs. A new wooden ramp leads down to the rock and the surrounding creek, which is a good place to take a dip.

Within the city center yet another cultural center and monument honors the island's Taíno heritage. From the plaza, hike up the steep staircase to reach a bust of the *cacique* Jayuya (Jayuya indian chief). Behind the bust, the small locked building contains the **Puerto Rican Indian tomb,** the bones of a Taíno indian lying on a bed of dirt accumulated from each of the island's 78 municipalities. Unfortunately, the monument is usually locked and difficult to see. Behind the tomb the Puerto Rican Department of Culture maintains a small **cultural center,** C. San Felipe 25, with an assortment of antiques, broken Taíno artifacts, and reproductions. (☎828-2220. Spanish only. Open M-F 8am-noon and 1-4:30pm. Free.)

Jayuya's largest festival is the annual **Festival Nacional Indígena** (National Indigenous Festival), celebrated over 3-5 days in mid-November. The festival focuses on Taíno culture with indigenous dances, *batey* games, and reproductions of an indigenous town. Contact the cultural center (see above) for exact dates. For the sake of sheer novelty, stop by Jayuya's annual **Tomato Festival,** which features local music, *artesanía*, and countless tomato-based dishes. The festival is held in April; contact the *Alcaldía* (☎ 828-0900) for exact dates.

BOSQUE ESTATAL DE GUILARTE

Directly west of Adjuntas, the Ruta Panorámica leads through Bosque Estatal de Guilarte, a protected area composed of seven distinct units of land. Visitors coming from the east first pass Lago Garzas, a popular **fishing** spot. Farther west, the official forest entrance is marked by a patrol unit at the intersection of Rte. 131 and Rte. 518. Drive up the hill across from the office to reach the **DRN office,** which provides information about the forest and nearby **swimming holes.** The **Area Recreativa,** just west of the DRN office on a narrow peak, does not have picnic tables but the observation point at the end provides superb views of the surrounding valley. (☎ 829-5767. Open M-F 7am-3:30pm, Sa-Su 9am-5:30pm.) The only **marked trail** in the forest is a well-marked 30min. dirt path leading up to a mountain summit; the trailhead is about 20 ft. west of the patrol unit on the right-hand side Rte. 131. The highlight of Guilarte is its exceptional **camping area ❶.** Like all DRN camping areas, Guilarte has bathrooms, rustic showers, trash cans, running water, and fire pits; however, this site also has five cabins with two sets of bunkbeds (bring your own bedding) for the same low, low price of $4 per person or $20 per cabin. To stay you here must have a DRN permit and a reservation (see **Camping,** p. 58).

UTUADO

This story starts a long, long time ago on a rocky island known as Boriken. At the time, the island was inhabited only by a peaceful and spiritual group of indigenous people who enjoyed playing ball. Then in 1493 Christopher Columbus landed on the island and dubbed the locals, "Taínos". The following events quickly tumbled to an unpleasant climax—the Spanish settled in, the Taínos fled to the center of the island, and within 150 years disease, slavery, and hostility had completely wiped out the native population. However, in 1915 two American archaeologists rekindled the story when they dug up some Taíno artifacts and a series of rectangular *batey* courts. It was the largest excavation of Taíno ruins on the island, but the neatly arranged rocks remained untouched for almost 50 years. Finally in 1956 the government excavated the

GIVING BACK

GOING GREEN

With a history of intense deforestation, Puerto Rico, one of the most densely populated areas in the world, is not known for its environmental activism. However, one organization in the small town of Adjuntas continues to fight environmental destruction on the island. **Casa Pueblo** (People's House) was created in 1980 when the government announced plans for a huge mineral excavation near Adjuntas that would have converted 37,000 acres of land into immense holes. For 15 years civil engineer Alexis Massol González, head of Casa Pueblo, led the fight against the excavation, and incredibly in 1995 he succeeded. The land was preserved and instead converted into **Bosque del Pueblo,** a protected reserve managed by Casa Pueblo. But Casa Pueblo did not disintegrate with its success—over the last 10 years the organization has worked on developing solar energy, studied the environmental damage on Vieques, and protested new development near Lago Garzas. The private company is funded entirely through the production of its own gourmet coffee, Café Madre Isla. For his incredible success, Massol González received the Goldman Environmental Prize, the Nobel Prize of environmentalism, in April 2002. To learn more about Casa's projects and check out the small museum and butterfly garden, stop by the office. Casa Pueblo also offers guided visits to Bosque del Pueblo for groups of 15 or more. (C. Rodulfo Gonzalez 30, 1½ blocks from the plaza, Adjuntas. ☎ 829-4842. Open daily 8am-4:30pm.)

TAÍNO TERMS 101 To fully understand Puerto Rico's rich Taíno heritage, there are a few common terms that everyone should be familiar with.

Batey: A traditional Taíno ball game that was used as both a sport and a religious rit-
ual. Two teams of 10-30 men try to keep a 3-5 lb. ball made of tree fiber in the air; the
first team to drop the ball loses. Played on a court also called a *batey.*

Bohio: Circular hut made of straw and wood that served as home for Taínos. *Caciques*
(chiefs) lived in rectangular huts.

Cemis: Stone idols shaped like a triangular cone that served as a Taíno object of worship. There are various theories about the design. Some state that it is in the shape of
a mountain; others say that it is a phallic symbol.

land and in 1965 the sight was opened to the public as **Parque Indígena Caguana.** This
is still the largest sight of Taíno ruins on the island, which leads archaeologists to
believe that it once served as some sort of social, religious, or ceremonial center.
Supposedly the Taínos came down the Río Tamaná, then chose to settle in this spot
when they saw that the surrounding mountains had the shape of their idol, the *cemí.*
Radioactive testing dates the ruins back to AD 1200, giving the natives ample time in
this area before Columbus came. The Institute of Culture maintains the site today,
which means that it has much better infrastructure than other Taíno sights, and
friendly workers frequently provide unofficial free guided tours. Even without a tour
it's enjoyable to wander around the picturesque botanical garden and attempt to
identify the petroglyphs in the rocks. A museum at the beginning provides the basics
of Taíno culture. (Rte. 111 Km 12.5, 6 mi. west of Utuado. ☎894-7325. Open daily
8:30am-4pm. $2, ages 6-12 $1, under 6 and over 60 free.)

Tanamá Expeditions, just past Parque Caguana, leads exhilarating hiking/kayaking
expeditions into the Camuy Caves (p. 166) so extreme that good physical health is a
prerequisite for participation. Choose from four different trips ranging from 3½hr. kayaking trips through the 700 ft. Arco Cave ($58) to two-day journeys that include tra-
versing two caves, hiking the Tanamá Trail, and visiting Arecibo Observatory ($195).
The tour includes all equipment (except lunch) and, if you're based far away, **free lodging** (basic rooms or camping space) at the owner's house/office. (Continue past Parque
Caguana to Rte. 111 Km 14.5, then turn left and follow signs to the office. ☎894-7685. 2-
day trips currently do not including camping supplies. Cash only.) For slightly more
subdued adventurers, **Hacienda de'l Lago,** Rte. 612 Km 0.3, across from Casa Grande
(see below), offers 2hr. guided adventure rides over the river and through the woods
on attractive horses. (☎894-0240. 4 person max. 12 and over. $55 per person.)

■☎ **TRANSPORTATION AND PRACTICAL INFORMATION. Públicos** go to
Adjuntas (40min., $2); **Arecibo** (45min., 5 per day, $2); and **Ponce** (2¾hr., $6). The city
center is divided by a river. Rte. 123 enters town on the same side as the plaza and
becomes Ave. Esteves. On the other side of the river, Rte. 111 runs parallel to the
water about two blocks away; several bridges connect the two sides. **Banco Popular,**
C. Doctor Cueto 93, is on the same side of the river as the plaza. (☎894-2700. 24hr.
ATM. Open M-F 8am-4pm.) The **police station,** Centro Gubermental 11, hides behind
the McDonald's near the intersection of Rte. 111 and Rte. 123. (☎894-2020. Open
24hr.) **Walgreen's,** at the intersection of Rte. 111 and Rte. 123, west of town, has an
ATM. (☎894-0100. Open daily 8am-10pm. AmEx/MC/V.) To reach **Hospital General de
Utuado,** on Ave. Isaac González, walk one block from the plaza away from the
church and cross the footbridge; the hospital is behind the parking lot. (☎894-6052.
Open M-F 7am-1pm. 24hr. emergency room.) **Utuado Web,** C. Perez Soto 2, may provide the only Internet service between Aibonito and Mayagüez. (Facing the church
walk 2 blocks past the plaza. ☎814-1621. $3 per hr. Open M-Sa 8am-4:30pm.) The
post office, Ave. Fernando Luis Rivas 41, is on Rte. 111. (☎894-2490. General Delivery. Open M-F 8am-4:30pm, Sa 8am-noon.) **Zip Code:** 00641.

⌐⌐ ACCOMMODATIONS AND FOOD. Former coffee plantation **Casa Grande Mountain Retreat ❹,** Rte. 612 Km 0.3, is one the premier mountain accommodations for wealthy Yankees looking to get away from it all. Located 30min. outside of town, this *parador* has an unbeatable location—cabins perch on the edge of the mountain with incredible views of the lush valley. (From Utuado take Rte. 111 east, turn left on Rte. 140, then turn left on Rte. 612. ☎894-3939, from the US 888-343-2272; fax 894-3900; www.hotelcasagrande.com. Check-in 3pm. Check-out noon. Pool. Yoga daily 8-9:15am $10. Doubles Nov.-Apr. $90-95; May-Oct. $80-85. Extra person $10, 2 children under 12 free. Tax not included. AmEx/D/MC/V.) If you just want a place to crash, look no farther than **Hotel Riverside ❷,** Ave. Fernando Rivas 1, near the intersection of Rte. 111 and Rte. 123. This tiny hotel is on the second floor of a store, and rooms crowd a disproportionate number of beds into a small space, but the price can't be beat. (☎814-0272. TV, fridge, and A/C. Doubles $40; 6-person room $50-60. Cash only.) The folks at **Valle Indigena Area de Acampar ❶,** Rte. 111 Km 14, allow travelers to camp in their large yard overlooking the river. Call ahead or the gate may be closed. (☎894-9434. $10 per tent. Cash only.) To be truly at one with nature, head to **Jungle Jane's Restaurant ❹,** at Casa Grande (see above). This *mesón gastronómico* serves unexceptional *comida criolla* in a truly exceptional setting. Candlelit tables on a balcony overlooking the forest with coquís chirping in the background create one of the most romantic scenes in Puerto Rico. (Entrees $12-25. Open M-F 8-10:30am and 6-9pm, Sa-Su 8-10:30am, noon-4pm, and 6-9pm. AmEx/D/MC/V.) Locals call **La Familia ❷,** Rte. 111 Km 12, the best eatery near Parque Caguana. After pondering the diversions of the Taínos, stop to ponder the varied options (*mofongo,* spaghetti, pizza) at this family restaurant. (☎894-7209. Entrees $4-15. Open M and W-Th 11am-9pm, F-Sa 11am-11pm, Su 1-10pm. MC/V.)

MARICAO

The primary attraction of this tiny mountain town is that it is the best place to rest after the long drive from Adjuntas. As possibly the only town on the main island without any fast food restaurants, it's also a refreshing glimpse at what Puerto Rico used to be. Yes, it sounds boring, but **Los Viveros Fish Hatchery,** Rte. 410 Km 1.7, is one of the most tranquil man-made sights along the Ruta Panorámica. This manicured functioning hatchery raises fish in several large pools to later be distributed in dammed lakes around the island. (From the east, turn right at the sign for Los Viveros and continue to the end of Rte. 410. ☎838-3710. Open Th-Su 8:30am-11:30am and 1-3:30pm. Free.) On the way to Los Viveros you will pass **La Gruta San Juan Bautista,** Rte. 410 Km 0.3, a tiny waterfall with a religious shrine. Maricao's largest festival, the **Fiesta del Café** (Coffee Festival) held in the plaza on the weekend of Washington's birthday in mid-February, includes traditional music, coffee samples, drama shows, *artesanía,* and folkloric dances.

Parador Hacienda Juanita ❹, Rte. 105 Km 23.5, is yet another attractive mountain *parador.* This 19th-century coffee plantation centers on a lush courtyard garden, and the grounds include a swimming pool, a tennis court, and a great restaurant (see below). Unfortunately the entire place feels rundown. (Take Rte. 120 east of town, then turn on Rte. 105. ☎838-2550; fax 838-2551. Cable TV. Singles $101; doubles $131; quads $164. Prices include dinner, breakfast, and tax. AmEx/MC/V.) Guests at Hacienda Juanita should not miss an idyllic meal at **La Casona de Juanita ❸**. Like most *mesones gastronómicos,* this restaurant serves succulent *comida criolla* on a back porch that makes you feel like you're sitting in the middle of the forest. (Entrees $9-18. Wine $20-180. Open Su-Th 8am-7pm, F-Sa 8am-10pm.) Those passing through town can grab a quick bite to eat at **El Buen Café ❶,** on the plaza. This is the type of place where local men congregate to discuss the weather, politics, and the mistakes of the Spanish-American war over a Medalla. There is no written menu, but you shouldn't pay more than $6 for a sandwich or a big plate of *comida criolla.* (☎838-4198. Open M-Sa 7am-10pm. MC/V.)

VIEQUES

When most people think of Vieques, the first thing that comes to mind is the US Navy occupation of the island and the vocal protests by locals. But as of May 1, 2003, the Navy officially left Vieques, closing one chapter of history and leaving *viequenses* with the prize that they had long been fighting for: their beautiful land. Once again, the only sounds heard on most of the island are the chirps of coquís and the crows of roosters—a marked contrast from the recent past, when it was common to hear the sounds of bombs falling less than 10 mi. away. Vieques's tumultuous history had almost made outsiders forget that this island is, to put it simply, incredible. Referred to by many Puerto Ricans as *La Isla Nena* (the little girl island), Vieques is covered with lush tropical forests and surrounded by crystalline seas that rival any in the Caribbean. The entire island feels a bit untamed—palm trees are scattered amidst gnarled jungle vegetation and herds of wild horses wander through the forest as if they own it. On the south coast, the island has been graced with two bioluminescent bays that are among the best in the world. Vieques is far more than a controversial Navy testing ground—it is one of the most beautiful and naturally rich islands in the Caribbean.

With 10,000 people, Vieques is just large enough to contain two small settlements. Isabel II (Isabel Segunda), the largest city, feels like any small Puerto Rican town, complete with a plaza, a busy main strip, and, when the ferry arrives, a bit of traffic congestion. Aside from two decent museums and the ferry terminal, visitors will find little of interest in Isabel II. Most travelers spend their time in Esperanza, a *barrio* on the south side of the island with a sizable US expat population. This primarily residential neighborhood has been invaded by several restaurants and guest houses lining the *malecón* (referred to as "the strip"). Along this quarter mile of land the language of operation is English and you might as well be in the US. Except in the US you can't walk 15min. and arrive at spectacular Sun Bay.

Like any Puerto Rican city, Vieques does have its share of issues. With the Navy gone, the island must figure out how to deal with one of the highest unemployment rates in the US, a budding tourism industry, and the allocation of hundreds of acres of valuable land. Locals have organized non-profit organizations to deal with these issues and to protect the island for future generations. But *viequenses* know that even if the island's future is a bit unsure, they live in paradise; along with Culebra, this is one of the last strongholds of undiscovered Caribbean culture, free of excessive tourism. But come before it's too late, because Vieques may not retain its newfound quiet forever.

HIGHLIGHTS OF VIEQUES

QUESTION LOGIC and watch the water glow as you swim in the world's most vibrant bioluminescent bay (see p. 292).

DO ABSOLUTELY NOTHING but lounge on the white sands of Sun Bay (see p. 291).

BRUSH UP on Vieques's fascinating history at the last Spanish fort in the new world, Fuerte de Conde de Marisol (see p. 289).

▐ INTER-ISLAND TRANSPORTATION

Flights: Aeropuerto Antonio Rivera Rodríguez (☎ 741-8358 or 741-0515), on Rte. 200, may be the most attractive airport in Puerto Rico. The following airlines sell tickets over the phone or at their airport desks. Reserve at least 24hr. in advance, more during high season and holidays. A *público* waiting on Rte. 200 when flights come in will take visitors anywhere on the island (see **Públicos,** below). Open 24hr.

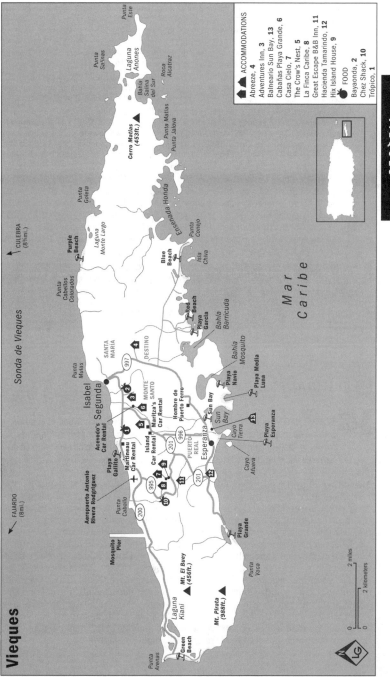

Vieques

VIEQUES

ACCOMMODATIONS

Abreeze, **4**
Adventures Inn, **3**
Balneario Sun Bay, **13**
Cabañas Playa Grande, **6**
Casa Cielo, **7**
The Crow's Nest, **5**
La Finca Caribe, **8**
Great Escape B&B Inn, **11**
Hacienda Tamarindo, **12**
Hix Island House, **9**

● **FOOD**

Bayaonda, **2**
Chez Shack, **10**
Trópico, **1**

Punta Este

Laguna Anones

Punta Salinas

Bahía Salina del Sur

Roca Alcatraz

Bahía Matías

Punta Matías

Punta Jalova

Cerro Matías (453ft.) ▲

Punta Goleta

CULEBRA (8½mi.)

Laguna Monte Largo

Purple Beach

Ensenada Honda

Punta Conejo

Punta Cabellos Colorados

Blue Beach

Isla Chiva

Mar Caribe

Red Beach

Playa García

Bahía Barracuda

Sonda de Vieques

Punta Mulas

SANTA MARIA

997

DESTINO ④

Bahía Mosquito

Isabel Segunda

MONTE SANTO

② ③ ⑥

Acevedo's Car Rental

Maritza's Car Rental

Hombre de Puerto Ferro

⑤

Playa Navio

Playa Media Luna

FAJARDO (8mi.)

Playa Galito

Martineau Car Rental

Island Car Rental

995

①

Aeropuerto Antonio Rivera Rodríguez

⑦ ⑨

⑧ ⑪

⑩

PUERTO REAL

996

Sun Bay ⑬

201

Esperanza

Cayo Tierra

Playa Esperanza

Cayo Afuera

201 ⑫

Mosquito Pier

Punta Caballo

200

Laguna Kiani

Mt. El Buey (456ft.) ▲

Mt. Pirata (988ft.) ▲

Playa Grande

Punta Vaca

Green Beach

Punta Arenas

0   2 miles
0   2 kilometers

Air Sunshine (☎ 741-7900, toll-free 888-879-8900; www.airsunshine.com) flies to: **San Juan International** (25min.; 3 per day; $62, round-trip $124) and **St. Croix, USVI** (25min.; 3 per day; $62, round-trip $124). Connections to St. Thomas, Tortola, and Virgin Gorda. Open daily 8am-6pm. AmEx/MC/V.

Isla Nena (☎ 741-1505, toll-free 877-812-5144) flies only on demand to: **Culebra** (8min.; $25, round-trip $40); **Fajardo** (8min.; $20, round-trip $35); and **San Juan International** (20min.; $70, round-trip $130). Open daily 5:30-10am and noon-6pm. MC/V.

M&N Aviation (☎ 741-3911, toll-free 877-622-5566) flies to: **Fajardo** (7min.; 3 per day; $25, round-trip $40); **San Juan Isla Grande** (19min.; 4 per day; $50, round-trip $90) and **San Juan International** (20min.; 2 per day; $70, round-trip $130). Open daily 6am-7pm. AmEx/MC/V.

Vieques Air Link (☎ 741-8331, toll-free 888-901-9247) flies to: **Culebra** (10min.; on demand; $20, round-trip $40); **Fajardo** (10min.; on demand; $19, round-trip $36); **San Juan International** (30min.; 3 per day; $69, round-trip $135); **San Juan Isla Grande** (30min.; 5 per day; $43, round-trip $80); **St. Croix, USVI** (30min.; 4 per day; $62, round-trip $123). Open M-F 7:30am-6:30pm, Sa 7:30am-5:30pm, Su 7:30am-4:30pm. AmEx/MC/V. Or stop by their **reservations office**, C. Antonio Mellado 258. Open M-F 7:30am-5:30pm.

Ferries: Puerto Rican Port Authority (☎ 741-4761 or 741-0233, in Fajardo 863-0705, 863-0852, or 863-4560) operates ferries between Vieques and Fajardo. In addition to the routes below, a recently added passenger ferry runs between Vieques and Culebra (M-F leaves Vieques 6am, returns from Culebra 5pm; round-trip $4). There is an additional charge for beach equipment, including tents ($2) and sleeping bags ($1). Reservations required to take a car on board, but not accepted for passengers. Show up at least 1hr. in advance. Open daily 8am-noon and 1-4pm. MC/V.

FERRIES	FAJARDO-VIEQUES	VIEQUES-FAJARDO	PRICE
PASSENGER	M-F 9:30am, 1pm, 4:30pm Sa-Su 9am, 3pm, 6pm	M-F 7, 11am, 3pm Sa-Su 7am, 1pm, 4:30pm	$2
CARGO	M-F 4am, 1:30, 6pm	M-F 6am, 1:30pm, 6pm	$15; round-trip $26.50

⊞ ORIENTATION

⚠ WARNING Vieques has its share of petty crime. Lock your hotel room and **never bring valuables to the beach.** Thieves have been known to grab cell phones, purses, or wallets from the beach while owners are in the water, or break into cars parked behind the beach. Sun Bay has been especially vulnerable to these crimes.

Measuring 20 by 4½ mi., Vieques looks like a mini, elongated version of Puerto Rico. As of May 2003, both the eastern and western thirds of the island, former US Navy lands, are controlled by the US Fish and Wildlife Service. Most of the area is open to the public as a natural reserve, although certain areas remain closed because they may still contain unexploded ordinance or other hazardous materials. Most people arrive in Isabel II, the island's largest town and home of the ferry dock. From the dock turn right, then take a left on C. Benítez Guzmán, then a right just past the plaza to reach Rte. 200 and leave town. The fastest route between Isabel II and Esperanza is Rte. 997; however, for a much more scenic route drive west on Rte. 200, then south along Rte. 995, one of the most beautiful roads on the island, then turn left on Rte. 201 and right on Rte. 996, which leads straight into Esperanza. Coming into Esperanza on Rte. 996, veer left as you hit La Tienda Verde and the road will reach the ocean and become **"the strip,"** home to almost all of the town's hotels. Most of the former Navy roads are unpaved.

LOCAL TRANSPORTATION

VIEQUES

> **ISLAND INFO** Several publications and web sites provide invaluable information about Vieques in English. Take a look at the following:
> **www.enchanted-isle.com.** Almost every tourist service on the island has a link on this comprehensive site. Resident expat Judy answers questions relating to tourism on Vieques in her online column, *Ask Judy.*
> **Vieques Events (www.vieques-events.com).** Another source for island news. On the first of every month this helpful newsletter appears on the web with a calendar of current events, articles about recent happenings, and a small classified section. Almost every tourist-related business on the island carries a hard copy.
> **www.Elenas-Vieques.com.** A longtime expat and owner of Blue Heron Kayak, Elena has compiled a personal web site with information about Vieques.

It is not easy to get around Vieques without a car. *Públicos* run between Isabel II and Esperanza but rarely head to any beaches except Sun Bay.

Car Rental: Several small companies rent jeeps, but there are no major chains. Make reservations during high season (Dec.-May) as it's not uncommon for every car on the island to be booked. There are two **gas stations** around Rte. 200 Km 1.5. The third station is at the intersection of Rte. 200 and Rte. 997.

Island Car Rental, Rte. 201 Km 1.1 (☎741-1666), sometimes provides pick-up and drop-off service. Jeeps $45-55, minivans $75. Discounts for 5 or more days. Insurance $10 per day. Driver's license required; no min. age. $500 deposit required. Open daily 8am-5pm. AmEx/MC/V.

Martineau Car Rental, Rte. 200 Km 3.2 (☎741-0087; www.enchanted-isle.com/martineaucar), rents shiny new jeeps ($45-65 per day). Insurance $12 per day. 25+. Ages 21-24 $5 per day surcharge. They also rent bikes ($30 per 24hr.) and scooters ($45 per 24hr. with helmets). Pick-up and drop-off available. Credit card required. Open daily 8am-6pm. AmEx/MC/V.

Maritza's Car Rental, Rte. 201 Km 1 (☎741-0078). Nov.-Apr. jeeps $40-60 per day; May-Oct. $35-55 per day. Insurance $12 per day. 25+ unless you have your own insurance on a credit card. No pick-up, but they will drop off cars at any hotel. Open daily 8am-5pm. AmEx/MC/V.

Acevedo's Car Rental, Rte. 201 Km 0.4 (☎741-4380), rents 3 types of jeeps ($40-60). 21+. No pick-up or delivery. Open M-Sa 9am-6pm, Su 10am-noon. AmEx/MC/V.

Steve's Car Rental (☎741-8135, cell 310-3455) rents several types of jeeps ($40-45 per day). No pick-up, but the car will be waiting when you arrive at your hotel or guest house. 21+. MC/V.

Acacia Car Rental (☎741-1856). The owners of Acacia Apartments also rent 4 jeeps ($40-50 per day). Driver's license required; no min. age. Rentals come with an orientation. No pick-up. MC/V.

Públicos: Shared vans travel the island, usually circulating between the airport, the ferry terminal in Isabel II, and the strip in Esperanza. If you flag down a *público,* it will usually take you anywhere on the island. Passengers traveling alone may have to pay the fare of 3 passengers. When ferries arrive, all of the operating *públicos* will be at the dock, then about 30min. later most will end up on the strip in Esperanza; plan your schedule accordingly. Transport anywhere on the major roads should cost $1-3 per person; transport to the beaches on former Navy lands runs $5; extra luggage costs $0.50 per item. The following drivers stand out for their exceptional English skills: **Lolo** (☎741-3444, cell 485-5447); **Ángel** (☎741-1370, cell 484-8796); **Anibal** (☎741-3024, cell 375-7027); **José** (☎741-0959, cell 568-1814).

Scooters: Extreme (☎435-9345), just uphill from the ferry terminal in Isabel II, rents 2 types of scooters ($40-50 per 24hr.) with helmets. Call ahead and they'll deliver. $60 deposit required. Cash only. **Martineau Car Rental** (see above) also rents scooters.

Bike Rental: La Dulce Vida (☎617-2453; www.bikevieques.com) rents 27 speed mountain bikes suitable for all athletes ($20 per day including helmet, lock, and delivery). The owner also leads ½-day bike tours around the western end of the island ($45-65 per person including snacks and water). Some tours include snorkeling stops. Reservations required. MC/V.

PRACTICAL INFORMATION

Unless otherwise stated, all services are located in Isabel II.

Tourist Office: Puerto Rico Tourism Company, C. Carlos LeBrun 449 (☎741-0800), on the corner of the plaza. Offers maps and a Vieques brochure. Open daily 8am-5pm.

Bank: Banco Popular, C. Muñoz Rivera 115 (☎741-2071). ATM. Open M-F 8am-3pm.

Equipment Rental: Extreme Scooters and Water Sports (☎435-9345), in Bo. Morro Pouse, rents jet skis from the Isabel II area. Call ahead. $40 for 30min. Cash only.

English-Language Bookstore: 18 Degrees North, C. Flamboyan 134 (☎741-8600), in Esperanza, has a large selection of used books. Usually open M-Tu 9:30am-noon, W-Su 9:30am-3pm. MC/V.

Supermarkets:

Super Descuentos Morales, Rte. 200 Km 1.3 (☎741-6701), is the largest grocery store on Vieques. Open M-Sa 6:30am-7pm, Su 6:30am-noon. MC/V. Another location at C. Baldorioty de Castro 15.

La Tienda Verde, C. Robles 273 (☎741-8711), Rte. 996, at the entrance to Esperanza. A glorified minimart and Esperanza's largest grocery store. Open daily 9am-9pm. MC/V.

Chef Michael's, C. Flamboyan 134 (☎741-0490), in Esperanza, sells specialty foods including fresh bread, fruits, veggies, fish, cheeses, meats, spices "by the pinch," and a shelf full of Asian foods. Open Th-M 10am-5pm. MC/V.

Colmado Lydia (☎741-8678), on C. Almendro in Esperanza. This small grocery store is close to the strip. Open M-Sa 7:30am-6pm, Su 7:30am-noon. Cash only.

Laundromat: Familia Rios, C. Benítez Castaño 1 (☎438-1846). Self-serve washers $1.50-6. Dryers $0.50 per 10min. Wash-and-fold $1 per lb.; usually same-day service. Change and detergent available. Open Su-M and W-F 6am-7pm, Tu and Sa 6am-5pm.

Police: Rte. 200 Km 0.2, at Rte. 997 (☎741-2020 or 741-2121). Open 24hr.

Late-Night Pharmacy: Isla Nena Pharmacy (☎741-1906), on C. Muñoz Rivera. Open M-F 7:30am-7pm, Sa 8am-6pm, Su 11am-3pm. AmEx/MC/V.

Hospital: Centro de Salud Familiar, Rte. 997 Km 0.4 (☎741-0392, emergency room 741-2151). Clinic open M-F 7am-3:30pm. Emergency room open 24hr.

Internet Access: Museo de Esperanza, C. Flamboyán 138 (☎741-8850), Esperanza, allows travelers to use their computer ($3 for 30min.). Open daily 11am-4pm.

Post Office: C. Muñoz Rivera 97 (☎741-3891). Address General Delivery mail to: General Delivery, Vieques, P.R. 00765. Open M-F 8am-4:30pm, Sa 8am-noon.

Zip Code: 00765

ISLAND TIME All hours and prices in Vieques are subject to change. Hours change with the season and owners frequently close down shop in the middle of the day to go to the beach. Make plans with a grain of salt and always retain a sense of flexibility.

ACCOMMODATIONS AND CAMPING

Vieques has excellent accommodations for travelers of all budgets. If you want to be in the middle of local action, stay in Isabel II; if you want to join the expat crowd and be close to the beaches, try Esperanza. If you just want to get away from it all, try one of the accommodations in the middle of the island (but you will need a car). Many hotels do not allow children.

REALTORS

The realtors below offer short-term vacation rentals around the island. All prices are for weekly rentals.

Connections Real Estate, C. Muñoz Rivera 117 (☎741-0023; www.viequesrealtor.com), in Isabel II. 1 week min. 50% deposit required. Houses vary in size; most rent for $300-1200. Open M-F 10am-5pm, Sa-Su by appointment. Credit card deposit required; payment accepted only in cash and check.

Rainbow Realty, C. Flamboyan 62 (☎/fax 741-4313; www.enchanted-isle.com/rainbow), in Esperanza. Most rentals have washer and dryer, some have pool and A/C. 1 week min. Nov.-May $650-3400; June-Nov. $500-2400. Open F-M and W 11am-1pm. MC/V.

Crow's Nest Realty, Rte. 201 Km 1 (☎741-0033 or 1-888-4VIEQUES (484-7837); fax 741-1294; www.crowsnestvieques.com). 1 week min. Rentals $1000-4000. AmEx/MC/V.

ISABEL II

■ **Casa de Amistad,** C. Benítez Castaño 27 (☎741-3758; www.casadeamistad.com). Come join the fun at this friendly *casa* in the heart of Isabel II. The owners wanted to create an affordable, attractive guest house and they succeeded marvelously. Renovated concrete house contains 7 rooms with A/C and wicker furniture. Rooftop deck. Tiny pool. Dog-lovers only. Common area with TV. Beach equipment, snorkels, and bikes available. Doubles $45, with bath $55; quads $65. Tax not included. MC/V. ❷

Waters Edge Guest House (☎741-1128; fax 741-3918; www.viequespuertorico.com), on North Shore Road. You wouldn't guess it from looking at this worn pink building, but the rooms

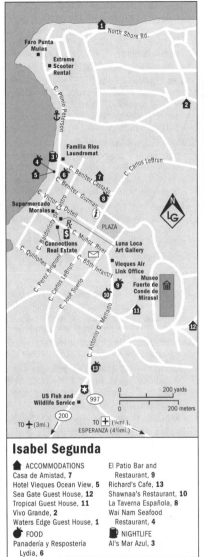

Isabel Segunda

🛏 ACCOMMODATIONS
Casa de Amistad, **7**
Hotel Vieques Ocean View, **5**
Sea Gate Guest House, **12**
Tropical Guest House, **11**
Vivo Grande, **2**
Waters Edge Guest House, **1**

🍴 FOOD
Panadería y Respostería Lydia, **6**

El Patio Bar and Restaurant, **9**
Richard's Cafe, **13**
Shawnaa's Restaurant, **10**
La Taverna Española, **8**
Wai Nam Seafood Restaurant, **4**

🍸 NIGHTLIFE
Al's Mar Azul, **3**

at Waters Edge are actually quite nice, with TV, balcony, fridge, A/C, and sometimes an ocean view. Mosquito nets hanging over the big beds add a fun tropical touch. Small pool. One corner of the guest house is a separate **villa**—a huge house with laundry machines, a private BBQ and pool, and 2 bedrooms. Check-out noon. Thanksgiving to Easter doubles $92-150; villa $300 per night, $200 per week. Easter to Thanksgiving doubles $76-125; villa $250/$1500. Extra person $15. Tax included. AmEx/MC/V. ❸

Sea Gate Guest House (☎ 741-4661), on the hill above the fort. Founded in 1977, comfortable Sea Gate claims to be the original Vieques guest house. The small rooms have been lovingly decorated with gauzy curtains and seashells. It's quite a walk, but the inconvenient location compensates with great views. All rooms have ceiling fan; some have a full kitchen. A few dogs run around. Large book exchange. Miniscule pool. Doubles Sept.-Apr. $50-70; May-Aug. $40-60; extra person $10. MC/V. ❷

Vivo Grande (☎ 845-758-8728). This 2-story vacation home on the hills above Isabel II is well-equipped and clean, but lacks any zest. Rooftop patio looks out over the town. Phone, kitchen, TV, washer, dryer, BBQ, bedroom A/C, and porch. Free pick-up and delivery. Weekly rates: Nov.-Apr. 2-bedroom apartment $700; 3-bedroom apartment $1000; 5-bedroom house $1500. May-Oct. $500/$700/$1000. No credit cards. ❹

Hotel Vieques Ocean View, C. Plinio Peterson 571 (☎ 741-3696), is Vieques's most institutional accommodation, falling somewhere between a run-down *parador* and an unkempt business hotel. Convenient to town. Doubles and quads have balconies; request an ocean view. All rooms have A/C and a small TV. Pool. Doubles $55-65; quads $75; 3 double beds $99; 4 beds $119. Prices rise in July. Tax not included. AmEx/MC/V. ❸

Tropical Guest House, C. Progreso 41 (☎ 741-2449). Leaving Isabel II on Rte. 200 take the first left after El Patio restaurant, then veer left; the hotel is on your left. Hidden in a residential neighborhood, this simple Puerto Rican-run guest house has all of the amenities (A/C, TV, hot water), but no charm. Rooms are clean, but a bit stuffy. Doubles $50-$60; quads $75. Tax included. No credit cards. ❷

ESPERANZA

▧ **Trade Winds Guest House,** C. Flamboyan 107 (☎ 741-8666; fax 741-2964; www.enchanged-isle.com/tradewinds). Spirited Trade Winds laughs in the face of traditional hotel monotony and offers colorful Caribbean rooms with bright wall murals. Some rooms share an ocean-view patio. Great value. All rooms have fridges, reading lights, and ceiling fans. Dec.-Apr. singles $50-65; doubles $60-75. May-Nov. $40-55/$50-65. Extra person $15. Tax not included. AmEx/MC/V. ❸

Bananas Guest House, C. Flamboyan 142 (☎ 741-8700; fax 741-0790; www.bananas-guesthouse.com). This cozy guest house looks and feels like an elegant wood cabin plopped down across the street from the beach. Friendly backpacker atmosphere. Lively restaurant. Check-in noon. Check-out 11am. Doubles $50, with A/C, fridge, and porch $65-75; extra person $10. Tax not included. MC/V. ❷

Pablo's Guest House, C. Piños 217 (☎ 741-8917). For those willing to forego the fun tourist-friendly atmosphere on the strip, Pablo offers the best deal in Esperanza. The 4 small rooms on the 2nd floor of his house are simple, but clean enough to eat off of. All include hot water and fridge. Triples $40, with A/C $55. Cash only. ❷

Ted's Guest House, C. Húcar 103 (☎ 741-2225; www.vieques-island.com/rentals/ted), ½ block from the strip. Another shining star in the world of private guest houses. Though they are located on the 2nd floor of the owner's home, these 3 immaculate apartments look like brand new hotel rooms. All come with a full kitchen, A/C, TV, and a kitchen table. Doubles $65; quads $100. Tax included. No credit cards. ❸

Acacia Apartments, C. Acacia 236 (☎ 741-1856 or 741-1059), 3 long blocks from the strip. This big white guest house looks overdressed for the party, as all the surrounding homes are modest private residences. On a clear day you can see St. Croix from the rooftop deck. Spotless apartments have ceiling fans, a kitchen, a separate bedroom, and a terrace. Call ahead; no on-site management. Free washing machine. 3 night min. 1-bedroom apartments $75-89; 2-bedroom $105. Tax not included. MC/V. ❸

Amapola Inn and Tavern, C. Flamboyan 144 (☎ 741-1382). Ignore the slightly fading lime green cement facade—Amapola's rooms are actually quite nice, with A/C, wicker furniture, and pretty blue tiles. They just lack that special touch to put them on par

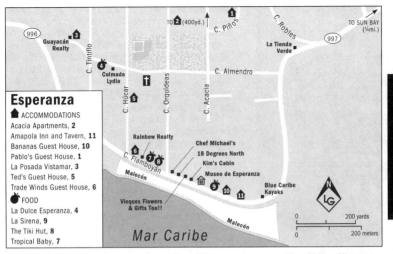

Esperanza

🏠 ACCOMMODATIONS
Acacia Apartments, **2**
Amapola Inn and Tavern, **11**
Bananas Guest House, **10**
Pablo's Guest House, **1**
La Posada Vistamar, **3**
Ted's Guest House, **5**
Trade Winds Guest House, **6**

🍴 FOOD
La Dulce Esperanza, **4**
La Sirena, **9**
The Tiki Hut, **8**
Tropical Baby, **7**

Mar Caribe

with Esperanza's other attractive options. Most rooms come with a fridge. All guests enjoy free coffee, a small backyard, and a pleasant common room. Doubles $70-80; extra person $10. Tax not included. AmEx/MC/V. ❸

La Posada Vistamar (☎741-5052), at the end of C. Almendro. Though it's only a 2min. walk from the strip, this 6-room hotel feels like it's in the middle of farmland. Small, generic rooms come with A/C, fan, private bath, and mosquito repellent. New management and new murals may spice things up a bit. Office in the chiropractor's office in back. Check-in 3pm. Check-out 11am. Doubles $55, students $45. Tax included. No credit cards. ❷

AROUND VIEQUES

The Crow's Nest, Rte. 201 Km 1 (☎741-0033 or 1-888-4VIEQUES; fax 741-1294; www.crowsnestvieques.com). Cross a cozy inn with a well-equipped hotel and you'll get The Crow's Nest, one of Vieques's most comfortable accommodations. Located on 5 acres of land just off busy Rte. 201, the hotel emits the feel of a clean, impersonal summer home. A/C, satellite TV, phone, and patio. Friendly staff. Internet $4 for 20min. No children under 12. Continental breakfast included. Doubles Dec. 20-May 1 $68-99; May 2-Dec. 19 $58-89. Extra person $15. Tax not included. AmEx/MC/V. ❸

La Finca Caribe, Rte. 995 Km 2.2 (☎741-0495; fax 741-3584; www.lafinca.com). If you enjoyed summer camp as a kid, come try this rustic wooden hotel hidden on a farm in the middle of Vieques. The tin-roofed house strives for tranquility and simplicity; most rooms share bathrooms and guests use outdoor solar-heated showers. All rooms have a loft bed. Friendly conversation ensues in the common kitchen area. Pool. Book exchange. The guest house is up for sale, so call ahead, as many details may change. Doubles $70, $60 for 3 nights or more. Small house $85, weekly $525. Large cabins with kitchen $800 per week. Tax not included. 4% credit card fee. AmEx/MC/V. ❸

Abreeze, Rte. 997 Km 1.6 (☎741-1856; www.vieques-island.com/rentals/abreeze). The owners of Acacia Apartments rent out 2 apartments in their beautiful yellow house. With 3½ acres of land on the top of a hill with nearly panoramic views, this house feels like a Caribbean country estate. Rooms include kitchens, private patios, phones, and some of Vieques's largest bathrooms. All guests can use coolers, washer, dryer, and grill. 1 week min. 2-person studio $750 per week; 4-person apartment $850. MC/V. ❹

ME, MYSELF, AND THE US NAVY

Vieques has made the worldwide press over the last 10 years for its vocal opposition to the US Navy presence, but the island's battle against Navy occupation began much earlier. The US first began expropriating land on Vieques for Naval training in the 1940s and by 1949 the marines controlled 72% of the island. In the early 1960s US President John F. Kennedy proposed taking over the rest of Vieques and moving all residents, alive and dead, to mainland Puerto Rico, but repercussions from the Cuban revolution quickly thwarted this plan. As early as 1964 locals spoke out against the Navy's plans for expansion. Protests erupted again in 1978-80 when several local fisherman were arrested for standing in the way of Naval exercises. Minor protests continued throughout the '80s, but it wasn't until 1999 that Vieques erupted. On April 19 two live bombs accidentally hit an observation post, killing resident patrol guard David Sanes Rodríguez. Vieques made international news as hundreds of Puerto Ricans camped out on Navy land, preventing military exercises from taking place. In 2000 Governor Sila M. Calderón was elected largely on her firm commitment to get the Navy out of Vieques. Reports circulated that due to the Navy's presence, the cancer rate on Vieques had grown as high as 26%. Protests continued, committees formed, and banners around Puerto Rico begged for "Paz Para Vieques" (Peace for Vieques).

Adventures Inn, Rte. 200 Km 1.5 (☎741-1564), about 50m off the main road. This immense green concrete structure looks like it dropped down from Mars and landed in the middle of a residential neighborhood. The highlight is the huge rooftop breakfast patio. Rooms lack inspiration, but all have A/C. Bike rental $15 per day. No daily maid service. Doubles $70-90; extra person $20. Tax not included. AmEx/MC/V. ❸

Cabañas Playa Grande, Rte. 201 Km 0.4 (☎741-4380), is one of the few truly Puerto Rican-style accommodations on Vieques. Like a government-run *centro vacacional* (see p. 58) Playa Grande has 2 options: well-equipped, clean apartments with 2 bedrooms, A/C, TV, VCR, and fully stocked kitchen, or rustic, dark wood cabins with nothing but some old mattresses and a tiny fridge. Cabanas are small and can get very hot. All rooms sleep up to 5 people. Uninspiring grounds; you essentially sleep in someone's messy backyard. Cabins $50; apartments $125. Tax included. AmEx/MC/V. ❹

Balneario Sun Bay (☎741-8198), on Rte. 997, ¼ mi. east of Esperanza, lets people camp in a large field next to the beach. Nothing compares to falling asleep to the sound of waves pounding the shore 20 ft. away from your tent. Except during major holidays, the camping area is not too crowded. Facilities include trash cans, picnic tables, fire pits, surprisingly nice bathrooms, showers, and a water fountain. $10 per tent. ❶

THE SKY'S THE LIMIT

Vieques has several beautiful high-end guest houses spread throughout the island.

Hacienda Tamarindo, Rte. 996 Km 4.5 (☎741-8525; fax 741-3215; www.enchanted-isle.com/tamarindo). Take a big, refined beach house, add a dash of charm, a pinch of convenience, and a dollop of taste and you get Tamarindo. The owner/interior decorator has personally adorned each room with murals and antiques. Gorgeous common library and lounge. A/C and ceiling fans. No children under 15. Honor bar. American breakfast included. Check-out 8:30-11am. Reception open 8am-6pm. Nov. 16-May 4 singles $145-170; doubles $155-225; extra person $25. May 5-Nov. 15 $115-140/$125-150/$15. Tax and 10% service charge not included. AmEx/D/MC/V. ❺

Casa Cielo, Rte. 995 Km 1.2 (☎741-2403; www.casa-cielo.net). Originally constructed as a private residence, this *casa* has since transformed into one of Vieques's most peaceful guest houses. The airy, spacious white house sits on 6 acres of land on a hill with views of both the northern and southern sides of the island. Most rooms have A/C and a private balcony. Tu morning yoga. Common kitchen, grill, and living area.

Beach equipment provided. Large bright blue swimming pool. No children. Continental breakfast included. Doubles Thanksgiving to Easter $178-238; Easter to Thanksgiving $148-208; extra person $25. Discounts with longer stays. Tax included. MC/V. ❺

Hix Island House, Rte. 995 Km 1.2 (☎741-2302; fax 741-2797; www.hixislandhouse.com). Designed by an architect and his fashion designer wife, hip Hix Island House may be the most unique accommodation in Puerto Rico. 3 concrete buildings contain breezy, completely open rooms (re: no walls), each with a fully stocked kitchen, breakfast supplies, an outdoor shower, homemade bread, mosquito nets, and long smock shirts. Concrete pool fits ingeniously into the landscape. You'll either love it or you'll hate it; not everyone wants to live in a work of art. Doubles late Dec.-Apr. $155-230; May-June $140-180; July-early Dec. $125-150. Tax not included. AmEx/MC/V.

Great Escape Bed & Breakfast Inn (☎741-2927; paradise@greatescape.ws), on Rte. 201 between Rte. 995 and Rte. 996. Follow signs and turn right after the pink concrete fence. Located on 3.8 acres of land in the middle of farm country, the appropriately named Great Escape offers fresh air, tranquility, and great mountain views. The big white house contains 10 rooms with high ceilings, wrought-iron beds, and private balconies. Pool. Breakfast included. Dec.-Apr. doubles $150; May-Nov. $125. Extra person $25. Apartments $200-400. Tax included. No credit cards. ❺

🍴 FOOD

Keep your ATM card handy; with the food prices on Vieques as high as they are, you may be making frequent withdrawals. Several American expats have opened delicious, but expensive restaurants. For cheaper eats, try the local restaurants that serve quality *comida criolla*. Many restaurants on Vieques, especially the American-run operations, request reservations.

ISABEL II

🍴 **El Patio Bar and Restaurant** (☎741-6381), on C. Antonio G. Mellado. Locals applaud El Patio as the best eatery in Isabel II, and it's easy to see why. With outdoor seating and tasty, affordable *comida criolla*, this relaxed restaurant shines in all areas. Breakfast $1.50-3. Lunch special 11am-2pm $5. Typical seafood, chicken, and meat entrees $5-15. Beer $1-2; mixed drinks $2-3. Open M-F 7am-8:30pm. MC/V. ❷

🍴 **La Taverna Española** (☎741-1175), at the corner of C. Carlos LeBrun and C. Benítez Castaño. The facade is fading, but perhaps this accounts for La Taverna's com-

In 2000 and 2001 over 150 people were arrested on charges of civil disobedience in relation to the Naval presence. Finally, the US Navy left the western half of the island and turned the land over to US Fish and Wildlife Service. But *viequenses* were not satisfied with only two-thirds of the island, and protests continued. In June 2001 President George W. Bush announced that the Navy would leave the eastern third of the island and completely discontinue all military operations on Vieques. A huge celebration on May 1-2, 2003 signified excitement over the departure, but the controversy wasn't close to ending.

Three of the beaches located on eastern Navy lands—Red, Blue, and Garcia—opened in May 2003, but it will take the Navy much longer to ensure that the rest of the area is safe for public use. A large portion of the eastern third of the island, mostly the area used for live ordinance training, may never open to the public. Furthermore, nobody can agree about what should be done with the land. Originally it was given to Fish and Wildlife Service to become part of the largest reserve in the Caribbean, but some locals claimed that it should be turned over to residents for development. When many of the island's environmental groups protested this, the island was divided once again. As of press time, Fish and Wildlife was managing both the western and eastern sides of the island, but Vieques continues to be wracked with controversy.

paratively low prices. Locals and foreigners rave about the fresh seafood inside. Get into the spirit of Spain; sit amidst red curtains and feast on seafood paella for 2 ($30) and a jar of fabulous sangria ($11). Entrees $8-14. Open daily 5-10pm. MC/V. ❸

Shawnaa's Restaurant (☎ 741-1434), on C. Antonio Mellado, demonstrates the benefit of doing one thing well. Open for lunch only, this cozy eatery serves up some superb buffet-style *comida criolla*. Choose between a clean indoor dining area and a small outdoor balcony. Delivery within Isabel II $1-2. Lunch $5. Open M-F 11am-3pm. MC/V. ❶

Richard's Cafe (☎ 741-5242), at the intersection of Rte. 997 and Rte. 200. Fake flowers, shiny counters, and a faux brick wall give Richard's the aura of a cheesy American pizzeria attempting to go classy. Except for this aesthetic identity crisis, Richard's seems to be doing just fine, with a variety of Puerto Rican food, pizza, hamburgers, and ice cream. Entrees $5-19. Large pizza $9. Open daily 11am-10pm. AmEx/MC/V. ❸

Wai Nam Seafood Restaurant, C. Plinio Peterson 571 (☎741-0622), under Hotel Ocean Front. Like any good Puerto Rico town, Isabel II must have the requisite Chinese/seafood/fried chicken restaurant. However, this may be the only one with a fantastic sea view. Lackluster Chinese entrees $6-13. Open daily 10:30am-10pm. Visa. ❷

Panadería y Repostería Lydia (☎ 741-8679), at C. Plinio Peterson and Benítez Guzmán, sells tasty sandwiches to eat on the go. There is no sitting area inside, but there are 2 plastic tables out front. Sandwiches $1.50-2.50. Pastries served M-F. Open M-F 5am-2pm, Sa 5am-noon, Su 5am-10:30am. Cash only. ❶

ESPERANZA

Trade Winds, C. Flamboyan 107 (☎741-8666; fax 741-2964). Like the guest house in back, Trade Winds restaurant is unpretentious but attractive. Soft music plays while you sit in a big wooden chair, gaze out over the water, and dine on some of the best food on the strip. Scrumptious breakfasts. Fish and pasta served with an island twist. Breakfast $4-9; lunch $4-9; dinner $12-19. Open daily 8am-2pm and 6-9:30pm. AmEx/MC/V. ❸

The Tiki Hut, C. Flamboyan 62 (☎741-4992). For a satisfying, affordable lunch on the strip, look no farther than The Tiki Hut. This simple outdoor sandwich/salad bar serves made-to-order sandwiches and salads with some of the friendliest service on Vieques. Full breakfast menu $2-3.50. Sandwiches $6. Open daily 8:30am-3pm. Cash only. ❶

Amapola Inn and Tavern, C. Flamboyan 144 (☎741-1382), spices up the generic strip food with a bit of Mexican flavor. Try the enchiladas, filled with everything from cheese to seafood ($10-18). Then grab a beer and enjoy the friendly parlance at the bar. Also serves burgers and *comida criolla* ($7-20). Open daily 11am-11pm. AmEx/MC/V. ❸

La Dulce Esperanza (☎ 741-7085), on C. Almendro, hides in a back neighborhood, and is one of the few affordable (but appetizing) restaurants in Esperanza. Serves pastries in the morning, sandwiches for lunch, and salty pizzas for dinner. Take your food to go and check for a baseball game down the street. Sandwiches $1.50-2.50. Small pizza $9-13.25. Usually open daily 7am-9pm. Cash only. ❶

Tropical Baby, C. Flamboyan 62 (☎608-4261), serves "global" food—primarily southeast Asian entrees made with fresh vegetables and fish. The menu changes regularly, but should always satisfy healthy eaters and vegetarians. A small casual restaurant with 2 outdoor picnic tables. BYOB. Lunch $6-16; dinner $15-18. Reservations required. Open Tu 11am-4pm, W-F 10am-2pm and 7-9:30pm, Su 10am-2pm. MC/V. ❹

La Sirena, C. Flamboyan 140 (☎741-4462; fax 741-4371), is one of the classiest restaurants on the strip. Bright yellow walls liven up the lower floor, while upstairs flames and twinkle lights create a romantic ambiance for nighttime dining. All outdoor seating, overlooking the water. Simple breakfast and lunch menu ($5.50-9), more elaborate French-Caribbean dinners ($15-25). Th live steel drum band 7:30pm. Open M-Tu and Th-F 11am-4pm and 6-10pm, Sa-Su 9am-10pm. Bar open until 1-2am. AmEx/MC/V. ❹

La Posada Vistamar Restaurant (☎ 741-5052), at the end of C. Almendro, has excellent food, but is lacking in the decor category. The rotating menu of refined *comida criolla* mixes flavorful spices in entrees guaranteed to please. However, the drab room is only mildly improved by dim lights and light music. Only in Puerto Rico can a romantic restaurant have plastic chairs. Entrees $8-19. Open W-Su 5:30-9:30pm. Cash only. ❸

Bananas, C. Flamboyan 142 (☎ 741-8700), at the guest house of the same name. "This is a Gin-U-Wine Sleazy Waterfront Dive," claims the sign at the front of this rustic wooden eatery. Well, it's not quite a dive any more, but Bananas does offer cheap (and mediocre) eats and a lively bar. Burgers $5-8; basic beach entrees $14-16.50. Beer $1.75-3; frozen drinks $5-6.50. Happy Hour daily 10pm-midnight. Occasional live music. Restaurant open daily 11am-9pm. Bar open later. MC/V. ❸

AROUND VIEQUES

Chez Shack, Rte. 995 Km 1.8 (☎ 741-2175). The name says it all. This kooky restaurant seems to exemplify the oxymorons of Vieques: Chez Shack literally sits in a tin-roofed open-air shack, but at night funky lanterns transform the restaurant into a classy eatery. The rotating French-Caribbean menu defies classification, but consistently comes out with first-rate food. Don't miss ▨ M grill night, when all food is cooked on a grill and a steel band creates an instant party. Entrees $13-18; grill night $18-24. Call ahead; hours change frequently. Open Th-M 6:30-10pm. MC/V. ❹

Bayaonda, Rte. 200 Km 1.5 (741-0312), is Vieques's newest and hippest restaurant. Though it's 20 ft. from the main road, Bayaonda maintains an aura of isolation with an intimate dining area surrounded by trees. The food, defined as Artisan Caribbean, is pricey but delicious. Try the organically fed roasted rabbit, or choose from one of the several vegetarian and vegan options. Entrees $14-25. Open F-M 6-10pm. MC/V. ❹

Trópico, Rte. 200 Km 3.0 (☎ 741-4000), changes its menu almost daily—W is grill night, Th is Mexican night, F is the shrimp festival, and Sa is the famous paella night. The open-air restaurant sits on 12 acres of land where the owners grow many of their own vegetables. Any dish can be modified for vegetarians. W-Sa Happy Hour 5-7pm. Beer $1.50-3. Entrees $9-15. Open W-Sa 11am-2pm and 5-10pm. AmEx/MC/V. ❸

◎ SIGHTS

Unlike Culebra, Vieques does have a fair share of cultural sights. It's worth an afternoon of missed beach time to check out the island's major museums.

MUSEO FUERTE DE CONDE DE MIRASOL. Vieques's most impressive sight was constructed in the 1840s as the last Spanish fort in the New World, then entered a long period of neglect and disrepair before the Puerto Rican Institute of Culture restored the fort and installed a museum inside. Even with this interesting history, the fort's past does not rival its turbulent present. In addition to unsurprising displays of historical memorabilia and archaeological artifacts, the museum also hosts rotating exhibits of local artwork, much of which has focused on the US Navy presence. A recent exhibit entitled "Queremos Paz Para Vieques," consisting of children's depictions of the naval presence on the island, was so controversial that some locals refused to enter the museum. The issue is complicated by the fact that the US government partially funds the museum. The controversy will likely subside with the Navy's departure, and the fort still merits a visit for both its architecture and its well-thought-out displays. Furthermore, this is the best place to learn about Vieques's long history, even if only about half of the exhibits have English signs. (*Rte. 989 Km 0.5. Follow signs to the Fuerte neighborhood. ☎ 741-1717; www.icp.gobierno.pr. Open W-Su 10am-4pm. $2, under 12 and over 65 free.*)

ROM THE ROAD

SAVING VIEQUES

Several organizations work to conserve the Vieques's resources and are happy to share their work.

Bio Bay Conservation Group, Rte. 996 Km 4.5 (☎741-0720; www.biobay.org). Run by American expat Sharon Grasso, this organization strives to preserve the bioluminescent bays and educate local students about the bay, as well as astronomy and other related fields. Recent projects include making educational signs for the bays and hosting an environmental fair. One of the world's leading research centers on bioluminescence.

The Vieques Conservation and Historical Trust (☎741-8850; www.vcht.com), in the Museo de Esperanza (see p. 290), on the strip in Esperanza. The Conservation Trust works to preserve the bio bays, but they also preserve archaeological artifacts, restore marine life, and educated students about Vieques. The organization has hosted a 4H summer camp, held marine life talks, and organized a recycling center.

US Fish & Wildlife Service, Rte. 200 Km 0.4 (☎741-2138; http://southeast.fws.gov/vieques), in the green building behind the Department of Education. This government organization is responsible for administering all of former Navy lands land (the largest reserve in the Caribbean) with the mission to conserve and protect the area's flora and fauna for future generations. The office has info about Vieques's wildlife and updates on beaches on the eastern half of the island. Open M-F 7:30am-5pm.

FARO PUNTA MULAS. From the ferry, the view of the Punta Mulas lighthouse crowning the hill is quite stunning. Unfortunately, this is as good as it gets. Up close the lighthouse doesn't compare to others in Puerto Rico and the ocean views, while impressive, are nothing special. The lighthouse was built by the Spaniards in 1895-96, but it was partially destroyed when the Americans attacked, and was only restored in 1992. Today the museum contains lots of historical photos with long descriptions, in addition to displays on everything from *santos* to famed Vieques boxer Nelson Dieppa. Most captions are in Spanish. *(On Calle A, uphill from the ferry dock. ☎741-0060. Free 15min. Spanish/English tour. Open daily 8am-4:30pm. Free.)*

MUSEO DE ESPERANZA. The home base of the Vieques Conservation and Historical Trust (see p. 290) has established a small museum in Esperanza to display artifacts and educate the public about their work. The front area focuses primarily on Taíno artifacts recovered from the island. Unfortunately, the exhibit is not particularly well displayed, and many signs are in Spanish only. Continue back past the gift shop to the **smallest aquarium on earth.** Or so they claim. The Trust collects baby animals from the ocean, then displays them in tanks for a few weeks before returning them to the sea. Previous fish have included starfish, yellow-tailed damsels, baby blue tang, and even small nurse sharks. Finally, the back room houses a series of rotating exhibits on the flora and fauna of Vieques. Talking to the volunteers and learning about their important work is usually more interesting than viewing the exhibits, but the museum does make a nice rainy-day stop. *(C. Flamboyán 138, Esperanza. ☎741-8850 or 741-2844; www.vcht.com. Open daily 11am-4pm. Free.)*

HOMBRE DE PUERTO FERRO. In 1990 archaeologists excavating on Vieques came across the remains of a 4000-year-old man, the oldest such finding in the Caribbean. They believe the so-called Hombre de Puerto Ferro was 5'10" and between the ages of 35 and 40 at the time of his death. In 2003 the famous man was on tour in the United States, but he should be housed in the Fort Museum upon being returned to the island. Visitors are welcome to stop by the excavation site, but there is not much left except some big boulders in a dry, empty field. *(Rte. 997 Km 6.5, on a dirt road.)*

BEACHES

Spectacular beaches surround Vieques. The southern Caribbean coast tends to be slightly more appealing than the northern Atlantic coast, but really, who's complaining? Major spots are listed below, but the best strategy is to go out and explore. Locals claim that some of Vieques's best beaches are located on the former Navy land on the eastern half of the island; however, at the time of publication only **Red, Blue, and Garcia beaches** were open to the public. Check with Fish and Wildlife (☎ 741-2138) for the current status of other eastern beaches.

BALNEARIO SUN BAY. At Vieques's only public beach, medium-sized waves of crystal clear water hit an enormous crescent of white sand lined with palm trees. Sound like paradise? It's not far off. The only Puerto Rican beaches that rival Sun Bay are located on Culebra, and if you haven't been there you'll never know the difference. Furthermore, Sun Bay receives far fewer visitors than Culebra's Playa Flamenco, so it's not uncommon to find the beach almost deserted, especially on weekdays. To avoid the excessive seaweed head to the area in front of the *balneario*, where the staff rakes every morning, or the far eastern edge of the bay. Like most public *balnearios*, Sun Bay contains picnic tables, fire pits, a huge parking area, a drinking fountain, trash cans, lifeguards during daylight hours, and a camping area. *(On Rte. 997, ¼ mi. east of Esperanza. ☎ 741-8198. Parking $2. Open W-Su 9am-6pm; the gates are always open, but during these hours you have to pay to park and lifeguards patrol the beach.)*

PLAYA MEDIA LUNA. Located directly east of Sun Bay, Half Moon Beach is technically part of the *balneario* complex, but it feels quite separate. This quiet bay has shallow water and soft waves, making it a good place for kids to play. The beach can become besieged by seaweed, but it's hard to find fault with the perfectly turquoise water. The only facilities are trash cans and a couple of covered picnic tables. This is a popular location for illegal camping. *(Enter the Sun Bay complex, then drive east on the dirt road for about ¼ mi. Parking $2 if you enter W-Su 9am-6pm.)*

PLAYA NAVIO. The third member of the Sun Bay *balneario* complex, Navio feels a bit more isolated than its western neighbors. This small bay is less protected by cliffs and thus waves pound directly against the shore, creating large waves great for boogie boarders but dangerous for small children. If you stand on the beach and look out to the left you'll see the waves breaking over a large reef near the cliffs. This is the Sun Bay complex's best **snorkeling site**. *(Continue ¼ mi. past Playa Media Luna on the bumpy dirt road. You may need 4WD. Parking $2 if you enter W-Su 9am-6pm.)*

GREEN BEACH. For a true jungle adventure, try the trek out to Green Beach, on the western tip of the island. Ever since the Navy relinquished this land, Fish and Wildlife has kept the area open to anyone intrepid enough to brave the roads. Green Beach actually consists of a series of small sandy areas running south from Punta Arenas. The crystal-clear water laps gently against the palm-lined beach, making for enjoyable swimming and picturesque sunsets. Mainland Puerto Rico is visible off in the distance. However, beware of the ferocious sand flies that attack around late afternoon. Green Beach is also known for some of the **best snorkeling** on Vieques. Continue to the far southern end of the beach until you hit the fence. Follow the fence into the water and all the way out to the small reef. *(To reach Green Beach take Rte. 200 west into the old Navy base, then continue onto the dirt road. Veer right at the fork, and cross 2 bridges. The road forms a T at the end—go left for snorkeling and right for Punta Arenas. Facilities include trash cans and 1 covered picnic table.)*

RED, BLUE, AND GARCIA BEACHES. These three popular beaches reopened to the public in May 2003 after the Navy determined that they were safe for public use. All three offer white sands and bright blue waters, although Blue Beach is by far the largest. Some of the beaches have covered cabanas. *(Take Rte. 997 to the Camp Garcia gate, then follow the dirt road east.)*

PLAYA GALLITO. Located between the airport and the new Wyndham resort, this long, narrow stretch of sand provides a place to rest in the sun if you don't mind the sound of traffic and the stares of passersby. Playa Gallito receives few visitors, but does have white sand, some shade, and small waves. *(Rte. 200 Km 3.8. Park on the side of the road. Trash cans.)*

PLAYA GRANDE. For a bit more privacy, head to Playa Grande. This long, narrow beach has course sand and no facilities but it is almost always deserted. Lay in the shade and listen to the big waves crash against the beach. The water also gets deep quickly, so this is not the best place for children. *(Drive west on Rte. 996 past Esperanza to Rte. 201, continue to the end of the road and turn left. Park in the dirt area.)*

⚡ OUTDOOR ACTIVITIES

BIOLUMINESCENT BAY

Nowhere on Puerto Rico does the water shine like it does in Bahía Mosquito. This large bay on the south coast of Vieques is the most impressive example of biolumi-nescence in Puerto Rico, if not in the world. When you jump into the dark waters, your entire body seems to glow. Local organizations (see p. 290) are working to continue the bay's preeminence by reducing artificial light pollution and educating locals about the bay's value, but Mosquito Bay continues to be threatened. For more information about bioluminescent bays, see p. 258. Barracuda Bay, the next inlet to the east, is also bioluminescent, but most tours don't head out that far. **Island Adventures** (see below) and several kayak operations (see **Boating,** below) offer bio bay tours, but individuals can also just drive east on the rough Sun Bay road and jump in the water. While cheap, this option means that you miss the guided tour and the opportunity to take a boat across the bay. Only choose this option if you have 4WD, and drive cautiously over the bumpy dirt road.

🏞 **Island Adventures,** Rte. 996 Km 4.5 (☎741-0720; www.biobay.com). Run by the Bio Bay Conservation Group (see p. 290), Island Adventures leads 1½ hr. tours through the bio bay. First groups listen to an informative talk, then they take the magic school bus to the bay for the electric boat tour and swimming. Call ahead for reservations. Trips almost every night, except during a full moon. $23, under 12 $12. MC/V.

BOATING

Blue Heron Kayaks (☎615-1625; www.Elenas-Vieques.com), leads several different kayak packages through the bio bay. The best trip departs at 1pm, traverses the man-grove channels, spends time at a deserted beach, provides sunset dinner, then returns to the bio bay ($94 including dinner). 4½ hr. beach/bio bay trip $69.50. 2½ hr. daytrip through the mangroves $49.50. Reservations with deposit required. No credit cards.

Blue Caribe Kayaks (☎741-2522), on C. Flamboyan in Esperanza. Sometimes employ-ees sit in front of Esperanza's pier. Offers 2hr. kayak tours of the bioluminescent bay with a chance to swim ($23). and 3½hr. kayaking/snorkeling trips around Cayo Afuera ($30). Single kayak rental $10 per hr. Open most days 8:30am-5pm. MC/V.

Aqua Frenzy Kayaks (☎741-0913) rents many single kayaks ($10 per hour or $40 per day) and 1 double kayak ($12.50/$50). 2hr. min. They allow renters to take the kayaks overnight, and provide information about kayaking into the bio bay. Delivery available.

DIVING AND SNORKELING

Like Culebra and Fajardo, the area around Vieques is flush with good, relatively shallow, diving opportunities. However, the island's only dive shop recently closed, so you can only dive here with a charter from the mainland. Vieques also has some great snorkeling, but the best areas are accessible by boat. The best place to snorkel from land is **Green Beach** (see p. 291). **Mosquito Pier,** which reaches out toward mainland Puerto Rico from the western reserve, has good snorkeling under the pier and on the four pile-ons just off the side. In **Esperanza,** the small dock in front of Playa Esperanza attracts a few fish. **Cayo Afuera,** the island in front of the strip, has some good reefs, but it's quite a swim.

FISHING

Caribbean Fly Fishing Co. offers half-day shoreline fly fishing trips ($35 per person plus $20 to rent the rods and reels) to catch chinook, tarpon, red snapper, grouper, and other fish. (☎741-1344. 2-person min. Cash only.)

HORSEBACK RIDES

Penny Miller at **Sea Gate Guest House** (see p. 284) leads horseback rides through both mountain and beach areas, depending on customer interest. (☎741-4661. Reservations requested. $40 per hr. MC/V.)

◤ SHOPPING

Vieques does not share Culebra's wealth of yuppie boutiques, but there are a few good places to get some local art or a classy souvenir.

Luna Loca Art Gallery, C. Baldorioty de Castro 500 (☎741-0264), Isabel II, has its fair share of cheesy tchotchkes, but also offers some quality local artwork. The owner makes attractive Vieques magnets. Open M-Sa 9am-5pm. AmEx/MC/V.

Vieques Flowers & Gifts Too!!, C. Flamboyan 134 (☎741-4197; www.viequesflowers.com), Esperanza, manages to stuff a complete flower store as well as many locally made arts and crafts, into its small space. Open daily 10am-4pm. AmEx/MC/V.

Kim's Cabin, C. Flamboyan 136 (☎741-3145), Esperanza, sells a variety of clothing, local art, and high-quality jewelry. Open daily 9am-5pm. AmEx/MC/V.

18 Degrees North, C. Flamboyan 134 (☎741-8600), Esperanza, carries a huge assortment of beach supplies. Forgot your shorts, beach toys, sunscreen, beach blankets, towel, or sandals? This large store probably has what you need, along with a collection of souvenir t-shirts. Usually open M-Tu 9:30am-noon, W-Su 9:30am-3pm. MC/V.

◧ FESTIVALS

The island of Vieques celebrates two annual festivals. During a long weekend in March or April, the Institute of Puerto Rican Culture hosts a cultural festival at the Fort with local artwork and music. Call ☎741-1717 for more info. Vieques's **fiestas patronales** are celebrated during the third weekend in July with five days of partying (W-Su). Contact the tourist office (☎741-0800) for exact dates.

◧ NIGHTLIFE

Vieques may be a major tourist area, but its nightlife scene lacks pizazz, to say the least. Most tourists spend the night at one of the bar/restaurants along the strip in Esperanza. Bananas has a popular evening crowd, but **Amapola Tavern,** C. Flamboyan 144, is the real winner. Throughout the day locals gather at the bar to discuss the day's events and relax in front of the TV. At night a fair number of travelers join in, creating a friendly, laid-back scene. (☎741-1382. Beer $1.75-3; frozen drinks $5-6. Open daily 11am-11pm. AmEx/MC/V.) For a bit more action, check out **Al's Mar Azul,** C. Plinio Peterson 577, in Isabel II. In spite of the honky-tonk American vibe, the bar hosts a lively crowd of both tourists and Puerto Ricans. Come early for a seat on the wooden patio overlooking the water. And whatever you do, **do not miss** the annual **Spam Cook-off,** held in May. This one-of-a-kind (in Puerto Rico at least) celebration features competitions for best entree, appetizer, and sculpture—at the end everyone eats the winning entries. Only in Vieques. (☎741-3400. Happy Hour daily 5-7pm. Beer $1.50-3; mixed drinks $4-5. Pool tables. Occasional live music. 18+ after 9pm. Open Su-Th 11am-1am, F-Sa 11am-2:30am. Cash only.)

CULEBRA

If you came to Puerto Rico in search of a gorgeous, picture-perfect beach, then look no farther than Culebra. Only on this small island will you find perfectly clear aquamarine ocean waves crashing gently against a long crescent of fine white sand. Culebra easily has the most beautiful beaches in Puerto Rico. And it has several snorkeling spots that rank among Puerto Rico's best. In addition to these attractions, Culebra retains a small-town charm that you wouldn't expect to find in such a prime tourist destination. With slightly over 2000 inhabitants, this is an island where people still stop and say hi to neighbors and the ferry arrival is the big event of the day. Culebra has one town with approximately six stop signs and zero traffic lights. And this may be the only place in Puerto Rico where you never have to worry about crime—Culebra simply does not have any. If you're looking for peace and quiet, welcome.

Culebra has not always been such a haven of tranquility. In 1901, two years after winning the Spanish-American war, the US government established military bases on Culebra, forcing residents to resettle in the area now known as Dewey. US President Theodore Roosevelt designated Culebra a National Wildlife Refuge in 1909, but the bombing practice continued on the northern half of the island, especially around Playa Flamenco. In 1975 the military left and moved all exercises to Vieques, which is only now escaping the Navy's presence (see p. 286).

The military may be gone, but Americans continue flocking to Culebra. The island houses a significant expat population, composed primarily of Americans who came on vacation and decided they couldn't leave. Culebra is the type of place where you get entrapped in the magic forever. The tiny island has few cultural attractions, and the dry vegetation is more similar to the Virgin Islands than tropical eastern Puerto Rico. However, the beaches alone are more than enough to keep any visitor happy. Of course any experience is what you make of it. During big holidays like Christmas and Holy Week the island's population can increase by as much as 15,000, as Puerto Ricans head east to take their own vacations. But for the majority of the year, Culebra continues at the slow pace that it was meant to live on, where nobody has anything to do but go to the beach. There may be no such thing as paradise, but Culebra comes awfully close.

HIGHLIGHTS OF CULEBRA

ESCAPE THE CROWDS with an adventurous hike down to the wild waves at isolated Playa Resaca (see p. 303).

JOIN THE CROWDS at the simply stunning Playa Flamenco (see p. 302).

SAMPLE Puerto Rico's best snorkeling at popular Playa Carlos Rosario (see p. 302).

TAKE A RIDE to the cays of Isla Peña or Culebrita, with their pristine beaches and prime snorkeling (see p. 303).

✈ INTER-ISLAND TRANSPORTATION

Flights: Aeropuerto Benjamin Rivera Noriega (☎ 742-0022), 2 mi. north of town at the intersection of Rte. 250 and Rte. 251. A 20min. walk or a $2 taxi ride. All of the airlines flying out of Culebra use tiny 6- to 8-seat planes and leave on demand. For reservations call or stop by the airport at least 1-2 days in advance. During major holidays reserve a few weeks in advance. Airport open daily 6am-7pm.

Air Flamenco (☎ 742-1040) flies to **Fajardo** (15min.; 4 per day; $25, round-trip $40) and **San Juan Isla Grande** (30min.; 2 per day; $40, round-trip $80). Open daily 6am-6pm. MC/V.

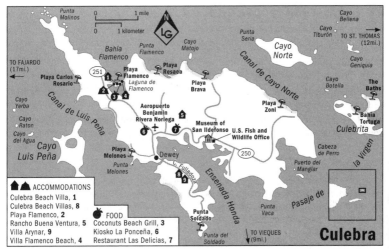

ACCOMMODATIONS
Culebra Beach Villa, **1**
Culebra Beach Villas, **8**
Playa Flamenco, **2**
Rancho Buena Ventura, **5**
Villa Arynar, **9**
Villa Flamenco Beach, **4**

FOOD
Coconuts Beach Grill, **3**
Kiosko La Ponceña, **6**
Restaurant Las Delicias, **7**

Culebra

Isla Nena (☎742-0872, reservations 863-4447) flies to **Fajardo** (15min.; 1-2 per day; $25, round-trip $45) and **San Juan International** (30min.; 4 per day; $70, round-trip $130). Also charters flights to **St. Thomas** ($550 per plane, round-trip $1000). Open daily 6am-6pm. MC/V.

Vieques Air Link (☎742-0254) flies to **Fajardo** (15min.; 3 per day; $20, round-trip $40) and **San Juan Isla Grande** (30min.; 2 per day; $40, round-trip $75). Open daily 6am-6pm. AmEx/MC/V.

Ferries: The **Puerto Rican Port Authority** (☎742-3161) runs ferries between Culebra and Fajardo. In addition to the routes below, a passenger ferry was recently added between Culebra and Vieques (M-F leaves Vieques 6am, returns from Culebra 5pm; round-trip $4). There is an additional charge for beach equipment, including tents ($2) and sleeping bags ($1). Reservations required for cars, but not accepted for passengers. Arrive 1hr. in advance. Reservation office open daily 8-11am and 1-3pm. MC/V.

FERRIES	FAJARDO-CULEBRA	CULEBRA-FAJARDO	PRICE
PASSENGER	M-F 9:30am, 3pm Sa-Su 9am, 2:30pm, 6:30pm	M-F 6:30am, 11:30am Sa-Su 6:30am, 11am, 4:30pm	$2.25
CARGO	M-F 3:30am, 4pm W and F 10am	M-F 7am, 6pm W and F 1pm	$15; round-trip $26.50

ORIENTATION

Culebra lies 17 mi. east of Puerto Rico and 12 mi. west of St. Thomas. Measuring 7 mi. in length and 3½ mi. in width, the island is tiny, and seems even smaller because almost all attractions are concentrated on the eastern side. The ferry arrives at the only town, **Dewey**, which is located on the southwest corner. From Dewey **Route 251** heads north past the airport to Playa Flamenco. **Route 250** goes east, past Fish and Wildlife, and the turn-offs for Playa Resaca and Brava, before finally ending up at Playa Zoni. The only other real road, **Calle Fulladoza,** heads south from town along Ensenada Honda to Punta Soldado. When people refer to Dewey's "main road" or "calle principal", they are usually talking about **Calle Pedro Márquez,** which originates at the ferry terminal and continues through town.

LOCAL TRANSPORTATION

Culebra's diminutive size makes it very easy to get around. Travelers staying in Dewey or Playa Flamenco can get by using only public transportation, but will be relatively stranded after dark. Those who want to explore the island should rent a jeep. Don't bring a rental car to Culebra; just rent a new one when you arrive. In theory biking seems like a good option, but the combination of hilly roads and hot afternoon sun can tire even the most fit travelers.

> **!** **PARKING WOES** Culebra police are extraordinarily vigilant about parking violations. Do not park in front of a fire hydrant, along a yellow curb, in a handicapped area, in a public vehicle spot, or along any curve in the road.

Públicos: Guaguas públicas, or shared taxi vans, run from the ferry terminal past the airport to Playa Flamenco, stopping at Culebra Beach Villa. Any trip between these points should cost $2-3. For an additional fee, vans will go almost anywhere on the island. During the day it is easy to hail down a taxi along Rte. 251; at night, or from a different location, try one of the following operators: **Kiko's Transportation Services** (☎509-3485), **Willy's Taxi** (☎742-3537), **Ruben** (☎405-1209), or **Eduardo** (☎438-3864).

Car Rental: Several companies rent jeeps, but during major holidays you should reserve 2-3 months in advance. Theoretically most companies require drivers to be at least 25, but in reality some companies do not rigidly enforce this requirement. The age and condition of jeeps varies greatly; if you get an older car, try bargaining down the price. Almost all companies offer airport/ferry pick-up service and weekly discounts.

Carlos Jeep Rental (☎742-3514 or 613-7049), on Rte. 250 at Vacation Property Realty. One of Culebra's more professional operations. $50-60 per day. Also rents snorkel equipment ($12 per day) and car seats ($3 per day). Weekly $5 per day discount. 25+. Open daily 8am-5pm. AmEx/MC/V.

Coral Reef Car Rental, C. Pedro Márquez 37 (☎/fax 742-0055). Jeeps $50-60 per day. 21+ with credit card; 25+ with cash. Open daily 8am-noon and 1-5pm. AmEx/MC/V.

Dick and Cathie Rentals (☎742-0062) rents VW Things. No pick-up service. $45 per day. 21+. No office; call ahead. No credit cards.

Jerry's Jeep Rental (☎742-0587), across from the airport. When you pick up the jeep Jerry spends 30min. explaining a map of Culebra. $45-60 per day. $5 per day discount with weekly rental. 25+. Open daily 8:30am-5pm. AmEx/MC/V.

Willy's Jeep Rental (☎742-3537), on Rte. 250. $40-45 per day. 25+. Open daily 8am-5pm. AmEx/MC/V.

Bike Rental: Culebra Bike Rental (☎742-2209; www.culebrabike.com), on C. Fulladoza, rents mountain bikes (21-speed bikes $15 per 24hr., $85 per week; 24-speed bikes $20/$100), boogie boards ($8 per day), and snorkel equipment ($12 per 24hr.). Open daily 9am-6pm. MC/V. **Dick and Cathie Rentals** (☎742-0062) delivers bikes ($15 per day). No credit cards. Reservations recommended.

PRACTICAL INFORMATION

Tourist Office: The municipal tourist office (☎742-3116 ext. 441 or 442), is on C. William Font, in the big yellow cement building on the way to the health clinic. Not much literature, but the staff can answer general questions. Open M-F 8am-4:30pm.

Bank: Banco Popular (☎742-3572), across from the ferry terminal at the corner of C. Pedro Márquez, is the only bank on the island. ATM. Open M-F 8:30am-3:30pm.

Publications: The Culebra Calendar, an invaluable monthly island publication, lists local events, advertisements, a tide table, classified ads, letters to the editors, and articles on current Culebra issues. Many island businesses distribute free copies.

Web Sites: Culebra has several very good web sites. Check out www.culebra-island.com, www.islaculebra.com, and www.culebra.org.

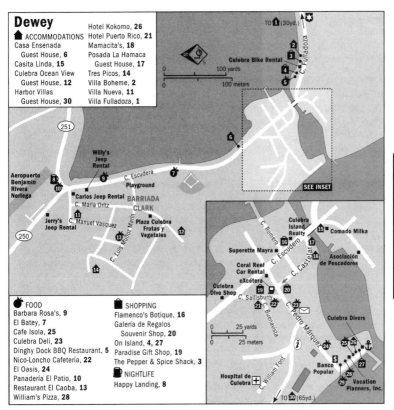

Dewey

🏠 ACCOMMODATIONS
Casa Ensenada
 Guest House, **6**
Casita Linda, **15**
Culebra Ocean View
 Guest House, **12**
Harbor Villas
 Guest House, **30**

Hotel Kokomo, **26**
Hotel Puerto Rico, **21**
Mamacita's, **18**
Posada La Hamaca
 Guest House, **17**
Tres Picos, **14**
Villa Boheme, **2**
Villa Nueva, **11**
Villa Fulladoza, **1**

🍴 FOOD
Barbara Rosa's, **9**
El Batey, **7**
Cafe Isola, **25**
Culebra Deli, **23**
Dinghy Dock BBQ Restaurant, **5**
Nico-Loncho Cafetería, **22**
El Oasis, **24**
Panadería El Patio, **10**
Restaurant El Caoba, **13**
William's Pizza, **28**

🛍 SHOPPING
Flamenco's Botique, **16**
Galería de Regalos
 Souvenir Shop, **20**
On Island, **4, 27**
Paradise Gift Shop, **19**
The Pepper & Spice Shack, **3**

🎵 NIGHTLIFE
Happy Landing, **8**

CULEBRA

Work Opportunities: The Culebra Calendar (see Publications, above) has a help-wanted section with short- and long-term job openings.

Supermarkets: Seertu **Food,** p. 300.

Laundromat: Mamacita's (☎ 360-9807; see **Accommodations,** p. 299) opens its laundromat to non-guests. Wash $2. Dry $0.25 per 6min. Change usually available in the office. Open daily 8am-9:30pm. **Dick and Cathie Rentals** (☎ 742-0062) provides wash, dry, and fold service ($1.25 per lb.). Call ahead. Cash only.

Police: ☎ 742-3501. On C. Fulladoza, about ¼ mi. past Dinghy Dock. Open 24hr.

Pharmacy: Culebra has no real pharmacies. The hospital (see above) has a pharmacy with prescription drugs only. **Superette Mayra** (see p. 300) and **eXcétera** (see **Internet Access,** below), both offer a small selection of over-the-counter toiletries. Bring your own tampons, contact lens supplies, condoms, and any other difficult to find supplies.

Medical Services: Hospital de Culebra (☎ 742-3511 or 742-0001, ambulance service ☎ 742-0208) at the end of C. William Font, in the building marked "recetas" at the top of the hill. A small health clinic. 24hr. **emergency room.** Clinic open M-F 7am-4:30pm.

Internet Access: eXcétera, C. Sallisburry 10 (☎ 742-0844; fax 742-0826) offers Internet ($5 for 15min. or $15 per hr.), **fax service,** and a long-distance telephone station. They also sell English-language travel guides. Open M-F 8am-5pm, Sa 9am-1pm. MC/V.

Post Office: C. Pedro Márquez 26 (☎ 742-3862). General Delivery available. Open M-F 8am-4:30pm, Sa 8am-noon.

Zip Code: 00775.

ACCOMMODATIONS & CAMPING

Culebra may play host to a plethora of visitors, but most of the accommodations are either lackluster or severely overpriced. An attractive room here will cost at least $90 per night. Most accommodations offer discounts for stays over a week or during low season (Aug.-Oct.).

REALTORS

The following realtors rent properties around the island equipped with linens, towels, and a kitchen. Check out the houses online, then call for rates and availability.

Vacation Planners, Inc. (☎742-3112, toll-free 866-CULEBRA; fax 742-1060; www.vplans.com), across from the ferry. Most properties have A/C, some have TVs. Free pick-up. 2-night min. 15% weekly discount. $125-$500 per night. Open M-Sa 9am-noon and 2-5pm, Su 3-5pm. MC/V.

Culebra Island Realty (☎742-0052; www.culebraislandrealty.com), at the intersection of C. Romero and Escudero. For over 6 years this operation has been renting out vacation homes around Culebra. Free pick-up. 1-week min. 50% deposit required. 2-6 person homes $800-2600 per week. Hours are sporadic; call ahead. Checks only.

DEWEY

▧ **Villa Fulladoza** (☎742-0807 or 396-2477), on C. Fulladoza. This waterside guest house charges some of the most affordable prices in town. Sparkling, brightly colored rooms come with a kitchen, fans, balconies, and some sort of ocean view. Room price varies by size. Spacious common patio filled with mango trees. Private dock. Book exchange. Check-in 2:30pm. Check-out 10am. $10 surcharge for 1 night stay. Doubles $55-75; weekly $350-475. Extra child (in larger rooms only) $10. Tax not included. MC/V. ❸

Villa Nueva, C. Manuel Vasquez 128 (☎742-0257), in a residential neighborhood north of town. 4 simple rooms come with a fridge. Unfortunately, the house is a bit dark. Common kitchen, living room, TV, VCR, and a movie collection. 15min. walk from town. Call ahead; the owner is rarely home. Free pick-up and drop-off. $20 surcharge for 1 night stay. Doubles $50, with A/C $65, with semi-private kitchen $85. MC/V. ❷

Casita Linda (☎742-0360 or 403-5292), across the bridge and to the right. This small 3-room guest house was clearly a labor of love. The friendly owners have hand-decorated every room with bright colors, flowers, and unique furniture. All rooms have a full kitchen, a balcony with canal views, a TV, and a VCR with movies. Some people have to sleep on fold-out futons. No office and the owners can be hard to reach; call ahead. Quad $99; 6-person suite $149; 8-person house $249. Tax included. MC/V. ❹

Posada La Hamaca Guest House, C. Castelar 68 (☎742-3516; fax 742-0181; www.posada.com). If you can live with the fact that Mamacita's next door is a lot more fun, this pretty pastel house offers comparable accommodations at a much better price. Small hotel-style rooms are acceptable but a bit dreary. A/C and ceiling fans. English-language book exchange. Snorkel gear $10 for 24hr. Check-out 10am. 10% surcharge for 1 night stay. Doubles $75-99; extra person $11. Tax included. MC/V. ❸

Villa Boheme, C. Fulladoza 368 (☎742-3508 or 370-4949; www.villaboheme.com), has great grounds; a large wall surrounds several buildings and a common patio area facing the bay. The rooms themselves are less inspiring, with generic decor and some futons and bunk beds. Fully equipped communal kitchen with direct TV. Also offers kayak rentals, a boat dock, and water taxi service (see p. 304). Management can be hard to reach. Check-in noon. Check-out 10:30am. 2 night min. on weekends. Doubles $95, with kitchen $119; quads $131-137. Tax included. AmEx/MC/V. ❹

Hotel Kokomo (☎742-0683), across from the ferry dock. New management has given this budget favorite a face-lift, with brightly colored walls and A/C in every room. Still the basic rooms are not always kept clean. Top-floor suites have ocean views. Prices may rise with future renovations. Check-out 11am. Doubles $45, with bath $60; triple $80; 8- to 10-person apartment with kitchen $125-150. Tax included. MC/V. ❷

Mamacita's, C. Castelar 64-66 (☎742-0090; fax 742-0301; www.mamacitaspr.com), feels like a fun European hostel painted in Caribbean colors. Rooms suffer from age, some mattresses are thin, and there are no TVs, but you can't beat the atmosphere and the location overlooking the canal. A/C. Check-in 2pm. Check-out 11am. Doubles $85-95; 2-person suites with kitchen $125; extra person $15. Tax not included. MC/V. ❹

Casa Ensenada Guest House, C. Escudero 142 (☎742-3559, toll-free 800-484-9659 code 6001; www.culebrarentals.com) consists of 3 hand-decorated rooms in the owners' home. All rooms come with 13" satellite TV, VCR, A/C, microwave, fridge, full utensils, and a guest info packet. Library. Common waterfront patio with picnic table and grill. Check-out 10am. $20 surcharge for 1 night stay. Doubles Nov. 26-Apr. 30 $100-150; May 1-Aug. 31 $90-130; Sept. 1-Nov. 25 $60-90; extra person $10. MC/V. ❹

Tres Picos (☎742-0048; tkagv@aol.com), in the hills above residential Barriada Clark. This well-equipped apartment on the first floor of a house seems like a pristine home away from home. Apartment includes a full kitchen, a living room with direct TV, a bathroom with a deluxe shower, and a bedroom with A/C, and a ceiling fan. Lots of space and privacy for a romantic retreat. Big porch area with great views of the town and the bay. 2 adults only. 1 week min. $775 per week. Tax included. Cash only. ❹

Coral Reef Car Rental, C. Pedro Márquez 37 (☎/fax 742-0055), rents 2 rooms in the Galería de Regalos building. You get exactly what you'd expect from a car rental agency: utilitarian, clean, functional, and utterly impersonal accommodations. Rooms include A/C, microwave, tiny fridge, and 13" TV. "Beds" sometimes consist of fold-out futons. 3-person studio $75; 6-person apartment $130. Tax included. AmEx/MC/V. ❸

Culebra Ocean View Guest House, C. Maria Ortíz 201 (☎360-9807 or 742-2601; www.culebraoceanview.com), perched high in the hills above Dewey, is located in someone's large orange house, but feels more like a hotel. Popular with Puerto Rican tourists. Big common balcony. Rooms have fridge, A/C, and TV. Miniscule plastic pool. Doubles $74-125; quads $104-125; extra person $10. Tax not included. MC/V. ❸

Hotel Puerto Rico (☎742-3372), on C. Buenavista, is the oldest hotel on Culebra, and it looks like it hasn't changed since it opened in 1945. The 3-story cement structure has dirt in the corners and chipping paint, but this is the cheapest place in town. No hot water and no TV. Rooms without A/C can get very hot. Spanish only. Reception 8am-6pm. Check-out 11am. Doubles $40, with A/C $50, with A/C and bath $60; quads with A/C and bath $80. Tax included. Cash only. ❷

Harbor Villas Guest House (☎742-3855 or 742-3171; www.culebrahotel.com), 1½ mi. west of town en route to Playa Melones. Look for the "Bienvenidos" sign and the 3 A-frame houses on the hill. Only at this unique hillside hotel can you cook dinner at an outdoor kitchen or shower beneath the stars. Quiet location with great views, but far from beaches and town. 1-2 bedroom suites have A/C in the bedroom and some sort of kitchen; only 1 has hot water. Villas are complete houses with kitchens. No office. Free pick-up and drop-off. Suites: doubles $125; quads $150. Winter 2-person villas $175; summer $125; extra person $25. Cash only. ❹

NORTH OF DEWEY

▧ **Culebra Beach Villa** (☎742-0319, reservations 754-6236), on the dirt road off Rte. 251 just before Playa Flamenco. This is the largest hotel located directly on the beautiful sands of Playa Flamenco. 'Nuff said. A 3-story wooden hotel faces the beach, and several brightly colored bungalows hide in back. Clean apartments vary in terms of set-up. All include A/C, cable TV, and a full kitchen. Book exchange. Reception 10am-2pm and 3:30-7pm. Check-in 3pm. Check-out noon. Doubles $125; quads $155-200; 6-person apartment $185; 8-person $250. Tax not included. MC/V. ❹

Villa Flamenco Beach (☎742-0023; www.culebra-island.com). Villa Flamenco Beach also boasts direct access to Playa Flamenco. However, with only 6 rooms, Flamenco feels much more personal than its neighbor. Neat and functional plain white rooms. Airy front studios have balconies and ocean view. All rooms have kitchenettes; only doubles have A/C. Doubles $100-115; 4-person apartments $120. Tax not included. MC/V. ❹

CULEBRA

Rancho Buena Ventura, Rte. 250 Km 2.7 (☎742-3374; fax 742-0638). Turn left at the sign, then right on the first long dirt driveway. With 2½ acres of grassy fields, this converted farm-house feels like it belongs in the central mountains. Pick some fresh fruit, then lie in the field and watch the stars. Private bathrooms located outside of the unadorned rooms. Huge common area with kitchen. Doubles $75; extra person $20. Tax not included. ❸

Playa Flamenco Campground (☎742-7000), at Playa Flamenco. Located just 20 ft. from the beach, this campground is easily the best in Puerto Rico. Unfortunately, it's also the most crowded; during high season (Apr.-Sept.) hundreds of people squeeze into the big field, leading to wild nights of booze and drugs. Facilities include toilets, outdoor showers, potable water, a bike rack, trash cans, and picnic tables. Reservations recommended during high season. $20 per tent; up to 6 people. Cash only. ❶

SOUTH OF DEWEY

Quiet C. Fulladoza receives little traffic and the accommodations on the hill offer tranquility and beautiful bay views. Unfortunately, there are no sandy beaches and it's quite a walk to town; if you're staying here, it's a good idea to splurge on a car.

Culebra Beach Villas, on C. Fulladoza, 1 mi. from town. These renovated vacation homes consist of shared wooden houses on a hill overlooking Ensenada Honda. Completed rooms charm with bright walls, wooden floors, and marble bathrooms. Most units come with a full kitchen, A/C, hot water, and a deck. Private dock. No office; contact Hotel Kokomo (see p. 298) for information and reservations. Doubles and quads $125; 2-bedroom units $160; prices may rise with renovations. Tax not included. MC/V. ❹

Villa Arynar (☎742-3145; www.arynar.com), on C. Fulladoza. The American couple running Culebra's only bed and breakfast welcomes guests as part of the family and does everything possible to help, from pointing out island attractions to reminding guests to wear sunscreen. The 2 cozy rental rooms feel like spare bedrooms and everyone sits down to breakfast together. Complimentary snorkel gear and beach towels. Shared bathroom. 1 rental car available ($40 per day). Free pick-up. Private pier. Adults only. 5-night min. Open Nov.15-May 15. Doubles $90; weekly $595. MC/V. ❹

⬛ FOOD

Food in Culebra tends to be expensive. Luckily many accommodations offer kitchen facilities and it's much more affordable to cook at home.

GROCERIES

Superette Mayra, C. Escudero 118 (☎742-3888) is Culebra's largest grocery store. Open M-Sa 9am-1:30pm and 3:30-6:30pm. MC/V.

Plaza Culebra Frutas & Vegetales (☎742-0596), on C. Maria Ortíz, has Culebra's best fruits and veggies. Sa-Su fresh baked goods. Open in the truck in front of the post office W 8:30-11:30am. Open in their home north of town W 1-5pm, Th 8:30-11:30am and 2:30-5:45pm, F 3:30-5:45pm, Sa-Su 9am-1pm. Cash only.

Asociación de Pescadores (☎742-0144 or 742-3506), across the bridge and to the right, sells frozen fish that come straight out of the waters around Culebra. Typically includes yellow tail, red snapper, conch, and octopus, among others. Fish $3-4 per lb. Lobster $7 per lb. Open M-Sa 7am-4:30pm, Su 7am-3pm. MC/V.

Colmado Milka (☎742-2253), across the bridge and to the right, is Culebra's 2nd largest grocery store. Open M-Sa 7am-6pm, Su 7am-noon. MC/V.

DEWEY

⬛ **Barbara Rosa's,** C. Escudero 189 (☎397-1923). Chef Barbara Rosa used to work at Club Seabourne, then decided to open her own restaurant with the perfect budget dining formula: a handwritten menu, counter service (no tip), and BYOB. The result is a collection of picnic tables around a trailer serving simple, but delicious, entrees. Meatless spaghetti $6. Lunch $6-7. Dinner $6-13. Open Tu-Su 11:30am-9pm. Cash only. ❷

Cafe Isola (☎742-0203), across from the ferry dock, under Hotel Kokomo. This trendy cafe seems to represent the changing times in Culebra. At Isola, good ol' *café con leche* is replaced with espresso, latte, and cappuccino ($1-3) and linoleum floors make way for a hip European-style decor. Reasonably priced and very tasty. Salads, sandwiches, and hamburgers $4-7. Breakfast $2-5. Beer $1.50-3. Open Th-M 8am-6pm. MC/V. ❶

El Oasis (☎742-3175), on C. Pedro Márquez. It's difficult to walk past The Oasis at night; if the smell doesn't draw you in, the raucous crowd certainly well. This is the best pizzeria on Culebra and Willy the bartender welcomes everyone like an old friend. Indulge on pizza or sample one of the salads with homemade dressing. Limited pasta entrees $7-10. Medium pizza $10-19. Open Th-M 6-10pm. Cash only. ❸

Nico-Loncho Cafetería, C. Sallisburry 56 (☎742-3372), across from eXcétera. Before you spend your life savings trying to eat, stop by Culebra's hidden lunchtime bargain. Few travelers realize that this small *cafetería* serves heaping Puerto Rican lunches at a reasonable price. Menu changes daily. Sandwiches $1.50-3.75. Breakfast $2-4.50. Lunch $6.50-8.50. Open M-F 6:30am-3:30pm. Cash only. ❷

Dinghy Dock BBQ Restaurant (☎742-0233), on C. Fulladoza. The name is not a metaphor; dinghies actually dock beside your table as you enjoy tasty Puerto Rican/American food at this expat favorite. Entrees are a bit spendy, but include a salad buffet. Try the specialty: baby back ribs with homemade BBQ sauce ($17). Breakfast and lunch $4-8. Dinner $10-17. Open daily 7:30am-9:30pm. Bar open noon-11pm. MC/V. ❸

El Batey, Rte. 250 Km 1.1 (☎742-3828), ½ mi. north of town, looks like a local joint but serves mostly foreigners. Meat, meat, and more meat. The interior is dreary, but the simple outdoor patio boasts a harbor view. Burgers $3-4.25. Dinner $8-15. Open Su-M 6-9pm, Tu-Th 10:30am-2:30pm and 6-9pm, F-Sa 10:30am-2:30pm. Cash only. ❸

Mamacita's, C. Castelar 64-66 (☎742-0090). When it's good, it's very good, but some locals claim that the food at Mamacita's varies greatly. Cozy patio overlooking the canal is consistently appealing. The rotating menu, written on a chalkboard, includes seafood, meats and 1 veggie option ($14-19). Lunch $6.50-8. Sa-Su breakfast buffet $8, children $5. Open daily noon-11pm. MC/V. ❹

Restaurant El Caoba (☎742-3235), on C. Luis Muñoz Marín. Locals refer to this traditional restaurant as "Tina's" after the amiable owner. The linoleum floor, plastic tablecloths, and abundant fans create a rustic charm. Big plates of genuine Puerto Rican food. No written menu. Entrees $8-15. Open M-Sa 11am-8:30pm, Su 11am-5pm. ❸

Panadería El Patio (☎742-0374), at the end of the airport runway. Culebra's version of the typical Puerto Rican sandwich shop. The small, dark restaurant has an outdoor seating area, but the sandwiches ($2.50-3.75) taste even better as a beach picnic. Serves sandwiches until noon, then sells prepackaged snacks only. Open daily 5:30am-6:30pm. Cash only. ❶

Culebra Deli, C. Pedro Márquez 26 (☎742-3277). This hole-in-the-wall deli dishes out fast, cheap Puerto Rican food. Choose between fried chicken ($3.25), sandwiches ($2-3), breakfast food ($2-3), and *empanadillas* ($1), then take your food to go; the 8 seats lining the wall are usually full. Open M-Sa 5:30am-2pm. Cash only. ❶

William's Pizza (☎742-7777), across from the ferry dock. This drab pizza place has a few redeeming qualities: it's cheap, it's open late, and it delivers. Slice $1.50-3; large pizza $10-22. Open Su-W 10am-10pm, Th-Sa 10am-11pm. Cash only. ❶

OUTSIDE OF TOWN

Restaurant Las Delicias, Rte. 250 Km 2.6 (☎742-3222). Relaxed Las Delicias serves up delicious seafood in a residential courtyard. Limited menu includes seafood salads and *ballenas,* crispy flour bowls filled with seafood. Also some chicken and meat options. Entrees $8-21. Open Th-Sa from 6pm till they run out of food. ❸

Kiosko La Ponceña, Rte. 250 Km 5.5 (☎608-7964). This little roadside kiosk makes an excellent stop between town and Playa Flamenco. The menu changes daily—call up the friendly owner and he'll tell you what's being served. Typical entrees include lasagna, meat, and fish ($6-8). Baked potatoes $3.75-5. Open M-Sa 11am-10pm. Cash only. ❷

Coconuts Beach Grill, in front of Culebra Beach Villa (see p. 299), is nothing more than an outdoor grill, but it's the only sit-down eatery near the beach. The chalkboard usually lists 3 sandwich options ($5-7) and a couple of mixed drinks. Tasty, simple food. Open Su-Th 11am-5:30pm, F-Sa 11am-7pm. Cash only. ❷

🌀 BEACHES

The water around the island is a translucent aqua that looks unmistakably Caribbean and invites swimmers to float beneath the sun for hours. While popular Playa Flamenco is undeniably amazing, it is worthwhile to venture out to other, less populated beaches, especially if you have a car. Regardless of where you travel, don't search for palm tree-lined beaches. Culebra has a very dry landscape and there are only a few scattered palms; shade-lovers should grab a spot early.

BEACHES	ACCESSIBILITY FROM DEWEY	CROWDS	ACTIVITIES	FACILITIES
Flamenco	8min. drive	Med.-Large	Swimming, snorkeling, boogie boarding	Bathrooms, picnic tables, trash cans, outdoor showers
Carlos Rosario	25min. walk from Flamenco	Med.-Large	Snorkeling	None
Culebrita	25min. boat ride	Small-Med.	Snorkeling, swimming, turtle-watching	None
Luis Peña	15min. boat ride	Small-Med.	Snorkeling, swimming	None
Zoni	15min. drive	Small-Med.	Swimming, boogie boarding	None
Brava	15min. drive plus 20min. walk	Small	Boogie boarding, turtle-watching	None
Resaca	15min. drive plus 30min. hike	Small	Boogie boarding, turtle watching	None
Punta Soldado	15min. drive	Small	Snorkeling	None
Melones	15min. walk	Small	Snorkeling, swimming	Trash cans

■ **PLAYA FLAMENCO.** In comparison to this exquisite beach every *balneario* on the mainland looks like a dirty swimming pool. Numerous media outlets, including the Travel Channel, have listed Culebra among the best beaches in the world. As you ascend the hill coming from Dewey, and Playa Flamenco spreads across the landscape, you'll no doubt agree. Playa Flamenco is Culebra's largest, most popular, and most accessible beach. It is also the only beach on the island with facilities, including bathrooms, picnic tables, and a campground. Because of these factors, and because Flamenco looks like it was created to be on a postcard, the beach can get crowded, especially on holidays when thousands of Puerto Ricans descend. Luckily Flamenco is huge and 99% of the time there's more than enough room for everyone. Flamenco also offers a few decent **snorkeling** opportunities. Facing the water, walk all the way to the left past the two deserted tanks (remnants of the US Navy's stint on Culebra) to the jetty, where you'll find a small reef. Alternatively, walk all the way to the right, just past the second rock jetty (actually old shark pens—another gift from the US Navy) for another small reef. *(Drive north on Rte. 251 until the road ends. A público from Dewey costs $2-3.)*

■ **PLAYA CARLOS ROSARIO.** Culebra's premier snorkeling beach can be full of people or completely empty. The crescent-shaped beach has coral on the right and boulders on the left, with a sandy passageway in the center. Enter the water in the middle, then swim about 15-30 ft. in either direction to find amazing schools of blue tang, sergeant majors, and the occasional barracuda. Don't forget to bring water and a snack, as Carlos Rosario has absolutely no facilities. *(From the Playa Flamenco parking lot, walk 25min. on the dirt path over the hill. Carlos Rosario is the second beach.)*

CULEBRITA. If you're looking for a deserted island, and Culebra doesn't quite do the trick, continue east to the tiny island of Culebrita. With adequate hiking, fabulous snorkeling, gorgeous beaches, and a lighthouse, Culebra's little sister easily merits a day of exploration. Most water taxis drop passengers at the pier on the west side of the island. This beach has great snorkeling, but continue along the marked trail for 10min. to reach **Bahía Tortuga,** the biggest and best beach on Culebrita. Few people make it out here during the week, so it's not uncommon to share the brilliant waters only with the other people on your boat. Culebrita is a protected wildlife refuge, and this is another popular turtle breeding ground. From the pier a different trail leads 15-20min. uphill to the lighthouse. This relic of the Spanish occupation was condemned in 2003, but there are plans to renovate and open it to the public. The peninsula on northeast Culebrita known as **The Baths** also has some great snorkeling. Culebrita is worth the transportation costs, but avoid the little island on weekends and holidays, when it turns into a zoo of private boats. *(From Dewey water taxis (see p. 305; $40) take 25min. to reach Culebrita.)*

LUIS PEÑA. For yet another quasi-deserted Caribbean beach with white sand, blue water, and lots of fish, head out to Luis Peña, a short 15min. water taxi ride from Dewey. On weekdays the long narrow beaches surrounding the island are almost always empty and the water is as calm as a lake. The snorkeling is superb all the way around the little island, especially in the channel facing Culebra. Like Culebra, Luis Peña is a designated wildlife refuge. *(15min. water taxi ride from Dewey (see p. 305; $25) or a short kayak ride from Playa Tamarindo.)*

PLAYA ZONI. Not many people make it out to the eastern side of the island, but those who do will be rewarded with acres of undeveloped land and a visit to Culebra's second most popular swimming beach, Playa Zoni. It seems impossible, but the water here tends to be an even more impressive color than the water at Flamenco. There are no facilities, and crowds are generally very small. The long, narrow, sandy beach affords views of the Culebrita lighthouse and, in the distance, St. Thomas. *(Take Rte. 250 all the way east to the end.)*

PLAYA BRAVA AND PLAYA RESACA. It's just you and the turtles at these two bays on Culebra's northern coast. Visitors rarely trek out to these secluded beaches and those who do will be rewarded with long stretches of beautiful white sand all for themselves. Both Brava and Resaca have strong waves that create conditions bad for swimming but decent for surfing. There are reefs on both sides of Resaca's bay, but the water is generally much too rough to snorkel. From March to August leatherback turtles lay their eggs on Resaca and Brava; never stay at these beaches after dark and if you see tracks during the day, try not to disturb them. *(To reach **Playa Brava** drive east on Rte. 250, continue past the cemetery, and turn left on the road just after the house with the "1908" sign. Park at the end of the pavement, then follow the dirt road 20min. downhill, veering left at the fork. Ignore the No Trespassing signs; all Puerto Rican beaches are public property. To reach **Playa Resaca** drive east on Rte. 250 and turn left on the road directly after the airport. Drive all the way to the top, stopping at the landing just before the radio tower. Follow the narrow trail downhill through the brush and mangroves until you reach the beach. Call Fish and Wildlife (☎ 742-0115) before attempting the difficult hike, because if it hasn't been marked recently you will get lost.)*

PUNTA SOLDADO. Located on the southern tip of Culebra, the coral beach at Punta Soldado has excellent snorkeling; some claim that it is even better than Carlos Rosario. Solitude and calm water more than compensate for the rocky shoreline. The shallow water makes it easy for even small children to snorkel—the best site is on the left-hand side of the beach, but reefs line the entire shore. *(Drive all the way down C. Fulladoza, past where the road turns to dirt. About 2½ mi.)*

PLAYA MELONES. Melones's claim to fame is that it is the most easily accessible beach from Dewey. The rocky beach's location on the Luis Peña Channel makes for good snorkeling and shallow, clear water. Unfortunately there are few shady areas and no facilities, so come prepared with lots of sunscreen.

C
U
L
E
B
R
A

GIVING BACK

TURTLE TIME

The Culebra archipelago serves as a major breeding ground for leatherback and hawksbill turtles. Throughout the year these enormous creatures, which can get as large as 3½ ft. and 400 lbs., drag themselves onto sandy beaches in the dead of night to lay eggs. Unfortunately, both species are endangered—humans, animals, and natural disasters have all contributed to the destruction of countless turtle egg nests. Furthermore, many traditional nesting sights have been developed and Culebra is one of the few places that still has deserted beaches where sea turtles can safely lay eggs. From March to August leatherback turtles nest on Playas Resaca, Brava, and Zoni. Hawksbill turtles lay eggs primarily between August and December although they can be found throughout the year) in pockets of sand on the north side of Culebra, Culebrita, and Cayo Norte. To protect the species, visitors should never disturb turtle nests and never bring lights to the beaches at night.

CORALations (www.coralations.org), a non-profit aimed at preserving Caribbean reefs, works with the DRN and Fish and Wildlife to protect the turtle breeding grounds. During breeding season they ask volunteers to spend the entire night on the beach, watching for turtles and assisting a technician. Participants must be in good physical condition. For more information contact Mary Ann at CORALations (☎877-772-6725) or Fish and Wildlife (☎742-0115).

The best snorkeling is on the right side of the beach. Swim all the way north, past the peninsula, and you'll end up at Playa Tamarindo, another good snorkeling beach. *(From town walk uphill past the tourist office, veer left, and continue walking for 15min. Melones is the second beach at the end of the road.)*

🔆 ⚐ SIGHTS AND FESTIVALS

Apart from the condemned lighthouse on Culebrita, Culebra does not have many traditional sights. However, the Culebra Foundation has been working to preserve the island's history by renovating abandoned buildings and promoting island culture. The first fruit of this project is the **Museum of San Ildefonso**, Rte. 250 Km 4, just behind the Department of Natural Resources office. Located in a 1905 US Navy magazine, the museum contains historical pictures and some pre-Taíno artifacts. The foundation plans to add an art museum and more historical markers. (In the building with the "1905" sign, next to the water. ☎742-0240. Open daily M-F 8am-noon and 1-3pm, Sa-Su on request. Free.) Culebra does not celebrate *fiestas patronales*, but Dewey hosts a large **artisans festival** every year over a weekend in late July. For information contact the tourist office (☎742-3116 ext. 441 or 442).

🏄 OUTDOOR ACTIVITIES

BOATING

Culebra Boat Rental (☎742-3559), at Casa Ensenada Guest House (see p. 299), rents 3 16-18' motorboats ($160-200 for the 1st day, $110-150 per additional day; $500 deposit; 25+) and a 14' Sunfish sailboat ($100 per day, $65 per ½ day; $200 deposit; 15+). Discounts for guests and multiday rentals. Call ahead. Limited fishing equipment for sale. Boats available 7am-6pm. MC/V.

Ocean Safari Kayaks (☎379-1973) rents kayaks for $40 per day (8hr.), including a free lesson. Most people go from Playa Tamarindo to LuisLuis Peña. Free pick-up and delivery.

Villa Boheme, C. Fulladoza 368 (☎742-3508 or 370-4949; www.villaboheme.com), rents single and double kayaks ($10 per hr., $40 per day) and windsurfers ($25 per hr.) $45 for a 1hr. beginning windsurfer lesson. AmEx/MC/V.

Buenadonga (☎235-7099), offers sailboat charters around Culebra ($100 per person per day, $60 per ½ day) and sailing lessons ($20 per hr.). Reservation with deposit required. Cash only.

DIVING AND SNORKELING

Over 50 attractive dive sights surround Culebra and its cays. Conditions here are very similar to those in Fajardo, with visibility around 30-80 ft. and plenty of shallow dives for beginners. This is a great place to get certified. Many beaches around Culebra have amazing snorkeling opportunities: see **Beaches,** p. 302, for more info.

Culebra Dive Shop (☎742-0566 or 501-4656; www.culebradiveshop.com), on Rte. 250, has a 30' boat. Offers 2-tank dives ($90), 1-tank night dives ($60), a 2-tank Discover Scuba package ($140), and a 4-day PADI open-water dive certification course ($460 includes 6 dives and all equipment). 5hr. snorkeling tour $45. Boat ride-along $25. Full-day trips include equipment and lunch. Snorkel equipment rental $10 for 24hr. Helpful staff provides info about island snorkel sites. ½-day deep sea fishing $450, full-day $600. Boogie board rental $10 for 24hr. Also sells souvenirs, artwork, clothing, and specialty foods. Open daily 9am-6pm. AmEx/D/MC/V.

Culebra Divers, C. Pedro Márquez 4 (☎742-0803; www.culebradivers.com), across from the ferry terminal, has two 26' boats that make dive trips in the morning (2-tank dive $85, equipment rental $15) and 3hr. snorkel trips in the afternoon ($45, ages 6-12 $30; min. 2 people). 1-tank night dive $70. 1-dive Discover Scuba package $90. NAUI Scuba Diver certification $495. During high season reserve up to 1 month in advance. All trips include beverages. Snorkel rental $12.50 for the 1st day (back by 9am the next day), $10 for additional days. High season open daily 9am-noon and 2-5:30pm. Low season open only Sa-Su reduced hours. MC/V.

HIKING

While most of Culebra's land is privately held, the US Fish and Wildlife Service protects over 1500 acres of the island, including all of the off-shore keys (except Cayo Norte), the majority of the Flamenco Peninsula, a large section of land around Playa Resaca, and all of the wetlands and mangroves. The **trail** down to Playa Resaca (see p. 303) is more than just a beach path; this intense 30min. hike descends Culebra's tallest hill. You must crawl over boulders and find your way through a mangrove grove before reaching the beach. Another path leads across Culebrita from the boat landing to Bahía Tortuga. The friendly staff at the **US Fish and Wildlife Service** is more than happy to answer questions about hikes, beaches, or the turtle-watching program. (Drive east on Rte. 250 and look for the sign just after the cemetery. ☎742-0115; www.fws.gov. Open M-F 7am-4pm.)

SURFING

Culebra's surf can't compete with the mainland's northern coast, but if you have your own board there are a few waves to be found. It's best to hit the beach from May to July, the beginning of hurricane season, when heavier winds create larger waves. Locals recommend **Carlos Rosario, Punta Soldado,** and **Zoni** as some of the best surfing beaches. Almost all of the beaches along the northern coast occasionally have big waves that are great for boogie boarding. **Culebra Dive Shop** (see above) rents boogie boards ($10 per 24hr.).

WATER TAXIS

Small motor boats take visitors on daytrips to Luis Peña and Culebrita. All certified boat captains (see below) charge $25 round-trip to Luis Peña and $40 to Culebrita. Trips do not leave every day; call ahead for a reservation.

Villa Boheme (Captain Rico's Water Taxi), C. Fulladoza 368 (☎742-3508 or 370-4949). Also offers trips to Carlos Rosario ($25 per person) and 3hr. fishing charters ($60-120 per person). AmEx/MC/V.

Tanama the Glass Bottom Boat (☎501-0011 or 397-7494). Just in case there's any confusion, this is Culebra's only glass-bottom boat. Tanama does a 2hr. harbor cruise ($25), a ½ mi. cruise over the reefs ($25), a 2-5hr. snorkeling trip ($40; equipment not included), and other trips upon request. Typically leaves from Dinghy Dock. Cash only.

Ocean View Water Taxi (☎360-9807) leaves from Mamacita's (see p. 299). 1hr. tour $25. Fully equipped snorkeling trip to Luis Peña with lunch, kayaks, snorkel equipment, beverages, and beer $45. Cash only.

■ SHOPPING

Over the past few years Culebra has experienced an influx of trendy little gift shops.

Paradise Gift Shop, C. Sallisburry 110 (☎742-3569), has the best selection on the island, including quite a few local gifts and artwork. Free English-language book exchange. Open Th-Tu 9am-6pm. MC/V.

On Island, C. Pedro Márquez 4 (☎742-0439), at the ferry landing, wins the prize for trendiest boutique store in town. The new age store sells island jewelry, Caribbean gifts, and hemp purses. Open daily 10am-noon and 3-6pmish. MC/V. Also at C. Fulladoza 372 (☎742-0704), above Dinghy Dock. Open daily 10am-6pmish.

The Pepper & Spice Shack (☎742-0705), on C. Fulladoza, sells spices and hot sauces from around the world ($6-8). Open daily 9am-6pm. MC/V.

Flamenco's Boutique (☎435-6654), on C. Romero, next to Superette Mayra. This cute shop sells ceramics, artwork, clothing, and souvenirs mostly made by Culebran or Puerto Rican artists. Open W-Su 10am-1pm and 3-4pm. AmEx/MC/V.

Galería de Regalos Souvenir Shop (☎742-2294), on C. Pedro Márquez, has a small room with generic clothing and another room full of knickknacks and souvenirs. Open daily 9am-noon and 1-4pm, sometimes later. AmEx/MC/V.

■ NIGHTLIFE

Don't come to Culebra for its nightlife. On weeknights the loudest sound is the song of crickets, and even on weekends most of the scant options shut down by 11pm. During holidays the biggest party may be at Flamenco's campground.

El Batey, Rte. 250 Km 1.1 (☎742-3828), a 5min. walk from town. Culebra's hotspot is actually the only place on the island to bust a move—or stay out past 11pm. This local favorite dominates the nightlife scene with a large dance floor and cheap beer. But don't expect glamour and glitz; the linoleum floor looks worn and decor is uninspiring. Beer $1.25-2; mixed drinks start at $3. F karaoke 10pm. Sa disco party 10pm. Open as a club F-Sa 10pm-2am. Cash only.

Mamacita's, C. Castelar 64-66 (☎742-0090). On weekend nights Mamacita's becomes a popular bar. Come on Sa when conga drummers shake the place up (8:30-11pm). Popular with foreigners. Serves interesting house drinks, such as the "Culebrita" ($6). Beer $3-4. Happy Hour M-F 4-6pm. 18+. Open F-Sa 6-11pm. MC/V.

El Oasis (☎742-3175), on C. Pedro Márquez. A long bar dominates the front of this popular pizzeria (see p. 301). Join the locals, pull up a stool, and watch the TV with a bottle of Medalla. Beer $1.50-3; mixed drinks $3-4. Happy Hour daily 6-7pm. Open Su-M and Th 6-10pm, F-Sa 6-11pm. Cash only.

Happy Landing, at the end of the airport strip. When even El Batey gets too touristy, saddle on up to Happy Landing, Culebra's own dive. Locals gather here for the cheapest beer in town. Foreigners come for an attempt at local flavor. Jukebox, electronic slot machines, and 2 pool tables. Beer $1-2. Open daily 9am-midnight. Cash only.

APPENDIX

SPANISH QUICK REFERENCE

PRONUNCIATION

Spanish pronunciation is pretty straightforward; Puerto Rican Spanish is a bit more complicated. Puerto Ricans have a notoriously strong accent and tend to speak very rapidly. Some also have a tendency to drop of the end of words—for example, "buenas días" becomes "buen día." In all Spanish each **vowel** has only one pronunciation: A ("ah" in father); E ("eh" in pet); I ("ee" in eat); O ("oh" in oat); U ("oo" in boot); Y, by itself, is pronounced the same as Spanish I ("ee"). Most **consonants** are pronounced the same as in English. Important exceptions are: J, pronounced like the English "h" in "hello" and Ñ, pronounced like the "gn" in "cognac." LL theoretically sounds like the English "y" in "yes", but in Puerto Rican Spanish it frequently comes out like "s" as in "pleasure." R at the beginning of a word or RR anywhere in a word is trilled. H is always silent. G before E or I is pronounced like the "h" in "hen"; elsewhere it is pronounced like the "g" in "gate." X has a bewildering variety of pronunciations: depending on dialect and word position, it can sound like English "h," "s," "sh," or "x."

Spanish words receive **stress** on the syllable marked with an accent (´). In the absence of an accent mark, words that end in vowels, "n," or "s" usually receive stress on the second-to-last syllable. For words ending in all other consonants, stress falls on the last syllable. The Spanish language has **masculine** and **feminine** nouns, and gives a gender to all adjectives. Masculine words generally end with an "o": *él es un tonto* (he is a fool). Feminine words generally end with an "a": *ella es bella* (she is beautiful). Pay close attention—slight changes in word ending can have drastic changes in meaning. For instance, when receiving directions, mind the distinction between *derecho* (straight) and *derecha* (right).

SPANISH PHRASEBOOK

ESSENTIAL PHRASES

ENGLISH	SPANISH	PRONUNCIATION
Hello	Hola	OH-la
Good morning	Buenos días	BWEN-as DEE-as
Good afternoon	Buenas tardes	BWEN-as TAR-des
Good night	Buenas noches	BWEN-as NO-tches
Goodbye	Adiós	ah-dee-OHS
Yes/No	Sí/No	SEE/NO
Please	Por favor	POOR fa-VOHR
Thank you	Gracias	GRA-see-ahs
You're welcome	De nada	DAY NAH-dah
At your service	A la orden	AH LA OR-den
Do you speak English?	¿Habla inglés?	AH-blah een-GLACE
I don't speak Spanish.	No hablo español.	NO AH-bloh ehs-pahn-YOHL
Excuse me.	Perdón.	pehr-DOHN

SURVIVAL SPANISH

ENGLISH	SPANISH	ENGLISH	SPANISH
Again, please.	Otra vez, por favor.	¿Can you repeat that?	¿Puede repetirlo?
I don't know.	No sé.	Can you speak more slowly?	¿Puede hablar más despacio?
I don't understand.	No entiendo.	Where is (the center of town)?	¿Dónde está (el centro)?
How do you say (beer) in Spanish?	¿Cómo se dice (cerveza) en español?	Where is (the bathroom)?	Dónde está (el baño)?
How are you?	¿Comó está?	I'm fine, thanks.	(Estoy) bien, gracias.
How much does it cost?	¿Cuánto cuesta?	That's too much.	Es demasiado.
That is very cheap/ expensive	Es muy caro/barato.	I want/would like (a sandwich).	Quiero/Me gustaría (un sandwich).
I'm sick/fine.	Estoy enfermo(a)/bien.	Let's go!	¡Vámanos!
Where can I make a phone call?	¿Dónde puedo hacer una llamada de teléfono?	Where can I check email?	¿Dónde puedo chequear el email?
I'm lost.	Estoy perdido/a.	Do you accept traveler's checks?	¿Accepta cheques de viaje?
What's up?	¿Qué pasa?	Stop/ that's enough.	Basta.
What?	¿Cómo?/¿Qué?	Why?	¿Por qué?
Who?	¿Quién?	What?	¿Qué?
When?	¿Cuándo?	Where?	¿Dónde?
Why?	¿Por qué?	Because	Porque

APPENDIX

GETTING AROUND

ENGLISH	SPANISH	ENGLISH	SPANISH
How do you get to (the público station)?	¿Cómo se va a (la terminal de guaguas públicas)?	Does this público go to (Río Piedras)?	¿Va este autobús para (Río Piedras)?
How do I get to...?	¿Cómo voy a...?	How far is...?	¿Qué tan lejos está...?
How long does the trip take?	¿Cuántas horas dura el viaje?	Is it near/far from here?	¿Está cerca/lejos de aquí?
I am going to the airport.	Voy para el aeropuerto.	I lost my baggage.	Perdí mi equipaje.

EMERGENCY

ENGLISH	SPANISH	ENGLISH	SPANISH
Help!	¡Ayúdame!/¡Socorro!	Call the police!	¡Llame a la policía!
I am hurt.	Estoy herido(a).	Leave me alone!	¡Déjame en paz!
It's an emergency!	¡Es una emergencia!	They robbed me!	¡Me han robado!
Fire!	¡Fuego!/¡Incendio!	Don't touch me!	¡No me toque!
Call a clinic/ambulance/ doctor!	¡Llame a una clínica/una ambulancia/un médico!	They went that way!	¡Fueron en esa dirección!

MEDICAL

ENGLISH	SPANISH	ENGLISH	SPANISH
I feel bad/better/worse.	Me siento mal/mejor/ peor.	I have a stomach ache.	Tengo dolor de estómago.
I have a headache.	Tengo dolor de cabeza.	It hurts here.	Me duele aquí.
I'm sick/ill.	Estoy enfermo(a).	I think I'm going to vomit.	Pienso que voy a vomitar.
What is this medicine for?	¿Para qué es esta medicina?	I haven't been able to go to the bathroom in (four) days.	No he podido ir al baño en (cuatro) días.
Where is the nearest hospital/doctor.	¿Dónde está el hospital/ doctor más cercano?	I have a cold/a fever/ diarrhea/nausea.	Tengo gripa/una calentura/diarrea/náusea.

DIRECTIONS

ENGLISH	SPANISH	ENGLISH	SPANISH
(to the) right	a la derecha	(to the) left	a la izquierda
Stay straight.	Siga derecho.	Turn right/left.	Doble a la derecha/ izquierda.
next to	al lado de	across from	en frente de
near	cerca	far	lejos
above	arriba	below	abajo
traffic light	semáforo	corner	esquina
street	calle/avenida	block	cuadra

ON THE ROAD

ENGLISH	SPANISH	ENGLISH	SPANISH
car	carro, auto	van	guagua
stop	pare	slow	despacio
lane (termina)	carril (ends)	yield	ceda
entrance	entrada	exit	salida
(narrow) bridge	puente (estrecho)	(maximum) speed	velocidad (máxima)
seatbelt	cinturón de seguridad	dangerous (curve)	(curva) peligrosa
narrow (lane)	(carril) estrecho	parking	estacionamiento, parking
toll (ahead)	peaje (adelante)	dead-end street	calle sin salida
authorized public buses only	transporte colectivo autorizado solamente	only (traffic only in the direction of the arrow)	solo
slippery when wet	resbala mojada	rest area	area de descansar
danger (ahead)	peligro (adelante)	do not park	no estacione
do not enter	no entre	do not turn right on red	no vire con luz roja
north	norte	south	sur
east	este	west	oeste

ACCOMMODATIONS

ENGLISH	SPANISH	ENGLISH	SPANISH
Is there a (cheap) hotel around here?	¿Hay un hotel (económico) por aqui?	Are there rooms with windows?	¿Hay habitaciones con ventanas?
Do you have any singles/ doubles?	¿Tiene habitaciones sencillas/dobles?	I am going to stay for (four) days.	Me voy a quedar (cuatro) días.
I would like to reserve a room.	Quisiera reservar una habitación.	Are there cheaper rooms?	¿Hay habitaciones más baratas?
Can I see a room?	¿Puedo ver una habitación?	Do they come with fans/ kitchen?	¿Vienen con abanico/ cocina?
I need another key/ towel/pillow.	Necesito otra llave/ toalla/almohada.	My bedsheets are dirty.	Mis sábanas están sucias.
The bathroom is broken.	El baño está roto.	I'll take it.	Lo tomo.

PERSONAL RELATIONSHIPS

ENGLISH	SPANISH	ENGLISH	SPANISH
Pleased to meet you.	Encantado(a)/Mucho gusto.	This is my first time in Puerto Rico.	Este es mi primera vez en Puerto Rico .
What is your name?	¿Cómo se llama?	Me llamo Carlos.	My name is Carlos
Where are you from?	¿De dónde es?	Soy de los Estados Unidos/Europa.	I am from the United States/Europe.
Do you have a boyfriend/ girlfriend/husband/wife?	¿Tiene un novio/novia/ esposo/esposa?	I have a boyfriend/girl-friend.	Tengo novio/novia.
How old are you?	¿Cuántos años tiene?	I'm (twenty) years old.	Tengo (viente) años.

NUMBERS, DAYS, AND MONTHS

ENGLISH	SPANISH	ENGLISH	SPANISH
0	cero	1000	un mil
1	uno	1 million	un millón
2	dos	Sunday	Domingo
3	tres	Monday	Lunes
4	cuatro	Tuesday	Martes
5	cinco	Wednesday	Miércoles
6	seis	Thursday	Jueves
7	siete	Friday	Viernes
8	ocho	Saturday	Sábado
9	nueve	today	hoy
10	diez	tomorrow	mañana
11	once	day after tomorrow	pasado mañana
12	doce	yesterday	ayer
13	trece	day before yesterday	antes de ayer/anteayer
14	catorce	weekend	fin de semana
15	quince	January	enero
16	dieciseis	February	febrero
17	diecisiete	March	marzo
18	dieciocho	April	abril
19	diecinueve	May	mayo
20	veinte	June	junio
21	veintiuno	July	julio
22	veintidos	August	agosto
30	treinta	September	septiembre
40	cuarenta	October	octubre
50	cincuenta	November	noviembre
100	cien	December	diciembre

EATING OUT

ENGLISH	SPANISH	ENGLISH	SPANISH
breakfast	desayuno	lunch	almuerzo
dinner	cena	dessert	postre
drink	bebida	Bon Apétit	Buen provecho
fork	tenedor	napkin	servilleta
knife	cuchillo	cup	copa/taza
spoon	cuchara	Check, please.	La cuenta, por favor.
I am hungry/thirsty.	Tengo hambre/sed.	Do you have hot sauce/ketchup?	¿Tiene salsa picante/ketchup?
Where is a good restaurant?	¿Dónde hay un restaurante bueno?	Table for (two), please.	Mesa para (dos, por favor.
Can I see the menu?	¿Podría ver el menú?	Do you take credit cards?	¿Aceptan tarjetas de crédito?
I'm allergic to (nuts).	Soy alérgico(a) a (las nuces).	Do you have anything vegetarian/without meat?	¿Hay algún plato vegetariano/sin carne?
I would like the crab.	Quisiera el juey.	Dáme el pollo.	Give me the chicken.
This is too spicy.	Pica demasiado.	Delicious!	¡Qué rico!

MENU READER

BASIC FOODS (COMIDAS BÁSICAS)

SPANISH	ENGLISH	SPANISH	ENGLISH
arroz	rice	pollo	chicken
pan	bread	carne	meat
vegetales	vegetables	ensalada	salad
fruta	fruit	queso	cheese
gandules	green pigeon peas	habichuelas	beans
amarillos	sweet fried plantains	tostones	dry fried plantains

BREAKFAST (DESAYUNO)

SPANISH	ENGLISH	SPANISH	ENGLISH
tostadas	toast with butter	café	coffee
huevos fritos	fried eggs	huevos revueltos	scrambled eggs
jamón	jam	tocineta	bacon
panqueques	pancakes	tostadas francesas	french toast
avena	oatmeal	tortilla española	Spanish omelet

SANDWICHES (SANDWICHES)

SPANISH	ENGLISH	SPANISH	ENGLISH
sandwich	sandwich	pan	bread
lechuga	lettuce	tomate	tomato
mayonesa	mayonaise	mantequilla	butter
pollo	chicken	pavo	turkey
atún	tuna	bistec/biftec	beef
jamón	jam	queso	cheese
juevo	egg	queso suiza	swiss cheese

MEATS (CARNES)

SPANISH	ENGLISH	SPANISH	ENGLISH
biftec encebollado	beef strips with onions	chuletas fritas	fried pork chops
pollo frito	fried chicken	biftec empanado	breaded Spanish steak
pechuga de pollo	chicken breast	churrasco	breaded steak
lechón	roasted pork	chicharrón	bite-sized pieces of meat

SEAFOOD (MARISCOS)

SPANISH	ENGLISH	SPANISH	ENGLISH
chillo	red snapper	camarones	shrimp
carrucho	conch	pulpo	octopus
chapin	trunk fish	langosta	lobster
cangrejo	crab	juey	crab

FRUITS (FRUTAS)

SPANISH	ENGLISH	SPANISH	ENGLISH
acerola	West Indian cherry	guayaba	guava
guineo	banana	manzana	apple
guanábana	soursop	aguacate	avacado
parcha	passion fruit	piña	pinapple
china	orange	pera	pear

APPENDIX

SPANISH GLOSSARY

abajo: below
abanico: fan
acerola: cherry
adelante: ahead
aduana: customs
aeropuerto: airport
agencia de viaje: travel agency
agua: water
aguacate: avacado
aguas termales: hot springs
ahora: now
ahorita: in just a little bit
aire acondicionado: air-conditioned (A/C)
ajo: garlic
a la orden: at your serivce
a la plancha: grilled
al gusto : as you wish
alcaldía: mayor's office
alcapuria: meat-filled fried plantains
almejas: clams
almuerzo: lunch
amarillos: fried sweet plantains
amigo/a: friend
area de descansar: rest area
arepas: corn dough patties, sometimes filled with meat, cheese or vegetables
arriba: above
arroz: rice
arroz con dule: sweet rice pudding
artesanía: arts and crafts
asada: roast
asopao: stew, thick soup
atún: tuna
auto: car
avena: oatmeal
avenida: avenue
ATH: ATM
bacalaíto: flat fritter fried in codfish oil
bahía: bay
balneario: public beach
baño: bathroom
barato/a: cheap
barrio: neighborhood
batidas: smoothies or milkshakes made from fresh fruit
béisbol: baseball
biblioteca: library
bistec/bistek/biftec: beefsteak
bocaditos: appetizers, at a bar
boletería: ticket counter
boleto: ticket
bomba: an African-influenced style of Puerto Rican music popular in Loíza
bonito/a: pretty, beautiful
Boriken: Taíno name for Puerto Rico

Boricuan: an affectionate term for a Puerto Rican
borracho/a: drunk
bosque (estatal): (state) forest
bueno/a: good
buena suerte: good luck
buen provecho: bon appetit
buenos días/tardes/ noches: good morning/afternoon/evening
burro: donkey
caballero: gentleman
caballo: horse
cabañas: cabins
café: coffee or cafe
cafetería: a small, informal restaurant
cajeros: cashiers
caldo: soup, broth, or stew
calle: street
cama: bed
camarones: shrimp
cambio: change
camino: path, track, road
camión: truck
campo: countryside
cangrejo: crab
capilla: chapel
carne: red meat

carrucho: conch
caro/a: expensive
carretera: highway
carril: lane
carro: car
casa: house
casado/a: married
cascada: waterfall
catedral: cathedral
ceda: yield
centro: city center
centro vacacional: government sponsored vacation center
cerca: near, nearby
cerro: hill
cerveza: beer
chapin: trunk fish
cheques de viaje: traveler's checks
chica/o: girl/boy, little
chicharrón: bite-sized pieces of meat
chillo: red snapper
china: orange
chuletas: pork chops
churrasco: steak
cigarillo: cigarette
cine: movie theater
cinturón de seguridad: seatbelt
ciudad: city
coche: car
cocina criolla: Puerto Rican food

coco: coconut
coliseo: coliseum, stadium
colmado: small store
comedor: dining room
comida criolla: regional dishes
comida típica: traditional Puerto Rican food dishes
con: with
consulado: consulate
correo: post office
cordillera: mountain range
CPN: Compañia de Parques Nacionales (National Parks Company)
cuadra: street block
cuarto: a room
cuatro: four, or a traditional Puerto Rican instrument similar to a guitar
Cuba Libre: rum and coke
cuenta: bill, check
cuento: story, account
cueva: cave
curva: curve
damas: ladies
derecha: right
derecho: straight
desayuno: breakfast
despacio: slow
dinero: money
disco: dance club
doblar: to turn
DRN: Departamento de Recursos Naturales (Department of Natural Resources)
dulce: sweet
edificio: building
embajada: embassy
empanado: breaded
embotellada: bottled
emergencia: emergency
empanadilla: fried fritter
encebollado: with onions
ensalada: salad
entrada: entrance
español: Spanish
esquina: corner
estacionamiento: parking
estacionar: to park
estadio: stadium
este: east
estrecho: narrow
estrella: star
extranjero: foreign/foreigner
farmacia: pharmacy
feliz: happy
fiesta: party, holiday
finca: farm, ranch
flan: egg custard
fresa: strawberry
friaje: sudden cold wind
frijoles: beans
frito: fried
fruta: fruit
fumar: to smoke

APPENDIX

Page 312.

gandules: green pigeon peas
gobierno: government
gordo/a: fat
gracias: thank you
gratis: free
gringo: American (sometimes derogatory)
guagua: van
guanábana: soursop
guaynabo (con queso): guava (with cheese)
guineo: banana
habichuelas: beans
habitación: a room
hacienda: ranch
helado: ice cream
hervido/a: boiled
hielo: ice
hola: hello
hombre: man
huevos: eggs
iglesia: church
impuestos: taxes
independentistas: supporters of the Puerto Rican independece movement
inglés: English
isla: island
izquierda: left
jamón: jam
jarra: 1-liter pitcher
jíbaro: a traditional man from the countryside
juevo: egg
juey: crab
jugo: juice
ladrón: thief
lago/laguna: lake
lancha: launch, small boat
langosta: lobster
larga distancia: long distance
lavandería: laundromat
leche: milk
lechón: roast pork
lechuga: lettuce
lejos: far
lento: slow
librería: bookstore
limber: frozen fruit juice
luz: light
mal: bad
malecón: seaside boardwalk
maleta: luggage, suitcase
mantequilla: butter
manzana: apple
mar: sea
mariscos: seafood
máxima: maximum
mayonesa: mayonnaise
mercado: market
mesón gastronómico: traditional restaurant endorsed by the Puerto Rican Tourism Company
mirador: an observatory or look-out point
mofongo: mashed plantain typically filled with meat

mojo: typical Puerto Rican sauce
muelle: dock
museo: museum
música (folklórica): (folk) music
nada: nothing
nevera: refridgerator
niño(a): child
norte: north
nuces/nuez: nuts/nut
Nuyorican: someone of Puerto Rican descent living in New York
obra: work of art/play
oeste: west
oficina de turismo: tourist office
ostiones: oysters
pan: bread
pana: breadfruit
panadería: bakery
panqueques: pancakes
parada: a bus or train stop (in San Juan "Parada" refers to old trolley stops that no longer exist; however, the term is still used for giving directions)
pare: stop
parador: "country inn" endorsed by the Puerto Rican Tourism Company
parcha: passion fruit
parilla: grilled (as in meat)
parque: park
pasaporte: passport
pavo: turkey
peaje: toll
pelea de gallos: cockfighting
peligroso/a: dangerous
pescado: fish
picante: spicy
piña: pinapple
pinono: fried plantain wrapped around ground beef
piragua: snow cone
plátano: plantain
playa: beach
plena: a form of Puerto Rican music that originated in sugar plantations around Ponce
población: population
policía: police
pollo: chicken
por favor: please
públicos: public vehicles
pueblo: town
puente: bridge
puerta: door
puerto: port
pulpo: octopus
queso: cheese
refrescos: refreshments, soft drinks
reloj: watch, clock
río: river
ropa: clothes
sábanas: sheets

sabor: flavor
sala: room
salida: exit
salsa: sauce, a type of music
santos: small hand-carved wooden religious figurines
seguro/a: insurance
semáforo: traffic light
semana: week
Semana Santa: Holy Week
sexo: sex
sí: yes
sin salida: without end (dead-end)
SIDA: the Spanish acronym for AIDS
solo/solamente: only
soltero/a: single, unmarried
sorullito: fried corn sticks
supermercado: supermarket
sur: south
Taíno: Native Americans living on Puerto Rico
tarifa: fee
té: tea
tembleque: cocnut milk custard
termina: ends
tiburón: shark
tienda: store
tiple: traditional Puerto Rican instrument similar to a guitar
tocineta: bacon
tortillas española: Spanish omelet
tostadas: toast with butter
tostadas francesas: french toast
tostones: dry fried plantains
trago: mixed drink/shot
tres leches: sweet, moist cake
turismo: tourism
turista: tourist
valle: valley
vegetales: vegetables
vejigante mask: a colorful mask with horns used during carnaval festivals
velocidad: speed
ventana: window
vereda: trail, path
vino: wine
virar: to turn
volcán: volcano
zoológico: zoo

APPENDIX

INDEX

INDEX

the ultimate
road trip

don't trip out planning your big road trip.
put contiki in the driver's seat with a hassle-free vacations
designed for 18 to 35 year olds. make new friends, enjoy
your free time and explore the sights in a convenient
vacation that gives you more bang for your buck... **from
only $70/day** including accommodations, sightseeing,
many meals and transportation. with contiki leading the
way, you can leave the road map at home!

> **7 days eastern discovery**
new york, washington d.c., us naval academy, kennedy space center

> **10 days canada & the rockies**
vancouver, calgary, banff national park

> **13 days wild western**
san francisco, grand canyon, las vegas, yosemite national park

*prices subject to change, land only.

for more info on our trips...
see your travel agent
call 1-888-CONTIKI
visit www.contiki.com

contiki
VACATIONS for 18-35 year olds

CST# 1001728-20

> europe > australia > new zealand > america > canada

FOUR-STAR HOTEL PAID FOR WITH MONEY FOUND IN COUCH.

Save up to 70%
on great hotels
with OrbitzSaver rates.*

ORBITZ.com

©2003 Orbitz, LLC. CST# 2063530-50 *Savings based on comparison with published rack rates.

Travel to another country by volunteering internationally

"You will feel the heartbeat of the country."

~ Judy, India volunteer

Participate in a Cross-Cultural Solutions short-term international volunteer program and get to know a country from the inside-out. Connect with local people while working side-by-side on locally designed and driven projects, participating in educational and cultural programming and reflecting on your experience during your free time.

It's your experience.

Make the most of it by participating in a Cross-Cultural Solutions international volunteer program either in Brazil, China, Costa Rica, Ghana, Guatemala, India, Peru, Russia, Thailand, or Tanzania. Programs run year-round from 2-12 weeks and the 2003 program fees start at $1,985. Contact us today to learn more about participating in your international volunteer program.

Cross-Cultural Solutions
AN INTERNATIONAL
VOLUNTEER PROGRAM

WWW.CROSSCULTURALSOLUTIONS.ORG
1-800-380-4777 · INFO@CROSSCULTURALSOLUTIONS.ORG

MAP INDEX

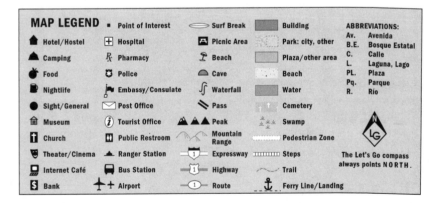